Positive
Psychological
Assessment

Positive Psychological Assessment

A Handbook of Models and Measures

Edited by
Shane J. Lopez and
C. R. Snyder

AMERICAN PSYCHOLOGICAL ASSOCIATION • *Washington, DC*

Published by
American Psychological Association
750 First Street, NE
Washington, DC 20002
www.apa.org

First Printing February 2003
Second Printing October 2003
Third Printing July 2004
Fourth Printing October 2006
Fifth Printing February 2009

To order
APA Order Department
P.O. Box 92984
Washington, DC 20090-2984
Tel: (800) 374-2721
Direct: (202) 336-5510
Fax: (202) 336-5502
TDD/TTY: (202) 336-6123
Online: www.apa.org/books/
E-mail: order@apa.org

In the U.K., Europe, Africa, and the Middle East, copies may be ordered from
American Psychological Association
3 Henrietta Street
Covent Garden, London
WC2E 8LU England

Typeset in Century Schoolbook by World Composition Services, Inc., Sterling, VA

Printer: Data Reproductions, Auburn Hills, MI
Cover Designer: Naylor Design, Washington, DC
Project Manager: Debbie Hardin, Carlsbad, CA

The opinions and statements published are the responsibility of the authors, and such opinions and statements do not necessarily represent the policies of the American Psychological Association.

Library of Congress Cataloging-in-Publication Data

Positive psychological assessment : a handbook of models and measures / edited by Shane J. Lopez and C.R. Snyder.—1st ed.
    p. cm.
  Includes bibliographical references and index.
  ISBN 1-55798-988-5 (alk. paper)
   1. Psychological tests. I. Lopez, Shane J. II. Snyder, C. R.

BF176.P67 2003
150'.28'7—dc21

2002043754

British Library Cataloguing-in-Publication Data
A CIP record is available from the British Library.

Printed in the United States of America

To Donald Clifton, for asking
"What would happen if we studied what is right with people?"

Contents

Contributors

Karen S. Basinger, Urbana University, Urbana, OH
Jennifer C. Bouwkamp, Bloomington, IN
David Caruso, Work-Life Strategies, New Canaan, CT
Charles S. Carver, University of Miami, Coral Gables, FL
Ed Diener, University of Illinois at Champaign–Urbana
Lisa M. Edwards, University of Kansas, Lawrence
Nancy Eisenberg, Arizona State University, Tempe
Robert A. Emmons, University of California, Davis
Lisa Y. Flores, University of Missouri, Columbia
Geneviève Fournier, Université Laval, Quebec, Canada
Camea Gagliardi, Tempe, AZ
John C. Gibbs, Ohio State University, Columbus
Jane Gillham, University of Pennsylvania, Philadelphia
Rebecca L. Grime, Columbus, OH
Todd F. Heatherton, Dartmouth College, Hanover, NH
Clyde Hendrick, Texas Tech University, Lubbock
Susan S. Hendrick, Texas Tech University, Lubbock
P. Paul Heppner, University of Missouri—Columbia
Alicia Ito, Lawrence, KS
Chantale Jeanrie, Université Laval, Quebec, Canada
Barbara Kerr, Arizona State University, Tempe
Corey L. M. Keyes, Emory University, Atlanta, GA
Nina Knoll, Freie Universität Berlin, Berlin, Germany
Randy J. Larsen, Washington University, St. Louis, MO
B. Leipold, Dresden, Germany
Paulo N. Lopes, New Haven, CT
Frederick G. Lopez, University of Houston, TX
Shane J. Lopez, University of Kansas, Lawrence
Richard E. Lucas, Michigan State University, East Lansing
Jeana L. Magyar-Moe, Lawrence, KS
Rod Martin, University of Western Ontario, London, Ontario, Canada
John D. Mayer, University of New Hampshire, Durham
Michael E. McCullough, University of Miami, Coral Gables, FL
Jason E. Neufeld, Lawrence, KS
Ezemenari M. Obasi, Columbus, OH
Karen M. O'Brien, University of Maryland, College Park
Kristin Koetting O'Byrne, Kansas City, MO
Jennifer Teramoto Pedrotti, Lawrence, KS
Stephanie Petersen, Lawrence, KS
M. J. Power, University of Edinburgh, Edinburgh, United Kingdom
Ellie C. Prosser, Lawrence, KS
Heather N. Rasmussen, Lawrence, KS

Karen Reivich, University of Pennsylvania, Philadelphia
Christine Robitschek, Texas Tech University, Lubbock
Jamie A. Ryder, Lawrence, KS
Peter Salovey, Yale University, New Haven, CT
Michael Scheier, Carnegie Mellon University, Pittsburgh, PA
Ralf Schwarzer, Freie Universität Berlin, Berlin, Germany
C. R. Snyder, University of Kansas, Lawrence
Susan Vehige Spalitto, Lawrence, KS
U. M. Staudinger, Dresden University of Technology, Dresden, Germany
Laura Yamhure Thompson, Harvard Medical School, Belmont, MA
Jo-Ann Tsang, Southern Methodist University, Dallas, TX
Jon C. Ulven, St. Cloud State University, St. Cloud, MN
Carlos Valiente, Tempe, AZ
Stephanie LaRue Walton, Lawrence, KS
Yu-Wei Wang, Columbia, MO
Carrie L. Wyland, Hanover, NH
Qing Zhou, Tempe, AZ

Foreword

Donald Clifton

Positive Psychological Assessment: A Handbook of Models and Measures supports a burgeoning revolution—a revolution of thought that moves us from a mode of explaining things in terms of deficits to explaining things in terms of positive perspectives. This volume provides the foundation of concepts and measurement experience to enable social scientists to make a leap forward in presenting a better way of life for future civilizations. The chapters included make it clear that positive personality characteristics can be measured just as readily as negative ones. For those of us who believe that no important change takes place without measurement, this book reinforces our hopes for the future. Furthermore, sound measurement and research may be the only conditions that bolster and maintain the respect for the movement as science-based rather than as a pop psychology fad of irrational euphoria. This handbook can provide the discipline the positive psychology movement needs to be more than short-lived.

Positive psychology as a discipline should not become a "this" rather than a "that" movement. The goal is to bring more balance to psychology, which during the past century has been skewed to pathologies rather than to well-being. Positive psychology encourages modes of perception that spontaneously observe the "good" but do not ignore the "bad" in human behavior. The mantra of positive psychology must be to *develop the strengths and manage the weaknesses*. Indeed, there still appears to be a need for correcting, even when the emphasis is on building the strengths. The proponents of positive psychology simply refuse to study and treat pathologies to the exclusion of building on human strengths.

This balanced view of the negative and positive is necessary in the social sciences, yet it is also imperative to address society's obsession with the negative. At Gallup we asked the question of a random sample across America: "Suppose your child came home with these grades: two As, a B, a C, and a low grade, such as a D or an F. Which of these grades would you deem worthy of considerable conversation?" Most (77%) said they would spend the most time on the lowest grade. Only 6% said they would spend the most time on the A.[1] I believe this bias on "fixing the negative" must be overcome. This handbook provides the tools for clinicians and researchers to use when developing a complementary view of strengths and weaknesses.

---

[1]Buckingham, M., & Clifton, D. O. (2001). *Now, discover your strengths.* New York: Simon & Schuster.

Lopez and Snyder have collected studies from competent and serious scientists. These studies provide the foundation for us to be confident and ready to celebrate the work of positive psychologists. The studies and measurements presented may be the classics of the future. They could set the standards for many studies in positive affect, optimism, emotional intelligence, work satisfaction, sense of humor, flow, and forgiveness. A new, positive language may develop in research journals—a language of gratitude, subjective well-being, love, and hope. And content analysis may be one of the most effective methods for measuring the positive psychology revolution.

I am very pleased to have been asked to write a foreword for this handbook. This is the kind of guide we need to transform our civilization and open the doors to a new, exciting quality of life—perhaps a world of abundance rather than scarcity and a world of peace for all. Positive psychologists can lead the way, showing with sound measurement that there are sufficient human strengths to create a productive, harmonious world.

Preface

"What would happen if we studied what is right with people?" This simple question posed nearly 50 years ago by Donald Clifton, an educational psychologist and former CEO of The Gallup Organization, can be answered only if we *measure* what is right with people. *Positive Psychological Assessment: A Handbook of Models and Measures* will give readers theoretically grounded measures that will help them answer Dr. Clifton's question.

Positive psychology is the scientific and practical pursuit of optimal human functioning. As professionals committed to helping people realize their potential by capitalizing on strengths and managing weaknesses, clinicians and researchers must be skilled at detecting the worst *and* the best in people. Our assumption is that most clinicians and researchers are more effective in examining illness or pathology than they are in evaluating health and well-being. This volume was written to help professionals bring balance to the assessment approach.

Organizing the Volume With a Purpose

We hope that this volume is thought-provoking and that it will help readers to incorporate assessment of the positive into their work. Indeed, we hope to stimulate our colleagues' scientific and practical pursuits of optimal human functioning. To this end we planned this volume so that it first establishes that a complementary view of human behavior—one that values the negative *and* the positive—yields a comprehensive understanding of the human pursuit of a fulfilling life. Chapters 1 and 2 promote this balanced view of psychology by highlighting the saliency and potency of human strength and by providing alternatives to traditional assessment and diagnostic models. Chapter 3 puts positive psychology and its assessment into a multicultural context. (Placement of this chapter is purposeful because we hope to encourage readers to critically examine the cross-cultural applicability of the models and measures described in the remainder of the volume.) Chapters 4 through 28 provide the resources necessary to transform research and practice by augmenting assessment of weakness and illness with the measurement of strength, healthy process, and well-being. Contributors of these chapters offer detailed descriptions of psychological models, then present psychometrically sound measures (some of which are gold standards and others of which are recently developed instruments with demonstrated utility). Finally, in chapter 29, we describe the future of positive psychological assessment, a future that we hope the readers of this volume will influence.

It is our contention that this volume reflects the state of the art and science of positive psychological assessment. Implementation of the Practice Model of Positive Psychological Assessment (see chapters 1 and 2) and modification of diagnostic frameworks will change how professionals gather and present psychological data. Selection of measures provided in this volume will help practitioners and researchers account for unexplained variance in human behavior. Most important, this volume should pique reader interest in the positive side of the human experience. As this interest grows through reading the book, questions about availability of additional measures of models included in this volume will arise, and queries about the exclusion or unavailability of other models and measures will be posed. We anticipate these inquiries because we grappled with our own questions about which constructs and processes should be highlighted. Ultimately, we decided to include coverage of human strengths that have been well researched and of healthy processes, life fulfillments, and environments that are theoretically grounded and empirically examined. As a review of the contents indicates, models and measures of human strengths are plentiful. Hence, we developed categories (cognitive models and measures, emotional models and measures, interpersonal models and measures, religious and philosophical models and measures; these are not necessarily mutually exclusive) to organize the 20 human strengths highlighted in the volume. Conversely, there is a paucity of models and measures that describe healthy human processes, positive outcomes, and nurturing environments. (Relevant measures are described in Part VI.) We hope readers will contribute to the development of a greater understanding of processes and environments that lead to the good life.

Thanking Visionaries and Supporters

Any new approach rests on the support of a few important people who see change not as a challenge but as a given part of life. This is true of our colleagues in our respective departments at the University of Kansas. Their support in our pursuits is unconditional. Likewise, Susan Reynolds and Vanessa Downing, our editors at the American Psychological Association, were unwavering in their support of this venture. We obviously could not have produced this volume without the solid backing of a first-rate publisher.

Many people shaped the ideas presented in this book, and we would like to acknowledge their contributions. Donald Clifton, through his work at the University of Nebraska, Selection Research International, and The Gallup Organization, showed us that positive psychological assessment has a place in the world. Beatrice Wright's scholarship, creativity, and passion have been infectious over the years. Her ideas about comprehensive assessment along four fronts repeatedly are reflected in our work. The same can be said about Karl Menninger's ideas as articulated in his book *The Vital Balance*. We think he would have been a vocal leader in the positive psychology movement. Hundreds of other scholars played a role in bringing this book to fruition. Indeed, we are indebted to the scholars who contributed their expertise to this volume and to our students over the years who have taught us about human strength.

Special thanks go to Heather Rasmussen. Her editorial assistance during the two-year process of organizing this book was invaluable. She is the future of positive psychology.

Finally, we recognize our families for allowing us the necessary time to devote to this project. Allison and Rebecca understand and share our fascination with positive psychology, and we thank them.

Part I

Searching for the Positive

1

Striking a Vital Balance: Developing A Complementary Focus on Human Weakness and Strength Through Positive Psychological Assessment

Shane J. Lopez, C. R. Snyder,
and Heather N. Rasmussen

Imagine walking into a great hall filled with grand wooden tables. On those tables are thousands of weights and hundreds of well-worn scales, some larger than others. Using the scales, all engraved with the names of age-old foibles, measure the success of your life.

Next, imagine a second hall with twice as many scales—all of the scales for human foibles *plus* scales labeled with antiquated names of human strengths. This huge system of scales measures all qualities essential to life and well-being. Now measure the success of your life.

We believe that the system of scales in the second hall would help to strike a vital balance in our measurement of life success. Indeed, psychological science has provided us with many theoretically grounded, psychometrically sound measures of human strength. Despite these recent developments in positive psychology involving operationalization of constructs and development of measures, however, no volume of these psychometric advances has been completed. This was the impetus for this volume.

Toward a Complementary Focus on Human Weaknesses and Strengths

As behavioral scientists and mental health practitioners craft questions about human behavior, we initiate a process of inquiry into what does and does not work in the lives of people. Determining the presence of weaknesses and strengths, and their existing associations, enables us to frame questions, to develop theories of human functioning, and to make recommendations for care. We contend that scientific and professional psychology have been biased toward identifying psychopathology and problems in everyday living, and thus we know a great deal about how to help people resolve concerns and alleviate symptoms. We know less, however, about the anatomy of optimal functioning and the enhancement of human strengths. Therefore, in this introductory chapter, we will briefly address conceptual issues related to identifying the human strengths that are considered the building blocks of positive psychology. We argue that such human strengths are "real" and that detecting these strengths is an important part of good science and practice. We also will identify the shortcomings in common assessment procedures and provide a new model of assessment and how-to information for addressing these shortcomings.

Conceptual and Practical Issues

We do not assume that the readers of this volume have completely ignored "the best in people" in your research plans or practice. On completing this volume, however, you may be even more compelled and better equipped to focus on human strengths and healthy processes. In the effort to refine your scholarly inquiries or practices by increasing the focus on human potentialities, we feel the need to offer a warning. Namely, your colleagues, insurance companies, journal editors, grant reviewers, and others may inquire about the authenticity and potency of human strengths. Furthermore, even if they accept a human strength as "real," they may contend that such a "fuzzy construct" cannot be measured reliably and accurately. Likewise, if you demonstrate how the particular strength can be measured, you then will have to balance the human strengths with the weaknesses. Moreover, you may be asked to substantiate information about the potency of strength by comparing it to the powerful effects of weakness and pathology. We have faced these issues in our own clinical practices and research programs, and we will address them briefly in subsequent sections of this chapter.

Human Strengths Are as Real as Weakness and Social Desirability

Psychological phenomena were discussed long before Sir Francis Galton performed mental measurement and Sigmund Freud called attention to psychodynamic processes. In our own work, we have found that Greek and Eastern philosophy, the Bible, historical accounts, and the linguistic origins of words provide important information about human strengths. We mention this because the topic of psychological strength is as old as humankind. Schimmel (2000) echoed this latter point and recommended that positive psychologists should explore their roots as exemplified in ancient philosophy and religious writings.

This "human strengths are as old as time" argument, however, is not always convincing to our colleagues. On this perplexing issue Seligman wrote,

> How has it happened that social science views the human strengths and virtues—altruism, courage, honesty, duty, joy, health, responsibility, and good cheer—as derivative, defensive, or downright illusions, while weakness

and negative motivations such as anxiety, lust, selfishness, paranoia, anger, disorder, and sadness are viewed as authentic? (1998, p. 6)

Though verification of the authenticity of human strengths may be rooted in subjectivity, potency of a human strength may be determined in a more objective manner. Indeed, we can answer questions about potency most directly. For example, do human strengths play an active, potent role in the attainment of health, happiness, and optimal functioning? We believe that this question has been addressed empirically. The vast literature dealing with the potency of human strengths has been summarized elsewhere (see Snyder & Lopez, 2002; Snyder & McCullough, 2000), but three examples may be helpful. First, what we know about hope is that high levels are related to better performances in academics and sports, as well as superior psychotherapy and physical health outcome. Second, college students with broad coping repertoires are able to perceive a potentially stressful event as a challenge rather than as a threat, and they use effective coping mechanisms to approach their problems rationally and effectively. Third, the capacity for social connectedness has been linked to lower mortality rates, increased resistance to communicable diseases, lower prevalence of heart disease, and faster recovery from surgery (Salovey, Rothman, Detweiler, & Steward, 2000). We cherry-pick these findings from the hundreds that could have been mentioned because each account focuses on the use of the strengths of hoping, coping, and connecting in our daily lives (lending evidence to their authenticity); moreover, these strengths have been linked to better immunosuppressance, health outcomes, and even mortality (lending credence to our potency claim).

Human strengths are as real as human weakness, so say history and science. But can we accurately measure these strengths given the tendency of respondents to provide socially desirable information about themselves? The answer is not a simple one. In essence, there are three schools of thought. First, some argue that one should measure and statistically control for the favorability bias in responding. Second, others suggest retaining the favorability bias after showing it is a substantive part of a given concept (i.e., the favorability bias is more content than confound [Taylor & Brown, 1988]). Third, yet others assume that a person's subjective report of strength forms the meaningful sources for analysis, not the objective accuracy of such report. These views on the extent to which social desirability undercuts, aids, or is irrelevant to the authenticity of a strength should be taken into account when considering the veracities of individuals' reports of their assets. The traditional view of social desirability as a confound is no longer widely held, and most scholars now believe that favorable self-presentation is part of the content that should not be taken out or corrected.

By only focusing on weaknesses, psychologists have perpetuated an assessment process that is out of balance. We will now identify shortcomings of psychological assessment and describe the practice model of positive psychological assessment and how-to information to address the imbalance. Thus, we hope to encourage researchers and practitioners to engage in a more balanced view of human life—a vital balance between weakness and strength of the person and the environment.

Figure 1.1. What do you see?

A Positive Psychology Perspective

Historically scholars and counseling theorists have argued about the *natural state of human behavior*. To reveal any implicit theories regarding this state, we encourage the readers to think about the assumptions they make about their research participants and their clients, their partners and their children, themselves and who they want to be. *Perspective* on human behavior determines the routes taken in pursuit of psychological data.

The information-gathering routes taken can yield data reflecting psychological weakness, psychological strength, or a combination of the two. It is the combination, the complementary bodies of knowledge, that will help resolve the shortcomings of common psychological assessment practices. We will illustrate the effects of making initial assumptions and entertaining both the negative and the positive with an exercise in perspective taking.

What determines what is *seen* when people are first presented with a novel stimulus? Look at Figure 1.1 and jot down what you see. Do you see anything else? Anything else?

Most people see either a rabbit (or some other rodent) or a bird of some kind (e.g., duck, goose, eagle) or both. What determines what is seen surely involves some visual scanning processes, but on a more basic level, experience influences response. Similarly, what is seen when people meet others is influenced by *experiences*, and in the professional realm, training also determines what is seen. The paradigm within which training occurs determines what is seen in human behavior and the routes taken to positively influence human change.

Did you see both a rodent and a bird during your first two glances at the picture? Do you see both of them now? Can you make the perceptual shift between the rodent and the bird? Once you have seen both, it should be easier to switch back and forth between what you see. After reading this handbook, it should be easier for you to see both the negative aspects of someone's presentation and the positive and to be able to switch back and forth between—and to integrate—the complementary views of psychology and bodies of psychological science.

Positive Psychological Assessment: Toward a Complementary Focus in Research

As mentioned previously, social scientists have demystified mental illness and its treatment. Thus, we have advanced a sound science on human weakness. The same approaches and types of tools used to make sense out of the presentation and experiences of mental illness can be used to highlight and measure potent elements of strengths. In the course of sharing ideas about how to tap human strengths, healthy processes, and fulfillments, we also will identify the following critical issues that should be addressed when undertaking the scholarly pursuit of optimal human functioning.

- Contextualize the examination of human strengths, healthy processes, and fulfillments.
- Balance the examination of hypotheses about strengths with testing hypotheses about weakness.
- Use/develop measurement procedures that account for the dynamics of healthy processes.
- Consider the universality of human fulfillments.

Measuring Human Strengths

Dozens of psychological strengths have been operationalized by psychologists committed to understanding the best in people. In this volume, the authors present their conceptualizations of particular human strengths, and they examine the psychometric properties and clinical utilities of observational techniques, physiological measures, scales, inventories, and interview and narrative techniques. We have asked the authors to elucidate the theoretical underpinnings of their measures and to critique their assessment strategies in light of today's stringent measurement standards. In our estimation, contributors did an excellent job of highlighting "gold standard" measures as well as assessment strategies that show promise for informing future research and practice. Whatever fuzziness in the operationalization of strengths that may have existed previously has been sharpened and clarified by our chapter authors.

Many of these measures of strengths are theoretically based, thus lending themselves to inclusion in explanatory models (such as those describing buffering processes that keep illness at bay and those models detailing how strengths facilitate healthy development). Furthermore, advancements in measurement of strength will provide the tools needed to examine the threshold effects (e.g., how much of a strength is enough to produce benefits in someone's life) and exponential effects of the positive (e.g., do four strengths combined yield more than double the beneficial effects of two strengths combined?).

Scientists conducting examinations of human strengths must be sensitive to the environmental, or contextual, influences that may determine how strength is manifested. More precisely, researchers should attempt to capture the essence of the interplay between the person and the environment (and culture). On this note, Menninger and colleagues (Menninger, Mayman, & Pruyser, 1963) stated that one measure of success in life is "the satisfactoriness to the individual and his environment of their mutual attempts to adapt themselves to each other" (p. 2).

As we are compelled to remind researchers to contextualize their examinations of strengths (i.e., how manifestations of strengths are dependent on environmental and cultural variables), we also want to remind scholars to balance any examination of the positive with consideration of the negative. That is, testing of hypotheses about human strength should be balanced by effort to test hypotheses regarding weakness.

Measuring Healthy Processes

Healthy human processes are those dynamic "means of living" that facilitate adaptation, growth, and the attainment of fulfillments. The dynamic, fluid nature of these processes render them difficult to observe and operationalize. Scholars studying coping possibly have made the most progress in developing understanding of healthy human processes, though much work is needed to harness the energy of positive processes (e.g., achieving mastery, being resilient).

Possibly scientists could incorporate the measurement tools used to elucidate the intricacies of unhealthy processes in their efforts to examine healthy processes. More likely, development and implementation of more dynamic measures of healthy processes would reveal the paths people take to attain fulfillments. For example, use of the experience sampling method (the process of collecting "in the moment" data by prompting participants via a pager or an alarm to record their mood or behavior on paper-and-pencil or computerized measures) would provide a wealth of data regarding how people deal with life events. Sociometric procedures also would generate what have been referred to as 360-degree assessments of human processes by asking members of an examinee's community (i.e., group, team, firm, neighborhood) to identify what works in a life.

Measuring Human Fulfillments

We use the phrase *human fulfillments* to refer to the aspects of the good life that many seek, such as well-being, meaningful work, love, and social connectedness. (Fulfillments exist in contrast to the "voids" of life that leave people feeling empty.) Fulfillments are quite complex in their makeup, thus rendering them difficult to operationalize. Unpacking fulfillment and the "good life" is necessary for scientific advancements because these outcomes ultimately are what we are trying to predict—fulfillments are the criterion variables of interest to positive psychologists.

The scholarly endeavor to operationalize the good life might be conceived as a noble one, yet the pursuit of definitions for good living is fraught with sociopolitical confounds. Universal fulfillments may be nonexistent, or optimal outcomes may be only subtly different across cultures. Therefore, we need to refrain from using research as a means to prescribe ways of living that possibly may be beneficial to some but detrimental to others (Lopez et al., 2002).

Despite these concerns and the complexities of defining the most positive of outcomes, this work is essential to advancing positive social science. Possibly the most meaningful fulfillment that needs attention is optimal mental health. Once we can operationalize what it is like to function optimally, we can establish it as a criterion variable of great interest to positive psychologists.

Interplay Among Positive and Negative Characteristics, Processes, and Life Outcomes

At least six dimensions need to be considered when scientifically testing hypotheses about psychological functioning. On the negative end of the continua characteristics, processes, and outcomes are represented as weaknesses, unhealthy processes, and voids. These are balanced on the positive end by strength, healthy processes, and fulfillments. We acknowledge that the foci of most research will not involve the operationalization of all six variables, yet it is important to consider how each of these variables manifests in the context of a person's environment and how each is influenced by the presence of the others. In time, talented researchers committed to advancing knowledge about optimal human functioning will have to examine the interplay of all six variables within the ever-changing context of the environment. Such research would provide practitioners with the information needed to develop more sophisticated conceptualizations of human change processes.

Positive Psychological Assessment: Toward a Complementary Focus in Practice

Practice communities have been interested in assessing human strengths for decades. Counselors and school counselors approach their work from a developmental perspective looking for the ways children successfully navigate transitions and effect changes in their lives. Some counseling psychologists subscribe to "hygiology" (Super, 1955), which emphasizes "normalities even of abnormal persons, with locating and developing personal and social resources and adaptive tendencies so that the individual can be assisted in making more effective use of them" (p. 5). Rehabilitation and health psychologists spotlight the resources needed to cope with physical changes, recover from illness, and find benefits in disability. Social workers, operating from a strengths perspective (Saleebey, 1996), value information about weakness *and* strength when making decisions about cases (Hwang & Cowger, 1998).

Professionals in these practice communities have attested to the value of capitalizing on the strengths they have identified in their clients (e.g., Saleebey, 2001; Wright & Fletcher, 1982). Nevertheless, there continue to be inherent problems with the standard assessment process. Indeed, "Two common short-comings of assessment procedures in agencies that deal with client problems and adjustment are the concentration on negative aspects of functioning, with insufficient attention to environmental aspects" (Wright & Fletcher, 1982, p. 229). The negative focus in psychology seems to perpetuate itself as researchers and practitioners enter the workforce with a negative bias. Explanations, other than tradition, for the negative emphasis include,

- Clients' presenting problems are regarded as negative; thus inferences about causes and effect also will be negative.
- Individuals detached from the situation (psychologists/counselors/social workers) are more likely to perceive more negatives in a difficult situation than the people directly affected by the situation (research participants/clients).

Environmental neglect in assessment has been addressed over the decades, yet researchers and practitioners do an inadequate job of scrutinizing the role of the environment in behavior and assessing it. This is because

- Professionals' decision making is influenced by the fundamental attribution bias.
- Professionals may justify the person's predicament by "blaming the victim."
- The person commands attention, and the environment is vague and less accessible.
- The environment is difficult to assess (see chapter 28, this volume).

Those interested in assessing human and environmental strengths and weakness have not, however, established a strategic approach to collecting data about the positive. To fill this void, we have developed the practice model of positive psychological assessment.

Figure 1.2a depicts the assessment approach that we use when working with clients. This model is based on Pepinsky and Pepinsky's (1954) view of counselor-as-scientist and Spengler, Strohmer, Dixon, and Shiva's (1995) scientist practitioner model of psychological assessment that is described as a "cognitive map" for practitioners engaging in the assessment process. Similarly, we encourage readers to walk through the model, or map, as we describe each aspect of it. Note that the headings in this section of the chapter correspond to steps of our approach. The first two steps make up the first phase of the approach, during which the practitioners set the stage for a comprehensive, scientific assessment by reexamining the experiences, values, biases, and assumptions (collectively referred to as the prerequisite attitudes and assumptions) that will influence the assessment process. The ongoing, cyclical process of assessment is the second phase of the approach, and it comprises numerous

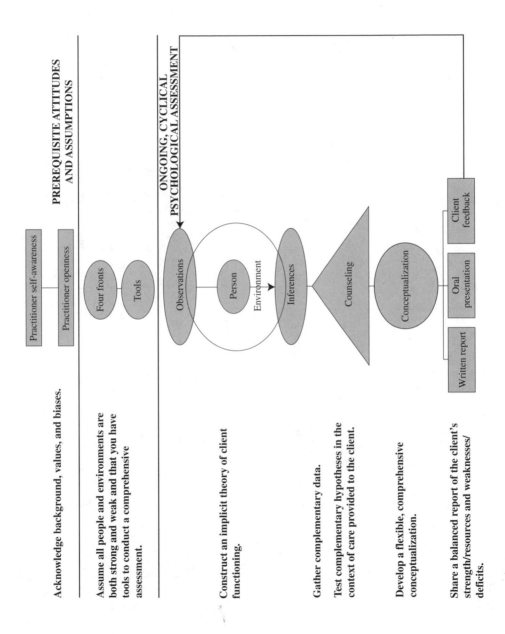

Figure 1.2a. The practice model of positive psychological assessment.

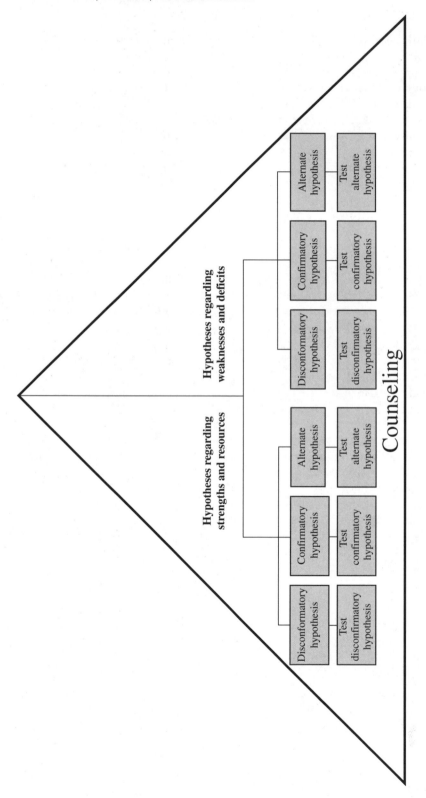

Figure 1.2b. Testing hypotheses in the context of counseling.

steps associated with developing a greater understanding of the client and his or her change process during the course of counseling.

The unique aspects of our model are the focus on complementary hypotheses (on strength and weakness); the attention paid to the environmental influences on client functioning; the framework for collecting balanced, comprehensive client data; and the fact-checking facilitated by sharing balanced data with clients and colleagues. This model also presents counseling and assessment processes as intricately intertwined. The open, flexible, and self-correcting quality of the approach is not unique. (See Spengler et al., 1995, for a model with similar flexibility.)

Acknowledge Background, Values, and Biases

As established in the beginning of this chapter, experiences influence what is seen. Personal background, values developed over a lifetime, and the biases that are part of all decision-making processes serve as the filters for the information gathered when working with clients. Acknowledging how background, values, and biases affect the assessment process is a goal that all practitioners should pursue. Neutralizing or de-biasing the effects of personal experiences and attitudes may serve as an aspirational goal, but it is important to note that we believe all assessments to be inherently flawed. This makes the self-correcting nature of this model valuable.

As local clinical scientists (Stricker & Trierweiler, 1995) or counselors-as-scientists (Pepinsky & Pepinsky, 1954), we are open to all explanations for behavior. In effect, we consider the simplest explanations for the most complex behaviors and the most complex explanations for the simplest of behaviors and everything in between. Values and biases that could influence assessment of behavior are made explicit, and implicit theories about personality are more thoroughly operationalized.

Assume All People and Environments Are Both Strong and Weak and That You Have Tools to Conduct a Comprehensive Assessment

Developing a complementary focus in practice requires practitioners to have particular beliefs and an awareness of professional resources. Specifically, practitioners must assume that all people and environments are both strong and weak. The reason for the assumption is simple: People only search for things they believe to exist.

Regarding awareness of resources, we hope that by the end of this volume readers are convinced that the practice community is well-equipped with tools designed to detect the best in people. Combining these tools with the tools used for detecting pathology would make it possible to conduct a balanced, comprehensive assessment.

Construct an Implicit Theory of Client Functioning

The assessment process begins the moment a practitioner sees a client's name on a schedule. From this data, guesses about sex and ethnicity are made.

Review of intake paperwork yields data that may influence, to some extent, the approach in the first session. These data along with observations of the client's behavior (as positively and negatively affected by the environment) serve as the initial layers of a multilayered, implicit theory of client functioning—a theory that reflects the unconscious, unsubstantiated assumptions about the client's functioning.

Constructing an implicit theory requires practitioners to make observations of the client in the context of the client's environment. Most practitioners do not interact with clients in their homes, schools, or workplaces; however, they do have the capacity to contextualize the client's presentation (determine how the client's functioning is dependent on environmental and cultural variables). Thus, as the model depicts, the practitioners make observations about how the client functions in his or her environment. To do this, practitioners must transcend the boundary of the client's context so that they can become more sensitive to the client's experience of the world.

Contextualizing inferences about a client's psychological status and capacity for change is the next focus in the construction of an implicit theory. These inferences should be focused on all domains of variables that are associated with client functioning. Making inferences along four fronts and gathering data along these fronts are essential aspects of constructing an implicit theory.

Wright's (1991; Wright & Lopez, 2002) four-front approach serves as the data-gathering and organizing method central to positive psychological assessment in practice situations. Practitioners' efforts to make meaningful observations of client status and propensity for growth is initiated by and organized by: (a) identifying undermining characteristics of the client, (b) identifying the client's strengths and assets, (c) identifying lacks and destructive factors in the environment, and (d) identifying resources and opportunities in the environment. Practitioners facilitate this approach by garnering responses to four questions: (a) What deficiencies does the person contribute to his or her problems? (b) What strengths does the person bring to deal effectively with his or her life? (c) What environmental factors serve as impediments to healthy functioning? (d) What environmental resources accentuate positive human functioning? Practitioners informally gathering data along the four fronts tend to generate a more complex set of inferences that ultimately evolve into formal clinical hypotheses to be tested directly.

Gather Complementary Data

Though strict adherence to scientific methodology would preclude the collection of formal data before clearly stating hypotheses, clinical work involves a process that is less of a lock-step approach and more of a simultaneous unfolding of multiple steps. Indeed, we believe that inferences are drawn from clinical data and an implicit theory about client functioning takes shape. Then, the creation of this theory triggers strategic and formal data collection efforts along the four fronts. Though these efforts at data gathering may not be directly linked to specific hypotheses at the onset, implicit views of clients become more explicit over time (possibly over the course of one session) and formal hypotheses (and disconfirmatory and alternative versions of these hypotheses) are refined and are tested directly (discussed in the section "Testing Complementary Hypotheses").

Strategic collection of complementary data involves using standard methods of detecting weakness (semistructured interviews, symptom checklists, objective and projective personality measures), and novel means of seeking out strengths. Also, a balanced, complementary approach to data collection would involve the identification of environmental resources and deficits. Because the detection of human weakness is the topic of most other assessment books, formal measures of strengths are presented throughout this volume, and environmental assessment is addressed in chapter 29, we will limit our subsequent discussion to the informal assessment of strengths.

"What Are Your Strengths?" and Beyond: Informal Means of Detecting Human Strengths

Wright and Fletcher (1982) noted that practitioners distort reality when they identify only problems without uncovering the positives in clients. In other words, practitioners should strive to uncover strengths along with problems when interviewing clients. Saleebey (1996) argued that all people possess strengths that can be extracted to improve the quality of their lives. In addition, focusing on client strengths help practitioners and clients discover how clients have managed to survive in even the most inhospitable environments and situations. Finally, Saleebey noted that all environments and clients contain resources; practitioners who engage in collaborative exploration with their clients can discover these strengths.

Unfortunately, few refined protocols for uncovering strengths via interviews are available. Instead, there has been a focus on diagnostic interviewing using pathology, treatment, medical, and dysfunction metaphors (Cowger, 1997). In the past decade, however, attempts have been made to focus on positive aspects of people rather than deficiencies.

Cowger (1997) emphasized the need to make assessment of clients and their strengths multidimensional. The focus of the interview should be on uncovering the client's external strengths as well as internal strengths. External strengths may include resources such as family networks, significant others, and community or church groups. The client's internal strengths may include psychological factors such as motivation, coping, and cognitive resources.

De Jong and Miller (1995) suggested using solution-focused interviewing (de Shazer, 1988) to uncover the strengths in clients. They stated that interviewing for solutions helps clients develop (a) well-formed, realistic goals that seek the presence of something rather than the absence and (b) solutions based on exceptions. Exceptions are "those occasions in the client's life when the client's problem could have occurred but did not" (De Jong & Miller, 1995, p. 729). The practitioner seeking out exceptions asks about the client's present and past successes in relation to the goals they have set to achieve through counseling. Once the exceptions are discovered, the practitioner attempts to clarify the contributions that the client made for the exception to occur. After the practitioner and client uncover an exception, along with the client's strengths, the practitioner aids the client in affirming and amplifying the strengths. The intended consequence of interviewing for strengths is empowerment of the client (De Jong & Miller, 1995; Saleebey, 1996). Thus, hope is stimulated as clients discover that they can create their own solutions and construct more satisfying lives. (A similar approach is used by the Wolins, 2001, in their work with adolescents.)

Test Complementary Hypotheses in the Context of Counseling

Facets of the implicit model of client functioning serve as the foundation for hypotheses to be tested during counseling. In the practice model of positive psychological assessment, the practitioner should generate parallel hypotheses addressing both strengths and resources and weaknesses and deficits. Moreover, practitioners should use a multiple-hypothesis testing strategy to ensure that she or he is considering all explanations for clinical presentations and life circumstances.

To clarify how this balanced, scientific approach to clinical data may unfold, consider the common initial presentation of a client who is "feeling blue." Of course, despite this being a common presenting complaint, the subtleties of each individual's experience of sadness needs to be carefully considered. Thus, information would be gathered about how symptoms developed and how severe the sadness is day to day. A parallel observation may involve a client's social well-being (i.e., the client has meaningful social interactions irrespective of how he or she is feeling). Both the "sadness" and the "doing well socially" hypotheses need to be put to the test during counseling sessions. Use of a multiple-hypothesis testing strategy (see Figure 1.2b for a detailed breakdown of what occurs during the "counseling" phase of the practice model of positive psychological assessement) would involve being open to and recording data that confirm and disconfirm the hypotheses. Furthermore, the possibility of alternative explanations of the client's mood or level of well-being need to be considered (i.e., alternative hypotheses have to be tested as well). By engaging in the scientific examination of hypotheses about strengths and weaknesses, practitioners can increase the possibility that unbiased, balanced determinations about psychological functioning are being made.

Develop a Flexible, Comprehensive Conceptualization

The scientific examination of complementary hypotheses generates a tremendous amount of data that needs to be organized, analyzed, and interpreted by the practitioner. Sifting through these data is made easier when the practitioner envisions the assessment process as cyclical and self-correcting. There is no "right" answer, but the goal of the process is to develop a conceptualization of how the client's strengths and weaknesses reverberate and contribute to psychological status.

Constructing this flexible, comprehensive conceptualization requires the practitioner to guard against bias entering their decision-making processes. Furthermore, metacognition functions as the scale that balances the information about human strength and human weakness that is incorporated into the working client model. Flexibility and comprehensiveness of the conceptualization are maintained over time by adding clinical information to the scale.

In addition, we believe that a conceptualization is incomplete if it is not accompanied by recommendations for counseling and change tailored for the client. Indeed, balanced descriptions of people still fall flat if they are not associated with relevant, meaningful suggestions for changing and growing.

Share a Balanced Report of the Client's Strengths / Resources and Weaknesses / Deficits

Fact-checking the information in the working model of a client is facilitated by sharing that information with others. This sharing occurs in different ways, including written reports, case presentations with colleagues, and feedback to the client.

Communicating with colleagues and people who provide support and care to the client can provide invaluable information that can enhance the accuracy of the conceptualization. Also, the conceptualization can become a cognitive map for others working directly with the client—it is hoped that this would result in support that is more sensitive to the needs of a client.

Information about client functioning often has been cloaked in psychological jargon and somewhat hidden from the client. In our approach to assessment, client opinions about the evolving conceptualization are gathered so that continued assessment can be refined by incorporating hypotheses pertinent to the client. Including the client's opinion establishes that his or her views on change are valued and that he or she is expected to be an active self-healer. (Guidelines for the feedback session of the therapeutic assessment model [Finn & Tonsager, 1997] also should be considered. The feedback rule of "equal space, equal time, equal emphasis" should be followed when sharing assessment information with clients, members of the clients' support systems, fellow practitioners, and mental health agencies and related organizations.)

Equal Space, Equal Time, Equal Emphasis

Wright (1991; Wright & Lopez, 2002) recommended that practitioners abide by the rule of giving equal space and equal time to the presentation of strengths and weaknesses (hence equal emphasis). It is important to remember to follow the rule of equal space and equal time when reporting client information.

When writing progress notes or other reports, it is important to convey a comprehensive view of the client. This comprehensive, balanced report can be constructed by giving equal space to clients' strengths and resources and weaknesses and deficits. An aspirational goal related to this end might involve devoting half of the clinical-impressions section of a report to psychological weaknesses and half to psychological strengths. For example, if the practitioner is accustomed to writing four-page reports—with one page addressing background information, one page presenting test results, and two pages describing clinical impressions and recommendations (i.e., the flexible, comprehensive conceptualization)—half of the last two pages of information should address client strengths and resources. Accordingly, if a practitioner is in the habit of writing one-page progress notes, half of the page should be devoted to the discussion of strengths and resources and how these can be used to promote change.

Though equal space in a report or progress note is considered the ideal within our model of assessment, we have realized through our clinical work and training of graduate students that initial "best practice" of this rule may involve appending a "strengths" section to a report or note. We consider this a step in the desired direction, but we encourage practitioners to build habits that lead them toward the reality of balancing the conceptualization of a client.

Similarly, equal time can be given to strengths and weaknesses when presenting cases to colleagues. If a practitioner has a five-minute presentation to give to clinical staff, a balanced presentation is the goal—allotting time to both strength and resources. When developing this habit, practitioners might experiment with the process by presenting strengths then weaknesses at one meeting, and then weaknesses then strengths at the next. Does the staff respond differently to reporting of strengths first? Do they offer different feedback depending on the initial focus? This may demonstrate the power of anchoring effects of information.

Another important part of any psychological assessment process is reporting test results to clients. Throughout this chapter, we have emphasized the need for psychologists to strive for a more balanced assessment of their clients; thus, test feedback offered to clients also must be balanced. At this time, however, there is a dearth of information about reporting test results to clients from a balanced strengths–deficiencies perspective. Drummond (1988) suggested that practitioners should emphasize the strengths in the test data while objectively reporting weaknesses. Hood and Johnson (1991) recommended discussing the test results in light of other information, including environmental resources and impediments. Finally, Drummond suggested that the practitioner should collaborate with the client to identify other information that supports or fails to support the test data. By actively involving the client in the feedback session, the practitioner and the client can work together to refine the conceptualization. The client's role of active self-healer could be reinforced and, by additional engagement in conceptualizing the functioning and counseling needs, a client could positively influence the ongoing process.

Balance of Struggles and Triumphs

As clients encounter struggles and triumphs when making efforts to change, so will practitioners trying to adopt a new approach to psychological assessment. The struggles may occur when practitioners try to break out of a habit of assessing pathology rather than all aspects of client functioning. Triumphs may be as simple as a client responding to a question with, "What are my strengths? . . . I have never been asked that before."

Aspiring to Strike a Vital Balance

The evolution of positive psychological science is predicated on sound measurement of strengths, healthy processes, and fulfillments. The vital balance in research can be achieved by developing diverse means of measuring positive aspects of the human experience.

The model of positive psychological assessment provides a cognitive map that can be followed to detect strengths and resources of all clients. Furthermore, the scientific approach provides de-biasing techniques that result in hypothesis testing, which in turn reveals meaningful findings. These findings, organized as a conceptualization, are shared with colleagues and the client, and feedback and subsequent interactions with the client serve to enhance the conceptualization.

Despite the benefits of the model, following the cognitive map through the steps of this model does not lead practitioners to a panacea. In fact, using the model may demonstrate that the assessment process is out of balance in other ways that need to be addressed.

Reconciling Subjective Experience With Collateral Reports

Some practitioners have steered clear of contacting collateral sources (such as family and friends) of client information. By neglecting collateral information we are unable to reconcile a client's subjective experience and report with how they are experienced by others in their work or relationships. Data from collateral sources would enhance the accuracy and external validity of the conceptualization and increase the internal validity of an assessment.

Diversifying Measurement Approaches

Paper-and-pencil measures are the primary means of data collection in positive psychology research and practice, and our reliance on this staid approach to measurement needs to be addressed. Structured interviews for strengths are sorely needed. Furthermore, existing measures need to be validated for use with all large ethnic groups in the United States—and any other group that serves as participants in positive psychological research.

The staid view of mental illness as progressive and refractory was challenged by Karl Menninger (Menninger et al., 1963) in the book *The Vital Balance*. Menninger and colleagues called for psychiatrists to view mental illness as amenable to change—thus this new view of mental illness would bring the old into balance. We call for a different type of balance—a balanced view of human life that puts weakness and strength in perspective.

References

Cowger, C. D. (1997). Assessment of client strengths. In D. Saleebey (Ed.), *The strengths perspective in social work practice* (pp. 139–147). New York: Longman.

De Jong, P., & Miller, S. D. (1995). How to interview for client strengths. *Social Work, 40*, 729–726.

de Shazer, S. (1988). *Clues: Investigating solutions in brief therapy*. New York: W. W. Norton.

Drummond, R. J. (1988). *Appraisal procedures for counselors and helping professionals*. Columbus, OH: Merrill.

Finn, S. E., & Tonsager, M. E. (1997). Information-gathering and therapeutic models of assessment: Complementary paradigms. *Psychological Assessment, 9*, 374–385.

Hood, A. B., & Johnson, R. W. (1991). *Assessment in counseling: A guide to the use of psychological assessment procedures*. Alexandria, VA: American Association for Counseling and Development.

Hwang, S-C., & Cowger, C. D. (1998). Utilizing strengths in assessment. *Families in society: The Journal of Contemporary Human Services, 79*, 25–31.

Lopez, S. J., Prosser, E., Edwards, L. M., Magyar-Moe, J. L., Neufeld, J., et al. (2002). Putting positive psychology in a multicultural perspective. In C. R. Snyder & S. J. Lopez (Eds.), *The handbook of positive psychology* (pp. 700–714). New York: Oxford.

Menninger, K., Mayman, M., & Pruyser, P. W. (1963). *The vital balance*. New York: Viking Press.

Pepinsky, H. B., & Pepinsky, N. (1954). *Counseling theory and practice*. New York: Ronald Press.

Saleebey, D. (1996). *A strengths perspective in social work practice* (2nd ed.). White Plains, NY: Longman.

Saleebey, D. (2001). The diagnostic strengths manual? *Social Work, 46*, 183–187.

Salovey, P., Rothman, A. J., Detweiler, J. B., & Steward, W. T. (2000). Emotional states and physical health. *American Psychologist, 55*, 110–121.

Schimmel, S. (2000). Vices, virtues and sources of human strength in historical perspective. *Journal of Social and Clinical Psychology, 19*, 137–150.

Seligman, M. E. P. (1998). Optimism: The difference it makes. *Science and Spirit, 9*, 6 & 19.

Snyder, C. R., & Lopez, S. J. (Eds.). (2002). *The handbook of positive psychology*. New York: Oxford University Press.

Snyder, C. R., & McCullough, M. E. (2000). A positive psychology field of dreams: "If you build it, they will come . . ." *Journal of Social and Clinical Psychology, 19*, 151–160.

Spengler, P. M., Strohmer, D. C. Dixon, D. N., & Shiva, V. A. (1995). A scientist-practitioner model of psychological assessment: Implications for training, practice and research. *Counseling Psychologist, 23*, 506–534.

Stricker, G., & Trierweiler, S. J. (1995). The local scientist: A bridge between science and practice. *American Psychologist, 50*, 995–1002.

Super, D. E. (1955). Transition: From vocational guidance to counseling psychology. *Journal of Counseling Psychology, 2*, 3–9.

Taylor, S. E., & Brown, J. D. (1988). Illusion and well-being: A social psychological perspective on mental health. *Psychological Bulletin, 103*, 193–210.

Wolin, S., & Wolin, S. (2001). Project Reselience, available May 2001 at www.Projectresilience.com

Wright, B. A. (1991). Labeling: The need for greater person-environmental individuation. In C. R. Snyder & D. R. Forsyth (Eds.), *Handbook of social and clinical psychology: The health perspective* (pp. 416–437). New York: Pergamon Press.

Wright, B. A., & Fletcher, B. L. (1982). Uncovering hidden resources: A challenge in assessment. *Professional Psychology, 13*, 229–235.

Wright, B. A., & Lopez, S. J. (2002). Widening the diagnostic focus: A case for including human strengths and environmental resources. In C. R. Snyder & S. J. Lopez (Eds.), *Handbook of positive psychology* (pp. 26–44). New York: Oxford University Press.

2

Measuring and Labeling the Positive and the Negative

C. R. Snyder, Shane J. Lopez, Lisa M. Edwards,
Jennifer Teramoto Pedrotti, Ellie C. Prosser,
Stephanie LaRue Walton, Susan Vehige Spalitto,
and Jon C. Ulven

As long as we have applied labels to each other, we probably have spoken of the degrees to which people have more or less of the characteristics reflected in those labels. This became more formal, however, when capitalism began to take root in Great Britain around the 19th century (Buss & Poley, 1976). With the need to quantify the prices of products for ease of sale, so too was there a need to attach value to different human skills or efforts. Work was divided into units, and value was attached to those units. Measurement thus allowed for trading, commerce, and the ensuing placement of value on everything— including what people did. The historical extreme to this process was servitude and slavery, wherein the entire person was priced and sold in a manner similar to that for other "commodities."

What happens when a person's worth is charted by using a pejorative term rather than a positive descriptor? The stakes are very high in regard to labeling and measuring people. In this chapter, we present our views on the inherent power and problems in the process of labeling (i.e., naming a person according to a characteristic) and measuring (i.e., identifying the degree to which a person possesses that characteristic). In the last portion of the chapter, we present an alternative—called the balanced dimension approach—to the pathology model for describing people. We also describe numerous modifications to the current diagnostic system and other small changes that all clinicians can make.

The Power in a Name

Why are we so impressed with something that is labeled? In this section, we will suggest that labels provide a heuristic communication device. In addition, by labeling we seemingly are gaining a better understanding of the targeted object or person.

Utility

A name provides a means for two or more people to communicate readily about the "named" entity. That is to say, a name is a symbol whose meaning lies in its utility to promote discourse. When applied to humans, such labels represent a shorthand means of conveying an assumed shared meaning. In turn, the term and its meaning shape such interchanges.

Unfortunately, we often assume that others hold the same definition for the label as we do. In reality, however, there are substantial variabilities in meanings that are ascribed to the same terms. (Ask 20 mental health workers, for example, to define the label "at risk," and you will get 20 different responses.) Undaunted or perhaps oblivious to this caveat, we nevertheless are likely to assume that others share our meanings.

In the applied arena, labels serve a gate-keeping role. A child must be labeled to receive "special" educational services, and a client must receive a label for the mental health professional to obtain reimbursement from third parties. Using labels as pathways to resources and treatment ascribes a power to a contrived name that is then reinforced by social institutions.

Psychological labels also form the lexicon wherein mental health professionals talk with each other. Moreover, terms that once were only in psychology textbooks are now common fare in popular magazines and everyday language. These terms believed to be rife with descriptive value often become watered-down versions of their former selves—"language light."

Understanding

One of the powers in naming something is that it facilitates our belief that we "understand" it. This is a slippery slope, however, because a name has only a surface reality and, as noted previously, others may not share our meaning. In its most fundamental sense, a name only initiates the process of understanding that which is labeled. More specifically, when something is given a name, we are explicitly placing it in a category of entities that differ from other categories and their associated entities. In a scientific sense, a label is part of a classification scheme that facilitates the investigation of additional, in-depth knowledge (e.g., the periodic table helps us to understand the distinctiveness of each of the chemical elements, and it highlights the nature of the elements' properties). Thus, scientists use names cautiously until they believe that some depth of understanding has been obtained after repeated empirical inquiries.

In our applications of labels to human beings, however, the tendency is to perceive that the named person is highly understood—more so than probably is warranted. In other words, by using a label, the protagonist often assumes that the name carries with it "deep" meaning. At best, however, such labels may only serve to differentiate the labeled person from others; even that premise, however, may be questionable when carefully scrutinized (see Wright & Lopez, 2002, for a discussion of de-individuation associated with labeling). For example, consider how the label "depressed" is used in practice parlance as well as in scholarly work. How often do we use the term with precision? When we describe a client as depressed we evoke thoughts of major depressive disorder, dysthymia, adjustment disorder, or bereavement—when the person may just be "feeling blue" and not experiencing any disorder. Our casual use of labels is commonplace in social science as well. For example, consider researchers who refer to their "depressed" samples, which are made up of individuals who have scored higher than a particular cutoff on a screening measure.

Another problem with rigid labels is that they tend to preclude the gathering of any subsequent "evidence" that is not consistent with the previously ascribed meaning for the label (Salovey & Turk, 1991). Given the seemingly "deep knowledge" already signified by one's being able to label another person, the label user may perceive little need to gather additional information.

In summary, labels always have represented shorthand phrases for conveying our understanding of others. Labels help sustain our illusions that we comprehend other people and can convey that knowledge in a facile manner. In truth, the potency of our language is decreasing as we use it with less and less precision. When a person conveys thoughts about another person, the ability to use the language in a full and exact manner—with a minimum of labels as verbal shortcuts—creates a complete understanding. Ironically, the trend seems to be toward the simplifying of spoken and written language, with labels taking on even greater power as they supplant phrases and entire sentences of vivid and precise description.

The Power in Measuring

If we are impressed with something that is labeled, we are even more impressed when some sort of measurement metric is attached to that named entity. In this section, we will describe how the measuring process augments the labeling process.

Utility

Rarely does the labeling process stop once a name has been applied to a person. Consider the following interchange between two people:

> **Person A:** Do you know Jack Epstein?
> **Person B:** No . . . I haven't met him.
> **Person A:** Well, believe me . . . he is a world-class liar!

In this example, we learn that Person A is not content with the pejorative label of "liar," and instead must add measurement information about the degree or extremity—in other words, "world-class." By applying such degree or qualifying information to a label, Person A is providing input that may be of use to Person B. That is to say, by knowing that Jack Epstein is a world-class liar, Person B may be better prepared to interact with Mr. Epstein.

If one is mired in the pathology or weakness model, the measurement information further clarifies how "bad" a person may be. Thus, within the weakness perspective, measurement allows only differentiating information about the degree of negativeness.

Understanding

Labels reach their greatest power when used in degrees. There supposedly is more communicative information when the label carries a qualifier. The users of such degree-based labels thereby perceive that they are discoursing at a refined level, one that carries a metric of precision that does not exist. For example, users of the *DSM-IV* (American Psychiatric Association, 1994) label people to two decimal places. Furthermore, once such a measurement device (e.g., a scale, a categorical system such as the *DSM-IV*, etc.) becomes available and recognized in a field, more professionals are likely to use that device, thereby enhancing its power. This is called instrument-driven usage. Because we readily can apply psychological instruments to measure some human characteristic, there is the potential for producing huge amounts of relatively vacuous research findings. In turn, the users of such instruments become even more enamored of the power of "their" instruments to yield precise measurements and insights about people. This can lead to an acceptance of measurements, without consideration of their scientific underpinnings. Whether we are measuring human weaknesses or strengths, the validity of our instruments must be scrutinized.

The Mismeasurement of Humans?

In our discussion to this point, we have presented disclaimers about the use of measurement-based labels as applied to people. We are not so naive, however, as to suggest that measurement-based labels can or should be eliminated. They simply are far too important for interpersonal commerce—both at the personal and professional levels. Our point, however, is that we need to be mindful of the various problems that are associated with measurement-based labels (and subsequently we argue that names and distinctions can be used to promote growth). They represent a form of categorizing and measuring that is filled with inaccuracies and imprecision. On this latter point, the measurement-based labeling of people always may be an inexact process, filled with "error variance."

The Obvious Limits of Diagnostic Systems

Ironies abound in the diagnostic systems that currently are part of the mental health field. Consider that our complex diagnostic systems, with the *DSM* representing the crown jewel, are not very reliable (see Garb, 1998, for a related discussion of lack of veracity in clinical judgment). As any expert in measurement will attest, without reliability, everything else about a measure is rendered suspect. Lack of reliability is not the only problem, however. Our diagnostic systems also are not well-validated. They often have reflected the ideas of the test constructors more so than a meaningful taxonomy for the characteristics of the people whom we seek to help.

The Myth of Diagnostic Meaningfulness

In health care, the label is meant to specify the problem. We even elevate this labeling process by giving it a special name: We are diagnosing. Perhaps the capstone of myths, however, is that our diagnoses really dictate our treatments. Unfortunately, this typically is not true. At best, there is a modest relationship between diagnoses and the subsequent treatments (Snyder & Ingram, 2000). It is as if clinical researchers each are pursuing their own interests without attending to the connections between their work. Small wonder then that our graduate students complain about seeing little relationship between their diagnostic and treatment training.[1]

The facts that our labels (otherwise known as diagnoses) are lacking in reliability and validity, and that they are not related to treatments, produces a collaborative illusion. On this point, we should not place the responsibility for this on practitioners, because they are doing that for which they were trained; in turn, the educators are conveying that which the researchers have suggested.

To the mismeasurements that we have described so far in this section, we must add yet another very troubling one. Why is it that we have focused in the mental health professions on the labeling of human weaknesses? At this point, the reader may be thinking, "Of course we have focused on weaknesses . . . people bring us their problems." It is true that people come to us with "repair" in mind. We also have been educated about diagnosing such problems from particular perspectives. But do these weaknesses need to dictate our helping actions? Is something fundamental being missed here? We think so. Surely we are guilty of yet another mismeasurement in that we have left out half of the human repertoire—*that which entails the strengths of people.*

The Potential Effects of Being Named and Measured

In today's education and mental health care systems, and society more broadly, we focus on labeling behaviors that are troublesome to us. Furthermore, because we sometimes label others to distance ourselves from them, names may carry negative connotations and be stigmatizing.

What happens to the person who is named and measured? Does a label really make much of a difference in the life of that person? To answer yes, it does matter would be an understatement. Thus, in considering this issue, we have not tackled some esoteric phenomenon that is of interest only to a few academicians. Rather, how we are labeled and measured guides the way that we are treated by powerful *other* people, how we come to see ourselves, and

---

[1]In fairness, however, credit should be given to the behaviorally trained mental health professionals. Their measurements are valid and closely tied to the actual treatments.

how we conduct our lives. It is this power to limit human potential that we will discuss next.

Labels and Self-Fulfilling Prophecy

Consider the well-known self-fulfilling prophecy notion as introduced by sociologist Robert Merton (1957) and refined by psychologist Robert Rosenthal (Rosenthal & Jacobson, 1968). The major emphasis in the self-fulfilling prophecy literature has been on how the perceiver treats the target of the perception. For example, an eighth-grade teacher perceives that boys are better at math than girls. Therefore, in math class and study sessions, the teacher spends less time with the girls. With the relatively greater attention and instruction, the boys then do better than the girls on math examinations. The girls in this example do not get their fair share of encouragement or instruction from the teacher. This all happens because the teacher has labeled the boys as being "very capable" in math, whereas the girls are "not very capable." To compound matters, the teacher probably is unaware of his or her differential behaviors toward the students.

The aforementioned description of the effect of labeling in the self-fulfilling prophecy is the standard approach to describing the dynamics of how the students' behaviors are shaped. A far less explored aspect of this self-fulfilling prophecy, however, involves the people who are the objects of the labeling— the eighth-grade boys and girls in this math example. With repeated treatments by the teachers as being either "smart" or "dumb" in math, the students come to see themselves in a mirror-like manner. They internalize the labels, and those labels influence their motivations and actions. In this sense, the labels have unleashed their full power in shaping both how the teacher treats the students and *how the students' self views drive their own efforts.*

The math example, along with similar ones, may be played out thousands of times daily. What makes such labeling even more troublesome is that the particular instantiations are happening in addition to, or on top of, other ongoing societal prejudices. With prejudice there are different rules and behaviors exhibited toward some subset of labeled people.

Generating Isms

The prejudices and the related "isms" (ageism, racism, sexism) operate via focusing on some dimension of personhood and thereafter ascribing different behaviors to identified subsets of those people. For example, the dimension of age can produce the prejudicial label of "old-timer" to signify older adults as being out of touch with the latest advances, and therefore somehow less capable of working and living in modern times. Thus, the prejudicial name leads to a discourse that potentially is damaging and casts the named person as someone who is less in terms of rights, freedoms, responsibilities, and powers. Once named, the target of that prejudicial naming is constrained in what she or he can do; moreover, that person is not allowed to play the game of life on a level playing field (Snyder & Feldman, 2000). The tragedy in such labeling is that a person can become stuck, unable to escape the powerful grip of the label in determining aspects of life. With the isms, for example, think of the enormous loss of talent when subgroups of the population are told *and come to believe* that they cannot do certain things.

Labeling and measuring processes have huge implications for people in general, and the professionals and clients of the mental health field in particular. Given the many caveats and concerns with the diagnostic system as it presently operates in the United States, what can be done? It is not enough to merely criticize without also offering some possible solutions. In the remaining portion of this chapter, we offer such solutions.

Reclaiming the Power of Labels and Measurement

Strategic attempts to identify and describe in detail are part of every science, and only in psychological science (and the related field of mental health practice) does labeling and measurement carry bad reputations and negative connotations. This was not always the case. In fact, it is a relatively new phenomenon. Early forms of assessment used by the Chinese empire in 2200 BC served as tools of selection for civil service jobs—in that case labeling simply was characterized as a means to an end. Alfred Binet, following centuries of European scientists' misguided efforts to categorize individuals according to intellect, used formal assessment methods to identify children who could benefit from remedial education; it was his successors who applied the scales universally, in an almost side-show manner, to differentiate among groups for the sake of doing so. Then, at some point in the 20th century, labeling and measurement became associated with the identification of ills and deficiencies, and stigmatization's association with psychology labels became more pronounced. It is time to destigmatize the labeling and measurement processes, and to reclaim their positive, enabling powers.

The Power of Naming and Expanding Our Categories of Human Strengths

When we give salience to a human strength by explicitly naming it, we are suggesting to the named person, and to those in the surrounding environment, that there is merit in this identified characteristic. It is something to be valued for both its intrinsic and extrinsic worth. On this point, we would suggest that the usual individualistic categories of meritorious behavior—achievements in academics and sports—are worthy of our attention. Perhaps more important, however, the communal human characteristics that make society more livable—courtesy, helping, sharing, humility, honesty, compassion, forgiveness, gratitude, and love—need to be singled out for our praise. By our attending to these latter characteristics in our children and our fellow adults (including our research participants and clients), we are suggesting that such virtues really do matter (McCullough & Snyder, 2000). As may be apparent in our suggestions in this paragraph, we are arguing that our individualistic American categories for praise (e.g., personal achievements) need to be augmented by a wider range of communal activities (see Snyder & Feldman, 2000).

The Power of Identifying the Best of the Best

In American education, with programs such as Head Start, the desire has been to give extra bolstering experiences to those young people who have been identified as disadvantaged in terms of their cognitive–intellectual functioning. Unfortunately, there has been a tendency to not want to give enriched experiences to those students who are labeled as intellectually or creatively endowed or gifted. Although there are programs for such children, the efforts on their behalf are small in comparison to those aimed at other students. The unspoken logic is that the talented students already can excel in our society, and therefore do not need extra benefits.

Whether it is in the context of school or elsewhere, we would suggest that those young people who are especially talented are natural resources for all of society. As such, it benefits all of us to foster the stretching of the talents of these youngsters. As we have learned (e.g., see Terman & Oden, 1947), the youth who are gifted are especially likely to make significant contributions in business, science, and academics in general. Furthermore, it is the case that the major contributions in science are made by people very early in their careers (Snyder & Fromkin, 1980). Accordingly, it makes sense to give extra stimulation to talented children, and to do so as early as is possible. We would suggest that we, as a society, should raise the bar for all students, that the special and unique talents of each child be nurtured, and that we use positive labels identifying the assets of children.

Balanced Dimensioning of Humans

To this point, we merely have hinted at a different approach to the naming and measurement process in the mental health profession. In this section, we unveil this alternative approach and consider how it may represent an improvement over the previous paradigm.

Assumptions

We begin with two foundational premises. First, we strongly believe that normality and abnormality are not constructs that apply *only to certain* people (Barone, Maddux, & Snyder, 1997). Rather, the processes that underlie adaptive and maladaptive functioning are the same for all people. Indeed, maladaptive and adaptive do not yield differences in kind but rather differences of degree (Maddux, 1993a).

Second, we reject the premise that the diagnostic process involves the identification of surface symptoms for the underlying diseases. We believe that the pathology model predisposes the helper to make errors in the subsequent gathering of information, as well as in making clinical decisions (Maddux,

1993b; Salovey & Turk, 1991). For example, the weakness model leads helpers into conceptual flowcharts wherein all options lead to "degree of pathology" inferences.

Dimensioning

We suggest a *dimensioning* approach to the labeling and measuring process. Instead of categories with inclusion/noninclusion criteria as typifies the pathology perspective, we advocate the use of those individual difference dimensions that appear to give a thorough coverage and overview of the specific person. Each individual differences dimension would range from one end of a continuum reflecting very low to very high levels. Various dimensions differ conceptually, but often may be correlated. We already have charted many of these individual difference dimensions, but there is more to be done in terms of adding new ones.

Some might argue that this suggested approach amounts to adding positive poles to previously pure pathology conceptualizations; however, we believe that it does not. As the pathology model presently operates, the closest that the diagnostician can come to reporting strength in a client is to note that "no pathologies were evident." Even when such a phrase is used, however, the diagnostician may intimate that the client was "covering up," "faking good," or that the instruments "may not have been sensitive to his particular symptom manifestation of the underlying pathology." (We have seen these phrases mentioned in actual reports.)

Considering various dimensions reveals to professionals that a person can display one or more strengths. This alone would force the diagnostician to consider these strengths. Remember, the pathology model does not allow any strengths to appear in the diagnostic process, and instead builds the diagnostic report on the basis of degree of pathology. Conceptualizing characteristics along dimensions also forces the diagnostician into using multiple inputs when forming ideas about a client. Rarely do people fit into neat categories anyway, and with dimensions the practitioner can use several applicable axes to fully chart the client's characteristics. Dimensions thus free the diagnostician to tailor assessment for the individual.

Balanced Dimensions

We suggest that all dimensions would have the inherent capability of yielding information that varies in content from maladaptive to adaptive. Admittedly, however, people often come to mental health professionals because of one or more problems that are no longer manageable for them. Therefore, the initial set may be a weakness. In our proposed approach, the diagnostician in such an instance would select several dimensions that seem to bear on the problem. In addition, however, the helper would ask the client about his or her personal strengths. On hearing these, the diagnostician would add dimensions to tap into those strengths. Such assets not only would help to form a more complete diagnostic impression of the client, but they also may become very important in the developing and implementing of treatments that are matched to the client's existing strengths. Accordingly, we would argue that the practitioner in training should be taught that finding people's psychological assets are essential to assessment.

Another means of injecting more balance into a diagnosis is to encourage diagnosticians to venture beyond the realm of personality. Most diagnosticians focus on the factors "inside" of a person to form an impression. This focus probably stems from the fundamental attributional error, wherein an observer forming an impression of a target person is prone to explain that target person's actions in terms of traits (Nisbett, Caputo, Legant, & Maracek, 1973). Conversely, we describe our own actions based on situational factors. Fortunately, experimental manipulations have shown that a diagnostician can learn to take the perspective of a person who is being judged (i.e., a client; Snyder, Shenkel, & Schmidt, 1976). Furthermore, one's graduate education can change the perspectives of budding mental health professionals so that they do not always explain their clients in terms of trait-like personality characteristics.[2]

Based on the predilection of diagnosticians to see clients in terms of their underlying personality dynamics, we believe that another necessary means of balancing a diagnosis is to make sure that the environmental contributions are examined. In this regard, we endorse the pioneering thinking of Beatrice Wright in regard to what she calls the four-front approach to diagnosis (Wright & Lopez, 2002). In addition to exploring the weaknesses and strengths that are inherent in clients (e.g., personality traits and abilities), in the four-front approach the diagnosticians also explore that which is lacking or counterproductive in the environment, along with the positive resources in environments. This 2 (CONTENT: liabilities, assets) × 2 (LOCUS: person, environs) matrix forms four cells in which the diagnostician would search for information about a client (see Figure 2.1). Accordingly, we advocate that a diagnostician investigate liabilities and assets within the client, as well as liabilities and assets in the client's environment.

---

[2]Langer and Abelson (1974) performed a study that illustrated the power of training on the perceptions formed of a client. They had behaviorally or psychodynamically educated mental health professionals view a tape of a man who was described as a job applicant or as a psychiatric patient (everyone in actuality saw the same tape). Using perceived maladjustment as the dependent variable, there was an interaction of rater training and tape label. In particular, the behaviorally trained raters saw no differences in the maladjustment when the man was labeled as a job applicant or patient. The psychodynamically trained raters, however, saw the man in the patient condition as being much more maladjusted than the man in the job applicant condition. Snyder (1977) took this same data set, and instead of perceived maladjustment, measured locus of the problem (from situational to within the person). The original maladjustment ratings correlated .64 with perceived locus, such that more maladjustment related to more perceived internal locus of the problem. Similar to the original maladjustment findings, the behaviorally trained raters saw no differences in locus of the problem when the man was labeled as a job applicant or patient. The psychodynamically trained raters, on the other hand, saw the man in the patient condition as compared to the job applicant condition as having problems that were much more "in" the person than the environment. Thus, consistent with their training backgrounds, the behaviorally trained raters were seeing the problems in terms of the environment, whereas the psychodynamically trained raters were seeing the problems as residing inside of the person.

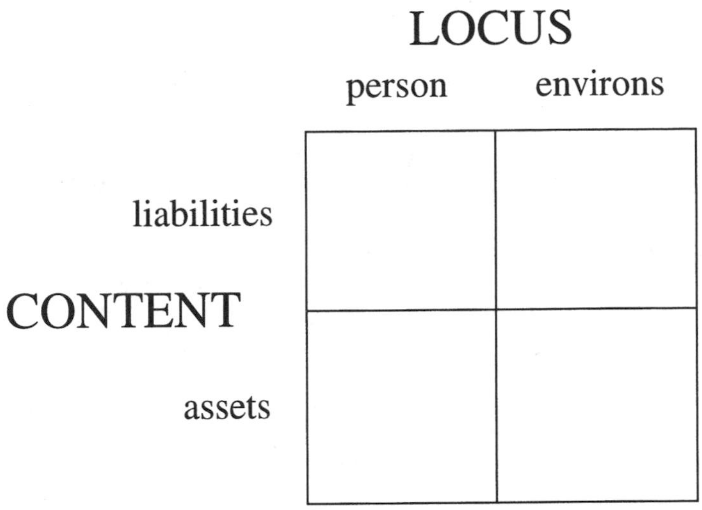

LOCUS

person   environs

liabilities

CONTENT

assets

Figure 2.1. The four-front approach of exploring liabilities and assets within the person and the environs.

Balanced Dimensions, Conceptualization, and Diagnosis

By creating a four-cell matrix of information, practitioners are able to offer more comprehensive descriptions of clients and of what they need to make changes in their lives. Determining the psychological liabilities of a person along dimensions might involve examining the client's negative affect, anxiety, depression, rigid thought patterns, functional limitations, physiological symptoms, somatization, social struggles, disengagement with life, and other "problems." Shades of dysfunction will become evident as details of dimensions are revealed. Then (not that there necessarily is an order by which you would cycle through the cells), the client's psychological assets would need to be explored. Aspects of human strength (e.g., wisdom, future-mindedness, transcendence), expectations about the future, level of social support, and coping skills should be targets of assessment. By creating dimensions on which to map these assets, the practitioner should have a more balanced view of a client whose make-up was once tightly linked to his or her presenting problem. Next, environmental liabilities and assets need to be taken into consideration. When first practicing the balanced dimension approach, filling these cells with dimensions may be challenging. In general, mental health practitioners are not well-trained to conduct environmental assessments (see chapter 28, this volume), however, through self-report scales the client can describe his or her view of the world, and through direct observation or collateral reports a more expansive view of the client's space can be gained.

Once all four cells are filled with information about the client's liabilities and assets, a difficult data synthesis process begins. In a scientific approach to the data (see chapter 1, this volume), a practitioner creates hypotheses about

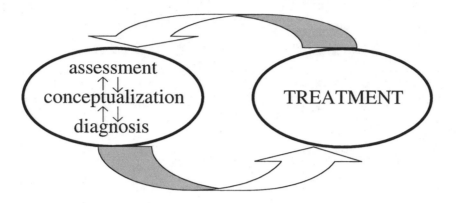

Figure 2.2.   Connecting conceptualization and treatment.

any given client and thereafter considers the evidence. As hypotheses and alternative hypotheses are tested and recast, a conceptualization of the client emerges and is refined by considering the diversity stemming from gender, race, age, sexual orientation, and so forth. This "tentative, working client model" (Spengler, Strohmer, Dixon, & Shiva, 1995, p. 518) incorporates the shades of pathology and of strengths, and the shades of environmental support and deficiencies. Once this conceptualization of the client's strengths and weaknesses is refined, the process of identifying those diagnostic criteria that do and do not align with the model begins.

Linking Conceptualization to Subsequent Interventions

Once clinical information has been gathered and tested against an evolving client understanding, the practitioner should arrive at a conceptualization that contains treatment recommendations. In our view, no conceptualization is complete without therapeutic suggestions.

Note that we stated that suggested interventions grow out of client conceptualization *and* diagnosis. We believe the disconnect between diagnosis and treatment occurs because diagnoses offer little information from which a practitioner would logically derive an intervention. The conceptualization that represents the data in the four-cell matrix gives clues to what the change process may look like for a particular client. That change process (as well as how it is facilitated and how effective it is) should be evaluated and this new information should be taken into consideration when refining the conceptualization and diagnosis. This ongoing process and connectedness between diagnosis and treatment are depicted in Figure 2.2.

Regarding the nature of treatment recommendations, interventions would build on the psychological and environmental assets of the client and curb or manage personal and environmental liabilities. Although at times there certainly will be the need to make reparative therapeutic suggestions, we advocate a model that draws on a client's strengths and includes future self-corrective actions. As such, the practitioner is looking for assets (psychological or environmental) that can help the person to be more resilient when encountering future challenges.

When a scientifically supported intervention is indicated, the diagnostician should recommend it. If a particular practitioner cannot perform the necessary treatment, we believe that there is an ethical responsibility to help the client in connecting with a therapist or treatment facility where that treatment can be obtained. When the conceptualization and diagnostic signals do not readily point to a specific intervention, and yet the diagnostician is able to form ideas about approaches that may be helpful, then the practitioner should describe those intervention strategies in the report.

Making Small Changes: *DSM-IV* Alterations

The *DSM-IV* diagnostic framework comprises five axes: clinical disorders and other conditions that may be a focus of clinical attention (Axis I), personality disorders and mental retardation (Axis II), general medical conditions (Axis III), psychosocial and environmental problems (Axis IV), and global assessment of functioning (Axis V). Diagnosis and conceptualization within this framework are grossly incomplete because environmental resources, well-being, and psychological strengths are not addressed. The *DSM*'s place in psychology is firm, however, and working within this diagnostic framework is necessary. Yet alterations to the system could serve to emphasize the positive side of functioning and provide a greater wealth of information that could be incorporated into a more comprehensive conceptualization.

Broadening Axis IV

When addressing psychosocial and environmental problems (Axis IV), clinicians log the problems that serve to add some context to the psychological disorders diagnosed along Axes I and II. The *DSM-IV* developers indicated that problems experienced would affect the diagnosis, prognosis, and treatment of mental disorders. In essence, the "problems" might initiate or exacerbate dysfunction. On reviewing the nine categories of problems listed in the *DSM-IV* (see Table 2.1), we were struck by the notion that if these everyday problems might serve as initiating and exacerbating factors of disorder, then everyday resources could serve as protective factors that would prevent the development of and would reduce the impact of disorder. Many of the resources in Table 2.1 can be measured with tools described in this volume.

Our recommendation for using a broadened Axis IV is to try to contextualize the view of the client and his or her functioning by considering psychosocial and environmental resources. Listing these resources alongside the "problems" might facilitate the conceptualization of the ways in which the client copes and solves problems in his or her life.

Table 2.1. Broadening Axis IV of the *DSM-IV* System

Psychosocial/environmental stressors	Psychosocial/environmental resources
Problems with primary support group	Attachment/love/nurturance with primary support group[a]
Problems related to the social environment	Connectedness/empathic relationships/ humor-filled interactions[b]
Educational problems	Accessible educational opportunities and support
Occupational problems	Meaningful work/career satisfaction/ self-efficacy[c]
Housing problems	Safe housing with essential elements that foster healthy development[d]
Economic problems	Financial resources adequate to meet basic needs and beyond
Problems with access to health care services	Access to high quality/reliable health care services
Problems related to interaction with the legal system–crime	Contributions made to society via donation of resources and time
Other psychosocial and environmental problems	Other psychosocial and environmental resources[e]

[a]See chapters 15 and 18, this volume.
[b]See chapters 17, 18, and 19, this volume.
[c]See chapters 7 and 24, this volume.
[d]See chapter 28, this volume.
[e]See chapters 8, 25, and 28, this volume.

Reanchoring Axis V

Axis V was incorporated into the *DSM-IV* system to assess client functioning. This is the only axis that does not focus exclusively on pathology, but it remains limited in assessing strengths. It is our contention that Axis V must be reorganized so that it is capable of capturing the absence of functional deficits and areas of optimal living. To create a functioning baseline, the current global assessment of functioning (GAF) level 100 (absence of symptomatology) would be rescaled as the midpoint (50) of the GAF scale. Levels 51 to 100 would be reserved for increasing levels of functioning. The GAF anchors of 1, 50, and 100 would be reflective of severely impaired functioning, good health, and optimal functioning, respectively. Having this type of assessment built into the diagnostic system would encourage clinicians to recognize and use strengths within clients and their environments.[3]

---

[3]A revised GAF is available from Shane J. Lopez.

Creating Axis VI

A third option for revising the current DSM-IV categorical system is including an additional axis. Personal strengths and facilitators of growth (Axis VI) presents an individual's strengths along dimensions, developing a more comprehensive picture of the client.

Axis VI (see Appendix 2.1) is designed to tap the psychological strengths associated with therapeutic change and positive functioning, thus serving the added function of creating a connection between diagnosis and treatment. Hope (Snyder et al., 1991; see also chapter 6, this volume), optimism (Scheier, Carver, & Bridges, 1994; see also chapter 5, this volume), and personal growth initiative (Robitschek, 1998) are measured with short scales, and strengths and social supporters identified by the client are listed in response to brief questions. In addition, the client's subjective well-being is measured by the Satisfaction With Life scale (Diener, Emmons, Larsen, & Griffin, 1985; see chapter 13, this volume).

As the field of psychology shifts to a balance model focusing on mental illness and mental health, practitioners and researchers must move beyond traditional deficit diagnosis. Modifying Axes IV and V and including an Axis VI are potential directions for growth.

Changing Day-to-Day Practice

On finishing this book, readers will have accumulated hundreds of recommendations about how to modify your work so that you are more sensitive to strengths. Yes, we have suggested changes to philosophies, data-gathering approaches, and language use. If you are not compelled to make major changes in your assessment approach, start by making these small changes:

1. Use people-first language when describing clients with diagnostic terms (e.g., a young man with a major depressive disorder).
2. Generate a conceptualization of a client by developing a balanced four-cell matrix of information.
3. Use precise language when describing client assets and liabilities as well as environmental resources and limitations.
4. Let the findings of positive psychological assessment guide your practice and research.

Values in Action Classification of Strengths

The Values in Action (VIA; Peterson & Seligman, 2001) classification of strengths serves as the antithesis of the *DSM* and holds the most promise for fostering additional understanding of psychological strengths. Peterson and Seligman make the point that although members of the field of psychology currently have a common language to use in speaking about the negative side of psychology, they have no such equivalent terminology to use in speaking about strengths of individuals. The VIA classification of strengths provides common language and at the same time encourages a more strength-based approach to diagnosis and treatment (treatment manuals focused on enhancing strengths will accompany the diagnostic manual).

In support of a less unilateral classification system, the VIA classification describes the individual differences of character strengths on continua and not as distinct categories. In this way, the authors contend that their classification approach is sensitive to the developmental differences in which character strengths are displayed and deployed (Peterson & Seligman, 2001). Six categories are delineated in the VIA classification system: wisdom, courage, humanity, justice, temperance, and transcendence, and these are thought to represent universal and cross-cultural virtues (Peterson & Seligman, 2001). This classification system, which is slated for publication in 2003, may become the gold standard for classifying the positive aspects of human life.

Power of Positive Psychological Assessment

By asking about strengths, the diagnostician is fostering several positive reactions in the client. First, the client can see that the helper is trying to understand the whole person. Second, the client is shown that she or he is not being equated with the problem. Third, the client is not reinforced for "having a problem" but rather is encouraged to look at her or his assets. Fourth, the client can recall and reclaim some of the personal worth that may have been depleted before coming to the mental health professional. Fifth, a consideration of the client's strengths can facilitate an alliance of trust and mutuality with the mental health professional; in turn, the client is open and giving of information that may yield a maximally productive diagnosis. By asking about strengths, therefore, a positive assessment is at once healing and buoyant in its focus.

In the weakness model, the diagnosis often may necessitate that the client starts anew to learn how to achieve mental health. In positive psychological assessment, however, a person's problem is viewed best through the lens of his or her already existing coping skills and talents. Contrary to the pathology model in which fairly major changes may be seen as necessary, the positive assessment approach takes a more minimalist approach. By discovering the strengths that already are in the repertoires of people and the support that they have in their environment, the diagnostic process then can help clients to use those strengths to return to mental health. Indeed, the guiding premise in positive psychological assessment is that fulfilling life journeys are built and maintained by considering personal and environmental assets. Positive psychology in general, and positive psychological assessment in particular, offer a perspective for working with the strengths in people. We owe nothing less to those who ask for our help.

Appendix 2.1

Axis VI:
Personal Strengths and Facilitating Factors of Growth

Information about your satisfaction with your life and your personal strengths is valuable when forming your individualized treatment plan. Please respond to the three questions presented below and to the four questionnaires attached to this form. When you are done, the scales will be scored and plotted below.

What are your goals for treatment? Be as specific as possible. _____

_____

_____

Who are the people in your life you will turn to for support while making changes in your life? List their first names here: _____

_____

What are your personal strengths? List all those that come to mind that are not listed above: _____

_____

_____

Now, please complete the attached measures of strengths.[4]

---

[4] Optimism and hope measures can be found in chapters 5 and 6, respectively. The Satisfaction With Life Scale can be found in chapter 13. The Personal Growth Initiate Scale can be found in Robitschek (1998).

References

American Psychiatric Association. (1994). *Diagnostic and statistical manual of mental disorders* (4th ed.). Washington, DC: Author.

Barone, D., Maddux, J., & Snyder, C. R. (1997). The social cognitive construction of difference and disorder. In D. Barone, J. Maddux, & C. R. Snyder (Eds.), *Social cognitive psychology: History and current domains* (pp. 397–428). New York: Plenum Press.

Buss, A. R., & Poley, W. (1976). *Individual differences: Traits and factors*. New York: Gardner Press.

Diener, E., Emmons, R. A., Larsen, R. J., & Griffin, S. (1985). Satisfaction With Life scale. *Journal of Personality Assessment, 49,* 71–75.

Garb, H. N. (1998). *Studying the clinician: Judgment research and psychological assessment*. Washington, DC: American Psychological Association.

Langer, E. J., & Abelson, R. P. (1974). A patient by any other name . . . : Practitioner group differences in labeling bias. *Journal of Consulting and Clinical Psychology, 42*, 4–9.

Maddux, J. E. (1993a). The mythology of psychopathology: A social cognitive view of deviance, difference, and disorder. *The General Psychologist, 29*, 34–45.

Maddux, J. E. (1993b). Social science, social policy, and scientific research. *American Psychologist, 48*, 689–691.

McCullough, M., & Snyder, C. R. (2000). Classical sources of human strength: Revisiting an old home and building a new one. *Journal of Social and Clinical Psychology, 19*, 1–10.

Merton, R. (1957). *Social theory and social structure* (Rev. ed.). Glencoe, IL: Free Press.

Nisbett, R. E., Caputo, C., Legant, P., & Maracek, J. (1973). Behavior as seen by the actor and as seen by the observer. *Journal of Personality and Social Psychology, 27*, 154–164.

Peterson, C., & Seligman, M. E. P. (2001). Values in action (VIA) classification of strengths. Retrieved May 2001, from http://www.psych.upenn.edu/seligman/taxonomy.htm

Robitschek, C. (1998). Personal growth initiative: The construct and its measure. *Measurement and Evaluation in Counseling and Development, 30*, 183–198.

Rosenthal, R., & Jacobson, L. (1968). *Pygmalion in the classroom: Teacher expectation and pupils' intellectual development*. New York: Holt, Rinehart, & Winston.

Salovey, P, & Turk, D. C. (1991). Clinical judgment and decision-making. In C. R. Snyder & D. R. Forsyth (Eds.), *Handbook of social and clinical psychology: The health perspective* (pp. 416–437). New York: Pergamon Press.

Scheier, M. F., Carver, C. S., & Bridges, M. N. (1994). Distinguishing optimism from neuroticism: A reevaluation of the Life Orientation Test. *Journal of Personality and Social Psychology, 67,* 1063–1078.

Snyder, C. R. (1977). "A patient by any other name" revisited: Maladjustment or attributional locus of problem? *Journal of Consulting and Clinical Psychology, 45*, 101–103.

Snyder, C. R., & Feldman, D. B. (2000). Hope for the many: An empowering social agenda. In C. R. Snyder (Ed.), *Handbook of hope: Theory, measures, and applications* (pp. 402–415). San Diego, CA: Academic Press.

Snyder, C. R., & Fromkin, H. (1980). *Uniqueness: The human pursuit of difference*. New York: Plenum Press.

Snyder, C. R., Harris, C., Anderson, J. R., Holleran, S. A., Irving, L. M., et al. (1991). The will and the ways: Development and validation of an individual-differences measure of hope. *Journal of Personality and Social Psychology, 60,* 570–585.

Snyder, C. R., & Ingram, R. E. (2000). Psychotherapy: Questions for an evolving field. In C. R. Snyder & R. E. Ingram (Eds.), *Handbook of psychological change: Psychotherapy processes and practices for the* 21st *century* (pp. 707–735). New York: Wiley.

Snyder, C. R., Shenkel, R. J., & Schmidt, A. (1976). Effects of role perspective and client psychiatric history on locus of problem? *Journal of Consulting and Clinical Psychology, 44*, 467–472.

Spengler, P. M., Strohmer, D. C., Dixon, D. N., & Shiva, V. A. (1995). A scientist-practitioner model of psychological assessment: Implications for training, practice and research. *Counseling Psychologist, 23*, 506–534.

Terman, L. M., & Oden, M H. (1947). *The gifted child grows up: Twenty-five years' follow-up of a superior group*. Stanford, CA: Stanford University Press.

Wright, B. A., & Lopez, S. J. (2002). Widening the diagnostic focus: A case for including human strengths and environmental resources. In C. R. Snyder & S. J. Lopez (Eds.), *Handbook of positive psychology* (pp. 26–44). New York: Oxford University Press.

3

Positive Psychological Assessment in an Increasingly Diverse World

Lisa Y. Flores and Ezemenari M. Obasi

Some readers may ask, "Why a chapter on cultural diversity[1] and positive psychological assessment?" We think the editors of this handbook were wise to include this topic in their vision of a comprehensive volume on positive psychological assessment. The United States and other industrialized countries are becoming increasingly diverse, and social scientists and mental health practitioners must be sensitive to the cultural nuances in the presentation of strength, healthy processes, and optimal living.

Thanks to the pioneering work of Black psychologists in the 1960s, social science has transformed steadily by integrating cross-cultural perspectives in research, training, and practice. Cross-cultural, or multicultural, psychologists have encouraged professionals to be mindful of the sociocultural context and worldview perspectives of the individuals with whom we study and work. Psychology has been criticized because theories have been based on White, middle-class values and research is conducted on "mainstream" samples. Cross-cultural psychology aims to redress these criticisms by focusing on the experiences of a broad range of people. Positive psychology, with its burgeoning body of science and its focus on promoting optimal human functioning, has the opportunity to acknowledge and strategically address ethnicity and culture while building its scholarly framework and practice armamentarium.

Assessment in an Increasingly Diverse World

Recent census data indicate that the demographic patterns within the United States are shifting to constitute an increasingly culturally diverse population (U.S. Bureau of the Census, 2001). This shift can be attributed to the high

---

[1]Throughout this chapter, we use the terms *culturally diverse, culturally different, multicultural,* and *cross-cultural populations* to refer to non-White and non-European racial and ethnic groups, both within the United States and across other countries. Cross-cultural assessment involves people who are culturally different from the clinician or researcher.

immigration and birth rates among racial–ethnic groups, and a population growth rate among European Americans that has been gradually decreasing. Given the increasing racial and ethnic diversity, it is imperative that researchers in positive psychology consider the cross-cultural applications of positive psychological constructs, evaluate the external validity of their research findings, and develop assessment instruments that are reliable and valid with culturally diverse populations. Including research samples that are representative of the expanding population will increase the relevance and significance of positive psychology research.

The purpose of this chapter is to discuss our capacity to assess positive characteristics of individuals from all populations and to examine the interpretation and generalizabilty of these findings from one culture to another. Specifically, we will review the history of cross-cultural psychological assessment, issues related to cross-cultural measurement, and the applications of positive psychological constructs across cultures. Finally, we will describe a model for positive psychological assessment with cross-cultural populations and provide recommendations for future developments in the assessment of positive psychological constructs.

History of Psychological Assessment With Culturally Diverse Populations

Before a scientist conducts an experiment, careful thinking ensures that she or he has prescribed the necessary steps to analyze the original hypothesis with some level of precision. These hypotheses are statements that can be tested to advance the current state of knowledge. Historically, psychological research with culturally diverse populations has produced questions and findings that were detrimental to the observed group and led to harmful consequences for the groups studied. To appreciate current approaches to assessing positive psychological traits in individuals, it is necessary to understand the context in which members of particular racial–ethnic groups historically have been assessed in psychology.

Sue and Sue (1999) have categorized historical and contemporary psychological research paradigms with racial–ethnic groups into the following three areas: genetically deficient, culturally deficient, and culturally different. The genetically deficient model highlighted biological differences to explain intellectual aptitudes between different racial groups. The aim of subscribers to this paradigm was to scientifically illustrate the intellectual superiority of the European race and to hierarchically categorize intellectual capacity as a function of race. This paradigm is evident in Darwin's *Origin of Species by Means of Natural Selection,* wherein theory supported the genetic intellectual superiority of Europeans and inferiority of other groups. Inferiority assertions (Jensen, 1969; Morton, 1839) continued in studies examining cranial capacities. The hypothesis that Africans had inferior brains and limited intellectual capacity was illustrated by measuring the differential amount of pepper corns held in the skulls of Africans and Europeans (Clark, 1975).

These notions of genetic inferiority were a prominent focus of scholarship in American psychology, where eugenics research was lead by prominent American psychologists such as G. Stanley Hall, Alexander Bell, Walter Cannon, Robert Yerkes, Edward Thorndike, Henry Goddard, and Lewis Terman (Hothersall, 1995). Stanley Hall "was a firm believer in 'higher' and 'lower' human races. He believed the 'Negro races' to be at an earlier stage of human development, dependent on the 'higher' white races for their development and supervision" (Hothersall, 1995, p. 360). Moreover, Goddard held similar views of what he called the "feebleminded." In his work with immigration screening procedures on Ellis Island in the early 1900s, he used psychological testing via the Binet and DeSanctis tests to increase deportation rates (Hothersall, 1995). Given that U.S. intelligence tests were being used with culturally and linguistically different European populations (i.e., Italians, Hungarians), we know today that these factors likely played a significant role in immigrants' poor performance.

A shift of focus in cross-cultural research from genetics to environmental factors characterized the next wave in psychological research. In the culturally deficient model, the communal lifestyles and values of various racial–ethnic groups were identified as the factors that perpetuated the mental and intellectual inferiority of certain racial and ethnic populations. Psychologists (e.g., Kardiner & Ovesey, 1951) looked to environmental, nutritional, psychological, sociocultural, and linguistic factors to explain how members from different groups were prevented from developing optimally. More specifically, Moynihan (1965) reported that the heart of cultural deterioration was attributed to the breakdown in family structure. Parham, White, and Ajamu (1999) detailed how this thinking led to the hypotheses of cultural deprivation, or "inadequate exposure to European American values, norms, customs, and life-styles," (p. 7) and European American cultural enrichment was proposed as a remedy. In essence, the culturally deficient model set the dominant European American middle-class cultural values and lifestyles as the ideal measuring stick and regarded anything that deviated from this norm as deficient.

With a change in terminology, from *deficient* to *different*, a major change in perspective in investigating differences followed. Those who subscribe to the culturally different model view alternative values and lifestyles as legitimate. Rather than comparing cultures to one another and placing one culture in a superior position in relation to other cultures, differences are appreciated, practices and behaviors are understood and interpreted within the context of the culture, and the benefits of living in a culturally diverse society are honored. Essentially, the strengths and values of multiple cultures are recognized and respected from a culturally different perspective.

Cross-Cultural Assessment Issues in Positive Psychological Assessment

Assessment is a *process* of understanding and helping people (Walsh & Betz, 2001). The importance of recognizing the reciprocal relationship between the person and his or her environment during the assessment process has been noted previously, and readers are encouraged to refer to chapters 1 and 2 in this volume for more on the interactionist perspective. Indeed, it is impossible to understand individual behavior without considering the environmental context in which the behavior occurs. What one group considers "normal" may be regarded as "abnormal" in another. For example, within the Latino culture, it is not unusual to hear about a person "communicating" with loved ones who have died. Although some mental health professionals may describe this person as experiencing hallucinations, among some Latino(as), it is regarded as a viable experience that is readily explained through cultural and religious beliefs. Thus, information regarding the cultural environment, explanations for behaviors, and characterizations of behaviors from the perspective of individuals who are part of the culture are essential components of cross-cultural assessment. Furthermore, we want to underscore the fact that assessment should be regarded as a process, whereby a question is asked, information is gathered, hypotheses are formulated, and then reformulated based on incoming information and feedback from the person and environment. A continual feedback loop between the individual or cultural group and researcher is necessary to validate evidence that is gathered and to support conclusions.

There are several methods through which the researcher or clinician gathers information. Assessment information can be obtained through both formal (i.e., paper and pencil tests) and informal (i.e., talking to the person, talking to person's family and friends) methods. We define cross-cultural assessment to include a process of gathering information in which the people (i.e., client, clinician, or researcher) involved in the process differ from one another along the dimensions of race, culture, or ethnicity. Most often, this situation includes a non-White person in the role of the client or the one being assessed for clinical or research purposes.

Culturally sensitive positive psychological assessment is a multifaceted process, and several issues must be taken into account in the construction of positive psychological measurements for use in research and practice. To begin, positive psychological researchers must understand the meaning of positive constructs among diverse cultural groups. It is essential that positive psychological measures are constructed from the worldview perspective of the cultural group for which it is intended to be used, and that interpretations from research studies are articulated in a manner that improves on a community's current condition in a culturally sensitive way and is validating to their sense of humanity. Moreover, researchers should recognize that every cultural group in not homogeneous.

Because of the scope of this handbook, we will primarily focus on assessment as it relates to selecting, administering, and interpreting measures with a culturally diverse population. However, it is sensible to consider matters related to measurement and test construction because this will have a direct influence on the validity of positive psychological measures with individuals across diverse cultures. In the following sections, we will delineate general concerns related to the use of positive psychological assessment in cross-cultural situations.

Construct: Etic Versus Emic Issues

When selecting an instrument, the foremost question is whether the construct being measured has the same meaning for all individuals; this measurement issue previously has been referred to as *conceptual equivalence* (Marsella & Leong, 1995). A researcher can assess conceptual equivalence by investigating whether the construct is defined similarly across cultures (etic) or whether the construct is culturally specific (emic). Several cultures may have a similar definition for well-being and may experience the feelings associated with well-being in the same way, but expressions may depend on cultural sanctions regarding what is socially appropriate (see Diener & Suh, 2000). For example, in Ghanaian culture it is taboo for a child to ask an elder how she or he is doing. It is understood that a certain level of wisdom is inherent in one's transition into eldership, and that a child will have little assistance to offer if the elder's reply to the question is "not good." However, this is a common inquiry among young people in the United States, and psychologists who are not sensitive to cultural differences may expect to see these same behaviors exhibited by members of diverse cultural groups.

Because of cultural variance in behaviors, customs, and norms, the selection of measures should consider not only the definition of the construct but also how the construct would be manifested in an individual's culture. It is important not to assume that the definition of constructs or the expressions of feelings, thoughts, or behaviors are universal across non-Western cultures or among racial and ethnic groups in the United States.

Standardization

A commonly discussed pitfall in cross-cultural assessment is the use of measures that lack adequate representation of individuals representing diverse U.S. racial–ethnic groups or individuals from different countries in the normative samples. Standardization data pertaining to average test scores and reliability and validity estimates often are derived from samples made up of predominately European American, middle-class, and college-educated individuals (Walsh & Betz, 2001). This becomes problematic when one's cultural values and life experiences, which may be different from the European American middle-class norm, elicit responses that are independent from what the testing instrument was constructed to measure. Much research is needed to examine the reliability and predictive validity of positive psychological constructs among the various racial and ethnic groups in the United States, along with international samples. Findings from studies that use positive psychological measures without normative psychometric data for particular groups should be considered with caution until data are provided that support the measure as being reliable and valid for the particular group under study.

Language

Linguistic equivalence refers to whether the test is administered in the preferred language of the individual being assessed (Marsella & Leong, 1995). In cases in which a bilingual individual is being assessed, the person's fluency in the language and preferred language under test-taking circumstances should be evaluated before the assessment process because this information may be critical when interpreting the validity of the test results. In cross-cultural research, it is common to find measures that have been translated for use in different languages. Indeed, this has occurred with hope scales (Lopez et al., 2000) and optimism scales (Perczek, Carver, Price, & Pozo-Kaderman, 2000). Although this practice may address the linguistic equivalence issues by administering assessment tools in the participant's preferred language, it creates another potential bias that has been referred to as *translation equivalence* (Brislin, 1993). Translation equivalence occurs when measures are translated into a different language without adequate consideration of whether concepts can be translated accurately into that particular foreign language. Using a bilingual expert to translate the measure into the foreign language, and then having another person skilled in both languages translate it back into the original language can minimize bias.

Scaling

How a person responds to scaled responses or forced-choice responses may vary across cultures and contributes to problems with the metric equivalence of a measure (Brislin, 1993). Scaling issues can be minimized when researchers understand the decision-making process of the individual. For example, European Americans' decision-making style may be described as a linear process with distinct opportunities. In this case, the use of a Likert scale may be appropriate. However, the use of the same scale may be inappropriate in other cultures in which decision making is markedly different and in which the options are seen dichotomously. To produce valid results, scaling must be understood by and reflect viable options for groups of interest.

Response Bias

A response style may exist across cultural groups such that emotions may consistently be reported at either extreme or at midlevels. These responses are likely to reflect cultural norms with regard to the expression of emotions. For example, in cultures that value collectivism and place higher value on group conformity, behaviors that draw attention to individuals may be frowned on (Sue & Sue, 1999). Thus, it is possible that individuals from these cultures may respond to Likert-scaled items in the mid-range. The importance of using measures that have used appropriate, culturally diverse samples in the standardization of the measure would provide information regarding the use of different cut-off scores across cultural groups.

Socially desirable behaviors may vary from one culture to another, and participants' responses to items may be influenced by these social norms. For example, it is not uncommon in some cultures to indicate that life is going well, when in fact it is not, to prevent placing one's burdens onto others. Alternatively, placing oneself in a bad light may be undesirable in some cultures because it reflects back on the family or cultural group. Researchers must develop a rapport with their research participants to get a full understanding of the barriers that may prevent them from answering questions truthfully or in a socially desirable manner.

Examiner Bias

Ethical cross-cultural assessment and research are conducted when the researcher or professional *understands the intricacies of the culture* and can appropriately interpret the responses and behaviors of the individual. It is important for researchers and practitioners to have a basic background on the particular culture of interest. Although reading relevant literature can give a macroscopic summary of a particular cultural group, another way of dealing with this bias is to personally engage in culture-specific activities that provide an invaluable atmosphere to learn about particulars that are meaningful to that culture. Moreover, researchers and practitioners must be aware of their personal biases when attempting to make constructive interpretations. Otherwise, the risk of misinterpreting the responses of an individual or groups of people exists.

Cultural Variables

Cultural variables, such as acculturation level, racial identity, socioeconomic status, and worldview, could influence the assessment process. These variables also may serve as moderating variables for positive psychological constructs and must be evaluated in the practice of positive psychological assessment. Because a person's worldview determines the way in which she or he is socialized to perceive, think, feel, and experience the world (Myers, 1993), a comprehensive understanding of this construct can be used to explain nonintuitive research findings. For example, one's cosmological relationship to a Supreme Being and ancestral community can affect the experience of well-being, hope, or optimism. The Yoruba understanding that one has an active role in choosing a destiny may mean that life's obstacles become an opportunity to work through spiritual imperfections. Within the culture, this is understood to mean that the Supreme Being and departed ancestors will not abandon the person with an unbearable task. In cultures where life experiences are viewed as opportunities for spiritual growth, individuals' perceptions of life conditions can be viewed favorably, whereas other cultures may regard these same life events in a negative light. Cultural components are critical in both assessment and research because culture can affect one's definition, evaluation, and explanation of behaviors.

Model of Cross-Cultural Positive Psychological Assessment

Because of the psychology profession's history of research and assessment with members of diverse racial and ethnic groups, it is essential that psychologists embrace stringent assessment and research procedures that are designed to maximize the exchange of knowledge between cultural groups. Ridley, Li, and Hill (1998) suggested a multicultural assessment procedure that involves identifying, interpreting, and incorporating cultural data that may contribute to sound decision making. In the following section, we propose a model of cross-cultural assessment that can be used in positive psychological assessment. We will adapt a culturally appropriate model for career assessment (Flores, Spanierman, & Obasi, in press) to positive psychological assessment and will outline the procedures for culturally sensitive positive psychological assessment. The model presented is adjunct to the model described in chapter 1.

Several assumptions undergirding the model include the ability to identify the positive and the negative aspects of human development, the ability to establish a professional relationship with the client, the acquisition of minimum competencies necessary to conduct appropriate assessment, and the application of minimum multicultural competencies. Development of multicultural competencies and general assessment skills serve as the foundation for culturally competent positive psychological assessment. Multicultural competencies have been conceptualized to include awareness of personal beliefs, knowledge, and skills in working with diverse populations (Sue, Arredondo, & McDavis, 1992; Sue et al., 1982). A psychologist must understand his or her cultural frame of reference before embarking on the assessment process with culturally different individuals (Sue & Sue, 1999). As such, psychologists should evaluate his or her worldview, values, prejudices, stereotypes, and reference group identity, because these will be influential when formulating research questions or clinical hypotheses for individuals from diverse cultural backgrounds. In addition to being aware of one's own cultural background, the psychologist also should take steps to examine the social–political realities, worldview, and values of the cultural groups with whom she or he works. This knowledge will facilitate assessment and decrease problems as a result of cultural differences. It is important to recognize that the information gathered from this process will permeate all aspects of assessment.

The culturally appropriate model for positive psychological assessment includes four interconnected steps: information gathering, selection of psychological instruments, administration of psychological instruments, and interpretation of psychological assessment results (see Figure 3.1). Gathering information that distinguishes the strengths of an individual that may bring about positive change in his or her life is the first step of the assessment process. Information gathering should incorporate data regarding the individual's sociocultural context, cultural identity, and worldview. Selection of instruments is culturally appropriate when the constructs being assessed are conceptually equivalent across cultures or has the same meaning in the culture the instrument was developed and in the culture of the individual taking the test. More specifically, psychologists should investigate the meaning of the construct to the person or group and compare this to the definition of the construct provided by the researcher who developed the theoretical model or the assessment measure. Culturally relevant assumptions reflected in the content of the items (i.e., cultural values), and any linguistic issues also may be important to investigate to establish linguistic and translation equivalence. Assessing the influences of

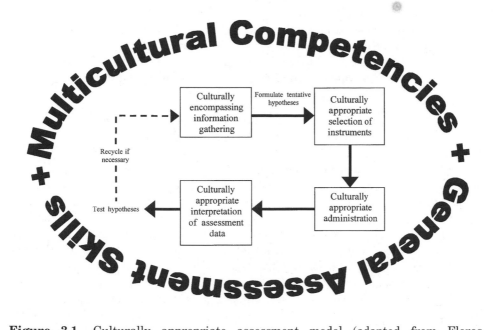

Figure 3.1. Culturally appropriate assessment model (adapted from Flores, Spanierman, & Obasi's [in press] culturally appropriate career assessment model).

cultural variables, such as acculturation level, racial identity, and worldview, which may moderate the magnitude of the psychological variables under investigation, should not be overlooked. Examining the standardized sample of the measures being considered for administration is a critical component in the selection of instruments. The psychometric properties of the assessment instrument for samples used in its development, as well as data from research studies that have used the instrument with diverse cultural groups, will provide evidence for the scale's reliability and validity. When these issues are taken into consideration, the psychologist should select the psychological measures that are most sensitive to the cultural assessment issues outlined previously in this chapter.

In the next step, culturally appropriate administration of assessment instruments, it is important to consider how scaling can affect a particular cultural group's response style to minimize problems with the metric bias. The manner in which a measure is scaled must reflect viable options for culturally different individuals. The assessment instruments should be administered in a fashion that is congruent with the client's familiarity with test administration and take into account the individual's history with test taking and anticipations about the process. This is particularly important with individuals from cultural groups that may be highly suspicious of how the data are going to be used.

Examiner bias must be minimized to ensure negligible error in appropriately interpreting the assessment data and the behaviors of the culturally different individual. The psychologist should be sensitive to possible response bias and to the respondent's interpretation of the process. This information can contribute to a more accurate depiction of the findings and should take into account issues such as responding in a socially desired manner. Finally, the interpretation of the results always should be presented to the individual to solicit feedback. The psychologist may recycle back through the cross-cultural assessment model to compensate for the new information gathered.

Applications of Positive Psychological Measurement Across Cultures

The cross-cultural positive psychology assessment model is difficult to apply to positive psychological assessment because research has not established a clear connection between the constructs and how these constructs are manifested in other cultures. As is the case with psychological research in general, there has been relatively limited research activity to validate positive psychological constructs among U.S. racial–ethnic groups or across nationalities. Hence, there are few well-established cross-cultural positive measures to use in today's increasingly diverse community. Indeed, Lopez and his colleagues (2002) have called for positive psychologists to integrate a cross-cultural perspective into their work to contribute to our current understanding of cross-cultural applications of positive psychology theories and measures. Such studies may provide evidence for the universal applicability of these constructs, and researchers are encouraged to generate additional studies that investigate the psychometric properties and predictive validity of various positive psychology measures across racial–ethnic groups. A few studies have made attempts to investigate how positive constructs are manifested in culturally diverse samples. In the following sections, we will review a few of the noteworthy research programs that have analyzed positive psychological constructs across cultures.

Hope

Although the Hope scale (Snyder et al., 1991), the most widely used scale to measure hope, has been translated into different languages and used with culturally diverse groups (Lopez et al., 2000), a review of the literature revealed no published studies to date with international populations or racial–ethnic groups in the United States. Scales that have been developed to assess hope in children and young children (Children's Hope scale: Snyder et al., 1997; Young Children's Hope scale (YCHS): McDermott, Gariglietti, & Hastings, 1998) have yielded preliminary findings with Latinos(as), African Americans, and Native Americans that provide support for the factor structures of each scale. Data on the YCHS indicate that Latino(a) and Native American children yield significantly lower hope scores than African American and White children (McDermott, Gariglietti, & Hastings, 1998). Hope was found to be related to Mexican immigrant students' social adjustment and language fluency (Gariglietti, 1999), racial or cultural identity among Jewish children (Sherwin, 1994) and African Americans (Sherwin, 1996), and safe-sex practices among gay men (Floyd & McDermott, 1998), thus providing some preliminary evidence for the applicability of hope theory with U.S. groups.

Problem Solving

Evidence regarding the cross-cultural applicability of problem-solving measures was provided with samples of African American (Neville, Heppner, & Wang, 1997) and Turkish college students (Sahin, Sahin, & Heppner, 1993). Specifically, Neville and her colleagues (1997) reported that African American students' scores on the Problem-Focused Style of Coping (Heppner, Cook, Wright, & Johnson, 1995) was comparable to those of other university/college students, and their scores on the Problem Solving Inventory (Heppner & Petersen, 1982) were slightly higher, reflecting a more negative problem-solving appraisal style. They found that higher immersion–emersion racial identity scores were predictive of negative problem-solving appraisal and avoidance of problem-focused coping. Finally, higher internalization racial identity scores were correlated with greater problem-solving appraisal.

Evidence for the generalizability of problem-solving theory was provided for a group of Turkish university students (Sahin et al., 1993). Using the most common assessment to measure perceived problem-solving abilities, Sahin and colleagues found that Turkish men did not differ from American men on total scores on the Problem Solving Inventory, but significant differences were found between Turkish and American women, with Turkish women reporting more positive problem-solving abilities. Negative problem-solving appraisal was related to higher levels of depression and anxiety among the Turkish students (and American students).

Subjective Well-Being

Perhaps the area in positive psychology that has been researched most often with ethnic groups and international samples is well-being (see Diener & Suh, 2000), with a vast amount of data collected by the World Values Study Group. Cross-cultural applications of some well-being measures have been provided. For example, Tepperman and Curtis (1995) provided construct validity for a measure of life satisfaction (taken from the World Values data set) with samples between the three North American countries and subgroups within each country, thus providing support that it may be a reliable and valid measure across cultural groups.

Differences in ratings of subjective well-being have been found across nations, with individualistic-oriented cultures scoring higher than collectivistic cultures, and wealthier nations scoring higher than poorer nations (Diener, Diener, & Diener, 1995). Some evidence for the universality of the relations between marital status and subjective well-being was provided by comparing data from 42 nations (Diener, Gohm, Suh, & Oishi, 2000). However, the relative strength of these relations may vary across cultures. This was supported in a comparison study between Asian Indians and Americans, which found that other factors (i.e., income, education) contributed a greater amount of variance in the prediction of well-being than marriage, whereas marriage was the strongest predictor of psychological well-being among Americans (Sastry, 1999). It appears that the cultural variables—in this case, the importance of improving one's position in the caste system—may moderate the relationship between marital status and well-being.

To summarize, some preliminary steps have been taken to validate positive psychology's constructs across ethnic and cultural groups. Initial data have shown that some constructs generalize across groups; however, multiple studies are needed before we can confidently state that positive psychology theories and measures are valid with non-European Americans and individuals in other countries. There is much room to improve the status of positive psychological assessment with regard to cultural applicability of measures and findings. Positive psychology is a relatively newly identified area in psychology, and there is promise and hope that the diversity-related issues that are currently being addressed in psychology as a whole will be attended to in the emergence of this body of knowledge. To be a force in the 21st century and to truly be able to say that positive psychology is for all, more research in positive psychology that integrates all perspectives is essential.

Future Developments in Global Assessment of Positive Psychological Measures

Researchers in positive psychology have made important contributions to the literature regarding individual strengths. As we noted previously, however, there are several areas that need to be improved. We provide the following recommendations to further the understanding of cultural factors in positive psychological assessment: (a) generate research that tests the applicability of positive psychological measures with racial–ethnic groups in the United States along with international samples, thus providing normative data to support the use of these measures;[2] (b) investigate the relationship of positive psychology constructs to other psychological variables in different cultural groups; (c) collaborate with cross-cultural psychologists from other areas of psychology who have expertise with particular groups and knowledge regarding cross-cultural research and assessment;[3] (d) encourage an increase in the number of scholars and graduate students in the field of positive psychology who express interests in studying positive psychological functioning in culturally diverse populations; and (f) apply the findings from positive psychology's research to improve the functioning and status of culturally diverse groups by building on the strengths and values within the culture.[4]

---

[2] Efforts should be made to examine the validity of these measures with samples that consist of one racial–ethnic group (i.e., only African Americans, Mexican Americans, or Chinese Americans), rather than combined groups (i.e, Latinos(as) or Asians), to more fully understand variations within a cultural group.

[3] Alternatively, healers within the culture could be consulted to understand individual and group assets that are currently recognized to facilitate healthy functioning.

[4] For a detailed discussion of perspectives on strengths across cultures, see chapter 6, particularly Table 6.1, p. 106, in Hays (2001).

References

Brislin, R. (1993). *Understanding culture's influence on behavior*. San Diego, CA: Harcourt Brace Jovanovich.

Clark, C. (1975). The Shockley-Jensen thesis: A contextual appraisal. *Black Scholar, 6*(10), 2–11.

Diener, E., Diener, M., & Diener, C. (1995). Factors predicting the subjective well-being of nations. *Journal of Personality and Social Psychology, 69*(5), 851–864.

Diener, E., Gohm, C. L., Suh, E., & Oishi, S. (2000). Similarity of the relations between marital status and subjective well-being across cultures. *Journal of Cross-Cultural Psychology, 31*(4), 419–436.

Diener, E. & Suh, E. M. (2000). *Culture and subjective well-being*. Cambridge: MIT Press.

Flores, L. Y., Spanierman, L. B., & Obasi, E. M. (in press). Professional and ethical issues in career assessment with diverse racial and ethnic groups. *Journal of Career Assessment*.

Floyd, R. K., & McDermott, D. (1998, Aug.). *Hope and sexual risk-taking in gay men*. Poster presented at the 106th annual convention of the American Psychological Association, San Francisco.

Gariglietti, K. P. (1999). *The role of hope in the academic success, social adjustment, and language proficiency of Hispanic immigrants*. Unpublished doctoral dissertation, University of Kansas, Lawrence.

Hays, P. A. (2001). *Addressing culture complexities in practice. A framework for clinicians and counselors*. Washington, DC: American Psychological Association.

Heppner, P. P., Cook, S. W., Wright, D. M., & Johnson, W. C., Jr. (1995). Progress in resolving problems: A problem-focused style of coping. *Journal of Counseling Psychology, 42*(3), 279–293.

Heppner, P. P., & Petersen, C. H. (1982). The development of implications of a personal problem-solving inventory. *Journal of Counseling Psychology, 29*(1), 66–75.

Hothersall, D. (1995). *History of psychology*. New York: McGraw-Hill.

Jensen, A. R. (1969). How much can we boost IQ and scholastic achievement? *Harvard Educational Review, 39*(1), 1–123.

Kardiner, A., & Ovesey, L. (1951). *The mark of oppression: A psychological study of the American Negro*. Norton: New York.

Lopez, S. J., Gariglietti, K. P., McDermott, D., Sherwin, E. D., Floyd, R. K., et al. (2000). Hope for the evolution of diversity: On leveling the field of dreams. In C. R. Snyder (Ed.), *Handbook of hope* (pp. 223–242). San Diego, CA: Academic Press.

Lopez, S. J., Prosser, E. C., Edwards, L. M., Magyar-Moe, J. L., Neufeld, J. E., et al. (2002). Putting positive psychology in a multicultural context. In C. R. Snyder & S. J. Lopez (Eds.), *The handbook of positive psychology* (pp. 700–714). New York: Oxford University Press.

Marsella, A. J., & Leong, F. L. (1995). Cross-cultural issues in personality and career assessment. *Journal of Career Assessment, 3*, 202–218.

McDermott, D., Gariglietti, K., & Hastings, S. (1998, Aug.). *A further cross cultural investigation of hope in children and adolescents*. Paper presented at the annual meeting of the American Psychological Association, San Francisco.

Morton, S. G. (1839). *Crania American*. Philadelphia: John Pennington.

Moynihan, D. (1965). *The negro family: The case of national action*. Washington, DC: Office of Policy Planning and Research, U.S. Department of Labor.

Myers, L. J. (1993). *Understanding the afrocentric world view: Introduction to optimal psychology* (2nd ed.). Dubuque, IA: Kendall/Hunt.

Neville, H. A., Heppner, P. P., & Wang, L.-F. (1997). Relations among racial identity attitudes, perceived stressors, and coping styles in African American college students. *Journal of Counseling & Development, 75*(4), 303–311.

Parham, T. A., White, J. L., & Ajamu, A. (1999). *The psychology of Blacks: An African centered perspective* (3rd ed.). Upper Saddle River, NJ: Prentice-Hall.

Perczek, R., Carver, C. S., Price, A. A., & Pozo-Kaderman, C. (2000). Coping, mood, and aspects of personality in Spanish translation and evidence of convergence with English versions. *Journal of Personality Assessment, 74*, 63–87.

Ridley, C. R., Li, L. C., & Hill, C. L. (1998). Multicultural assessment: Reexamination, reconceptualization, and practical application. *Counseling Psychologist, 26,* 827–910.

Sahin, N., Sahin, N. H., & Heppner, P. P. (1993). Psychometric properties of the Problem Solving Inventory in a group of Turkish university students. *Cognitive Therapy & Research, 17*(4), 379–396.

Sastry, J. (1999). Household structure, satisfaction and distress in India and the United States: A comparative cultural examination. *Journal of Comparative Family Studies, 30*(1), 135–152.

Sherwin, E. D. (1994). *Hope and social identity: An investigation into the relationship between the self and the environment.* Unpublished doctoral dissertation, Virginia Commonwealth University, Richmond.

Sherwin, E. D. (1996). *Hope and culture: The role of religion and spirituality in African American identity.* Unpublished manuscript.

Snyder, C. R., Harris, C., Anderson, J. R., Holleran, S. A., Irving, L. M., et al. (1991). The will and the ways: The development and validation of an individual differences measure of hope. *Journal of Personality and Social Psychology, 60*(4), 570–585.

Snyder, C. R., Hoza, B., Pelham, W. E., Rapoff, M., Ware, L., et al. (1997). The development and validation of the Children's Hope scale. *Journal of Pediatric Psychology, 22,* 399–421.

Sue, D. W., Arredondo, P., & McDavis, R. J. (1992). Multicultural competencies/standards: A call to the profession. *Journal of Counseling and Development, 70(4),* 477–486.

Sue, D. W., Bernier, J. B., Durran, M., Feinberg, L., Pedersen, P., et al. (1982). Position paper: Cross-cultural counseling competencies. *The Counseling Psychologist, 10,* 45–52.

Sue, D. W., & Sue, D. (1999). *Counseling the culturally different: Theory and practice* (3rd ed.). New York: John Wiley & Sons.

Tepperman, L., & Curtis, J. (1995). A life satisfaction scale for use with national adult samples from the USA, Canada and Mexico. *Social Indicators Research, 35*(3), 255–270.

U.S. Bureau of the Census. (2001). *Population estimates program, population division.* Washington, DC: Government Printing Office.

Walsh, W. B., & Betz, N. E. (2001). *Tests and assessment* (4th ed.). Upper Saddle River, NJ: Prentice-Hall.

Part II

Cognitive Models and Measures

4

Learned Optimism: The Measurement of Explanatory Style

Karen Reivich and Jane Gillham

Dictionary definitions of optimism encompass two related concepts. The first of these is a hopeful disposition or a conviction that "good" will ultimately prevail. The second conception of optimism refers to the belief, or the inclination to believe, that the world is the best of all possible worlds. In psychological research, *optimism* has referred to hopeful expectations in a given situation (Scheier & Carver, 1988) and, recently, to general expectancies that are positive (Scheier & Carver, 1993). This more generalized expectancy, or "dispositional optimism," is related to a variety of indexes of health. Individuals who score high on measures of dispositional optimism report fewer depressive symptoms, greater use of effective coping strategies, and fewer physical symptoms than do pessimists (for reviews see Scheier & Carver, 1992, 1993).

Consistent with the second, broader definition of optimism, the terms *optimism* and *pessimism* recently have been applied to the ways in which people routinely think about *causes* of events in their lives (Seligman, 1991). People are optimistic when they attribute problems in their lives to temporary, specific, and external (as opposed to permanent, pervasive, and internal) causes. An optimistic explanatory style is associated with higher levels of motivation, achievement, and physical well-being and lower levels of depressive symptoms (for reviews see Buchanan & Seligman, 1995; Peterson & Steen, 2001).

Psychologists interested in optimism tend to reside in one of two parallel universes. In each, similar terms apply and similar findings are obtained. Until recently, however, there has been surprisingly little discussion of the relationship between dispositional optimism (see chapter 5) and explanatory style (see Gillham, Shatté, Reivich, & Seligman, 2001). Carver and Scheier (2002) argued that dispositional optimism and explanatory style theories are conceptually linked. However, several researchers caution that causal attributions and predictions can be unrelated (Abramson, Alloy, & Metalsky, 1989; Hammen & Cochran, 1981). Given these conflicting views, it is important to clarify the link between explanations and expectations.

In this present chapter, we will describe the explanatory style construct of optimism as grounded in two theories of explanatory style, review the three most common methods for assessing explanatory style, and present some of the major research findings from this literature.

Explanatory Style Theories

The Reformulated Learned Helplessness Theory

When positive and negative situations occur we search for an explanation. According to the reformulated learned helplessness theory (RLHT: Abramson, Seligman, & Teasdale, 1978), the manner in which we routinely explain events in our lives can drain or enhance our motivation, reduce or increase our persistence, and render us vulnerable to depression or protect us from it. The RLHT describes three dimensions on which explanations can vary: internal versus external, stable versus unstable, and global versus specific. Optimistic explanations for negative events are those that are more external, unstable, and specific. That is, problems are believed to be caused by other people or situational factors, the causes are seen as fleeting in nature, and are localized to one or a few situations in one's life. Pessimistic explanations for negative events are those that are more internal, stable, and global. In explaining a conflict with a colleague, for example, an optimist might tell herself, "She's going through a rough time right now" (external, unstable, specific), whereas a pessimist may speculate, "I'm not good at making relationships work" (internal, stable, global). When explaining positive events, pessimistic and optimistic patterns reverse. Optimistic explanations for positive events are internal, stable, and global. That is, the source of success and good fortune is seen as caused by the self, lasting, and likely to affect many domains in one's life. In contrast, pessimistic explanations for good events are external, unstable, and specific, such as, "I got lucky this time."

According to the RLHT, pessimistic and optimistic explanations will lead to different expectations about the future. Individuals who attribute negative events to stable and global causes will expect outcomes to be uncontrollable in the future. These individuals will be vulnerable to helplessness in the face of adversity. In contrast, individuals who attribute negative events to unstable or specific causes will expect to exert control in the future and hence will be more resilient. The RLHT proposes that the stability of the cause is related to the duration of helplessness symptoms; the globality of the cause is related to the generalization of helplessness across situations; and the internality of the cause is related to self-esteem deficits in depression.

The Hopelessness Theory of Depression

Abramson et al. (1989) argued that the stable and global dimensions of explanatory style have a stronger impact on motivation and depression than does the internal dimension. Thus, blaming a conflict with one's spouse on the belief that "love never endures" (an external, stable, and global attribution) will lead to helplessness even though the attribution is not internal. According to the hopelessness theory (HT), a revision of the RLHT, three types of interpretations can put one at risk for depression following a negative event. First, the event may be attributed to stable and global causes. Second, negative or catastrophic consequences of the event may be inferred. Third, negative characteristics about the self may be inferred. When these interpretations are made frequently, they lead to negative expectations about the occurrence of highly valued outcomes (a negative outcome expectancy) and to negative expectations about one's ability to change the likelihood of these outcomes (a helplessness expectancy). According to the HT, these negative expectations are the proximal cause of a subtype of depression characterized by retarded initiation of voluntary response, sad affect, lack of energy, and apathy.

The Measurement of Explanatory Style

In this chapter, we will discuss three methods for assessing explanatory style: the Attributional Style Questionnaire, the Content Analysis of Verbatim Explanations technique and the Children's Attributional Style Questionnaire. The majority of researchers focusing on adults have used the Attributional Style Questionnaire (ASQ: Peterson et al., 1982; Seligman, Abramson, Semmel, & von Baeyer, 1979). It is important to note, however, that over the past 10 years, explanatory-style researchers have begun to use two expanded Attributional Style Questionnaires (E–ASQ: Peterson & Villanova, 1988; E–ASQ: Metalsky, Halberstadt, & Abramson, 1987). The extended ASQs have been the favorite measures in investigations of the HT (Metalsky & Joiner, 1992; Metalsky, Joiner, Hardin, & Abramson, 1993). These scales contain more negative events, and are therefore more reliable than the original ASQ. Because the extended ASQs do not sample positive events, only explanatory style for negative events can be assessed. Recently, Abramson, Metalsky, and Alloy (1998b) developed the Cognitive Styles Questionnaire to assess the tendency to infer stable and global causes, negative consequences, and negative characteristics about the self.

Other studies have assessed explanatory style by analyzing speeches, statements, journal entries, and other written materials using the content analysis of verbatim explanations (CAVE) technique (Peterson, Bettes, & Seligman, 1985). In CAVE, causal explanations for positive and negative events are extracted and then coded for their internality, stability, and globality.

The Children's Attributional Style Questionnaire (CASQ: Kaslow, Tannenbaum, & Seligman, 1978) is the most widely used measure of explanatory style in children. The CASQ presents 48 hypothetical events (24 positive and 24 negative events) in a forced-choice format. This instrument yields the same composite and subscale scores as the original ASQ. Recently, Thompson and colleagues developed a revised version of the CASQ (CASQ–R: Thompson, Kaslow, Weiss, & Nolen-Hoeksema, 1998). The CASQ–R is derived from the CASQ but contains 24 items (12 related to positive events and 12 for negative events). The CASQ–R is somewhat less reliable than the original CASQ, but may be particularly useful for assessing explanatory style in younger children or in time-limited situations.

The Attributional Style Questionnaire

The ASQ was developed in 1979 by Seligman et al. to investigate the central prediction of the RLHT: Those who tend to explain bad events with internal, stable, and global explanations will be more prone to depression than those who offer external, unstable, and specific explanations for bad events (Abramson et al., 1978). The ASQ is a self-report instrument containing 12 hypothetical situations: six negative events (e.g., "You can't get all the work done that others expect of you") and six positive events (e.g., "Your spouse [boyfriend/girlfriend] has been treating you more lovingly"). It was developed to maximize the degree to which the respondent projects his or her idiosyncratic belief system onto the stimuli, rather than reports the true causes of an event by containing simple, ambiguous, hypothetical events. These events require the respondent to construct the context surrounding the situations, which increases the likelihood that the respondent will project his or her subjective interpretation onto the ambiguous situations. For each situation, respondents are asked to vividly imagine it happening to them and to decide what they believe would be the one major cause. The respondents then indicate, on 7-point rating scales, the degree to which the cause is internal or external, stable or unstable, and global or specific (1 = external/unstable/specific, 7 = internal/stable/global).

Of the 12 situations, six have an affiliation orientation and six have an achievement orientation. Affiliation items are those that present an event revolving around interpersonal relationships, whereas achievement items are those that present events regarding work, academic success, and sports. An example of an item used to assess explanatory style in the affiliation domain is, "You meet a friend who acts hostilely toward you." An example of an item used to assess explanatory style in the achievement domain is, "You do a project that is highly praised." Both affiliative- and achievement-oriented items were included for two reasons. First, by including situations across a broad spectrum, a cross-situational "style" can be measured. Second, the inclusion of both types of items allows for the possibility that an individual may have an affiliative style that differs from his or her achievement style.

SCORING. The ASQ yields six individual dimension scores and three composite scores. The individual dimension scores are the following: the average of the internality ratings for the six negative events (IN), the average of the stability ratings for the six negative events (SN), and the average of the six globality ratings for the six negative events (GN). Individual dimension scores are also formed in a similar manner based on the six positive events (internal positive, IP; stable positive, SP; and global positive, GP). Three composite scores also are derived: composite negative explanatory style (CN), which is the composite score for the six negative events, summing across internal, stable, and global dimensions and dividing by the number of events; composite positive explanatory style (CP), the composite score for the six positive events; and a total score, composite positive minus composite negative (CP–CN).

Three other scores for hopelessness and hopefulness have been derived from the ASQ, although these are not used as frequently. Hopelessness (HN) is determined by averaging the stability and globality dimensions for negative events, whereas hopefulness (HP) is the average of the stability and globality dimensions for positive events. That is, HN is taken to be the belief that the causes of negative events are permanent and pervasive (e.g., "The audience reacted negatively because people are competitive and like to see others fail"). Hopefulness, in comparison, is the belief that when things go right, it is a result of forces that will persist and affect many areas of our lives (e.g., "The project was highly praised because people are generally supportive and generous"). Just as CP–CN is a composite measure formed by subtracting a respondent's CN score from his or her CP score, some researchers also form the composite HP–HN.

In summary, the ASQ can be scored by forming composite variables or through the individual attributional dimensions. Both scoring procedures have been used in explanatory style research. The question of when to form composite scores versus when to rely on the individual dimensions remains a critical issue. Composite scores boost reliability. Exploring the individual dimensions enables the researcher or clinician to more critically assess the relationship between specific attributional dimensions and an array of deficits and/or outcomes.

INTERNAL CONSISTENCY. Internal consistency measures are used to determine the homogeneity of items—that is, whether the items measure the same property. Several studies have investigated the internal consistency of the ASQ. Based on these findings, the ASQ subscales have modest reliability; however, when composite scores are formed, substantially higher and satisfactory levels of internal consistency are found (Peterson et al., 1982; Seligman et al., 1979).

CONSISTENCY ACROSS VALENCE. Peterson et al. (1982) found that the attributional composites for positive versus negative events are unrelated to each other. Schulman, Castellon, and Seligman (1989), on the other hand, found a small, significant correlation between CN and CP, $-.24$ ($p < .002$, $n = 160$). That is, in their sample, the more pessimistic an individual was regarding failures, the less optimistic he or she was regarding successes. These data highlight the importance of analyzing explanatory style for positive events separately from the style for negative events.

TEST–RETEST RELIABILITY. According to the RLHT, individuals have a fairly enduring explanatory style. This is not to say that explanatory style cannot be changed. Indeed, the primary goal of cognitive therapy is to teach the client how to evaluate whether his or her thoughts are accurate, and if they are not accurate, how to change them.

Golin, Sweeney, and Schaeffer (1981) have investigated the test–retest reliability of the ASQ. Golin et al. administered the ASQ to 206 undergraduate students and readministered the questionnaire to 180 of these students. For positive events, test–retest reliability coefficients were .66 for internality, .56 for stability, .51 for globality, and .67 for composite. For negative events, the test–retest correlations were .47 for internality, .61 for stability, .65 for globality, and .67 for composite.

Although explanatory style may be stable, it is important to note that intervention can significantly change ASQ scores. For example, in a recent study of treatments for severely depressed outpatients, explanatory style improved significantly for patients treated with cognitive therapy or antidepressant medications (Hollon, 2001).

Based on these findings, adults' explanatory style is stable although not immutable. It can be changed through therapies for depression and through cognitive interventions. Moreover, there may be individual differences in the extent to which someone has a true style. That is, some individuals may be more consistent in projecting their idiosyncratic explanations onto diverse situations, whereas others may be more situation- and reality-based.

CONSTRUCT VALIDITY. Studies of construct validity are conducted to validate the theory underlying the instrument. To test construct validity, the researcher posits relationships that should and should not exist between the construct and other measures, and determines whether these relationships are empirically supported. In one test of construct validity, Schulman et al. (1989) administered the ASQ to 169 undergraduates. For this study, each hypothetical event and the cause the respondent wrote down was extracted from the ASQ and rated by three raters. The raters did not know who the respondent was and what other explanations they gave. (This technique, CAVE, is discussed in detail later in the chapter.) The ratings of the explanations were moderately to highly correlated with the respondents' ratings on the ASQ. Correlations were .71 for CPCN, .48 for CN, and .52 for CP ($ps < .001$, $n = 159$).

CRITERION VALIDITY. Criterion-related validity is established by comparing test scores with one or more criteria known to measure the attribute being examined. The predictive and concurrent validity of the ASQ has been supported in a variety of domains. An optimistic explanatory style has been shown to predict lower levels of depression, greater achievement, as well as improved physical health (e.g., Peterson & Seligman, 1984a; Schulman, Keith, & Seligman, 1991).

Content Analysis of Verbatim Explanations

A second method for assessing explanatory style is the CAVE technique. The CAVE technique, developed by Peterson, Luborsky, and Seligman (1983), enables researchers to assess explanatory style by analyzing documents such as interviews, diaries, letters, essays, newspaper articles, therapy transcripts, speeches, and so forth. The CAVE technique yields the same scores as the ASQ.

The CAVE technique involves two independent steps: extraction of verbatim event–causal explanation couplets and rating of the causal statements on the internality, stability, and globality dimensions of explanatory style. Both steps are completed by trained researchers who do not know the identity of the respondent as well as to the outcome measures. Both extracting and rating steps have proven highly reliable.

This approach may be more ecologically valid than a self-report questionnaire. The events described in the material are more relevant and meaningful to the individuals than the events presented in the ASQ. Furthermore, these spontaneous explanations are more likely to be honest because demand characteristics associated with completing a questionnaire will not be present.

REALITY VERSUS STYLE. Unlike the ASQ, the events used in the CAVE technique are not hypothetical; rather, they are occurrences from the person's life. Therefore, reality can be a major determinant of the explanation offered. If the material from which the attributions are extracted is mainly reality-driven, little will be learned about the idiosyncratic style of the individual. Events, however, are often complex and the causes of the events are usually many and varied. For example, suppose an employee has an argument with his boss regarding how to prioritize his tasks. Although usually a quiet man, in this conflict, the employee turns red in the face and raises his voice in anger. In addition, imagine that the employee recently learned that he would not be promoted and that his boss described a presentation he made as "underwhelming." In addition, before the conflict, the employee's wife called to tell him that she was asked to transfer to a prestigious new position in a different city and that their daughter refused to go to school because she hated her friends. It is possible that all of these factors contributed to the conflict with his boss. But, when explaining to himself the cause of the fight, it is not likely that he will take into account (or even be aware of) all of these factors. Most likely, he will explain the fight by only one or two of the many contributing variables, and the ones that occur to him may be those driven by his explanatory style. For example, if he tends to see the causes of problems as stable, he is more likely to focus on the contributing factors that are permanent rather than those that are temporary. Therefore, although the CAVE technique relies more on actual versus hypothetical events, these events are often as ambiguous as those found on the ASQ.

CONSISTENCY IN EXPLANATIONS. Although explanatory style is regarded as a cognitive trait, it is not expected that people will maintain consistency in their style at all times. Fluctuations occur across time and across situations. To use the CAVE technique effectively, several causal explanations must be found for an individual, and the events should span achievement and affiliation situations. Moreover, Peterson and Seligman (1984a) suggested that the term *style* should be reserved for individuals whose causal explanations are stable.

EXTRACTING EVENT-EXPLANATION UNITS. An *event* is defined as any stimulus that occurs in an individual's environment or within the individual (e.g., thoughts or feelings) that is positive or negative from that individual's point of view. Events can be mental (e.g., "I can't stop thinking about him"), social (e.g., "We were invited to a posh restaurant"), or physical (e.g., "I was diagnosed with cancer"). Events may occur in the past, present, or hypothetical future, but they must be unambiguously positive or negative from the respondent's point of view. This latter point is often difficult to assess. For example, "My wife and I started seeing a therapist" may be experienced as a negative event or a positive event, depending on the individual. This should only be extracted if it is clear how this man views being in therapy. Events that have positive and negative elements ("I am seeing a doctor for my weight problem"), and neutral events ("I took a walk around the block") should not be extracted.

To be extracted, the respondent must express his or her own explanation for the event. The respondent cannot simply agree with or quote another person's explanation. For example, "My boss put me on an important project. She said she wants me to do the job because I have the best writing skills in the firm" would not be an acceptable extraction because the causal explanation comes from the employer, not the respondent. Although explanations must be in the respondent's own words, there are times when the event itself may be spoken by someone else. In addition, there must be a clear causal relationship between the explanation and the event (not simply a sequence of events that describe without explaining), and the explanation must be perceived as causal by the respondent. Possible causes can include other events, behaviors, dispositions, and so on.

The procedure begins by searching through any verbatim material, audio-taped, videotaped, or written, for event-explanation units. Even if the word "because" or its synonyms are missing, event-explanation units can be extracted if an intended causal relationship can be inferred. Examples of acceptable event-explanation units (E = event, A = attribution) are,

> **E:** I lost my temper with my son.
> **A:** He doesn't listen to a word I say.
> **E:** My sister was rude to me.
> **A:** She doesn't care about my feelings at all.

Following is an example of unacceptable extraction:

> **E:** I must be getting sick.
> **A:** because I feel lethargic and I have a bad cough.

"Because" does not always mean a causal explanation will follow. In this case, the respondent is giving a definition of what she means by "getting sick" and is not giving the cause of her illness.

Once event-explanation units have been extracted, these units are randomized within and between respondents before they are presented to the raters. The randomization procedure is important because it ensures that the raters are not biased by previous ratings for the same person and do not fall into entrenched rating patterns.

Finally, it has been found that independent judges agree more than 90% of the time whether or not an extraction should be included as a causal explanation (Peterson et al., 1985). This level of agreement occurs when a stringent criterion for the identification of causal explanations is used. Poor extractions degrade the data.

RATING OF EXTRACTIONS. As with the ASQ, ratings of explanations are assigned to the three dimensions (internal versus external, stable versus unstable, global versus specific) using a 7-point scale. Ratings range from 1 to 7 for each dimension, with a 7 representing the most internal, stable, and global explanations; and a 1 representing the most external, unstable, and specific.

THE INTERNAL VERSUS EXTERNAL SCALE. The internal versus external dimension reflects the degree to which the explanation is about the self or about others or circumstance. The internal versus external scale should not be confused with blame, credit, control, and so forth. Although these constructs are often expressed, the purpose of this scale is to distinguish between self-caused versus other-caused attributions only—not to distinguish between subcategories of the internal dimension.

Examples of a 1 rating on this dimension include explanations that invoke the actions of another person, the difficulty or ease of a task, or time and environmental factors (such as a natural disaster, the weather, or economics). Examples of a 7 rating include references to the individual's own personality or physical traits, behavior, decisions, ability or inability, motivation, knowledge, disability, illness, injury, age, and social or political classifications (such as widow, liberal, etc.). Ratings in the 2 through 6 range apply to explanations in which the cause shares both internal and external elements and is an interaction between self and another person or between self and the environment. Following are some examples:

> **E:** I won the debate
> **A:** because the other guy could barely put a sentence together. (Rating = 1)
> **E:** My husband and I have been fighting a lot
> **A:** because he can't come to terms with my work schedule (Rating = 2 or 3)
> **E:** My daughter and I fight all the time.
> **A:** We never seem to give each other the benefit of the doubt. (Rating = 4)
> **E:** I need surgery on my knee.
> **A:** It's in bad shape from all that skiing I do. (Rating = 4 or 5)
> **E:** I didn't get the promotion
> **A:** because I'm a woman. (Rating = 7)

THE STABLE VERSUS UNSTABLE SCALE. This dimension refers to the persistence in time of the cause, whether the cause of the event is chronic (stable) or temporary (unstable). It is crucial to distinguish between the stability of the cause and the stability of the events; we are concerned with the former. A useful framework from which to assess the stability of the cause is, "Given this event has occurred, how permanent is this cause?" The RLHT theory would indicate that individuals who consistently offer stable causes will suffer chronic deficits. Therefore, to test this hypothesis we must rate only the stability of the attribution, regardless of the event stability.

There are four interacting criteria that help to determine the appropriate stability rating:

1. The tense of the cause. If the cause of an event is phrased in the past tense, then the rating would tend to be less stable than if the cause is in the present or progressive tense.

2. The probability of future reoccurrence of the cause. A cause that is unlikely to occur again would be less stable than a cause that is likely to occur again.
3. An intermittent versus a continuous cause. A cause that is intermittent, such as the weather, would be less stable than a continuous cause, such as a physical trait.
4. A characterological versus a behavioral cause. Explaining an event by a character trait is more stable than attributing an event to a behavior. These criteria should be used as guidelines when rating. They will not all be relevant in all cases, nor should they be weighted equally. For instance, the tense of the attribution should be used as a way to fine-tune the rating, knocking it up or down a point depending on the tense in which it is stated. Following are examples:

> **E:** I can't attend the conference
> **A:** because I am going to a wedding. (Rating = 1; this cause is in the present tense but is unlikely to occur again.)
> **E:** I always have trouble falling asleep
> **A:** when it is hot. (Rating = 3; this cause is likely to occur again but only intermittently.)
> **E:** I've been afraid to go out in the dark
> **A:** since I was attacked. (Rating = 4; this cause occurred in the past, has a small probability of a future occurrence, but may exert an ongoing influence on behavior.)
> **E:** It's difficult for me to express my anger.
> **A:** That's just the way I was raised. (Rating = 5; this cause occurred continuously in the past and has an ongoing influence on behavior.)
> **E:** I didn't get the job
> **A:** because I'm Latino. (Rating = 7; this cause is unalterable and continuous.)

THE GLOBAL VERSUS SPECIFIC SCALE. This dimension measures the extent to which a cause affects the entire life of an individual (global) or just a few areas (specific). Typically, there is not enough information to indicate the pervasiveness of the effects of the cause, nor do we always know which domains of the individual's life are particularly important. For example, poor cooking ability would have a greater effect on a chef than on a carpenter; quality of friendships would tend to be more important to a gregarious person than to a recluse; and physical grace would have a more global impact on a ballet dancer than a mechanic. In the absence of such intimate knowledge, it is useful to consider the impact of a cause on the scope of an "average" individual's life in terms of two general categories—*achievement* and *affiliation,* each comprising subcategories. Clearly, this is an artificial distinction and is neither exclusive nor exhaustive, but as a heuristic it helps keep the rater from projecting biases onto the rating of globality.

Achievement, for instance, would include occupational or academic success, accumulation of knowledge or skills, sense of individuality or independence, and social status. Affiliation includes intimate relationships, sense of belongingness, play, and marital or familial health. An attribution may affect just one category, part of one category, parts of both categories (such as mental or physical health), all of one category, or all of both categories.

It is crucial when rating globality that the stability dimension is held constant. That is, the rater is assessing at this point in time, not across time, how much of the individual's life is affected by the cause. Although the stable and global dimensions are significantly intercorrelated and probably often overlap in reality, it is important to rate each of these two dimensions independently of the other. Consider the following examples:

> **E:** I got a speeding ticket
> **A:** I guess the cop had to fill her quota for the day. (Rating = 1; this attribution only affects this situation.)
> **E:** My friends are annoyed with me
> **A:** because I'm not very spontaneous. (Rating = 2 or 3; this cause affects part of the affiliative category and possibly part of the achievement category.)
> **E:** I feel more confident about myself
> **A:** since I had the plastic surgery. (Rating = 4 or 5; this cause will probably affect some of affiliative and some achievement situations.)
> **E:** I've had to cut back on my level of activity
> **A:** since my radiation treatment began. (Rating = 5 or 6; this cause affects many aspects of a person's life.)
> **E:** I've been in a funk for weeks.
> **A:** Nothing in life seems to matter anymore. (Rating = 7)

INTERRATER RELIABILITY. Schulman et al. (1989) found interrater reliability for the CAVE technique to be satisfactory .89 for CN and .80 for CP. Alphas for negative events were .93 for internal, .63 for stable, and .73 for global. For positive events, alphas were .95 for internal, .66 for stable, and .48 for global. Because reliabilities for the composites are better than for individual dimensions, as with the ASQ, researchers are encouraged to focus on composites.

CONSTRUCT VALIDITY. Peterson and Seligman (1981) first used the CAVE technique in a study of the relationship between explanatory style and depression. In this study, the CAVE technique was used with therapy transcripts, and the researchers found that as a patient's optimism increased his or her depression decreased. This study supports similar research findings with the ASQ (Hamilton & Abramson, 1983; Persons & Rao, 1985) that indicate that explanatory style is an index of improvement in depression during the course of psychotherapy.

To validate the CAVE further, Peterson et al. (1985) asked 66 undergraduates to write essays about the two worst events that had occurred to them during the past year. After writing the essays, respondents completed the ASQ and the Beck Depression Inventory (BDI). Two primary results from this study further support the validity of the CAVE technique. First, causal explanations were significantly correlated with the BDI scores as predicted by the RLHT. Second, CAVE scores significantly correlated with the corresponding scales on the ASQ.

Peterson and Seligman (1984b) conducted a study of morbidity and mortality using CAVE and narrative samples from members of the St. Louis Baseball Hall of Fame between 1900 and 1950 to investigate the effect of optimism on later health and longevity. Although this may seem like an odd population to use, it is one of the few that meets the criteria to conduct a study of this sort— That is, (a) the respondents should be already dead or very old so that the study can be conducted retrospectively, rather than prospectively; (b) the respondents must have left enough recorded statements while young to extract; (c) the respondents should have been physically healthy when the statements were made to partially control for the effects of ill health on explanations; (d) to control for hardship on physical health, the respondents should have been successful when the statements were made; and (e) there must be enough individuals that meet the other criteria to test the hypothesis statistically. The investigators extracted and rated players' sports page interviews. Peterson and Seligman (1984b) correlated the players' composite style for both positive and negative events with age at death (or age in 1984, if still living). The results suggest that an optimistic style for positive events predicted longevity ($r = .45$, $p < .01$), whereas a pessimistic style for negative events showed the opposite relationship ($r = -.26$, $p < .08$). These results, though tentative because of a small sample size, do suggest that the CAVE technique might make predictive psychohistory possible.

In a similar study, Peterson, Seligman, and Valliant (1988) predicted morbidity from explanatory style for individuals who had participated in the Grant Study, a longitudinal investigation of the Harvard classes of 1939 to 1942. The 99 respondents in this study gave interviews in 1946 about war experiences. Peterson et al. extracted and rated this material and found that the more optimistic an individual was in 1946, the better his physical health in 1970, even when physical health and mental health at age 25 were controlled. These studies, taken together, show the CAVE technique to be a valid and reliable tool.

The Children's Attributional Style Questionnaire (CASQ)

The CASQ was developed for use with children approximately ages 8 to 14 (Kaslow et al., 1978). The CASQ contains 48 items, each of which consists of a hypothetical positive or negative event involving the child and two possible causes of the event. Respondents are instructed to choose the cause that best describes why the event occurred. The two causes provided hold constant two of the attributional dimensions while varying the third. For example, the following sample item from the CASQ measures internality versus externality (while holding constant stability and globality): "You go on a vacation with a group of people and you have a good time: (a) I was in a good mood (internal); (b) The people I was with were in good moods (external)." Sixteen questions pertain to each of the three dimensions. Half of the questions provide positive events to be explained and half provide negative events.

SCORING. The CASQ is scored by assigning a value of 1 to each internal, stable, or global response and a value of 0 to each external, unstable, specific response. Subscales are formed by summing these scores across the appropriate questions for each of the three causal dimensions. Items are scored separately for positive events and negative events. Thus, the same scores can be derived from the CASQ as from the ASQ.

PSYCHOMETRIC PROPERTIES OF THE CASQ. CASQ subscale scores, like the ASQ, possessed only modest reliabilities. Internal consistencies mostly exceeded scale intercorrelations, however, indicating that the scales were empirically distinguishable and that they were not high. Higher reliabilities were obtained by combining the subscales (separately for positive events and for negative events) to form a composite, as is done with the ASQ. The CASQ scores were consistent over the six-month interval (composite rs = .71, .66, ps < .001), showing style to be stable among children.

Children exhibiting depressive symptoms were more likely than nondepressed children to endorse internal, stable, global explanations for negative events. Furthermore, a pessimistic explanatory style predicted depressive symptoms in children at a six-month follow-up, when initial levels of depression were controlled for. Several other studies using the CASQ have corroborated these findings (e.g., Kaslow, Rehm, Pollack, & Siegel, 1988).

Future Developments in the Measurement of Explanatory Style

Research on Explanatory Style and Expectations

Despite the role of expectations in the RLHT and HT, and the parallel findings for dispositional optimism and explanatory style, few investigations of explanatory style have assessed expectations for the future. One exception is a study by Metalsky and colleagues. In this study, among students who received a low grade, those who attributed negative achievement events to stable and global factors expected to perform poorly in the future. These expectations predicted changes in mood (Metalsky et al., 1993).

A handful of studies have assessed both explanatory style and dispositional optimism, using the Life Orientation Test (LOT: Scheier & Carver, 1985). These have yielded inconsistent findings. Carver and Scheier (1992) reported correlations between the ASQ CP–CN composite and the LOT that are in the high .10s and low .20s. Kamen (1989) reported a correlation of –.25 between the LOT and the ASQ CN composite. In contrast, Hjelle and colleagues reported a correlation of .41 between the LOT and the ASQ CP–CN (Hjelle, Belongia, & Nesser, 1996). Gillham found correlations of .63 and .41 between the LOT and the ASQ CP–CN composite at two different assessment points. These correlations rose to .77 and .49, respectively, after they were corrected for attenuation (Gillham, Tassoni, Engel, DeRubeis, & Seligman, 1998). Thus, across these studies, correlations have ranged from below .20 to .77. Clearly more research is needed that directly examines the relationship between the two constructs.

Clarifying the Optimism Construct

OPTIMISM VERSUS EXPLANATORY STYLE. Another obvious area of confusion results from the use of the terms *optimism* and *pessimism* to refer to explanatory style. The following arguments have been made for the use of these terms by researchers investigating explanatory style. First, optimism and pessimism are terms from ordinary language. Second, it is optimistic to view the causes of negative events as external, temporary, and affecting few areas of life. Explanatory style is associated with many outcomes, which are linked to pessimism, such as depression, lowered expectancies, passivity, poor achievement, and poor health. In contrast, Abramson and colleagues argued that the use of optimism and pessimism to denote causal attributions is potentially misleading because our intuitive notion of optimism concerns expectations (Abramson, Dykman, & Needles, 1991). Although optimism and pessimism may be useful modifiers of terms like attributions and explanatory style, we agree with the suggestion by Abramson and colleagues that these terms in isolation be reserved for the expectational components of the RLHT and HT (Abramson et al., 1991). This suggestion also applies to the terms *hopeful* and *hopeless,* which recently have been applied to explanatory style (Abramson et al., 1989). Although explanatory style and pessimism are associated with many of the same outcomes, this does not mean we should equate the constructs. In most studies, measures of explanatory style are only weakly to moderately correlated with measures of dispositional optimism (Scheier & Carver, 1992).

DIMENSIONS. Most research on explanatory style uses composite scores that sum across three dimensions (internality, stability, and globality) of explanatory style. There is considerable debate among researchers regarding the validity of this practice. Correlations between the different explanatory style dimensions, particularly correlations between the internal dimension and other dimensions, are often quite low. This raises questions about whether these dimensions reflect a single construct (explanatory style) and should be weighted equally (Carver, 1989).

Overlap With Other Psychological Constructs

Recently, researchers have become interested in the uniqueness of optimism as a psychological construct. Watson and Clark proposed that several seemingly diverse personality and cognitive constructs actually reflect facets of two broad underlying constructs: positive affectivity (PA) and negative affectivity (NA; Watson & Clark, 1984). Thus, constructs such as neuroticism, self-esteem, optimism, and explanatory style may correlate with each other and "predict" depressive symptoms simply because they each reflect NA. In support of this view, Smith and colleagues found that the correlation between optimism and depressive symptoms disappeared when NA was partialed out (Smith, Pope, Rhodewalt, & Poulton, 1989). In contrast, Chang, Maydeu-Olivares, and D'Zurilla (1997) found that optimism and pessimism remained significant predictors of psychological well-being even after controlling for PA and NA. Lucas, Diener, and Suh (1996) found that optimism could be discriminated from negative affectivity and life satisfaction using a multitrait–multimethod matrix analysis. More research is needed to evaluate this hypothesis with regard to both optimism and explanatory style.

Accuracy

Most researchers investigating explanatory style and dispositional optimism have assumed that the more optimistic individuals are, the better off they will be. The research, in general, indicates that individuals with an optimistic explanatory style will have greater well-being and greater physical health than their pessimistic peers. But is being more optimistic always beneficial? Existing research on explanatory style and dispositional optimism has largely ignored the role of accuracy. Taylor and Brown (1998) and others argue that optimistic biases are adaptive. For example, nondepressed individuals overestimate their ability to control events whereas depressed individuals provide more negative (and accurate) estimates of control (Alloy & Abramson, 1979). Yet clinicians specializing in depression often report that clients overestimate the negative consequences of events and underestimate their influence over environments.

It seems likely that an optimism that is out of touch with reality will backfire. Individuals who underestimate the likelihood of negative events may find themselves unprepared. Individuals who overestimate the likelihood of success may waste energy pursuing goals they have little chance of achieving. Similarly, individuals who focus on inaccurate, albeit optimistic, explanations for problems will not be in a good position to solve problems. Thus, future research should examine the role accuracy plays in performance and health.

Conclusion

We have learned a tremendous amount about explanatory style over the past 20 years, but important questions remain. Optimism and explanatory style must be more precisely defined and differentiated from each other and from other constructs. Further work is needed to test whether the dimensions of explanatory style reflect a single construct and should be weighted equally, or whether they reflect different constructs. The use of composite scores versus individual dimensions requires more research. In addition, the value of explanatory accuracy, the relationship between explanatory style and accuracy, and methods for assessing the accuracy attributions are areas ripe for research. Finally, the mechanisms through which optimism and explanatory styles affect well-being need to be identified and the sources of optimism and explanatory style need to be discovered. If optimism and explanatory style are causally related to well-being, future research may enable us to improve the quality of life for many people.

References

Abramson, L. Y., Alloy, L. B. & Metalsky, G. I. (1989). Hopelessness depression: A theory-based subtype of depression. *Psychological Review, 96,* 358–372.

Abramson, L. Y., Alloy, L. B., & Metalsky, G. I. (1998a). *The Cognitive Style Questionnaire: A measure of the vulnerability featured in the hopelessness theory of depression.* Manuscript in preparation, University of Wisconsin-Madison.

Abramson, L. Y., Alloy, L. B., & Metalsky, G. I. (1998b). Unpublished, untitled manuscript, University of Wisconsin–Madison.

Abramson, L. Y., Dykman, B. M., & Needles, D. J. (1991). Attributional style and theory: Let no one tear them asunder. *Psychological Inquiry, 2,* 11–49.

Abramson, L. Y., Seligman, M. E. P., & Teasdale, J. D. (1978). Learned helplessness in humans: Critique and reformulation. *Journal of Abnormal Psychology, 87,* 49–74.

Alloy, L. B., & Abramson, L. Y. (1979). Judgment of contingency in depressed and nondepressed students: Sadder but wiser? *Journal of Experimental Psychology: General, 108,* 441–485.

Buchanan, G. M., & Seligman, M. E. P. (1995). *Explanatory style.* Hillsdale, NJ: Erlbaum.

Carver, C. S. (1989). How should multi-faceted personality constructs be tested? Issues illustrated by self-monitoring, attributional style, and hardiness. *Journal of Personality and Social Psychology, 36,* 1501–1511.

Carver, C. S., & Scheier, M. F. (2002). Optimism. In C. R. Snyder & S. J. Lopez (Eds.), *Handbook of positive psychology* (pp. 231–243). London: Oxford University Press.

Chang, E. C., Maydeu-Olivares, A., & D'Zurilla, T. J. (1997). Optimism and pessimism as partially independent constructs: Relationship to positive and negative affectivity and psychological well-being. *Personality and Individual Differences, 23,* 433–440.

Gillham, J. E., Shatté, A. J., Reivich, K. J., & Seligman, M. E. P. (2001). Optimism, pessimism, and explanatory style. In E. C. Chang (Ed.), *Optimism & pessimism* (pp. 53–75). Washington, DC: American Psychological Association.

Gillham, J. E., Tassoni, C. J., Engel, R. A., DeRubeis, R .J., & Seligman, M. E. P. (1998). *The relationship of explanatory style to other depression relevant constructs.* Unpublished manuscript, University of Pennsylvania, Philadelphia.

Golin, S., Sweeney, P. D., & Schaeffer, D. E. (1981). The causality of causal attributions in depression: A cross-lagged panel analysis. *Journal of Abnormal Psychology, 90,* 14–22.

Hamilton, E. W., & Abramson, L. Y. (1983). Cognitive patterns and major depressive disorder: A longitudinal study in a hospital setting. *Journal of Abnormal Psychology, 92,* 173–184.

Hammen, C., & Cochran, S. (1981). Cognitive correlates of life stress and depression in college students. *Journal of Abnormal Psychology, 90,* 23–27.

Hjelle, L., Belongia, C., & Nesser, J. (1996). Psychometric properties of the Life Orientation Test and Attributional Style Questionnaire. *Psychological Reports, 78,* 507–515.

Hollon, S. D. (2001, July). Cognitive therapy and the prevention of relapse in severely depressed outpatients. In D. M. Clark (Chair), *Cognitive therapy versus medications in the treatment of severely depressed outpatients: Acute response and the prevention of relapse.* Symposium held at the World Congress of Behavioral and Cognitive Therapies, Vancouver, Canada.

Kamen, L. P. (1989). *Learned helplessness, cognitive dissonance, and cell-mediated immunity.* Unpublished doctoral dissertation, University of Pennsylvania, Philadelphia.

Kaslow, N. J., Rehm, L. P., Pollack, S. L., & Siegel, A. W. (1988). Attributional style and self-control behavior in depressed and nondepressed children and their parents. *Journal of Abnormal Child Psychology, 16,* 163–175.

Kaslow, N. J., Tannenbaum, R. L., & Seligman, M. E. P. (1978). *The KASTAN: A children's attributional style questionnaire.* Unpublished manuscript, University of Pennsylvania, Philadelphia.

Lucas, R. E., Diener, E., & Suh, E. (1996). Discriminant validity of well-being measures. *Journal of Personality and Social Psychology, 71,* 616–628.

Metalsky, G. I., Halberstadt, L. J., & Abramson, L. Y. (1987). Vulnerability to depressive mood reactions: Toward a more powerful test of the diathesis-stress and causal mediation components of the reformulated theory of depression. *Journal of Personality and Social Psychology, 52*, 386–393.

Metalsky, G. I., & Joiner, T. E. (1992). Vulnerability to depressive symptomatology: A prospective test of the diathesis-stress and causal mediation components of the hopelessness theory of depression. *Journal of Personality and Social Psychology, 63*, 667–675.

Metalsky, G. I., Joiner, T. E., Hardin, T. S., & Abramson, L. Y. (1993). Depressive reactions to failure in a naturalistic setting: A test of the hopelessness and self-esteem theories of depression. *Journal of Abnormal Psychology, 102*, 101–109.

Persons, J. B., & Rao, P. A. (1985). Longitudinal study of cognitions, life events, and depression in psychiatric inpatients. *Journal of Abnormal Psychology, 94*, 51–63.

Peterson, C., Bettes, B. A., & Seligman, M. E. P. (1985). Depressive symptoms and unprompted causal attributions: Content analysis. *Behavior Research and Therapy, 23*, 379–382.

Peterson, C., Luborsky, L., & Seligman, M. E. P. (1983). Attributions and depressive mood shifts: A case study using the symptom-context method. *Journal of Abnormal Psychology, 92*, 96–103.

Peterson, C., & Seligman, M. E. P. (1981). Helplessness and attributional style in depression. *Tiddsskrift for Norsk Psykologforening, 18*, 3–18, 53–59.

Peterson, C., & Seligman, M. E. P. (1984a). Causal explanations as a risk factor for depression: Theory and evidence. *Psychological Review, 91*, 347–374.

Peterson, C., & Seligman, M. E. P. (1984b). *Content analysis of verbatim explanations: The CAVE technique for assessing explanatory style.* Unpublished manuscript, Virginia Polytechnic Institute and State University.

Peterson, C., Seligman, M. E. P., & Valliant, G. E. (1988). Pessimistic explanatory style is a risk factor for physical illness: A thirty-five year longitudinal study. *Journal of Personality and Social Psychology, 55*, 23–27.

Peterson, C., Semmel, A., von Baeyer, C., Abramson, L. Y., Metalsky, G. I., & Seligman, M. E. P. (1982). The Attributional Style Questionnaire. *Cognitive Therapy and Research, 6*, 287–299.

Peterson, C., & Steen, T. (2001). Optimistic explanatory style. In C. R. Snyder & S. J. Lopez (Eds.), *The handbook of positive psychology* (pp. 244–256). London: Oxford University Press.

Peterson, C., & Villanova, P. (1988). An Expanded Attributional Style Questionnaire. *Journal of Abnormal Psychology, 97*, 87–89.

Scheier, M. F., & Carver, C. S. (1985). Optimism, coping and health: Assessment and implications of generalized outcome expectancies. *Health Psychology, 4*, 219–247.

Scheier, M. F., & Carver, C. S. (1988). A model of behavioral self-regulation: Translating intention into action. In L. Berkowitz (Ed.), *Advances in experimental social psychology* (Vol. 21, pp. 303–346). San Diego, CA: Academic Press.

Scheier, M. F., & Carver, C. S. (1992). Effects of optimism on psychological and physical well-being: Theoretical overview and empirical update. *Cognitive Therapy and Research, 16*, 201–228.

Scheier, M. F., & Carver, C. S. (1993). On the power of positive thinking: The benefits of being optimistic. *Current Directions in Psychological Science, 2*, 26–30.

Schulman, P., Castellon, C., & Seligman, M. E. P. (1989). Assessing explanatory style: The Content analysis of verbatim explanations and the Attributional Style Questionnaire. *Behavior Research and Therapy, 27*, 505–512.

Schulman, P., Keith, D., & Seligman, M. E. P. (1991). Is optimism heritable? A study of twins. *Behavior Research and Therapy, 31*, 569–574.

Seligman, M. E .P. (1991). *Learned optimism.* New York: Knopf.

Seligman, M. E. P., Abramson, L. Y., Semmel, A., & von Baeyer, C. (1979). Depressive attributional style. *Journal of Abnormal Psychology, 88*, 242–247.

Smith, T. W., Pope, M. K., Rhodewalt, F., & Poulton, J. L. (1989). Optimism, neuroticism, coping, and symptom reports: An alternative interpretation of the Life Orientation Test. *Journal of Personality and Social Psychology, 56*, 640–648.

Taylor, S., & Brown, J. (1998). Illusion and well-being: A social psychological perspective on mental health. *Psychological Bulletin, 103*, 193–210.

Thompson, M., Kaslow, N. J., Weiss, B., & Nolen-Hoeksema, S. (1998). Children's Attributional Style Questionnaire–Revised: Psychometric examination. *Psychological Assessment, 10,* 166–170.

Watson, D., & Clark, L. A. (1984). Negative affectivity: The disposition to experience aversive emotional states. *Psychological Bulletin, 96,* 465–490.

5

Optimism

Charles S. Carver and Michael Scheier

Optimists are people who expect good things to happen to them; pessimists are people who expect bad things to happen to them. Does this difference among people matter? It certainly does. Optimists and pessimists differ in several ways that have a big impact on their lives. They differ in how they approach problems and challenges they encounter, and they differ in the manner and the success with which they cope with life's difficulties.

Definitions of optimism and pessimism rest on people's expectations for the future. This grounding in expectations links optimism and pessimism to a long tradition of expectancy–value models of motivation. As a result, the optimism construct is grounded in decades of theory and research on human motives and how motives become expressed in behavior. We begin this chapter with a brief outline of the expectancy–value approach to motivation, to make clear the dynamics we believe underlie optimism and pessimism.

Expectancy–Value Models of Motivation

Expectancy–value theories begin by assuming that behavior is aimed at the pursuit of goals. Goals have a variety of labels, but in this chapter we want to emphasize what goals have in common (for broader discussion, see Carver & Scheier, 1998). Goals are actions, end states, or values that people see as either desirable or undesirable. People try to fit their behaviors—indeed fit their very selves—to what they see as desirable. They try to stay away from what they see as undesirable (think of the undesirable as "antigoals"). The more important a goal is, the greater its value in the person's motivation. Without having a goal that matters, there is no reason to act.

The second element in expectancy–value theories is expectancy—a sense of confidence or doubt about the attainability of the goal value. If the person lacks confidence, again there will be no action. Doubts can impair effort before

Preparation of this chapter was facilitated by support from the National Cancer Institute (grants CA64710, CA64711, CA78995, and CA84944) and the National Heart, Lung, and Blood Institute (grants HL65111 and HL65112).

the action starts or while it is ongoing. Only if people have enough confidence will they act and keep acting. When people are confident about an eventual outcome, effort continues even in the face of great adversity.

Goals Vary in Breadth and Abstractness

Goals vary in specificity—from the very concrete and narrow, to those that pertain to a particular domain of life, to the very general. This suggests that expectancies have a comparable range of variation (Armor & Taylor, 1998; Carver & Scheier, 1998). You can be confident about having a fulfilling life, about making good impressions in social situations, about finding a nice place to vacation, about winning a particular tennis game, or about tying your shoes.

Which expectancies matter? Probably all of them. Expectancy-based theories generally suggest, explicitly or implicitly, that behavior is predicted best when the level of expectancy fits that of the behavior being predicted. Sometimes it is argued that prediction is best when you take into account several levels of specificity that pertain to the behavior (e.g., action-specific, domain-specific, and generalized). Many events in life, however, are new, or evolve over time. In such situations, generalized expectations may be particularly useful in predicting behavior.

The principles that apply to a focused confidence also apply to the generalized sense of confidence we think of as optimism. When we talk about optimism and pessimism, the confidence is just diffuse and broad in scope. When confronting a challenge (whatever it is), optimists should tend to approach it with confidence and persistence (even if progress is difficult or slow). Pessimists should be doubtful and hesitant.

This divergence may even be amplified when things get difficult. Optimists should assume that the adversity can be handled successfully, whereas pessimists are more likely to anticipate disaster. These differences are likely to have important implications for how people cope with stress (see, e.g., Carver & Scheier, 1999; Scheier & Carver, 1992).

Optimism as Confidence Rather Than Control

One more conceptual issue that should be addressed is the extent to which optimism overlaps with the concept of control (Thompson & Spacapan, 1991) or personal efficacy (Bandura, 1986). All of these constructs have strong overtones of expecting desired outcomes to take place. However, there is an important difference in the assumptions that are made (or not made) regarding how the desired outcomes are expected to come to pass. Self-efficacy would appear to represent a construct in which the self as a causal agent is paramount. If people have high self-efficacy expectancies, they presumably believe that their personal efforts (or personal skills) are what will determine the outcome. The same is true of the concept of control. When people perceive themselves as in control, they are assuming that the desired outcome will occur through their personal efforts (for discussion see Carver et al., 2000; Carver & Scheier, 1998).

In contrast to this emphasis, our view of the optimism construct always has been that it is broader than personal control. People who are optimistic can be optimistic because they believe they are immensely talented, because they are hard-working, because they are blessed, because they are lucky, because they have friends in the right places, or any combination of these or other factors that produce good outcomes (cf. Murphy et al., 2000). Clearly there are some circumstances in which personal efficacy is the key determinant of a desired outcome. There are also circumstances in which the goal is explicitly to do something yourself. In the latter case, *only* a personally determined success is the desired endpoint, so personal control over the outcome is critical. However, there are also many cases in which the causal determinant of the outcome is far less important than the occurrence of the outcome. We believe those cases also should be included under the umbrella of the optimism construct.

This position has sometimes caused people to question whether optimists can really be expected to exert efforts toward attainment of desired goals, as was argued previously. Why should optimists not just sit quietly waiting for all good things to happen to them from out of the sky? (As is described shortly, they do not appear to do this.) Our answer is that the expectation of good outcomes appears to be held contingent on remaining in pursuit of those good outcomes. It may be one's own efforts that turn the tide, or it may be that by remaining involved the person is able to take advantage of breaks that fall his or her way. In either case, the optimist expects the best but also understands the need to be part of the matrix of influences on the outcome.

Effects of Optimism on Coping Responses and Well-Being

A fairly substantial body of research has investigated various hypotheses that derive from this conceptual analysis (for a broad review see Scheier, Carver, & Bridges, 2001). Optimists differ from pessimists in the subjective well-being they enjoy when experiencing various kinds of adversity. The two sorts of people also differ from one another in the manner with which they attempt to cope with difficulties in their lives: Optimists are quicker to accept the reality of a challenge to their current lives. They appear to engage in more focused, active coping when such efforts are likely to be productive. They are less likely to display signs of disengagement or giving up pursuit of their goals (see also Scheier & Carver, 2001). Indeed, there is also evidence that optimism is related to better health outcomes in certain circumstances.

Assessment of Individual Differences

Individual differences in optimism versus pessimism can be measured by several different devices that have their origins in this expectancy–value model of behavior. The measures have different focuses and characteristics, but in large part they share the same underlying conception.

Life Orientation Test

We began our own work on this topic by developing a measure called the Life Orientation Test, or LOT (Scheier & Carver, 1985) to assess personal differences in optimism and pessimism. The LOT consists of eight coded items, plus fillers. Half the items are framed in an optimistic manner, half in a pessimistic manner, and respondents indicate their extent of agreement or disagreement with each item on a multipoint scale. The LOT was used in our earliest studies of the effects of optimism and pessimism. It has good psychometric properties in most respects. However, it has been criticized on the grounds that the optimistic and pessimistic item sets form two factors that are not always strongly interrelated (Chang, D'Zurilla, & Maydeu-Olivares, 1994; Marshall & Lang, 1990). Further, after having used the LOT for some years, we became aware that some of the items were assessing constructs other than expectations per se.

Accordingly, the LOT has been superseded by a newer form, called the Life Orientation Test–Revised, or LOT–R (Scheier, Carver, & Bridges, 1994). The LOT–R (see Appendix 5.1), is briefer than the original (six coded items, three framed in each direction). In revising, we omitted or rewrote items from the original if they did not focus explicitly on expectancies for the future. The LOT–R has good internal consistency (Cronbach's alpha runs in the high .70s to low .80s) and is stable over time. Because of the extensive item overlap between the original scale and the revised scale, correlations between the two scales are very high (Scheier et al., 1994). However, the positive and negative item subsets of the LOT–R are more strongly related to each other than were those of the LOT.

Both the LOT and the LOT–R provide continuous distributions of scores. Distributions tend to be skewed toward the optimistic, but not greatly so. We often refer to optimists and pessimists as though they were distinct groups, but that is really a matter of linguistic convenience. We have no specific criterion for saying that a person is an optimist or a pessimist. Rather, people range from very optimistic to very pessimistic, with most falling somewhere in the middle. Most research using these instruments uses them to create continuous distributions, with optimists and pessimists being defined relative to each other.

Hopelessness Scale

Another measure that assesses an optimistic versus pessimistic orientation to life is the Hopelessness scale (Beck, Weissman, Lester, & Trexler, 1974). This 20-item scale is similar in some respects to the pessimistic side of the LOT. However, it uses a true–false response format and it is somewhat farther ranging in its focus. In addition to items concerning pessimism per se, it also includes items that measure affective experiences and giving-up tendencies (which form separate factors but are usually not separated from each other in using the scale). We believe that both of these experiences are important concomitants of pessimism, but we also believe that they should be distinguished from pessimism per se. In addition, as Chang et al. (1994) have pointed out, many of this scale's items are fairly extreme in their expression of pessimism. This may make the measure less sensitive to variations in degree of optimism and pessimism within the less extreme part of the distribution.

The Hopelessness scale has been used in a variety of research applications, including a study of the prediction of eventual suicide from earlier pessimism (Beck, Steer, Kovacs, & Garrison, 1985). In our own early work (Scheier & Carver, 1985) we found that the full scale correlated –.47 with the LOT. Chang et al. (1994) reported correlations between the Hopelessness scale and the two subsets of LOT items of –.53 and –.67, suggesting more convergence. Lucas, Diener, and Suh (1996) also found a correlation of –.53 between the scale and the LOT, but from a variety of other data concluded that the two are not measuring the same thing. In the absence of additional information, we are inclined to regard the subset of items from the scale that bear on expectancies for the future as being a reasonable measure of optimism but to regard the other items as distinct from optimism.

Generalized Expectancy of Success Scale

Another measure that is potentially relevant to the assessment of optimism is the Generalized Expectancy of Success scale (GESS; Fibel & Hale, 1978). This scale presents respondents with a series of situations, some fairly specific, others more general, and asks them to evaluate their likelihood of experiencing a success in each. The stem for each item is, "In the future I expect that I will . . . ," with response options ranging from "highly improbable" to "highly probable." Most of the items refer to successful outcomes, with a few (reverse-scored) relating to failures. The situations range fairly widely. Perhaps in part for this reason, its authors found the GESS to have four factors, each of which focused around one domain (Fibel & Hale, 1978).

One criticism of the GESS has been that some of the original items (e.g., "be a good parent," "have a successful marital relationship") are not appropriate for some populations (Mearns, 1989). In part for this reason, the GESS has recently undergone a minor revision (Hale, Fiedler, & Cochran, 1992). In the revision process, the items just named were rewritten, several new items were created, and the resulting item set was distilled to 25 items by examining item–total correlations. Reliance on this procedure rather than factor analysis, however, leaves open the question of how many factors the GESS–R contains.

Smith, Pope, Rhodewalt, and Poulton (1989) reported correlations of .51 and .55 between the original GESS and the LOT in two samples. Hale et al. (1992) reported a correlation of .40 between the GESS–R and the LOT. Taken together, these data suggest that the two scales are assessing somewhat different qualities. The original GESS was correlated with the Hopelessness scale –.69 (among men) and –.31 (among women) in two small samples reported by Fibel and Hale (1978). Although the former association suggests considerable convergence between measures, the latter does not.

Optimism–Pessimism Scale

Yet another measure that might be used in this domain is the Optimism–Pessimism scale (OPS; Dember, Martin, Hummer, Howe, & Melton, 1989). The OPS is considerably longer than the measures just described, with 18 items reflecting optimism, 18 items reflecting pessimism, and 20 fillers. Dember et al. reported a separation among the subsets of items representing optimism and pessimism, but they did not conduct a factor analysis of the item set. Chang et al. (1994) did so, and found multiple factors. On statistical grounds they suggested that three factors be retained, but found the factors not to be readily interpretable. After further analysis, they concluded that the OPS is a complex, multidimensional instrument that is difficult to interpret theoretically.

An Alternative Conceptualization

Expectancies are pivotal in theories of optimism, and as indicated in the previous section we prefer to assess expectancies directly by self-report. However, there is also a second way to view expectancies and to measure them indirectly. This approach to optimism relies on the assumption that expectancies for the future derive from people's view of the causes for events in the past (Peterson & Seligman, 1984; Seligman, 1991). If explanations for past failures emphasize causes that are stable, the expectancy for the future in the same domain will be for bad outcomes, because the cause is seen as relatively permanent and thus likely to remain in force. If attributions for past failures emphasize causes that are unstable, then the outlook for the future may be brighter, because the cause may no longer be in force. If explanations for past failures are global (apply across aspects of life), the expectancy for the future across *many* domains will be for bad outcomes, because the causal forces are at work everywhere. If the explanations are specific, the outlook for other areas of life may be brighter, because the causes do not apply there.

Just as expectancies vary in breadth, so do attributions about causes. Attributions can be made to a particular area of action (e.g., good and bad outcomes in skiing) or to a moderately broad domain (e.g., good and bad sports performances), but they usually are assessed even more broadly. It is often assumed that people have "explanatory styles," which bear on the person's whole life space. The theory behind explanatory style (Peterson & Seligman, 1984; Seligman, 1991) holds that optimism and pessimism are defined by patterns of explanation for bad outcomes that are unstable and specific versus stable and global, respectively.

Attributional style (see chapter 4, this volume) is indexed by a questionnaire that asks people to imagine a series of hypothetical negative events happening to them (Peterson et al., 1982). Respondents then write down what they would see as the likely cause for the event and they rate that cause on attributional dimensions. A second method of assessing attributional style is called content analysis of verbatim explanations (CAVE; Peterson, Luborsky,

& Seligman, 1983; Peterson, Schulman, Castellon, & Seligman, 1992). This procedure involves assembling a sample of written or spoken material from a person—letters, diaries, interviews, speeches, and so on—that contain statements about explanations for negative outcomes. The statements are then analyzed for their attributional qualities. The CAVE technique is quite flexible; it can be applied to archival data, even records pertaining to people who are no longer alive.

Although the two approaches to conceptualizing and measuring optimism have important differences, they share the assumption that expectations help determine people's actions and experiences. In both approaches optimism is the expectation of good outcomes; pessimism is the expectation of bad outcomes. The approaches differ in measuring variables that logically precede and may underlie the expectancy (attributions) versus measuring the expectancy itself.

These two approaches to optimism and pessimism have led to their own research literatures, each of which sheds light on the nature and function of optimism and pessimism (see also the literature on hope, another member of this theoretical family, which is discussed by Lopez et al. in this volume and Snyder, 1994). In this chapter, however, we focus largely on optimism as we have operationalized it (Scheier & Carver, 1985, 1992; Scheier et al., 1994)—that is, in terms of self-reports of generalized expectancies.

Construct Measurement Issues

As in the assessment of any psychological construct, several issues have been raised over the years concerning the measurement of optimism and pessimism. Indeed, several such issues were raised in the preceding sections.

Direct Versus Indirect Assessment

Is it preferable to measure optimism directly, by asking people to report their expectancies, or is it preferable to measure optimism indirectly, by asking people about their attributions for adverse events? One potential advantage of direct assessment is that it explicitly targets the precise construct of interest: expectancies. In contrast, attributions are always a step away in the logical sequence from the expectancies that are critical. A potential disadvantage of direct assessment is that the items are face-valid. It is quite apparent what they are assessing. As such, they are potentially more vulnerable to response sets such as social desirability, and even faking of responses, than are items that are less face-valid (Schulman, Seligman, & Amsterdam, 1987).

This is not the only research domain in which there are both direct and explicit assessment techniques and indirect and implicit techniques. There has been some suggestion from other domains that direct and indirect measures of a given construct can both be valid but may assess different aspects of the construct (McClelland, Koestner, & Weinberger, 1989). Perhaps that will turn out to be the case in the optimism literature as well.

Operationalization of Generality

Another issue that is relevant to the assessment of optimism is how best to operationalize the breadth of applicability presumed for the expectancy. That is, optimism is considered to be a generalized expectancy, one that is broad in scope. There are at least two ways in which that generality can be assessed.

One approach is to survey broadly among specific life domains (e.g., social interaction, professional achievement), assessing expectancies in each of those domains. One can then aggregate or integrate the expectancy ratings across the various domains. If the domains making up people's life space are adequately represented in this survey, the aggregate index that results is a reasonable measure of optimism. This is the approach taken in the GESS (Fibel & Hale, 1978). (It also is the approach embodied in questionnaire measures of attributional style.)

The other approach is to frame the items not in terms of restricted domains, but rather in terms of the broad generality of life as a whole. Items written using this approach are necessarily more abstract in their content. They are intrinsically high in the generality that each item implies. This is the strategy that most measures of optimism have taken.

Each of these approaches has advantages and disadvantages, which stem from differences underlying what respondents are asked to report on. The aggregation approach asks about specific domains (though there is a degree of generalization within a given domain). Respondents must integrate information across at least a few events before making the response, but they do not have to integrate very far. As long as people can accurately report their expectancies in each specific domain (each of which is fairly concrete), it is fairly easy to make the reports accurately. In contrast, the approach using the more abstract general items appears to make the assumption that people can merge expectancies across multiple domains and report accurately on that overall sense of confidence versus doubt about life.

The disadvantage of the aggregation approach is that it makes two assumptions that may not be correct: First, it assumes that the generalized sense of optimism is equivalent to the summation of a set of specific expectancies. This may not be true. There is evidence that global self-esteem is different from the sum of specific areas of self-esteem (Marsh, 1986), and the same question can be raised about expectancies. Generalized optimism may instead be an emergent quality, which is different from the sum of the contributors that lie behind it. There is evidence from several studies that generalized expectancies do not relate strongly to various specific expectancies (Scheier et al., 1989; Taylor et al., 1992), which tends to support this argument.

The other assumption made in the aggregation approach is that different individuals weight the various domains of life in approximately the same way. If, however, a domain matters much to one person and not at all to another, confidence of success in that domain should have a stronger impact on the overall sense of optimism in the person for whom the domain matters a great deal.

Dimensionality of Optimism and Pessimism

Yet another issue, also alluded to previously in the chapter, can be seen as a methodological issue, but it may also represent a conceptual issue. This is the fact that the items of the LOT typically yield two factors, one defined by the positively framed items, the other defined by the negatively framed items. It has been shown that the two subscales have somewhat different personality correlates (Marshall, Wortman, Kusulas, Hervig, & Vickers, 1992), and some studies (though not others) have found that one subscale is more important than the other in the prediction of relevant outcomes (Robinson-Whelen, Kim, MacCallum, & Kiecolt-Glaser, 1997), though which subscale is more important varies from study to study.

The question is what to make of this difference between the two subsets of items. Is this purely a methodological artifact, caused by the reverse phrasing of half the items together with the tendency to acquiesce in responding? Or does the negative item set provide a more valid measure of the underlying construct? That is, when the item subsets have differed in their prediction, it generally (though not always) has been the negative items that predicted better.

Relevant to this issue, Scheier et al. (1994) observed that two items from the positively framed subset of the original LOT were not as explicitly focused on expectancies as were the remainder of the items. These two items were discarded in the revision. It is perhaps telling, in this regard, that the corresponding item subsets of the LOT–R are consistently more highly intercorrelated than those of the original LOT. It is also the case that the LOT–R's items are more likely to load on a single bipolar factor than were the original items.

Nonetheless, there remains at least some basis for wondering if there might not be two separate dimensions. One precedent for this possibility is the repeated finding that subjectively experienced affect forms two dimensions, one commonly termed positive affect, the other negative affect (Watson & Tellegen, 1985). Although the question remains open as to whether these dimensions are actually unipolar versus both being bipolar (see Carver, 2001), the dimensions do appear to be distinct.

There is reason to believe that the dimension termed positive affect relates to the functioning of a biobehavioral approach system, whereas the dimension called negative affect relates to the functioning of a biobehavioral withdrawal system (Carver, 2001). These biological systems themselves are apparently separate from one another (Davidson, 1992; Gray, 1990). This raises the possibility that there might be one kind of optimism that relates to the attainment of desired incentives and another kind of optimism that relates to the avoidance of threats. Each sort of optimism would relate to a distinct aspect of life (though threats and incentives certainly are often interwoven in real life). Each sort of optimism (in this view) would also imply a corresponding pessimism (relating to doubts about attaining incentives and doubts about avoiding threats, respectively).

This issue is a complex one. As yet, there is no clear resolution to it. The original LOT has been used in more studies to date than the LOT–R, and it is unclear whether the same issue of differential prediction exists with respect to the LOT–R. If future work determines that the LOT–R does not display the differential prediction that has come from the LOT, the answer would apparently be that the problem was artifactual. If the pattern of differential prediction continues, it would tend to imply that the problem is more substantive.

Discriminant Validity

Yet another issue that should be considered regarding the assessment of optimism is the extent to which this construct differs from other constructs in the lexicon of personality psychology (cf. Lucas et al., 1996). As noted earlier, we derived our view of optimism from the perspective of an expectancy–value model of motivation. There are, however, many different perspectives on personality (cf. Carver & Scheier, 2000), which derive from diverse lines of thought. Might some of those perspectives lead to constructs that are nearly the same as optimism?

One suggestion, in that regard, has been that pessimism has a strong resemblance to the construct of neuroticism (Smith et al., 1989). Neuroticism (or emotional instability) is defined by a tendency to worry, to experience unpleasant emotions, and to be pessimistic. Smith et al. found that the LOT was strongly related to a measure of neuroticism, a finding that was replicated by Marshall and Lang (1990). Smith et al. also found that correlations between optimism and outcome variables were sharply reduced when neuroticism was controlled.

Does this imply that pessimism is essentially the same as neuroticism? Does it mean we should be studying neuroticism instead of pessimism? No. When asking about the predictive overlap between optimism and neuroticism, it is just as important to examine the issue the other way around. Neuroticism is a broader construct than is pessimism. It incorporates the quality of pessimism, but other qualities as well. To ask the question of whether an effect attributed to pessimism is really an effect of neuroticism also raises the question of whether any aspect of neuroticism other than its pessimism component is important to such effects.

Furthermore, subsequent research has made it clear that measures of neuroticism do not always have such a large effect on associations between optimism and other relevant variables. Scheier et al. (1999) found that optimism predicted disease-related rates of rehospitalization after coronary artery bypass graft surgery, even when the effects of self-esteem, neuroticism, and depression were controlled. Räikkönen, Matthews, Flory, Owens, and Gump (1999) showed that optimism predicted ambulatory diastolic blood pressure and negative daily mood, controlling for differences in trait anxiety. Aspinwall and Taylor (1992) found that optimism retained its predictive power after controlling for self-esteem and other variables. And Scheier, Carver, and Bridges (1994) found that optimism retained predictive power after controlling for neuroticism, trait anxiety, self-mastery, and self-esteem.

Future Development in Measurement

How will efforts to assess optimism evolve in future years? At least three possibilities stand out in our minds as being likely directions for further work.

Further Discriminant Validity

One issue that always remains, in measuring any construct, is the issue of discriminant validity. The theorist–researcher is always fighting a holding action against the potential erosion of confidence in a measure by the challenges of new constructs. Indeed, even if we were absolutely certain that optimism is distinct from every single related construct that now exists, the problem would still remain. Why? Because the psychologists of the 21st century doubtlessly will come up with new constructs that have not yet been envisioned. When those constructs arrive, one or more of them may pose a challenge to optimism as a key variable. When that happens, people who are interested in optimism will have another discrimination to examine.

State Measures of Optimism

Another issue concerning the assessment of optimism that is sure to receive attention in the future derives from the broad issue of state versus trait measures. It has long been recognized in the literature of emotions that any person can have a transient emotion, but people also vary in the chronic tendencies they have to experience a particular emotion. Thus, there is merit in developing a way to assess both state anxiety and the trait disposition to become anxious (Spielberger, Gorsuch, & Lushene, 1970). Although the point may have been made first with respect to emotions (and proneness to a particular sort of emotional experience), in principle the same issue can be raised for any characteristic of a person that varies over time and situations and also varies as a disposition. We became interested in optimism as a disposition that remains fairly stable across time. However, there is little doubt that even a serious pessimist varies somewhat in his or her pessimism over changing circumstances, as does the optimist. To measure such changes over time and situations requires a state measure.

Relation Between Domain and Generalized Expectancies

A final issue that seems likely to receive additional attention concerns the fact that expectancies exist at multiple levels of abstraction. As was noted earlier, there is some reason to believe that these expectancies are not strongly related to each other. An important methodological question—and a potentially important theoretical question as well—is how these various levels of abstraction function in the creation of relevant outcomes. Does the best prediction come from taking a combination of expectancies into account? Does the best prediction come from a level of abstraction that is chosen as close to that of the outcome? Might the answers to such questions differ from outcome to outcome? These are some of the questions to be addressed in future work.

Future Applications

Although the focus of this chapter is on assessment, it seems appropriate to close with a few brief comments on future applications of the LOT–R and the optimism construct more broadly. We are personality and health psychologists. As such, we have been interested primarily in how this basic quality of personality relates to behavior and affect, and how it differentiates people's responses to stressful circumstances. We intend to continue to investigate mechanisms by which these differences between people are manifested in their experiences.

We have devoted less attention to the question of how pessimism might be changed into optimism. There is, however, research evidence that such changes can indeed occur (Antoni et al., 2001), though the magnitude of the change in that study was not great. One avenue for further exploration is whether such recently acquired optimism functions in the same way as optimism that develops by more typical pathways. Investigating such questions will require research that takes place over longer time spans than has been true of past work. Yet the questions invite study. We look forward to finding out how they are answered.

Appendix 5.1
Items of the Life Orientation Test–Revised (LOT–R), a
Measure of Generalized Optimism Versus Pessimism

1. In uncertain times, I usually expect the best.
2. It's easy for me to relax. (Filler)
3. If something can go wrong for me, it will.[a]
4. I'm always optimistic about my future.
5. I enjoy my friends a lot. (Filler)
6. It's important for me to keep busy. (Filler)
7. I hardly ever expect things to go my way.[a]
8. I don't get upset too easily. (Filler)
9. I rarely count on good things happening to me.[a]
10. Overall, I expect more good things to happen to me than bad.

Note. Respondents indicate the extent of their agreement with each item using a 5-point Likert scale ranging from "strongly disagree" to "strongly agree." After reverse-coding the negatively worded items (those identified with the superscript "a"), the six nonfiller items are summed to produce an overall score. From Scheier, Carver, & Bridges (1994). Copyright © 1994 by the American Psychological Association. Reproduced with permission.

References

Antoni, M. H., Lehman, J. M., Kilbourn, K. M., Boyers, A. E., Culver, J. L., et al. (2001). Cognitive–behavioral stress management intervention decreases the prevalence of depression and enhances benefit finding among women under treatment for early-stage breast cancer. *Health Psychology, 20,* 20–32.

Armor, D. A., & Taylor, S. E. (1998). Situated optimism: Specific outcome expectancies and self-regulation. In M. Zanna (Ed.), *Advances in experimental social psychology* (Vol. 30, 309–379). San Diego, CA: Academic Press.

Aspinwall, L. G., & Taylor, S. E. (1992). Modeling cognitive adaptation: A longitudinal investigation of the impact of individual differences and coping on college adjustment and performance. *Journal of Personality and Social Psychology, 63,* 989–1003.

Bandura, A. (1986). *Social foundations of thought and action: A social cognitive theory.* Englewood Cliffs, NJ: Prentice-Hall.

Beck, A. T., Steer, R. A., Kovacs, M., & Garrison, B. (1985). Hopelessness and eventual suicide: A 10-year prospective study of patients hospitalized with suicidal ideation. *American Journal of Psychiatry, 142,* 559–563.

Beck, A. T., Weissman, A., Lester, D., & Trexler, L. (1974). The measurement of pessimism: The Hopelessness scale. *Journal of Consulting and Clinical Psychology, 42,* 861–865.

Carver, C. S. (2001). Affect and the functional bases of behavior: On the dimensional structure of affective experience. *Personality and Social Psychology Review, 5,* 345–356.

Carver, C. S., Harris, S. D., Lehman, J. M., Durel, L. A., Antoni, M. H., et al. (2000). How important is the perception of personal control? Studies of early stage breast cancer patients. *Personality and Social Psychology Bulletin, 26,* 139–150.

Carver, C. S., & Scheier, M. F. (1998). *On the self-regulation of behavior.* New York: Cambridge University Press.

Carver, C. S., & Scheier, M. F. (1999). Optimism. In C. R. Snyder (Ed.), *Coping: The psychology of what works* (pp. 182–204). New York: Oxford University Press.

Carver, C. S., & Scheier, M. F. (2000). *Perspectives on personality* (4th ed.). Needham Heights, MA: Allyn & Bacon.

Chang, E. C., D'Zurilla, T. J., & Maydeu-Olivares, A. (1994). Assessing the dimensionality of optimism and pessimism using a multimeasure approach. *Cognitive Therapy and Research, 18,* 143–160.

Davidson, R. J. (1992). Emotion and affective style: Hemispheric substrates. *Psychological Science, 3,* 39–43.

Dember, W. M., Martin, S. H., Hummer, M. K., Howe, S. R., & Melton, R. S. (1989). The measurement of optimism and pessimism. *Current Psychology: Research & Reviews, 8,* 102–119.

Fibel, B., & Hale, W. D. (1978). The Generalized Expectancy for Success scale—A new measure. *Journal of Consulting and Clinical Psychology, 46,* 924–931.

Gray, J. A. (1990). Brain systems that mediate both emotion and cognition. *Cognition and Emotion, 4,* 269–288.

Hale, W. D., Fiedler, L. R., & Cochran, C. D. (1992). The revised Generalized Expectancy for Success scale: A validity and reliability study. *Journal of Clinical Psychology, 48,* 517–521.

Lucas, R. E., Diener, E., & Suh, E. (1996). Discriminant validity of well-being measures. *Journal of Personality and Social Psychology, 71,* 616–628.

Marsh, H. W. (1986). Global self-esteem: Its relation to specific facets of self-concept and their importance. *Journal of Personality and Social Psychology, 51,* 1224–1236.

Marshall, G. N., & Lang, E. L. (1990). Optimism, self-mastery, and symptoms of depression in women. *Journal of Personality and Social Psychology, 59,* 132–139.

Marshall, G. N., Wortman, C. B., Kusulas, J. W., Hervig, L. K., & Vickers, R. R., Jr. (1992). Distinguishing optimism from pessimism: Relations to fundamental dimensions of mood and personality. *Journal of Personality and Social Psychology, 62,* 1067–1074.

McClelland, D. C., Koestner, R., & Weinberger, J. (1989). How do self-attributed and implicit motives differ? *Psychological Review, 96,* 690–702.

Mearns, J. (1989). Measuring self-acceptance: Expectancy for success vs. self-esteem. *Journal of Clinical Psychology, 45,* 390–397.

Murphy, P. E., Ciarrocchi, J. W., Piedmont, R. L., Cheston, S., Peyrot, M., et al. (2000). The relation of religious belief and practices, depression, and hopelessness in persons with clinical depression. *Journal of Consulting and Clinical Psychology, 68*, 1102–1106.

Peterson, C., Luborsky, L., & Seligman, M. E. P. (1983). Attributions and depressive mood shifts: A case study using the symptom-context method. *Journal of Abnormal Psychology, 92*, 96–103.

Peterson, C., Schulman, P., Castellon, C., & Seligman, M. E. P. (1992). The explanatory style scoring manual. In C. P. Smith (Ed.), *Handbook of thematic analysis* (pp. 383–392). New York: Cambridge University Press.

Peterson, C., & Seligman, M. E. P. (1984). Causal explanations as a risk factor for depression: Theory and evidence. *Psychological Review, 91*, 347–374.

Peterson, C., Semmel, A., von Baeyer, C., Abramson, L. Y., Metalsky, G. I., et al. (1982). The Attributional Style Questionnaire. *Cognitive Therapy and Research, 6*, 287–299.

Räikkönen, K., Matthews, K. A., Flory, J. D., Owens, J. F., & Gump, B. B. (1999). Effects of optimism, pessimism, and trait anxiety on ambulatory blood pressure and mood during everyday life. *Journal of Personality and Social Psychology, 76*, 104–113.

Robinson-Whelen, S., Kim, C., MacCallum, R. C., & Kiecolt-Glaser, J. K. (1997). Distinguishing optimism from pessimism in older adults: Is it more important to be optimistic or not to be pessimistic? *Journal of Personality and Social Psychology, 73*, 1345–1353.

Scheier, M. F., & Carver, C. S. (1985). Optimism, coping and health: Assessment and implications of generalized outcome expectancies. *Health Psychology, 4*, 219–247.

Scheier, M. F., & Carver, C. S. (1992). Effects of optimism on psychological and physical well-being: Theoretical overview and empirical update. *Cognitive Therapy and Research, 16*, 201–228.

Scheier, M. F., & Carver, C. S. (2001). Adapting to cancer: The importance of hope and purpose. In A. Baum & B. L. Andersen (Eds.), *Psychosocial interventions for cancer* (pp. 15–36). Washington, DC: American Psychological Association.

Scheier, M. F., Carver, C. S., & Bridges, M. W. (1994). Distinguishing optimism from neuroticism (and trait anxiety, self-mastery, and self-esteem): A reevaluation of the Life Orientation Test. *Journal of Personality and Social Psychology, 67*, 1063–1078.

Scheier, M. F., Carver, C. S., & Bridges, M. W. (2001). Optimism, pessimism, and psychological well-being. In E. C. Chang (Ed.), *Optimism and pessimism: Implications for theory, research, and practice* (pp. 189–216). Washington, DC: American Psychological Association.

Scheier, M. F., Matthews, K. A., Owens, J. F., Magovern, G. J., Lefebvre, R. C., et al. (1989). Dispositional optimism and recovery from coronary artery bypass surgery: The beneficial effects on physical and psychological well-being. *Journal of Personality and Social Psychology, 57*, 1024–1040.

Scheier, M. F., Matthews, K. A., Owens, J. F., Schulz, R., Bridges, M. W., et al. (1999). Optimism and rehospitalization following coronary artery bypass graft surgery. *Archives of Internal Medicine, 159*, 829–835.

Schulman, P., Seligman, M. E. P., & Amsterdam, D. (1987). The Attributional Style Questionnaire is not transparent. *Behavior Research and Therapy, 25*, 391–395.

Seligman, M. E. P. (1991). *Learned optimism.* Knopf: New York.

Smith, T. W., Pope, M. K., Rhodewalt, F., & Poulton, J. L. (1989). Optimism, neuroticism, coping, and symptom reports: An alternative interpretation of the Life Orientation Test. *Journal of Personality and Social Psychology, 56*, 640–648.

Snyder, C. R. (1994). *The psychology of hope: You can get there from here.* New York: Free Press.

Spielberger, C. D., Gorsuch, R. L., & Lushene, R. E. (1970). *Manual for the State-Trait Anxiety Inventory.* Palo Alto, CA: Consulting Psychologists Press.

Taylor, S. E., Kemeny, M. E., Aspinwall, L. G., Schneider, S. G., Rodriguez, R., & Herbert, M. (1992). Optimism, coping, psychological distress, and high-risk sexual behavior among men at risk for Acquired Immunodeficiency Syndrome (AIDS). *Journal of Personality and Social Psychology, 63*, 460–473.

Thompson, S. C., & Spacapan, S. (1991). Perceptions of control in vulnerable populations. *Journal of Social Issues, 47*, 1–21.

Watson, D., & Tellegen, A. (1985). Toward a consensual structure of mood. *Psychological Bulletin, 98*, 219–235.

6

Hope: Many Definitions, Many Measures

*Shane J. Lopez, C. R. Snyder,
and Jennifer Teramoto Pedrotti*

Do you have hope? It is a simple question. If your answer is "yes," then how much hope do you have? and do you have enough? If the answer to the initial question is "no," then would you describe yourself as "hopeless" or have you pursued "false hope" down difficult paths? These questions and many others have been grappled with over the centuries by philosophers, spiritual leaders, psychologists, and each of us as we conduct our individual lives.

In the late-20th century, social scientists have turned their attentions to hope. In this regard, we have located at least 26 theories or definitions, and a handful of validated measures. In this chapter, we have decided to focus on conceptualizations of hope that have been scrutinized by social scientists and practitioners. Therefore, we present information about views of hope, and in the process we will address a widely debated question: Is hope an emotion or a cognition? Measures linked to these conceptualizations also will be discussed, and thoughts about future directions in hope measurement will be shared.

Conceptualizations of Hope

Most theories and ideas regarding the concept of hope can be grouped into either an emotion-based or cognition-based category. These two perspectives are beginning to merge to some degree, imbuing hope with both affective and cognitive qualities. For the purposes of this portion of the chapter, we will discuss each separately, though the reader may notice overlap.

Hope: The Emotion

Contrary to what one might intuitively postulate, models that operationalize the construct of hope from an affective point of reference are fewer in number than those that are more cognitive in nature. Furthermore, many of the researchers who put forth emotion-based models include some sort of cognitive component. For example, Averill, Catlin, and Chon (1990) described their theory of hope as an emotion, though governed by cognitions. Environment was named in this theory as having an effect on the development, and deterioration, of hope as well. These researchers see hope as most appropriate when goals are (a) reasonably attainable, (b) under control, (c) viewed as important by the individual, and (d) acceptable at a social and moral level. Derived from a social–constructionist background, this viewpoint relies on the norms and rules of the intended society to help define the true meaning of hope. Thus, Averill and colleagues believe that hope only can be understood within a social and cultural context.

Mowrer's (1960) conceptualization of hope is based on a more behavioral point of view, with hope as an affective form of secondary reinforcement. In his research with animals, for example, Mowrer noticed that when working in a stimulus–response paradigm, the emotion of hope seemed to appear in these subjects when a stimulus associated with something pleasurable occurred. Once this affective ingredient was induced, the animals seemed to anticipate the eventual pleasurable occurrence, as shown by increased activity. In this way, hope sustained desirous behavior by contributing to the reinforcement of the original stimulus. In these cases, the emotion of hope seemed to propel animals toward their goal.

In contrast to Mowrer's stimulus–response paradigm, Marcel advanced from a more philosophical approach by suggesting that the construct was exemplified in the phrase, "I hope in thee for us" (as cited in Godfrey, 1987, p. 103). This view is less individualistic, and looks at hope as it applies to society as a whole. Based on his work with prisoners of war from World War II, Marcel proposed that hope was an affective form of coping that could be used in the most dire circumstances of imprisonment. According to his theory, the feeling of hope must be present to face the despair that is inherent in such interments (see Godfrey, 1987). Marcel's view defines hope as being applicable only in seemingly helpless situations.

Hope: The Cognition

In popular literature and prose, hope often is treated solely as an emotion, a particular feeling that allows one to sustain belief in dire circumstances. The cognitive side of hope, however, receives more research attention. The work of Erikson, for example, suggests that hope is an element of healthy cognitive development. Accordingly, he defines hope as "the enduring belief in the attainability of fervent wishes, in spite of the dark urges and rages which mark the beginning of existence" (1964, p. 118). Thus, hope is a thought or belief that allows individuals to sustain movement toward goals. Erikson places hope in a developmental context, positing that we hope from birth; moreover, he discusses the conflicts that arise internally because of hope. Our "fervent wishes" may come into conflict with those of others, especially when we are infants.

Breznitz (1986) also takes a cognitive slant in defining hope, suggesting that hope "relates to a fleeting thought or to a description of a cognitive state" (p. 296). For hope to have influence on the individual, he posits that it must be of sufficient strength and persistence to induce a physiological response. In this sense, a momentary thought such as a soothing self-statement ("I will be fine") has less chance of fully invoking the same type of response that the true process of *hoping* will have on the body. On this point, Breznitz distinguishes between *hope* and the *work of hoping,* with the *work of hoping* being an active process in which one must be engaged to truly experience the essence of hope. Breznitz also identifies hope as an illusion and struggles with the differences between hope and denial. This conundrum is evident in the works of many writers who question the inclusion of hope alongside the evils in Pandora's box.

Other theorists (e.g., Stotland, Gottschalk, Godfrey) have emphasized how perspective and expectancy are involved in hoping. Stotland conceptualized hope as "an expectation greater than zero of achieving a goal" (1969, p. 2). Borrowing from his background in social psychological theory and cognitive schemas, Stotland added that the degree of hope was to be determined by the perceived probability of achieving the goal, and the importance of the goal itself. If a sufficient level of importance is attached to the particular goal, then hope is *ignited*, mediating between the desire and the actual movement toward the goal.

Gottschalk (1974) viewed hope in terms of positive expectancy, defining it as an amount of optimism that particular favorable outcomes are likely to occur. Gottschalk also posits that hope can occur about larger, more global issues, including "cosmic phenomena and . . . spiritual or imaginary events" (1974, p. 779). Hope is thus believed to be a provocative force that impels an individual to move through psychological problems. To Godfrey, hope is the belief in some probability of a pleasant outcome. Such hope is guided by the person's perception of resources or the resources that he or she perceives another as possessing (1987). Though such hope is begun by an affective jolt, it is a cognitive process of weighing the likely outcomes in an individual's life. In addition, Godfrey distinguishes between ultimate and fundamental hope. Ultimate hope is directed at a particular outcome, and it is often prosocial in nature rather than being purely individualistic. An example might be a hope for society at large. Fundamental hope is, in contrast, defined as a mental set related to goal pursuit.

In Staats's view, hope is seen as "the interaction between wishes and expectations" (1989, p. 367). This view combines tenets of Erikson's view with those of the theorists who emphasized expectancy. Staats defined hope as having an affective component as well as cognitive aspects. Indeed, she terms it "the affective cognition" (Staats & Stassen, 1985, p. 235). On the affective side, hope is operationalized by Staats as "the difference between expected positive and expected negative affect" (1989, p. 367). Cognitively, hope is seen as the communication between these expectations and the desires behind them. Again, hope is seen as a mediating force that weighs expectations of achievement and the affective intensity of the wish or desire.

Hope, Cognitions, and Emotions

A theory of hope by Snyder and his colleagues (Snyder, 1994; Snyder et al., 1991) has received considerable attention in the past two decades. Originally built almost solely on cognitions, this theory has evolved to include roles for emotions. Within this theory, hope is defined as goal-directed thinking in which people perceive that they can produce routes to desired goals (pathways thinking) and the requisite motivation to use those routes (agency thinking).

Goals may vary temporally from short- to long-term; moreover, a given goal must be of sufficient value before a person will pursue it. In addition, goals may be approach-oriented in nature (i.e., something positive that we want to happen), or preventative in nature (i.e., something negative that we want to stop from happening). Last, goals can vary in difficulty of attainment. Even seemingly "impossible" goals may at times be attained through supreme planning and efforts. Accordingly, Snyder has warned that we should be careful in criticizing goals that seem to be based on "false hopes" (Snyder, Rand, King, Feldman, & Taylor, in press).

Pathways thought reflects the actual production of alternate routes when impeded, as well as positive self-talk about being able to find routes to desired goals (e.g., "I'll find a way to solve this"; Snyder, LaPointe, Crowson, & Early, 1998). Agency thinking is the motivational component of hope theory. On this point, high-hopers endorse agentic personal self-talk phrases (e.g., "I won't give up"; Snyder, LaPointe, et al., 1998). Such agency thought is especially important in applying the motivation to the appropriate alternate pathway when confronted by impediments.

Hope theory expressly addresses the roles of barriers, stressors, and emotions. When encountering barriers that impede goal pursuits, people appraise such circumstances as stressful. According to the postulates of hope theory, positive emotions result because of perceptions of successful goal pursuit. Conversely, negative emotions typically reflect the perceived lack of success under unimpeded, and especially impeded, circumstances. Thus, the perceptions regarding the success of goal pursuits causally drive subsequent positive and negative emotions (see Snyder, Sympson, et al., 1996). Furthermore, these emotions serve as reinforcing feedback.

Given their histories of successfully dealing with stressors and attaining their desired goals, high-hopers generally have positive emotions, as well as zest and confidence (Snyder, Sympson, Michael, & Cheavens, 2000); conversely, low-hopers have histories of not dealing successfully with stressors, along with negative emotions and affective flatness. Depending on their trait hope levels, people should bring these emotional sets to their goal-related activities.

To give the reader an overview of the various interactions of the components in hope theory, we have constructed Figure 6.1. To the left, the iterative relationship of pathways and agency thoughts is shown. (For the reader who would like detailed descriptions of the developmental antecedents of the hope process, we would recommend Snyder [1994, pp. 75–114]; and Snyder, McDermott, Cook, & Rapoff [1997, pp. 1–32].) Immediately to the right of agency-pathways thoughts, we see the emotional sets that each individual brings to the particular goal-pursuit process. Together, these learning histories and mood predispositions reflect the beginning context for goal pursuit thinking in regard to specific goals.

Turning our attentions to the pre-event analysis phase of Figure 6.1, we see the values related to particular goal pursuits. Assuming that there is sufficient value attached to a given goal pursuit, the person next moves into the event sequence analysis phase. Here, the person initiates behaviors for achieving the desired goal. If the goal pursuit seems to be going well at this stage, the feedback loop involves positive emotions that reinforce the goal pursuit process. As such, these positive emotions sustain motivation. If the person is not doing well, negative emotions and self-critical ruminations should arise, thereby undermining the goal pursuit process. It should be noted that Snyder and colleagues adopt a functional view of emotions. On this point, Levenson (1994) wrote, "Emotions serve to establish our position vis-à-vis our environment, pulling us toward certain people, objects, actions, and ideas, and pushing us away from others" (p. 123).

Returning to Figure 6.1, note the point at which a stressor—a barrier to the progression of the actual goal pursuit—is met. High-hope persons interpret such barriers as challenges, and thereafter seek alternate routes and rechannel their motivation to those routes. Often successful in bridging the impeding stressor, positive emotions thus reinforce hopeful thinking. On the other hand, low-hope people typically become "stuck" and experience ruminative thoughts and negative emotions—the result being that they are likely to abandon their goal pursuits.

The most recent addition to hope theory involves surprise events (see Figure 6.1, lower center). Such surprises may be negative (e.g., watching your 6-year-old bicycle rider hit a bump and fly headfirst over the handlebars) or positive (e.g., watching your child finally learn to ride a bike). Surprises typically are quick to produce emotions because of their sheer contrast (positive or negative) in relation to ongoing events. Such surprise-based emotions elicit arousal that is transformed almost immediately into motivation (i.e., agency). This agency then is "attached" to a goal and pathways that befit the situation (e.g., rushing to the aid of the child who has had an accident). Though such surprise-based emotions begin outside the typical goal-pursuit "corridor," it should be noted how readily they are incorporated into goal pursuits.

In summary, it can be seen that hope theory has both feed-*forward* and feed*back* emotion-laden mechanisms that modulate the person's success in attaining a given goal. Thus, hope theory is an interrelated system of goal-directed thinking that responds to emotionally laden feedback throughout goal pursuit. As such, thoughts and emotions work hand-in-hand in hope theory to help the person pursue the coveted goals that are crucial in day-to-day living.

Self-Report Measures of Hope

Researchers have had different views on the topic of measuring hope. Stotland, for example, did not believe that asking individuals about their levels of hope could provide accurate information. He contended that self-report leads to confusion, or to socially desirable responses, making it more feasible to ask

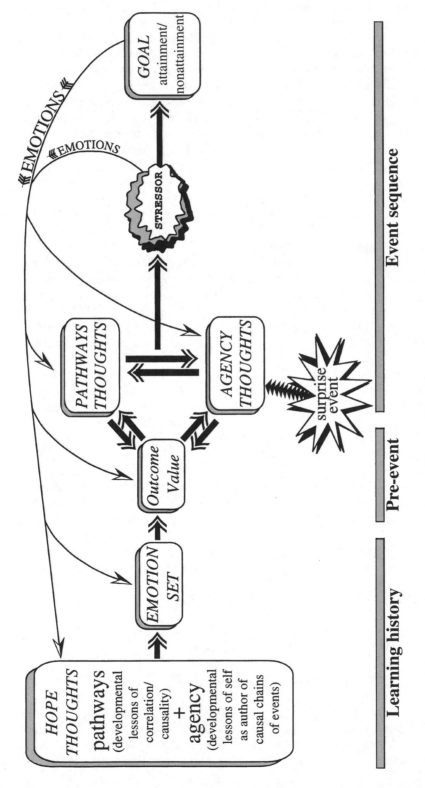

Figure 6.1. Hope theory.

questions regarding such topics as the individual's perceived probability of success. Affective conceptualizations do not easily lend themselves to measurement via self-report. This may be attributed to historical difficulties operationalizing hope and a scholarly neglect of models of positive emotions. Cognitive conceptualizations, however, have been operationalized to produce brief, valid self-report measures of hope.

The 1975 Hope Scale

Erickson, Post, and Paige (1975) devised a scale that operationalized Stotland's (1969) view of hope. The 1975 Hope scale consists of a list of 20 focused goals that are not situation-specific in nature and that are intended to span an array of common goals in our society. Participants are asked to rate each goal using a 7-point Likert scale ranging from "I don't care if this happens or not" (1) to "It's extremely important. Without it I'd rather be dead" (7). Next, each individual is asked to go back through the list, assigning numbers reflective of the probability that the goal would be attained by the individual using a rating scale of 0 to 100 (0 = impossible; 100 = certain). Scores obtained include mean importance (I) and mean probability (P) across these goals. Psychometrics for this measure appear adequate with test–retest reliability coefficients of .79 (I) and .80 (P) over a one-week period and moderate internal consistency.

The Expected Balance Scale and the Hope Index: Measuring Two Sides of Hope

Staats and colleagues separated the "two sides of hope" for measurement purposes, with each being based theoretically on Beck's depressive triad. The Expected Balance scale (EBS; Staats, 1989) assesses the affective side of this construct and uses an 18-item (nine positive and nine negative) self-report measure. Answers are spread on a 5-point Likert scale. The Hope Index (Staats & Stassen, as cited in Staats, 1989) is designed to measure the cognitive side of hope. This measure has a specific focus on particular events and outcomes, instead of a more general focus, and contains four subscales: hope–self, hope–other, wish, and expect (see Appendix 6.1). Both measures demonstrated moderate test–retest reliabilities and internal consistency, with an alpha of .83 for the EBS and alphas ranging from .72 to .85 for the Hope Index (Staats, 1989). In addition, construct validity was determined based on correlations with related scales.

Snyder's Hope Scales

Snyder's two-factor hope model is reflected in several direct and indirect measures of the construct. The availability of sound measures of this model of hope has facilitated the generation of basic and applied hope research.

ADULT DISPOSITIONAL HOPE SCALE. The Hope scale (Snyder, Harris, et al., 1991) is a self-report, 12-item inventory designed to tap dispositional hope in adults, ages 15 and older (see Appendix 6.2). The 4-point continuum (from 1 = definitely false to 4 = definitely true) was used in the original studies, although an 8-point scale has been used recently to encourage diverse responding. Total Hope scale scores range from 8 to 32 when the 4-point continuum is used (8 to 64 with the 8-point version). Four items reflect agency, four reflect pathways, and four are distracters. Agency and pathways items are summed to yield a total score.

Regarding the psychometric properties of the Hope scale, Cronbach alphas for the total score have ranged from .74 to .84 for six samples of undergraduate college students and two samples of individuals in psychological treatment. Test–retest correlations have been .80 or higher over time periods exceeding 10 weeks (Snyder, Harris, et al., 1991). Responses to the Hope scale are highly correlated with responses to several scales tapping similar psychological processes (Snyder, Harris, et al., 1991). For example, scores from the Hope scale have correlated from .50 to .60 with scores on measures of optimism (Life Orientation Test: Scheier & Carver, 1985), expectancy for attaining goals (Generalized Expectancy for Success scale: Fibel & Hale, 1978), and self-esteem (Self-Esteem scale: Rosenberg, 1965). Moreover, Hope scale scores have correlated negatively with Minnesota Multiphasic Personality Inventory subscale scores (Hathaway & McKinley, 1951; Irving, Crenshaw, Snyder, Francis, & Gentry, 1990). As a test of discriminant validity, the Hope scale scores were correlated with a measure (the Self-Confidence scale: Fenigstein, Scheier, & Buss, 1975) in which the content was believed to be unrelated to hope. As predicted, no significant correlations resulted with hope scores and the subscales of public and private self-consciousness (rs of .06 and –.03, respectively) (Snyder, Harris, et al., 1991).

CHILDREN'S HOPE SCALE. The Children's Hope scale (CHS; Snyder, Hoza, et al., 1997) is a 6-item self-report measure that is based on the premise that children are goal-directed and that their goal-directed thoughts can be understood according to agency and pathways. The CHS has been validated for use with children ages 7 to 16. Three of the six items reflect agency and three reflect pathways thinking. Children respond to a 6-point Likert scale regarding the applicability of each item. Total scores can range from 6 to 36. The administrator can have the child read the scale without guidance or read the items aloud and mark their responses.

Reliabilities for the CHS have been acceptable, with Cronbach alphas for the CHS total score ranging from .72 to .86, with a median alpha of .77 (Snyder, Hoza, et al., 1997); moreover, the test–retest correlations over the one-month interval were both positive and significant (rs of .70 to .80; Snyder, Hoza, et al., 1997). The scores on the CHS correlated positively (with one exception) with the five subscales of the Self-Perception Profile for Children (SPP–C; Harter, 1985) and with overall SPP–C self-worth (ranging from .23 to .55). In correlating responses to the CHS and the Children's Attributional Style Questionnaire (Kaslow, Tanenbaum, & Seligman, 1978), the children scoring higher on the CHS exhibited an attributional attachment to positive outcomes and a slight disposition to distance themselves from negative outcomes. Finally, scores on the Children's Depression Inventory (CDI; Kovacs, 1985) and the CHS correlated negatively (rs of −.27 to −.48). Together, these findings offer support for the concurrent validity of the CHS.

ADULT STATE HOPE SCALE. The State Hope scale (Snyder, Sympson, et al., 1996) is a 6-item self-report scale (response range of 1 = definitely true to 8 = definitely false) that assesses goal-directed thinking at a given moment in time. This scale can be administered in two to five minutes, and hand-scored in a minute or less. The scale is written at approximately a sixth-grade reading level and includes the agency and pathways subscales, as well as a total score that is attained by summing responses to all six items. The agency and pathways subscale scores are derived by summing their respective three items, with total scores ranging from 6 to 48.

In four studies involving college students, the alphas for the overall State Hope scale ranged from a low of .79 to a high of .95. Alphas for the agency subscale varied from .76 to .95, and from .59 to .93 for the pathways subscale (Snyder, Sympson, et al., 1996). Overall, there is strong support for the internal reliability. Test–retest correlations, which should vary because of the differing situations in which the State Hope scale is taken, ranged from a low of .48 to a high of .93 comparing any two days across a four-week study (Snyder, Sympson, et al., 1996). Based on a principal components analysis, the two-factor structure of state hope was supported.

Over a one-month period, State Hope scale scores and the daily scores from the State Self-Esteem scale (Heatherton & Polivy, 1991) correlated positively and significantly (rs = .45 to .75). Similarly over the 30-day interval, the daily State Hope scale scores correlated: (a) positively (rs = .48 to .65) with scores on the Positive Affect scale of the State Positive and Negative Affect Schedule (PANAS; Watson, Clark, & Tellegen, 1988), and (b) negatively (rs = −.37 to −.50) with the scores on the Negative Affect scale of the PANAS (Snyder, Sympson, et al., 1996).

OTHER MEASURES. Sympson (1999) and McDermott, Hastings, Gariglietti, and Callahan (1997) have responded to calls for a domain-specific measure of hope and for a young children's hope scale. Sympson's Domain-Specific Hope scale for adults and McDermott et al.'s Young Children's Hope scale (YCHS) have undergone preliminary validation procedures and show promise (see Lopez, Ciarelli, Coffman, Stone, & Wyatt, 2000, for details on these new scales).

Detecting Hope in Action: Observational Measures of Hope

Observing hope in action may be one of the most meaningful ways to determine if individuals have the intangible qualities that connect them to their goals, and this can be accomplished with some reliability. Review of work on observational methods suggests that there is moderate correspondence between self-ratings and observational ratings generated by someone who knows the client–participant well (Snyder, Harris, et al., 1991).

Considering Stories of Hope: Detecting Hope in the Spoken and Written Word

Through their daily conversation, letters, stories, poems, diaries, journal entries, and client–clinician exchanges, people tell their stories of hope. Gottschalk's Hope scale (1974) was devised to analyze the content of individuals' speech as a method of measuring levels of hope. This measure requires the use of five-minute speech samples given by the participants, which were then assessed for hopefulness using a weighted scale across various content categories. Sections with "references to feelings of hopelessness" (p. 780) or other correlates are given a rating of –1, and references that suggest optimism, good fortune, and other positive ideas are assigned a rating of +1 (Gottschalk). Because the ratings achieved are situational in nature and may change from one time to another, it may be necessary to collect numerous samples of speech. A composite score can be calculated by averaging scores across a number of different samples taken at different times. Psychometrics for this test appear to be adequate, with concurrent validity being demonstrated through positive and significant correlations between hope and (a) human relations ($r = .51$) and (b) achievement strivings ($r = .55$). Negative and significant relationships were found between hope and anxiety scores ($r = -.46$), as well as outward hostility ($r = -.45$).

Using hope theory, Snyder and his colleagues have made suggestions about inferring hope level via a person's writing. Snyder et al. (1997) offer techniques for tapping hope of children through prose. For adults, Snyder (1994) and McDermott and Snyder (1999) described how to extract hope levels from the writing products. Finally, Vance (1996) developed the Narrative Hope scale to gauge the agency and pathways elements of hope in adults' stories. Using the Vance scale, raters identify hope markers by selecting from a menu of descriptors that reflect high- versus low-hope thoughts and behaviors. Also, Lopez et al. (2000) have generated lists of questions about goals, pathways, agency, and barriers that can be posed to help clients find the hope they already possess.

Selecting Hope Measures

When deciding among the many self-report hope scales, one should consider the theoretical conceptualization, the scale administration, the psychometric properties, and the age of the client (see Tables 6.1 and 6.2 for measure characteristics). While the self-report hope measures are easy to use, such direct questioning may not always be feasible. Thus, the modes for reviewing written or spoken language or observing hopeful behavior should be considered.

Measuring Hope Across Cultures

As suggested by historical writing and anthropological accounts, hope is a universal construct—all peoples during all times have valued the role hope plays in their lives. Definitions of hope, however, vary within and across

Table 6.1. Characteristics of Often-Used Hope Measures

Name of Hope Index	Target age	Number of items	Administration time (min.)	Internal consistency	Test–retest reliability	Construct validation
Hope scale Erickson, Post, and Paige (1975)	Adult	20	Brief		.793** (I) .787** (P)	Some support
Gottschalk Hope scale Gottschalk (1974)	Adult	7 categories	5 (per speech sample)		—	Some support
Herth Hope scale Herth (1991)	Adult	32		.75–.94	.89–.91	Some support
Nowotny Hope scale Nowotny (1991)	Adult	47		.90		Some support
Miller Hope scale Miller and Powers (1988)	Adult	40		.93	.82	Some support
Expected Balance scale Staats (1989)	Adult	18	Brief		.66**	Strong support
Hope Index Staats and Stassen (1985)	Adult	16	Brief		.74**	Strong support

*$p < .05$ **$p < .01$

Table 6.2. Characteristics of Snyder Hope Scales

Name of Hope Index	Target age	Number of items	Administration time (min.)	Internal reliability	Construct validation
Hope scale	15–100	12[a]	2–5	.70–.80	Excellent
Domain Specific Hope scale	15–100	48	7–15	.93	Strong
Children's Hope scale	7–16	6	2–5	.72–.86	Excellent
Young Children's Hope scale	5–7	6	2–5	.88	Some Support
State Hope scale	15–100	6	2–5	.90s	Strong
Hope scale-Observer	15–100	8	2–5	—	—
CHS-Observer	7–16	6	2–5	—	Some Support
YCHS-Observer	5–7	6	2–5	—	Some Support

[a]The Hope scale has 12 items: four reflect pathways, four reflect agency, four are distracters.

Note. —indicates that data regarding psychometric properties are not available because the reliability and validity of these measures have not been examined rigorously.

cultures, and the assumption that hope "looks and behaves" the same across all groups is a risky one. Given that cultures hold different values in which hope is imbedded, the cross-cultural applicability of hope needs to be considered.

Issues of Measurement and Assessment of Hope

The fact that hope has been given so many definitions by so many researchers and scholars results in a multifaceted picture of this construct. At the same time, it leads to confusion and ambiguity. Although some theorists carefully operationalize hope, others rely on vague impressions, further muddying our understanding of this concept. Enigmatic and philosophical definitions do not lend themselves well to either quantitative or qualitative measures of hope. How to gain access to individuals' views of their own level of hope is another assessment concern. Stotland (1969) suggested that asking directly will not lead to the answers desired, whereas theorists such as Gottschalk (1974) measure purely by observation. Other researchers (Staats, 1989) use more than one measure of hope, attempting to access both the affective and cognitive features of hope as they see them. In addition, the discreteness of some of the theories in holding to either a purely cognitive or affective model may limit progress in measurement. As we move toward new models offering both cognitive and affective components, combining them in a more integrated way (e.g., Snyder, in press), a delicate balance must be devised between a parsimonious model and one that attends to the fundamental complexity of the hope construct.

Appendix 6.1
Staats Hope Scale

Instructions

Read the item below and circle 0, 1, 2, 3, 4, or 5 on the left-hand side to indicate the extent that you would wish for the item mentioned. Then circle 0, 1, 2, 3, 4, or 5 on the right-hand side to indicate the extent to which you expect the thing mentioned to occur.

To what extent would you wish for this?	[Insert proper time frame here]	To what extent do you expect this?
0 = not at all 5 = very much		0 = not at all 5 = very much

Item

0 1 2 3 4 5	1. To do well in school, in job, or in daily tasks.[a]	0 1 2 3 4 5
0 1 2 3 4 5	2. To have more friends.	0 1 2 3 4 5
0 1 2 3 4 5	3. To have good health.	0 1 2 3 4 5
0 1 2 3 4 5	4. To be competent.	0 1 2 3 4 5
0 1 2 3 4 5	5. To achieve long range goals.	0 1 2 3 4 5
0 1 2 3 4 5	6. To be happy.	0 1 2 3 4 5
0 1 2 3 4 5	7. To have money.	0 1 2 3 4 5
0 1 2 3 4 5	8. To have leisure time.	0 1 2 3 4 5
0 1 2 3 4 5	9. Other people to be helpful.	0 1 2 3 4 5
0 1 2 3 4 5	10. The crime rate to go down.	0 1 2 3 4 5
0 1 2 3 4 5	11. The country to be more productive.	0 1 2 3 4 5
0 1 2 3 4 5	12. Understanding by my family.	0 1 2 3 4 5
0 1 2 3 4 5	13. Justice in the world.	0 1 2 3 4 5
0 1 2 3 4 5	14. Peace in the world.	0 1 2 3 4 5
0 1 2 3 4 5	15. Personal freedom.	0 1 2 3 4 5
0 1 2 3 4 5	16. Resources for all.	0 1 2 3 4 5

[a]Use the item most appropriate to sample—for example, daily tasks for retired persons.

Note. Sara Staats of The Ohio State University at Newark 1179 University Drive, Newark, Ohio 43055-1797. Email: Staats.1@osu.edu. Reprinted with permission.

Appendix 6.2
Adult Dispositional Hope Scale Items and Directions for Administering and Scoring the Goals Scale

Directions

Read each item carefully. Using the scale shown below, please select the number that best describes YOU and put that number in the blank provided.

1 = definitely false   2 = mostly false   3 = mostly true   4 = definitely true

_____ 1. I can think of many ways to get out of a jam.
_____ 2. I energetically pursue my goals.
_____ 3. I feel tired most of the time.
_____ 4. There are lots of ways around any problem.
_____ 5. I am easily downed in an argument.
_____ 6. I can think of many ways to get the things in life that are most important to me.
_____ 7. I worry about my health.
_____ 8. Even when others get discouraged, I know I can find a way to solve the problem.
_____ 9. My past experiences have prepared me well for my future.
_____ 10. I've been pretty successful in life.
_____ 11. I usually find myself worrying about something.
_____ 12. I meet the goals that I set for myself.

Notes: When administered, we have called this the "Goals scale" rather than the "Hope scale" because on some initial occasions when giving the scale, people became sufficiently interested in the fact that hope could be measured that they wanted to discuss this rather than taking the scale. No such problems have been encountered with the rather mundane title "Goals scale." Items 3, 5, 7, and 11 are distracters and are not used for scoring. The pathways subscale score is the sum of items 1, 4, 6, and 8; the agency subscale is the sum of items 2, 9, 10, and 12. Hope is the sum of the four pathways and four agency items. In our original studies, we used a 4-point response continuum, but to encourage more diversity in scores in our more recent studies, we have used the 8-point scale:

1 = definitely false   2 = mostly false   3 = somewhat false   4 = slightly false
5 = slightly true   6 = somewhat true   7 = mostly true   8 = definitely true

Scores using the 4-point continuum can range from a low of 8 to a high of 32. For the 8-point continuum, scores can range from a low of 8 to a high of 64.

Note. From Snyder, Harris, Anderson, Holleran, Irving, et al. (1991). The scale can be used for research or clinical purposes without contacting the author. Reprinted with permission of the American Psychological Association and the senior author of the scale.

References

Averill, J. R., Catlin, G., & Chon, K. K. (1990). *Rules of hope.* New York: Springer-Verlag

Breznitz, S. (1986). The effect of hope on coping with stress. In M. H. Appley & P. Trumbull (Eds.), *Dynamics of stress: Physiological, psychological, and social perspectives* (pp. 295–307). New York: Plenum Press.

Erickson, R. C., Post, R. D., & Paige, A. B. (1975). Hope as a psychiatric variable. *Journal of Clinical Psychology, 31,* 324–330.

Erikson, E. H. (1964). *Insight and responsibility.* New York: W. W. Norton.

Fenigstein, A., Scheier, M. F., & Buss, A. H. (1975). Public and private self-consciousness: Assessment and theory. *Journal of Consulting and Clinical Psychology, 43,* 522–527.

Fibel, B., & Hale, W. D. (1978). The Generalized Expectancy for Success scale—A new measure. *Journal of Consulting and Clinical Psychology, 46,* 924–931.

Godfrey, J. J. (1987). *A philosophy of human hope.* Dordrecht: Martinus Nijhoff.

Gottschalk, L. (1974). A hope scale applicable to verbal samples. *Archives of General Psychiatry, 30,* 779–785.

Harter, S. (1985). *Manual for the Self-Perception Profile for Children: Revision of the Perceived Competence Scale Score for Children.* Denver, CO: University of Denver Press.

Hathaway, S. R., & McKinley, J. C. (1951). *The MMPI manual.* New York: Psychological Corporation.

Heatherton, T. F., & Polivy, J. (1991). Development and validation of a scale for measuring state self-esteem. *Journal of Personality and Social Psychology, 60,* 895–910.

Herth, K. (1991). Development and refinement of an instrument to measure hope. *Scholarly Inquiry for Nursing Practice: An International Journal, 5,* 39–51.

Irving, L. M., Crenshaw, W., Snyder, C. R., Francis, P., & Gentry, G. (1990, May). *Hope and its correlates in a psychiatric inpatient setting.* Paper presented at the 62nd annual meeting of the Midwestern Psychological Association, Chicago.

Kaslow, N. J., Tanenbaum, R. L., & Seligman, M. E. P. (1978). *The KASTAN–R: A children's attributional style questionnaire (KASTAN–R–CASQ).* Unpublished manuscript, University of Pennsylvania, Philadelphia.

Kovacs, M. (1985). The Children's Depression Inventory (CDI). *Psychopharmacology Bulletin, 21,* 995–998.

Levenson, R. W. (1994). Human emotion: A functionalist view. In P. Ekman & R. J. Davidson (Eds.), *The nature of emotion: Fundamental questions* (pp. 123–126). New York: Oxford University Press.

Lopez, S. J., Ciarlelli, R., Coffman, L., Stone, M., & Wyatt, L. (2000). Diagnosing for strengths: On measuring hope building blocks. In C. R. Snyder (Ed.). *Handbook of hope* (pp. 57–85). San Diego, CA: Academic Press.

McDermott, D., Hastings, S. L., Gariglietti, K. P., & Callahan, B. (1997). *The development of the Young Children's Hope scale.* Unpublished manuscript, University of Kansas, Lawrence.

McDermott, D., & Snyder, C. R. (1999). *Making hope happen: A workbook for turning possibilities into reality.* Oakland, CA: New Harbinger Press.

Miller, J. F., & Powers, M. J. (1988). Development of an instrument to measure hope. *Nursing Research, 37,* 6–10.

Mowrer, O. H. (1960). *Learning theory and behavior.* New York: Wiley and Sons.

Nowotny, M. L. (1991). Every tomorrow, a vision of hope. *Journal of Psychologocial Oncology, 9,* 117–126.

Rosenberg, M. (1965). *Society and adolescent self-image.* Princeton, NJ: Princeton University Press.

Scheier, M. F., & Carver, C. S. (1985). Optimism, coping, and health: Assessment and implications of generalized outcome expectancies. *Health Psychology, 4,* 219–247.

Snyder, C. R. (1994). *The psychology of hope: You can get there from here.* New York: Free Press.

Snyder, C. R. (in press). Hope theory: Rainbows of the mind. *Psychological Inquiry.*

Snyder, C. R., Harris, C., Anderson, J. R., Holleran, S. A., Irving, L. M., et al. (1991). The will and the ways: Development and validation of an individual-differences measure of hope. *Journal of Personality and Social Psychology, 60,* 570–585.

Snyder, C. R., Hoza, B., Pelham, W. E., Rapoff, M., Ware, L., et al. (1997). The development and validation of the Children's Hope scale. *Journal of Pediatric Psychology, 22,* 399–421.

Snyder, C. R., LaPointe, A. B., Crowson Jr., J. J., & Early, S. (1998). Preferences of high- and low-hope people for self-referential input. *Cognition & Emotion, 12,* 807–823.

Snyder, C. R., McDermott, D., Cook, W., & Rapoff, M. (1997). *Journeys of hope: Giving children stories to grow on.* Boulder, CO: Westview/HarperCollins.

Snyder, C. R., Rand, K., King, E., Feldman, D., & Taylor, J. (in press). "False" hope. *Journal of Clinical Psychology.*

Snyder, C. R., Sympson, S. C., Michael, S. T., & Cheavens, J. (2000). The optimism and hope constructs: Variants on a positive expectancy theme. In E. C. Chang (Ed.), *Optimism and pessimism* (pp. 103–124). Washington, DC: American Psychological Association.

Snyder, C. R., Sympson, S. C., Ybasco, F. C., Borders, T. F., Babyak, M. A., et al. (1996). Development and validation of the State Hope scale. *Journal of Personality and Social Psychology, 2,* 321–335.

Staats, S. R. (1989). Hope: A comparison of two self-report measures for adults. *Journal of Personality Assessment, 53,* 366–375.

Staats, S. R., & Stassen, M. A. (1985). Hope: An affective cognition. *Social Indicators Research, 17,* 235–242.

Stotland, E. (1969). *The psychology of hope.* San Francisco, CA: Jossey-Bass.

Sympson, S. (1999). *Validation of the Domain Specific Hope scale: Exploring hope in life domains.* Unpublished doctoral dissertation, University of Kansas, Lawrence.

Vance, M. (1996). *Measuring hope in personal narratives: The development and preliminary validation of the Narrative Hope Scale.* Unpublished doctoral dissertation, University of Kansas, Lawrence.

Watson, D., Clark, L. A., & Tellegen, A. (1988). Development and validation of brief measures of positive and negative affect: The PANAS scales. *Journal of Personality and Social Psychology, 54,* 1063–1070.

7

Measuring Career Self-Efficacy: Promoting Confidence and Happiness at Work

Karen M. O'Brien

Freud suggested that healthy functioning could be operationalized as the ability to love and to work. Similarly, a recent gathering of social scientists identified love, intimacy, and satisfying work–occupation as salient characteristics that contribute to a positive life (Clifton, 2000). For many years, counseling psychologists assisted individuals in maximizing their ability to select careers that will allow them to succeed and, thus, lead happy and healthy work lives. Hackett and Betz (1981) advanced the work of counseling psychologists when they applied Bandura's cognitive theory to the study of vocational development. Specifically, they hypothesized that women who were confident in their ability to pursue career-related tasks (i.e., demonstrated strong levels of career self-efficacy) would be likely to consider a wide range of careers and be satisfied with their vocational choice. Since that time, career-related self-efficacy has been studied extensively and shown to be predictive of variables related to vocational development and occupational success (Bandura, Barbaranelli, Vittorio Caprara, & Pastorelli, 2001; Brown, Reedy, Fountain, Johnson, & Dichiser, 2000; Donnay & Borgen, 1999; Flores & O'Brien, 2002; Lent, Brown, & Hackett, 1994). To further assist researchers and practitioners in promoting health and happiness in the workplace, this chapter will provide information regarding the measurement of career-related self-efficacy.

Self-Efficacy: A Theory Unfolds

Bandura (1977) provided researchers and clinicians with a meaningful tool to assist people in their pursuit of positive and productive lives when he advanced the self-efficacy component of his social cognitive theory. Self-efficacy, defined as "beliefs in one's capabilities to organize and execute the courses of action required to produce given attainments" (Bandura, 1997, p. 3), leads to initiation of behaviors, amount of effort expended, persistence despite obstacles, and eventual success. Bandura also indicated that self-efficacy beliefs influence resilience to adversity, the presence of helpful or hindering cognitions, and the degree to which depression and stress occur when difficult situations are encountered. Moreover, he suggested that self-efficacy is domain-specific and that "efficacy beliefs should be measured in terms of particularized judgments of capability that may vary across realms of activity, under different levels of task demands within a given activity domain, and under different situational circumstances" (1997, p. 42). The precursors of self-efficacy, according to Bandura, include previous performance accomplishments, vicarious experiences, verbal persuasion, and affective reactions.

Career Self-Efficacy: Multiple Constructs and Myriad Measures

The application of Bandura's social cognitive theory and related research to clinical interventions has assisted people to lead healthy and productive lives in myriad ways. For example, researchers have studied the role of career self-efficacy in vocational development and occupational achievement. Career self-efficacy can be broadly defined as confidence in one's ability to manage career development and work-related tasks. This construct has been shown to relate to vocational interests (Nauta, Kahn, Angell, & Cantarelli, 2002), self-esteem (Brown et al., 2000), career indecision (Betz & Klein Voyten, 1997) and vocational aspirations (O'Brien, Friedman, Tipton, & Linn, 2000). Recently, Bandura and his colleagues (2001) found that children's perceived occupational self-efficacy was more predictive of career choice than academic performance. Moreover, because this construct is malleable, numerous researchers have developed vocational interventions aimed at enhancing career-related self-efficacy beliefs to promote healthy vocational development and occupational success (e.g., Betz & Schifano, 2000; Juntunen, 1996; Krieshok, Ulven, Hecox, & Wettersten, 2000; Sullivan & Mahalik, 2000). This chapter will focus on several career-related self-efficacy measures that have been used successfully in interventions designed to enhance the career functioning of adults.

Career Decision Self-Efficacy: Scale Purpose and Uses

The Career Decision Self-Efficacy scale–Short Form (CDSES; Betz, Klein, & Taylor, 1996; Betz & Taylor, 2000) is a self-report, 25-item inventory developed to assess confidence in making career-related decisions and engaging in tasks related to career decision making (see Appendix 7.1). This instrument can be used to promote confidence and happiness at work by identifying areas in which adults lack confidence and then developing interventions to increase confidence in the career development process. Individuals who feel confident in pursuing career-related tasks exhibit lower levels of career indecision (Betz & Klein Voyten, 1997) and feel more confident in exploring careers (Blustein, 1989) that may, in turn, lead to healthier career choices and eventual success and satisfaction at work.

This scale was formerly known as the Career Decision-Making Self-Efficacy scale and is the most widely used measure of career-related self-efficacy (Betz,

2000); the instrument was shortened from the original 50-item Career Decision Self-Efficacy scale developed by Taylor and Betz (1983) through item, split-scale, and factor analyses. The authors based the development of the original scale (and five subscales) on Crites's (1978) model of career maturity, which identified five career choice competencies believed to underlie healthy career decision making (i.e., accurate self-appraisal, gathering occupational information, goal selection, making future plans, and problem-solving).

ADMINISTRATION AND SCORING. The instrument can be administered to individuals or groups and takes fewer than 10 minutes to complete. A 10-level confidence continuum, ranging from no confidence at all (1) to complete confidence (10), or a 5-point continuum, ranging from no confidence at all (1) to complete confidence (5) can be used. All items are summed to obtain the total score on the CDSES–SF. Subscale scores are calculated by summing the scores on the five items for each subscale, and they can range from 5 to 50, or 5 to 25. High scores reflect strong levels of confidence in completing career-related tasks.

DESCRIPTIVE STATISTICS. Betz et al. (1996) reported the following descriptive data for a sample of college students: mean scores ranged from 34.0 (SD = 6.9) to 36.7 (SD = 7.1) for females and from 35.5 (SD = 6.7) to 38.4 (SD = 6.6) for males (corresponding to a confidence level of 7–7.5 on a 10-point scale).

RELIABILITY ESTIMATES. A total score reliability estimate of .94 was obtained and subscale reliabilities ranged from .73 (self-appraisal) to .83 (goal selection; Betz et al., 1996). Additional research found reliability estimates of .93 for the total score and a range of .69 (problem solving) to .83 (goal selection) for the subscales (Betz & Klein Voyten, 1997).

FACTOR STRUCTURE. Betz et al. (1996) noted that factor analyses marginally supported the 5-factor structure of this measure. They found that the occupational information and goal selection factors emerged as clear subscales (although planning items were included on each of these factors); problem solving and self-appraisal items loaded on two other factors, and only one self-appraisal item made up the fifth factor. Nevertheless, Betz and her colleagues suggested using the 5-factor solution because of the derivation of these subscales from theory and their usefulness in applied settings (e.g., designing interventions). Alternatively, the total score may be used as an indicator of career decision self-efficacy.

VALIDITY ESTIMATES. Support for the validity of this instrument has been demonstrated through negative correlations with measures of career indecision (Betz et al., 1996; Betz & Klein Voyten, 1997) and positive correlations with vocational identity (Betz et al., 1996). Career beliefs related to control, responsibility, and working hard were related to the CDSES–SF in the expected positive direction (Luzzo & Day, 1999).

The Occupational Questionnaire: Scale Purpose and Uses

The Occupational Questionnaire was developed by Teresa (1991) to assess confidence in students' ability to learn to successfully perform 31 occupations (i.e., self-efficacy for mastering a range of vocations; see Appendix 7.2). This instrument can be used to promote confidence and happiness at work by enabling researchers and clinicians to accurately assess students' confidence levels for various occupations and then develop interventions to assist these students in pursuing careers that match their abilities, interests, and values. For example, the instrument was used in a study of the career confidence and occupational consideration of 85 minority students enrolled in a high school equivalency program (Church, Teresa, Rosebrook, & Szendre, 1992). The use of this measure with a minority sample is particularly salient because students of color may underestimate their ability to succeed in numerous careers and thus limit their vocational and educational aspirations (Post, Stewart, & Smith, 1991).

ADMINISTRATION AND SCORING. Students complete this measure individually or in groups, in English or Spanish, and in approximately 10 minutes. They rate their confidence in learning to successfully perform each occupation on the following 6-point scale: very unsure (1), fairly unsure (2), somewhat unsure (3), somewhat sure (4), fairly sure (5), and very sure (6). The instrument provides an index of confidence in each of 31 occupations and a generality rating of confidence across all occupations. To obtain the generality rating, scores on the items are summed and averaged. High scores correspond to strong levels of confidence.

The Occupational Questionnaire was modified by Flores and O'Brien (2002) to assess nontraditional career self-efficacy in a study of 364 Mexican American high school women. They selected seven male-dominated occupations from the occupational self-efficacy questionnaire based on recent (1998) data from the U.S. Bureau of the Census. The participants rated their confidence in their ability and skills to successfully learn to do each of the jobs on a 4-point scale ranging from very unsure (1) to very sure (4). High scores indicated confidence in learning nontraditional occupations.

DESCRIPTIVE STATISTICS. Church et al. (1992) reported the following mean scores (and standard deviations) for women and men respectively on the female-dominated (3.94, $SD = 1.10$; 3.13, $SD = 1.01$), male-dominated (3.14, $SD = 0.98$; 3.74, $SD = 1.05$), and gender-balanced (3.77, $SD = 1.02$; 3.37, $SD = 0.91$) occupations. The Flores and O'Brien (2002) sample evidenced low levels of confidence in succeeding in nontraditional occupations ($M = 1.75$, $SD = .68$).

RELIABILITY ESTIMATES. Church et al. (1992) found an internal consistency reliability estimate of .95 for their sample of high school equivalency students. Teresa (1991) reported a 7-day test–retest reliability estimate of .84 for the generality ratings in a sample of 87 undergraduate education majors. The modified measure used by Flores and O'Brien (2002) evidenced an internal consistency reliability estimate of .81.

FACTOR STRUCTURE. The original measure was not factor analyzed, but occupations included on the instrument were chosen to represent each of Holland's (1985) occupational themes and included female-dominated, male-dominated, and gender-balanced occupations (according to the U.S. Bureau of the Census, 1998). Occupations that would be considered too easy or unrealistic by high school equivalency students were not included on the measure. Also, all occupations listed on the instrument could be translated into Spanish.

VALIDITY ESTIMATES. Gender differences provided support for the validity of the measure as both women and men reported more confidence in occupations traditionally held by their gender (Church et al., 1992). Flores and O'Brien (2002) reported that nontraditional occupational self-efficacy was related to nontraditional interests and career choice traditionality as expected.

Career Counseling Self-Efficacy Scale: Scale Purpose and Uses

The Career Counseling Self-Efficacy scale (CCSES: O'Brien, Heppner, Flores, & Bikos, 1997) was developed to assess counselors' level of confidence in providing vocational interventions to people who struggle with career concerns. In addition, this instrument can be used when training career counselors to identify areas of strength and possible limitations, which may then inform interventions to improve counseling skills and effectiveness. For example, Heppner, Multon, Gysbers, Ellis, and Zook (1998) used the CCSES when evaluating graduate-level practicum training and found that confidence in students' ability to perform career counseling increased after training. Moreover, the relationship of career counseling self-efficacy to outcome variables in career counseling was complex, and their findings suggested that high self-efficacy is not always related to the most favorable counseling outcomes.

The CCSES also has been used with school counselors. Perrone, Perrone, Chan, and Thomas (2000) administered a modified CCSES to more than 500 school counselors to assess efficacy in performing career counseling. School counselors felt least confident in understanding special issues related to gender, culture, ethnicity, and sexual orientation in career decision making. The researchers articulated a need for interventions to address this area of inefficacy and to assist school counselors in enhancing their effectiveness with a wide range of career clients.

ADMINISTRATION AND SCORING. The 25-item scale can be administered to individuals or groups and takes less than 10 minutes to complete. Ratings are made on a 5-point scale that includes not confident (0), moderately confident (2), and highly confident (4). Four factors make up the scale: therapeutic process and alliance skills (TPAS; 10 items); vocational assessment and interpretation skills (VAIS; 6 items); multicultural competency skills (MCS; 6 items); and current trends in the world of work, ethics, and career research (TWER; 3 items). A total score is calculated by summing all items, and items loading on each subscale can be summed for subscale scores. High scores indicate confidence in career counseling ability.

DESCRIPTIVE STATISTICS. Mean total scores on the CCSES ranged from 60.44 (SD = 23.20) for a sample of graduate students to 79.03 (SD = 11.05) for practicing psychologists (O'Brien et al., 1997). Scale scores also ranged for students and psychologists, respectively, as follows: TPAS, 26.56 (SD = 8.25) to 34.90 (SD = 4.37); VAIS, 13.50 (SD = 7.55) to 18.97 (SD = 3.94); MCS, 13.56 (SD = 5.50) to 17.79 (SD = 4.03); TWER, 6.03 (SD = 2.72) to 7.38 (SD = 2.31).

RELIABILITY ESTIMATES. Internal consistency reliability estimates were obtained for the total scale score (.96) and for each subscale (TPAS = .93; VAIS = .94; MCS = .92; and TWER = .76) with a sample of 289 students enrolled in doctoral or master's programs in counseling (O'Brien et al., 1997). Adequate reliability estimates also were reported with the sample of graduate students in the Heppner et al. (1998) study. Using a sample of 33 graduate students in counseling, the test–retest reliability estimates for a two-week period were as follows: total score = .86, TPAS = .87, VAIS = .87, MCS = .72, and TWER = .69 (O'Brien et al., 1997).

FACTOR STRUCTURE. The 4-factor structure was obtained through a principal components exploratory factor analysis using an oblique rotation and a randomly selected sample of half of the participants in the initial O'Brien et al. (1997) study. This structure accounted for 73% of the variance, and the factor structure was replicated with the second half of the sample. In a sample of 567 school counselors, Perrone and her colleagues (2000) replicated the first three factors of the CCSES. They suggested that school counselors use only these factors (i.e., TPAS, VAIS, and MCS) when administering this instrument, because the fourth factor (i.e., Current Trends in the World of Work, Ethics, and Career Research) was not replicated.

VALIDITY ESTIMATES. Support for the validity of this measure was demonstrated through relations in the expected direction between scores on the CCSES and years of career counseling experience and several subscales of a measure of counseling self-efficacy (O'Brien et al., 1997). Moreover, discriminant validity was demonstrated through no correlations between the CCSES total score and years of emotional–social counseling experience, scores on an emotional–social counseling self-efficacy scale, and a research self-efficacy scale (O'Brien et al., 1997). In addition, students who completed a career counseling course had higher levels of career counseling self-efficacy at the end of the course than at the beginning (Heppner et al., 1998; O'Brien et al., 1997). Finally, O'Brien and her colleagues found that practicing psychologists held higher career counseling self-efficacy beliefs than did counseling graduate students.

Construct Measurement Issues

When measuring self-efficacy (or selecting measures of self-efficacy) it is critical to keep the following four points in mind. First, according to Bandura (1997), self-efficacy is domain-specific and must be contextualized. "Analyses of how efficacy beliefs affect actions rely on microanalytic measures rather than global indices of personality traits or motives of effectance. It is no more informative to speak of self-efficacy in general terms than to speak of nonspecific social behavior" (p. 14). For example, if a graduate student who specialized in career counseling was asked about her global sense of counseling efficacy, she may think not only of her ability to perform career counseling but also her ability to counsel victims of domestic violence and children who have been sexually abused. Averaged self-efficacy across all types of counseling (when compared to the student's career counseling self-efficacy) should not be as predictive of the student's ability to assist a client in finding a career that matches his or her interests and allows him or her time to care for children. Thus, accurate assessment relies on the clear and comprehensive operationalization and measurement of the domain being assessed.

Second, Bandura (1997) indicated that self-efficacy measurement should not be broken down into subskills, but rather assess the person's belief in her or his capability to perform a function (i.e., link a number of subskills) in a variety of challenging situations related to the domain of interest. For example, a career search self-efficacy scale might include items that assess confidence in scheduling an informational interview in a variety of challenging situations. The measurement of this construct should not include items assessing confidence in finding the professional's number or asking to speak to the professional because these items would not assess the construct as a whole, as Bandura (1997) intended. Including challenging items ensures variability in scores and guards against ceiling effects.

Third, as to specific instructions regarding the wording of items, Bandura (1995) indicated that items should not inquire about future plans to complete a task (thus assessing intention), but rather should be phrased to assess thoughts regarding current ability to perform the task. Specifically, items should be written to assess what individuals think they can do now versus what they will do or what they plan to do. Moreover, individuals must understand what they are rating to obtain an accurate assessment of self-efficacy. If a participant does not know what an ophthalmologist is, she cannot accurately rate her ability to complete the tasks necessary for this career. Also, items should be written at the appropriate reading level and should not assess more than one task per item. For example, an item should not read, "Rate your confidence in your ability to ask your boss for a raise and to describe your many work accomplishments" because the employee may have different levels of efficacy for asking for a raise and articulating her successes at work. In addition, Bandura recommended including a sample item and suggested that self-efficacy be rated on a 100- or a 10-point scale to obtain variability in scores.

Fourth, at times the measurement of self-efficacy has been confused with other constructs (e.g., self-esteem, outcome expectations). For example, Bandura (1997) noted that self-efficacy addresses feelings regarding abilities, whereas self-esteem focuses on one's sense of self-worth. An individual might have low self-efficacy for pursuing a career as a physician, yet these beliefs may not negatively affect his sense of self if he has no interest in medicine.

Future Directions for the Measurement
of Career-Related Self-Efficacy

Researchers and practitioners have used measures of career-related self-efficacy to facilitate knowledge about, and interventions to enhance, the vocational development of many people. Continued research is needed to develop and use career-related self-efficacy measures with people from varied cultures, backgrounds, and occupations. In addition, the use of these measures in the evaluation of vocational interventions is strongly recommended.

First, many career-related self-efficacy measures have been used without attention to the reliability and validity of these instruments with diverse samples. Given the changing demographics of American society, researchers must attend to the psychometric properties of these instruments with people of color. This call to action presents challenges because self-efficacy measures must be domain-specific. Although it is unlikely that measures of every construct could be developed and tested with every diverse group, attention to the proper development of self-efficacy measures and accurate assessment of the psychometric properties of these instruments with people of color could result in a greater number of measures for use in research and practice.

Second, the research on career-related self-efficacy often reports on the confidence levels of college students. Similar to Brown and her colleagues (2000) in their investigation of the career decision-making self-efficacy of battered women, researchers must study a wide variety of individuals who may, in fact, need career assistance more than college students. Notable examples include the interventions developed for veterans to strengthen self-efficacy expectations for job searching, decision making, and integrating a new understanding of one's problems in future vocational decisions and work experiences (Krieshok et al., 2000).

Third, researchers should be encouraged to use self-efficacy measures when evaluating vocational interventions designed to enhance career-related self-efficacy. For example, recent studies highlighted effective interventions for improving vocational exploration and commitment in college women (Sullivan & Mahalik, 2000), increasing women's self-efficacy in pursuing traditionally male-dominated occupations (Betz & Schifano, 2000), and enhancing the career self-efficacy and vocational considerations of minority students in at-risk environments (O'Brien, Dukstein, Jackson, Tomlinson, & Kamatuka, 1999). Continued research is needed to inform the development of successful career interventions that are based in theory and previous research.

Fourth, Lent and Hackett (1987) called for career self-efficacy research that integrates environmental factors into the study of this individually focused construct. Given that self-efficacy was born from a theory that posits the reciprocal interaction of person, environment, and behavior, it seems timely to echo their call for continued research involving contextual variables.

Conclusion

Career-related self-efficacy is related to success and satisfaction in making vocational decisions and is predictive of occupational satisfaction (Betz & Luzzo, 1996; Donnay & Borgen, 1999; Flores & O'Brien, 2002). Continued attention to the measurement of this construct could assist researchers and practitioners in improving the quality of life for those who seek employment, strive to succeed in work, and aspire to lead positive and productive lives.

Appendix 7.1
Career Decision Self-Efficacy Scale

Career Questionnaire

Instructions: For each statement below, please read carefully and indicate how much confidence you have that you could accomplish each of these tasks by marking your answer according to the key. Mark your answer by filling in the correct circle on the answer sheet.

No confidence at all	Very little confidence	Moderate confidence	Much confidence	Complete confidence
1	2	3	4	5

Example: How much confidence do you have that you could:

   a. Summarize the skills you have developed in the jobs you have held?

If your response was "moderate confidence," you would fill out the number **3** on the sheet.

How much confidence do you have that you could:

1. Find information in the library about occupations you are interested in.
2. Select one major from a list of potential majors you are considering.
3. Make a plan of your goals for the next five years.
4. Determine the steps to take if you are having academic trouble with an aspect of your chosen major.
5. Accurately assess your abilities.
6. Select one occupation from a list of potential occupations you are considering.
7. Determine the steps you need to take to successfully complete your chosen major.
8. Persistently work at your major or career goal even when you get frustrated.
9. Determine what your ideal job would be.
10. Find out the employment trends for an occupation over the next ten years.
11. Choose a career that will fit your preferred lifestyle.
12. Prepare a good resume.
13. Change majors if you did not like your first choice.
14. Decide what you value most in an occupation.
15. Find out about the average yearly earnings of people in an occupation.
16. Make a career decision and then not worry about whether it was right or wrong.
17. Change occupations if you are not satisfied with the one you enter.
18. Figure out what you are and are not ready to sacrifice to achieve your career goals.

19. Talk with a person already employed in the field you are interested in.
20. Choose a major or career that will fit your interests.
21. Identify employers, firms, institutions relevant to your career possibilities.
22. Define the type of lifestyle you would like to live.
23. Find information about graduate or professional schools.
24. Successfully manage the job interview process.
25. Identify some reasonable major or career alternatives if you are unable to get your first choice.

Note. Reprinted with permission of Nancy E. Betz and Karen M. Taylor.

Appendix 7.2
The Occupational Questionnaire

For each of the following occupations, please indicate *how sure* you are that you have the *ability to learn to successfully do* the occupation. Please circle one answer for each question.

	very unsure	fairly unsure	somewhat unsure	somewhat sure	fairly sure	very sure
1. I have the ability to learn to be a floral designer (arranges flowers for sale).	very unsure	fairly unsure	somewhat unsure	somewhat sure	fairly sure	very sure
2. I have the ability to learn to be a probation officer (supervises persons released from prison).	very unsure	fairly unsure	somewhat unsure	somewhat sure	fairly sure	very sure
3. I have the ability to learn to be a drafter of plans for machinery and buildings (technical drawing).	very unsure	fairly unsure	somewhat unsure	somewhat sure	fairly sure	very sure
4. I have the ability to learn to be a food service manager in a cafeteria.	very unsure	fairly unsure	somewhat unsure	somewhat sure	fairly sure	very sure
5. I have the ability to learn to be a pharmacist (prepare medicines according to doctor's prescription).	very unsure	fairly unsure	somewhat unsure	somewhat sure	fairly sure	very sure
6. I have the ability to learn to be a manager of a bank loan department.	very unsure	fairly unsure	somewhat unsure	somewhat sure	fairly sure	very sure
7. I have the ability to learn to be a music teacher.	very unsure	fairly unsure	somewhat unsure	somewhat sure	fairly sure	very sure
8. I have the ability to learn to be a computer data entry operator (types information into a computer).	very unsure	fairly unsure	somewhat unsure	somewhat sure	fairly sure	very sure
9. I have the ability to learn to be a nurse.	very unsure	fairly unsure	somewhat unsure	somewhat sure	fairly sure	very sure
10. I have the ability to learn to be a life insurance salesperson.	very unsure	fairly unsure	somewhat unsure	somewhat sure	fairly sure	very sure
11. I have the ability to learn to be a landscape gardener (plans and maintains grounds of private homes and businesses, including seeding, planting, mowing and spraying).	very unsure	fairly unsure	somewhat unsure	somewhat sure	fairly sure	very sure
12. I have the ability to learn to be a repairer of electronic equipment such as computers and TV sets.	very unsure	fairly unsure	somewhat unsure	somewhat sure	fairly sure	very sure
13. I have the ability to learn to be a firefighter.	very unsure	fairly unsure	somewhat unsure	somewhat sure	fairly sure	very sure

	very unsure	fairly unsure	somewhat unsure	somewhat sure	fairly sure	very sure
14. I have the ability to learn to be a social worker.	very unsure	fairly unsure	somewhat unsure	somewhat sure	fairly sure	very sure
15. I have the ability to learn to be a forester (helps maintain trees for wood products, manages water, wildlife, grazing and recreational areas).	very unsure	fairly unsure	somewhat unsure	somewhat sure	fairly sure	very sure
16. I have the ability to learn to be a military officer.	very unsure	fairly unsure	somewhat unsure	somewhat sure	fairly sure	very sure
17. I have the ability to learn to be a fish hatchery manager (supervises the trapping, breeding, raising, and transfer of game fish to rivers and lakes).	very unsure	fairly unsure	somewhat unsure	somewhat sure	fairly sure	very sure
18. I have the ability to learn to be an interior designer (plans, designs, and furnishes the inside of homes and buildings).	very unsure	fairly unsure	somewhat unsure	somewhat sure	fairly sure	very sure
19. I have the ability to learn to be a bookkeeper.	very unsure	fairly unsure	somewhat unsure	somewhat sure	fairly sure	very sure
20. I have the ability to learn to be a police officer.	very unsure	fairly unsure	somewhat unsure	somewhat sure	fairly sure	very sure
21. I have the ability to learn to be a travel agent.	very unsure	fairly unsure	somewhat unsure	somewhat sure	fairly sure	very sure
22. I have the ability to learn to be a physical therapist (plans and teaches physical exercises to the disabled).	very unsure	fairly unsure	somewhat unsure	somewhat sure	fairly sure	very sure
23. I have the ability to learn to be a park ranger (enforces regulations, provides information to visitors, and supervises park maintenance in state and national parks).	very unsure	fairly unsure	somewhat unsure	somewhat sure	fairly sure	very sure
24. I have the ability to learn to be a mechanical engineer (designs machinery and equipment).	very unsure	fairly unsure	somewhat unsure	somewhat sure	fairly sure	very sure
25. I have the ability to learn to be a manager of a department in a large retail store.	very unsure	fairly unsure	somewhat unsure	somewhat sure	fairly sure	very sure
26. I have the ability to learn to assist scientists with laboratory work.	very unsure	fairly unsure	somewhat unsure	somewhat sure	fairly sure	very sure
27. I have the ability to learn to be a high school teacher.	very unsure	fairly unsure	somewhat unsure	somewhat sure	fairly sure	very sure
28. I have the ability to learn to be a recreation director in a nursing home.	very unsure	fairly unsure	somewhat unsure	somewhat sure	fairly sure	very sure

	very unsure	fairly unsure	somewhat unsure	somewhat sure	fairly sure	very sure
29. I have the ability to learn to be a personnel manager.	very unsure	fairly unsure	somewhat unsure	somewhat sure	fairly sure	very sure
30. I have the ability to learn to be a librarian.	very unsure	fairly unsure	somewhat unsure	somewhat sure	fairly sure	very sure
31. I have the ability to learn to be a dietician (plans and supervises the preparation and serving of meals, often including special diets).	very unsure	fairly unsure	somewhat unsure	somewhat sure	fairly sure	very sure

Note. Reprinted with permission of Judy Teresa.

Appendix 7.3
The Career Counseling Self-Efficacy Scale

Below is a list of activities regarding counseling. Indicate *your confidence in your current ability to perform each activity* according to the scale defined below. Please answer each item based on how you feel now, not on your anticipated (or previous) ability.

0	1	2	3	4
Not confident		Moderately confident		Highly confident

1. Select an instrument to clarify a career client's abilities.
2. Provide support for a client's implementation of her/his career goals.
3. Assist a client in understanding how his/her nonwork life (e.g., family, leisure, interests, etc.) affects career decisions.
4. Understand special issues related to gender *in career decision making*.
5. Develop a therapeutic relationship with a career client.
6. Select an instrument to clarify aspects of a career client's personality which may influence career planning.
7. Explain assessment results to a career client.
8. Terminate counseling with a career client in an effective manner.
9. Understand special issues related to ethnicity *in the workplace*.
10. Understand special issues that lesbian, gay and bisexual clients may have *in career decision making*.
11. Provide knowledge of local and national job market information and trends.
12. Choose assessment inventories for a career client which are appropriate for the client's gender, age, education, and cultural background.
13. Assist the career client in modulating feelings about the career decision-making process.
14. Apply knowledge about current ethical and legal issues which may affect the career counseling process.
15. Understand special issues present for lesbian, gay, and bisexual clients *in the workplace*.
16. Communicate unconditional acceptance to a career client.
17. Select an instrument to assess a career client's interests.
18. Select an instrument to clarify a career client's values.
19. Understand special issues related to gender *in the workplace*.
20. Understand special issues related to ethnicity in *career decision making*.
21. Listen carefully to concerns presented by a career client.
22. Synthesize information about self and career so that a career client's problems seem understandable.
23. Help a career client identify internal and external barriers that might interfere with reaching her/his career goals.

24. Use current research findings to intervene effectively with a career client.
25. Be empathic toward a career client when the client refuses to accept responsibility for making decisions about his/her career.

References

Bandura, A. (1977). Self-efficacy: Toward a unifying theory of behavioral change. *Psychological Review, 84,* 191–215.

Bandura, A. (1995). *Guide for constructing self-efficacy scales.* Unpublished manuscript, Stanford University.

Bandura, A. (1997). *Self-efficacy: The exercise of control.* New York: W. H. Freeman.

Bandura, A., Barbaranelli, C., Vittorio Caprara, G., & Pastorelli, C. (2001). Self-efficacy beliefs as shapers of children's aspirations and career trajectories. *Child Development, 72,* 187–206.

Betz, N. E. (2000). Self-efficacy theory as a basis for career assessment. *Journal of Career Assessment, 8,* 205–222.

Betz, N. E., Klein, K., & Taylor, K. M. (1996). Evaluation of a short form of the Career Decision-Making Self-Efficacy scale. *Journal of Career Assessment, 4,* 47–57.

Betz, N. E., & Klein Voyten, K. (1997). Efficacy and outcome expectations influence career exploration and decidedness. *Career Development Quarterly, 46,* 179–189.

Betz, N. E., & Luzzo, D. A. (1996). Career assessment and the Career Decision-Making Self-Efficacy scale. *Journal of Career Assessment, 4,* 413–428.

Betz, N. E., & Schifano, R. S. (2000). Evaluation of an intervention to increase realistic self-efficacy and interests in college women. *Journal of Vocational Behavior, 56,* 35–52.

Betz, N. E., & Taylor, K. M. (2000). *Manual for the Career Decision Self-Efficacy Scale and CDMSE–Short form.* Unpublished instrument, Ohio State University, Columbus.

Blustein, D. L. (1989). The role of goal instability and career self-efficacy in the career exploration process. *Journal of Vocational Behavior, 35,* 194–203.

Brown, C., Reedy, D., Fountain, J., Johnson, A., & Dichiser, T. (2000). Battered women's career decision-making self-efficacy: Further insights and contributing factors. *Journal of Career Assessment, 8,* 251–265.

Church, A. T., Teresa, J. S., Rosebrook, R., & Szendre, D. (1992). Self-efficacy for careers and occupational consideration in minority high school equivalency students. *Journal of Counseling Psychology, 39,* 498–508.

Clifton, D. O. (2000). Mapping the wellsprings of a positive life: The importance of measurement to the movement. *The Gallup Review, 3,* 8–13.

Crites, J. O. (1978). *Career Maturity Inventory.* Monterey, CA: CTB/McGraw Hill.

Donnay, D. A. C., & Borgen, F. H. (1999). The incremental validity of vocational self-efficacy: An examination of interest, self-efficacy, and occupation. *Journal of Counseling Psychology, 46,* 432–447.

Flores, L. Y., & O'Brien, K. M. (2002). The career development of Mexican American adolescent women: A test of social cognitive career theory. *Journal of Counseling Psychology, 49,* 14–27.

Hackett, G., & Betz, N. E. (1981). A self-efficacy approach to the career development of women. *Journal of Vocational Behavior, 18,* 326–339.

Heppner, M. J., Multon, K. D., Gysbers, N. C., Ellis, C. A., & Zook, C. E. (1998). The relationship of trainee self-efficacy to the process and outcome of career counseling. *Journal of Counseling Psychology, 45,* 393–402.

Holland, J. L. (1985). *Making vocational choices: A theory of vocational personalities and work environments* (2nd ed.). Englewood Cliffs, NJ: Prentice-Hall.

Juntunen, C. (1996). Relationship between a feminist approach to career counseling and career self-efficacy beliefs. *Journal of Employment Counseling, 33,* 130–143.

Krieshok, T. S., Ulven, J. C., Hecox, J. L., & Wettersten, K. (2000). Resume therapy and vocational test feedback: Tailoring interventions to self-efficacy outcomes. *Journal of Career Assessment, 8,* 267–281.

Lent, R. W., Brown, S. D., & Hackett, G. (1994). Toward a unifying social cognitive theory of career and academic interest, choice, and performance. *Journal of Vocational Behavior, 45,* 79–122.

Lent, R. W., & Hackett, G. (1987). Career self-efficacy: Empirical status and future directions. *Journal of Vocational Behavior, 30,* 347–382.

Luzzo, D. A., & Day, M. A. (1999). Effects of Strong Interest Inventory feedback on career decision-making self-efficacy and social cognitive career beliefs. *Journal of Career Assessment, 7,* 1–17.

Nauta, M. M., Kahn, J., Angell, J., & Cantarelli, E. A. (2002). Identifying the antecedent in the relation between career interests and self-efficacy: Is it one, the other, or both? *Journal of Counseling Psychology, 49,* 290–301.

O'Brien, K. M., Dukstein, R. D., Jackson, S. L., Tomlinson, M. J., & Kamatuka, N. A. (1999). Broadening career horizons for students in at-risk environments. *Career Development Quarterly, 47,* 215–229.

O'Brien, K. M., Friedman, S. M., Tipton, L. C., & Linn, S. G. (2000). Attachment, separation, and women's vocational development: A longitudinal analysis. *Journal of Counseling Psychology, 47,* 301–315.

O'Brien, K. M., Heppner, M. J., Flores, L. Y., & Bikos, L. H. (1997). The Career Counseling Self-Efficacy scale: Instrument development and training applications. *Journal of Counseling Psychology, 44,* 20–31.

Perrone, K. M., Perrone, P. A., Chan, F., & Thomas, K. R. (2000). Assessing efficacy and importance of career counseling competencies. *Career Development Quarterly, 48,* 212–225.

Post, P., Stewart, M. A., & Smith, P. L. (1991). Self-efficacy, interest, and consideration of math/science and non-math/science occupations among Black freshmen. *Journal of Vocational Behavior, 38,* 179–186.

Sullivan, K. R., & Mahalik, J. R. (2000). Increasing career self-efficacy for women: Evaluating a group intervention. *Journal of Counseling & Development, 78,* 54–62.

Taylor, K. M., & Betz, N. E. (1983). Applications of self-efficacy theory to the understanding and treatment of career indecision. *Journal of Vocational Behavior, 22,* 63–81.

Teresa, J. S. (1991). *Increasing self-efficacy for careers in young adults from migrant farmworker backgrounds.* Unpublished doctoral dissertation, Washington State University, Pullman.

U.S. Bureau of the Census. (1987). *Statistical abstract of the United States: 1988* (108th ed.). Washington, DC: U.S. Government Printing Office.

U.S. Bureau of the Census. (1998). *Statistical abstract of the United States: 1998* (118th ed.). Washington, DC: U.S. Government Printing Office.

8

Problem-Solving Appraisal

P. Paul Heppner and Yu-Wei Wang

Applied real-life problem solving is of special interest to professionals who help others plan and strive toward goals, as well as struggle with transitions and difficult problems that they have been unable to resolve. People typically face a complex web of goal-setting decisions, daily hassles, major life events, and continually changing situations.

A persistent problem within applied problem-solving research has been the operationalization of actual problem-solving skills, effectiveness, or competence (Kendall & Fischler, 1984). As a result, the measurement of applied problem solving generally has been categorized into two categories: (a) self-report or verbal and (b) observational (D'Zurilla, 1986). Observational methods are useful for assessing overt problem-solving performances or the product of problem-solving processes. Despite the appeal of observational approaches, this strategy encounters complex measurement issues; see D'Zurilla (1986) for a more thorough discussion of the advantages and limitations of this assessment approach. The self-report method has been the most common method of assessment and will be the focus of this chapter.

People respond to applied personal problems in different ways. Some people bring a wealth of resources to coping with their problems, whereas others have significant problem-solving deficits. Much research suggests that how people appraise their problem-solving style is directly related to not only the manner in which they cope with their problems but also the extent to which they resolve their problems as well as their psychological adjustment (see Heppner & Baker, 1997; Heppner, Cooper, Mulholland, & Wei, 2001; Heppner & Lee, 2002). For example, consider Pauline, who had been working for a large high-tech firm as director of research. Her company was downsized, and she was laid off with little warning. Naturally, she was disappointed, but also confident she could find employment, maybe even a position that would be more satisfying. In fact, after a few days Pauline saw this as an opportunity to make a career change. Within a few weeks of her dismissal, Pauline had updated her resume, arranged informational interviews, and was making progress toward resolving career problems. As depicted, having confidence in problem solving typically results in making progress in coping.

Conversely, consider Tom, who moved to a new city when his wife was relocated. Tom, who had worked as an accountant, was experiencing more fear in looking for a new position than he thought he would. Tom slept and drank more than usual, and did other, less important, tasks than seeking new employment. Tom found himself applying for jobs well below his experience level in hopes that someone would find him competent. Tom's lack of confidence in his ability to find employment impeded his progress in resolving his career problem.

These scenarios not only highlight how people respond to personal problems in different ways but also how one's self-assessment (a type of self-report) of his or her problem-solving skills (e.g., problem-solving confidence) affects subsequent coping with life transitions. This chapter focuses on applied problem solving, and particularly problem-solving appraisal, or how people evaluate their problem-solving capabilities as well as their style of approaching (or avoiding) problems. Identifying how a client appraises his or her problem-solving style is a critical step in developing interventions to help clients resolve troublesome problems. The next section provides a brief history of applied problem-solving work, followed by a description of a model of problem-solving appraisal. We will briefly discuss alternative conceptions of applied problem solving, complex measurement issues, and future developments.

Brief History of Applied Problem Solving

The bulk of the early focus on applied problem solving was on impersonal laboratory problems, such as solving water jar or string problems (Wicklegren, 1974). Some of the earliest and most significant programmatic research in applied problem solving was conducted by Shure, Spivack, and colleagues (e.g., Shure & Spivack, 1972; see Platt & Spivack, 1975, for a description of the means–end problem-solving procedure). Conceptualizing problem solving as a constellation of relatively discreet thought processes, Spivack and Shure pioneered research on cognitive problem-solving skills within interpersonal situations, such as problem sensitivity, alternative solution thinking, causal thinking, and means–end thinking (see Shure, 1982). This line of research found that the number of means generated for solving hypothetical problems was positively correlated with developing better solutions and related to better psychological adjustment (Shure, 1982). Other early models of applied problem solving conceptualized problem solving within stage-sequential models, most notably D'Zurilla and Goldfried's (1971) five-stage model (general orientation, problem definition and formulation, generation of alternatives, decision making, and verification). In the 1970s, more attention was given to how people grapple with ambiguous, real-life problems (e.g., Janis & Mann, 1977), as well as the implications for those in the helping professions (e.g., Dixon & Glover, 1984; Heppner, 1978). The stage sequential models were particularly useful in developing interventions for enhancing problem solving in general as well as particular problems such as drug abuse (see D'Zurilla, 1986).

Later advances in understanding the complexities of information processing spawned the development of dynamic and nonlinear models of problem solving (Heppner & Krauskopf, 1987). The 1990s witnessed additional refinement of applied problem-solving models and training (e.g., Nezu, Nezu, Fried-man, Faddis, & Houts, 1998), as well as the incorporation of problem-solving effectiveness that resulted in the conceptualization of problem-solving resolution (e.g., Heppner et al., 2002; Heppner, Cook, Wright, & Johnson, 1995).

Problem-Solving Appraisal

Within the cognitive revolution of the 1970s and 1980s, Butler and Meichenbaum (1981) focused on higher order or metacognitive variables within applied problem solving; they suggested that a crucial construct is not just "the specific knowledge or processes that individuals may apply directly to the solution of problems, but with higher order variables that affect how (and whether) they will solve problems" (p. 219). More specifically, Butler and Meichenbaum emphasized the centrality of an individual's self-appraisal of their problem-solving ability. At this time, the coping scholars (e.g., Antonovsky, 1979) made similar suggestions that appraisal of one's ability is related to coping with stress. In short, the appraisal of one's problem-solving skills may well be an important component of how one approaches life and its circumstances.

Following the notion of appraisal of one's problem-solving skills, Heppner and Petersen (1982) developed the Problem Solving Inventory (PSI) to assess problem-solving appraisal. The PSI has been one of the most widely used self-report inventories in applied problem-solving research and has been translated into at least eight languages (Nezu, Nezu, & Perri, 1989). In essence, the PSI research literature has confirmed Butler and Meichenbaum's hypothesis that problem-solving appraisal is an important construct in applied problem solving (see Heppner & Baker, 1997; Heppner & Lee, 2002). Thus, the primary focus of this chapter is on problem-solving appraisal and the PSI—the only measure of problem-solving appraisal.

Instrument Structure

The PSI assesses perceptions of one's problem-solving ability, as well as behaviors and attitudes associated with problem-solving style (Heppner, 1988; Heppner & Baker, 1997). The inventory does not assess problem-solving skills but rather perception of problem-solving beliefs and style. The PSI consists of 35 items (including three filler items) with a 6-point Likert scale (1 = strongly agree to 6 = strongly disagree). The term *problems* refers to issues that many people experience, such as depression, inability to get along with friends, or deciding whether to get a divorce. This inventory can be completed in 10 to 15 minutes at a counseling session, in class, or at home. It can be hand scored in fewer than five minutes or computer scored. The PSI should be administered and interpreted by professionals with training in assessment and knowledge of problem-solving literature and who have normative information on PSI.

The PSI contains three factors: (a) problem-solving confidence (PSC, 11 items), (b) approach–avoidance style (AAS, 16 items), and (c) personal control

(PC, 5 items); the PSI total score is the sum of these three subscales. Specifically, PSC is defined as an individual's self-assurance, a belief, and trust in one's ability to effectively cope with a wide range of problems (e.g., "When faced with a novel situation, I have confidence that I can handle problems that may arise"). Lower scores on the PSC reflect higher levels of problem-solving confidence. AAS refers to a general tendency to approach or avoid different problem-solving activities (e.g., "When making a decision, I weigh the consequences of each alternative and compare them against each other"). Lower scores are associated with a style of approaching rather than avoiding problems. The PC is defined as believing one is in control of one's emotions and behaviors while solving problems (e.g., "Even though I work on a problem, sometimes I feel like I am groping or wandering, and am not getting down to the real issue"). Lower scores indicate more positive individual perception of control in handling problems. The intercorrelation among these three factors ranged between .39 to .69 across a range of studies on PSI (see Heppner, 1988)—suggesting that the factors are interrelated and independent.

There are three existing forms of the PSI, and there is considerable support for the factor structure across the three forms and different populations. The inventory published with the testing manual is labeled Form B (see Table 8.1 for sample items), in which 18 of the original PSI items were reworded to make them easier to understand. All previous versions of the PSI items are referred to as Form A. The adolescent version of the PSI was created by reducing the reading levels of the items in Form B from a 9.25 grade reading level to approximately a fourth-grade reading level (Heppner, Manley, Perez, & Dixon, 1994), and is available from the first author. Previous studies suggest that the PSI structure replicated well across these three forms, and it seem to be generalizable across different age groups from various backgrounds such as midwestern high school students (Heppner et al., 1994), midwestern White college students (e.g., Heppner, Baumgardner, Larson, & Petty, 1988), military personnel consisting of mostly Whites and African Americans (Chynoweth, 1987), French Canadian adults (Laporte, Sabourin, & Wright, 1988), Turkish college students (Sahin, Sahin, & Heppner, 1993), and South African college students (Heppner, Pretorius, Wei, Wang, & Lee, 2000).

Reliability

The PSI has acceptable internal consistency; this has been demonstrated across a number of populations and cultures (e.g., Heppner, 1988; Heppner et al., 1994, 2000). Summing across the studies using PSI Form A, B, or Adolescent version, the PSI total obtains average alpha coefficients in the high .80s, whereas two of the factors (PSC and AAS) obtain average alpha coefficients in the low to mid .80s, and the third factor (PC) obtains average alpha coefficients in the low .70s. These results suggest that the PSI is internally consistent even with different forms of the PSI used across quite different cultural groups. Five studies provided estimates of stability of the PSI over various time intervals, from two weeks to two years across different samples. Total PSI scores

Table 8.1. Sample Items From the Problem-Solving Inventory–Form B (PSI)

Subscales	Sample items
Problem-solving confidence	Given enough time and effort, I believe I can solve most problems that confront me.
	I trust my ability to solve new and difficult problems.
Approach-avoidance style	When confronted with a problem, I usually first survey the situation to determine the relevant information.
	*When confronted with a problem, I tend to do the first thing that I can think to solve it.
Personal control	*There are times when I become so emotionally charged that I can no longer see the alternative for solving a particular problem.
	*I make snap judgments and later regret them.

Note. *Indicates reversed scoring.

are correlated .80 over two weeks, .81 over three weeks and also for four months, and .60 over two years across samples of White college students, Black college students, and French Canadian adults (e.g., Heppner, 1988). In essence, the results suggest that the PSI scores are stable over time across different populations and cultures.

Validity

A wide range of studies provide a wealth of data supporting the validity of the PSI (see Heppner, 1988; Heppner & Baker, 1997; Heppner & Lee, 2002). First of all, the three scale scores and the total PSI score were correlated with students' ratings of their level of problem-solving skills and their perceived level of satisfaction with skills (Heppner & Petersen, 1982). Second, the PSI scores do not seem to be strongly correlated with aptitude measures or social desirability (Heppner & Petersen, 1982), which in turn helped to establish the discriminant validity. Also, judges, blind to the research participants' PSI scores, independently and successfully differentiated higher and low scorers on the PSI (Heppner & Petersen, 1982), which provided additional support for the construct validity of the PSI. Finally, the PSI has been found to relate to a wide range of cognitions, affective responses, and problem-solving behaviors, as well as to numerous indexes of psychological health. For example, students who had completed a motivation course reported an increase in problem-solving appraisal, whereas those who did not take the course reported a more negative appraisal (Chynoweth, Blankinship, & Parker, 1986). Also, Sabourin, Laporte, and Wright (1990) found that PSI factors were related to marital coping. The lack of problem-solving confidence was associated with resignation in women, and avoiding problems was associated with less negotiation in men. Also, data indicate that people who appraise their problem-solving ability negatively tend to report having a wide range of distress on a number of indexes (see Heppner & Baker, 1997; Heppner & Lee, 2002).

Normative Information

The means suggest that clinical populations have higher PSI means than do nonclinical populations. For college students, measures of central tendency for nonclincial samples had a mean around 88 (e.g., Heppner, 1988), whereas for clinical college student samples the PSI mean tended to be around 100 (e.g., Nezu, 1986). Likewise for adults, measures of central tendency for nonclinical samples had a PSI mean in the low 80s (e.g., Sabourin, Laporte, & Wright, 1990), whereas for clinical adult samples the mean tended to be around 100 (Reis & Heppner, 1993). Although PSI means represent approximations (i.e., sample sizes were not taken into account), the distributions suggest rather impressive differences between clinical and nonclinical samples.

Applications

The PSI has a wide range of applications. In terms of working with clients, the PSI can provide an assessment of a client's problem-solving style that may facilitate or hinder his or her daily functioning or provide relevant information underlying a client's presenting problem. Thus, the PSI can provide relevant diagnostic information, which can be used to inform interventions. Several studies have indicated that people who perceive themselves to be less effective problem solvers on the PSI tend to disengage from problem solving (see Heppner & Baker, 1997); thus, it can be helpful for practitioners to monitor the self-appraised negative problem solvers, or to build on self-appraised positive problem solvers' tendency to approach situations. In addition, the PSI can be a very good outcome measure for evaluating service delivery in general, but especially for problem-solving training interventions.

The PSI has been used successfully as a training tool to enhance participants' awareness of their problem-solving attitudes, knowledge, and skills (e.g., Heppner & Reeder, 1984). The PSI also has applications in school settings, such as identifying students at risk for academic failure or as a measure of problem-based learning (see Heppner & Baker, 1997).

Alternative Conceptualizations of Problem Solving

Four other strategies to assess verbal measures of applied problem solving will be briefly mentioned because they are based on alternative conceptualizations. One strategy to assess applied problem solving has been to assess the nature and frequency of personal problems. The basic assumption has been that fewer problems in one's life suggest effective problem solving, whereas more problems reflect ineffective problem solving. Perhaps one of the earliest problem checklists was the Mooney Problem Checklist (MPC: Mooney & Gordon, 1950). The MPC consists of 330 items asking participants to identify problems, which constitute 11 scales on major problem areas (e.g., health and physical development, social–psychological relations). It has been used extensively in studies examining college student problems (e.g., Hartman, 1968). A slightly different type of problem assessment is the Computerized Assessment System for Psychotherapy Evaluation and Research (CASPER: McCullough & Farrell, 1983), which is a branching system to assess the presence and severity of common problems across 13 categories.

Another problem checklist is the Inventory of Interpersonal Problems (IIP: Horowitz, Rosenberg, Baer, Ureño, & Villaseñor, 1988). The IIP consists of 127 items that ask participants to rate how distressing a particular problem has been (0 = not at all, 4 = extremely). Factor analyses revealed that the IIP consists of problems related to six scales: assertive, sociable, intimate, submissive, responsible, and controlling. Higher scores indicate a higher degree of self-reported distress related to the problem in one's life. In sum, the MPC provides a broad assessment of the number of problems across a broad range of categories. The IIP adds another dimension by assessing the distress to the number of problems confronting an individual.

A second strategy has been to attempt to assess both problem-solving attitudes and skills through self-report assessments. D'Zurilla and Nezu (1990) developed a theory-driven Likert type item questionnaire (with 70 items) called the Social Problem Solving Inventory (SPSI). The SPSI is organized into two major subscales, a problem orientation scale (POS) and problem solving skills scale (PSSS). The POS has three subscales: cognitive subscale, emotion subscale, and behavior subscale. The PSSS scale has four subscales: problem definition and formulation subscale, generation of alternative solution subscale, decision-making subscale, and solution implementation and verification subscale. Each scale has 10 items rationally derived from social problem-solving theory. The psychometric data suggest that the internal consistency of each scale and subscale range from .75 to .94, with test–retest correlations of .83 to .88 over three weeks. Validity estimates with adults suggest that scores correlate with measures of psychological health and are sensitive to problem-solving training. The developers of this strategy propose that the verbal reports on the PSSS assess problem-solving skills associated with the skill components of social problem-solving theory; the validity estimates would serve to support this assumption.

Another strategy to assess verbal reports of applied problem solving is to examine the degree to which one's problem-solving activities facilitate or inhibit progress toward resolution of problems. Rather than assessing whether a person reports typically engaging in a particular problem-solving activity, the assessment focuses on whether the reported consequences of the problem-solving activities facilitate or inhibit progress toward resolving the problem. This strategy provides more of an assessment of the perceived effectiveness of the problem-solving activities. Heppner et al. (1995) used the construct of problem resolution to develop the Problem-Focused Style of Coping scale (PF–SOC). The PF–SOC integrates problem-solving constructs with traditional coping constructs such as problem-focused coping, and thus straddles both the traditional applied problem solving and coping literatures. The PF–SOC consists of 18 items, and asks participants, on a 5-point Likert scale (1 = almost never, 5 = almost all of the time) how frequently each item describes how they deal with problems. Analysis revealed three factors: reflective style (emphasizes cognitive activities such as planning, reflection, and causal analyses); reactive style (emphasizes emotional and cognitive activities that deplete the individual or distort problem-solving activities); and suppressive style (indicates an avoidance and denial of problem-solving activities; Heppner et al., 1995). The PF–SOC thus integrates the perceived outcome of problem-solving activities within items to assess the extent that a person's efforts altered the problem or stressor. Psychometric information suggests a stable factor structure; acceptable internal consistency and stability estimates; and very good estimates of discriminant, concurrent, and construct validity. Psychometric findings also suggest that the PF–SOC adds a unique dimension to the assessment of applied problem solving (and coping as well).

The construct of problem resolution has been further operationalized within a therapeutic context. Heppner et al. (2001) developed a problem-based psychotherapy outcome measure that assesses the extent that clients have resolved the problems for which they sought therapeutic assistance. The Problem Resolution Outcome Survey (PROS) consists of 24 items that provide a multidimensional assessment of clients' resolution of their presenting problems. Four factors were derived from factor analysis: problem solving strategies (which represents critical problem-solving strategies for resolving problems with specific goals, plans, and actions), problem-solving self-efficacy (which represents a motivational component, or agency, in resolving clients' presenting problems), problem impact on daily functioning (which reflects the extent of impairment on a broad range of daily functioning domains), and general satisfaction with therapy (which provides an index of satisfaction with how counseling helped the clients resolve their problems). The total score reflects a multidimensional assessment of client resolution of presenting problems, from very specific problem-solving strategies to very global satisfaction. The validity estimates suggest that the PROS is related to process, outcome, and problem-solving measures in theoretically consistent ways and is sensitive to change over time.

In summary, there are a number of strategies to assess verbal reports of applied problem solving. Moreover, different strategies have focused on assessing different aspects of the problem-solving process. For example, some assessment strategies have focused solely on examining the frequency of problems, or the amount of distress associated with current problems confronting an individual. Perhaps the most common strategy has been to assess primarily reported cognitive (but to some extent affective and behavioral) activities within applied problem solving, such as reflected in the PSI, PSP–R, PF–SOC, and PROS. More recently, investigators have added a perceived effectiveness component to the items to assess the perceived or implied impact of problem-solving activities on resolution, such as with the PF–SOC and PROS. The multiple assessment strategies reflect the multifaceted nature of assessing applied problem solving.

Complexity in Measuring Applied Problem Solving

The focus of this chapter has been on assessing verbal reports of applied problem solving. One advantage of assessing verbal reports of applied problem solving is that reports are efficient and practical. For example, completing the PSI generally takes 15 minutes or less, and even a 330-item questionnaire (the Mooney Problem Checklist; Mooney & Gordon, 1950) assessing the frequency of current problems typically can be completed in 25 minutes. Perhaps more important, however, verbal reports provide assessments about complex and dynamic internal as well as covert problem-solving processes that often are hidden to outside observers, even close friends. Thus, verbal report assessments garner hard-to-access information about how people solve applied problems.

The manner in which people struggle and cope with stressful personal difficulties, however, is an exceedingly complex process and has defied description for years in the problem-solving literature. A critical issue pertains to the accuracy of an individual's report on the various measures of applied problem solving. Perhaps an individual has some motivation to under- or over-rate him- or herself, either consciously or unconsciously. Or maybe an individual's selective attention of his or her performance causes a distorted assessment. To address this validity issue, earlier writers have called for observational tests of problem-solving behaviors to assess actual problem-solving skill, ability, or effectiveness (e.g., Butler & Meichenbaum, 1981). Various strategies have been suggested and tried, such as role-playing problematic situations, using think-aloud or process-recall techniques of data collection, self-monitoring charts, and examining responses to hypothetical or staged interpersonal problems (see Larson, Potenza, Wennstedt, & Sailors, 1995). Unfortunately, this strategy of examining the relationship between verbal reports and actual problem-solving skill or effectiveness has encountered numerous conceptual and methodological problems, such as sampling and generalizability issues, criterion validity issues, and external validity concerns related to fabricated problem-solving trials.

Perhaps the most critical measurement issue pertains to individual differences within the complex process of applied problem solving. For example, there is some evidence to suggest people engage in different problem-solving activities across different types of problems (see Heppner & Hillerbrand, 1991). Moreover, after reviewing a wide range of problem-solving research, Heppner and Krauskopf (1987) concluded that "problem solving cannot be well understood without reference to a person's knowledge bases, how they are acquired, and how they are internally represented" (p. 433). Moreover, people differ greatly from one another in their knowledge bases, and people have greatly different knowledge bases from one topic to another. The notion of individual differences and knowledge bases introduces tremendous complexity in problem-solving assessment. Thus, it seems like it might be particularly useful to examine individual differences and particularly contextual issues (such as knowledge bases and cultural context) in applied problem solving. For example, examining the role of problem-solving appraisal across different problem domains, sex, gender socialization, race, ethnicity, all within the context of cultural norms, might increase understanding of this complex topic. Moreover, appraisal of problem solving might include appraisal of different activities across cultures, such as appraisal of one's individual problem-solving skills versus appraisal of one's family problem-solving skills. In short, the complexity and diversity in applied problem solving suggest that research in applied problem solving must include more complex assessment tools.

Future Developments in Measurement of the Construct

There is considerable evidence that supports the generalizability of the PSI factor structure across quite different populations and cultures; data from a number of PSI samples from other racial–ethnic minority groups and various cultures are encouraging. Nonetheless, more research with different ethnic and race samples is still needed (cf. Leong, 1990). Thus, more work needs to be done to develop an understanding of culture-specific as well as universal problem-solving constructs. More cross-cultural normative data is needed for adequate comparisons. Also, it is important to emphasize that there may be other components of problem solving that are not assessed by the PSI that may play a significant role in approaching life. Research that integrates indigenous ways of coping used by various cultural groups (e.g., traditional spiritual practices) may be useful for identifying culture-specific ways of coping.

Furthermore, future research is needed to clarify the relationships among PSI factors and psychological health. There has been a range of studies that have examined the link between problem-solving appraisal and psychological health in the United States (e.g., Heppner & Lee, 2002) and other countries (e.g., Heppner et al., 2000; Pretorius, 1993; Sahin et al., 1993). It has been suggested that a more complete understanding of problem-solving appraisal might occur by examining the role of specific PSI factors in predicting psychological health (e.g., Dixon, Heppner, & Anderson, 1991). Witty, Heppner, Bernard, and Thoreson (2001) found that problem-solving confidence (PSC) mediated the relationship between approach–avoidance style (AAS) and three separate psychological adjustment indexes (depression, hopelessness, and general psychosocial adjustment) in people with chronic low-back pain in the United States. Recently, a study conducted with Black South African samples also partially supported this finding (Heppner et al., 2000). In essence, the results suggested that although a person's tendency to approach or avoid problems was directly related to adjustment (depression, hopelessness, trait anxiety, and trait anger), that tendency had a much stronger impact by affecting problem-solving confidence and subsequently psychological adjustment. In sum, studies that use more sophisticated statistical analyses (e.g., structural equation modeling) are needed to investigate the complex relationships among the PSI factors and other psychological adjustment constructs.

Finally, more research is needed to develop effective methods for enhancing problem-solving appraisal (see Heppner & Hillerbrand, 1991). Moreover, problem-solving training is needed not only to prevent physical and psychological distress in children and adults but also to maximize people's potential in their academic achievement, relationships, parenting, and occupations. In essence, problem solving can play an important role in developing a positive psychology that actively promotes the positive development of a broad range of individuals across many aspects of their lives.

References

Antonovsky, A. (1979). *Health, stress, and coping*. San Francisco: Jossey-Bass.

Butler, L., & Meichenbaum, D. (1981). The assessment of interpersonal problem-solving skills. In P. C. Kendall & S. D. Hollen (Eds.), *Assessment strategies for cognitive-behavioral interventions* (pp. 197–225). New York: Academic Press.

Chynoweth, G. H. (1987). *Problem solving: A rational process with an emotional matrix*. Unpublished manuscript, Kansas State University, Manhattan.

Chynoweth, G. H., Blankinship, D. A., & Parker, M. W. (1986). The binomial expansion: Simplify the evaluation process. *Journal of Counseling Development, 64*, 645–647.

Dixon, D. N., & Glover, J. A. (1984). *Counseling: A problem solving approach*. New York: Wiley & Sons.

Dixon, W. A., Heppner, P. P., & Anderson, W. P. (1991). Problem-solving appraisal, stress, hopelessness, and suicide ideation in a college population. *Journal of Counseling Psychology, 38*, 51–56.

D'Zurilla, T. J. (1986). *Problem-solving therapy: A social competence approach to clinical intervention*. New York: Springer.

D'Zurilla, T. J., & Goldfried, M. R. (1971). Problem solving and behavior modification. *Journal of Abnormal Psychology, 78*, 107–126.

D'Zurilla, T. J., & Nezu, A. M. (1990). Development and preliminary evaluation of the Social Problem Solving Inventory (SPSI). *Psychological Assessment: A Journal of Consulting and Clinical Psychology, 2*, 156–163.

Hartman, B. J. (1968). Survey of college student's problems identified by the Mooney Problem Checklist. *Psychological Reports, 22*, 715–716.

Heppner, P. P. (1978). A review of the problem-solving literature and its relationship to the counseling process. *Journal of Counseling Psychology, 25*, 366–375.

Heppner, P. P. (1988). *The Problem-Solving Inventory*. Palo Alto, CA: Consulting Psychologist Press.

Heppner, P. P., & Baker, C. E. (1997). Applications of the Problem Solving Inventory. *Measurement and Evaluation in Counseling and Development, 29*, 229–241.

Heppner, P. P., Baumgardner, A. H., Larson, L. M., & Petty, R. E. (1988). The utility of problem-solving training that emphasizes self-management principles, *Counseling Psychology Quarterly, 1*, 129–143.

Heppner, P. P., Cook, S. W., Wright, D. M., & Johnson, C. (1995). Progress in resolving problems: A Problem-Focused Style of Coping. *Journal of Counseling Psychology, 42*, 279–293.

Heppner, P. P., Cooper, C., Mulholland, A., & Wei, M. (2001). A brief, multidimensional, problem solving psychotherapy outcome measure. *Journal of Counseling Psychology, 48*, 330–343.

Heppner, P. P., & Hillerbrand, E. T. (1991). Problem-solving training: Implications for remedial and preventive training. In C. R. Snyder & D. R. Forsyth (Eds.), *Handbook of social and clinical psychology: The health perspective* (pp. 681–698). Elmsford, NY: Pergamon Press.

Heppner, P. P., & Krauskopf, C. J. (1987). An information processing approach to personal problem solving. *Counseling Psychologist, 15*, 371–447.

Heppner, P. P., & Lee, D. (2002). Problem-solving appraisal and psychological adjustment. In C. R. Snyder & S. J. Lopez (Eds.), *Handbook of positive psychology* (pp. 288–298). New York: Oxford University Press.

Heppner, P. P., Manley, C. M., Perez, R. M., & Dixon, W. A. (1994). *An adolescent version of the Problem Solving Inventory: Initial reliability and validity estimates*. Unpublished manuscript.

Heppner, P. P., & Petersen, C. H. (1982). The development and implications of a personal problem-solving inventory. *Journal of Counseling Psychology, 29*, 66–75.

Heppner, P. P., Pretorius, T. B., Wei, M., Wang, Y.-W., & Lee, D. (2000, Aug.). *Associations between problem solving and psychological adjustment in South Africa*. Paper presented at the annual meeting of the American Psychological Association, Washington, DC.

Heppner, P. P., & Reeder, B. L. (1984). Training in problem-solving for residence hall staff: Who is most satisfied? *Journal of College Student Personnel, 25*, 357–360.

Horowitz, L. M., Rosenberg, S. E., Baer, B. A., Ureño, G., & Villaseñor, V. S. (1988). Inventory of interpersonal problems: Psychometric properties and clinical applications. *Journal of Consulting and Clinical Psychology, 56*, 885–893.

Janis, I. L., & Mann, L. (1977). *Decision making: A psychological analysis of conflict, choice, and commitment*. New York: Free Press.

Kendall, P. C., & Fischler, G. L. (1984). Behavioral and adjustment correlates of problem solving: Validational analyses of interpersonal cognitive problem solving measures. *Child Development, 55*, 227–243.

Laporte, L., Sabourin, S., & Wright, J. (1988). L'inventaire de resolution de problemes personels: Une perspective metocognitvie (The inventory of personal problem solving: A metacognitive perspective). *International Journal of Psychology, 23*, 569–581.

Larson, L. M., Potenza, M. T., Wennstedt, L. W., & Sailors, P. J. (1995). Personal problem solving in a simulated setting: Do perceptions accurately reflect behavior? *Cognitive Therapy and Research, 19*, 241–257.

Leong, F. T. L. (1990). Problem Solving Inventory. In D. J. Keyser & R. C. Sweetland (Eds.), *Test Critiques, Volume VIII* (pp. 574–582). Austin, TX: PRO-ED.

McCullough, L., & Farrell, A. D. (1983). *The computerized assessment for psychotherapy evaluation and research (computer program)*. New York: Beth Israel Medical Center, Department of Psychiatry.

Mooney, R. L., & Gordon, L. V. (1950). *Manual: The Mooney Problem Checklists*. New York: Psychological Corporation.

Nezu, A. M. (1986). Efficacy of a social problem solving therapy approach for unipolar depression. *Journal of Consulting and Clinical Psychology, 54*, 196–202.

Nezu, A. M., Nezu, C. M., Friedman, S. H., Faddis, S., & Houts, P. S. (1998). *Helping cancer patients cope*. Washington, DC: American Psychological Association.

Nezu, A. M., Nezu, C. M., & Perri, M. G. (1989). *Problem-solving therapy for depression: Theory, research, and clinical guidelines*. New York: Wiley.

Platt, J. J., & Spivack, G. (1975). *Manual for the Means-Ends Problem Solving Procedure: A measure of interpersonal cognitive problem solving skill*. Philadelphia: Department of Mental Health Sciences, Hahnemann Medical College and Hospital.

Pretorius, T. B. (1993). Assessing the problem-solving appraisal of Black South African students. *International Journal of Psychology, 28*, 861–870.

Reis, S. D., & Heppner, P. P. (1993). Examination of coping resources and family adaptation in mothers and daughters of incestuous versus nonclinical families. *Journal of Counseling Psychology, 40*, 100–108.

Sabourin, S., Laporte, L., & Wright, J. (1990). Problem-solving self-appraisal and coping efforts in distressed and non-distressed couples. *Journal of Marital and Family Therapy, 16*, 89–97.

Sahin, N., Sahin, N. H., & Heppner, P. P. (1993). Psychometric properties of the Problem Solving Inventory (PSI) in a group of Turkish university students. *Cognitive Therapy and Research, 17*, 379–396.

Shure, M. B. (1982). Interpersonal problem solving: A cog in the wheel of social cognition. In F. C. Serafica (Ed.), *Social-cognitive development in context* (pp. 133–166). New York: Guilford Press.

Shure, M. B., & Spivack, G. (1972). Means-ends thinking, adjustment and social class among elementary school–aged children. *Journal of Consulting and Clinical Psychology, 38*, 348–353.

Wicklegren, W. A. (1974). *How to solve problems*. San Francisco: Freeman.

Witty, T. E., Heppner, P. P., Bernard, C. B., & Thoreson, R. W. (2001). Problem solving appraisal and psychological adjustment of chronic low back pain. *Journal of Clinical Psychology in Medical Settings, 8,* 149–160.

9

Locus of Control: Back to Basics

Geneviève Fournier and Chantale Jeanrie

Since its operationalization in 1966 by Julian Rotter, the locus of control concept has been examined in an impressive number of studies across a wide range of disciplines (psychology, education, economy, medicine, etc.). Likewise, the dependent variables with which researchers have linked locus of control are extremely diverse, including adjustment ability, professional success, marital success, smoking cessation, mental health, self-efficacy, and so forth. This diversity shows just how much this concept, despite all the controversy surrounding it, is still considered to be central to the understanding of human behavior as well as to the optimization of one's strengths and capacity to adapt to various situations. Locus of control clearly fits into the positive psychology paradigm because it emphasizes the identification of those areas in which the individual can exercise control over his or her own development and psychological well-being while recognizing that some situations or events are out of his or her control (and may not be worth fighting against). This perspective also recognizes the importance of subjectivity in the perception of the external and internal intertwining forces that determine what happens to someone (and which behaviors he or she can choose to cope.) Thus, one of the objectives of the practitioner focusing on locus of control is to help people to discover and gain access to their strengths and, meanwhile, to choose health-promoting actions.

Though locus of control has been widely studied, there is, nonetheless, little convergence in the results. This lack of convergence might be explained by the variability in instruments, a variability that is analogous to the different ways in which authors understand the construct. Indeed, the very concept of locus of control raises several theoretical and psychometric questions. The goal of this chapter is to briefly review the evolution of this concept, the main conceptual and empirical issues concerning it, and to present diverse instruments tapping various iterations of this construct.

The Locus of Control Construct: Definition and Interpretation Difficulties

Basing his ideas on social learning theories, Rotter (1954) suggested that the probability that one engages in a behavior to satisfy a need rests on the expectation of a specific reinforcement and the value attributed to this reinforcement. He also pointed out that this expectation depends much more on the person's attitude toward the situation than on the situation itself. This attitude is shaped by people's perceptions of their capacities to influence the outcome of the desired reinforcement. Some people believe that they can have a certain impact on the course of events, whereas others believe they have little ability to influence situations. Rotter (1966) described locus of control as follows:

> When a reinforcement is perceived by the subject as following some action of his own but not being entirely contingent upon his action, then, in our culture, it is typically perceived as the result of luck, chance, fate, as under the control of powerful others, or as unpredictable because of the great complexity of the forces surrounding him. When an individual interprets the event in this way, we have labeled this a belief in *external control* [emphasis added]. If the person perceives that the event is contingent upon his own behavior or his own relatively permanent characteristics, we have termed this a belief in *internal control*. (Rotter, 1966, p. 1)

Over the course of its evolution, the locus of control construct has been incorrectly considered to be a stable personality dimension (Phares, 1976). Similar to Phares, Lefcourt (1976) argued that the locus of control is not a specific psychological characteristic that manifests itself uniformly across situations and time. The view of locus of control as characterological has not been the only misconception about the construct. Indeed, locus of control often has been regarded as being either intrinsically positive (internal) or negative (external). In keeping with this conceptualization, many researchers and practitioners have associated numerous positive consequences with internality. This rather Manichean view of locus of control and this glorification of internality gave rise to many debates about the nature of the construct, its unidimensional character as defined by Rotter, its generalizability, and its vulnerability to dominant social norms.

In 1975, Rotter addressed this misconception, as well as certain erroneous interpretations about the results of locus of control tests. Among these, he mentioned that researchers did not consider the reinforcement value as a separate variable, which can, in certain cases, bias the interpretation of the results. Thus, if people attribute a low value to the reinforcement, they can obtain a high internality score and still display the passive attitudes and behavior generally associated with externality. Conversely, if a high value is attributed to reinforcement, a person who obtains a high externality score can just as likely work energetically to reach a goal (generally associated with internality) just to conform to a group. Rotter also criticized the oversimplified conceptualization of locus of control that implies that internality is invariably associated with positive elements and that externality is only associated with negative elements. Rotter attempted to counteract this oversimplification of locus of control and to illustrate the possible biases in the interpretation of the results by emphasizing the difficulty of determining whether or not a high internality score indicates adjustment difficulties. For instance, a high internality score might mean that people think they have more power to influence events than is actually the case. This high score might indicate an inability to recognize one's failures rather than an ability to confront them. Similar to Dubois (1987), who asserted that the perception of the locus of control has been studied out of context, Rotter (1989) restated the importance of understanding and interpreting locus of control results by seeing them in the larger context of social learning theories. He observed that many researchers had a poor understanding of social learning theories and that "they regarded these individuals differences as fixed traits, or types" (1989, p. 490).

To better qualify and clarify our understanding of locus of control, Rotter (1975) suggested the possible existence of two distinct categories of external people—namely defensive externals and passive externals. The former become very active when they find themselves in competitive situations because they are afraid of failure; the latter adopt a more passive attitude toward events. Even though two different external persons could similarly value a specific reinforcement, these two individuals would not react to it with the same behavior. Likewise, other researchers have called into question the internal–external dichotomy, and they have criticized the reinforcement of this polarization by focusing on the differences between the two (e.g., Lefcourt, 1991; Marks, 1998; Strickland, 1989).

Dimensionality of the Locus of Control Construct

Though Strickland (1989) noted that the factor analyses of Rotter's scale reflected more specific factors than 20 years ago, Rotter (1975, 1989) always defended the unidimensional characteristic of locus of control while recognizing the presence of these subfactors. Other authors have examined this dimensionality question and have proposed some various distinctions. For example, Wong and Sproule (1984) suggested a bidimensional view of locus of control, echoing both Rotter's concerns about the potentially negative character of an overly high internality and his 1962 observations about the existence of a sizable group of people in the center of the external–internal continuum. This conception is in contrast to the linear vision of locus of control, and it presupposes a more realistic division of the influence of personal responsibility and the environment on events. People who believe that both internal and external forces exercise control are called *bilocal*. According to Wong and Sproule, people who are bilocal are better adjusted to real life, mostly because they accept that they cannot exercise control over all events or situations. In other words, "they attempt to alter what can be changed but accept what cannot be changed" (1984, p. 325).

Factor analyses carried out on the various locus of control scales support its multidimensional characteristics (e.g., Gurin, Gurin, & Morisson, 1978; Lefcourt, 1981, 1982; Levenson, 1974; Paulhus, 1983; Strickland, 1989). For example, Coombs and Schroeder (1988) compared three locus of control scales, and the factor analyses clearly demonstrated the presence of several specific factors in each scale. Other authors previously had considered the possibility that locus of control could be composed of more than a single factor represented by a bipolar scale. As early as 1974, Levenson proposed a three-factor model of locus of control. She suggested the idea that people can believe in luck while also believing in the influence that their personal efforts can have on events in their lives, thus implicitly introducing a distinction between individual responsibility (potentially passive internality) and context-related behavior (analytical and active internality). She developed a scale in which she divided the external locus of control concept into a chance locus (C) and powerful others locus (P). This three-part instrument (with I, P, and C scales) has proven to be a valid representation of control (Levenson, 1981; Ward, 1994), with relatively independent factors (Lefcourt, 1991). Finally, Fournier and Jeanrie (1999) proposed a typology for a vocational locus of control scale in which they conceived of different levels of internality and externality. External beliefs are subdivided into three levels: defeatist (the belief that an outcome is determined by the context and others); dependent (the belief that an outcome is determined by chance and fate); and prescriptive (the belief that social norms and dictates determine the outcome). Internality is subdivided into two levels—namely responsible (the belief that an outcome is contingent on one's actions) and proactive (the belief that both one's efforts and environmental contingencies influence the course of events). Using factor analysis to examine their scale, they identified two general factors (internal–external), subdivided into a total of five relatively independent subfactors. These results support the idea that people can simultaneously believe that they are influenced by chance, fate, or certain environmental contingencies, and still believe in the impact of their personal efforts.

The Locus of Control Construct: General or Specific

Even though Rotter (1975) acknowledged that a general measure of control has certain limitations, in particular that it has a low degree of prediction for a wide range of situations, he restated in 1989 that the concept illustrates a general tendency among people that is relatively independent of behavioral domains. He further emphasized that

> numerous articles were written and published challenging the notion of generality because some specificity could be demonstrated. The theory does not specify independent traits, faculties, or types . . . , and concluded mistakenly that the concept had no generality because some specificity could be demonstrated. Generality-specificity is a matter of degree, not kind. (1989, p. 490)

Contrary to Rotter's view, other authors have suggested that the locus of control can be considered as a domain-specific construct (Mischel & Mischel, 1979). Indeed, several researchers have developed domain-specific locus of control scales (e.g., Lefcourt, 1991; Paulhus, 1983; Spector, 1988). Paulhus (1983), for instance, developed a Spheres of Control scale (SOC) in which he measured locus of control according to different situations and spheres of life. This scale is subdivided into three spheres of control: personal, interpersonal, and sociopolitical control. With regard to this scale, Paulhus and Christie (1981) pointed out that "the SOC battery provides a profile of a person's perception of control across three important behavioral domains. . . . Each of the eight types of internal–external combinations may be associated with a different syndrome" (1981, pp. 179–180). More recently, Friedrich (1987) stated that his Vocational Locus of Control scale, seen as domain-specific, is a better predictor of success and attitudes in job-hunting activities than the general Rotter scale. Furthermore, Trice, Haire, and Elliot (1989) found a better prediction of career-development activities using their domain-specific instrument (Career Locus of Control scale) than with the general Rotter scale. Finally, based on his work on the stability of the locus of control over time, Lachman (1986) suggested that examining control beliefs in certain specific domains such as academic achievement and careers seems to be more relevant than examining more general control beliefs, particularly with young people. Moreover, results from such studies allow us to establish the truly situational nature of the locus of control, with the same people achieving either internal or external scores, depending on the content of the scale used. The predictive utility and validity of these specific scales has contributed to their increased use by researchers (Shapiro, Schwartz, & Astin, 1996). In fact, since 1980, more than 30 new locus of control measurement scales have been developed and adapted to different domains such as health (Georgiou & Bradley, 1992), work (Spector, 1988; Taylor, Boss, Bédard, Thibault, & Evans, 1990), and finances (Furnham, 1986).

Though locus of control has sometimes been interpreted incorrectly over the years, numerous authors have taken care to reestablish the theoretical and empirical basis of the concept. This reestablishment has made it clear that most of the misconceptions about locus of control have arisen as a result of the gap between Rotter's initial conception and later interpretations. It is now agreed that the locus of control concept can vary according to the situation and does not refer to a fixed, innate personality trait. If we are to understand and predict a person's behavior, locus of control must be examined in context and take into account the associated reinforcements. As a consequence, if the notion of a general locus of control can furnish useful information about a person, making it specific to a particular domain does not distort the way in which Rotter explained and reexplained this concept over the past 40 years. It is the dimensionality of locus of control that would seem to be the sole issue that is contrary to Rotter's position. However, even if multidimensionality has been confirmed by numerous studies, the problem concerning the number of internal and external factors still need to be explored to reach a clear, theoretically and empirically based solution.

Locus of Control Scales: Different Definitions, Different Formats

The definition that a particular researcher gives to locus of control has a considerable effect on the way the construct can later be used in interventions aimed at the optimal development of strengths. The construct, as it has evolved, reflects the principles of positive psychology. To illustrate the evolution of the construct, this second part of the chapter will present different conceptualizations of locus of control. As a consequence, both a unidimensional and a multidimensional general scale will be presented in addition to two domain-specific scales.

INTERNAL–EXTERNAL LOCUS OF CONTROL SCALE. Rotter's Internal–External Locus of Control scale (I–E scale: 1966) is the most often used and cited locus of control questionnaire. In a 1991 literature review, Lefcourt noted that 50% of the studies had used the Rotter scale. This general measure comprises 23 items, and it makes it possible to evaluate people's general control expectancies from a unidimensional viewpoint. Each item has two statements that respectively describe an external and internal locus. People are asked to decide which ones represent their control expectancies in diverse situations. Six filler items are included to camouflage the goal of the measure and to limit the effect of social desirability. The use of forced-choice items may reduce socially desirable responding. The results of this scale are expressed by a single score that indicates the level of externality. Norms are reported in several publications (Lefcourt, 1982, 1991; Phares, 1976).

The I–E scale was based on two previous scales developed, respectively, by James (1957) and Phares (1955). Rotter's first attempt to develop a measure of locus of control involved the construction of a test made up of subscales that evaluated control expectancy in relation to various domains such as performance, affection, and social and political attitudes. Various psychometric analyses contributed to reducing the number of items in the I–E scale from 100 to 23. During the development, the correlations observed among the items of the various domains led Rotter to give up on the idea of developing a domain-specific locus of control scale. Indeed, the factor analyses conducted by Rotter brought to light a first large factor plus a series of small factors that were impossible to interpret.

The reliability analyses conducted by Rotter (1966) indicated that the I–E scale had an acceptable internal consistency ($r = .70$). With a subgroup of students, test–retest reliability was $r = .72$ after one month ($n = 60$) and $r = .55$ after two months ($n = 177$). The low correlations observed between the external and internal statements imply a relatively high independence of these two factors. Therefore, it also means that one person can entertain both external and internal beliefs about a single issue. Over the years, several factor analyses conducted with the I–E scale have indicated that this scale is more multidimensional than Rotter had suggested (Coombs & Schroeder, 1988; Smith, Trompenaars, & Dugan, 1995). Although the I–E scale is into its fifth decade, validation studies are not that common. Most studies have linked the locus of control variable to a specific construct. In addition, some researchers do use Rotter's scale but divide it into subfactors. As a consequence, as implied by Lefcourt (1991), who qualified this scale as "impure" (p. 422), it cannot be concluded that the scale validity has been firmly established.

INTERNALITY, POWERFUL OTHERS, AND CHANCE SCALES. Consisting of 24 items, Levenson's IPC scale (1974, 1981) was one of the first to be based on a multidimensional conception of locus of control. This scale, which was derived from social learning theories (Ward, 1994), made it possible to analyze the profiles of people's causal beliefs by distinguishing, in addition to internality (I), two types of external forces—namely chance (C) and powerful others (P). Recognizing the influence of specific situations and cultural contexts, Levenson's conception of locus of control was both situational (as opposed to dispositional) and general.

Each of these subscales has eight items presented on a 7-point Likert scale that goes from −3 (strongly disagree) to +3 (strongly agree). A constant is added to the points of each scale to eliminate overall negative scores. A high score in one of the scales indicates that the respondents see the source of control as having considerable influence over what they experience, whereas a low score indicates that the source of control is seen as having little impact.

Even though some items were reformulated to better determine the three control attributions, the items of Levenson's scale originate from Rotter's scale (Lefcourt, 1991). In response to Gurin, Gurin, Lao, and Beattie's (1969) criticisms of the I–E scale, items were revised so that they would refer clearly to individual rather than ideological control and to unmodifiable situations. The initial version of IPC comprised 36 items; it was later reduced to 24 items.

The internal consistencies (KR-20) reported by Levenson were .64 (I), .77 (P), and .78 (C) for a sample of 152 students, whereas those reported for an adult group were slightly less. These moderately high coefficients were relatively comparable to those found with Rotter's I–E scale (1966). The stability index varied from $r = .60$ to .79 over a one-week interval to $r = .66$ to .73 after seven weeks (Lefcourt, 1991). Several studies (e.g., Levenson, 1981; Ward, 1994) have supported the overall three-factor structure suggested by the author, even though the relation between certain items and the three factors was not as strong as expected. The correlations established with the Rotter scale (respectively, $r = -.41$, .25, and .56 for the I, P, and C subscales) also provided evidence of validity.

WORK LOCUS OF CONTROL SCALE. The Work Locus of Control scale (WLCS: Spector, 1988), comprising 16 items, is a specific scale that refers to diverse sources of control related to the workplace (self, powerful others, and chance). The answers are noted on a 6-point Likert scale that goes from "strongly disagree" to "strongly agree." Half of the answers are expressed in an external form and the other half in an internal form to decrease the influence of social desirability. The overall score has a maximum possible value of 96, with a high score indicating an external locus of control.

The initial scale was composed of 49 items and was reduced on the basis of an item analysis ($n = 149$) and on the correlations between the results and a social desirability scale. Even though WLCS was conceived of as a unidimensional measure of locus of control, the results of some studies (e.g., Spector, 1988) led to the identification of two factors (internal and external) that were fairly or weakly independent, depending on the study. Alpha coefficients ranged from .75 to .85. The internal consistency of the two factors was not reported. A more recent study (Lu, Kao, Cooper, & Spector, 2000) also obtained results reaching moderate or higher internal consistency level (Robinson, Shaver, & Wrightsman, 1991). A study of temporal stability showed an $r = .70$ for six months (Spector, 1992).

The convergent validity of WLCS was studied by determining its correlations with other locus of control measures, as well as with work-domain related variables. Though acceptable mean correlations of $r = .38$ to $.54$ with the I–E scale and $r = .33$ with the IPC (Spector, 1988) were established, the relational patterns between scales were not identical to those postulated.

VOCATIONAL LOCUS OF CONTROL SCALE. The Vocational Locus of Control scale (VLCS: Fournier, Jeanrie, & Drapeau, 1996) proposes a specific multidimensional conception of locus of control. The measure (Appendix 9.1) is based on a typology comprising five hierarchical control levels (Fournier, Pelletier, & Pelletier, 1993), including three external levels (defeatist, dependent, and prescriptive) and two internal levels (responsible and proactive). The scale comprises 90 statements, each referring to one of the five postulated locus of control levels. Answers are given according to a 4-point scale that ranges from "totally disagree" to "totally agree." Six scores are calculated—one for each of the five types and the overall score, with the latter indicating the degree of internality (Fournier & Jeanrie, 1999).

This scale was developed to empirically examine five levels of locus of control in the career domain. These levels were identified through a content analysis of interviews with a large number ($n = 70$) of young people concerning their beliefs about the workplace and job hunting and later served as a basis for the production of the original 206 items. In a second step, the number of items was reduced to 140 by the use of an item analysis ($n = 142$). A second item analysis conducted after a massive administration of the scale ($n = 1100$) brought the questionnaire down to the current 90 statements (for more details on scale development, see Fournier & Jeanrie, 1999).

Reliability was measured using the internal consistency analyses. The coefficients obtained ranged from fair to high (Robinson, Shaver, & Wrightsman, 1991, p. 13: $r = .85, .78, .69; .77,$ and $.85$ for Type 1 to Type 5) and an overall alpha of .90. No stability analyses are reported.

The VLCS content validity was first validated using experts who had to associate each item to the corresponding type and theme. The interjudge agreement proved to be satisfactory, surpassing by far the agreement rate attributable to chance, with $r = .74$ and $.61$ for the types and themes, respectively. The scale's multidimensional character was supported using a factor analysis. The results showed that there was an internal and external factor. A subsequent factor analysis empirically revealed the presence of the postulated five types. The middle externality type would seem to be the most ambiguous and the least independent of the factors. The intercorrelations among the subfactors and the correlation between the overall score and Rotter's I–E scale ($r = -.40$) provided supplementary evidence of the scale's validity.

Construct Measurement Issues and Future Developments

Though the numerous theoretical and empirical advancements have refined the conceptualization of locus of control, there are recurrent problems that need to be addressed.

MISMATCH BETWEEN THEORY AND MEASUREMENT. Rotter (1975, 1989), Lefcourt (1981), and Phares (1976) all insisted that the theory at the basis of the locus of control concept must furnish the framework for the interpretation of locus of control measure results. Unfortunately, often authors of empirical articles have discussed the results without considering the precise definition of their concepts. Thus, a confusion in the work of some authors between the locus of control and several related constructs (desire for control, self-efficacy, etc.; Lefcourt 1982; Reid & Ware, 1974) might explain the divergence observed in the results of several scales. Self-efficacy, for example, refers to one's perception of his or her capacity to exhibit specific observable behaviors and explicitly avoids any reference to the reinforcements that can be tied to them (Bandura, 1997). The attribution that is made by the individual thus refers to the source of the constraints that prevent him or her to display a given level of performance or attainment related to specific behaviors. This confusion between the theoretical boundaries of those concepts may have led to a lack of uniformity in the interpretation of locus of control scale results.

CULTURAL DEPENDENCE OF LOCUS OF CONTROL. Several authors clearly have demonstrated the influence of cultural and socioeconomic factors on the results of different locus of control measures. On the one hand, the results of numerous studies have shown that respondents from certain countries (e.g., Japan, China) or cultures (e.g., Hispanic) obtain higher external scores (e.g., Chia, Cheng, & Chuang, 1998; Smith et al., 1995) than do respondents from the American or Western cultures. In 1966, however, Rotter mentioned (p. 25) that locus of control represented, for "people in American culture" the expectation concerning the source of reinforcements. Similarly, Marks (1998) pointed out that such differences in scores do not allow us to conclude that groups that obtain a more external score have less control expectations concerning their own lives. Such differences cannot, indeed, lead to the conclusion that Japanese, Africans, Spaniards, or Muslims, for example, have less expectations about the control they can have on their own life or of their representation of what a positive or "good" life should be. They do emphasize, however, that one's way to express control is closely tied to his or her cultural norms, and that it is extremely important to interpret data of a locus of control scale from the point of view of the given culture. These differences also call into question the intercultural generalization of the interpretation of locus of control measure results. Furthermore, other studies have noted significant relationships between externality and the fact of belonging to a majority or a less socioeconomically privileged group (Gurin et al., 1978; Levenson, 1981). As stated by Lefcourt (1982) and Marks (1998), these significant relationships testify to the impact that genuine opportunities have on people's control beliefs, as revealed through responses to different instruments.

ANOTHER LOOK AT THE NATURE OF DIMENSIONALITY. Though the multidimensionality of locus of control is no longer controversial, the nature of the dimensions that make it up has not yet been clarified. Lefcourt's (1982) text clearly outlined the various facets that a measure's different dimensions can embody. The most notable would seem to be those facets that distinguish between the external sources of control (Levenson, 1974) and between the contexts to which the control beliefs apply (e.g., Paulhus & Christie, 1981; Reid & Ware, 1974). These two facets, however, each have very different implications. If, in fact, a scale dimension corresponds to different types of situations, it would be important to verify if unidimensional scales of these specific situations would not represent a better assessment approach. Given how difficult it is to neatly distinguish between the control sources and the specific domains to which the control situations are related, it would be reasonable to believe that the concept of control situations refers more to issues of general or specific measures, and that the concept of control sources refers to questions of the construct's dimensionality. Paulhus and Christie (1981) explicitly mention that the three control spheres proposed in their test do not represent a substitute for control sources but rather complement them. They suggest, moreover, that the systematic and integrative approach to locus of control recommended by Lefcourt (1976) and Phares (1976) be adopted by simultaneously using the two conceptions of dimensionality. The advantage of this approach would be to maximize the generalizability of a scale's results. Its disadvantage, of course, is that such a scale would have to be quite long to contain enough statements to ensure the stability of each dimensional combination.

Final Thoughts

Over the past 35 years, the locus of control measure has suffered from substantial misconceptions about the construct. Paradoxically, these misconceptions have helped to refine our understanding and assessment of the concept. The theoretical basis set down by Rotter (1966) is still helping us to understand the subtleties and limits of locus of control and its measure. Lefcourt's work and numerous empirical studies carried out using different scales have facilitated our understanding of the gaps that are still hindering the analysis of this concept. If the concept is to remain as popular in future decades, attempts to improve locus of control measures must be closely linked to the concept's theoretical foundations. Over the years, the locus of control has developed into a construct taking into account the interinfluences of the external and internal sources of control. Clearly, such a locus of control grants the individual with a contextualized action capacity and a higher degree of autonomy, two essential conditions to his or her genuine participation to a fulfilled and meaningful life.

Appendix 9.1
The Vocational Locus of Control Scale: Questionnaire

The goal of this questionnaire is to find out what you think about the job market. Everything that you write here will be kept strictly confidential. This questionnaire contains ninety (90) statements dealing with various aspects of careers and the working world.

1. Read each statement carefully and *answer spontaneously*.
2. *Based on your first impression,* indicate how much you agree or disagree with each statement by circling the number that best corresponds to your choice.
3. There are no right or wrong answers.
4. It is important to answer all the questions.

The possible answers are:

1. Totally disagree   TD
2. Disagree   D
3. Agree   A
4. Totally agree   T

1. Even a job that doesn't satisfy your career expectations can offer worthwhile challenges.	1 2 3 4
2. You decide by and for yourself.	1 2 3 4
3. Job forecasting specialists are in the best position to help you with career choices.	1 2 3 4
4. School is boring.	1 2 3 4
5. You don't always have complete control over decisions concerning your choice of careers.	1 2 3 4
6. You should follow your family's advice if you want to succeed in what you do.	1 2 3 4
7. Everything you learn at school is useful.	1 2 3 4
8. Having a job is a matter of luck and not choice.	1 2 3 4
9. A job is only interesting when the work involved is enjoyable.	1 2 3 4
10. All you have to do to find a job is develop good job hunting strategies.	1 2 3 4
11. If teachers were more competent, you would learn more at school.	1 2 3 4
12. When you put enough energy into it, all work can be fulfilling.	1 2 3 4
13. School allows you to develop important work skills.	1 2 3 4
14. It's no good planning for next year, because anything can happen.	1 2 3 4
15. You have to be lucky to find a fulfilling job.	1 2 3 4

16. You have to know the right people to find a job.   1 2 3 4

17. The world is run by a small group of powerful people and there's nothing you can do about it.   1 2 3 4

18. You only work to put in time.   1 2 3 4

19. The best way to plan your career is to consult employment statistics.   1 2 3 4

20. Next year will bring its share of surprises in your career.   1 2 3 4

21. Job hunting should be based on openings in the job market.   1 2 3 4

22. You alone are responsible for your success in school.   1 2 3 4

23. Rich people get all the best jobs.   1 2 3 4

24. Work is slavery.   1 2 3 4

25. You need a specialist's help to plan your career.   1 2 3 4

26. You alone are responsible for your future.   1 2 3 4

27. What counts most for an employer is your school marks.   1 2 3 4

28. You have to take work limitations into account and be ready to make compromises in your career.   1 2 3 4

29. You have to use available resources if you want to make an informed decision about your career.   1 2 3 4

30. You depend on your friends' support to succeed in projects that you start.   1 2 3 4

31. When planning your career, you should choose from job sectors of the future.   1 2 3 4

32. Professional success depends on your capacity for developing your personal abilities.   1 2 3 4

33. It's pure coincidence when you find information on a career.   1 2 3 4

34. Above all, an interesting job is one that matches your career choice.   1 2 3 4

35. Good intentions aren't enough. You have to know how to use job hunting strategies.   1 2 3 4

36. Career choices are forced on you and there's nothing you can do about it.   1 2 3 4

37. If school were more interesting, students would do better.   1 2 3 4

38. There's only one job in life that is meant for you.   1 2 3 4

39. School is a good place to develop personal abilities and job skills.   1 2 3 4

40. You have to count on others if you want to make good decisions.   1 2 3 4

41. Finding a job depends mainly on how much effort you put into it.   1 2 3 4

42. Fate or luck couldn't possibly play an important role in decision making.   1 2 3 4

43. Only the very best people can hope to succeed in their careers.   1 2 3 4

44. To play the game well, you have to know how to use available resources.   1 2 3 4

45. You can find out what your work capabilities are by taking a test.   1 2 3 4

46. There's aren't many decisions to make in life because time takes care of everything.   1 2 3 4

47. It's not necessary to lay down career goals.   1 2 3 4

48. Every job can provide personal growth opportunities.   1 2 3 4

49. No matter what the context is, it's important to achieve your career goals.   1 2 3 4

50. Finding a job depends on fate and luck.   1 2 3 4

51. It's not difficult to play the job market if you know it well.   1 2 3 4

52. Other peoples' opinions don't matter in career development, because only you know what you want.   1 2 3 4

53. A job is only interesting when it matches your career training.   1 2 3 4

54. It's not worth trying different strategies for career development.   1 2 3 4

55. It's by integrating different life experiences that you develop yourself.   1 2 3 4

56. Even if a job has some limitations, it can still be beneficial.   1 2 3 4

57. Finding a job depends both on how much effort you put into it and employment possibilities.   1 2 3 4

58. School provides a valuable learning environment when you apply yourself.   1 2 3 4

59. You have to rely on others as little as possible if you want to achieve your career goals.   1 2 3 4

60. Making choices doesn't get you anywhere because others decide for you anyway.   1 2 3 4

61. Your career development depends directly on the various influences that your friends, family, and the society have on you.   1 2 3 4

62. People stay in school because they have nothing else to do.   1 2 3 4

63. Working is boring.   1 2 3 4

64. Your success in the working world depends on luck.   1 2 3 4

65. Becoming informed about different careers is essential but it doesn't automatically lead to success in the job market.   1 2 3 4

66. Social pressure can keep you from succeeding in the working world.   1 2 3 4

67. You need to be organized to follow the career path that you have chosen.   1 2 3 4

68. If you try hard enough, there's always a way to reach your career goals.   1 2 3 4

69. The success or failure of your career depends on family support.   1 2 3 4

70. All you have to do to find a job is be in the right place at the right time.   1 2 3 4

71. Taking courses is a waste of time.   1 2 3 4

72. An interesting job is one that has no limitations.   1 2 3 4

73. Good career planning implies that you leave room for the unexpected.   1 2 3 4

74. You can only get a good job with a diploma.   1 2 3 4

75. The job market is closed. Trying doesn't get you anywhere.   1 2 3 4

76. Career satisfaction depends on the advice you receive from people in positions of authority.   1 2 3 4

77. You have no control over your future in the working world.   1 2 3 4

78. To succeed at school, all you have to do is work hard.   1 2 3 4

79. Choosing a saturated line of work leads nowhere.   1 2 3 4

80. Alternative solutions must be part of a career plan.   1 2 3 4

81. There are so many limitations in the workplace that it's not worth starting anything at all.   1 2 3 4

82. School is a necessary evil.   1 2 3 4

83. Above all, an interesting job is one that meets your career expectations.   1 2 3 4

84. To get ahead in your career, you have to show initiative, even if conditions aren't always favorable. 1 2 3 4

85. Work skills are innate, they can't be developed.   1 2 3 4

86. You have to be lucky to succeed at school.   1 2 3 4

87. You shouldn't let yourself be influenced by the limitations of your environment.   1 2 3 4

88. To plan your career, you have to choose short- and long-term goals.   1 2 3 4

89. Finding a job that matches your abilities is a matter of luck.   1 2 3 4

90. The only reason you work is to gain a certain social standing.   1 2 3 4

References

Bandura, A. (1997). *Self-efficacy: The exercise of control.* New York: Freeman.

Chia, R. C., Cheng, B. S., & Chuang, C. J. (1998). Differentiation in the source of internal control for Chinese. *Journal of Social Behavior and Personality, 13, 4,* 565–578.

Coombs, W. N., & Schroeder, H. E. (1988). Generalized locus of control: An analysis of factor analytic data. *Personality and Individual Differences, 9*(1), 79–85.

Dubois, N. (1987). *La psychologie du contrôle: Les croyances internes et externes (Psychology of control: Internal and external beliefs).* Grenoble: Presses Universitaires de Grenoble.

Fournier, G., & Jeanrie, C. (1999). Validation of a five-level locus of control scale. *Journal of Career Assessment, 7*(1), 63–89.

Fournier, G., Jeanrie, C., & Drapeau, S. (1996). *Échelle de Locus de contrôle relié à la carrière (Vocational locus of control scale).* Québec, Canada: Université Laval.

Fournier, G., Pelletier, R., & Pelletier, D. (1993). Typologie des croyances entretenues par les jeunes de 16 à 25 ans à l'égard de l'insertion socio-professionnelle (Typology of socioprofessional integration beliefs among 16–25-year-old young adults). *L'orientation Scolaire et Professionnelle, 22*(1), 65–83.

Friedrich, J. R. (1987). Perceived control and decision making in a job hunting context. *Basic and Applied Social Psychology, 8*(1–2), 163–176.

Furnham, A. (1986). Economic locus of control. *Human Relations, 39*(1), 29–43.

Georgiou, A., & Bradley, C. (1992). Development and validation of the safety locus of control scale. *Perceptual and Motor Skills, 61*(1), 151–161.

Gurin, P., Gurin, G., Lao, R. C., & Beattie, M. (1969). Internal–external control in the motivational dynamics of Negro youth. *Journal of Social Sciences, 25,* 29–53.

Gurin, P., Gurin, G., & Morrison, B. M. (1978). Personal and ideological aspects of internal and external control. *Social Psychology, 41(4),* 275–296.

James, W. H. (1957). *Internal versus external control of reinforcement as a basic variable in learning theory.* Unpublished doctoral dissertation, Ohio State University, Columbus.

Lachman, M. E. (1986). Locus of control in aging research: A case for multidimensional and domain-specific assessment. *Journal of Psychology and Aging, 1*(1), 34–40.

Lefcourt, H. M. (1976). *Locus of control: Current trends in theory and research.* Hillsdale, NJ: Erlbaum.

Lefcourt, H. M. (1981). *Research with the locus of control construct. Vol. 1. Assessment methods.* New York: Academic Press.

Lefcourt, H. M. (1982). *Locus of control: Current trends in theory and research.* Hillsdale, NJ: Erlbaum.

Lefcourt, H. M. (1991). Locus of control. In J. P. Robinson, P. R. Shaver, & L. S. Wrightsman (Eds.), *Measures of personality and social psychological attitudes* (pp. 413–499). New York: Academic Press.

Levenson, H. (1974). Activism and powerful others: Distinctions within the concept of internal–external control. *Journal of Personality Assessment, 38,* 377–383.

Levenson, H. (1981). Differentiating among internality, powerful others, and chance. In H. M. Lefcourt (Ed.), *Research with the locus of control construct. Vol. 1. Assessment methods* (pp. 15–63). New York: Academic Press.

Lu, L., Kao, S. F., Cooper, C. L., & Spector, P. E. (2000). Managerial stress, locus of control, and job strain in Taiwan and USA comparative study. *International Journal of Stress Management, 7,* 209–226.

Marks, L. I. (1998). Deconstructing locus of control: Implications for practitioners. *Journal of Counseling and Development, 76,* 251–260.

Mischel, W., & Mischel, H. N. (1979). Self control and the self. In T. Mischel (Ed.), *The self: Psychological and philosophical issues* (pp. 31–64). New York: Holt, Rinehart and Winston.

Paulhus, D. L. (1983). Sphere-specific measures of perceived control. *Journal of Personality and Social Psychology, 44(6),* 1253–1265.

Paulhus, D., & Christie, R. (1981). Spheres of control: An interactionist approach to assessment of perceived control. In H. M. Lefcourt (Ed.), *Research with the locus of control construct. Vol. 1. Assessment methods* (pp. 161–188). New York: Academic Press.

Phares, E. J. (1955) *Changes in expectancy in skill and chance situations.* Unpublished doctoral dissertation, Ohio State University, Columbus.

Phares, E. J. (1976). *Locus of control in personality.* Morristown, NJ: General Learning Press.

Reid, D., & Ware, E. E. (1974). Multidimensionality of internal versus external control: Addition of a third dimension and nondistinction of self vs. others. *Canadian Journal of Behavioral Science, 6,* 131–142.

Robinson, J. P., Shaver , P. R., & Wrightsman, L. S. (1991). *Measures of personality and social psychological attitudes.* San Diego, CA: Academic Press.

Rotter, J. B. (1954). *Social learning and clinical psychology.* Englewood Cliffs, NJ: Prentice Hall.

Rotter, J. B. (1966). Generalized expectancies for internal versus external control of reinforcement. *Psychological Monographs, 80*(1, whole No. 609).

Rotter, J. B. (1975). Some problems and misconceptions related to the construct of internal versus external control of reinforcement. *Journal of Counsulting and Clinical Psychology, 48,* 56–67.

Rotter, J. B. (1989). Internal vs. external control of reinforcement. *American Psychologist, 45,* 489–493.

Shapiro, D. H., Schwartz, C. E., & Astin, J. A (1996). Controlling ourselves, controlling our world. *American Psychologist, 51(12),* 1213–1230.

Smith, P. B., Trompenaars, F., & Dugan, S. (1995). The Rotter Locus of control scale in 43 countries: A test of cultural relativity. *International Journal of Psychology, 30(3),* 377–400.

Spector, P. E. (1988). Development of the Work Locus of Control scale. *Journal of Occupational Psychology, 61,* 335–340.

Spector, P. E. (1992). *Summated rating scale construction: An introduction.* Beverly Hills, CA: Sage.

Strickland, B. R. (1989). Internal–external control of reinforcement. In T. Blass (Ed.), *Personality variables in social behavior* (pp. 219–279). Hillsdale, NJ: Erlbaum. (Original published 1977)

Taylor, M. C., Boss, M. W., Bédard, R., Thibault, C. J., & Evans, K. (1990). Variables related to the transition of youth from school to work. *Canadian Journal of Counselling, 24(3),* 153–164.

Trice, A. D., Haire, J. R., & Elliott, K. A. (1989). A career locus of control scale for undergraduate students. *Perceptual and Motor Skills, 69,* 555–561.

Ward, E. A. (1994). Construct validity of need for achievement and locus of control scales. *Educational and Psychological Measurement, 54*(4), 983–992.

Wong, P. T. P., & Sproule, C. F. (1984). An attribution analysis of the Locus of Control Construct and the Trent Attribution Profile. In H. Lefcourt (Ed.), *Research with the Locus of Control Construct* (Vol. 3, pp. 310–360). New York: Academic Press.

10

Measuring Creativity in Research and Practice

Barbara Kerr and Camea Gagliardi

Creativity is that characteristic of human behavior that seems the most mysterious and yet most critical to human advancement. The capacity to solve problems in new ways and to produce works that are novel, appropriate, and socially valued has fascinated people for centuries. Most creativity research concerns the nature of creative thinking, the distinctive characteristics of the creative person, the development of creativity across the individual life span, and the social environments most strongly associated with creative activity (Simonton, 2000). This research can help counselors who are committed to a positive psychology to assess creative thinking and to identify creative traits in their clients. Counselors can use this knowledge to help clients overcome internal and environmental barriers to the development of creative lives.

Many of the studies of creativity have been driven by the desire to identify those children who are most likely to profit from programs for developing giftedness or the desire to identify adults who are likely to be innovative in science, business, and industry. Counselors who want to respond to clients' strengths and who want to seek positive directions for counseling often focus on creativity. Assessment plays a part in all of these activities.

In this chapter we will address numerous challenges that counselors measuring creativity must consider, including the multiplicity of definitions and measures of creativity, the psychological and contextual variables that enhance or block it, and the need to use measurement appropriately in the broader context of assessing creativity. Then we will identify measures of the creative process and the creative person, apply creativity measurement and assessment to counseling, and discuss future directions for the field.

Measurement Issues to Consider

There are several issues to be addressed before selecting instruments to measure creativity. First, the definition of creativity may vary from one instrument to another. Second, it is sometimes unclear what creativity instruments actually predict. Third, creativity always needs to be assessed in the context of other psychological and environmental variables.

Many Definitions, Many Measures

The definition of creativity is elusive. Although most researchers agree on such aspects of creativity as originality, appropriateness, and the production of works of value to society, they have had difficulty agreeing on appropriate instruments and methods in operationalizing these concepts. The insufficiency of most creativity measures to capture the complex concept of creativity has been well-established. Three decades ago, Treffinger, Renzulli, and Feldhusen (1971) argued that as a result of the lack of a unified, widely accepted theory of creativity, researchers and educators

> have been confronted with several difficulties: establishing a useful operational definition, understanding the implications of differences among tests and test administration procedures, and understanding the relationship of creativity to other human abilities. (p. 107)

Sternberg (2001) argued that creativity should not be considered in isolation from other constructs of human abilities; rather, it is best understood in a societal context. He suggests that the "common thread" in the prolific research literature is the interrelations or "dialectic" among intelligence, wisdom, and creativity, where intelligence advances existing societal agendas, creativity questions them and proposes new ones, and wisdom balances the old with the new. Yet the many challenges in operationalizing and assessing creativity are still being confronted today. And the proliferation of hundreds of creativity tests, some of which hold up better under psychometric scrutiny than others, exacerbate the criterion problem. These concerns leave us asking an important question. What is it exactly that creativity researchers are studying?

Some researchers in the field choose to consider the multiplicity of measures as indicative of a viable, dynamic, creative field. Houtz and Krug (1995) suggested, "Multiple instruments and methods permit flexibility and adaptability to new problems and situations, maximum theory development, and application to real-world problems" (p. 273). Irrespective of one's position on whether criterion variation is problematic, the evaluation of creativity tests fare much better when considered in light of recent advances and when they are interpreted in light of limitations.

What Do Creativity Instruments Predict?

Many of the available creativity instruments identify divergent thinking or ideational fluency but fail to predict future creative behavior. In many cases, children identified by creativity measures have not produced significant creative works as adults. However, Plucker and Runco (1998) argued that the "death of creativity measurement has been greatly exaggerated" (p. 36), discussing advancements not only in the predictive validity of the measurements in existence but, more important, in the utility of broadening the scope of creativity measurement to include personal definitions and theories of creativity. Weak predictive validity coefficients may be attributed to weak methodology (e.g., studies too short in duration, inadequate statistical procedures for nonnormally distributed data, and poorly operationalized outcome criteria in longitudinal studies) rather than weak psychometrics. Moreover, explicit definitions and theories of creativity, although useful in many traditional studies, do not access the wealth of information inherent in individuals' personal beliefs about creativity. Plucker and Runco (1998) suggested that when people engage in creative activity "their thoughts and actions are guided by personal definitions of creativity and beliefs about how to foster and evaluate creativity that may be very different from the theories developed by creativity experts" (p. 37). Creating instruments that correspond well with the implicit theories of the people completing them not only addresses the definitional problem but also yields a socially valid technique for instrument design that is particularly sensitive to cross-cultural and discipline-specific research questions.

Creativity in Context

Measuring creativity in isolation from other psychological and contextual variables also is problematic. In a groundbreaking examination of creative people, Csikszentmihalyi (1996) studied 100 individuals who had produced works that were publicly acknowledged as creative and who had all affected their culture in some important way. In this comprehensive study of scientists, artists, writers, educators, politicians and social activists, engineers, and religious leaders, he found that the first and foremost characteristic of creative individuals is mastery of a domain of knowledge or skill. Without mastery of a domain, diverse thinking or ideational fluency are not likely to lead to creative products. These creative individuals, for the most part, had normal childhoods and families that provided them with a solid set of values. They, however, differed significantly from others in the high proportion of them whom had suffered a parental loss, particularly the loss of a father. Commonly, they had other supportive adults in their lives who encouraged them to use their loss as an opportunity to create their own identities. Creative individuals had little good to say about school; in many ways, general schooling was irrelevant to these profoundly curious and self-guided young people. Only in college and advanced training did they find a match between their interests and those of others, in mentors and significant teachers who provided the knowledge they desired so intensely. As adults, these creative people had circuitous paths to their careers. What was most extraordinary, according to Csikszentmihalyi, was that these creative people seized on whatever opportunities they had been given and then shaped them to meet their own ends, rather than being shaped by genes or events.

Csikszentmihalyi (1990, 1996) has concluded that the major distinguishing characteristic of creative people is the capacity to experience "flow," that experience of timelessness and oneness with the activity in which one is engaged. In a flow state, people have a sense that their abilities are only just equal to the challenge that the project provides; therefore, they are caught up in the process of creating to enhance the flow state.

In addition to these characteristics and life conditions that enhance creativity, certain psychological conditions can block creativity. Although creative individuals often are considered to "live on the edge" and generally choose more independent lifestyles, this may lead to substance abuse and other self-destructive behaviors that dull creativity. Pritkzer (1999) proposed that creative people use alcohol because their work, uncertain and plagued by rejection, is difficult, stressful, and anxiety-provoking. Whether self-medicating as a response to depression or succumbing to a genetic predisposition, creative people often have long periods of time alone to drink and develop addictions without the knowledge of others. Although it has not yet been proven that creativity *causes* drug use (Kerr, Shaffer, Chambers, & Hallowell, 1991), the belief that substance use enhances creativity may be the result of inaccurate perceptions.

There is also evidence that a high proportion of creative writers, artists, and musicians suffer from symptoms of mood disorders, especially bipolar disorder (Andreasen, 1987; Jamison, 1989; Richards & Kinney, 1990). Although much of the evidence is correlational, Bowden (1994) proposed several characteristics that are associated with creativity in bipolar disorder that may reflect causal relationships and that offer direction for further experimental research. These include increased range and speed of associated concepts, perseverance, increased energy, reduced sleep, overt focus on the self, and heightened sexual interests. Unfortunately, whatever gifts that moderate manic states might bestow on the individual, manic psychosis and depression destroy all motivation and productivity. No one understands fully the connection between bipolar disorder and creativity; however, when creativity is studied in isolation from personality and lifestyle, it is difficult to assess the capacity for original production.

Finally, environmental variables interact in important ways with cognitive variables to produce creative behavior (Piirto, 1998). It has long been observed that certain communities at particular times in history seemed to give rise to a great many creative individuals: 15th-century Florence, the Harlem Renaissance, and San Francisco in the 1960s are examples. The presence of patrons, the support of a subculture of creative individuals, the possibility of freedom of expression, and the availability of materials and resources necessary for creative products all play a part in the emergence of creative behavior in individuals of talent. Gender, race, and class can all be barriers to the expression of creativity when low expectations and stereotypes discourage otherwise talented individuals from pursuing their ideas and fulfilling their gifts. Amabile (2001) encouraged creativity researchers to go beyond the assumption that individual creativity depends primarily on talent and to consider environmental influences. Her componential model of creativity, which proposes three major components of creativity—skills specific to the task domain, general creativity-relevant skills, and task motivation—provides a useful way to conceptualize the importance of the social environment in creativity (which can support or undermine the intrinsic motivation to create).

Using Measures Appropriately

Different creativity tests measure different constructs within the complex intel-lectual and affective concept of creativity; problems arise when one measure is inappropriately compared against another. Torrance (1984), the originator of the best known standardized creativity tests, cautioned against exclusivity of objective measurement in assessment. He recommended that creativity not be the sole criterion for decision making, that multiple talents be evaluated, and that culturally different individuals be given tasks that evaluate "the kinds of excellence that are valued by the particular culture or subculture" (pp. 155–156) of the individuals being evaluated. Even within the limited context of objective measurement, using multiple measures helps to ensure that the assessment discriminates between individuals and not against them. Hocevar and Bachelor (1989) offered a taxonomy of measurements used in the study of creativity. The categories include tests of divergent thinking, attitude and interest inventories, personality inventories, biographical inventories, judg-ments of products, the study of eminent people, and self-reported creative activities and achievements. Readers interested in comprehensive discussions of psychometric approaches to creative thinking are directed toward recent reviews (Hocevar & Bachelor, 1989) and criticisms (Houtz & Krug, 1995).

Measures of Creativity

Most measures of creativity fall into just a few categories. Divergent thinking is considered to be the critical component of creative process; therefore, the major assessments attempt to measure this kind of thinking. Most personality tests are paper-and-pencil tests that measure aspects of self-descriptions that seem to be related to creative behavior. However, projective tests purport to measure creative personality by assessing unconscious motivations and needs that may energize creative behavior.

Measures of the Creative Process: Divergent Thinking

Traditional intelligence tests do not require much creative or divergent-produc-tion thinking, which leads to the hypothesis that creativity and intelligence are separate constructs, requiring separate measures. Traditional intelligence tests primarily measure convergent thinking, the kind of thinking used when a person must "converge" on one right answer to a question or problem. Divergent thinking, in contrast, is the sort of thinking that produces multiple responses to a question and that produces novel ideas and unusual responses to questions. Divergent thinking is cognition that leads in various directions, some conven-tional and some original. As explained by Runco (1999), "Because some of the resulting ideas are original, divergent thinking represents the potential for creative thinking and problem solving" (p. 577). Thus, to the degree that these tests are reliable and valid, they can be taken as estimates of the potential for creative thinking, but cautions should be taken when inferring estimates of future creative production.

Tests of divergent thinking are available. In the 1960s, J. P. Guilford and E. Paul Torrance developed and used batteries of divergent thinking tests used in the early study of creativity, which are widely used today.

THE GUILFORD BATTERY. Guilford's battery of tests, based on his Structure of the Intellect model (Guilford, 1962), differentiated among 180 different kinds of thinking, including many forms of divergent thinking. The abilities most relevant for creative thinking are to be found in the divergent production abilities that allow new information to be generated from information; and transformation abilities, which involve revision of what one experiences or knows, thereby producing new forms and patterns.

The Guilford Battery consists of 10 individual tests measuring different aspects of divergent production. These tests are (a) names for stories (divergent production of semantic units); (b) what to do with it (divergent production of semantic classes); (c) similar meanings (divergent production of semantic relations); (d) writing sentences (divergent production of semantic systems); (e) kinds of people (divergent production of semantic implications); (f) make something out of it (divergent production of figural units); (g) different letter groups (divergent production of figural classes); (h) making objects (divergent production of figural systems); (i) hidden letters (divergent production of figural transformations); and (j) adding decorations (divergent production of figural implications). Each of the tasks is timed and scored on fluency (number of responses) and originality (statistical infrequency). Both verbal (semantic) and nonverbal (figural) content are included. Although Guilford's Structure of the Intellect model has earned support over the decades, his battery of tests does not have the extensive validity research to compare with the Torrance tests (described later). Meeker (1978) engaged in a number of follow-up studies of children tested with Guilford's measures and found that children who were identified as creative in elementary school maintained high creativity scores in high school. Michael and Bachelor (1990), however, used factor analytical procedures to reexamine a correlation matrix of 27 divergent thinking tests from Guilford's (1962) study of 204 junior high school students, and found only modest agreement with the original solution. Therefore, it is not clear that the factor structure underlying these measures is still valid, and it may be that these tests have only moderate usefulness in assessing creativity.

THE TORRANCE TESTS. Although Torrance would later acknowledge that creativity "defies precise definition" (Parkhurst, 1999, p. 13), his early attempts at operationalizing creativity for research purposes centered on problem-solving. He wrote,

> I have tried to describe creative thinking as taking place in the process of sensing difficulties, problems, gaps in information, missing elements; making guesses or formulating hypotheses about these deficiencies; testing and retesting them; and finally in communicating the results. (Torrance, 1965, p. 8)

The Torrance Tests of Creative Thinking (TTCT) consist of nonverbal and verbal forms, Thinking Creatively With Pictures and Thinking Creatively With Words, which are suitable for students in kindergarten through graduate school to assess four creative abilities: fluency, flexibility, originality, and elaboration. The nonverbal forms consist of three sets of activities that require respondents to draw lines to elaborate on a single shape, to draw lines to complete a picture, and to draw as many different pictures as possible using the same shape. The verbal forms consist of six activities that require respondents to generate questions, alternative uses, and guesses. Each of the activities in each of the nonverbal and verbal forms is timed and scored for fluency, flexibility, and originality. The nonverbal forms are scored also for elaboration.

Not only are the TTCT the most widely used tests to measure creativity, but their use is supported by more evidence of validity than any other creativity tests. They have been translated into numerous languages, data on the TTCT have been gathered on an international scale (Houtz & Krug, 1995), and they have been critically reviewed (Cooper, 1991; Hocevar & Bachelor, 1989; Torrance, 1988). Treffinger's (1985) analysis of several studies of test–retest reliability attest to moderate to high reliability and posit a range extending from .50 to .93. Torrance (1988) reported on a 22-year longitudinal study in which scores were correlated with accomplishments in adulthood, with validity coefficients of .62 for males and .57 for females. Although these coefficients demonstrate only moderate predictive validity, Torrance noted that they are commensurate with coefficients for intelligence in predicting achievement. Two decades of research establish validity and reliability of the TTCT and demonstrate the appropriateness of including divergent measures in a multifaceted approach to assessing creativity.

CRITICISM OF DIVERGENT THINKING TESTS. Treffinger et al. (1971) aptly described a primary criticism of divergent thinking tests when he cautioned us to not make inferences about the complex and multifaceted construct of creativity from measures that are distinctly cognitive. This, however, does not imply rejection of the usefulness of tests of divergent thinking; on the contrary, "while divergent-thinking measures certainly do not tell the entire story about creativity, it is quite likely that these measures do assess intellectual abilities which play an important role in creativity" (Treffinger et al., 1971, p. 108). Moreover, the perceived lack of predictive validity for divergent thinking tests is problematic. Divergent thinking, or critical thinking therein defined, does not necessarily correspond to creative production or eminence. Plucker and Runco (1998) challenged this long-standing criticism by suggesting that weak predictive validity may be the result of poor methodology, including ineffective outcome criteria in longitudinal studies. They argued that studies including both quantity and quality of creative achievement in outcome variables, as opposed to the traditional reliance on quantity, provide improved support for the predictive validity of divergent thinking tests. Also, Parkhurst (1999) maintained that it is specious to argue that divergent thinking is equivalent to creativity because real-life creativity—that is, creative production—has not been shown to be highly correlated with divergent thinking. Researchers and practitioners specializing in intellectual assessment do not assume, for example, that a test measuring an individual's scientific ability will be a predictor of observable later scientific accomplishments. Rather, "all that is expected is that the [individual] will have the scientific knowledge and ability when and if he or she needs to use them" (Parkhurst, 1999, p. 6).

Finally, a serious problem with all the major tests of creative cognitive process is that they are lengthy in administration and that they require an expert who is trained in the specific use and interpretation of the tests. Simple forms of these instruments have not been developed or have been unsuccessful in predicting creativity.

Measures of the Creative Person: Distinguishing Traits

Some researchers view creativity entirely as a cognitive process, whereas others see it as a set of personality traits. When individuals are evaluated as creative thinkers but do not manifest such characteristics as endurance and independence, they may not become creatively productive. A valid assessment procedure should consider both cognitive and personality components.

Attitudes and personality, like divergent thinking, are observable and measurable. Personality inventories, self-report adjective checklists, biographical surveys, interest and attitude measures, self- and peer-nomination procedures, and interviews are all methods used to study the creative person; however, personality assessments and projective tests are the primary measures used. As King and Pope (1999) pointed out, creativity has long been associated with a number of psychological traits (p. 201), the most prominent of which include autonomy, introversion, and openness to experience. As Feist (1999) wrote, "One of the most distinguishing characteristics of creative people is their desire and preference to be somewhat removed from regular social-contact, to spend time alone working on their craft . . . to be autonomous and independent of the influence of a group" (p. 158). Closely related to the tendency toward autonomy, creative people tend to be more introverted than extroverted; that is, they tend to avoid excessive social stimulation. Piirto (1998) reviewed the characteristics of creative adults in particular domains in *Understanding Those Who Create*. Artists tend to be more impulsive and spontaneous than other creative people; writers tend to be more nonconforming than other types; architects tend to be less flexible than others; musicians are more introverted than others; and inventors and creative engineers tend to be more well-adjusted on the whole than other types. Therefore, it may be important to consider personality characteristics associated with particular domains in attempting to predict creative behavior, rather than seeking one creative personality type that fits all creative occupations.

Birth order and attachment are two important early influences on the development of autonomy. Sulloway (1999) argued that birth order causes siblings to experience the family environment in dissimilar ways that underlie differences in personality development and, subsequently, creative achievement. Although evidence does not exist to suggest that firstborns and laterborns differ in overall levels of creativity, they tend to demonstrate their creativity in different ways. Specifically, Feist (1999) argued that laterborns tend to be more open to experience and tend to express their creativity in unconventional, nonconformist, independent ways, whereas firstborns are more likely to resist new experiences and tend to express their creativity in conventional, cultured, and intellectual ways. Moreover, "security of attachment and parental facilitation of autonomy and independence are likely to lead to greater curiosity, confidence, achievement, and creativity in children" (Feist, 1999, p. 159).

PERSONALITY INVENTORIES: ADJECTIVE CHECK LIST, MYERS–BRIGGS, AND NEO PI–R. Gough's Adjective Check List (1960) comprises 300 descriptor words that a person checks as being self-descriptive. Gough identified a subscale of 30 adjectives that reliably differentiated more creative people from less creative people. Gough's Creative Personality Scale for the Adjective Check List is based on 12 samples in a variety of fields, made up of 1,701 respondents whose creativity had been assessed by experts in those fields. Of those 30 distinguishing adjectives, 18 of them are positively related to creativity, as follows: *capable, clever, confident, egotistical, humorous, individualistic, informal, insightful, intelligent, interests wide, inventive, original, reflective, resourceful, self-confident, sexy, snobbish,* and *unconventional.* Three other slightly different sets of adjectives have been used in creativity research. Domino (1994) examined the use of the four different Adjective Check Lists (ACL; also called the Domino, Gough, Schaefer, and Yarnell scales) in assessing creativity, with two samples of creative adults. He found that all four scales had adequate levels of reliability and all correlated significantly with the criterion measures.

The Myers–Briggs Type Indicator (Briggs & Myers, 1998) is a self-report measure designed to assess individuals' preferences for different types of information processing. Composed of nearly 300 forced-choice items, individuals are rated on four dimensions: introversion–extraversion, intuitive–sensing, thinking–feeling, and perceiving–judging. The Creativity Index is a pattern among the four dimensions that is closely associated with creativity. A person whose scores show him or her to be introverted, intuitive, thinking, and perceiving in personality style may be more likely to be a creative individual. The Creativity Index of the Myers–Briggs has been associated with creative styles in teachers (Houtz, LeBlanc, Butera, & Arons, 1994), psychotherapists (Buchanan & Bandy, 1984), and many other professionals.

The NEO Five Factor Personality Inventory (Costa & McCrae, 1991) is named after the first three factors of the model of personality on which it is based: neuroticism, extraversion, and openness to experience. Conscientiousness and agreeableness are the last two factors. This self-report personality inventory requires respondents to rate themselves on 9-step bipolar scales using adjective pairs. The factor structure underlying the NEO has impressive validity across cultures, lifespan, and gender (Costa & McCrae, 1992). There is only indirect evidence pointing to patterns of responding that might be associated with creativity. Typically, laterborn siblings, who are found to be more creative, are evaluated as conscientious, more agreeable, and more open to experience (Sulloway, 1999). In addition, certain of these factors may facilitate the attainment of the flow states, the sine qua non of creativity productivity, according to the research of Csikszentmihalyi (1996). These include introversion, because flow tends to happen in solitude, and openness to experience, because flow requires a profound receptivity in the present moment. This author also makes it clear that creative people are often disagreeable when faced with resistance to their work, as well as low in the sort of conscientiousness that leads most people to conform. It may be that introversion, low conscientiousness, low agreeableness, and openness to experience as measured by the NEO will be shown to be associated with creativity. The value of this instrument is its basis in clear and well-supported constructs that make additional research along these lines possible.

PROJECTIVE TESTS: RORSCHACH INKBLOT TEST. The psychodynamic model is the basis for projective test techniques that were developed to interpret an individual's instinctual drives, motives, and defenses. The basic assumption of projective tests is that participants' responses to vague stimuli will tend to portray personality style. Inkblots and pictures of human situations are commonly used. As described by Walsh and Betz (1995), because an inkblot is ambiguous, "the interpretation a person gives must come from the way that individual perceives and organizes the world . . . one is said to project into the picture one's own emotional attitudes and ideas about life" (p. 128). The interpreter seeks to gain a general impression of an individual's personality by focusing on the outstanding features in a pattern of responses and finding consistencies therein. Projective tests differ from personality inventories in several important ways: Not only are they less obvious in their intent, they are less structured, and they rely on qualitative interpretation for meaning. Projective tests are more difficult to interpret than objective measures of personality assessment, and even the most rigorous scoring systems yield only modest reliability and validity; however, they can be used to collect important information about people.

Hermann Rorschach developed the Rorschach Inkblot Test in 1921 as a subtle means of exploring personality. It consists of 10 cards, each containing an inkblot. Five of the cards are black or gray and five are colored. The cards are presented one at a time, and the respondent is asked to report what he or she sees in the inkblot or what might be represented by the inkblot. The administrator records the responses and repeats the procedure, asking the respondent to identify the location of the responses and the characteristics or determinants of the inkblot that led to the responses. Although all scoring systems require considerable training and practice, generally more original responses are interpreted as reflecting more creativity and productivity. King and Pope (1999) cited multiple studies that support their contention that creative individuals produce original and often elaborate responses to the Rorschach inkblots, and challenge other researchers to examine Rorschach protocols for responses that are complex, novel, and indicate autonomy. In fact, they have produced a preliminary scale of creativity for the Rorschach responses that is based on content and on the hypotheses that "creative responses would probably be either overly elaborated common percepts or unusual percepts," that "form quality would likely be unusual, indicating a novel approach to the stimulus," and that "movement and color would frequently be seen" (p. 203). Ferracuti, Cannoni, Burla, and Lazzari (1999) found strong correlations between the Figural Form test of the TTCT and the Developmental Quality-

Synthesized Responses of the Rorschach, a scale that clinicians have long considered to be related to creativity. (Murray and Morgan developed the Thematic Apperception Test [TAT; Murray, 1943], which has been used to measure creativity. Gieser and Stein [1999] traced six decades of history of the TAT, showing how it has been used successfully to evoke the motive to create.)

There exists renewed interest in the use of projective tests in understanding creativity. Gregory (2000) suggested "reversing the test" in such a way as to identify those patterns that seem to elicit creative responses. He supported the idea that instead of focusing on pathology, the Rorschach can help to uncover the sources of creativity in clients' personalities. He suggested "reversing the test" (i.e., from kinds of people to kinds of patterns) might show what stimulates creativity. He also posed a clear experimental question: "Which kinds of pattern evoke the richest variety of perceptions?" (p. 19).

Using Creativity Measurement in Counseling

Given the many methods of assessing creativity, what is the most useful approach to assessing creativity in counseling? First, one must consider the reason for the assessment. If a client has been referred for educational assessment, for example, for the purpose of placement in gifted classes or for a special program, then the counselor should investigate the nature of that program. The method always should "match" the program. That is, if the curriculum is one that emphasizes the ability to brainstorm ideas and to use creative problem solving, then the TTCT may be appropriate. If, on the other hand, the curriculum focuses on a particular domain, then it may be more effective to use personality tests such as the Adjective Check List to attempt to identify individuals with personalities most similar to those of artists.

What does it mean if a client who has been referred for educational testing scores very high on the TTCT? It means that the client *thinks* creatively but not necessarily that the client had produced creative works. It does mean that the individual has the cognitive "building blocks" of creativity: ideational fluency, flexibility, and originality. However, these must be combined with motivation to achieve, above average intelligence, and endurance as well as a great number of other characteristics to predict creative behavior. If the client is to be placed in a program that will require creative writing and art work as well as creative problem solving, then the TTCT may help support that placement if it is used in combination with tests of ability in the critical domains and personality tests that yield information about the need for achievement and the need for endurance. The child who is a creative thinker but lacks intelligence, motivation to achieve, and persistence may have many interesting ideas but be unable to carry them through or to evaluate them critically. Even the creative thinker is likely to become an academic dilettante without the personality characteristics that permit concentration in the pursuit of a goal.

Meeker (1978) advocated measuring creativity from the child's point of view and showed how Guilford's scales can be used to help a child to understand his or her own creativity. A child is assessed according to the Structure of Intellect model, and then is helped to understand intellectual strengths and weaknesses. The resulting profile is used to help place children in gifted education classes that build on the students' strengths and remediate weaknesses.

Both the TTCT and Guilford tests can be useful in advocating for the bright child who is highly creative but only slightly above average in intelligence. Because creativity and intelligence overlap but are not perfectly correlated, many children who are highly creative and only moderately intelligent also can benefit from gifted education if they are also persistent and motivated to complete tasks. Those gifted programs that are based on the Renzulli (1999) Three Ring method of identification—requiring evidence of intelligence, creativity, and task commitment—will be particularly open to objective measures of the creative process.

If the client is requesting vocational guidance, then a much broader approach to creativity assessment may be appropriate. Rather than a battery of creativity instruments, the creativity scale of the Adjective Check List, or subscales of other personality inventories that are correlated with creativity to identify creative potential, might be the measures of choice. The personality tests can be combined with vocational interest tests and values inventories to yield a profile of the particular domains in which the client might be most creative. An approach to assessing the multipotential, creatively gifted was developed at the University of Iowa's Counseling Laboratory for Talent Development (Kerr & Erb, 1991). The Counseling Laboratory was a series of activities that integrated assessment into both group and individual counseling. Adolescent clients took the Vocational Preference Inventory (VPI: Holland, 1996); the Personality Research Form (PRF: Jackson, 1991) and a values inventory. The PRF, like the Adjective Check List, yields scores on the need for autonomy, achievement, endurance, affiliation, dominance, and several other scales that had been found to be positively or negatively correlated with creative productivity. Together with vocational interests and values, these scores were very useful to clients in determining the probability of satisfaction and success in creative fields. In this study, more than half of the college-age clients changed college majors to majors that were more creative and more in keeping with their own values.

It is intriguing to consider the possible uses of projective tests for creativity assessment in counseling. Counseling often focuses on negative situations, personality and mood disorders, and behavioral deficits. It may be that the use of projective tests can help not only the client but also the counselor to refocus on the positive psychology of the client. As the counselor administers the Rorschach or the TAT, he or she often finds that the process is often both surprising and intuitively satisfying. The counselor has an opportunity to see the creative processes of the client in a more immediate way than one can in using an objective instrument.

In addition, a biographical approach in which the client's own history is compared to the life histories of creative people in Piirto's (1998) or Csikszentmihalyi's (1996) summaries of creative lives can be fruitful. One of the most affirming experiences for a client can be that of having a counselor show how the conflicts that he or she is enduring, the polarities of emotions that are felt, and the barriers to productivity that arise are common to creative lives. Too often, characteristics of autonomy, nonconformity, spontaneity, and expressiveness are devalued by society; yet these are the very traits that lead individuals to produce great art, literature, music, and science. Counselors who are sensitive to this paradox can help creative individuals to recognize themselves and to value their gifts.

Future Directions for Creativity Measurement

It is clear from a review of the research in creativity assessment that the bulk of the work in this area has been on instrument development. With the exception of the TTCT, there seems to have been little follow-through in terms of instrument validation. More longitudinal studies of predictive validity of tests of cognitive processes and personality characteristics would be useful in culling out the many mediocre tests of creativity. In addition, more attention to reliability would strengthen current tests and make them useful to clinicians.

The search for shorter, more easily administered means of measurement also is necessary. Tests need to be simplified so that they are more easily scored. The most commonly used instrument for measuring creative thinking, the TTCT, has the unfortunate quality of being long and difficult to administer and to score. As a result, many educators and counselors sour on the use of a strategy that requires such an investment of time.

Perhaps the most obvious need is that of integration of creativity assessment into both education and counseling. Although ways of measuring creativity abound, few practitioners understand how to make the creative aspects of personality and intellect a part of their evaluation. Teachers need preservice training in the nature of creativity and the means for identifying it. Counselors need training in ways of evaluating and selecting creativity tests and in ways of using them in counseling. To date, there are very few counselors who are qualified to train others in the uses of these instruments. However, those who are willing to help counselors and teachers to learn efficient ways of identifying the creative strengths of their clients and students will find an eager and enthusiastic audience.

References

Amabile, T. M. (2001). Beyond talent: John Irving and the passionate craft of creativity. *American Psychologist, 56,* 333–336.

Andreasen, N. C. (1987). Creativity and mental illness: Prevalence rates in writers and their first-degree relatives. *American Journal of Psychiatry, 144,* 1288–1292.

Bowden, C. L. (1994). Bipolar disorder and creativity. In M. P. Shaw & M. A. Runco (Eds.), *Creativity and affect* (pp. 73–86). Westport, CT: Ablex.

Briggs, K. C., & Myers, I. B. (1998). *Myers–Briggs Type Indicator.* Palo Alto, CA: Author.

Buchanan, D., & Bandy, C. (1984). Jungian typology of prospective psychodramatists: Myers–Briggs Type Indicator analysis of applicants for psychodrama training. *Psychological Reports, 55,* 599–606.

Cooper, E. (1991). A critique of six measures for assessing creativity. *Journal of Creative Behavior, 25,* 194–217.

Costa, P. T., & McCrae, R. R. (1991). *NEO Five-Factor Inventory.* Odessa, FL: Psychological Assessment Resources.

Costa, P. T., & McCrae, R. R. (1992). Four ways five factors are basic. *Personality and Individual Differences, 13,* 655–656.

Csikszentmihalyi, M. (1990). *Flow: The psychology of optimum experience.* New York: Harper-Collins.

Csikszentmihalyi, M. (1996). *Creativity: Flow and the psychology of discovery and invention.* New York: Harper-Collins.

Domino, G. (1994). Assessment of creativity with the ACL: An empirical comparison of four scales. *Creativity Research Journal, 7,* 21–33.

Feist, G. J. (1999). Autonomy and independence. *Encyclopedia of Creativity* (Vol. 1, pp. 157–163). San Diego, CA: Academic Press.

Ferracuti, S., Cannoni, E., Burla, F., & Lazzari, R. (1999). Correlations for the Rorschach with the Torrance Tests of Creative Thinking. *Perceptual and Motor Skills, 89,* 863–870.

Gieser, L., & Stein, M. (1999). *Evocative images: The Thematic Apperception Test and the art of projection.* Washington, DC: American Psychological Association.

Guilford, J. P. (1962). Potentiality for creativity. *Gifted Child Quarterly, 6,* 87–90.

Gough, H. G. (1960). The Adjective Check List as a personality assessment research technique. *Psychological Reports, 6,* 107–122.

Gregory, R. (2000, March 2). Reversing Rorschach. *Nature, 404,* 19.

Hocevar, D., & Bachelor, P. (1989). A taxonomy and critique of measurements used in the study of creativity. In J. A. Glover, R. R. Ronning, & C. R. Reynolds (Eds.), *Handbook of creativity* (pp. 53–76). New York: Plenum Press.

Holland, J. (1996). *Vocational Preference Inventory.* Odessa, FL: Psychological Assessment Resources.

Houtz, J. C., & Krug, D. (1995). Assessment of creativity: Resolving a mid-life crisis. *Educational Psychology Review, 7,* 269–299.

Houtz, J. C., LeBlanc, E., Butera, T., & Arons, M. F. (1994). Personality type, creativity, and classroom teaching style in student teachers. *Journal of Classroom Interaction, 29,* 21–26.

Jackson, D. (1991). *The Personality Research Form.* Port Huron, MI: Sigma Assessment Systems.

Jamison, K. (1989). Mood disorders and seasonal patterns in British writers and artists. *Psychiatry, 52,* 125–134.

Kerr, B. A., & Erb, C. (1991). Career counseling with academically talented students: Effects of a value-based intervention. *Journal of Counseling Psychology, 38,* 330–314.

Kerr, B., Shaffer, J., Chambers, C., & Hallowell, K. (1991). Substance use of creatively talented adults. *Journal of Creative Behavior, 25,* 145–153.

King, B. J., & Pope, B. (1999). Creativity as a factor in psychological assessment and healthy psychological functioning. *Journal of Personality Assessment, 72,* 200–207.

Meeker, M. (1978). Measuring creativity from the child's point of view. *Journal of Creative Behavior, 12,* 52–62.

Michael, W. B., & Bachelor, P. (1990). Higher-order structure-of-intellect creativity factors in divergent production tests: A re-analysis of the Guilford data base. *Creativity Research Journal, 3,* 58–74.

Murray, H. A. (1943). *Thematic Apperception Test.* Cambridge: Harvard University Press.

Parkhurst, H. B. (1999). Confusion, lack of consensus, and the definition of creativity as a construct. *Journal of Creative Behavior, 33,* 1–21.

Piirto, J. (1998). *Understanding those who create.* Scottsdale: Gifted Psychology Press.

Plucker, J. A., & Runco, M. A. (1998). The death of creativity measurement has been greatly exaggerated: Current issues, recent advances, and future directions in creativity assessment. *Roeper Review, 21,* 36–39.

Pritzker, S. R. (1999). Alcohol and creativity. In M. A. Runco, & S. Pritzker (Eds.), *Encyclopedia of Creativity* (Vol. 2, pp. 699–708). San Diego, CA: Academic Press.

Renzulli, J. S. (1999). What is this thing called giftedness, and how do we develop it? A twenty-five year perspective. *Journal for the Education of the Gifted, 23,* 3–54.

Richards, R., & Kinney, D. K. (1990). Mood swings and creativity. *Creativity Research Journal, 3,* 202–217.

Runco, M. A. (1999). Divergent thinking. In M. A. Runco & S. Pritzker (Eds.), *Encyclopedia of creativity* (Vol. 1, pp. 577–582). San Diego, CA: Academic Press.

Simonton, D. K. (2000). Creativity: Cognitive, personal, developmental, and social aspects. *American Psychologist, 55,* 151–158

Sternberg, R. J. (2001). What is the common thread of creativity? Its dialectical relation to intelligence and wisdom. *American Psychologist, 56,* 360–362.

Sulloway, F. J. (1999). Birth order. In M. A. Runco & S. Pritzker (Eds.), *Encyclopedia of creativity* (Vol. 1, p. 701). San Diego, CA: Academic Press.

Torrance, E. P. (1965). *Rewarding creative behavior: Experiments in classroom activity.* Englewood Cliffs, NJ: Prentice-Hall.

Torrance, E. P. (1984). The role of creativity in identification of the gifted and talented. *Gifted Child Quarterly, 28,* 153–156.

Torrance, E. P. (1988). The nature of creativity as manifest in its testing. In R. J. Sternberg (Ed.), *The nature of creativity* (pp. 43–75). New York: Cambridge University Press.

Treffinger, D. J. (1985). Review of the Torrance Tests for Creative Thinking. In J. Mitchell (Ed.), *Ninth mental measurements yearbook* (pp. 1633–1634). Lincoln, NE: Buros Institute of Mental Measurement.

Treffinger, D. J., Renzulli, J. S., & Feldhusen, J. F. (1971). Problems in the assessment of creative thinking. *The Journal of Creative Behavior, 5,* 104–111.

Walsh, B. W., & Betz, N. (1995). *Tests and assessment* (3rd ed.). Englewood Cliffs, NJ: Prentice-Hall.

11

The Assessment of Wisdom-Related Performance

U. M. Staudinger and B. Leipold

Since the beginnings of human culture, wisdom has been viewed as the ideal endpoint of human development. Certainly, the psychological study of wisdom is still rather young compared to its philosophical treatment considering that the very definition of philosophy is "love or pursuit of wisdom." Important to recognize is that in the general historical wisdom literature, the identification of wisdom with the mind and character of individuals is not the preferred mode of analysis. The identification of wisdom with individuals (such as wise persons), the predominant approach in psychology, is but one of the ways by which wisdom is instantiated. More often wisdom is described as a knowledge system that is instantiated in religious and constitutional texts or collections of proverbs. Wisdom is considered an ideal that is difficult to be fully represented in the isolated individual.

Throughout history, the interest in the topic of wisdom has waxed and waned (Baltes, in press). In the Western world, the question of whether wisdom is divine or human was at the center of wisdom-related discourse during the Renaissance. An initial conclusion of this debate was reached during the later phases of the Enlightenment when worldly wisdom took center stage. Archeological–cultural work dealing with the origins of religious and secular bodies of wisdom-related texts in China, India, Egypt, Old Mesopotamia, and the like has revealed many similarities in the definition of wisdom across cultures and historical time (Baltes, in press): Wisdom (a) addresses important and difficult questions and strategies about the conduct and meaning of life; (b) includes knowledge about the limits of knowledge and the uncertainties of the world; (c) represents a truly superior level of knowledge, judgment, and advice; (d) constitutes knowledge with extraordinary scope, depth, measure, and balance; (e) involves a perfect synergy of mind and character—that is, an orchestration of knowledge and virtues; (f) represents knowledge used for the good or well-being of oneself and that of others; (g) is easily recognized when manifested, though difficult to achieve and to specify. These shared characteristics suggest that wisdom and its related body of knowledge and skills have been culturally selected because of their adaptive value for humankind (e.g., Staudinger, 1996).

The interest in the concept of wisdom has been growing recently. It has been suggested that this strong interest is related to the fact that Western industrialized societies have become pluralistic societies. It is not obvious any more how to lead one's life and thus a need for guidance and orientation emerges. The concept of wisdom seems ideally suited to fulfilling such needs. Concern for the topic of wisdom is evident in a wide spectrum of disciplines, ranging from philosophy and religious studies to cultural anthropology, political science, education, and psychology (e.g., Arlin, 1993; Nichols, 1996). Among the major reasons for the emergence of the psychological study of wisdom in the late 1970s and early 1980s was the search for domains or types of intellectual functioning that would not show age-related decline.

Psychological Definitions of Wisdom

When struggling with how to define wisdom scientifically, a major source to consult are dictionaries. The major German historical dictionary (Grimm & Grimm, 1854/1984), for instance, defines wisdom as "insight and knowledge about oneself and the world . . . and sound judgment in the case of difficult life problems." Similarly, the *Oxford Dictionary* includes in its definition "good judgment and advice in difficult and uncertain matters of life." Definitions of wisdom in encyclopedias emphasize knowledge or judgment as key characteristics.

The psychologists who define wisdom must specify the content and formal properties of wisdom-related thought, judgment, and advice in terms of psychological categories; moreover, they must describe the characteristics of persons who have approached a state of wisdom and are capable of transmitting such wisdom to others. For the most part, these initial efforts by psychologists were theoretical and speculative. In his pioneering piece on senescence, G. Stanley Hall (1922) associated wisdom with the emergence of a meditative attitude, philosophic calmness, impartiality, and the desire to draw moral lessons that emerge in later adulthood. Furthermore, writers emphasized that wisdom involves the search for the moderate course between extremes, a dynamic between knowledge and doubt, a sufficient detachment from the problem at hand, and a well-balanced coordination of emotion, motivation, and thought (e.g., Hartshorne, 1987; Labouvie-Vief, 1990). In line with dictionary definitions, such psychological definitions typically include that wisdom is knowledge about the human condition at its frontier, knowledge about the most difficult questions of the meaning and conduct of life, and knowledge about the uncertainties of life, about what cannot be known, and how to deal with that limited knowledge. Birren and Fisher (1990) reviewed a number of psychological conceptualizations of wisdom, and proposed the definition, "Wisdom is the integration of the affective, conative, and cognitive aspects of human abilities in response to life tasks and problems. Wisdom is a balance between the opposing valences of intense emotion and detachment, action and inaction, and knowledge and doubts" (p. 326). In varying degrees, most conceptions of wisdom represent such multidimensionality.

Although wisdom has been described as the ideal integration of mind and virtue for millennia, only recently has it been investigated empirically. One reason for this dearth of empirical conceptualization and study may reflect the serious doubts whether a concept as rich in ideational history and connotations as wisdom is even amenable to scientific study. Admittedly, any of the current empirical attempts only captures parts of this highly complex phenomenon. Yet we believe that the current operationalizations of wisdom have demonstrated that it can be studied and is worth the effort. A selection of wisdom measures is described in Appendix 11.1.

Two Major Approaches to the Psychological Study of Wisdom

Two major approaches to the psychological study of wisdom, grounded in either implicit or explicit theories of wisdom, can be distinguished. Implicit theories and focus on the assessment of subjective, commonsense beliefs about wisdom or a wise person abound (e.g., Clayton & Birren, 1980; Holliday & Chandler, 1986; Sowarka, 1989; Sternberg, 1985).

Implicit Theories of Wisdom

Most psychological research on wisdom so far has focused on further elaborating the definition of wisdom. Moving beyond the dictionary definitions of wisdom, research assessed the nature of everyday beliefs, folk conceptions, or implicit (subjective) theories of wisdom. The pursuit of answers to questions such as, What is wisdom? How does wisdom differ from other forms of intelligence? Which situations require wisdom? What is a wise act? What are the characteristics of wise people? are at the center of this approach (see Staudinger & Baltes, 1994).

Wisdom in these studies is "assessed" in two ways. Either participants are asked to sort adjectives according to the degree to which they reflect wisdom (Clayton, 1975) or their probability of co-occurring in one person (Sternberg, 1985). Such ratings subsequently are analyzed using multidimensional scaling. In other studies, participants are asked to rate items to which degree they reflect their prototype of a wise person (Holliday & Chandler, 1986). Those items either describe a wise person, a nonwise person, and nonrelevant characteristics. These ratings then are factor analyzed. In both cases, the stimulus materials (adjectives, items) have been developed based on pilot studies in which participants described their concept of a wise person. Characteristics that were mentioned most often were then turned into scale items.

Clayton (1975) defined wisdom as an ability to grasp paradoxes, reconcile contradictions, and develop compromises. She used multidimensional scaling to identify words that are related to wisdom for persons from different age groups. Three dimensions of wisdom were identified: (a) affective (e.g., empathy, compassion); (b) reflective (e.g., intuition, introspection); and (c) cognitive (e.g., experience, intelligence). Clayton also found that the concept of wisdom became more differentiated with increasing age of respondents.

In her dissertation, Sowarka (1989) examined the reconstruction of commonsense concepts about wise persons by content-analyzing interviews with elderly participants about their notions of wisdom. Participants' responded to the following questions: "Have you ever known someone that you consider a wise person?" and "What was it about this person that made you say that this is a wise person?" Results indicated that wise people exhibit excellent character, are intellectually competent (personality traits), exert influence on others, and have professional skills (social role). One of the major findings was that it seems easy for participants to generate nominations of wise persons from their acquaintance.

From a series of studies, Sternberg (1985) concluded that investigating implicit theories was useful for studying the meaning of wisdom. In a pilot study, professors of art, business, philosophy, and physics were asked to list behaviors that characterized an ideally wise person in his or her respective field of scholarship. Based on these characteristics of an ideally wise person, laypersons (nonacademicians) as well as academicians from several disciplines were asked to rate the prototypicality of each of the behaviors with respect to their conception of an ideally wise person. Mean ratings for wisdom on a 9-point scale ranged from 6.3 to 7.1. The results suggest that the listed items were quite characteristic for wise persons in each of the groups. Furthermore, the ratings were highly consistent across participants (.86 to .96) and items (.89 to .97). Hence, results indicate reliability within occupational group and within the item set.

More recently, Sternberg (1998) integrated his work on implicit theories of wisdom and of practical intelligence and tacit knowledge, and suggested that the notion of balance was central in defining wisdom. Wisdom is seen as being inherently linked to the interaction between the individual and the situation. It is defined as the application of tacit knowledge with the goal of achieving a common good. In particular, tacit knowledge is applied to balance interests (intrapersonal, interpersonal, extrapersonal), as well as responses to environmental context (adaptation, shaping, selection). Wisdom in this sense is a special form of practical intelligence that requires balancing of interests to achieve a common good.

From this research on implicit theories of wisdom and wise persons, it is evident that Westerners apparently hold fairly clearcut images of the nature of wisdom. Four findings are especially noteworthy. First, wisdom seems to be closely related to wise persons and their acts as "carriers" of wisdom. Second, wise people are expected to combine features of mind and character and to balance multiple interests and choices. Third, wisdom carries a very strong interpersonal and social aspect with regard to both its application (advice) and the consensual recognition of its occurrence. Fourth, wisdom exhibits overlap with other related concepts such as intelligence, but in aspects such as sagacity, prudence, and the integration of cognition, emotion, and motivation, it also carries unique variance. To date, there are only very few studies (and unfortunately of unclear scientific quality) that compare implicit theories of wisdom between cultures (e.g., Takahashi & Bordia, 2000). This area of research needs additional study.

Explicit Theories of Wisdom

In contrast to the implicit theories, the other approach to the psychological study of wisdom involves explicit theories. They are grounded in theoretical conceptions of wisdom that subsequently are operationalized and tested. Behavioral expressions of wisdom are the unit of analysis in this tradition. Within the explicit approaches three different lines of work can be distinguished: (a) assessment of wisdom as a personal characteristic (Erikson, 1959); (b) assessment of wisdom in the neo-Piagetian tradition of postformal operations and mature thought (e.g., Kramer & Woodruff, 1986; Labouvie-Vief, 1990); and (c) assessment of wisdom as an expert system (e.g., Baltes & Smith, 1990; Staudinger & Baltes, 1994).

Within theories of personality development, wisdom usually is conceptualized as an advanced if not the final stage of development. For Erikson, wisdom implies accepting one's life without major regrets, and accepting death as the inevitable end. Whereas integrity versus despair constitutes the final psychosocial crisis of human existence, integrity can only be attained in a dynamic balance with despair. The individual regards death with equanimity, sees wisdom as a major value orientation, and generally has an accepting attitude toward humankind. A related aspect of personality development is transcendence (Orwoll & Perlmutter, 1990), or moving beyond individualistic concerns to more collective or universal issues.

Informed by the Piagetian tradition of studying cognitive development, several investigators have proposed a postformal stage of adult thinking. In these theories of postformal thought, wisdom is conceptualized as increasing complexity and dialectic thinking. Criteria for postformal thinking include awareness of multiple causes and solutions, awareness of paradoxes and contradictions, and the ability to deal with uncertainty, inconsistency, imperfection, and compromise. Recently, dialectical thinking also has been investigated cross-culturally. Peng and Nisbett (1999) have found that Eastern (in this case Chinese) cultures seem to foster dialectic thinking much more than do Western cultures (in this case the United States and Australia).

Finally, wisdom also is conceptualized as a special kind of expert-level knowledge and skill. Consistent with the idea that expertise is grounded in years of acquiring domain-specific knowledge, research within this framework demonstrates that experts excel mainly in a special domain—namely the "fundamental pragmatics of life" (e.g., Baltes & Staudinger, 2000; see subsequent section for a more detailed description).

Individual-Differences Measures of Wisdom

In this section, the assessment procedures related to each of the three explicit approaches to the study of wisdom are presented.

The Assessment of Wisdom as a Personality Characteristic

Within personality theories, wisdom usually is conceptualized as an advanced if not the final stage of personality development. In this context, wisdom is comparable to "optimal maturity." A wise person is characterized, for instance, as integrating rather than ignoring or repressing self-related information by having coordinated opposites and by having transcended personal agendas in favor of collective or universal issues. Because "optimal maturity" is highly desirable, most operationalizations are skewed toward the socially desirable end of the scale.

For instance, Walaskay, Whitbourne, and Nehrke (1983–1984) and Ryff and Heincke (1983) have developed self-report questionnaires based on the Eriksonian notions of personality development, especially integrity or wisdom. The scale "integrity" developed by Ryff and Heincke (1983) consists of 16 items. A high scorer is described as adapting to triumphs and disappointments of being; accepting personal life as something that had to be; viewing past life as inevitable, appropriate, and meaningful; being emotionally integrated; having resolved past conflicts and having a sense of having taken care of things. The Adult Ego-Development scale (Walaskay et al., 1983–1984) is a refinement of two previous assessment instruments (Boylin, Gordon, & Nehrke, 1976; Constantinople, 1969). Items refer to Erikson's three final developmental tasks (i.e., intimacy vs. isolation, generativity vs. self-absorption, integrity vs. despair); five items measure the positive and five items measure the negative resolution of the crises.

Other approaches have used recombinations of extant personality questionnaires to operationalize wisdom in the sense of self-development and maturity. For instance, Wink and Helson (1997) used a personality measure and open-ended responses to assess practical (i.e., interpersonal skill and interest, insight, clear thinking, reflectiveness, tolerance, etc.) and transcendent wisdom (i.e., transcending the personal, recognizing the complexities and limits of knowledge, integrating thought and effort, spiritual depth). The Practical Wisdom scale, for example, consists of 14 indicative items (e.g., mature, insightful, tolerant) and four contraindicative items (e.g., immature, reckless, shallow). The final wisdom score is computed by subtracting the number of the contraindicative items from the number of indicative items. In addition to self-reported wisdom, participants also are asked, "Many people hope to become wiser as they grow older. Would you give an example of wisdom you have acquired and how you came by it?" A panel of trained judges evaluates the answers using a 5-point scale. More recently, Ardelt (1997) used Haan's (1969) Ego Rating scale and Block's (1961) California Q-sort to operationalize a cognitive, reflective, and affective component of wisdom. The cognitive component of wisdom was measured by one Q-sort item and four items from Haan's Ego Ratings— that is, objectivity, intellectuality, logical analysis, and concentration. The reflective component was operationalized by three items from Haan's measure and six items from the Q-sort (e.g., no denial, no projection, and "is introspective"). Finally, the affective component of wisdom consisted of 10 items from the Q-sort (e.g., behaves in a sympathetic or considerate manner or has no hostility toward others) and one item from the Ego Rating scale (empathy).

The Assessment of Wisdom as Postformal Thinking

Central to Neopiagetian theories of adult thought is the transcendence of the universal truth criterion that characterizes formal logic. This transcendence is common to conceptions such as dialectical, complementary, and relativistic thinking. Such tolerance of multiple truths—that is, tolerance of ambiguity— also has been mentioned as a crucial feature of wisdom. A number of different approaches all linked to this basic understanding can be distinguished: dialectical thinking; complementary thinking; relativistic thinking; and reflective judgment. Usually, these kinds of mature thoughts are assessed as performances. Thus, participants are asked to respond to a fictitious problem. The answers subsequently are coded according to respective coding schemes reflecting ascending levels of mature thought (e.g., Blanchard-Fields, 1986; Kitchener & Brenner, 1990; Kramer & Woodruff, 1986; Labouvie-Vief, 1980). Reported interrater agreements usually range between Cronbach alpha .75 and .85.

Kramer (1983) suggested the following three features of mature thinking to summarize a number of models of postformal thinking: awareness of the relativistic nature of knowledge; acceptance of contradiction; and integration of contradiction into the dialectical whole. In a study by Kramer and Woodruff (1986), these features were operationalized as sequentially ordered levels of mature thinking and, at the same time, as coding categories for the analysis of response protocols. To assess postformal thinking, participants each were presented with two dilemmas. The career dilemma centered on a woman's decision about whether to enter the workforce for the first time full-time. The second dilemma centered around a hostage crisis set in the future, where both parties involved had potentially "constructive" and "deconstructive" intentions or actions. Coders rated each protocol for instances of responses that revealed each of the categories of thought. On the basis of coding, each participant was assigned a frequency score and a rating score that indicated the quality of the responses with regard to dialectical thinking on a 4-point scale.

Ill-structured social dilemmas usually are used to examine postformal thought. In another study, the role of emotions in social reasoning was investigated (Blanchard-Fields, 1986). Three age groups were presented with three fictitious situations, each of which offered two opposing accounts (fictional war, visit to the grandparents conflict, pregnancy dilemma). The tasks varied in emotional saliency and the degree of interpersonal conflict. Participants were asked to give their accounts of the situation, and afterward some probing questions were asked (e.g., Who was at fault in this situation? How was the conflict resolved?). Responses were scored according to levels of dialectical thinking (Perry, 1970) and judgment under uncertainty (Kitchener & King, 1981). Interrater reliability ranged from Cronbach alpha .92 to .94.

The Assessment of Wisdom as Expert-Level Knowledge and Judgment in the Fundamental Pragmatics of Life

Besides these measures of wisdom as a personality characteristic, or as a feature of mature thought, there also is work that attempts to assess wisdom-related performance in tasks dealing with the interpretation, conduct, and management of life. This approach is based on lifespan theory, the developmental study of the aging mind and aging personality, research on expert systems, and cultural–historical definitions of wisdom (Baltes, Smith, & Staudinger, 1992). Integrating these perspectives, wisdom is defined as an expert knowledge system in the fundamental pragmatics of life permitting exceptional insight, judgment, and advice involving complex and uncertain matters of the human condition.

The body of knowledge and skills associated with wisdom as an expertise in the fundamental pragmatics of life entails insights into the quintessential aspects of the human condition, including its biological finitude and cultural conditioning. Wisdom involves a fine-tuned and well-balanced coordination of cognition, motivation, and emotion. More specifically, wisdom-related knowledge and skills can be characterized by a family of five criteria: (a) rich factual knowledge about life; (b) rich procedural knowledge about life; (c) lifespan contextualism; (d) value relativism; and (e) awareness and management of uncertainty (see Baltes & Staudinger, 2000, for an extensive definition).

To elicit and measure wisdom-related knowledge and skills in this approach, participants are presented with difficult life dilemmas such as, "Imagine, someone receives a call from a good friend who tells him/her that he/she can't go on anymore and has decided to commit suicide. What would the person/what would you do and consider in this situation?" (see Appendix 11.1). Participants then are asked to "think aloud" about such dilemmas. The five wisdom-related criteria are used to evaluate these protocols. To do so, an age-heterogeneous expert panel of raters is selected based on their life experience. These raters are extensively trained and calibrated in using the five criteria to evaluate the response protocols. Every rater is trained on only one criterion to avoid halo affects. Two raters always apply the same criterion to establish interrater reliability. Across more than 3000 response protocols, the reliabilities of the five criteria have ranged between .72 and .93. Reliability of the wisdom score averaged across the five criteria even reaches a Cronbach alpha of .98. The exact training procedure and the calibration protocols are described and included in the *Rater Manual* that can be obtained from the authors (Staudinger, Smith, & Baltes, 1994).

INDICATORS OF EXTERNAL AND INTERNAL VALIDITY. When using this wisdom paradigm to study people who were nominated as wise according to nominators' subjective beliefs about wisdom, it was found that wisdom nominees also received higher wisdom scores than comparable control samples of various ages and professional backgrounds (Baltes & Staudinger, 2000). Convergent and discriminant validity was established with regard to extant measures of cognitive and personality functioning. In line with the historical wisdom literature that portrays wisdom as the ideal combination of mind and virtue, it was found that wisdom-related performance was best predicted by measures located at the interface of cognition and personality, such as a judicious cognitive style, creativity, and moral reasoning. Neither intelligence (fluid, crystallized) nor personality (Big Five, psychological-mindedness) made a significant *indepen-*

dent contribution to wisdom-related knowledge and judgment (Staudinger, Lopez, & Baltes, 1997).

ONTOGENESIS OF WISDOM. A working model of the development of wisdom-related knowledge specifies a set of conditions and processes that need to "cooperate" for wisdom to develop (e.g., Baltes et al., 1992; Staudinger et al., 1997). The development of wisdom is dependent on *general person factors* (e.g., cognitive mechanics, openness to experience, social competence), *expertise-specific factors* (e.g., experience in life matters, receiving mentorship, motivational dispositions such as strive for excellence, etc.), and *facilitative experiential contexts* (e.g., age, education, profession, period). Furthermore, three processes have been specified that may support the acquisition of wisdom: *life review, life management, and life planning*. These processes refer to the three-fold perception of time, organize the experiences and impressions, and provide an avenue to measure wisdom-related knowledge. An effective constellation of context-related, person-related, and expertise-specific factors is assumed to maximize the likelihood of attaining expertise in the fundamental pragmatics of life.

Tests of this ontogenetic model demonstrated that *age-related* increases of wisdom-related performance only occur between the ages of 14 and approximately 25 years of age (Pasupathi, Staudinger, & Baltes, 2001). After that age until later adulthood (approx. 75 years), it is not enough to grow older to become "wiser" (Staudinger, 1999). During adulthood, other factors than chronological age predict wisdom performance. Empirical studies supported the important role of experiential settings, as well as guidance and mentorship in dealing with difficult life issues (e.g., Smith, Staudinger, & Baltes, 1994; Staudinger, Smith, & Baltes, 1992). In the same vein, it was found that wisdom-related knowledge and judgment does not follow a simple cumulative function, but rather it is related to the contexts of everyday life. It was demonstrated that young and old respondents gave best responses when asked about a problem relevant to their own life phase (for a review Staudinger, 1999).

FACILITATING WISDOM-RELATED PERFORMANCE. Besides finding evidence for the ontogenetic model, it also was shown that wisdom-related performance can be facilitated. Wisdom-related performance was enhanced by one standard deviation if participants had a chance to discuss the life problem with a self-selected partner before responding (Staudinger & Baltes, 1996). In a second study, teaching participants a thinking strategy that encourages switching between perspectives resulted in significant increases in wisdom-related performances (Böhmig-Krumhaar, Staudinger, & Baltes, 2002).

Future Developments in the Measurement of Wisdom

The concept of wisdom represents a fruitful topic for psychological research because (a) the study of wisdom emphasizes the search for continued optimization and the additional evolution of the human condition; and (b) in a prototypical fashion, it allows for the study of collaboration among cognitive, emotional, and motivational processes.

Future research on wisdom will be expanded in at least four ways: (a) the identification of more social and personality factors as well as life processes relevant for the ontogeny of wisdom; (b) attempts to further develop less labor-intensive assessment tools; (c) gaining better understanding of the interplay between self-related wisdom and wisdom about others; and (d) comparing antecedents and correlates of wise judgment or wise advice as compared to wise acts. Within the emerging field of positive psychology, wisdom may be considered one of the central human strengths, and attempts will be made to facilitate its development (see also Aspinwall & Staudinger, 2002).

Appendix 11.1
Illustration of a Wisdom-Related Task With Examples
of High-Level Responses (Abbreviated)

Life Planning: *A 14-year old girl absolutely wants to move out of her family home immediately. What should one/she do and consider?*

First, I would ask why it is that the girl wants to move out. There can be reasons like violence or abuse, but it can also be more emotional reasons due to adolescence. If it is the case that there are real problems at home, it depends on their severity. There can be cases where it is absolutely necessary to help the girl to move out right away. . . . But in the case of emotional disturbances on the part of the girl, I would first try to talk to the girl and the parents as well. If no compromise can be reached, one could also think about a temporary separation. Often, time helps. . . . Any solution to the problem needs to take into account that circumstances and attitudes are likely to change and that modification after a certain amount of time should be possible. . . . One also has to consider that these things become fads among teenagers. . . . Also, times have changed, and girls at 14 nowadays are more grown up than girls at 14 were 20 years ago.

Life Management: *Somebody gets a phone call from a good friend who says that he/she can't go on any more and that he/she has decided to commit suicide. What should one/the person do and consider?*

On one hand, this problem has a pragmatic side—one has to react one way or other. On the other hand, it also has a philosophical side—whether human beings are allowed to kill themselves, etc. . . . First, one would need to find out whether this decision is the result of a longer process or whether it is a reaction to a momentary life situation. In the latter case, it is uncertain how long this condition will last. There can be conditions that make suicide conceivable. But I think no one should be easily released from life. They should be forced to "fight" for their death if they really want it. . . . It seems that one has a responsibility to try to show the person alternative pathways. Currently, for example, there seems to be a trend in our society that it becomes more and more accepted that old people commit suicide. This can also be viewed as dangerous. Not because of the suicide itself but because of its functionality for society.

Life Review: *In reflecting over their lives, people sometimes realize that they have not achieved what they had once planned to achieve. What should one/they do and consider?*

First, I would want to say that only very few and most likely uncritical people would say that they are completely satisfied with what they have achieved. . . . It depends very much on the type of goals we are considering, whether they are more of the materialistic or more of the idealistic kind. It also depends on the age of the person and the life circumstances in which he/she is embedded.

. . . Next, one would start to analyze possible reasons for why certain goals are not attained. Often, it is the case that multiple goals were pursued at the same time without setting priorities and, therefore, in the end, things get lost. . . . It is important to gradually become realistic about goals. Often, it is helpful to talk to others about it. . . . Conditions external and internal to the person could be at work or sometimes it is also the match between the two that can lead to difficulties in life.

References

Ardelt, M. (1997). Wisdom and life satisfaction in old age. *Journal of Gerontology, 52B*, 15–27.

Arlin, P. K. (1993). Wisdom and expertise in teaching: An integration of perspectives. *Learning and Individual Differences, 5*, 341–349.

Aspinwall, L. G., & Staudinger, U. M. (2002). A psychology of human strengths: Some central issues of an emerging field. In L. G. Aspinwall & U. M. Staudinger (Eds.), *A psychology of human strengths: Perspectives on an emerging field* (pp. 9–22). Washington, DC: American Psychological Association.

Baltes, P. B. (in press). *Wisdom: The orchestration of mind and character*. Boston: Blackwell.

Baltes, P. B., & Smith, J. (1990). The psychology of wisdom and its ontogenesis. In R. J. Sternberg (Ed.), *Wisdom: Its nature, origins, and development* (pp. 87–120). New York: Cambridge University Press.

Baltes, P. B., Smith, J., & Staudinger, U. M. (1992). Wisdom and successful aging. In T. Sonderegger (Ed.), *Nebraska symposium on motivation* (Vol. 39, pp. 123–167). Lincoln: University of Nebraska Press.

Baltes, P. B., & Staudinger, U. M. (2000). Wisdom: A metaheuristic (pragmatic) to orchestrate mind and virtue toward excellence. *American Psychologist, 55*, 122–136.

Birren, J. E., & Fisher, L. M. (1990). The elements of wisdom: Overview and integration. In R. J. Sternberg (Ed.), *Wisdom: Its nature, origins, and development* (pp. 317–332). New York: Cambridge University Press.

Blanchard-Fields, F. (1986). Reasoning on social dilemmas varying in emotional saliency: An adult developmental perspective. *Psychology and Aging, 1*, 325–333.

Block, J. (1961). *The Q-sort method in personality assessment and psychological research*. Springfield, IL: Charles C. Thomas.

Böhmig-Krumhaar, S., Staudinger, U. M., & Baltes, P. B. (2002). Mehr Toleranz tut Not: Läßt sich wert-relativierendes Denken und Urteilen verbessern? (In need of more tolerance: Is it possible to facilitate value relativism?). *Zeitschrift für Entwicklungspsychologie und Pädagogische Psychologie, 36*, 30–43.

Boylin, W., Gordon, S. K., & Nehrke, M. F. (1976). Reminiscence and ego integrity in institutionalized elderly males. *Gerontologist, 16*, 118–124.

Clayton, V. P. (1975). Erikson's theory of human development as it applies to the aged: Wisdom as contradictory cognition. *Human Development, 18*, 119–128.

Clayton, V. P., & Birren, J. E. (1980). The development of wisdom across the life span: A reexamination of an ancient topic. In P. B. Baltes & J. O. G. Brim (Eds.), *Life-span development and behavior* (Vol. 3, pp. 103–135). New York: Academic Press.

Constantinople, A. (1969). An Eriksonian measure of personality development in college students. *Developmental Psychology, 1*, 357–372.

Erikson, E. H. (1959). *Identity and the life cycle*. New York: International University Press.

Grimm, J., & Grimm, W. (1984). *Deutsches Wörterbuch* (German dictionary). München: Deutscher Taschenbuch. (Original published 1854)

Haan, N. (1969). A tripartite model of ego functioning: Values and clinical research applications. *Journal of Nervous and Mental Diseases, 148*, 14–30.

Hall, G. S. (1922). *Senescence: The last half of life*. New York: Appleton.

Hartshorne, C. (1987). *Wisdom as moderation: A philosophy of the middle way*. Albany: State University of New York Press.

Holliday, S. G., & Chandler, M. J. (1986). Wisdom: Explorations in adult competence. In J. A. Meacham (Ed.), *Contributions to human development* (Vol. 17, pp. 1–96). Basel: Karger.

Kitchener, K. S., & Brenner, H. G. (1990). Wisdom and reflective judgement: Knowing in the face of uncertainty. In R. J. Sternberg (Ed.), *Wisdom. Its nature, origins, and development* (pp. 212–229). New York: Cambridge University Press.

Kitchener, K. S., & King, P. M. (1981). Reflective judgment: Concepts of justification and their relationship to age and education. *Journal of Applied Developmental Psychology, 2*, 89–116.

Kramer, D. A. (1983). Postformal operations? A need for further conceptualization. *Human Development, 26*, 91–105.

Kramer, D. A., & Woodruff, D. S. (1986). Relativistic and dialectical thought in three adult age-groups. *Human Development, 29*, 280–290.

Labouvie-Vief, G. (1980). Beyond formal operations: Uses and limits of pure logic in life-span development. *Human Development, 23*, 141–161.

Labouvie-Vief, G. (1990). Wisdom as integrated thought: Historical and developmental perspectives. In R. J. Sternberg (Ed.), *Wisdom: Its nature, origins, and development* (pp. 52–83). New York: Cambridge University Press.

Nichols, R. (1996). Maxims, "practical wisdom," and the language of action. *Political Theory, 24*, 687–705.

Orwoll, L., & Perlmutter, M. (1990). The study of wise persons: Integrating a personality perspective. In R. J. Sternberg (Ed.), *Wisdom: Its nature, origins, and development* (pp. 160–177). New York: Cambridge University Press.

Pasupathi, M., Staudinger, U. M., & Baltes, P. B. (in press). Adolescents' knowledge and judgment about difficult matters of life. *Developmental Psychology*.

Peng, K., & Nisbett, R. E. (1999). Culture, dialectics, and reasoning about contradiction. *American Psychologist, 54*, 741–754.

Perry, W. G. (1970). *Forms of intellectual and ethical development in the college years*. New York: Rinehart & Winston.

Ryff, C. D., & Heincke, S. G. (1983). The subjective organization of personality in adulthood and aging. *Journal of Personality and Social Psychology, 44*, 807–816.

Smith, J., Staudinger, U. M., & Baltes, P. B. (1994). Occupational settings facilitating wisdom-related knowledge: The sample case of clinical psychologists. *Journal of Consulting and Clinical Psychology, 62*, 989–999.

Sowarka, D. (1989). Weisheit und weise Personen: Common-Sense-Konzepte älterer Menschen (Wisdom and wise persons: Common-sense concepts of older adults). *Zeitschrift für Entwicklungspsychologie und Pädagogische Psychologie, 21*, 87–109.

Staudinger, U. M. (1996). Wisdom and the social-interactive foundation of the mind. In P. B. Baltes & U. M. Staudinger (Eds.), *Interactive minds* (pp. 276–315). New York: Cambridge University Press.

Staudinger, U. M. (1999). Older and wiser? Integrating results from a psychological approach to the study of wisdom. *International Journal of Behavioral Development, 23*, 641–664.

Staudinger, U. M., & Baltes, P. B. (1994). The psychology of wisdom. In R. J. Sternberg (Ed.), *Encyclopedia of intelligence* (pp. 1143–1152). New York: Macmillan.

Staudinger, U. M., & Baltes, P. B. (1996). Interactive minds: A facilitative setting for wisdom-related performance? *Journal of Personality and Social Psychology, 71*, 746–762.

Staudinger, U. M., Lopez, D., & Baltes, P. B. (1997). The psychometric location of wisdom-related performance: Intelligence, personality, and more? *Personality and Social Psychology Bulletin, 23*, 1200–1214.

Staudinger, U. M., Smith, J., & Baltes, P. B. (1992). Wisdom-related knowledge in a life review task: Age differences and the role of professional specialization. *Psychology and Aging, 7*, 271–281.

Staudinger, U. M., Smith, J., & Baltes, P. B. (1994). *Manual for the assessment of wisdom-related knowledge* (Technical Report). Berlin: Max Planck Institute for Human Development.

Sternberg, R. J. (1985). Implicit theories of intelligence, creativity, and wisdom. *Journal of Personality and Social Psychology, 49*, 607–627.

Sternberg, R. J. (1998). A balance theory of wisdom. *Review of General Psychology, 2*, 347–365.

Takahashi, M., & Bordia, P. (2000). The concept of wisdom: A cross-cultural comparison. *International Journal of Psychology, 35*, 1–9.

Walaskay, M., Whitbourne, S. K., & Nehrke, M. F. (1983–1984). Construction and validation of an ego integrity status interview. *International Journal of Aging and Human Development, 18*, 61–72.

Wink, P., & Helson, R. (1997). Practical and transcendent wisdom: Their nature and some longitudinal findings. *Journal of Adult Development, 4*, 1–15.

12

Profiling Courage

Shane J. Lopez, Kristin Koetting O'Byrne,
and Stephanie Petersen

Courage is difficult to operationalize but not hard to find. Did a child you know stand up to a bully so that her siblings would not be confronted by the same treatment? That is courage. Did a client of yours say, "I will try," even though she was very scared? That is courage too. Courage is all around us. It can reflect extraordinary acts in extraordinary circumstances (thus rendering it a rare occurrence), but we believe that two positive psychology scholars have it right: Courage is "extraordinary behavior in ordinary times" (C. R. Snyder, personal communication, Sept. 2001) and "rising to the occasion" (M. E. P. Seligman, personal communication, Jan. 2001) no matter what that occasion may be.

Arguing that courage manifests itself more often than you think and that you will know it when you see it (sometimes) does not qualify as scholarly treatment of this topic. Scholarship in philosophy, psychology, and associated health fields has not taken us too far beyond the question that Socrates posed to Laches so many centuries ago, "What is courage?" In *Laches*, Socrates discusses the nature of courage with the Athenian generals Nicias and Laches, who focus on intellectual qualities and endurance in their respective views of courage. We still grapple with that definitional issue, but this core question has left us with many means to examine how courage looks and acts—we can now profile courage. Given the scientific state of affairs in this area, it may be best for us to share the many answers to the question "What is courage?" Before addressing this core question, we will distill the varied perspectives on the many brands of courage. Finally, we will address how we can better measure courage in research and practice.

The Many Brands of Courage

Courage historically has been regarded as a great virtue because it helps people to face their intrapersonal and interpersonal challenges. Philosophers offered the earliest views on understanding courage. Over the past centuries, efforts to construct a socially relevant view of courage transported it from the heart of the brave soldier on the battlefield to the experience of daily life and the mind of every person.

Centuries ago, Socrates wanted to determine the nature of courage, as well as how young men could attain this quality. Aristotle analyzed the physical courage of his "brave soldier," and Plato marveled at the moral courage of his mentors. Some of the focus of philosophy seemed to shift to the deeds and traits of veterans of moral wars with Aquinas's focus on steadfastness in the face of difficulty and Tillich's interpretation of courage as the reaffirmation of self and being. These two "brands" of courage (physical and moral) have captured most of the attention of philosophers. Physical courage, or valor, has been identified as the ability to overcome the overwhelming fear of harm or death, whereas moral courage has been discussed in terms of the behavioral expression of authenticity in the face of dissension (Larsen & Giles, 1976). A modern applied philosopher, Daniel Putman (1997), drew distinctions between moral and physical courage, and even described psychological courage. Though he acknowledged that all courage stems from a psychological process, he offered a definition of psychological courage that focused on the strength to confront destructive habits and irrational anxiety. This psychological courage may be the forebearer of what we refer to as the vital courage that is displayed daily in people's perseverance in the pursuit of mental and physical health.

Physical Courage: The Battlefield and Beyond

Andreia, or military courage, defined the "brave soldier" in ancient Greece. Finding the rugged path between cowardice and foolhardiness distinguished a Greek soldier as courageous, and hence more valuable to the force. That disposition to act appropriately in situations involving fear and confidence on the battlefield seems to be universally valued—from ancient times to present day (Rorty, 1988).

Ernest Hemingway was a primary purveyor of literature on courage in 20th-century America. His fascination with physical courage displayed in a variety of arenas (the battlefield, the open sea, the bull-fighting arena) seemed to mirror the fascination that Americans had with staring danger in the face and persevering. In fact, the "Hemingway code" (living a life characterized by strength, knowledge, and courage) provided a code of conduct for many Americans.

Fear became the focus of Jack Rachman's research after he realized that physical courage was the mirror image of the fear associated with physical jeopardy, and some people deal with the perceived danger better than others. Rachman (1984) worked with paratroopers, decorated soldiers, and bomb squad members to gather information on the nature of courage. He found that the courageous persevere and make a quick physiological recovery. He also suggested that courageous acts are not necessarily confined to a special few, nor do they always take place in public. In regard to this latter point, he became intrigued by the inner battles and private courage displayed by his psychotherapy clients. He concluded that there clearly was more to courage than *andreia* and related physical conquests over danger.

Moral Courage: Doing What Is Best and Authentic

It is apparent from the writings of Plato on Socrates's moral courage that a person can display physical as well as moral courage. As Putman (1997) noted, Socrates endured in the fight to protect Athens from conquest, but he fought a more difficult battle when he defended "a greater moral good *against* society" (p. 1). Other writers and laypersons have noted that summoning and sustaining moral courage requires incredible strength.

John F. Kennedy was fascinated by courage. He spent years gathering stories of statesmen who followed their hearts and principles when determining what was "best" for the American people—even when constituents did not agree with their decision making or value their representation. Although Kennedy himself was a military hero, he lauded moral courage, not physical courage, in his *Profiles in Courage* (1956).

Authenticity and integrity may be the fulfillments most closely associated with the expression of personal views and values in the face of dissension and rejection. Though valued aspects of "the good life," there is no guide for doing what is best or most authentic. Exactly when should one take a stand? In one example, Rosa Parks said that she took a seat at the front of a bus because it was time to do so. In another example, respondents to our five-question survey (O'Byrne, Lopez, & Petersen, 2000) noted that they valued the moral courage needed to face prejudice and hold firm to ideas when situations demanded such. Others (e.g., Finfgeld, 1998; Shelp, 1984) maintain that in a health-care context, courage should be facilitated by health-care providers in part by being truthful and straightforward. Not only does it take courage to speak the truth (Finfgeld, 1998), but it also takes courage to hear the truth. Moral courage can take on still another face when an individual stands up to someone with power over him or her (e.g., boss) for the greater good, and individuals displaying moral courage often are at risk for social disapproval (Putman, 1997).

This moral courage may be more germane to the readership of this volume than physical courage. Although physical courage may be applicable in certain circumstances, such as during psychological assessment when determining someone's readiness to perform particular occupational tasks, moral courage (and what has been referred to as vital courage, health/change courage, or psychological courage) is the platform on which positive mental health rests.

Vital Courage: Fighting for Life

Hospitals are akin to the battlefields of old. Well-trained, well-equipped professionals fight the enemy alongside their wounded brethren—together facing the fear of losing life. In our estimation, vital courage is at work as the patient battles illness through surgery, medication, and treatment regimens. Physicians, nurses, and other allied health professionals use their expertise to save lives or to improve quality of life of those they serve. Many researchers have examined vital courage (though not calling it such) and their work has captured the phenomenon that captivates us when we hear about someone facing chronic illness.

Haase (1987) used a phenomenological approach to study the subjective experiences of courage in nine chronically ill adolescents. An eight-step process of analysis was used to address the answer to the question, "What is the essential structure of the lived-experience of courage in chronically ill adolescents?," and to uncover the essential structure of courage in the face of illness. Through this process Haase found that the "lived experience" (p. 69) of courage is an interpersonally assigned attribute that results from living in a specific manner through the experience of having a health condition. Initially, the lived experience involves a struggle for personal awareness of the nature and impact of the situation. Through daily encounters with "minisituations" of courage (e.g., treatment, procedures, physical changes, and others that result from having this illness), the adolescent comes to awareness and resolution of the experience as one of courage. Increasingly, the situation is viewed as difficult, but not impossible. Coping strategies are developed and other aspects of life unrelated to the illness are actively pursued. Through resolution of the situation of courage, the adolescent develops a sense of mastery, competence and accomplishment, and a feeling of growth.

In interviews about courage with middle-aged adults with illnesses, Finfgeld (1998) determined that courage involves becoming aware of and accepting of the threat of a long-term health condition, solving problems through insight, and developing enhanced sensitivities to self and others. Finfgeld (1995) also interviewed older adults who were demonstrating courage in the face of chronic illness, and concluded that being courageous is a lifelong process involving factors such as significant others, values, and hope. Participants in Finfgeld's (1995) study indicated that struggle or threat elicited courage in their lives. She purports that courageous behaviors take place following the identification of a threat and problem solving, which lead one to shift from struggle to challenge. Behavioral expectations, the existence of role models, and value systems also appear to determine if and how courage unfolds. This courageous behavior may result in a sense of equanimity and absence of regret about one's life, along with a sense of personal integrity.

According to Shelp (1984), courage is a prerequisite for physicians as well as patients. Shelp stated that in addition to the "virtues" of competence and compassion, courage is an essential virtue physicians must have to effectively treat patients. Moreover, instilling courage via "encouragement" (p. 358) is required of anyone in a profession that exemplifies care and concern. Shelp stated that necessary components of courage are freedom of choice, fear of a situation, and the willingness to take risks in a situation with an uncertain, but morally worthy end. According to Shelp, when deeming an act courageous, it is important to look at the nobleness of the outcome (i.e., the more noble the end, the more appropriate it is to deem it as a courageous act). Finfgeld (1995, 1998) also echoed many of Shelp's sentiments that courage can be facilitated by health-care providers.

Psychological courage, as Putman (1997) described it, is strength in facing one's destructive habits. This form of vital courage may be quite common as we all struggle with psychological challenges in the forms of stress, sadness, and dysfunctional–unhealthy relationships. In light of these threats to our psychological stability, we stand up to our dysfunction by restructuring our beliefs or systematically desensitizing ourselves to the fears. One striking argument that Putman made about psychological courage is that there is a paucity of training for psychological courage compared to physical and moral courage. Putman goes on to say that in pop culture, we have many physically courageous and morally courageous icons presented in literary works and movies, but exemplars of psychologically courageous individuals are few and far between. Perhaps this is a result of the negative stigma surrounding mental health problems and destructive behaviors. However, it is also possible that the language surrounding vital courage is new relative to moral and physical courage, which have been acknowledged since the time of Plato and Aristotle.

The Multidimensional Nature of Courage

Although different brands of courage have come in and out of vogue, the classification of courage has yet to become more expansive. *Andreia* is not the only meaningful form of courage today. Standing up for beliefs and fighting for physical and psychological health clearly have become valued by society and scholars. Scholarship and classic literature to date have provided us with the means by which to organize our knowledge of courage. Subsequent to extensive reviews of work on courage, two groups of researchers developed similar classifications of courage. O'Byrne et al. (2000) identified three brands of courage: physical, moral, and health–change (now referred to as vital courage). Physical courage involves the attempted maintenance of societal good by the expression of physical behavior that is grounded in the pursuit of socially valued goals (e.g., a fireperson saving a child from a burning building). Moral courage is the behavioral expression of authenticity in the face of the discomfort of dissension, disapproval, or rejection (e.g., a politician invested in a "greater good" voting in an unpopular manner in a meeting). Vital courage refers to the perseverance through a disease/disability, even when the outcome is ambiguous (e.g., a child with a heart transplant maintaining her intensive treatment regimen even though her prognosis is uncertain).

In the Values in Action Classification system, a similar categorization of dimensions of courage exists. Peterson and Seligman's (2001) courage is conceptualized as a core human virtue comprising such strengths as authenticity (i.e., representing oneself to others and the self in a sincere fashion), enthusiasm–zest (i.e., thriving/having a sense of vitality in a challenging situation), industry–perseverance (i.e., taking on tasks and challenges and finishing them), and valor (i.e., taking physical, intellectual, and emotional stances in the face of danger). All of these strengths are trait-like, fulfilling, morally valued, and specific to the individual.

Though we have been able to parse out the different types of courage by establishing between-brand differences, we have been less successful at determining the elements or components of courage. Thus, what is common to all brands of courage remains unclear. Closer inspection of the answers to the question "What is courage?" may move us toward a parsimonious operationalization of the phenomenon.

What Is Courage? Moving Toward Operationalization

Socrates: "Then, Laches, suppose we set about determining the nature of courage and in the second place, proceed to inquire how the young men may attain this quality by the help of study and pursuits. Tell me, if you can, what is courage" (Plato, 1953, p. 85).

In the last few decades, scholars (e.g., Finfgeld, 1995; Haase, 1987; Putman, 1997; Rachman, 1984; Shelp, 1984) have established a theoretical and scientific springboard needed to launch a more comprehensive examination of courage. In fact, scholarly definitions of courage provide a rich database from which to draw as we attempt to operationalize the construct. See Table 12.1 for 17 different conceptualizations of courage. Perhaps Hemingway's definition is the most parsimonious description of courage. Certainly Hobbes's (cited in Rorty, 1988) view is the most critical of courageous action. Each of the other definitions provides a glimpse into what the scholars and society valued in terms of persevering in the face of fear at different times in history.

To more closely examine how laypersons view courage, O'Byrne et al. (2000) queried 97 people and found that people's views of this virtue varied considerably. For example, as seen in Table 12.2, some individuals perceive courage as an attitude (e.g., optimism), others as a behavior (e.g., saving someone's life). Some refer to mental strength, others write of physical strength. Participants discuss scenarios that can be classified as vital courage, moral courage, and physical courage, providing some support for the multidimensional nature of this virtue. Some claim that courage involves taking a risk, whereas others mention fear. However, neither of these components is found in all responses.

Attempts at Measuring Courage

Researchers and clinicians have used many different means for measuring courage. Rachman, a pioneer in courage research, measured the physiological responses associated with courageous responses to fear or stress. Finfgeld (1995, 1998) developed a system of interviews that highlighted the process of becoming and being courageous in the face of chronic illness. Buss and Craik's (1983) act–frequency approach and related sociometric procedures lend themselves to identifying courage exemplars and their qualities. And, of course, paper and pencil scales serve as quick and easy means of measurement. Each of the approaches will be discussed in turn, and the extent to which the generated discoveries have clarified courage will be highlighted.

Measuring Physiological Responses Associated With Courage

Rachman (1984) questioned the link between fearlessness and courage, asserting that frightened people can perform courageous acts. Although courage and fearlessness often are regarded as synonymous, many (see Table 12.1) have argued that perseverance despite fear is the purest form of courage. Indeed,

Table 12.1. Selected Scholarly Definitions of Courage

Scholar	Definition
Aquinas	Defined *fortitudo* as "firmness in mind in enduring or repulsing whatever makes steadfastness outstandingly difficult, that is, particularly serious dangers, primarily sustaining action to overcome fears of bodily harm and death and secondarily in persevering in attacking" (1948, p. 123).
Aristotle	Defined *andreia* (military courage) as the disposition to act appropriately in situations that involve fear and confidence—a rationally determined mean between cowardice and foolhardiness (cited in Rorty, 1988).
Finfgeld	"Being courageous involves being fully aware of and accepting the threat of a long-term health concern, solving problems using discernment, and developing enhanced sensitivities to personal needs and the world in general. Courageous behavior consists of taking responsibility and being productive" (1998, p. 153).
Gergen and Gergen	"To be courageous, then, is to remain steadfast within the bosom of those relationships from which one's sense of personal esteem and identity are derived" (1998, p. 144).
Haitch	"Courage is two-sided: there is an aspect of standing firm or fighting, and an aspect of accepting intractable realities . . . courage is the psychic strength that enables the self to face danger and death" (1995, p. 86).
Hemingway	Grace under pressure. (1995, 1996)
Hobbes	"The contempt of wounds and violent death. It inclines men to private revenges, and sometimes to endeavor the unsettling of public peace" (cited in Rorty, 1988, p. 307).
Kant	Defined *fortudido* as the "capacity and the resolved purpose to resist a strong but unjust opponent; and with regard to the opponent of the moral disposition within us" (Rorty, 1988, p. 65).
Kennedy	(Describing senators with political courage) "men whose abiding loyalty to their nation triumphed over personal and political considerations" (1956, p. 21).
Kohut	"Oppose the pressures exerted on them and remain faithful to their ideals and themselves" (1979, p. 5).
O'Byrne et al.	"Dispositional psychological courage is the cognitive process of defining risk, identifying and considering alternative actions, and choosing to act in spite of potential negative consequences in an effort to obtain "good" for self or others recognizing that this perceived good may not be realized" (2000, p. 6).
Plato	The ability to remember what is worth prizing and what is worth fearing (cited in Rorty, 1988).

(continued)

Table 12.1   *(continued)*

Scholar	Definition
Putman	Facing the fears associated with the loss of psychological stability (1997).
Rachman	Persevering in the face of fear (1984).
Seligman	The capacity to rise to the occasion (personal communication, Sept. 2001).
Shelp	"The disposition to voluntarily act, perhaps fearfully, in a dangerous circumstance, where the relevant risks are reasonably appraised, in an effort to obtain or preserve some perceived good for oneself or others recognizing that the desired perceived good may not be realized" (1984, p. 354).
Snyder	Extraordinary behavior in ordinary times (personal communication, Sept. 2001).

Rachman proposed that true courage is being willing and able to approach a fearful situation despite the presence of subjective fear. In this case, physiological responses may be measured to assess the presence of fear or stress in a given situation to determine how the courageous respond.

Rachman's (1978) research before his work on courage focused on subjective fear and one's bodily responses. When he became interested in courage, he and his colleagues (Cox, Hallam, O'Connor, & Rachman, 1983; O'Connor, Hallam, & Rachman, 1985) studied the distinction between courage and fearlessness with bomb operators, as well as the distinction between courageous acts and courageous actors. Operators who had received decorations for "gallantry" were compared to undecorated operators with comparable training and years of service. The decoration served as a method of identifying individuals with the experience of a courageous act. The individuals' performance under stress was determined by various subjective, behavioral, and psychophysiological measures. Experimental results (Cox et al., 1983) provided indications of distinctive physiological responses under stress for decorated and nondecorated bomb operators, though there were no subjective differences found. The identified courageous actors (i.e., decorated bomb operators) reported similar bodily sensations under stress to other participants. In a replication, O'Connor et al., (1985) demonstrated that decorated operators maintained a lower cardiac rate under stress than other participants. Rachman (1984) found that paratroopers reported a moderate amount of fear at the beginning of their program, but this fear subsided within five jumps. The execution of a jump despite the presence of fear (i.e., courage) was followed by a reduction of fear.

Becoming and Being Courageous

Several researchers have attempted to measure courage and determine how people "become" courageous through the use of open-ended questions/ interviews asking the individual to describe a situation involving courage

Table 12.2. Laypersons' Responses to the Question, "What Is Courage?"

- Taking action (either mental, physical, or spiritual) that is difficult because it makes you uncomfortable (because it is dangerous, threatening, or difficult).
- Doing something outside of one's comfort zone—fine line between courage and stupidity.
- Taking risks in the face of possible failure and uncertainty.
- Ability to take what life gives and make the best out of one's life (positive attitude involved).
- Initiate risk-taking behavior in the face of a threatening situation toward one's emotional/psychological/spiritual/physical health.
- Standing up for what one believes in, even if others don't feel the same.
- Standing up for oneself in the face of adversity or harm, even when the consequences are known.
- Willingness to take risks, not knowing if one may fail or succeed (being brave).
- Sacrificing, working, or helping a cause; faith.
- Proceeding in a situation even when one is unsure about the outcome; challenging the norm in the best interest of society.
- Ability to face threats/fears/challenges and overcome obstacles.
- Ability to contain one's fear enough to progress with a task.
- Self-confidence, belief in self and situations, making a choice and acting on it, strength.
- Bravery; act of strength/wisdom in moments of crisis.
- Defending a viewpoint that is different from the norm; standing up for what one believes in.
- Having the power and strength to face difficulties or challenges.
- Taking responsible risks, sacrificing part of oneself.
- Facing challenges rather than running away or pretending they don't exist.
- Displaying actions that go along with one's beliefs.
- Risking failure; determination in the face of failure.
- Form of assistance during a dangerous or life-threatening event.
- Selfless behavior; displaying concern for others rather than oneself.
- Committing act of perceived bravery that ordinary person might not do.
- Being mentally/physically strong.
- Under strenuous situations/circumstances, an individual engages in a behavior knowing that negative consequences may occur because of that behavior/action taken.

Note. Major themes: taking risks (possible failure, negative consequences, uncertainty), particular attitude, facing challenges, and defending beliefs.

(Finfgeld, 1995, 1998; Haase, 1987; Szagun & Schauble, 1997). Haase (1987) used a phenomenological, descriptive method of assessment. In an unstructured interview format with chronically ill adolescents, each participant identified and described his or her courageous experience. Specifically, the participants were asked to think about a situation of courage that they experienced before the interview and were given a written copy of instructions stating, "Describe a situation in which you were courageous. Describe your experience as you remember it, include your thoughts, feelings, and perceptions as you remember experiencing them. Continue to describe the experience until you feel it is fully described" (p. 66). This statement demonstrates an assumption that all individuals have the capacity for, and past experience with courage. Haase's findings regarding courage point to the development of attitudes and coping methods rather than descriptions of so-called "born heroes." Clarifying questions also were posed at appropriate times during the interview. She then used an eight-step process of data analysis that involved listening and transcribing tapes, extracting significant statements and formulating more general restatements, and organizing theme clusters and categories.

Finfgeld (1995) examined courage in older adults with chronic illnesses using a grounded theory methodology. Interview questions were generated from Haase's research on courage of adolescents, and other questions were developed from hypotheses that emerged throughout the study. In a 1998 study with chronically ill middle-age adults Finfgeld again used grounded theory, with qualitative data analysis methods. Potential participants were selected based on theoretical sampling procedures; some individuals were recruited by finding support group meetings and identifying individuals demonstrating courageous behavior.

Evans and White (1981) developed a methodology to determine attributions for being courageous, then correlated attributed fear and attributed bravery (they viewed bravery and courage as synonymous). Adolescent participants were asked to view videotaped sequences and then answer questions. The three questions asked were, (a) "How frightened did you think the person in the film was?"; (b) "How would you have felt about picking up the snake?"; and (c) "How brave did you think the person in the film was?" They found that correlations moved from negative to positive with increasing age of the participant, which reflects a more sophisticated concept of bravery, allowing for some amount of fear.

Regarding younger children's conceptualizations of courage, Szagun (1992) studied 5- to 12-year-olds using structured individual interviews asking them to rate the degree of courage for 12 different risks (on a 5-point scale ranging from not courageous to very courageous) and asking them to judge courage vignettes. It was not surprising that younger children (5- to 6-year olds) likened courage to the difficulty of the task at hand and being fearless, whereas older children (8- to 9-year-olds) likened courage to subjective risk taking and overcoming fear. Still older children (11- to 12-year-olds) reported that being fully aware of a risk at the time of acting is a necessary component of courage (Szagun, 1992). Not surprising given their developmental stage, the younger group rated physical risks as more courageous than other risks (e.g., psychological risks).

More recently, Szagun and Schauble (1997) investigated courage using an interview technique for younger children and an open-ended questionnaire for adolescents and adults. The researchers asked participants to recall and describe a situation in which they had acted courageously, focusing on the thoughts and feelings of that situation. Children were asked about courage through the use of a short story focusing on a specific character. Young children did not consider fear or overcoming fear in describing the experience of courage, but equating courage with the experience of fear increased with age. Similar to past research (Szagun, 1992), younger respondents conceptualized courage as more physical risk taking, whereas older respondents focused on psychological risk taking as a requisite to courage. Older respondents also conceptualized courage as a multifaceted emotional experience with overcoming fear, self-confidence, and an urge to act.

The Act–Frequency Approach and Sociometric Methodology

Buss and Craik's (1983) act–frequency approach serves as a means of having people identify individuals who demonstrate a particular trait and supporting the nomination with details of the behaviors the nominee has engaged in that are consistent with the state or the trait. For instance, the chapter authors are in the process of having schoolteachers identify students who show the most courage. The teachers are then asked to list five actions or behaviors that the nominees have performed that reflect or exemplify courage. This process is valuable because it identifies exemplars of courage and the structure of their courage. In addition, the approach can provide the information needed to create an individual-differences measure of courage.

Sociometric methodology also may be instrumental in the detection of people with courage who are part of a particular group (e.g., a family, team, and firm). This is a simple approach in which all members of a group are asked choice (e.g., Who would you recruit to join you in a demonstration against a company's unfair hiring practices?) and rejection (e.g., Who would you not look to when seeking support in a dispute?) questions. Via this interview process (see Hale, 1985, for details), group members use their interpersonal experiences to collectively determine who might possess the courage necessary to occupy a leadership role in the group.

Brief Scales

In the context of the positive psychology movement in the field, efforts are being made to measure aspects of a positive life. Brief questionnaires are being developed or revised to effectively tap the strengths within every individual. This psychometric work, as suggested in other chapters in this volume, has been going on for decades. Specifically regarding measures of courage, efforts to devise a brief scale have been somewhat sporadic. In 1976, Larsen and Giles developed a scale to measure two types of courage: existential (akin to moral courage) and social courage (related to physical courage). Twenty-two items tap the social-courage domain and 28 examine existential courage. Psychometric support for this measure is limited, and little if any work has been done to refine the scale.

More recent scale development has been completed by positive psychology research teams working on what has been called "wellsprings" measures. The first version of a wellsprings measure included five items (e.g., "I have taken a stand in the face of strong resistance") that tap courage. Because courage is identified as one of six core virtues being assessed in the second version of the wellsprings, much work is going into creating a psychometrically sound instrument (Peterson & Seligman, 2001).

Conceptual and Measurement Issues

The psychology of courage is not well-understood. We have no consensus on the initiating forces for courage (fear or fearlessness), uncertainty about whether it is a dispositional variable, and little understanding of how it fits into the larger framework of psychological strength and healthy processes. Without a theoretical framework that outlines testable tenets we will have difficulty identifying the true spark for courage. (In fact, a comprehensive theory that addresses the different brands of courage is needed because physical, moral, and vital courage may have different eliciting forces.) The *tonic* versus *phasic* element of courage also needs to be clarified. If courage is a tonic phenomenon, demonstrating a trait-like quality found within an individual, then scales could yield a meaningful representation of this strength. On the other hand, if courage is phasic, only emerging in its pure form when "needed" in a given situation, observation, narrative reports, experience-sampling methods, and critical incident techniques would be needed to tap this strength. Finally, subsequent to validation of a theoretically based measurement system, we must determine how courage relates to other characteristics, processes, and fulfillments. In other words, do we truly need courage to be, to create, and to heal as suggested by psychologists and popular authors?

Conclusion

Courage has been referred to as a neglected virtue (Shelp, 1984) because it has received so little attention by scholars. Although there has been relatively little scholarly attention given to courage, one could argue that it is much more commonly expressed in individual's lives than previously thought. Courage is an important part of living life and dealing with the challenges and stresses that inevitably accompany life. Courage may be viewed as an important part of coping, and even as necessary to the coping process, depending on the circumstances. With a view such as this, courage may be thought of as attainable for any person. We hope that by profiling courage we have intrigued you and given you some tools to find courage in your everyday world and to contribute to the scholarship that will become the psychology of courage.

References

Aquinas, T. (1948). *Introduction to St. Thomas Aquinas: The Summa theologica, The Summa contra gentiles* (Trans. and Ed. A Pegis). New York: Random House.

Buss, D. M., & Craik, K. H. (1983). The act–frequency approach to personality. *Psychological Review, 90*, 105–126.

Cox, D., Hallam, R., O'Connor, K., & Rachman, S. (1983). An experimental analysis of fearlessness and courage. *British Journal of Psychology, 74*, 107–117.

Evans, P. D., & White, D. G. (1981). Towards an empirical definition of courage. *Behavior Research and Therapy, 19*, 419–424.

Finfgeld, D. L. (1995). Becoming and being courageous in the chronically ill elderly. *Issues in Mental Health Nursing, 16*, 1–11.

Finfgeld, D. L. (1998). Courage in middle-aged adults with long-term health concerns. *Canadian Journal of Nursing Research, 30*(1), 153–169.

Gergen, M. M., & Gergen, K. J. (1998). The relational rebirthing of wisdom and courage. In S. Srivastva & D. L. Cooperrider (Eds.), *Organizational wisdom and executive courage* (pp. 134–153). San Francisco: New Lexington Press.

Haase, J. E. (1987). Components of courage in chronically ill adolescents: A phenomenological study. *Advances in Nursing Science, 9*(2), 64–80.

Hale, A. E. (1985). *Conducting clinical sociometric explorations. A manual for psychodramatists and sociometrists.* Roanoke, VA: Royal.

Haitch, R. (1995). How Tillich and Kohut find courage in faith. *Pastoral Psychology, 44,* 83–97.

Hemingway, E. (1995). *The sun also rises.* New York: Scribner's. (Original published 1926)

Hemingway, E. (1996). *The old man and the sea.* New York: Scribner's. (Original published 1952)

Kennedy, J. F. (1956). *Profiles in courage.* New York: Harper and Brothers.

Kohut, H. (1979). *Self-psychology and the humanities: Reflections on a new psychoanalytic approach.* New York: W. W. Norton.

Larsen, K. S., & Giles, H. (1976). Survival or courage as human motivation: Development of an attitude scale. *Psychological Reports, 39,* 299–302.

O'Byrne, K. K., Lopez, S. J., & Petersen, S. (2000, Aug.). *Building a theory of courage: A precursor to change?* Paper presented at the 108th Annual Convention of the American Psychological Association, Washington, DC.

O'Connor, R., Hallam, R., & Rachman, S. (1985). Fearlessness and courage: A replication experiment. *British Journal of Psychology, 76,* 187–197.

Peterson, C., & Seligman, M. E. P. (2001). Values in action (VIA) classification of strengths. Retrieved July 7, 2001, from http://psych.upenn.edu/seligman/taxonomy.htm

Plato. (1953). *The dialogues of Plato, Volume 1: Laches* (Trans. B. Jowett). New York: Appleton.

Putman, D. (1997). Psychological courage. *Philosophy, Psychiatry and Psychology, 4*(1), 1–11.

Rachman, S. J. (1978). Human fears: A three-systems analysis. *Scandinavian Journal of Behaviour Therapy, 7,* 237–245.

Rachman, S. J. (1984). Fear and courage. *Behavior Therapy, 15,* 109–120.

Rorty, A. O. (1988). *Mind in action: Essays in the philosophy of mind.* Boston: Beacon Press.

Shelp, E. E. (1984). Courage: A neglected virtue in the patient-physician relationship. *Social Science and Medicine, 18*(4), 351–360.

Szagun, G. (1992). Age-related changes in children's understanding of courage. *Journal of Genetic Psychology, 153,* 405–420.

Szagun, G., & Schauble, M. (1997). Children's and adults' understanding of the feeling experience of courage. *Cognition and Emotion, 11*(3), 291–306.

Part III

Emotional Models and Measures

13

Measuring Positive Emotions

Richard E. Lucas, Ed Diener, and Randy J. Larsen

The diverse chapters in this handbook illustrate that the field of positive psychology encompasses areas of research that extend beyond the psychology of positive subjective experience. Positive psychologists value characteristics such as creativity, wisdom, and empathy, even if these characteristics do not always lead to feelings of happiness. Yet the field would be incomplete if it failed to incorporate individuals' subjective experiences. It would be hard to argue that an individual had a positive, fulfilling life if he or she did not have the sense that life was rewarding. One central feature of the subjectively rewarding life is the experience of pleasant emotions. Judgments of happiness and life satisfaction are consistently and moderately to strongly correlated with the frequency with which one experiences pleasant emotions such as joy, contentment, excitement, affection, and energy (Diener & Lucas, 2000). These emotions often indicate that one's life is going well.

Yet the role of positive emotions extends beyond a simple signal that one's life is on the right track. Positive emotions also may serve specific functions and may play a role in helping individuals achieve positive outcomes. Research suggests that positive emotions cause people to become more creative (e.g., Estrada, Isen, & Young, 1994; Isen, Daubman, & Nowicki, 1987) and more affiliative (e.g., Cunningham, 1988; Isen, 1987). Happy people even make more money than unhappy people (Diener, Nickerson, Lucas, & Sandvik, 2002). Furthermore, individual differences in the tendency to experience positive emotions have implications for personality traits: Some researchers claim that positive emotionality forms the core of the extraversion personality dimension (Lucas, Diener, Grob, Suh, & Shao, 2000; Tellegen, 1985; Watson & Clark, 1997). Therefore, positive emotions must assume a central role, both as an outcome variable and an input variable, in a comprehensive positive psychology.

To understand positive emotions, it is essential that our measures of positive emotions are adequate. However, it is not enough simply to examine the reliability and validity of our emotion scales. Emotions are complex phenomena with a broad array of components that range from purely subjective feelings to action tendencies, and from observable behaviors to specific physiological changes. Often, these various components are only modestly related, and by measuring only one or two of these components, researchers may miss part of the picture. In this chapter, we will discuss some of the issues surrounding the measurement of positive emotions. This will enable psychologists to understand, evaluate, and select positive emotion measures.

Definition and Models of Positive Emotions

What is an *emotion*? Unfortunately, there is no single, widely agreed on answer to this question (see, e.g., Frijda, 1999; Kleinginna & Kleinginna, 1981; Larsen & Fredrickson, 1999; Ortony & Turner, 1990). Instead, most theorists define emotions in terms of multiple components, each of which is included in some, but not all definitions of the construct. Frijda (1999), for example, argued that emotions are made up of the following components: (a) affect, or the experience of pleasure or pain; (b) appraisal of an object or event as good or bad; (c) action readiness, or the readiness for changes in behavior toward the environment; (d) autonomic arousal; and (e) cognitive activity changes. Yet some researchers have included certain nonvalenced feeling states in their lists of basic emotions even though these states do not meet these criteria. For example, Ortony and Turner (1990) pointed out that surprise, interest, and desire often are included in lists of basic emotions, even though these feelings are not clearly affectively valenced. Surprise, interest, and desire can all be pleasant, unpleasant, or completely neutral. Similarly, Fredrickson (1998) noted that many positive emotions do not have easily identifiable action tendencies. Therefore, the components that Frijda listed can be seen as a description of possible components rather than a definition of emotions.

It may seem that some of these definitional issues are made moot by this chapter's focus on positive emotions. One may argue that a positive emotion by definition must be affectively valenced. Unfortunately, there also are disagreements about what is positive about positive emotions. For some, positive emotions are simply those that have a pleasant valence (e.g., Larsen & Diener, 1992). For others, however, positive emotions result from a behavioral activation system that motivates approach behavior. According to this approach, positive emotions are not simply pleasant. Instead, they are positive if they lead to approach behavior. Affectively neutral feelings like interest would be considered positive emotions, whereas pleasantly valenced feelings like contentment and relaxation would not. These definitional issues become measurement issues when psychologists have specific hypotheses about the nature of the positive emotions they are investigating. If psychologists are interested in approach behavior and activity in approach systems, they may want to assess emotions such as interest or engagement; whereas if they are interested solely in pleasantness, they may want to ensure that their measures include such emotions as contentment and relaxation. In our experience, however, different types of positive emotion scales often behave similarly (e.g., Lucas & Fujita, 2000), and the use of these different emotion scales may not make much practical difference as long as a broad range of positive emotions are sampled.

Structural Models of Positive Emotions

Emotion researchers often try to develop models that can organize the large number of emotions that exist into a smaller list of basic emotions or emotional dimensions. There are a number of alternative approaches to accomplishing this goal. Some researchers, for example, argue for the existence of a small number of basic emotions. Among the various advocates of the basic emotions approach, there is some disagreement about what constitutes a basic emotion and which emotions satisfy these requirements (Ekman, 1992a, 1992b; Izard, 1992; Ortony & Turner, 1990; Panksepp, 1992; Turner & Ortony, 1992). Fortunately, only a few distinct positive emotions have been proposed to be basic. In Ortony and Turner's (1990) review, most theorists only included a single general pleasantness emotion (e.g., joy, happiness, elation, or pleasure). More specific emotions such as courage, hope, love, and wonder (along with the questionably positive emotions of interest, surprise, and desire) were included as basic emotions less frequently. If basic emotions do exist, basic positive emotions seem to be fewer in number than basic negative emotions.

An alternative to the basic emotion approach is the dimensional approach to understanding the associations among different emotions (e.g., Russell, 1980; Watson & Tellegen, 1985). According to the dimensional approach, the covariance among distinct emotions can be reduced to a small number of important dimensions through factor analysis. Some researchers suggest that three dimensions are necessary to account for the covariance (e.g., Schimmack & Grob, 2000), but there is somewhat greater consensus that two dimensions satisfactorily account for the variability in emotion terms (e.g., Russell, 1980; Watson & Tellegen, 1985). In some of the two-factor approaches, emotion terms are described as having a circumplex structure: The emotions are thought to be equally spaced in a circle around a point formed from the intersection of the two independent emotion dimensions (for a review of circumplex approaches see Larsen & Diener, 1992; for recent evidence on the circumplex structure, see Watson, Wiese, Vaidya, & Tellegen, 1999).

Among the two-dimensional models of emotion, there are alternative approaches to understanding the specific dimensions that emerge. Specifically, within any factorial representation of mood terms, the factors can be rotated differently, and the dimensions that emerge will have different interpretations. Russell and his colleagues (Russell, 1980; Russell & Feldman Barrett, 1999), for example, argued that the factor space can be described well by independent pleasantness and arousal dimensions. Watson, Tellegen, and their colleagues (Watson & Tellegen, 1985; Watson et al., 1999), on the other hand, argued that these dimensions should be rotated 45 degrees to create independent positive affect or positive activation and negative affect or negative activation dimensions. Positive affect is a combination of high pleasantness and high arousal and includes such emotions as interested, engaged, and active; negative affect is a combination of high unpleasantness and high arousal and includes such emotions as nervous, distressed, and afraid (for a similar view see Thayer, 1978). These researchers argue that these rotated dimensions are aligned with the major clusters of emotions, and that they represent fundamental emotional systems.

It also is possible that the structure of affect and emotions may be hierarchical. Watson (2000) argued that although positive and negative affect formed two higher level factors in a hierarchy, a larger number of correlated lower order factors were needed to fully describe emotion structure. In his model, positive affect can be broken down into three distinct facets: joviality, self-assuredness, and attention. Similarly, in a theoretical analysis of positive emotions, Fredrickson (1998) argued that there were at least four distinct types of positive emotions: joy, interest, contentment, and love. Diener, Smith, and Fujita (1995) took a more systematic, empirical approach and selected emotion terms from a variety of research traditions (including cognitive approaches to emotion, biological/evolutionary approaches, and empirical approaches). Their analyses suggested that two distinct types of positive emotion were necessary to account for the variability: joy and love. All three groups of researchers (Diener et al., 1995; Fredrickson, 1998; Watson & Clark, 1992) noted, however, that positive emotions are often strongly correlated and relatively undifferentiated.

One other debate concerns whether positive emotions and negative emotions represent opposite poles of a single dimension or whether they are in fact independent dimensions. In other words, there is a question about whether one could experience positive emotions at the same time as negative emotions, or whether the presence of one indicates the absence of the other. A number of studies have investigated this issue (e.g., Diener & Emmons, 1984; Diener & Iran-Nejad, 1986; Feldman Barrett & Russell, 1998; Green, Salovey, & Truax, 1999), yet we do not believe that any resolution has been proposed that can satisfy all sides of the debate. The independence of positive and negative emotions probably depends on the time frame during which emotions are measured (e.g., Diener & Emmons, 1984), the response scale that is used, and whether multiple methods are used to measure the constructs (Green, Goldman, & Salovey, 1993). We recommend that researchers and clinicians explicitly measure positive emotions and not take the absence of negative emotions as evidence for the existence of the positive. At least in certain cases, the two are independent; and in fact, positive and negative emotions may result from different brain systems (Cacioppo, Gardner, & Berntson, 1999).

One final structural issue concerns the time frame in which positive emotions are measured. Emotions can be short-lasting responses to specific events and objects or long-lasting responses that may not be associated with anything specific. In general, the term "emotion" refers only to the former (Frijda, 1999), whereas the term "mood" refers to the latter (Morris, 1999). However, the terms have sometimes been used interchangeably, and when we talk about positive emotions in the current chapter, we refer to both emotions and moods. Both researchers and practitioners should be aware, however, that the structure and processes of emotions may differ when they are assessed during a single moment versus over long periods of time. Psychologists must decide which types of emotional reactions are of interest when they choose specific response scales and measures.

Summary and Implications of Emotion Models

Each of the approaches to understanding the nature of emotional experience has resulted in a slightly different model of positive emotions. Our discussion of these issues has necessarily been brief, and readers are advised to consult the sources cited previously if they believe that these issues will affect their assessment of positive emotions. We must point out, however, that there are a number of similarities among the different models, and for most psychologists, the major debates in the field will have few practical implications for the assessment of positive emotions. At most, there are a small number of highly correlated basic positive emotions or positive emotional dimensions. There are many short emotion questionnaires available (which we review subsequently), and most provide a broad sampling of these emotions. If one is unsure whether to measure activated positive emotions versus unactivated positive emotions, he or she could reliably assess both with only a few extra items. If the two types of positive emotions exhibited different correlations, researchers could keep them separate in their analyses; if they exhibited similar correlations, researchers could combine them to form a single measure. Of course, psychologists who are interested in the dynamics of a specific positive emotion (e.g., love, joy, contentment) should make sure that they use reliable, multiple item scales.

Methods of Assessment

Emotions are complex phenomena that comprise multiple components ranging from the purely subjective to the purely physiological. No single method of emotion assessment can possibly capture the entirety of emotional phenomena, and a complete understanding of emotion phenomena can only be gained through multiple-method investigations. Therefore, psychologists interested in positive emotions always should use multiple methods when possible. In this section, we review the different methods that have been used, and we discuss the promises and problems of using these methods for the assessment of positive emotions.

Self-Reports of Positive Emotions

Self-report emotion scales generally require respondents to indicate how frequently or intensely they are experiencing or have experienced positive emotions. The specific format of the scales can vary along a number of dimensions, and these differences can profoundly affect the measurement properties of the scale.

NUMBER OF ITEMS. The simplest way to assess positive emotions is to ask how a respondent feels using a single, broad positive emotion. For example, he or she could be asked, "How pleasant are you feeling in general" or "How happy do you feel in general?" Alternatively, if a psychologist was interested in a specific positive emotion such as excitement, he or she could ask, "How excited do you feel right now?" Scales such as these have some amount of validity and have the advantage of brevity. Unfortunately, they might suffer from low reliability.

Multiple-item scales offer the advantage of greater reliability and, in many cases, greater breadth of coverage. Multiple aspects of a single basic emotion can be assessed (e.g., contentment, happiness, joy, and elation all reflect various intensities of a single basic emotion), or multiple basic emotions can be included so that a broad range of positive emotions is sampled.

Although emotion scales can run as long as 132 items (e.g., Zuckerman & Lubin's [1985] Multiple Affect Adjective Checklist–Revised [MAACL–R]), most scales are much shorter. Because the various positive emotions are highly correlated, even scales as short as four or five items often exhibit very strong reliability (see, e.g., Diener et al., 1995; Watson & Clark, 1994).

RESPONSE SCALE. A variety of response scales have been used to measure positive emotions. Many instruments use a simple checklist approach in which participants are presented with a list of emotions and are asked to check which ones they are experiencing or have experienced during some discrete period of time (e.g., Zuckerman & Lubin, 1985). A variation of this approach asks participants to indicate, using a yes–no response scale, whether they agree with various statements that describe their emotional states (e.g., Bradburn & Caplovitz, 1965). In both cases, checks or "yes" responses are summed for an overall positive emotion score. Checklists may be more likely than other response scales to be influenced by certain response sets, and some researchers caution against their use (e.g., Green et al., 1993).

An alternative to the checklist is the Likert response scale. Again, participants are presented with a list of emotion terms or statements describing their emotional states. They are then asked to indicate how strongly they feel the emotion, how frequently they have felt the emotion in the past or how much they agree with the statement using a numbered Likert scale.

The number of points on the scales varies (generally, from five to nine points), and the specific anchors change depending on the focus of the measure. Some scales assess the strength with which a respondent has experienced an emotion, and these scales often use labels that range from "not at all or slight," "a little," "moderately," "quite a bit," to "very much" (e.g., Watson, Clark, & Tellegen, 1988). Other scales assess the frequency with which a respondent has experienced an emotion, and these scales may use anchors that refer to specific percentages of time (e.g., "0% of the time," "10% of the time," etc.) or general frequency descriptors (e.g., "never," "about half the time," "always"; Diener et al., 1995). Frequency and intensity are separable components of emotional experience and they may reflect different processes (Schimmack & Diener, 1997).

Diener, Sandvik, and Pavot (1991), for example, argued that overall happiness reflects the frequency, but not the intensity, of positive versus negative affect over time. Because these components are separable, we recommend using response scales that refer to the frequency or intensity of emotion (or both measured separately) and to avoid response scales that ambiguously measure both (e.g., "not much" or "a lot").

A variation of the Likert response scale is the visual analog scale. This approach uses a visual representation of the response options on the Likert scale. For example, participants may be presented with a series of faces that range from frowning to neutral to smiling. They can then circle the face that best reflected their own feeling state. Similarly, participants may be presented with a line separating two opposing adjectives, or a thermometer indicating intensity of an emotion. Participants can indicate how they feel by making a mark somewhere on the visual analog. Visual analog scales are a useful alternative to traditional emotion measures when participants are likely to have difficulty understanding the words on a scale. For example, research with young children or with participants who speak different languages would benefit from the use of visual analog scales.

TIME FRAME. Perhaps the most important feature to consider when deciding how to assess emotion is the time frame of the instructions. As noted previously, most theorists distinguish between the short-lived reactions to specific stimuli (emotions) and the long-lasting feelings that tend to be unrelated to specific objects and events (moods). Furthermore, long-term individual differences in emotions and moods may reflect one's underlying personality dispositions. The processes that underlie moods, emotions, and temperament may differ and may be differentially related to other phenomena. Therefore, it is essential for researchers and clinicians to decide which aspect of emotional experience they wish to study and to select appropriate measures.

Many emotion questionnaires have different instructions for measuring different types of emotional experiences. For example, Watson et al. (1988) noted that their Positive And Negative Affect Schedule (PANAS) scale can be administered with instructions that ask participants to indicate how they feel "right now," "today," "in the last week," "in the last month," or "in the last few months." The shorter the time frame, the more likely one is to capture emotional responses; the longer the time frame, the more likely one is to capture mood or personality differences in emotionality. The instructions for most emotion questionnaires can be altered to assess various aspects of emotional experience.

ON-LINE VERSUS RETROSPECTIVE REPORTS. The issue of time frame should alert researchers to a related problem in emotion assessment: The dynamic nature of emotional experience. Emotions vary considerably over time. We may feel angry if we are cut off in traffic, and this event may significantly affect our mood for the rest of the day. Yet the intensity and subjective experience of anger would change dramatically in the hours following the event. Asking participants to retrospectively evaluate their emotions requires participants to remember their feelings and to accurately aggregate across this dynamic experience, a task that may be very difficult (Fredrickson & Kahneman, 1993). Often researchers who wish to capture the temporal dimension of emotional experience use on-line measures of emotion and mood (e.g., Kahneman, 1999). For example, researchers can ask participants to carry palm-top computers programmed to assess positive emotions at random times throughout the day. A low-cost alternative to this procedure can be undertaken using inexpensive watches that have alarms to remind participants to complete paper-and-pencil emotion questionnaires (though compliance cannot be assessed with paper-and-pencil inventories). Alternatively, psychologists who are interested in shorter emotional experiences can use a variety of new techniques to assess changes in emotion over time in the laboratory. For example, sliding meters and rotating dials can be used to assess emotional experience over time. Participants can change the dials and meters as their emotions change.

By assessing emotions over time, psychologists can examine a number of features of emotional experience. Multiple emotion reports can be decomposed into distinct components. For example, separate frequency and intensity scores can be calculated; and emotional reactivity can be examined by calculating variability in emotions or peak levels of emotional experience. Similarly, different sampling strategies can be used to emphasize emotions versus mood. An event-sampling strategy, where participants are asked to complete a report any time a significant emotional even takes place, is likely to capture emotional reactions to specific events. A random-sampling strategy, where participants are signaled randomly throughout the day, may capture context-free mood to a greater extent. The use of different strategies allows different aspects of emotional experience to be investigated. Furthermore, participants often have difficulty remembering and accurately aggregating across multiple affective experiences when they are asked how much positive emotion they have experienced over long periods of time (Robinson & Clore, 2000). On-line experience can be compared to retrospective judgments of positive emotions to assess how well participants can remember and report the emotions they experienced. On-line emotion assessment is becoming an increasingly important part of a comprehensive study of positive emotional experience.

SPECIFIC POSITIVE EMOTION MEASURES. Table 13.1 presents a list of 12 widely used self-report positive emotion scales. Most are embedded within larger emotion questionnaires that assess a broad range of emotional experiences. Some were designed specifically to measure individual differences in emotionality (e.g., Tellegen & Waller's [1994] Multidimensional Personality Questionnaire), whereas most can be used to measure individual differences or momentary experience of emotion depending on the specific instructions and response scales. As noted previously, theories about the structure of positive emotions differ, and the measures described in Table 13.1 reflect these differences. Some measures focus on basic positive emotions or lower level facets of positive emotional experience; whereas others focus on broad pleasantness or activated positive emotion dimensions. Most lower order scales can be combined to form a single higher order positive emotion scale. Because most positive emotions are highly intercorrelated (especially at an individual difference level; see Zelenski & Larsen, 2000), all of the scales listed in Table 13.1 exhibit strong internal consistency and strong evidence of validity (with the possible exception of the Affect Balance scale; see Larsen, Diener, & Emmons, 1985). Also included is a measure of cognitive well-being, the Satisfaction With Life scale (Diener, Emmons, Larsen, & Griffin, 1985). Measures of cognitive well-being are

Table 13.1. Summary of Positive Emotion Measures

Measure items	Authors	Subscales	Items	Positive emotions subscales
Activation–deactivation Adjective checklist	Thayer (1967)	2	28	Energetic arousal
Affect balance scale	Bradburn and Caplovitz (1965)	2	10	Positive emotions
Affect grid	Russell, Weiss, and Mendelsohn (1989)	2	1	Pleasantness
Differential emotion scale	Izard, Dougherty, Bloxom, & Kotsch (1974)	10	30	Surprise, interest, enjoyment
Intensity and time affect scale	Diener, Smith, and Fujita (1995)	6	24	Love, joy
Mood adjective checklist	Nowlis and Green (1957)	12	130	Surgency, elation, social affection, vigor
Multiple affect adjective checklist	Zuckerman and Lubin (1985)	5	132	Positive affect
Multidimensional personality questionnaire	Tellegen and Waller (1994)	11	300	Positive emotionality
Positive and negative affect schedule	Watson, Clark, and Tellegen (1988)	2	20	Activated positive affect
Positive and negative affect schedule (expanded)	Watson and Clark (1994)	11	55	Joviality, self-assurance, attentiveness
Profile of mood states	McNair, Lorr, and Droppleman (1971)	6	72	Vigor
Satisfaction with life scale	Diener, Emmons, Larsen, and Griffin (1985)	1	5	Life satisfaction

moderately correlated with the experience of positive emotions (Lucas, Diener, & Suh, 1996). Appendix 13.1 and 13.2 show examples of standard positive emotion and life satisfaction scales.

SUMMARY. Self-report methods of assessment are probably the easiest and most efficient way to assess positive emotions. These methods are reliable and valid, and they map closely on to the layperson's understanding of what a positive emotion actually is. Furthermore, by changing the specific items, response scales, time frames, or the specific method of assessment, self-report scales are quite flexible. Separate intensity, frequency, reactivity, and variability scores (as well as other components) can be easily computed from various emotion measures.

These separable components allow for a rich understanding of emotional experience. Yet self-reports do not provide the only insight into emotional processes, and they are certainly not infallible. Participants may be unable or unwilling to report on their true emotional experiences. Their responses may be influenced by social desirability, extreme responding, or other response styles and response sets. Furthermore, there may be aspects of emotional experience that are simply not available to subjective awareness. Therefore, self-report emotion scales should be supplemented with non–self-report measures when possible.

Non–Self-Report Methods

Most non–self-report measures of positive emotions are based on the assumption that an emotional experience comprises multiple components. For example, emotion theorists argue that emotions have an expressive component that can be recognized by others. Therefore, informant reports of emotional experience can provide a useful alternative to self-reports. Similarly, most emotion theorists argue that there are physiological correlates of emotional experience. By assessing physiological processes, researchers may be able to tap aspects of emotions that cannot be recognized by the person who is experiencing the emotion. In this section, we review the various non–self-report measures of positive emotions that have been proposed.

OBSERVER REPORTS. One simple and easily administered alternative to self-reports is the observer report. Most self-report positive emotion measures can be easily altered to create reliable and valid observer measures of emotion. By asking friends and family members to rate how frequently or intensely a target participant has experienced an emotion, researchers can get additional information about emotional experience. Informants likely have different response sets, response styles, and memory biases, and the combination of self- and informant-reports of emotion may provide more valid measures of positive emotions (Diener et al., 1995).

Although it may seem difficult for informants to judge the private and subjective emotional feelings experienced by a target, research shows that informants and targets generally agree fairly well about a target's emotional experiences. For example, Diener et al. (1995) found that self- reports of positive emotions correlated over .50 with informant reports of positive emotions.

An alternative to the known-informant approach is the expert-rater approach. Using this technique, informants who do not know the target can be trained to interpret specific signs of emotional experience (e.g., Gottman, 1993). Alternatively, untrained judges can simply be asked to judge a person's emotion after observing the target in an emotion-provoking situation. The former approach involves extensive training of raters but provides more valid and reliable emotion reports than the latter.

FACIAL MEASURES. In addition to training raters to judge emotional experience holistically, it is possible to train raters to look for specific signs of emotions in the facial expressions that targets exhibit. For example, the Facial Action Coding System (FACS; Ekman & Friesen, 1975, 1978) allows raters to make judgments about emotions based on specific muscle movements in the face. Substantial training is required, and facial coding of temporal sequences can be very time-consuming. Nonetheless, reliable and valid measures of individual differences in positive emotions can be obtained from static pictures such as yearbook photos (e.g., Harker & Keltner, 2001). Furthermore, the measurement of facial expressions can be automated using electromyographical techniques (Cacioppo, Berntson, Larsen, Poehlmann, & Ito, 2000; Cacioppo & Tassinary, 1990). These techniques measure muscle contractions in the face and compare these muscle contractions to known changes that occur when emotions are expressed.

Electromyography has the added advantage of being able to capture muscle changes that may be too small to be noticed by the naked eye. We should note that although facial measures of positive emotions offer a promising alternative to self-reports, it is unlikely that differentiated measures of positive emotions can be obtained from facial measures (Fredrickson, 1998). Instead, these techniques can probably only reliably measure general pleasantness.

PHYSIOLOGICAL MEASURES. Other psychophysiological measures have been used to measure emotion, but again, these tend to distinguish general happiness from negative emotions or to distinguish among various negative emotions. For example, Cacioppo et al. (2000) presented a meta-analysis of the literature examining the physiological correlates of different emotional experiences. The studies they reviewed measured such variables as heart rate, heart rate acceleration, blood pressure, bodily temperature, finger temperature, respiration amplitude, skin conductance, and many others. Several of these variables were able to distinguish positive from negative emotions, but they had limited success in discriminating among discrete emotions.

Other researchers have noted that certain brain regions tend to be involved in the experience and expression of distinct types of emotions and that the measurement of activity in these regions may provide a useful measure of emotional activity (either on an individual difference or momentary state level). For example Davidson (1992) reviewed evidence that the left anterior region of the brain may be responsible for positive emotions, whereas the right anterior region may be involved in the expression of negative emotions. Electroencephalogram (EEG) measures as well as PET scans and functional MRI can index this differential activity to assess positive emotional experience. Again, however, discrete emotions are unlikely to be captured by this psychophysiological approach.

EMOTION-SENSITIVE TASKS. Because emotions affect cognitive processing and action tendencies, researchers can sometimes take advantage of these effects to measure emotions themselves. Seidlitz and Diener (1993), for example, simply asked people to recall as many happy experiences from their lives as they could in a short amount of time. The number of recalled experiences was positively correlated with happiness reports. Thus, recall of positive events can be used as an indicator of elevated mood. Other studies have used other cognitive tasks such as word-completion and word-recognition tasks. Happy participants are quicker than participants in neutral states to identify positive words as words, and happy participants are more likely than unhappy participants to complete word stems to form positive words. When researchers are concerned about social desirability or other issues that may make respondents answer in untruthful ways, cognitive tasks such as these may help identify how happy the respondent really is. Rusting (1998) reviewed evidence that these cognitive tasks are sensitive to both individual differences in positive emotions as well as positive emotional states.

SUMMARY. Because emotions are known to involve more than just subjective experience, non–self-report measures are essential to our understanding of emotions and emotional processes. There is much work that is needed, however, before the various non–self-report measures can be incorporated into standard assessment batteries. Although there are a number of facial and physiological indicators that have been shown to be associated with self-reports of emotion, these indicators also are associated with other nonemotional processes. Therefore, they often are only weakly correlated with the subjective experience of emotion. Nonphysiological measures such as informant reports, behavioral tasks, and cognitive measures can easily be incorporated into research programs. However, they are often only weakly to moderately correlated with self-reports. Therefore, although we encourage multiple-method investigations, researchers should not expect strong convergence across these diverse methods.

Future Developments in the Measurement of Positive Emotions

There are four main challenges regarding the measurement of positive emotions. First, a number of the debates regarding the definition and structure of positive emotions will need to be settled. Studies are beginning to take advantage of multiple methods of assessment and modern analytical techniques such as structural equation modeling and hierarchical linear modeling to address the structure of emotions between persons and within persons over time. These sophisticated measurement approaches will help us understand the nature of emotional experience and the processes that underlie emotions themselves.

Second, psychologists must develop a better understanding of the ways that the various components of positive emotions converge. Most emotion theorists believe that emotions have multiple components including subjective experience, cognitive changes, action tendencies, and physiological changes. Yet measures of the various components are only modestly intercorrelated. Future research must determine when the components converge and why.

Third, research on the measurement of positive emotions will benefit from a closer examination of the structure of discrete positive emotions. Although many theorists argue that there are distinct basic positive emotions or at least discriminable positive emotion facets, the specific positive emotions that are identified vary across different models. Furthermore, most research shows that these different positive emotions are strongly intercorrelated. Future research must determine whether there are distinct, discriminable, basic positive emotions, and what features (appraisal patterns, physiological changes, action tendencies, etc.) can distinguish among them. Fredrickson (1998) suggested that to accomplish this goal, researchers may need to shift their strategy from the methods and theories that have been used to study negative emotions. Fredrickson argued that positive emotions are fundamentally different from negative emotions, and theories of positive emotions may need to focus on different characteristics to distinguish among and explain the various ways of feeling positive.

Fourth, clinicians and other practitioners must determine what implications these theoretical debates have for practical issues associated with the experience of positive emotions. For example, although distinct positive emotions may be strongly intercorrelated, they may exhibit differential relations with other psychological problems or clinical treatments. Understanding these relationships can help researchers and practitioners alike understand the mechanisms underlying the experience of positive emotions.

Conclusion

Positive psychologists can confidently assess positive emotions using a variety of well-validated measurement techniques. The simplest and most flexible are self-reports of emotions; and self-reports probably provide the best insight into the experience of emotion within individuals over time. In general, any reasonably diverse collection of positive emotion adjectives will capture the positive emotion dimension with a fair amount of reliability and validity. However, these self-reports must be complemented with a broad array of non–self-report measures including informant reports, facial coding, and psychophysiological measures before a complete understanding of emotional experience can be attained.

Appendix 13.1
Intensity and Time Affect Survey (ITAS)

Instructions: [During the past month/During the past week/During the past day/Right now], how [frequently/intensely] [did you experience/are you experiencing] each of the following emotions?

1	2	3	4	5	6	7
Never			About half the time			Always

1. Affection
2. Joy
3. Fear
4. Anger
5. Shame
6. Sadness
7. Love
8. Happiness
9. Worry
10. Irritation
11. Guilt
12. Loneliness
13. Caring
14. Contentment
15. Anxiety
16. Disgust
17. Regret
18. Unhappiness
19. Fondness
20. Pride
21. Nervous
22. Rage
23. Embarrassment
24. Depression

Note. Items 1, 7, 13, and 19 make up the "love" subscale; items 2, 8, 14, and 20 make up the "joy" subscale. The love and joy subscales can be combined to form an overall positive emotions scale. Different response options can be used to measure affect over different lengths of time. Frequency and intensity instructions can be used to measure different components of affective experience.

Appendix 13.2
The Satisfaction With Life Scale

Instructions: Please use one of the following numbers from 1 to 7 to indicate how much you agree or disagree with the following statements.

7   Strongly agree
6   Agree
5   Slightly agree
4   Neither agree nor disagree
3   Slightly disagree
2   Disagree
1   Strongly disagree

1. _____ In most ways my life is close to my ideal.
2. _____ The conditions of my life are excellent.
3. _____ I am satisfied with my life.
4. _____ So far I have gotten the important things I want in my life.
5. _____ If I could live my life over, I would change almost nothing.

Note. Scores for all items are summed to calculate a total score.

References

Bradburn, N. M., & Caplovitz, D. (1965). *Reports on happiness.* Chicago: Aldine.

Cacioppo, J. T., Berntson, G. G., Larsen, J. T., Poehlmann, K. M., & Ito, T. A. (2000). The psychophysiology of emotion. In M. Lewis & J. M. Haviland-Jones (Eds.), *Handbook of emotions* (2nd ed., pp. 173–191). New York: Guilford Press.

Cacioppo, J. T., Gardner, W. L., & Berntson, G. G. (1999). The affect system has parallel and integrative processing components: Form follows function. *Journal of Personality and Social Psychology, 76,* 839–855.

Cacioppo, J. T., & Tassinary, L. G. (1990). Inferring psychological significance from physiological signals. *American Psychologist, 45,* 16–28.

Cunningham, M. R. (1988). Does happiness mean friendliness? Induced mood and heterosexual self-disclosure. *Personality and Social Psychological Bulletin, 14,* 283–297.

Davidson, R. J. (1992). Anterior cerebral asymmetry and the nature of emotion. *Brain and Cognition, 20,* 125–151.

Diener, E., & Emmons, R. A. (1984). The independence of positive and negative affect. *Journal of Personality and Social Psychology, 47,* 1105–1117.

Diener, E., Emmons, R. A., Larsen, R. J., & Griffin, S. (1985). The Satisfaction With Life scale. *Journal of Personality Assessment, 49,* 71–75.

Diener, E., & Iran-Nejad, A. (1986). The relationship in experience between various types of affect. *Journal of Personality and Social Psychology, 50,* 1031–1038.

Diener, E., & Lucas, R. E. (2000). Subjective emotional well-being. In M. Lewis & J. M. Haviland-Jones (Eds.), *Handbook of emotions* (2nd ed., pp. 325–337). New York: Guilford Press.

Diener, E., Nickerson, C., Lucas, R. E., & Sandvik, E. (2002). Dispositional affect and job outcomes. *Social Indicators Research, 59,* 229–259.

Diener, E., Sandvik, E., & Pavot, W. (1991). Happiness is the frequency, not the intensity, of positive versus negative affect. In F. Strack, M. Argyle, & N. Schwarz (Eds.), *Subjective well-being: An interdisciplinary perspective. International series in experimental social psychology* (pp. 119–139). Oxford: Pergamon Press.

Diener, E., Smith, H., & Fujita, F. (1995). The personality structure of affect. *Journal of Personality and Social Psychology, 50,* 130–141.

Ekman, P. (1992a). An argument for basic emotions. *Cognition and Emotion, 6,* 169–200.

Ekman, P. (1992b). Are there basic emotions? *Psychological Review, 99,* 550–553.

Ekman, P., & Friesen, W. (1975). *Unmasking the face.* Englewood Cliffs, NJ: Prentice-Hall.

Ekman, P., & Friesen, W. (1978). *Facial Action Coding System.* Palo Alto, CA: Consulting Psychologists Press.

Estrada, C. A., Isen, A. M., & Young, M. J. (1994). Positive affect improves creative problem solving and influences reported source of practice satisfaction in physicians. *Motivation and Emotion, 18,* 285–299.

Feldman Barrett, L., & Russell, J. A. (1998). Independence and bipolarity in the structure of affect. *Journal of Personality and Social Psychology, 74,* 967–984.

Fredrickson, B. L. (1998). What good are positive emotions? *Review of General Psychology, 2,* 300–319.

Fredrickson, B. L., & Kahneman, D. (1993). Duration neglect in retrospective evaluations of affective episodes. *Journal of Personality and Social Psychology, 65,* 45–55.

Frijda, N. H. (1999). Emotions and hedonic experience. In D. Kahneman, E. Diener, & N. Schwarz (Eds.), *Well-being: The foundations of hedonic psychology* (pp. 190–210). New York: Russell Sage Foundation.

Gottman, J. M. (1993). Studying emotion in social interaction. In M. Lewis & J. M. Haviland (Eds.), *Handbook of emotions* (pp. 475–487). New York: Guilford Press.

Green, D. P., Goldman, S. L., & Salovey, P. (1993). Measurement error masks bipolarity in affect ratings. *Journal of Personality and Social Psychology, 64,* 1029–1041.

Green, D. P., Salovey, P., & Truax, K. M. (1999). Static, dynamic, and causative bipolarity of affect. *Journal of Personality and Social Psychology, 76,* 856–867.

Harker, L., & Keltner, D. (2001). Expressions of positive emotion in women's college yearbook pictures and their relationship to personality and life outcomes across adulthood. *Journal of Personality and Social Psychology, 80*, 112–124.

Isen, A. M. (1987). Positive affect, cognitive processes, and social behavior. In L. Berkowitz (Ed.), *Advances in experimental social psychology* (Vol. 20, pp. 203–253). San Diego, CA: Academic Press.

Isen, A. M., Daubman, K. A., & Nowicki, G. P. (1987). Positive affect facilitates creative problem solving. *Journal of Personality and Social Psychology, 52*, 1122–1131.

Izard, C. E. (1992). Basic emotions, relations among emotions, and emotion–cognition relations. *Psychological Review, 99*, 561–565.

Izard, C. E., Dougherty, F. E., Bloxom, B. M., & Kotsch, W. E. (1974). *The differential emotions scale: A method of measuring the subjective experience of discrete emotions.* Unpublished manuscript, Vanderbilt University, Nashville, TN.

Kahneman, D. (1999). Objective happiness. In D. Kahneman, E. Diener, & N. Schwarz (Eds.), *Well being: The foundations of hedonic psychology* (pp. 3–25). New York: Russell Sage Foundation.

Kleinginna, P. R., & Kleinginna, A. M. (1981). A categorized list of emotion definitions, with suggestions for a consensual definition. *Motivation and Emotion, 5*, 345–379.

Larsen, R. J., & Diener, E. (1992). Promises and problems with the circumplex model of emotion. In M. S. Clark (Ed.), *Review of personality and social psychology: Emotion* (Vol. 13, pp. 25-59). Newbury Park, CA: Sage.

Larsen, R. J., Diener, E., & Emmons, R. A. (1985). An evaluation of subjective well-being measures. *Social Indicators Research, 17*, 1–17.

Larsen, R. J., & Fredrickson, B. L. (1999). Measurement issues in emotion research. In D. Kahneman, E. Diener, & N. Schwarz (Eds.), *Well-being: The foundations of hedonic psychology* (pp. 40–60). New York: Russell Sage Foundation.

Lucas, R. E., Diener, E., Grob, A., Suh, E. M., & Shao, L. (2000). Cross-cultural evidence for the fundamental features of extraversion. *Journal of Personality and Social Psychology, 79*, 452–468.

Lucas, R. E., Diener, E., & Suh, E. M. (1996). Discriminant validity of subjective well-being measures. *Journal of Personality and Social Psychology, 71*, 616–628.

Lucas, R. E., & Fujita, F. (2000). Factors influencing the relation between extraversion and pleasant affect. *Journal of Personality and Social Psychology, 79*, 1039–1056.

McNair, D. M., Lorr, M., & Droppleman, L. F. (1971). *Manual: Profile of Mood States.* San Diego, CA: Educational and Industrial Testing Service.

Morris, W. N. (1999). The mood system. In D. Kahneman, E. Diener, & N. Schwarz (Eds.), *Well-being: The foundations of hedonic psychology* (pp. 169–189). New York: Russell Sage Foundation.

Nowlis, V., & Green, R. (1957). *The experimental analysis of mood.* Technical report, contract no. Nonr-668 (12). Washington, DC: Office of Naval Research.

Ortony, A., & Turner, T. J. (1990). What's basic about basic emotions? *Psychological Review, 97*, 315–331.

Panksepp, J. (1992). A critical role for "affective neuroscience" in resolving what is basic about basic emotions. *Psychological Review, 99*, 554–560.

Robinson, M., & Clore, G. L. (2000). *Belief and feeling: Evidence for an accessibility model of emotional self-report.* Manuscript submitted for publication. University of Illinois at Urbana-Champaign.

Russell, J. A. (1980). A circumplex model of affect. *Journal of Personality and Social Psychology, 39*, 1161–1178.

Russell, J. A., & Feldman Barrett, L. (1999). Core affect, prototypical emotional episodes, and other things called emotion: Dissecting the elephant. *Journal of Personality and Social Psychology, 76*, 805–819.

Russell, J. A., Weiss, A., & Mendelsohn, G. A. (1989). The Affect Grid: A single-item scale of pleasure and arousal. *Journal of Personality and Social Psychology, 57*, 493–502.

Rusting, C. L. (1998). Personality, mood, and cognitive processing of emotional information: Three conceptual frameworks. *Psychological Bulletin, 124*, 165–196.

Schimmack, U., & Diener, E. (1997). Affect intensity: Separating intensity and frequency in repeatedly measured affect. *Journal of Personality and Social Psychology, 73*, 1313–1329.

Schimmack, U., & Grob, A. (2000). Dimensional models of core affect: A quantitative comparison by means of structural equation modeling. *European Journal of Personality, 14*, 325–345.

Seidlitz, L., & Diener, E. (1993). Memory for positive versus negative life events: Theories for the difference between happy and unhappy persons. *Journal of Personality and Social Psychology, 64*, 654–663.

Tellegen, A. (1985). Structures of mood and personality and their relevance to assessing anxiety, with an emphasis on self-report. In A. H. Tuma & J. D. Maser (Eds.), *Anxiety and the anxiety disorders* (pp. 681–706). Hillsdale, NJ: Erlbaum.

Tellegen, A., & Waller, N. (1994). Exploring personality through test construction: Development of the Multidimensional Personality Questionnaire. In S. R. Briggs & J. M. Cheek (Eds.), *Personality measures: Development and evaluation* (Vol. 1, pp. 133–161). Greenwich, CT: JAI Press.

Thayer, R. E. (1967). Measurement of activation through self-report. *Psychological Reports, 20*, 663–678.

Thayer, R. E. (1978). Toward a psychological theory of multidimensional activation (arousal). *Motivation and Emotion, 2*, 1–34.

Turner, T. J., & Ortony, A. (1992). Basic emotions: Can conflicting criteria converge? *Psychological Review, 99*, 566–571.

Watson, D. (2000). *Mood and temperament*. New York: Guilford Press.

Watson, D., & Clark, L. A. (1992). On traits and temperament: General and specific factors of emotional experience and their relation to the five-factor model. *Journal of Personality, 60*, 441–476.

Watson, D., & Clark, L. A. (1994). *The PANAS-X: Manual for the Positive and Negative Affect Schedule Expanded Form*. Unpublished manuscript, University of Iowa, Iowa City.

Watson, D., & Clark, L. A. (1997). Extraversion and its positive emotional core. In R. Hogan, J. Johnson, & S. Briggs (Eds.), *Handbook of personality psychology* (pp. 767–793). San Diego, CA: Academic Press.

Watson, D., Clark, L. A., & Tellegen, (1988). Development and validation of brief measures of positive and negative affect: The PANAS scales. *Journal of Personality and Social Psychology, 54*, 1063–1070.

Watson, D., & Tellegen, A. (1985). Toward a consensual structure of mood. *Psychological Bulletin, 98*, 219–235.

Watson, D., Wiese, D., Vaidya, J., & Tellegen, A. (1999). The two general activation systems of affect. Structural findings, evolutionary considerations, and psychobiological evidence. *Journal of Personality and Social Psychology, 76*, 820–838.

Zelenski, J. M., & Larsen, R. J. (2000). The distribution of basic emotions in everyday life: A state and trait perspective from experience sampling data. *Journal of Research in Personality, 34*, 178–197.

Zuckerman, M., & Lubin, B. (1985). *Manual for the MAACL-R: The multiple affect adjective check list revised*. San Diego, CA: Educational and Industrial Testing Service.

14

Assessing Self-Esteem

Todd F. Heatherton and Carrie L. Wyland

It is generally believed that there are many benefits to having a positive view of the self. Those who have high self-esteem are presumed to be psychologically happy and healthy (Branden, 1994; Taylor & Brown, 1988), whereas those with low self-esteem are believed to be psychologically distressed and perhaps even depressed (Tennen & Affleck, 1993). Having high self-esteem apparently provides benefits to those who possess it: They feel good about themselves, they are able to cope effectively with challenges and negative feedback, and they live in a social world in which they believe that people value and respect them. Although there are negative consequences associated with having extremely high self-esteem (Baumeister, 1998), most people with high self-esteem appear to lead happy and productive lives. By contrast, people with low self-esteem see the world through a more negative filter, and their general dislike for themselves colors their perceptions of everything around them. Substantial evidence shows a link between self-esteem and depression, shyness, loneliness, and alienation—low self-esteem is aversive for those who have it. Thus, self-esteem affects the enjoyment of life even if it does not have a substantial impact on career success, productivity, or other objective outcome measures. Given the choice, however, most people would prefer to have high self-esteem.

That self-esteem is vital for psychological health is evident in the popular media and in educational policy. Indeed, some educators have changed course curricula in their attempts to instill children with high self-esteem, even to the point that in some states students are promoted to a higher grade even when they have failed to master the material from the previous grade. These social promotions are based on the belief that positive self-esteem is of cardinal importance, and that many societal ills—such as teenage pregnancy and drug use, violence, academic failure, and crime—are caused by low self-esteem. Accordingly, California enacted legislation that encouraged schools to develop self-esteem enhancement programs, the general idea being that high self-esteem would act something like a "social vaccine" that would prevent many of the serious behavioral problems facing the state (Mecca, Smelser, & Vasconcellos, 1989). Although societal ills are not caused by low self-esteem, it is easy to understand why policy makers and educators are concerned with the emotional consequences of negative self-views. Those who feel ostracized or rejected experience a variety of negative reactions, including physical illness, emotional problems, and negative affective states. Furthermore, social support is known to be a key ingredient of mental and physical health (Cohen & Wills, 1985), and people who feel disliked may be less likely to receive support from others. Thus, even if the benefits of having high self-esteem have been exaggerated (see Dawes, 1994), there is little doubt that low self-esteem is problematic for those who have it. But how exactly is self-esteem measured? This chapter examines the various ways in which self-esteem is measured and the implications that these methods have on our understanding of what it means for a person to have high or low self-esteem.

Understanding the Construct of Self-Esteem

Self-esteem is the evaluative aspect of the self-concept that corresponds to an overall view of the self as worthy or unworthy (Baumeister, 1998). This is embodied in Coopersmith's (1967) classic definition of self-esteem:

> The evaluation which the individual makes and customarily maintains with regard to himself: it expresses an attitude of approval and indicates the extent to which an individual believes himself to be capable, significant, successful and worthy. In short, self-esteem is a personal judgment of the worthiness that is expressed in the attitudes the individual holds towards himself. (pp. 4–5)

Thus, self-esteem is an attitude about the self and is related to personal beliefs about skills, abilities, social relationships, and future outcomes.

It is important to distinguish *self-esteem* from the more general term *self-concept,* because the two terms often are used interchangeably. Self-concept refers to the totality of cognitive beliefs that people have about themselves; it is everything that is known about the self, and includes things such as name, race, likes, dislikes, beliefs, values, and appearance descriptions, such as height and weight. By contrast, self-esteem is the emotional response that people experience as they contemplate and evaluate different things about themselves. Although self-esteem is related to the self-concept, it is possible for people to believe objectively positive things (such as acknowledging skills in academics, athletics, or arts), but continue to not really like themselves. Conversely, it is possible for people to like themselves, and therefore hold high self-esteem, in spite of their lacking any objective indicators that support such positive self-views. Although influenced by the contents of the self-concept, self-esteem is not the same thing.

Throughout the history of research on self-esteem, there have been concerns that the concept was poorly defined and therefore badly measured (Blascovich & Tomaka, 1991). Jackson (1984) noted that "After thirty years of intensive effort . . . what has emerged . . . is a confusion of results that defies interpretation" (p. 2). Wylie (1974), one of the chief critics of self-esteem research, blamed the area's difficulties on a lack of rigor in experimentation and a proliferation of instruments to measure self-esteem. For example, there are a large number of self-esteem instruments, and many of the scales correlate poorly with one another. Indeed, in reviewing the history of the measurement of self-esteem, Briggs and Cheek (1986) stated, "it was obvious by the mid-1970s that the status of self-esteem measurement research had become something of an embarrassment to the field of personality research" (p. 131).

How a construct is defined has obvious implications for how it is measured. As a term that is widely used in everyday language and heavily laden with social value, perhaps it should not be surprising that idiosyncratic and casual definitions have contributed to the chaos of defining and measuring self-esteem. There is not nearly enough space in this chapter to consider all of the various ways in which self-esteem has been defined. In this chapter we touch on some of the central conceptual issues that are relevant to the measure of self-esteem, including the proposed source of self-esteem, possible gender differences in which factors are most important, and differential views of the dimensionality and stability of self-esteem.

Sources of Self-Esteem

There are many theories about the source of self-esteem. For instance, William James (1890) argued that self-esteem developed from the accumulation of experiences in which people's outcomes exceeded their goals on some important dimension, under the general rule that *self-esteem = success/pretensions*. From this perspective, assessment has to examine possible discrepancies between current appraisals and personal goals and motives. Moreover, self-perceived skills that allow people to reach goals are also important to assess. Thus, measures ought to include some reference to personal beliefs about competency and ability.

Many of the most popular theories of self-esteem are based on Cooley's (1902) notion of the *looking-glass self*, in which self-appraisals are viewed as inseparable from social milieu. Mead's (1934) *symbolic interactionism* outlined a process by which people internalize ideas and attitudes expressed by significant figures in their lives. In effect, individuals come to respond to themselves in a manner consistent with the ways of those around him. Low self-esteem is likely to result when key figures reject, ignore, demean, or devalue the person. Subsequent thinking by Coopersmith (1967) and Rosenberg (1965, 1979), as well as most contemporary self-esteem research, is well in accord with the basic tenets of symbolic interactionism. According to this perspective, it is important to assess how people perceive themselves to be viewed by significant others, such as friends, classmates, family members, and so on. Some recent theories of self-esteem have emphasized the norms and values of the cultures and societies in which people are raised. For instance, Crocker and her colleagues have argued that some people experience *collective* self-esteem because they are especially likely to base their self-esteem on their social identities as belonging to certain groups (Luhtanen & Crocker, 1992).

Leary, Tambor, Terdal, and Downs (1995) have proposed a novel and important social account of self-esteem. Sociometer theory begins with the assumption that humans have a fundamental need to belong that is rooted in our evolutionary history (Baumeister & Leary, 1995). For most of human evolution, survival and reproduction depended on affiliation with a group. Those who belonged to social groups were more likely to survive and reproduce than those who were excluded from groups. According to the sociometer theory, self-esteem functions as a monitor of the likelihood of social exclusion. When people behave in ways that increase the likelihood they will be rejected, they experience a reduction in state self-esteem. Thus, self-esteem serves as a monitor, or sociometer, of social acceptance–rejection. At the trait level, those with high self-esteem have sociometers that indicate a low probability of rejection, and therefore such individuals do not worry about how they are being perceived by others. By contrast, those with low self-esteem have sociometers that indicate the imminent possibility of rejection, and therefore they are highly motivated to manage their public impressions. There is an abundance of evidence that supports the sociometer theory, including the finding that low self-esteem is highly correlated with social anxiety. Although the sociometer links self-esteem to an evolved need to belong rather than to symbolic interactions, it shares with the earlier theories the idea that social situations need to be examined to assess self-esteem.

Gender Differences in Self-Esteem

A number of studies suggest that boys and girls diverge in their primary source of self-esteem, with girls being more influenced by relationships and boys being more influenced by objective success. Stein, Newcomb, and Bentler (1992) examined participants in an eight-year study of adolescent development. During adolescence, an agentic orientation predicted heightened self-esteem for males but not for females, whereas a communal orientation predicted heightened self-esteem for females but not for males. Men and women show this same pattern. Josephs, Markus, and Tafarodi (1992) exposed men and women to false feedback indicating that they had deficits either on a performance dimension (e.g., competition, individual thinking) or on a social dimension (e.g., nurturance, interpersonal integration). Consistent with predictions, men high in self-esteem enhanced their estimates at being able to engage successfully in future performance behaviors, whereas women high in self-esteem enhanced their estimates at being able to engage successfully in future social behaviors. Overall, then, it appears that males gain self-esteem from getting ahead whereas females gain self-esteem from getting along.

In terms of another salient gender difference in feelings about the self across the lifespan, women tend to have lower body image satisfaction than men. Women are more likely than men to evaluate specific body features negatively, to attempt weight loss, to report anxiety about the evaluation of their physical appearance, and to have cosmetic surgery (Heatherton, 2001). Body image dissatisfaction among women usually is related to perceiving oneself to be overweight. More than three quarters of American women would like to lose weight and almost none would like to gain weight. Believing oneself to be overweight, whether one is or is not, is closely related to body image dissatisfaction. Beginning in early adolescence, women compare their body shape and weight with their beliefs about cultural ideals. A discrepancy from the ideal often motivates people to undertake dieting to achieve a more attractive body size. Dieting is rarely successful, with fewer than 1% of individuals able to maintain weight loss over five years (NIH Technology Assessment Conference Panel, 1993). Repeated failures may exacerbate body image dissatisfaction and low self-esteem (Heatherton & Polivy, 1992). Women with perfectionistic tendencies and low self-esteem are particularly affected by dissatisfaction, such that these personality traits in combination have been linked to increased bulimic symptoms (Vohs, Bardone, Joiner, Abramson, & Heatherton, 1999). Black women are less likely to consider themselves obese and are more satisfied with their weight than are White women despite the fact that Black women are twice as likely to *be* obese. These women also rate large Black body shapes more positively than do White women rating large White body shapes (Hebl & Heatherton, 1998). In contrast to women, men are more likely view their bodies as instruments of action and derive self-esteem from self-perceived physical strength (Franzoi, 1995). Therefore, in terms of assessing personal feelings about body-esteem issues, researchers need to be sensitive to the differential determinants of body image for women and men.

Dimensionality of Self-Esteem

Self-esteem can refer to the overall self or to specific aspects of the self, such as how people feel about their social standing, racial or ethnic group, physical features, athletic skills, job or school performance, and so on. An important issue in the self-esteem literature is whether self-esteem is best conceptualized as a unitary global trait or as a multidimensional trait with independent subcomponents. According to the global approach, self-esteem is considered an overall self-attitude that permeates all aspects of people's lives. In this regard, Robins, Hendin, and Trzesniewski (2001) developed a single-item measure of global self-esteem. It merely consists of the statement, "I have high self-esteem," with a 5-point scale. They found that this single item correlated to a similar extent as the most widely used trait scale with a variety of measures, including domain-specific evaluations, personality factors, and psychological well-being.

Self-esteem also can be conceptualized as a hierarchical construct such that it can be broken down into its constituent parts. From this perspective, there are three major components: *performance* self-esteem, *social* self-esteem, and *physical* self-esteem (Heatherton & Polivy, 1991). Each of these components, in turn, can be broken down into smaller and smaller subcomponents. Performance self-esteem refers to one's sense of general competence and includes intellectual abilities, school performance, self-regulatory capacities, self-confidence, efficacy, and agency. People who are high in performance self-esteem believe that they are smart and capable. Social self-esteem refers to how people believe others perceive them. Note that it is perception rather than reality that is most critical. If people believe that others, especially significant others, value and respect them, they will experience high social self-esteem. This occurs even if others truly hold them in contempt. People who are low in social self-esteem often experience social anxiety and are high in public self-consciousness. They are highly attentive to their image and they worry about how others view them. Finally, physical self-esteem refers to how people view their physical bodies, and includes such things as athletic skills, physical attractiveness, body image, as well as physical stigmas and feelings about race and ethnicity.

How are these subcomponents of self-esteem related to global self-esteem? William James (1892) proposed that global self-esteem was the summation of specific components of self-esteem, each of which is weighted by its importance to the self-concept. In other words, people have high self-esteem to the extent that they feel good about those things that matter to them. Not being good at tennis is irrelevant to the self-concept of the nonathlete, whereas doing poorly in school may have little impact on some innercity youth who have disidentified from mainstream values (Steele, 1997). On this point, Brett Pelham (1995) and Herbert Marsh (1995) have debated the value of global versus specific component models. Pelham's research has generally supported the Jamesian view that the centrality of self-views is an important predictor of the emotional response to self (i.e., one's feelings of self-esteem), whereas Marsh has claimed that domain importance does not relate strongly to self-esteem. Although the jury is still out on this issue, the concept of domain importance is a central feature of most theories of self-esteem.

Stability of Self-Esteem

Another issue in the measurement and definition of self-esteem is whether it is best conceptualized as a stable personality trait or as a context-specific state. Most theories of self-esteem view it as a relatively stable trait: if you have high self-esteem today, you will probably have high self-esteem tomorrow. From this perspective, self-esteem is stable because it slowly builds over time through personal experiences, such as repeatedly succeeding at various tasks or continually being valued by significant others. A number of studies, however, suggest self-esteem serves as the dependent rather than the independent or classification variable (Wells & Marwell, 1976). These studies assume that self-esteem can be momentarily manipulated or affected. Others suggest that self-esteem is not manipulable *by definition*.

According to subsequent views, however, self-esteem can be viewed as a "state" as well as a trait (Heatherton & Polivy, 1991). Around a stable baseline are fluctuations; although we might generally feel good about ourselves, there are times when we may experience self-doubt and even dislike. Fluctuations in state self-esteem are associated with increased sensitivity to and reliance on social evaluations, increased concern about how one views the self, and even anger and hostility (Kernis, 1993). In general, those with a fragile sense of self-esteem respond extremely favorably to positive feedback and extremely defensively to negative feedback.

Individuals Difference Measures of Self-Esteem

Given the importance attached to self-esteem by many people and the fact that it also has defied consensual definition, it is not surprising that there are many measures of self-esteem Unfortunately, the majority of these measures have not performed adequately, and it is likely that many of them measure very different constructs because the correlations between these scales range from zero to .8, with an average of .4 (Wylie, 1974).

Some self-esteem measures are better than others. Crandall (1973) reviewed 33 self-esteem measures in detail and judged four to be superior: Rosenberg's Self-Esteem scale (Rosenberg, 1965), the Janis–Field Feelings of Inadequacy scale (Janis & Field, 1959), the Coopersmith Self-Esteem Inventory (1967); and the Tennessee Self-Concept scale (Fitts, 1964). Except for the Rosenberg, which measures global self-esteem, the others are multidimensional and measure various affective qualities of self-concept. In a test of eight measures of self-esteem (including projectives, interviews, self-report, and peer ratings), Demo (1985) found that the Rosenberg and Coopersmith scales performed best in factor analysis.

Blascovich and Tomaka's (1991) careful examination of numerous measures of self-esteem led them to conclude that no perfect measure exists and that few of the conceptual and methodological criticisms had been answered. They recommended a revision of the Janis–Field scale (described shortly) as one of the better measures of trait self-esteem. They noted, however, that the Rosenberg scale is the most widely used in research. We next describe both measures as well as the State Self-Esteem scale (Heatherton & Polivy, 1991).

Revised Janis–Field Feelings of Inadequacy

The original Janis–Field Feelings of Inadequacy scale (JFS) was a 23-item test developed in 1959 to be used in attitude change research (Janis & Field, 1959). This multidimensional scale measures self-regard, academic abilities, social confidence, and appearance (Fleming & Watts, 1980). The split-half reliability estimate by Janis and Field was .83, and the reliability was .91.

The items from the JFS have been modified a number of times (e.g., Fleming & Courtney, 1984; Fleming & Watts, 1980), such as changing the format of the responses (5- or 7-point scales, etc.) or adding questions for other dimensions of self-esteem, such as academic ability (Fleming & Courtney, 1984). A thorough review by Robinson and Shaver (1973) identified the JFS as one of the best for use with adults, and Blascovich and Tomaka (1991) selected the Fleming and Courtney (1984) version as one of the best measures to use. We recommend it for studies in which researchers wish to examine multiple components of self-esteem (see the JSF in Appendix 14.1).

Rosenberg Self-Esteem Scale

The Rosenberg Self-Esteem scale (RSE; Rosenberg, 1965) is the most widely used measure of global self-esteem (Demo, 1985). It was used in 25% of the published studies reviewed in the previously mentioned review by Blascovich and Tomaka (1991). The RSE is a 10-item Guttman scale with high internal reliability (alpha .92). Rosenberg (1979) reported that the scale is correlated modestly with mood measures. Carmines and Zeller (1974) identified one potential problem with the RSE; they identified separate "positive" and "negative" factors. Unfortunately, those questions that were worded in a negative direction loaded on the "negative" factor and those that were worded in a positive manner loaded most heavily on the "positive" factor, thereby suggesting a response set. Because both factors correlated almost identically with a criterion variable (in strength, direction, and consistency), however, they seem to be tapping the same general construct (Rosenberg, 1979; see the RSE in Appendix 14.2).

State Self-Esteem Scale

The State Self-Esteem scale (SSES: Heatherton & Polivy, 1991) is a commonly used measure that is sensitive to laboratory manipulations of self-esteem. The SSES consists of 20 items that tap momentary fluctuations in self-esteem. The scale (see Appendix 14.3) has acceptable internal consistency (alpha = .92) and it is responsive to temporary changes in self-evaluation (see Crocker, Cornwell, & Major, 1993). Psychometric studies show the SSES to be separable from mood (Bagozzi & Heatherton, 1994). Confirmatory factor analysis reveals that the SSES is made up of three factors: performance, social, and appearance self-esteem (Bagozzi & Heatherton, 1994). The SSES is labeled "current thoughts" to minimize experimental demands. Of course, measures of trait and state self-esteem are highly correlated, and therefore in neutral settings scores on the SSES will be highly related to trait measures. The decision to use a trait or state measure of self-esteem, therefore, depends on whether one is interested in predicting long-term outcomes or in the immediate effects associated with feelings about the self.

Alternative Conceptualizations: Implicit Self-Esteem

The validity of explicit measures increasingly has come under challenge because, by definition, such measures rely on individuals' potentially biased capacity to accurately report their attitudes and feelings. As a result, implicit measures of attitudes, including self-esteem, attempt to tap into the unconscious, automatic aspects of self. People do not necessarily have access to their internal mental states, and therefore self-presentational motives or other beliefs may produce bias or distortion, both intended and unintended. Greenwald and Banaji (1995) defined implicit self-esteem as "the introspectively unidentified (or inaccurately identified) effect of the self-attitude on evaluation of self-associated and self-dissociated object" (p. 10). A variety of evidence supports the idea of implicit positive attitudes about the self. For instance, people show a positive bias for information about the self, such as preferring their own initials (Koole, Dijksterhuis, & van Knippenberg, 2001) and preferring members of their in-group more than those from an out-group, even when the groups are determined arbitrarily (Greenwald & Banaji, 1995). In essence, anything associated with the self is generally viewed as being especially positive.

A number of different methods have been developed to assess implicit self-esteem (Bosson, Swann, & Pennebaker, 2000), but the most widely known and used is the Implicit Associates Test (IAT; Greenwald, McGhee, & Schwarz, 1998). The IAT involves making paired-word associations; when used to measure self-esteem, the distinctions are between self-related words, such as *me,* and other-related words, such as *your,* and between pleasant words, such as *sunshine,* and unpleasant ones, such as *death.* Self-esteem is a function of difference between the reaction time to make self-pleasant (and other-unpleasant) associations and the reaction time to make self-unpleasant (and other-pleasant) associations. The IAT has been shown to be modestly reliable, and correlates positively but weakly with explicit measures. A factor analysis indicated that they are different constructs (Greenwald & Farnham, 2000).

The validities of the IAT and other implicit measures of self-esteem are unknown. There are reasons to favor implicit measures, given their immutability to self-presentation or cognitive processes, but available evidence does not exist to justify selecting them over the more widely used explicit measures. At another conceptual level, it is difficult to know what to expect from implicit measures. There are thousands of studies in which explicit measures have been used to predict specific outcomes, with reasonable consistency obtained when similar scales are used. This has allowed researchers to make generalizations about what it means to have high or low self-esteem (Baumeister, 1998). Should implicit measures lead to the same conclusions? If so, there is little need of them. But if implicit measures lead to different conclusions than explicit measures, how can we know which is really the better way to assess self-esteem?

Future Developments

Despite the popularity of the self-esteem construct and its potential value to understanding the positive aspects of human nature, the measurement of self-esteem has been problematic for decades. A proliferation of poorly validated scales has posed significant challenges for scholars trying to investigate the consequences of self-esteem for behavior, thought, and emotion. A major problem inherent in the measure of self-esteem is the extent to which self-reports are influenced by self-presentational concerns. One strategy might be to use measures of defensiveness or social desirability to tease out the variance associated with self-report biases. Although some researchers have pursued this approach, no single method has established itself to be empirically useful. Indeed, it may well be that socially desirable responding is a legitimate component of self-esteem and therefore separating it out using statistical procedures would create an artifactual situation. The development of implicit measures may address self-presentational concerns. Much work remains to be done, however, before we know whether implicit measures are valid. At minimum, research on implicit self-esteem has forced researchers to reflect on what exactly a good measure of self-esteem ought to predict in terms of behavioral or cognitive outcomes. This reassessment of the basic definitional issues related to the construct of self-esteem is long overdue.

Appendix 14.1
Revised Janis and Field Scale

Each item is scored on a scale from 1–5 using terms such as "very often, fairly often," "sometimes," "once in a great while," or "practically never" or "very confident," "fairly confident," "slightly confident," "not very confident," "not at all confident." Most items are reverse-scored so that a high self-esteem response leads to higher scores. Items with (R) are not reverse-scored. Some researchers use 7-point scales with different anchors, depending on the wording of the item.

1. How often do you feel inferior to most of the people you know?
2. How often do you have the feeling that there is nothing you can do well?
3. When in a group of people, do you have trouble thinking of the right things to talk about?
4. How often do you feel worried or bothered about what other people think of you?
5. In turning in a major assignment such as a term paper, how often do you feel you did an excellent job on it? (R)
6. How confident are you that others see you as being physically appealing? (R)
7. Do you ever think that you are a worthless individual?
8. How much do you worry about how well you get along with other people?
9. When you make an embarrassing mistake or have done something that makes you look foolish, how long does it take you to get over it?
10. When you have to read an essay and understand it for a class assignment, how worried or concerned do you feel about it?
11. Compared with classmates, how often do you feel you must study more than they do to get the same grades?
12. Have you ever thought of yourself as physically uncoordinated?
13. How confident do you feel that someday the people you know will look up to you and respect you? (R)
14. How often do you worry about criticisms that might be made of your work by your teacher or employer?
15. Do you often feel uncomfortable meeting new people?
16. When you have to write an argument to convince your teacher, who may disagree with your ideas, how concerned or worried do you feel about it?
17. Have you ever felt ashamed of your physique or figure?
18. Have you ever felt inferior to most other people in athletic ability?
19. Do you ever feel so discouraged with yourself that you wonder whether you are a worthwhile person?
20. Do you ever feel afraid or anxious when you are going into a room by yourself where other people have already gathered and are talking?
21. How often do you worry whether other people like to be with you?
22. How often do you have trouble expressing your ideas when you have to put them into writing as an assignment?
23. Do you often feel that most of your friends or peers are more physically attractive than yourself?

24. When involved in sports requiring physical coordination, are you often concerned that you will not do well?
25. How often do you dislike yourself?
26. How often do you feel self-conscious?
27. How often are you troubled with shyness?
28. How often do you have trouble understanding things you read for class assignments?
29. Do you often wish or fantasize that you were better looking?
30. Have you ever thought that you lacked the ability to be a good dancer or do well at recreational activities involving coordination?
31. In general, how confident do you feel about your abilities? (R)
32. How much do you worry about whether other people regard you as a success or failure in your job or at school?
33. When you think that some of the people you meet might have an unfavorable opinion of you, how concerned or worried do you feel about it?
34. How often do you imagine that you have less scholastic ability than your classmates?
35. Have you ever been concerned or worried about your ability to attract members of the opposite sex?
36. When trying to do well at a sport and you know other people are watching, how rattled or flustered do you get?

Note. From Fleming and Courtney (1984). Copyright 1984 by the American Psychological Association. Adapted with permission of the publisher.

Appendix 14.2
Rosenberg Self-Esteem Scale

3	2	1	0
strongly agree	agree	disagree	strongly disagree

1. I feel that I am a person of worth, at least on an equal plane with others.
2. I feel that I have a number of good qualities.
3. All in all, I am inclined to feel that I am a failure. (R)
4. I am able to do things as well as most people.
5. I feel I do not have much to be proud of. (R)
6. I take a positive attitude toward myself.
7. On the whole, I am satisfied with myself.
8. I wish I could have more respect for myself. (R)
9. I certainly feel useless at times. (R)
10. At times I think that I am no good at all. (R)

For the items marked with an (R), reverse the scoring (0 = 3, 1 = 2, 2 = 1, 3 = 0). For those items without an (R) next to them, simply add the score. Add the scores. Typical scores on the Rosenberg scale are around 22, with most people scoring between 15 and 25.

Note. Copyright 1965 by the Morris Rosenberg Foundation.

Appendix 14.3
Current Thoughts

This is a questionnaire designed to measure what you are thinking at this moment. There is, of course, no right answer for any statement. The best answer is what you feel is true of yourself at this moment. Be sure to answer all of the items, even if you are not certain of the best answer. Again, answer these questions as they are true for you RIGHT NOW.

1 = not at all   2 = a little bit   3 = somewhat   4 = very much   5 = extremely

1. I feel confident about my abilities.
2. I am worried about whether I am regarded as a success or failure. (R)
3. I feel satisfied with the way my body looks right now.
4. I feel frustrated or rattled about my performance. (R)
5. I feel that I am having trouble understanding things that I read. (R)
6. I feel that others respect and admire me.
7. I am dissatisfied with my weight. (R)
8. I feel self-conscious. (R)
9. I feel as smart as others.
10. I feel displeased with myself. (R)
11. I feel good about myself.
12. I am pleased with my appearance right now.
13. I am worried about what other people think of me. (R)
14. I feel confident that I understand things.
15. I feel inferior to others at this moment. (R)
16. I feel unattractive. (R)
17. I feel concerned about the impression I am making. (R)
18. I feel that I have less scholastic ability right now than others. (R)
19. I feel like I'm not doing well. (R)
20. I am worried about looking foolish. (R)

Note. From Heatherton and Polivy (1991). Copyright 1991 by the American Psychological Association. Adapted with permission of the publisher and author.

References

Bagozzi, R. P., & Heatherton, T. F. (1994). A general approach to representing multifaceted personality constructs: Application to self-esteem. *Structural Equation Modelling, 1,* 35–67.

Baumeister, R. F. (1998). The self. In D. Gilbert, S. Fiske, & G. Lindzey (Eds.), *The handbook of social psychology* (pp. 680–740). New York: Random House.

Baumeister, R. F., & Leary, M. R. (1995). The need to belong: Desire for interpersonal attachments as a fundamental human motivation. *Psychological Bulletin, 117,* 497–529.

Blascovich, J., & Tomaka J. (1991). Measures of self-esteem. In J. P. Robinson & P. R. Shaver (Eds.), *Measures of personality and social psychological attitudes* (pp. 115–160). San Diego, CA: Academic Press.

Bosson, J., Swann, W. B., Jr., & Pennebaker, J. (2000). Stalking the perfect measure of implicit self-esteem: The blind men and the elephant revisited? *Journal of Personality and Social Psychology, 79,* 631–643.

Branden, N. (1994). *The six pillars of self-esteem.* New York: Bantam Books.

Briggs, S. R., & Cheek, J. M. (1986). The role of factor analysis in the development and evaluation of personality scales. *Journal of Personality, 54,* 106–148.

Carmines, E. G., & Zeller, R. A. (1974). On establishing the empirical dimensionality of theoretical terms: An analytical example. *Political Methodology, 1,* 75–96.

Cohen, S., & Wills, T. A. (1985). Stress, social support, and the buffering hypothesis. *Psychological Bulletin, 98,* 310–357.

Cooley, C. H. (1902). *Human nature and social order.* New York: Charles Scribner & Sons.

Coopersmith, S. (1967). *The antecedents of self-esteem.* San Francisco: Freeman.

Crandall, R. (1973). The measurement of self-esteem and related constructs. In J. P. Robinson & P. Shaver (Eds.), *Measurements of social psychological attitudes* (pp. 45–167). Ann Arbor, MI: Institute for Social Research.

Crocker, J., Cornwell, B., & Major, B. (1993). The stigma of overweight: Affective consequences of attributional ambiguity. *Journal of Personality and Social Psychology, 64,* 60–70.

Dawes, R. (1994). Psychological measurement. *Psychological Review, 101,* 278–281.

Demo, D. H. (1985). The measurement of self-esteem: Refining our methods, *Journal of Personality and Social Psychology, 48,* 1490–1502.

Fitts, W. H. (1964). *Tennessee Self-Concept scale.* Los Angeles: Western Psychological Services.

Fleming, J. S., & Courtney, B. E. (1984). The dimensionality of self-esteem: II. Hierarchical facet model for revised measurement scales. *Journal of Personality and Social Psychology, 46,* 404–421.

Fleming, J. S., & Watts, W. A. (1980). The dimensionality of self-esteem: Some results for a college sample. *Journal of Personality and Social Psychology, 39,* 921–929.

Franzoi, S. (1995). The body-as-object versus the body-as-process: Gender differences and gender considerations. *Sex Roles, 33,* 417–437.

Greenwald, A. G., & Banaji, M. R. (1995). Implicit social cognition: Attitudes, self-esteem, and stereotypes. *Psychological Review, 102,* 4–27.

Greenwald, A. G., & Farnham, S. D. (2000). Using the Implicit Associate Test to measure self-esteem and self-concept. *Journal of Personality and Social Psychology, 79,* 1022–1038.

Greenwald, A. G., McGhee, D. E., & Schwarz, J. L. K. (1998). Measuring individual differences in implicit cognition: The implicit association test. *Journal of Personality and Social Psychology, 74,* 1464–1480.

Heatherton, T. F. (2001). Body image and gender. In N. J. Smelser & P. B. Baltes (Eds.), *International Encyclopedia of the Social and Behavioral Sciences* (Vol. 2, pp. 1282–1285). Oxford, UK: Elsevier.

Heatherton, T. F., & Polivy, J. (1991). Development and validation of a scale for measuring state self-esteem. *Journal of Personality and Social Psychology, 60,* 895–910.

Heatherton, T. F. & Polivy, J. (1992). Chronic dieting and eating disorders: A spiral model. In J. H. Crowther & D. L. Tennenbaum (Eds.), *The etiology of bulimia nervosa: The individual and familial context* (pp. 133–155). Washington, DC: Hemisphere.

Hebl, M., & Heatherton, T. F. (1998). The stigma of obesity in women: The difference is black and white. *Personality & Social Psychology Bulletin, 24,* 417–426.

Jackson, M. R. (1984). *Self-esteem and meaning*. Albany: State University of New York Press.

James, W. (1890). *Principles of psychology, Volume 1*. New York: Henry Holt.

James, W. (1892). *Psychology: The briefer course*. New York: Henry Holt.

Janis, I. L., & Field, P. B. (1959). Sex differences and factors related to persuasibility. In C. I. Hovland & I. L. Janis (Eds.), *Personality and persuasibility* (pp. 55–68). New Haven, CT: Yale University Press.

Josephs, R. A., Markus, H. R., & Tafarodi, R. W. (1992). Gender and self-esteem. *Journal of Personality and Social Psychology, 63*, 391–402.

Kernis, M. H. (1993). The roles of stability and level of self-esteem in psychological functioning. In R. F. Baumeister (Ed.), *Self-esteem: The puzzle of low self-regard* (pp. 167–172). New York: Plenum Press.

Koole, S. L., Dijksterhuis, A., & van Knippenberg, A. (2001). What's in a name: Implicit self-esteem and the automatic self. *Journal of Personality and Social Psychology, 80*, 669–685.

Leary, M. R., Tambor, E. S., Terdal, S. K., & Downs, D. L. (1995). Self-esteem as an interpersonal monitor: The sociometer hypothesis. *Journal of Personality and Social Psychology, 68*, 518–530.

Luhtanen, R., & Crocker, J. (1992). A collective self-esteem scale: Self-evaluation of one's social identity. *Personality and Social Psychology Bulletin, 18*, 302–318.

Marsh, H. (1995). A Jamesian model of self-investment and self-esteem: Comment on Pelham. *Journal of Personality & Social Psychology, 69*, 1151–1160.

Mead, G. H. (1934). *Mind, self, and society*, Chicago: University of Chicago Press.

Mecca, A. M., Smelser, N. J., & Vasconcellos, J. (Eds.). (1989). *The social importance of self-esteem*. Berkeley: University of California Press.

NIH Technology Assessment Conference Panel. (1993). Methods for voluntary weight loss and control. *Annals of Internal Medicine, 199*, 764–770.

Pelham, B. W. (1995). Self-investment and self-esteem: Evidence for a Jamesian model of self-worth. *Journal of Personality and Social Psychology, 69*, 1141–1150.

Robins, R. W., Hendin, H. M., & Trzesniewski, K. H. (2001). Measuring global self-esteem: Construct validation of a single-item measure and the Rosenberg self-esteem scale. *Personality and Social Psychology Bulletin, 27*, 151–161.

Robinson, J., & Shaver, P. R. (1973). *Measures of social psychological attitudes*. Ann Arbor, MI: Institute for Social Research.

Rosenberg, M. (1965). *Society and the adolescent self-image*. Princeton, NJ: Princeton University Press.

Rosenberg, M. (1979). *Conceiving the self*. New York: Basic Books.

Steele, C. (1997). Race and the schooling of Black Americans. In L. H. Peplau & S. E. Taylor (Eds.), *Sociocultural perspectives in social psychology: Current readings* (pp. 359–371). Upper Saddle River, NJ: Prentice-Hall.

Stein, J. A., Newcomb, M. D., & Bentler, P. M. (1992). The effect of agency and communality on self-esteem: Gender differences in longitudinal data. *Sex Roles, 26*, 465–483.

Taylor, S. E., Brown, J. D. (1988). Illusion and well-being: A social psychological perspective on mental health. *Psychological Bulletin, 103*, 193–210.

Tennen, H., & Affleck, G. (1993). The puzzles of self-esteem: A clinical perspective. In R. F. Baumeister, (Ed.), *Plenum series in social/clinical psychology* (pp. 241–262.) New York: Plenum Press.

Vohs, K. D., Bardone, A. M., Joiner, T. E., Abramson, L. Y., & Heatherton, T. F. (1999). Perfectionism, perceived weight status, and self-esteem interact to predict bulimic symptoms: A model of bulimic symptom development. *Journal of Abnormal Psychology, 108*, 695–700.

Wells, L. E., & Marwell, G. (1976). *Self-esteem: Its conceptualization and measurement*. Beverly Hills, CA: Sage.

Wylie, R. C. (1974). *The self-concept: A review of methodological considerations and measuring instruments*. Lincoln: University of Nebraska Press.

15

Romantic Love: Measuring Cupid's Arrow

Clyde Hendrick and Susan S. Hendrick

Love is one of the central characteristics of positive psychology, and it is linked in a dynamic system with other core concepts represented in this volume. As Seligman and Csikszentmihalyi (2000) noted, positive psychology is concerned with "valued subjective experiences: well-being, contentment, and satisfaction . . . flow and happiness . . . the capacity for love and vocation" (p. 5).

Love in all its forms—love of romantic partner, parents, children, and friends—is centrally important to human society. Although the current chapter focuses on the measurement of romantic or partnered love specifically, we recognize the fundamental importance of all forms and manifestations of love.

This chapter initially discusses historical conceptions of love, including its assignment in the "general" sense as a biological phenomenon, part of our hard-wiring as humans, and in its "specific" sense as a societal construction that is shaped and nuanced by historical period, culture, and so forth. We consider love as a primary emotion, exemplified most clearly in its romantic or partnered form as passionate love and in its corollary of companionate love. We discuss in detail two measures of love—the Love Attitudes scale and the Passionate Love scale—and we review in less detail several other conceptions and measures of love. Finally, we sketch our views about the most compelling future directions in the study of love.

Historical Considerations

Philosopher Irving Singer wrote a comprehensive history of love (1984a, 1984b, 1987) and proposed four primary conceptual traditions: eros (the search for the beautiful); philia (love in friendship); nomos (submission and obedience, frequently to the divine will); and agape (bestowal of love by the divine). Such conceptual–philosophical perspectives on love generally take little note of the romantic–partnered love so attended to by contemporary Western societies. Romantic love is thought by some scholars to have developed only in recent centuries as an accompaniment to marriage by choice (Gadlin, 1977). Until people developed a sense of a unique "self" that was capable of loving another self, romantic love (particularly with a life partner as opposed to a more transient paramour) was less common than it is today (S. Hendrick & Hendrick, 1992a).

Some scholars, however, view romantic and passionate love as existing in all cultures and across all historical periods (Hatfield & Rapson, 1996). Indeed, Cho and Cross (1995) found evidence that both passionate love and free mate choice (as well as other manifestations of love) dated back several thousand years as explicit themes in Chinese literature. More recently, Doherty, Hatfield, Thompson, and Choo (1994) compared Japanese American, European American, and Pacific Islander residents of Hawaii and found them to be very similar in terms of both passionate and companionate love.

Although there may well be universal aspects to love, the impact of culture and historical period on the particular manifestations and expressions of love is undeniable. Sprecher et al. (1994), in comparing Russian, Japanese, and American approaches to love, found both similarities and differences. For example, Russians were less likely to view love as a necessary precursor to marriage, Japanese respondents did not subscribe to certain romantic beliefs, and Americans were more likely to subscribe to a secure attachment style. Furthermore, cultural norms such as individual mate selection versus arranged marriages may accompany other cultural differences in love and romantic beliefs (deMunck, 1998).

Therefore, even though love may be a cultural universal, and its specific expression in romantic love may be "near-universal" (Jankowiak & Fischer, 1992), it is expressed differently depending on culture and historical era. So how should love be envisioned?

Visions of Love

As discussed previously, the *emotion* of love has many manifestations, only one of which is the romantic, partnered love considered in this chapter. Indeed, scholars (e.g., Shaver, Morgan, & Wu, 1996) have argued convincingly that love should be considered a "basic emotion," one that is fundamental to all of the more complex and nuanced emotions. Shaver et al. detailed a number of reasons why love meets the criteria for such basic emotion status, including distinctive facial expressions and distinctive universal signals. The authors also pointed out the inappropriateness of dividing love into "emotions" and "dispositions." In this regard, Shaver et al. noted that emotions are indeed trait-like, but with state-like or "surge" qualities that reflect "moments when we feel especially in-love or loving" (p. 86). "What all love surges have in common, however, is that they move the person toward proximity, touch, and openness to intimacy. These common behavioral tendencies . . . cause people in many different cultures to use the same term, 'love,' for all such instances" (p. 93). Thus Shaver et al. argue eloquently for love's importance as they argue for its status as a basic emotion.

Although we agree with Shaver et al. that love is important for a psychology of emotion (see also Taraban, Hendrick, & Hendrick, 1998), we are less concerned that love be considered primary in the sense of meeting criteria for "basicness" or purity than that it be considered fundamental and foundational to human experience. Consistent with the perspective on the centrality of love, Baumeister and Leary (1995) have described the "fundamental need to belong" as a need for attachment and connection that is part of our evolutionary heritage. Similarly, Harlow many years ago (1974) emphasized the importance of physical contact and interaction as part of the primate (and human) systems of infant–mother bonding. Such phenomena are surely a part of the broader emotion of love.

It is likely that there is a bonding phenomenon in primates that is designed to facilitate effective mating, infant survival, group defense, and so forth. That bonding is expressed in human experience as the emotion we call love. Love is expressed in various ways, depending on who is doing the giving and receiving. Thus, the romantic–partnered love that is elaborated in this chapter is rooted in the emotions and behaviors that sustain our very survival. This latter statement may sound dramatic, but love *is* dramatic—at least in some forms. Drama is in fact one differentiating characteristic between types or styles of love, and this point is clearly drawn in the contrast between passionate and companionate love.

Passionate and Companionate Love

Ancient Chinese, Egyptian, and Hebrew writings (to name just a few) all contain evocative descriptions of passionate sentiments. The social scientific categorization of romantic love into passionate and companionate forms, however, is relatively recent. Berscheid and Walster (1978) were among the first scholars to organize love into the primary categories of passionate love (the intense, aroused bonfire that typically fuels the beginning of a romantic union) and companionate love (the steady, quiet, soothing, glowing embers that sustain a relationship over time). These were conceptualized as two "stages" of love, with passionate love often blazing brightly and then consuming itself, only in the most fortunate of cases ripening into companionate love. We have referred elsewhere to this perspective as the "either/or theory of love" (S. Hendrick & Hendrick, 2000, p. 204).

More recently, Hatfield (1988) has envisioned passionate and companionate love as simultaneous rather than necessarily sequential, noting that people "are *capable* of passionate/companionate love and are likely to experience such feelings intermittently throughout their lives" (p. 193). In support of this perspective, we (S. Hendrick & Hendrick, 1993) have found that friendship-type love was the love theme most often mentioned in respondents' written accounts of their own romantic relationships. In addition, nearly half the college students, when asked to name their closest friends, named their romantic partners. Thus, even in the presumably initial stages of relationships when passion is raging, respondents highlighted the friendship aspects of their love. The corollary of this study is research by Contreras, Hendrick, and Hendrick (1996), who found that even for couples married as long as 40 years, passionate love was the strongest predictor of relationship satisfaction. So both passion and companionship coexist in many, perhaps most, romantic, partnered relationships.

This dual perspective on passion and friendship has informed considerable research and has strong empirical underpinnings (e.g., C. Hendrick & Hendrick, 1989). It is unlikely, however, that current romantic relationships can be conceptualized in terms of just two love orientations, no matter how compelling those orientations may be. We consider next a multidimensional approach that offers six different orientations to or "styles" of love.

The Love Styles

Sociologist John Alan Lee (1973) used the metaphor of a color wheel to develop his conception of love as available in different and equally beautiful colors—similar to colors on a color wheel. Although Lee described love (like color) as having primary, secondary, and even tertiary mixes, most of the research based on Lee's approach has concentrated on six relatively independent love styles.

Lee (1973) developed these styles from extensive research using an interview questionnaire format (the Love Story Card Sort). Out of this research came Lee's concept of the love styles, described subsequently as "ideal types." In fact, no one person is an "ideal," and no one person has just one love style. All persons have some of each love style in their love profile.

Eros is an intense, passionate love. The erotic lover prefers particular physical attributes in a partner, becomes intense quickly, wants to communicate and "know" the loved one on all levels, and is both confident and willing to become committed.

Ludus is love played as a game, albeit a serious one. The ludic lover wants love to be a pleasant pastime for everyone involved, may "balance" several love relationships at the same time, and avoids emotional intensity and commitment.

Storge is love based in friendship, much like the companionate love discussed previously. A storgic lover wants a steady, secure, and comfortable relationship with a love partner who has similar attitudes and values and who can be both a lover and a "best friend."

Pragma is a love that "goes shopping" (complete with list) for an appropriate partner. A pragmatic lover wants to make a good match and thus might seek help from a matchmaker or a computer dating service.

Mania is a love characterized by emotional ups and downs. A manic lover is obsessive, dependent, and insecure (the downside), supportive, loving, and devoted to the partner (the upside), and yearning for love with an expectation that it may even be painful (S. Hendrick & Hendrick, 1992b).

Agape is a spiritual love that reflects selflessness and altruism. The agapic lover is concerned for the partner's welfare, solicitous of the partner's needs, and relatively undemanding for the self. True agapic lovers are very rare, though some degree of agapic qualities is necessary if a relationship is to endure.

These six love styles offer a broader set of options for conceptualizing romantic love (more than previously available), and they provide the basis for a measure of love discussed in the next section.

Measurement of Love

As discussed previously, there are several approaches to the study of love, each with its own definition. Space precludes consideration of the history of love measurement scales, and we focus instead on the recent era. For our purposes, the "modern era" of love measurement began with Rubin's (1970) attempt to measure and distinguish between liking and loving. Rubin developed two 13-item rating scales to measure liking and loving, and these scales were widely used for a decade or more, and are still used occasionally. Kelley (1983) pointed out that the liking scale appeared to measure respect, and the love scale appeared to measure the concepts of needing, caring, trust, and tolerance. Experimental work did indeed confirm these constructs within Rubin's love scale (Steck, Levitan, McLane, & Kelley, 1982).

The complexity discovered in Rubin's scale also characterizes most of the subsequent instruments. Love is a complicated concept, and thus instruments usually, though not always, are multidimensional. For example, the two love scales used most frequently today, the Love Attitudes scale (LAS; C. Hendrick & Hendrick, 1986) and the Passionate Love scale (PLS; Hatfield & Sprecher, 1986) differ widely; the PLS measures the single construct of intense erotic love, whereas the LAS measures five other constructs in addition to passionate love. We devote most of our attention to these two scales, with other approaches discussed only briefly.

Love Attitudes Scale

The LAS was developed as a quantitative measure of love as conceptualized by Lee (1973). Lee's approach to measurement was qualitative and labor-intensive. Our quantitative approach was based on initial measurement work by Lasswell and Lasswell (1976). We developed a set of 42 items to measure the six constructs of Eros, Ludus, Storge, Pragma, Mania, and Agape (C. Hendrick & Hendrick, 1986). Six factors, representing the six love constructs, were routinely extracted from the 42 items using principal components analysis, typically accounting for nearly 45% of the variance. The seven-item sets representing each of the scales showed alphas ranging from .69 for Storge to .83 for Agape, and test–retest reliabilities ranging from .70 for Mania to .82 for Ludus (based on a 4- to 6-week interval; see C. Hendrick & Hendrick, 1986, for more details). The LAS has been used widely, and it has been translated into many languages. In conceptualizing the LAS, we decided to treat the six love constructs as variables rather than as a typology as construed by Lee (1973). With the variable approach, each person obtains six scores on the LAS that can be correlated with relevant relationship and personality constructs.

The LAS has not been immune to criticism. Johnson (1987) pointed out that many of the items were general in reference, whereas other items referred to a specific love partner, and that the relative proportion of general to specific items differed widely across the six scales. In response to this criticism, we rewrote 19 general items to create a 42-item relationship-specific version of the LAS (C. Hendrick & Hendrick, 1990). (Results from this version were fully consistent with the 1986 version, as we hypothesized.)

Results tend to be similar for people who currently are either in or not in a relationship. We exclude research participants who have never been in love because their responses tend to be different on numerous relationship variables. Admittedly, however, a detailed study of people who have never been in love would be valuable.

We soon discovered that success breeds revisionism. The LAS is not proprietary, and researchers used it as they saw fit. The most common change was to drop items to create an even shorter scale. Finally, we decided that we had to join the revisionists! We examined several of our large data collections and selected the best four items from each of the six scales, thereby creating a 24-item short form of the LAS (C. Hendrick, Hendrick, & Dicke, 1998). The psychometrics on the four-item subscales were excellent, and in some respects superior to the seven-item subscales. Coefficient alphas ranged from .75 for Mania to .88 for Agape, and test–retest correlations from .63 for Pragma to .76 for Storge (approximately seven-week interval).

Although the LAS was developed for research rather than clinical use, it can be used creatively in couple counseling. The scores should not be interpreted as positive or negative relational functioning, although research is consistent in showing that passionate love is positively related to relationship satisfaction, whereas game-playing love produces a negative relationship. Optimal use of the scale probably would involve using partners' scores on the LAS to stimulate discussion about how the partners view love within their relationship. The measure might be administered twice to each partner—once for the "real" relationship and once as they would "ideally" like their love to be. This exercise could clarify some aspirational goals for the partners as they rework their relationship with a therapist's help.

A copy of the 24-item version of the LAS is shown in Appendix 15.1. Eros (the first scale shown) is passionate love, and it is perhaps the closest to the traditional stereotype of romantic love. The unidimensional romantic love approach has been developed successfully by Hatfield with a set of items that measures passionate love.

Passionate Love Scale

Hatfield and Sprecher (1986), construing passionate love as an intense longing for union with another specific person, developed a 30-item Passionate Love scale (PLS) to tap cognitive and emotional components of this longing. They also posited a behavioral component, but in pretesting found "that passionate love appeared to be a phenomenon more of the mind and the heart than of actual behavior" (p. 390). (The authors also validated a 15-item short version of the PLS, using half of the 30-item set.)

The PLS was exceptionally well-constructed. It factored as a unidimensional scale with coefficient alphas of .94 for the 30-item version and .91 for the 15-item version. Hatfield and Rapson (1987) reviewed data supporting the validity of the PLS. They made a powerful case that passionate love occurs across cultures, and even in children before puberty. Furthermore, passionate love appears to have existed from the beginning of recorded history. The authors suggested that the experience of passionate love is a human universal.

Independent research supports the quality and validity of the PLS. For example, C. Hendrick and Hendrick (1989) factored a number of love measures, including the 30-item version of the PLS, and found that only a single factor emerged for the PLS, and it accounted for 54% of the variance. In addition, the PLS correlated well with several other scales designed to assess passionate love or a closely related concept. For example, scores for the PLS and Eros from the LAS were correlated positively at .53. Clearly, good measurement of passionate love is necessary for the study of romantic love. Because there appear to be types of romantic love other than passion (or Eros), however, numerous other scales have been developed.

Alternative Approaches to Love and Its Measurement

In this section, we describe the four most recent and popular approaches to conceptualizing and measuring love.

TRIANGULAR THEORY OF LOVE. Sternberg (1986) proposed that romantic love is a mix of three components: passion, intimacy, and commitment. Various mixes of presence–absence of the three components yield eight kinds of love ranging from nonlove (absence of all three components) to consummate love (full combination of all three components). This theory is elegant and simple; many implications can be derived from it. Unfortunately, there have been difficulties in devising scales that adequately measure the three constructs. An early 36-item rating scale developed by Sternberg has shown very high intercorrelations among the three component subscales in several studies (e.g., Acker & Davis, 1992; Chojnacki & Walsh, 1990; C. Hendrick & Hendrick, 1989). Sternberg (1997) reported an extensive validation study of the scale, including revision of several items, and consistently found that three orthogonal factors fit the data. These factors were best interpreted as representing passion, intimacy, and commitment. Even with the revised scale, however, subscale correlations remained quite high (ranging from .46 to .73).

Conceptually, it is unclear whether the concepts of passion, intimacy, and commitment are independent concepts still searching for a proper measure, or whether the measure is appropriate in that the meanings of the three concepts may be intrinsically confounded. More research is needed.

PROTOTYPE THEORY. In numerous studies, Beverly Fehr (e.g., 1988, 1993, 1994) developed a prototype theory of love, along with various measurement devices. The prototype approach is one way to study lay conceptions of love. Participants in research typically were asked to list types of love, resulting in about 15 types (e.g., friendship, sexual, mother, romantic). In other studies, participants listed attributes for each kind of love (e.g., candlelight dinners, taking walks, caring). Still other studies required ratings of these attributes on characteristics such as similarity, importance, agreement, and so forth. Fehr's research generally shows that companionate love is more prototypical of love than is passion (e.g., Fehr, 1988). Regan, Kocan, and Whitlock (1998) had one group list features of *romantic* love and another group rate the centrality of those features. Sexual attraction and passion were indeed on the list of features; however, these features ranked well below other features such as trust, honesty, and happiness. One would expect that for romantic love, passionate features would rank highest, but results showed otherwise. Aron and Westbay (1996) factor-analyzed all 68 features originally used by Fehr (1988). They identified three underlying dimensions of passion, intimacy, and commitment; moreover, they found that the features on the intimacy factor were rated as more central to love than features on the other two factors.

Aron and Westbay's (1996) research on the prototype perspective thus suggests a convergence between Fehr's work and Sternberg's (1986) triangular theory. We should note that the approaches of Fehr and Sternberg differ widely in concepts, and even more so in methods. Thus, the convergence found by Aron and Westbay is all the more remarkable.

SELF-EXPANSION THEORY. In addition to assessing other theories, the Arons have developed their own theory. Based on a metaphor from Eastern traditions, A. Aron and Aron (1986) proposed a theory that humans have a basic motivation to expand the self. "The idea is that the self expands toward knowing or becoming that which includes everything and everyone, the Self. The steps along the way are ones of including one person or thing, then another, then still another" (E. Aron & Aron, 1996, pp. 45–46). Romantic love derives from the basic motivation for self-expansion and the reciprocal inclusion of other in self, and usually, self in other.

Research using the self-expansion metaphor has been fruitful. A variety of measures has been used, including free descriptions, self-efficacy ratings, and various types of questionnaires. An interesting approach to scaling was developed by A. Aron, Aron, and Smollan (1992), who had people rate a relationship by the degree of overlap of two circles representing the two persons in the relationship. This scale—the Inclusion of Other in Self scale—is a very effective measure of closeness, and it at least equals and often surpasses more traditional questionnaires in psychometric properties. Self-expansion theory appears to have a prosperous future.

ATTACHMENT PROCESSES. Bowlby (1969) developed attachment theory in studying mother–infant relationships. He noted three types of infant attachment: secure, anxious, and avoidant. Hazan and Shaver (1987) extended attachment theory to adult romantic relationships. A variety of measures have been developed to study attachment processes in children and adults, including both interview and self-report measures. The literature on attachment is massive, and just the literature on self-report scales for adult romantic attachment is now voluminous. An excellent summary of the many issues involved in adult attachment measures is given in Crowell, Fraley, and Shaver (1999) and in chapter 18 (this volume).

Measurement Issues

This survey of love measures indicates that there is no agreed on methodology to study love. Approaches range from overlapping of circles to standard questionnaires. Perhaps this state of affairs is desirable as long as there exists such a wide divergence in the theories of love. The current diversity of theory exists against the backdrop (some would say "threat") of social constructivism. Gergen and Gergen (1995) applied this approach to the concept of love. They detected three eras of love in the past few centuries: romanticist, modernism, and postmodernism. Modernism is the era of rationality and pragmatism, with some carryover of the romantic strains from the previous era. The instrumental practicality of the modern era makes possible the analytical study of love (and sex) in detail by quantitative scales. Such analytical scrutiny would have been unthinkable in the intensity of the romantic era. As we move into the postmodern era, rationality becomes just one approach to life among many. The notion of a coherent self will dissolve as different identities are assumed across relational contexts.

In such a postmodern world with its multidimensional identities, the notion of "one true love" would have little meaning. Accordingly, we should keep in mind that the current prolific theorizing and research on love occurs within a certain cultural context that sanctions and supports it. If and when there are substantial cultural changes, the relevance of *all* current work may come into question.

On a more positive note, Singer (1984a) distinguished *appraisal* (an everyday behavior of setting a value) from *bestowal* (an unqualified emotional valuing of another). Bestowal is a gift—a gift of love, freely given. As S. Hendrick and Hendrick (1992b) noted, the concept of bestowal is quite dramatic because it provides a means for new creation within the world. That is, bestowal creates a new value: love. At the same time, a concept such as bestowal creates real measurement problems. How does one measure something that is a new, free creation of the human spirit? The answer is not yet clear.

Larger theoretical measurement issues loom on the horizon. Michell (1999) developed the interesting argument that the founding fathers of measurement, people such as Fechner, Thurstone, and S. S. Stevens, simply *assumed* that psychological attributes are measurable. Michell (1999) contended that whether an attribute is quantifiable is an empirical question; quantifiability should not simply be assumed. (An excellent review of Michell's book is provided by Luce, 2000.) The arguments can become quite abstract, and this issue is much larger, of course, than measurement of attributes such as love, liking, closeness, and so forth. The outcome of the abstruse arguments about the nature of measurement, however, may well affect the type of theories of love and measurement scales we will develop in the future.

Future Directions

As we pursue new directions for the study of love (see S. Hendrick & Hendrick, 2002), we also will need to develop and validate the related measures. Many of the research approaches to love discussed previously (e.g., prototypes, self-expansion) emphasize the *process* by which people love, whether it is through exemplifying a central form of love or expanding the self by including another. Such research should continue so that scholars better understand the complex cognitions and affects that describe the wider phenomena of love. The love styles and passionate love approaches emphasized in this chapter, however, are much more concerned with the *content* of love, at least romantic love. The questions explored have to do with what love is—in all its romantic forms—and how it relates to other aspects of the individual and the romantic dyad. Such research should continue. Far from having too much research on love, we believe that we have too little.

As we have noted elsewhere (S. Hendrick & Hendrick, 2002), love in its romantic form often is related to sexuality, though research on the two phenomena often has bifurcated. Love and sex are linked for many couples, and they need to be linked by more researchers. Broadening love research to include sex should be accompanied by widening the current research on "young, attractive, heterosexual" love to include more gay, lesbian, and bisexual persons; more persons with physical disabilities; and more mature and even "senior" persons in partnered relationships. Surveys indicate that people continue to have sex well into their later years if blessed with reasonably good health and an appropriate love–sex partner (Levy, 1994). As photographer Keri Pickett consulted with her grandmother about what content was appropriate for Pickett's compilation of letters, photographs, and commentary that were to become a book about her grandparents' 60+ years of marital love, she asked her grandmother whether she would be comfortable having the couple's sexual relationship mentioned. Her grandmother replied, "Well, the book would need to have some sex in it or it wouldn't be natural" (Pickett, 1995, p. 5).

If romantic love is the cultural universal that we believe it to be, then scholars need to examine love across societies, within societies, and across groups within societies. Though love may indeed be biologically hard-wired, it is culturally expressed, and in a future where the global village will more and more become reality, love needs to be measured more diversely in terms of respondents as well as measures.

Finally, love needs to be studied in the context of other positive psychology concepts such as hope. It is interesting, yet unsurprising perhaps, that "Saint Paul and Martin Luther held hope, along with love, as the essence of what is good in life" (Snyder, 2000, p. 3). Although the measurement of love and the other positive psychology constructs is substantive, more work remains.

> Thus, we view love as a central concept within a linked, dynamic structure of other positive concepts. The concepts are fundamentally related, their relational nature mirroring the relational nature of the human community. With this view, a much broader, more fully integrated understanding of the human condition is possible, one which will allow a complete positive psychology to emerge. (S. Hendrick & Hendrick, 2002, p. 481)

Appendix 15.1
Love Attitudes Scale–Short Form

Eros

1. My partner and I have the right physical "chemistry" between us.
2. I feel that my partner and I were meant for each other.
3. My partner and I really understand each other.
4. My partner fits my ideal standards of physical beauty/handsomeness.

Ludus

5. I believe that what my partner doesn't know about me won't hurt him/her.
6. I have sometimes had to keep my partner from finding out about other partners.
7. My partner would get upset if he/she knew of some of the things I've done with other people.
8. I enjoy playing the "game of love" with my partner and a number of other partners.

Storge

9. Our love is the best kind because it grew out of a long friendship.
10. Our friendship merged gradually into love over time.
11. Our love is really a deep friendship, not a mysterious, mystical emotion.
12. Our love relationship is the most satisfying because it developed from a good friendship.

Pragma

13. A main consideration in choosing my partner was how he/she would reflect on my family.
14. An important factor in choosing my partner was whether or not he/she would be a good parent.
15. One consideration in choosing my partner was how he/she would reflect on my career.
16. Before getting very involved with my partner, I tried to figure out how compatible his/her hereditary background would be with mine in case we ever had children.

Mania

17. When my partner doesn't pay attention to me, I feel sick all over.
18. Since I've been in love with my partner, I've had trouble concentrating on anything else.

19. I cannot relax if I suspect that my partner is with someone else.
20. If my partner ignores me for a while, I sometimes do stupid things to try to get his/her attention back.

Agape

21. I would rather suffer myself than let my partner suffer.
22. I cannot be happy unless I place my partner's happiness before my own.
23. I am usually willing to sacrifice my own wishes to let my partner achieve his/hers.
24. I would endure all things for the sake of my partner.

Note. Each item is rated on a five-point basis: 5 = strongly disagree, 4 = disagree, 3 = neutral, 2 = agree, 1 = strongly agree.

References

Acker, M., & Davis, M. H. (1992). Intimacy, passion and commitment in adult romantic relation-ships: A test of the triangular theory of love. *Journal of Social and Personal Relationships, 9*, 21–50.

Aron, A., & Aron, E. N. (1986). *Love and the expansion of self: Understanding attraction and satisfaction.* New York: Hemisphere.

Aron, A., Aron, E. N., & Smollan, D. (1992). Inclusion of Other in the Self scale and the structure of interpersonal closeness. *Journal of Personality and Social Psychology, 63*, 596–612.

Aron, A., & Westbay, L. (1996). Dimensions of the prototype of love. *Journal of Personality and Social Psychology, 70*, 535–551.

Aron, E. N., & Aron, A. (1996). Love and expansion of the self: The state of the model. *Personal Relationships, 3*, 45–58.

Baumeister, R. F., & Leary, M. R. (1995). The need to belong: Desire for interpersonal attachments as a fundamental human motivation. *Psychological Bulletin, 117*, 497–529.

Berscheid, E., & Walster, E. (1978). *Interpersonal attraction* (2nd ed.). Reading, MA: Addison-Wesley.

Bowlby, J. (1969). *Attachment and loss: Vol. 1 Attachment.* New York: Basic Books.

Cho, W., & Cross, S. E. (1995). Taiwanese love styles and their association with self-esteem and relationship quality. *Genetic, Social, & General Psychology Monographs, 121*, 283–309.

Chojnacki, J. T., & Walsh, W. B. (1990). Reliability and concurrent validity of the Sternberg Triangular Love scale. *Psychological Reports, 67*, 219–224.

Contreras, R., Hendrick, S. S., & Hendrick, C. (1996). Perspectives on marital love and satisfaction in Mexican American and Anglo couples. *Journal of Counseling and Development, 74*, 408–415.

Crowell, J. A., Fraley, R. C., & Shaver, P. R. (1999). Measurement of individual differences in adolescent and adult attachment. In J. Cassidy & P. R. Shaver (Eds.), *Handbook of attachment: Theory, research, and clinical applications* (pp. 434–465). New York: Guilford Press.

deMunck, V. C. (1998). Lust, love, and arranged marriages in Sri Lanka. In V. C. deMunck (Ed.), *Romantic love and sexual behavior: Perspectives from the social sciences* (pp. 285–300). Westport, CT: Praeger.

Doherty, R. W., Hatfield, E., Thompson, K., & Choo, P. (1994). Cultural and ethnic influences on love and attachment. *Personal Relationships, 1*, 391–398.

Fehr, B. (1988). Prototype analysis of the concepts of love and commitment. *Journal of Personality and Social Psychology, 55*, 557–579.

Fehr, B. (1993). How do I love thee? Let me consult my prototype. In S. Duck (Ed.), *Individuals in relationships* (pp. 87–120). Newbury Park, CA: Sage.

Fehr, B. (1994). Prototype-based assessment of laypeople's views of love. *Personal Relationships, 1*, 309–331.

Gadlin, H. (1977). Private lives and public order: A critical view of the history of intimate relations in the United States. In G. Levinger & H. L. Raush (Eds.), *Close relationships: Perspectives on the meaning of intimacy* (pp. 33–72). Amherst: University of Massachusetts Press.

Gergen, M. M., & Gergen, K. J. (1995). What is this thing called love? Emotional scenarios in historical perspective. *Journal of Narrative and Life History, 5*, 221–237.

Harlow, H. F. (1974). *Learning to love.* New York: Jason Aronson.

Hatfield, E. (1988). Passionate and companionate love. In R. J. Sternberg & M. L. Barnes (Eds.), *The psychology of love* (pp. 191–217). New Haven, CT: Yale University Press.

Hatfield, E., & Rapson, R. L. (1987). Passionate love: New directions in research. In W. H. Jones & D. Perlman (Eds.), *Advances in personal relationships: Vol. 1* (pp. 109–139). Greenwich, CT: JAI Press.

Hatfield, E., & Rapson, R. L. (1996). *Love and sex: Cross-cultural perspectives.* Boston: Allyn & Bacon.

Hatfield, E., & Sprecher, S. (1986). Measuring passionate love in intimate relations. *Journal of Adolescence, 9*, 383–410.

Hazan, C., & Shaver, P. (1987). Romantic love conceptualized as an attachment process. *Journal of Personality and Social Psychology, 52*, 511–524.

Hendrick, C., & Hendrick, S. S. (1986). A theory and method of love. *Journal of Personality and Social Psychology, 50*, 392–402.

Hendrick, C., & Hendrick, S. S. (1989). Research on love: Does it measure up? *Journal of Personality and Social Psychology, 56*, 784–794.

Hendrick, C., & Hendrick, S. S. (1990). A relationship-specific version of the Love Attitudes Scale. *Journal of Social Behavior and Personality, 5*, 239–254.

Hendrick, C., Hendrick, S. S., & Dicke, A. (1998). The Love Attitudes scale: Short Form. *Journal of Social and Personal Relationships, 15*, 147–159.

Hendrick, S. S., & Hendrick, C. (1992a). *Liking, loving & relating* (2nd ed.). Pacific Grove, CA: Brooks/Cole.

Hendrick, S. S., & Hendrick, C. (1992b). *Romantic love.* Newbury Park, CA: Sage.

Hendrick, S. S., & Hendrick, C. (1993). Lovers as friends. *Journal of Social and Personal Relationships, 10*, 459–466.

Hendrick, S. S., & Hendrick, C. (2000). Romantic love. In C. Hendrick & S. S. Hendrick (Eds.), *Close relationships: A sourcebook* (pp. 203–215). Thousand Oaks, CA: Sage.

Hendrick, S. S., & Hendrick, C. (2002). Love. In C. R. Snyder & S. J. Lopez (Eds.), *Handbook of positive psychology* (pp. 472–484). New York: Oxford University Press.

Jankowiak, W. R., & Fischer, E. F. (1992). A cross-cultural perspective on romantic love. *Ethnology, 31*, 149–155.

Johnson, M. P. (1987, Nov.). Discussion of papers on love styles and family relationships. In K. E. Davis (Chair), *New directions in love style research.* Symposium conducted at the Pre-conference theory construction and research methodology workshop, National Council on Family Relations, Atlanta, GA.

Kelley, H. H. (1983). Love and commitment. In H. H. Kelley, E. Berscheid, A. Christensen, J. H. Harvey, T. L. Huston, et al. (Eds.), *Close relationships* (pp. 265–314). New York: Freeman.

Lasswell, T. E., & Lasswell, M. E. (1976). I love you but I'm not in love with you. *Journal of Marriage and Family Counseling, 38*, 211–224.

Lee, J. A. (1973). *The colors of love: An exploration of the ways of loving.* Don Mills, Ontario: New Press.

Levy, J. A. (1994). Sex and sexuality in later life stages. In A. S. Rossi (Ed.), *Sexuality across the life course* (pp. 287–309). Chicago: University of Chicago Press.

Luce, R. D. (2000). Empirical quantification is the key to measurement—including psychological measurement. [Review of the book *Measurement in psychology: A critical history of a methodological concept* by Joel Michell.] *Contemporary Psychology: APA Review of Books, 45*, 499–502.

Michell, J. (1999). *Measurement in psychology: Critical history of a methodological concept.* Cambridge: Cambridge University Press.

Pickett, K. (1995). *Love in the 90's: B.B. and Jo: The story of a lifelong love.* New York: Warner Books.

Regan, P. C., Kocan, E. R., & Whitlock, T. (1998). Ain't love grand! A prototype analysis of the concept of romantic love. *Journal of Social and Personal Relationships, 15*, 411–420.

Rubin, Z. (1970). Measurement of romantic love. *Journal of Personality and Social Psychology, 16*, 265–273.

Seligman, M. E. P., & Csikszentmihalyi, M. (2000). Positive psychology: An introduction. *American Psychologist, 55*, 5–14.

Shaver, P. R., Morgan, H. J., & Wu, S. (1996). Is love a "basic" emotion? *Personal Relationships, 3*, 81–96.

Singer, I. (1984a). *The nature of love: Vol. 1. Plato to Luther* (2nd ed.). Chicago: University of Chicago Press.

Singer, I. (1984b). *The nature of love: Vol. 2. Courtly and romantic.* Chicago: University of Chicago Press.

Singer, I. (1987). *The nature of love: Vol. 3. The modern world.* Chicago: University of Chicago Press.

Snyder, C. R. (2000). Hypothesis: There is hope. In C. R. Snyder (Ed.), *Handbook of hope: Theory, measures, and applications* (pp. 3–21). San Diego, CA: Academic Press.

Sprecher, S., Aron, A., Hatfield, E., Cortese, A., Potapova, E., et al. (1994). Love: American style, Russian style, and Japanese style. *Personal Relationships, 1*, 349–369.

Steck, L., Levitan, D., McLane, D., & Kelley, H. H. (1982). Care, need, and conceptions of love. *Journal of Personality and Social Psychology, 43*, 481–491.

Sternberg, R. J. (1986). A triangular theory of love. *Psychological Review, 93*, 119–135.

Sternberg, R. J. (1997). Construct validation of a triangular love scale. *European Journal of Social Psychology, 27*, 313–335.

Taraban, C. B., Hendrick, S. S., & Hendrick, C. (1998). Loving and liking. In P. A. Andersen & L. K. Guerrero (Eds.), *Handbook of communication and emotion* (pp. 331–351). San Diego, CA: Academic Press.

16

Measuring Emotional Intelligence as a Set of Abilities With the Mayer–Salovey–Caruso Emotional Intelligence Test

Peter Salovey, John D. Mayer, David Caruso, and Paulo N. Lopes

Psychologists and other thinkers have been reluctant throughout history to admit that the emotions might actually function to sharpen cognitive activities and to motivate adaptive behavior (e.g., Woodworth, 1940; Young, 1936, 1943). When we first proposed the term *emotional intelligence* (Salovey & Mayer, 1990), we knew it would strike some people—especially those steeped in this historical tradition—as an oxymoron. Nonetheless, we thought it would call attention to the view that emotions can serve rationality rather than interfere with it (cf. Damasio, 1994) and that the traditional view of what constitutes intelligence is probably too narrowly specified (cf. Gardner, 1983, especially the *personal intelligences*). Since that time, we have tried to provide a more precise definition of emotional intelligence, furnish a structural model of those abilities and competencies that it includes, and develop ways of measuring it as a set of abilities. The construct of emotional intelligence became part of the layperson's lexicon after some of this work was popularized in a best-selling book by psychologist–journalist Daniel Goleman (1995).

Emotional intelligence is the ability to perceive and express emotions, to understand and use them, and to manage them to foster personal growth. More formally, we define emotional intelligence as the ability to perceive, appraise, and express emotions accurately; the ability to access and generate feelings to facilitate cognitive activities; the ability to understand affect-laden information

The preparation of this chapter was facilitated by grants from the American Cancer Society (RPG-93-028-05-PBP), the National Cancer Institute (R01-CA68427), the National Institute of Mental Health (P01-MH/DA56826), and the Donaghue Women's Health Investigator Program at Yale to Peter Salovey. We thank the graduate students, undergraduates, and research staff associated with the Health, Emotion, and Behavior (HEB) Laboratory in the Department of Psychology at Yale University.

and use emotion-relevant knowledge; and the ability to manage one's own emotions and the emotions of others to promote emotional and intellectual growth, well-being, and adaptive social relations (Mayer & Salovey, 1997; Salovey, Bedell, Detweiler, & Mayer, 1999, 2000; Salovey, Mayer, & Caruso, 2002; Salovey, Woolery, & Mayer, 2001). Our view of emotional intelligence is that it is ability- or competency-based (cf. Saarni, 1999), as distinguished from being rooted in personality traits (see Mayer, Salovey, & Caruso, 2000a, 2000b, for more about this distinction).

Modeling Emotional Intelligence

As implied by our definition of emotional intelligence, we conceive of it along four dimensions or branches, as illustrated in Table 16.1.

Perceiving Emotion

The first branch is perceiving (sometimes termed *identifying*) emotion, although it encompasses more than is implied by this term. It is defined as the ability to perceive and identify emotions in oneself and others, as well as to appreciate the emotional dimension of other stimuli such as works of art, music, and stories. When focused on the self, this dimension of emotional intelligence is related to emotional awareness (Lane & Schwartz, 1987) and to not being alexithymic (Apfel & Sifneos, 1979) or ambivalent about emotional expressivity (King, 1998; King & Emmons, 1990). When focused on other people, this dimension of emotional intelligence encompasses what is meant by affect sensitivity (Campbell, Kagan, & Krathwohl, 1971), affect-receiving ability (Buck, 1976), nonverbal sensitivity (Rosenthal, Hall, DiMatteo, Rogers, & Archer, 1979), and

Table 16.1. The Four-Branch Model of Emotional Intelligence

Branch name	Brief description of skills involved
Perceiving emotion (Branch 1)	The ability to identify emotions in oneself and others, as well as in objects, art, stories, music, and other stimuli.
Using emotion to facilitate thought (Branch 2)	The ability to generate, use, and feel emotion as necessary to communicate feelings, or use them in other cognitive processes.
Understanding emotion (Branch 3)	The ability to comprehend emotional information, how emotions combine and progress through relationship transitions, and to appreciate such emotional meanings.
Managing emotion (Branch 4)	The ability to be open to feelings, to regulate them in oneself and others to promote personal understanding and growth.

empathy (e.g., Batson, Fultz, & Schoenrade, 1987; Buck, 1984; Mehrabian & Epstein, 1972).

Using Emotion to Facilitate Thought

The second branch of emotional intelligence concerns the ability to use emotions to focus attention and think more rationally. Using emotions may require the ability to harness feelings that assist in certain cognitive enterprises such as reasoning, problem-solving, creativity, and communication. Different emotions may create different mental sets that prove more and less adaptive for various kinds of reasoning tasks (Isen, 1987; Palfai & Salovey, 1993; Schwarz, 1990; Schwarz & Clore, 1996). Some emotions may be more useful in stimulating creative thought (Isen & Daubman, 1984; Isen, Daubman, & Nowicki, 1987), and there may be a feedback loop wherein some people are especially creative in their experiencing of emotion (Averill, 1999, 2000; Averill & Nunley, 1992).

Understanding Emotion

This third branch of emotional intelligence can be thought of as one's intelligence about the emotional system. It includes an understanding of the emotional lexicon and the manner in which emotions combine, progress, or transition from one to the other. Individuals who are skilled at understanding emotions have a particularly rich feelings vocabulary and understand the relationships among terms describing different feeling states. They may be especially sensitive to the manner in which emotion terms are arranged as fuzzy sets organized around emotional prototypes (Ortony, Clore, & Collins, 1988) and in identifying the core meaning or themes behind various emotional experiences (Lazarus, 1991).

Managing Emotion

The ability to regulate moods and emotions in oneself and in other people constitutes the fourth branch of emotional intelligence. When managing one's own feelings, people must be able to monitor, discriminate, and label their feelings accurately, believe that they can improve or otherwise modify these feelings, use strategies that will alter their feelings, and assess the effectiveness of these strategies. Individuals differ in their abilities along these lines; several investigators have identified clear differences at least in individuals' self-perceptions of these abilities (Catanzaro & Greenwood, 1994; Salovey, Mayer, Goldman, Turvey, & Palfai, 1995).

Perhaps there is even greater variability in the skill with which individuals can regulate the feelings of other people. Some individuals always know just the right thing to say or do to cheer up a despondent friend, motivate a partner in an athletic competition, or charismatically inspire others (e.g., Wasielewski, 1985). Although the benefits of social support are widely documented, some people may be especially gifted at providing social support and building social capital.

Measuring Emotional Intelligence as an Individual Difference With the Mayer–Salovey–Caruso Emotional Intelligence Test

We have argued that if emotional intelligence is more than a mere metaphor and, in fact, should be taken seriously as a set of abilities or competencies, then it is best measured as such (Mayer, DiPaolo, & Salovey, 1990; Mayer & Salovey, 1993; Mayer, Salovey, Caruso, & Sitarenios, 2001). So, although self-report scales capturing one's beliefs about one's skills in this arena have proliferated, we believe that the best predictor of actual behavior at school, work, and in social relationships will be measures of actual skills and abilities. Along these lines, we have developed two batteries to assess emotional intelligence, both organized in accord with the four-branch model. The first measure is called the Multifactor Emotional Intelligence scale (MEIS; Mayer, Caruso, & Salovey, 1999), which served as the basis for a shorter and more professionally produced measure, the Mayer–Salovey–Caruso Emotional Intelligence Test (MSCEIT; Mayer, Salovey, & Caruso, 2001).

Development and Structure of the MSCEIT

Similar to the MEIS, the MSCEIT operationalizes the four dimensions of our model of emotional intelligence. Each branch is assessed with two sets of tasks. The two tasks concerned with perceiving emotion ask respondents to identify the emotions expressed in photographs of faces (faces) as well as the feelings suggested by artistic designs and landscapes (pictures). For using emotions, respondents are asked to describe feelings using nonfeeling vocabulary (sensations) and to indicate the feelings that might facilitate or interfere with the successful performance of various cognitive and behavioral tasks (facilitation). Understanding emotions is assessed with questions concerning the manner in which emotions evolve and transition over time (changes) and how some feelings are produced by blends of emotions (blends). The ability to manage emotions is assessed with a series of scenarios eliciting the most adaptive ways to regulate ones own feelings (emotion management) and feelings arising in social situations and in other people (social management). The items developed for the MEIS served as the starting point for the MSCEIT, but there have been several iterations (the current MSCEIT is called Version 2.0). As of this writing, responses from various versions correlate very highly.

Scoring Systems

Unlike traditional analytical intelligence tests, it may not be obvious how one determines the "correct" answer on an ability-based test of emotional intelligence. We have considered three approaches: consensus scoring, expert scoring, and target scoring.

In consensus scoring, the MSCEIT items are given to a large, heterogeneous sample of individuals. Responses are tallied from this normative sample, and respondents are given "credit" for "correct" answers to the extent that their answers match those provided by the normative sample. Response scores are weighted by the proportion of the normative sample who also provided that answer. The consensus scoring approach measures the extent to which a respondent's performance on the MSCEIT matches that of the general public. The assumption is made that large samples of individuals converge on correct answers. At present, Multi-Health Systems (the publisher of the MSCEIT) has collected a sample of more than 5,000 individuals (and still growing) worldwide who serve as the basis for consensus scoring. The consensus sample for the MEIS was smaller, containing about 500 individuals (Mayer et al., 1999).

Expert scoring relies on properly identified experts to indicate what they feel are the correct answers. Respondents receive credit for correct answers to the extent that they match those of the experts. These responses also can be weighted based on the proportion of the expert sample who responded similarly. Because of the length of the original MEIS and the burden that would have placed on any group of experts, two of the authors of the test (Mayer and Caruso) served as experts, so that we could explore the relationships between scores determined in this way and those based on consensual norms. Of course, a broader expert sample would have been desirable. So, for the MSCEIT, approximately 20 members of the International Society for Research on Emotion (ISRE), a prestigious organization of scholars and researchers who study emotions in humans and other animals, served as the expert sample. Many of these individuals have spent lifetimes studying such phenomena as how emotions are conveyed in facial expressions, blending of emotion, the phenomenological (conscious) experience of emotion, and coping with and managing emotion.

Target-based scoring is possible for some items. For example, one can ask the person whose facial expressions are depicted what, in fact, he or she was feeling when the photograph was taken. Similarly, one might ask the artist who developed items based on nonrepresentational works of art what feelings he or she was trying to convey. To the extent that respondents' answers match those of these individuals, they would be scored as correct.

We have looked at the correlations among emotional intelligence scores based on these different scoring methods expecting that they may produce convergent but also somewhat distinct findings. The first test of expert versus consensus scoring was conducted with the MEIS (Mayer et al., 1999). In that study, a single expert rating (a composite of the judgments of Mayer and Caruso) was compared with the general consensus. Given the form of the expert ratings (a single rating), only a dichotomous version of the data was used (single best answer or not), thus reducing the potential agreement between group common and expert scoring. Even so, substantial agreement was found between the two rating approaches. On a subset of four tasks, one drawn from each of the four branches and representing a total of 127 items, the correlations between expert and consensus scoring ranged between $r = .61$ and .80. The actual consensus and expert test scores (e.g., participants' responses matched against the criteria) had lower correlations. Although scoring of six of the tasks had correlations of $r = .52$ or greater, a number of tasks showed less agreement. It should be noted, however, that correlations may have been weakened because expert and normative sample answers were tabulated in different ways. For example, the two experts judged faces and other pictures on a computer screen, whereas the members of the normative sample judged colored photocopies (Mayer et al., 1999).

The introduction of the MSCEIT permitted a far more powerful comparison of scoring methods. Because the test is much shorter, it is easier to ask experts for their time in evaluating the correct answers; accordingly, a more appropriate expert sample could be recruited. For the expert group, we enlisted researchers attending the 11th annual meeting of the International Society of Research in Emotion. These scores certainly represent a better expert sample than what was available for the MEIS. Analyses of these data are ongoing, but it appears that among the more than 5,000 individuals who have taken the MSCEIT, full-scale MSCEIT scores based on the consensus norms correlate with those based on the experts quite highly, $r > .90$ (Mayer et al., 2001, in press). We view these findings of substantial agreement between consensus-based and expert-based MSCEIT scores as encouraging.

Factorial Validity

A principal axis factor analysis based on the first 1,700 or so members of the normative sample using consensus scoring indicated that the eight subtasks of the MSCEIT (Version 2.0) mapped nicely on to the four branches of the theoretical model, two per branch, and all of the subtasks were positively correlated with each other. The four branches appeared to be measured with adequate internal consistency (alphas of .87, .76, .73, .82, for perceiving, using, understanding, and managing branches, respectively, in this sample), and the branch scores generally produced normal distributions. Women often scored somewhat higher than men, but there were no systematic differences related to ethnicity (Mayer, Salovey, & Caruso, 2002; see also Mayer et al., 2001, in press, for analyses based on even larger samples).

Although data still are being collected on this issue, the MSCEIT appears to show appropriate discriminant validity from measures of analytical intelligence and many personality constructs. In a data set collected from 103 college undergraduates (Lopes, Salovey, & Straus, in press), the MSCEIT was administered along with various other measures. As can be seen in Table 16.2, MSCEIT scores do not appear to be associated with social desirability or mood. They are not related to scores on many personality scales, such as public and private self-consciousness and self-esteem. Verbal intelligence, as assessed by the WAIS–III vocabulary subscale and Verbal SAT scores (ranges on both were somewhat restricted in this sample) correlated modestly with the understanding emotions branch of the MSCEIT (which relies on knowledge of emotional vocabulary), but verbal intelligence did not correlate significantly with any of the other branches or with the total score.

With respect to the Big Five model (Costa & McCrae, 1992) of personality (which includes the constructs of extraversion, neuroticism, agreeableness,

Table 16.2. Convergent and Discriminant Validity of the MSCEIT: Correlations With Other Measures

	MSCEIT: Perceiving emotions	MSCEIT: Using emotions	MSCEIT: Under-standing emotions	MSCEIT: Managing emotions	MSCEIT: Total score
Positive relations with others	−.01	−.06	.20	**.27**	.11
NRI negative interaction factor/close friend	**−.25**	**−.33**	**−.36**	**−.36**	**−.45**
NRI negative interaction factor/parent	−.05	−.08	−.03	−.10	−.09
NRI social support factor/best friend	−.09	−.05	.02	.10	−.03
NRI social support factor/parent	−.14	−.07	.09	**.22**	.01
Verbal intelligence (WAIS–III vocabulary)	.06	−.03	**.39**	.05	.17
Verbal SAT (self-reported)	−.10	**−.22**	**.36**	−.10	−.04
Math SAT (self-reported)	−.09	−.06	.19	−.13	−.03
TMMS–attention	.05	−.10	.04	.05	.01
TMMS–clarity	.08	−.13	.09	.04	.04
TMMS–mood repair	.00	.00	**.21**	**.27**	.15
Neuroticism	−.07	−.03	−.09	−.15	−.12
Extraversion	−.04	−.01	.10	.06	.03
Agreeableness	.19	**.24**	.15	**.33**	**.32**
Openness	−.13	**−.28**	−.01	**−.22**	**−.22**
Conscientiousness	.11	.12	**.22**	**.24**	**.23**
Self-esteem	.01	−.07	−.05	.08	−.01
Private self-consciousness	.00	−.11	−.16	−.12	−.12
Public self-consciousness	.02	.08	.04	.05	.06
Social anxiety	.02	−.02	−.07	.02	−.01
Social desirability	.09	.01	.08	.15	.11
Mood	−.01	−.09	.03	.12	.01

Note. Significant correlations are shown in boldface type ($p < .05$, two-tailed). $90 < N < 102$, because of missing data.

MOOD = a mood composite based on the circumplex model of emotion.

MSCEIT (emotional intelligence, ability-based) = MSCEIT Version 2.0 (Mayer et al., 2001).

NRI SOCIAL SUPPORT AND NEGATIVE INTERACTION = Network of Relationship Inventory (Furman, 1996).

NEUROTICISM, EXTRAVERSION, OPENNESS, AGREEABLENESS, AND CONSCIEN-TIOUSNESS = NEO Five-Factor Inventory (Costa & McCrae, 1992).

POSITIVE RELATIONS WITH OTHERS = Scales of Psychological Well-Being (Ryff, 1989, 14-item version).

PUBLIC-PRIVATE SELF-CONSCIOUSNESS INVENTORY = (Fenigstein, Scheier, & Buss, 1975).

SAT = Scholastic Aptitude Test, self-reported.

SELF-ESTEEM (Rosenberg, 1965) = Rosenberg Self-Esteem Inventory Abridged to four items and adapted to avoid restriction of range among students (alpha in this sample = .81).

SOCIAL DESIRABILITY = The Marlowe-Crowne Social Desirability Scale (Crowne & Marlowe, 1960).

TMMS ATTENTION, CLARITY, AND REPAIR = Trait Meta-Mood Scale (Salovey et al., 1995); abridged 12-item version; alphas in this sample .70 to.75.

VERBAL INTELLIGENCE = Wechsler Adult Intelligence Scale–Third edition (Wechsler, 1997) vocabulary subscale.

conscientiousness, and openness), the branch scores from the MSCEIT did not correlate significantly with neuroticism or extroversion (Costa & McCrae, 1992). Using and managing emotions were modestly associated with agreeableness and, to some extent, negatively associated with openness. Understanding and managing emotions were modestly associated with conscientiousness. None of these correlations with scores on the NEO Five Factor Inventory (Costa & McCrae, 1992), however, exceeded .33, and most of the significant ones were in the .2 to .3 range (Lopes et al., in press).

Two self-report measures tapping the quality of one's social interactions provide some evidence for the convergent validity of the MSCEIT. The managing emotions branch of the MSCEIT was associated with the positive relations with others subscale of Ryff's (1989) Scales of Psychological Well-Being. This scale assesses satisfaction with the quality of one's engagement in, and support obtained from, the social domain of life. The perceiving, using, understanding, and managing emotions branches of the MSCEIT were inversely associated with the negative interaction (with close friend) factor of the Network of Relationship Inventory (NRI; Furman, 1996). This scale assesses conflict and antagonism in the relationship. The managing emotions branch of the MSCEIT also was related to the social support factor of the NRI in relation to a parent. This scale measures the companionship, intimacy, and affection provided by the parent to the respondent (Lopes et al., in press).

There were relatively weak associations between the MSCEIT and self-report measures of the meta-mood experience (the way individuals reflect on their moods). We found correlations in the .2 to .3 range between the MSCEIT branches of managing and understanding emotions and the mood repair factor of the Trait Meta-Mood scale (TMMS: Salovey et al., 1995), which taps into the use of optimistic thinking to regulate negative moods. However, only an abbreviated (although reliable) version of the TMMS was used in this study (Lopes et al., in press).

Construct and Predictive Validity

Because the MSCEIT was published only recently, there are few completed studies in which it has been used to predict outcomes in the laboratory, workplace, home, or school. However, the precursor to the MSCEIT, the MEIS, was used in many studies in several different laboratories, and these findings suggest that the four-branch theory of emotional intelligence has predictive validity.

Trinidad and Johnson (2002), for example, explored the relationship between emotional intelligence and substance abuse among southern California teenagers. Youths with higher emotional intelligence scores were less likely to have ever smoked cigarettes or to have smoked recently, and were less likely to have used alcohol in the recent past. School children scoring higher on the MEIS were rated as being less aggressive by their peers and as more prosocial by teachers than those students with low emotional intelligence (Rubin, 1999). The leaders of insurance company customer claim teams with higher as compared to lower MEIS scores were rated by their managers as being more effective, and overall team performance for customer service was also correlated with the teams' average MEIS scores (Rice, 1999). Emotional intelligence, as measured by the MEIS, also is associated with scores on measures of empathy (Ciarrochi, Chan, & Caputi, 2000; Mayer et al., 1999; Rubin, 1999) and life satisfaction (Ciarrochi et al., 2000). Although these findings must be viewed as preliminary, they represent promising suggestions that emotional intelligence can predict relevant behaviors in various life domains, such as school, work, and family. Whether the interesting relationships involving the MEIS are replicated with the MSCEIT awaits reports of ongoing research.

Other Approaches to Measuring Emotional Intelligence

Thus far, we have emphasized the measurement of emotional intelligence as a set of abilities, but self-report inventory and observer rating scale approaches to measuring individual differences in emotional intelligence (or, at least, a personality construct given the label *emotional intelligence*) also have proliferated in recent years.

Self-Report Inventories

Among the many recent self-report inventories purporting to measure emotional intelligence, we will review the two that have appeared most frequently in the literature.

A brief self-report scale based on our original model of emotional intelligence (Salovey & Mayer, 1990) was developed by Schutte et al. (1998; see also Petrides & Furnham, 2000). Its subscales include appraisal and expression of emotion, regulation of emotion, and use of emotions to facilitate problem solving and other cognitive activities. The 33-item scale is internally consistent and has high test–retest reliability. The Schutte et al. scale correlates with measures of theoretically related constructs, including the Toronto Alexithymia scale (Bagby, Parker, & Taylor, 1994), the attention, clarity, and repair subscales of the Trait Meta-Mood scale (Salovey et al., 1995), and measures of openness to experience from the Big Five model of personality (Costa & McCrae, 1992). Scores on the scale are positively associated with first-year college grades and were higher for therapists than for therapy clients or prisoners. Emotional intelligence scores on this measure were associated with supervisors' ratings of student counselors working at various mental health agencies (Malouff & Schutte, 1998).

The most widely used self-report measure of emotional intelligence—defined as a broad range of adaptive personality traits—is Bar-On's (1997) Emotional Quotient Inventory (EQ–i). This is a 133-item instrument in which respondents must indicate on 5-point scales the degree to which items apply to themselves. The EQ–i is organized into five composite scales and 15 subscales: (a) intrapersonal EQ made up of self-regard, emotional self-awareness, assertiveness, independence, and self-actualization; (b) interpersonal EQ made up of empathy, social responsibility, and interpersonal relationship; (c) stress management EQ made up of stress tolerance and impulse control;

(d) adaptability EQ made up of reality testing, flexibility, and problem solving; and (e) general mood EQ made up of optimism and happiness. It should be emphasized that the EQ–i includes many attributes that we would not consider abilities (e.g., assertiveness, optimism, happiness) or necessarily emotion-related (e.g., independence, social responsibility, reality testing, problem solving). Significant differences have been reported in the EQ–i scores of successful and unsuccessful military recruits, prisoners and nonprisoners, and other relevant comparison samples (reviewed in Bar-On, 2000).

We have discussed elsewhere the limitations of these kinds of self-report measures of emotional intelligence (e.g., Mayer et al., 2000a, 2000b). Our concern is whether individuals have the ability to assess their emotion-related competencies accurately. Likewise, there is the likely problem that self-reported emotional intelligence is highly correlated with personality measures. Perhaps those individuals who are most compromised in their emotional intelligence are precisely those who believe they are actually quite gifted in this domain.

More important, when measured through self-report scales, it has been difficult to demonstrate that emotional intelligence is distinct from standard measures of personality (Davies, Stankov, & Roberts, 1998; reviewed by Hedlund & Sternberg, 2000; Mayer, Caruso, & Salovey, 2000). For example, studies with the EQ–i suggest that it is highly correlated with standard Big Five measures of personality (e.g., Dawda & Hart, 2000) and measures of constructs such as alexithymia (Parker, Taylor, & Bagby, 2001). Part of the problem is that broad definitions of what constitutes emotional intelligence— any noncognitive trait, deemed important for daily living and not measured by analytical intelligence tests (e.g., Bar-On, 1997; Goleman, 1995)—have included many personality traits that are typically organized by the Big Five taxonomy (McCrae, 2000; see especially his Table 12.1, p. 265). It is for this reason that we termed these definitions of emotional intelligence as *mixed models* to distinguish them from ability models (Mayer et al., 2000b). To his credit, Bar-On (2000, p. 364) noted that the EQ–i "may . . . be described as a self-report measure of emotionally and socially competent behavior that provides an estimate of one's emotional and social intelligence."

Observer Ratings

Another approach to the measurement of emotional intelligence is to rely on the composite ratings of a target individual by all the people in that individual's social environment. This procedure, common in organizational development, is sometimes referred to as a 360-degree assessment. Boyatzis, Goleman, and Rhee (2000) developed the Emotional Competence Inventory (ECI) to operationalize the skills included in Goleman's (1998) model of emotional intelligence for workplace settings. This Goleman model describes 25 competencies arrayed in five clusters. The ECI measures 20 such competencies using self-report or 360-degree assessment forms. Many of the competencies included in the ECI appear to have little to do with emotional intelligence, although they are likely important and not well-captured by traditional measures of analytical intelligence (e.g., initiative, organizational awareness, change catalyst). The ECI is used extensively by the Hay/McBer Group, a management and human resources consulting firm. The subscales of both the self-assessment and the others' (360-degree) assessment versions of the ECI appear to have adequate internal consistency (Boyatsis et al., 2000), although little in the way of concurrent, discriminant, or predictive validity data have been published (see also Dulewicz & Higgs, 2000, in press, for another approach to the 360-degree assessment of emotional intelligence).

Future Directions

First, although we believe that the MSCEIT is a promising measure of emotional intelligence, much work needs to be done to answer unaddressed issues in this field. Most obvious is the lack of studies on the predictive validity of the MSCEIT. Similar to others working on this construct, we have many ideas about what emotional intelligence *should* predict, but we only now have begun to explore such associations. Part of the problem is that emotional intelligence, even when measured as an ability, is unlikely to predict single instances of behavior. As an example of this challenge, consider Major League Baseball. It takes nearly a whole season of plate appearances before the differences between the best and merely average hitters are obvious. The best hitters get about 40 more hits per season than average hitters, which is only one extra hit every fourth game or so. So, trying to use a baseball aptitude test to predict what a hitter will do at a single at-bat is not easy to do; one needs to aggregate over plate appearances and games. Unfortunately, analogous studies in schools, workplaces, and relationships designed to assess the predictive validity of emotional intelligence will be costly.

Second, studies of predictive validity will need to show that emotional intelligence relates to important outcomes over and above known constructs such as analytical intelligence (IQ) and standard measures of personality (captured by the Big Five model). It will not be enough to show correlations between emotional intelligence and these outcomes. The strongest case for the utility of emotional intelligence will come from those studies demonstrating that it accounts for variance in important outcomes that previously could not be predicted (Salovey & Pizarro, in press).

Third, issues of scoring remain challenging. There is disagreement about whether it makes sense to assess emotional intelligence against consensual norms, especially if one is not convinced that individuals, on the whole, are especially insightful in this domain (Roberts, Zeidner, & Matthews, 2001). If data continue to show a strong overlap between scores based on general, consensual norms and experts, however, this issue may become less worrisome (Mayer et al., 2001, in press).

Fourth, we discussed three different ways to measure emotional intelligence—as a set of abilities, as a self-reported personality construct, and as observed by others. The relations among these approaches, including the crucial issue of whether all are actually measuring something that could be called emotional intelligence, have not been adequately addressed. It is possible that all three are important, although it is not completely clear that all three show adequate discriminant and convergent validity with respect to already available constructs.

Conclusion

One of us (P. S.) plays bass in a band called "The Professors of Bluegrass." Before deciding whether to give up his day job and become a touring musician, it is probably helpful for him to try to assess whether he is a poor, adequate, or excellent bass player. One might do this in three ways: assess his musicianship as an ability by asking him to play difficult pieces of music in front of an audience (or, better yet, a panel of experts); ask his fellow musicians in the band what they think of his playing; or ask him to assess his own playing. These three approaches tell us different things that all might be important: whether he has any bass playing ability; whether his peers enjoy playing music with him; and his degree of confidence in his own ability to play the bass. Without self-confidence, our bass player may be unwilling to perform in public or even practice. If his peers do not like his playing, they may be unwilling to continue to perform with him. However, we would submit that his actual bass-playing ability is the assessment approach that would provide the best guidance about giving up a lucrative career as a professor of psychology in favor of the vagaries of life as a road musician. This holds whether he plays well according to consensual norms (audience response) or experts (Mike Bub, Tom Gray, Todd Phillips, and Missy Raines). Similarly, we believe that conceptualizing and measuring emotional intelligence as an ability holds out the greatest hope for demonstrating the validity of this construct and its utility in predicting psychologically relevant behavior.

References

Apfel, R. J., & Sifneos, P. E. (1979). Alexithymia: Concept and measurement. *Psychotherapy and Psychosomatics, 32,* 180–190.

Averill, J. R. (1999). Individual differences in emotional creativity: Structure and correlates. *Journal of Personality, 67,* 331–371.

Averill, J. R. (2000). Intelligence, emotion, and creativity: From trichotomy to trinity. In R. Bar-On & J. D. A. Parker (Eds.), *The handbook of emotional intelligence* (pp. 277–298). San Francisco: Jossey-Bass.

Averill, J. R., & Nunley, E. P. (1992). *Voyages of the heart: Living an emotionally creative life.* New York: Free Press.

Bagby, R. M., Parker, J. D. A., & Taylor, G. J. (1994). The twenty-item Toronto Alexithymia Scale: I. Item selection and cross-validation of the factor structure. *Journal of Psychosomatic Research, 38,* 23–32.

Bar-On, R. (1997). *BarOn Emotional Quotient Inventory (EQ–i): Technical manual.* Toronto: Multi-Health Systems.

Bar-On, R. (2000). Emotional and social intelligence: Insights from the Emotional Quotient Inventory. In R. Bar-On & J. D. A. Parker (Eds.), *The handbook of emotional intelligence* (pp. 363–388). San Francisco: Jossey-Bass.

Batson, C. D., Fultz, J., & Schoenrade, P. A. (1987). Distress and empathy: Two qualitatively distinct vicarious emotions with different motivational consequences. *Journal of Personality, 55,* 19–39.

Boyatzis, R. E., Goleman, D., & Rhee, K. S. (2000). Clustering competence in emotional intelligence: Insights from the Emotional Competence Inventory. In R. Bar-On & J. D. A. Parker (Eds.), *The handbook of emotional intelligence* (pp. 343–362). San Francisco: Jossey-Bass.

Buck, R. (1976). A test of nonverbal receiving ability: Preliminary studies. *Human Communication Research, 2,* 162–171.

Buck, R. (1984). *The communication of emotion.* New York: Guilford Press.

Campbell, R. J., Kagan, N. I., & Krathwohl, D. R. (1971). The development and validation of a scale to measure affective sensitivity (empathy). *Journal of Counseling Psychology, 18,* 407–412.

Catanzaro, S. J., & Greenwood, G. (1994). Expectancies for negative mood regulation, coping, and dysphoria among college students. *Journal of Consulting Psychology, 41,* 34–44.

Ciarrochi, J. V., Chan, A. Y. C., & Caputi, P. (2000). A critical evaluation of the emotional intelligence construct. *Personality and Individual Differences, 28,* 539–561.

Costa, P. T., Jr., & McCrae, R. R. (1992). *NEO–PI–R Professional Manual–Revised NEO Personality Inventory (NEO–PIR) and NEO Five-Factor Inventory (NEO–FFI).* Odessa, FL: Psychological Assessment Resources.

Crowne, D. P., & Marlowe, D. (1960). A new scale of social desirability independent of psychopathology. *Journal of Consulting Psychology, 24,* 349–354.

Damasio, A. (1994). *Descartes' error: Emotion, reason, and the human brain.* New York: Putnam.

Davies, M., Stankov, L., & Roberts, R. D. (1998). Emotional intelligence: In search of an elusive construct. *Journal of Personality and Social Psychology, 75,* 989–1015.

Dawda, D., & Hart, S. D. (2000). Assessing emotional intelligence: Reliability and validity of the Bar-On Emotional Quotient Inventory (EQ–i) in university students. *Personality and Individual Differences, 28,* 797–812.

Dulewicz, V., & Higgs, M. (2000). Emotional intelligence: A review and evaluation study. *Journal of Managerial Psychology, 15,* 341–372.

Dulewicz, V., & Higgs, M. (in press). A study of 360-degree assessment of emotional intelligence. *Selection and Development Review.*

Fenigstein, A., Scheier, M. F., & Buss, A. H. (1975). Public and private self-consciousness: Assessment and theory. *Journal of Consulting and Clinical Psychology, 43,* 522–527.

Furman, W. (1996). The measurement of children and adolescents' perceptions of friendships: Conceptual and methodological issues. In W. M. Bukowski, A. F. Newcomb, & W. W. Hartup (Eds.), *The company they keep: Friendships in childhood and adolescence* (pp. 41–65). New York: Cambridge University Press.

Gardner, H. (1983). *Frames of mind: The theory of multiple intelligences.* New York: Basic Books.

Goleman, D. (1995). *Emotional intelligence.* New York: Bantam.

Goleman, D. (1998). *Working with emotional intelligence.* New York: Bantam.

Hedlund, J., & Sternberg, R. J. (2000). Too many intelligences? Integrating social, emotional, and practical intelligence. In R. Bar-On & J. D. A. Parker (Eds.), *The handbook of emotional intelligence* (pp. 136–167). San Francisco: Jossey-Bass.

Isen, A. M. (1987). Positive affect, cognitive processes, and social behavior. *Advances in Experimental Social Psychology, 20,* 203–253.

Isen, A. M., & Daubman, K. A. (1984). The influence of affect on categorization. *Journal of Personality and Social Psychology, 47,* 1206–1217.

Isen, A. M., Daubman, K. A., & Nowicki, G. P. (1987). Positive affect facilitates creative problem solving. *Journal of Personality and Social Psychology, 52,* 1122–1131.

King, L. A. (1998). Ambivalence over emotional expression and reading emotions in situations and faces. *Journal of Personality and Social Psychology, 74,* 753–762.

King, L. A., & Emmons, R. A. (1990). Conflict over emotional expression: Psychological and physiological correlates. *Journal of Personality and Social Psychology, 58,* 864–877.

Lane, R. D., & Schwartz, G. E. (1987). Levels of emotional awareness: A cognitive–developmental theory and its application to psychopathology. *American Journal of Psychiatry, 144,* 133–143.

Lazarus, R. S. (1991). *Emotion and adaptation.* New York: Oxford University Press.

Lopes, P. N., Salovey, P., & Straus, R. (in press). Emotional intelligence, personality, and the perceived quality of social relationships. *Personality and Individual Differences.*

Malouff, J., & Schutte, N. (1998, Aug.). *Emotional intelligence scale scores predict counselor performance.* Paper presented at the Annual Convention of the American Psychological Society, Washington, DC.

Mayer, J. D., Caruso, D., & Salovey, P. (1999). Emotional intelligence meets traditional standards for an intelligence. *Intelligence, 27,* 267–298.

Mayer, J. D., Caruso, D., & Salovey, P. (2000). Selecting a measure of emotional intelligence: The case for ability scales. In R. Bar-On & J. D. A. Parker (Eds.), *The handbook of emotional intelligence* (pp. 320–342). San Francisco: Jossey-Bass.

Mayer, J. D., DiPaolo, M. T., & Salovey, P. (1990). Perceiving affective content in ambiguous visual stimuli: A component of emotional intelligence. *Journal of Personality Assessment, 54,* 772–781.

Mayer, J. D., & Salovey, P. (1993). The intelligence of emotional intelligence. *Intelligence, 17,* 443–442.

Mayer, J. D., & Salovey, P. (1997). What is emotional intelligence? In P. Salovey & D. Sluyter (Eds.), *Emotional development and emotional intelligence: Implications for educators* (pp. 3–31). New York: Basic Books.

Mayer, J. D., Salovey, P., & Caruso, D. (2000a). Emotional intelligence as Zeitgeist, as personality, and as a mental ability. In R. Bar-On & J. D. A. Parker (Eds.), *The handbook of emotional intelligence* (pp. 92–117). San Francisco: Jossey-Bass.

Mayer, J. D., Salovey, P., & Caruso, D. (2000b). Models of emotional intelligence. In R. J. Sternberg (Ed.), *The handbook of intelligence* (pp. 396–420). New York: Cambridge University Press.

Mayer, J. D., Salovey, P., & Caruso, D. (2001). *The Mayer-Salovey-Caruso Emotional Intelligence Test (MSCEIT).* Toronto: Multi-Health Systems.

Mayer, J. D., Salovey, P., & Caruso, D. (2002). *Test manual for the MSCEIT V.2.* Toronto: Multi-Health Systems.

Mayer, J. D., Salovey, P., Caruso, D., & Sitarenios, G. (2001). Emotional intelligence as a standard intelligence. *Emotion, 1,* 232–242.

Mayer, J. D., Salovey, P., Caruso, D., & Sitarenios, G. (in press). Measuring emotional intelligence with the MSCEIT V2.0. *Emotion.*

McCrae, R. R. (2000). Emotional intelligence from the perspective of the five-factor model of personality. In R. Bar-On & J. D. A. Parker (Eds.), *The handbook of emotional intelligence* (pp. 263–276). San Francisco: Jossey-Bass.

Mehrabian, A., & Epstein, N. (1972). A measure of emotional empathy. *Journal of Personality, 40,* 525–543.

Ortony, A., Clore, G. L., & Collins, A. (1988). *The cognitive structure of emotions.* Cambridge: Cambridge University Press.

Palfai, T. P., & Salovey, P. (1993). The influence of depressed and elated mood on deductive and inductive reasoning. *Imagination, Cognition, and Personality, 13,* 57–71.

Parker, J. D. A., Taylor, G. J., & Bagby, R. M. (2001). The relationship between alexithymia and emotional intelligence. *Personality and Individual Differences, 30,* 107–115.

Petrides, K. V., & Furnham, A. (2000). On the dimensional structure of emotional intelligence. *Personality and Individual Differences, 29,* 313–320.

Rice, C. L. (1999). *A quantitative study of emotional intelligence and its impact on team performance.* Unpublished master's thesis, Pepperdine University, Malibu, CA.

Roberts, R. D., Zeidner, M., & Matthews, G. (2001). Does emotional intelligence meet traditional standards for an intelligence? Some new data and conclusions. *Emotion, 1,* 196–231.

Rosenberg, M. (1965). *Society and the adolescent self-image.* Princeton, NJ: Princeton University Press.

Rosenthal, R., Hall, J. A., DiMatteo, M. R., Rogers, P., & Archer, D. (1979). *Sensitivity to nonverbal communication: A profile approach to the measurement of individual differences.* Baltimore: Johns Hopkins University Press.

Rubin, M. M. (1999). *Emotional intelligence and its role in mitigating aggression: A correlational study of the relationship between emotional intelligence and aggression in urban adolescents.* Unpublished manuscript, Immaculata College, Immaculata, PA.

Ryff, C. D. (1989). Happiness is everything, or is it? Explorations on the meaning of psychological well-being. *Journal of Personality and Social Psychology, 57,* 1069–1081.

Saarni, C. (1999). *Developing emotional competence.* New York: Guilford Press.

Salovey, P., Bedell, B. T., Detweiler, J. B., & Mayer, J. D. (1999). Coping intelligently: Emotional intelligence and the coping process. In C. R. Snyder (Ed.), *Coping: The psychology of what works* (pp. 141–164). New York: Oxford University Press.

Salovey, P., Bedell, B. T., Detweiler, J. B., & Mayer, J. D. (2000). Current directions in emotional intelligence research. In M. Lewis & J. M. Haviland-Jones (Eds.), *Handbook of emotions* (2nd ed., pp. 504–520). New York: Guilford Press.

Salovey, P., & Mayer, J. D. (1990). Emotional intelligence. *Imagination, Cognition, and Personality, 9,* 185–211.

Salovey, P., Mayer, J. D., & Caruso, D. (2002). The positive psychology of emotional intelligence. In C. R. Snyder & S. J. Lopez (Eds.), *The handbook of positive psychology* (pp. 159–171). Oxford: Oxford University Press.

Salovey, P., Mayer, J. D., Goldman, S. L., Turvey, C., & Palfai, T. P. (1995). Emotional attention, clarity, and repair: Exploring emotional intelligence using the Trait Meta-Mood Scale. In J. W. Pennebaker (Ed.), *Emotion, disclosure, and health* (pp. 125–154). Washington, DC: American Psychological Association.

Salovey, P., & Pizarro, D. A. (in press). The value of emotional intelligence. In R. J. Sternberg, J. Lautrey, & T. Lubart (Eds.), *Models of intelligence for the next millennium.* Washington, DC: American Psychological Association.

Salovey, P., Woolery, A., & Mayer, J. D. (2001). Emotional intelligence: Conceptualization and measurement. In G. Fletcher & M. Clark (Eds.), *The Blackwell handbook of social psychology: Interpersonal processes* (pp. 279–307). London: Blackwell.

Schutte, N. S., Malouff, J. M., Hall, L. E., Haggerty, D., Cooper, J. T., et al. (1998). Development and validation of a measure of emotional intelligence. *Personality and Individual Differences, 25,* 167–177.

Schwarz, N. (1990). Feelings as information: Informational and motivational functions of affective states. In E. T. Higgins & E. M. Sorrentino (Eds.), *Handbook of motivation and cognition* (Vol. 2, pp. 527–561). New York: Guilford Press.

Schwarz, N., & Clore, G. L. (1996). Feelings and phenomenal experiences. In E. T. Higgins & A. W. Kruglanski (Eds.), *Social psychology: Handbook of basic principles* (pp. 433–465). New York: Guilford Press.

Trinidad, D. R., & Johnson, C. A. (2002). The association between emotional intelligence and early adolescent tobacco and alcohol use. *Personality and Individual Differences, 32,* 95–105.

Wasielewski, P. L. (1985). The emotional basis of charisma. *Symbolic Interaction, 8,* 207–222.

Wechsler, D. (1997). *WAIS–III: Wechsler Adult Intelligence Scale* (3rd ed.). San Antonio, TX: Psychological Corporation.

Woodworth, R. S. (1940). *Psychology* (4th ed.). New York: Holt.

Young, P. T. (1936). *Motivation of behavior.* New York: Wiley.

Young, P. T. (1943). *Emotion in man and animal: Its nature and relation to attitude and motive.* New York: Wiley.

Part IV

Interpersonal Models and Measures

17

Empathy and Its Measurement

Qing Zhou, Carlos Valiente, and Nancy Eisenberg

The empathy construct has received considerable attention by psychologists interested in positive behavior. Empathy motivates helping others and the desire for justice for others, as well as inhibits aggression toward others (Batson, 1991; Hoffman, 2000; Miller & Eisenberg, 1988). Empathy also facilitates people's socially competent interactions (Eisenberg et al., 1996; Saarni, 1990) and provides a sense of connection among people. Thus, it is an aspect of human responding that is critical for understanding positive development.

Empathy has, and continues to be, defined in various ways. In social and developmental psychology, empathy-related responding is defined as an affective response to the cognitive processing of information about another's state or condition. Similar to Feshbach (1978) and Hoffman (1982), Eisenberg and her colleagues have defined empathy as a state of emotional arousal that stems from the apprehension or comprehension of another's affective state; moreover, it is similar to, or congruent with, the feeling of other people (Eisenberg, Shea, Carlo, & Knight, 1991). For instance, if an observer sees another person who is sad and in response feels sad, that individual is experiencing empathy. Empathy can occur in response to cues of positive emotion as well as negative emotion. To qualify as empathy, the empathizer must recognize, at least on some level, that the emotion she or he is experiencing is a reflection of the other's emotional, psychological, or physical state. That is, there must be at least a minimal degree of self–other distinction in regard to the emotion; otherwise, the affective reactions would be a primitive form or precursor of empathy.

It is useful to distinguish, at least at a conceptual level, between pure empathy and other empathy-related responses such as sympathy and personal distress (Batson, 1991). Sympathy is an other-oriented, emotional response that is based on the apprehension or comprehension of another's negative emotional condition; it involves feelings of concern and the desire to alleviate the other's negative emotion (sometimes in combination with empathic sadness). Sympathy stems from the experience of empathy, or from cognitive processes

Work on this chapter was supported by grants from the National Institutes of Mental Health (R01 HH55052 and R01 MH 60838), as well as a Research Scientist Award to Nancy Eisenberg.

such as perspective taking, mental associations, and accessing information about the other's situation from memory (Eisenberg, Shea, et al., 1991).

Personal distress involves a negative reaction such as anxiety or discomfort on perceiving cues related to another's distress (Batson, 1991). Similar to sympathy, personal distress may stem primarily from empathy or empathic overarousal, but it also can arise solely through cognitive processes (e.g., through an association between cues related to another's sadness and distressing memories from one's own past). Scholars have suggested that empathic overarousal (Hoffman, 1982) or personal distress (Batson, 1991) is associated with a self rather than other focus. Consistent with this idea, researchers have found evidence that aversive emotional arousal induces self-focused attention (Wood, Saltzberg, & Goldsamt, 1990). Consequently, a person experiencing personal distress is believed to be concerned with reducing his or her own aversive vicarious emotional arousal (Batson, 1991).

In empirical research, some investigators have tried to differentiate empathy, sympathy, and personal distress; others have assessed only one construct or a combination of them. It is very difficult to distinguish between empathy and either personal distress or sympathy because the former is believed to elicit at least one of the latter two in most contexts. Thus, in many cases, measures of empathy-related responding could assess more than one construct.

In early work, before these distinctions were discussed, most relevant research pertained to global empathy or a combination of what we defined as empathy, sympathy, and personal distress (e.g., Bryant, 1982; Mehrabian & Epstein, 1972). However, Batson (1991) demonstrated that sympathy (labeled empathy by Batson), but not personal distress, is related to behaviors that appear to be altruistic (i.e., voluntary actions intended to benefit another that are not based on some form of self-gain). Thus, there has been considerable interest in empirically differentiating sympathy and personal distress.

Of course, definitions of empathy-related responding, as well as its correlates, vary as a function of the operational notion of the construct. In this chapter, we briefly review some of the methods that have been used to assess empathy-related responding. We present illustrative examples of findings and discuss advantages and disadvantages of the various approaches.

Self-Report of Empathy-Related Responding

Self-report is one of the most commonly used techniques for assessing empathy-related responding. Here we review three types of self-report measures—self-report on picture-stories, on questionnaires, and in stimulated experimental situations.

Self-Report on Pictures–Stories Measures

During the 1960s and 1970s, picture–story measures of empathy commonly were used for assessing children's empathy. With these measures, the child typically is told brief stories while being shown pictures (usually photos or drawings) depicting hypothetical protagonists in emotion-eliciting situations. The most frequently used measure of this type is the Feshbach and Roe Affective Situations Test for Empathy (FASTE; Feshbach, 1978), which was designed to assess empathy in preschoolers and young, school-age children. The FASTE consists of a series of eight stories (each accompanied by three slides) depicting events that would be expected to make the story protagonist happy, sad, fearful, or angry (there are two stories for each of these emotions). After exposure to each scenario, the child is asked, "How do you feel?" or "How did that story make you feel?" Empathic responsiveness is operationalized as the degree of match between the child's and the story character's emotional states.

The FASTE has been modified by many researchers to fit their studies. For example, the stories may have been altered or replaced, or only a subset of the emotions (e.g., only happiness and sadness) has been assessed (e.g., Eisenberg-Berg & Lennon, 1980). In some studies, the procedures have been augmented so that children can indicate their reactions nonverbally by pointing to pictures of facial expressions (e.g., Eisenberg-Berg & Lennon, 1980; Iannotti, 1985).

Although picture–story measures were an important early instrument for the study of affective empathy, especially for young children, there has been considerable concern about their psychometric properties (see Eisenberg & Miller, 1987; Lennon, Eisenberg, & Carroll, 1983). First, the stories typically are so short that they may not induce sufficient affect to evoke empathy, especially over repeated trials. Using longer stories, however, did not improve the validity of the measure in one study (Eisenberg-Berg & Lennon, 1980). Second, children's self-reports of empathy in reaction to picture–story indexes have related positively to public and requested prosocial behavior but negatively to spontaneous prosocial behavior (e.g., Eisenberg-Berg & Lennon, 1980), suggesting that self-reported empathy is generally affected by social demands (i.e., the need to behave in a socially approved manner).

Related to the last point, children's reports of empathy appear to be influenced by the interaction between sex of the child and sex of the experimenter. In this regard, researchers found that children scored higher on the picture–story measure (e.g., the FASTE) when interviewed by same-sex rather than other-sex experimenters (Eisenberg & Lennon, 1983; Lennon et al., 1983). Children also may be more concerned with providing socially desirable responses when interviewed by same-sex experimenters. In addition, in most studies using the picture–story measures of empathy, scores on children's empathic responses were combined across situations involving different emotions and only the global index of empathy was used in the analyses. As pointed out by Hoffman (1982), however, empathy with one emotion (e.g., happiness) may not be equivalent to empathy with another emotion (e.g., sadness). Moreover, researchers using picture–story procedures generally have not differentiated between sympathy and empathy. Given these problems with picture–story measures, it is not surprising that meta-analyses have found weak associations between them and prosocial behavior and aggression (Eisenberg & Miller, 1987; Miller & Eisenberg, 1988).

Self-Report on Questionnaires

Questionnaire measures of empathy are believed to assess the trait of empathy (empathic responding across a range of settings). One of the most commonly used is Mehrabian and Epstein's (1972) scale of emotional tendency, which has been used mostly with older adolescents and adults. The measure consists of 33 items requiring a response to each item on a 9-point Likert scale (from "very strong agreement" to "very strong disagreement"). The items pertain to susceptibility to emotional contagion (e.g., "People around me have a great influence on my moods"), appreciation of the feelings of unfamiliar and distant others (e.g., "Lonely people are probably unfriendly"), extreme emotional responsiveness (e.g., "Sometimes the words of a love song can move me deeply"), the tendency to be moved by others' positive emotional experiences (e.g., "I like to watch people open presents"), sympathetic tendencies or the lack thereof (e.g., "It is hard for me to see how some things upset people so much"), and willingness to have contact with others who have problems (e.g., "When a friend starts to talk about his/her problem, I try to steer the conversation to something else"). The internal consistency of the Mehrabian and Epstein measure is .79 among adults (Kalliopuska, 1983) and .48 among seventh graders (Bryant, 1982). A split-half reliability of .84 has been reported (Mehrabian & Epstein, 1972).

Bryant (1982) modified the Mehrabian and Epstein scale for children. Bryant's empathy scale consists of 22 items assessing global sympathy (e.g., "I get upset when I see a girl being hurt," "It makes me sad to see a boy who can't find anyone to play with"). Seventeen of the items were adapted from Mehrabian and Epstein's (1972) scale. Three formats have been used in administering the resulting children's version of empathy assessment (Bryant, 1987). Younger children place cards (one empathy item per card) in a "me" or "not me" box; older children circle "yes" or "no" in response to each item; and adolescents or adults respond to the Mehrabian and Epstein 9-point format. The alpha of Bryant's measure was .54 for first graders, .68 for fourth graders, and .79 for the seventh graders (Bryant, 1982).

A major problem with Mehrabian and Epstein's and Bryant's self-report measures is that items seem to tap various aspects of empathy-related responding such as sympathy, susceptibility to emotional arousal, perspective taking, and personal distress. Davis's (1983, 1994) Interpersonal Reactivity scale (see Davis, 1994) resolves this concern because it contains separate scales designed to differentiate among empathic concern (i.e., sympathy), personal distress, fantasy empathy (i.e., vicarious responding to characters in books for film), and perspective taking. This measure has been used primarily with adolescents and adults. Internal reliabilities for the four subscales ranged from .70 to .78, and test–retest reliabilities over two months range from .61 to .81 in research with adults (Davis, 1983, 1994). Test–retest reliabilities over two years in adolescence ranged from .50 to .62 (Davis & Franzoi, 1991).

In addition, Eisenberg and her colleagues developed a simplified 3-item scale of dispositional sympathy for use with children (Eisenberg, Fabes, Schaller, Carlo, & Miller, 1991): "I feel sorry for people who don't have the things that I have," "When I see someone being picked on, I feel kind of sorry for them" and "I often feel sorry for other children who are sad or in trouble" (alpha = .67). This scale was enlarged to seven items in Eisenberg et al. (1996; alpha =.73 with kindergarten to second graders) and six items in Spinrad et al. (1999; alpha =.63 with children aged 5 to just turning 8; see Appendix 17.1).

Compared to picture–story measures, questionnaire assessments of empathy-related responding are more convenient and economical to administer. Moreover, because the questionnaires tap individuals' empathic or sympathetic reactions over a much broader range of behaviors and situations, they likely provide more stable and consistent estimates of empathic responding than measures pertaining to specific situations (Eisenberg & Miller, 1987). Indicative of their validity, questionnaire measures of empathy consistently have been found to relate positively to participants' prosocial behavior, and negatively to aggression in middle childhood to adulthood (Eisenberg & Fabes, 1998; Eisenberg & Miller, 1987; Miller & Eisenberg, 1988). Researchers and practitioners, however, should be aware of the disadvantages of self-report questionnaire measures of empathy. One of the weaknesses is that social desirability has been related to children's reports of empathy and sympathy on questionnaires (e.g., Eisenberg, Fabes, Schaller, Miller, et al., 1991). In adulthood, the desire to see oneself in ways consistent with one's own values, needs, and self-perceptions, including those stemming from one's same-sex gender role (e.g., men might prefer to present themselves as unemotional to others whereas women might not be concerned with being viewed as emotional) may be more likely than social desirability to influence participants' reports of empathy and sympathy (Losoya & Eisenberg, 2001).

Self-Report in Stimulated Experimental Situations

With this set of measures, the emotion-evoking stimuli usually are presented via audiotapes, videotapes, or realistic enactments that aim to make participants believe that the events and people involved in the stimuli are real, not hypothetical. After the exposure to the evoking stimuli (e.g., a distress film), participants are asked to report their emotional reactions by means of self-ratings on a mood scale with adjectives reflecting empathy (e.g., empathic, concerned, warm, softhearted, compassionate; Batson, 1991), positive and negative affect, or other empathy-related responses such as sympathy and personal distress (e.g., Batson, 1991; Holmgren, Eisenberg, & Fabes, 1998; Zahn-Waxler, Friedman, & Cummings, 1983). Depending on the age of the participants, the responses may be obtained with paper or pencil measure, verbal reports, or by pointing to pictorial scales indicating how much an adjective applies. In general, a moderate association has been found between prosocial behavior and self-report of empathy in empathy-evoking situations for adolescents and adults (Eisenberg & Miller, 1987), albeit weak relations for children (Eisenberg & Fabes, 1990, 1998).

Strayer and Schroeder (1989; see also Strayer, 1993) developed a set of procedures to measure children's empathic responding to a series of videotaped emotionally evocative vignettes. After viewing the vignettes, the children were asked to identify the kind and intensity of emotions felt by the vignette characters, and to report any self-experienced emotion (e.g., happy, sad, angry, afraid, surprised, disgusted, or neutral). Empathy was rated in two ways. First, empathy was scored as a generally dysphoric or euphoric emotion shared by the character and child, as a more specific match of emotion (in kind but not intensity) for self and the character, or as an identical match in both kind and intensity of emotion reported for self and the character. Second, if children reported an emotion for the self, they were asked what it was about the vignette witnessed that made them feel that way. Empathy was then scored on the Empathy Continuum (EC) scoring system. The EC, which organizes scores at seven different levels of cognitive mediation, consolidates the degree of affective sharing reportedly experienced with the child's cognitive attributions for these emotions.

Almost all types of self-report measures, including self-report in experimentally induced situations, may be affected by study participants' verbal ability and comprehension, particularly when used with children. For example, children may not be able to correctly label an emotion they observe, accurately report how they feel, or differentiate among emotion states with similar affective valence (Strayer, 1987).

Other-Reports of Empathy-Related Responding

To obtain information about participants' empathy-related responding from parents, teachers, or peers, research on other-reports of empathy often uses items similar to those in the Mehrabian and Epstein (1972) empathy scale, Davis's (1983) empathy subscales, or Eisenberg and colleagues' (1991) self-report sympathy scales (e.g., Eisenberg, Carlo, Murphy, & Van Court, 1995; Eisenberg et al., 1998; see Appendix 17.2 for the scale). As suggested by Losoya and Eisenberg (2001), there are several benefits of using other-report measures. First, other-reports can be used to obtain data on children too young to provide accurate self-reports. Second, other-reports are less likely than self-reports to be biased by social desirability, especially if someone other than a family member is the respondent. Third, it is possible to use multiple reporters to obtain information about participants' empathy-related responding in a variety of settings, which is likely to provide more reliable data than that obtained from a single reporter. There is modest agreement between parents' and teachers' reports of children's sympathy, although this agreement appears to decrease to nonsignificance as children enter adolescence (Eisenberg, Fabes, et al., 1996, 1998; Murphy, Shepard, Eisenberg, Fabes, & Guthrie, 1999). This may be because junior high teachers do not know their students as well as do elementary school teachers, or because adolescents may be more private or guarded about their emotional experience. In studies examining the associations between other-reports of empathy and children's prosocial behavior, the correlations were high when the same person who rated the child's empathy also provided data on prosocial behavior. This pattern of association may, of course, reflect raters' tendencies to assume that relations exist between empathy and prosocial behavior. Moderate associations were found between other-reported empathy and prosocial behavior when independent measures of these two variables were used (Eisenberg & Miller, 1987). Moreover, other-reports of sympathy tend to be related to children's social competence more generally (Eisenberg et al., 1996; Murphy et al., 1999).

Facial, Gestural, and Vocal Indices of Empathy-Related Responding

Participants' facial, gestural, and vocal reactions to experimentally induced empathy-evoking stimulus (while they are watching videotapes of others in need or distress—e.g., Holmgren et al., 1998—or responding to someone in distress—e.g., Zahn-Waxler et al., 1983) have been obtained and coded as markers of empathy-related reactions. Alternatively, Zahn-Waxler, Radke-Yarrow, Wagner, and Chapman (1992) asked mothers to describe in detail their young children's reactions to naturally occurring instances of another's distress that the children either caused or witnessed.

A variety of emotions can be coded from the facial, gestural, and vocal responses to empathy-inducing stimulus. For example, in Zahn-Waxler and colleagues' study (1992), participants' reactions to naturally occurring instances of another's distress were coded for: (a) empathic concern (i.e., emotional arousal that appeared to reflect sympathetic concern for the victim (e.g., sad looks, sympathetic statements such as "I'm sorry" said in a soothing or reassuring tone of voice, or gestures such as rushing to the victim while looking worried); (b) self-distress (i.e., emotions evoked by the other's distress that were more intense, negative, and reflective of personal distress; e.g., the target child sobs, cries, frets, or whimpers); and (c) positive affect when viewing another's distress. While coding individuals' facial and gestural reactions to viewing empathy-inducing films, Eisenberg and colleagues tried to differentiate among facial expressions that likely reflect sympathy, empathy, and personal distress. Expressions of concerned attention (e.g., eyebrows pulled down and inward over the nose, head forward, intense interest in evocative events in the film) are believed to indicate sympathy during exposure to empathy-inducing stimuli; signs of empathic sadness (sad expressions) in response to sad events likely tap empathy and may be likely to engender sympathy; fearful and anxious expression and lip-biting are likely to indicate personal distress (Eisenberg, Schaller, et al., 1988; Eisenberg & Fabes, 1990).

A clear strength of facial, gestural, and vocal indexes of empathy is that they are less subject to the self-presentational biases inherent in self-report measures, particularly for younger children who have yet to learn socially appropriate facial display rules (Cole, 1986) or for participants who are video-taped unobtrusively. Therefore, facial, gestural, and vocal measures of empathy-related responding have been used with children from as young as 15 months old through elementary school (e.g., Miller, Eisenberg, Fabes, & Shell, 1996; Zahn-Waxler et al., 1992), as well as with adults (Eisenberg et al., 1994).

It should be noted, however, that facial and gestural measures also have limitations. First, the facial expressions in situations involving vicarious emotion reflect not only empathy but also the participants' emotional expressivity. Expressive children are likely to be identified as more empathic with facial, gestural, and vocal measures than less expressive children, although the levels of their empathic arousal might be the same. Moreover, as children age, they increasingly become able to mask their expression of negative emotion (Cole, 1986), and to do so in a variety of situations (Eisenberg, Fabes, et al., 1988). Thus, as in the case of self-reports, self-presentational biases and demand characteristics may affect older children's and adults' willingness to display negative emotions (Losoya & Eisenberg, 2001). Therefore, facial indexes may not be accurate markers of empathy-related responding for older children and adults, especially if facial expressions are assessed when individuals are in view of others.

The relations of facial, gestural, and vocal indexes of empathy to participants' prosocial behavior and aggression seem to differ by the type of empathy stimuli used. In Eisenberg and Miller's (1987) meta-analyses, a significant positive relation of empathy to prosocial behavior was found for studies in which children's reactions to movies, television, film, or lifelike enactments were examined. There was no consistent relation between prosocial behavior and facial, gestural, and vocal reactions to the picture–story indexes. Moreover, no consistent relations were found between facial, gestural, and vocal reactions of empathy (both to pictures–stories and to films) and aggression across studies (Miller & Eisenberg, 1988). In a recent study, however, boys' (but not girls') negative facial reactions to slides of empathy-evoking negative events were negatively related to their externalizing problem behaviors (Eisenberg et al., in press).

Physiological Measures of Empathy-Related Responses

Researchers increasingly have used physiological indexes, especially heart rate (HR) and skin conductance (SC), as markers of empathy-related responses (e.g., Eisenberg, Fabes, Schaller, Carlo, & Miller, 1991; Zahn-Waxler, Cole, Welsh, & Fox, 1995). These measures have been validated by examining their occurrence in response to different types of evocative stimuli (sympathy- or distress-inducing) and in regard to their ability to predict prosocial behavior. Although these measures have distinct advantages, they also have some disadvantages in regard to ease of use and interpretation.

Heart Rate

There is growing evidence that differential patterns of HR are related to empathy-related responses. In psychophysiological studies, HR deceleration has been associated with the intake of information and the outward focus of attention (Cacioppo & Sandman, 1978; Lacey, Kagan, Lacey, & Moss, 1963). Therefore, when individuals exhibit HR deceleration in an empathy-inducing context, they are likely to be focusing on information about another's emotional state or situation and experiencing sympathy. In contrast, acceleration of HR is likely to occur when individuals experience anxiety, distress, and active coping (Cacioppo & Sandman, 1978; Lazarus, 1975); thus, HR acceleration is believed to be associated with experiencing personal distress.

In initial studies, investigators examined whether HR varied when individuals were exposed to sympathy-inducing films (or were talking about sympathy-inducing events) and when they were watching or discussing events that were likely to be more distressing. In general, HR deceleration has occurred in situations likely to evoke sympathy (e.g., during exposure to sympathy-inducing films) whereas HR acceleration has been associated with activities likely to evoke distress (e.g., during a scary film; Eisenberg, Fabes, et al., 1988; Eisenberg, Schaller, et al., 1988). Moreover, consistent with theory on the relation of sympathy to altruism, HR deceleration generally has been positively associated with prosocial behavior (in circumstances where it is likely to be motivated by altruism), whereas HR acceleration sometimes has been negatively related to prosocial behavior (see Eisenberg & Fabes, 1990). For example, in a sample of 4- to 5-year-old children at risk for behavior problems, HR deceleration was associated with prosocial behaviors and empathetic concern (Zahn-Waxler et al., 1995). It is important to note that it is HR deceleration during the evocative period, not mean HR over a longer period of time, that tends to be associated with prosocial tendencies (e.g., Zahn-Waxler et al., 1995).

Skin Conductance

Skin conductance (SC) has been used as a marker of empathy-related responding (Eisenberg, Fabes, Schaller, Miller, et al., 1991; Fabes, Eisenberg, & Eisenbud, 1993) and tends to be exhibited when people are anxious or fearful (MacDowell & Mandler, 1989; Wallbott & Scherer, 1991). Because SC is often associated with physiological arousal, SC is believed to be a marker of personal distress rather than sympathy (Eisenberg & Fabes, 1990). In fact, adults and children tend to exhibit high levels of SC to films likely to induce vicarious distress (Eisenberg, Fabes, Schaller, Carlo, et al., 1991; Eisenberg, Fabes, Schaller, Miller, et al., 1991).

SC has been related to prosocial and antisocial behavior in ways consistent with theory. For example, Fabes et al. (1993) found an inverse relationship between girls' dispositional helpfulness and SC to response to an empathy-inducing film, and their reports of general distress were positively related to SC. Moreover, preschool girls classified as having the most problem behaviors (both externalizing and internalizing) experienced the greatest increase in SC in response to an empathy-inducing stimulus (Zahn-Waxler et al., 1995).

Advantages and Disadvantages of Physiological Data

There are a number of advantages to collecting physiological data to assess empathy-related responses. First, because it is unlikely that most individuals will consciously control their physiological reactions (although HR can be controlled to some degree), such data probably are relatively free from social desirability biases. Second, given that children tend to have difficulty reporting their vicariously induced emotional reactions (Eisenberg & Lennon, 1983; Eisenberg & Miller, 1987), physiological data provide an alternative way to tap their empathy-related reactions. Third, including physiological data in the study allows one to overcome the disadvantages of using the same reporter to report on empathy-related responses and other variables included in the study.

There also are methodological and practical disadvantages to the use of physiological data. First, a potentially serious drawback to the use of physiological data is that individuals can experience both personal distress and sympathy concurrently, and presently it is unclear how these reactions would be reflected physiologically. Second, analyses with physiological data can be complicated. The investigator has to decide if the data points just after the evocative event are of most interest or the mean levels across a longer period of time. Third, it is usually necessary to control for baseline responses because of individual differences in physiological responding. Fourth, age can influence children's physiological reactions, which makes examining physiological data longitudinally more difficult.

At a practical level, the participants, especially young children, may react to the use of the physiological equipment (see Wilson & Cantor, 1985). Even after familiarizing children with the electrodes, they may feel uncomfortable. Gottman, Katz, and Hooven (1997) and their colleagues, however, have developed a creative way to minimize this problem. In their lab, children put on a space suit, which contains the electrodes, and they are then strapped into a space capsule. Using such a procedure has the added advantage of minimizing the child's movement, which is known to interfere with the collection of physiological data. Because speaking also influences physiological reactions, it is necessary to have participants refrain from speaking when collecting data (or somehow covary the effects of amount of speech). It also is necessary to have the laboratory somewhat isolated because unexpected sounds as well as changes in temperature can affect physiological reactions.

Conclusion

In this chapter we have outlined four (e.g., self-report, other-report, facial, and physiological) methods for assessing empathy-related responses. There is a need for more information about how these methods relate to one another. In some studies, the measures tend to be modestly positively related (e.g., Eisenberg, Fabes, et al., 1988); however, other data suggest that there are few relations among the measures (Eisenberg, Fabes, Schaller, Carlo, et al., 1991; Zahn-Waxler et al., 1995; see also Cacioppo et al., 1992). HR and SC may be more likely to relate to one another when the emotion-eliciting stimulus is relatively evocative (Eisenberg et al., 1996). To explain the lack of correspondence, some theorists have discussed the differential role socialization may play on influencing external (e.g., self-reports and facial expressions) versus internal (physiological responding) expressions of emotion (Cacioppo et al., 1992). Others have hypothesized that some individuals mainly express emotion externally, whereas others tend to express emotion internally (Buck, 1984). However, the type and quality of data that are needed to directly examine the nature and determinants of individual differences in expressing empathy-related emotional responses are scant.

If some people tend to show their emotion (including empathy-related responding) whereas others tend to keep it inside, it is important to use a multimethod approach to assessing empathy-related responding when possible. Such an approach also is important because every measure of empathy-related responding has strengths and weaknesses. In addition, because sympathy and personal distress related differently to prosocial behavior, it is important to move beyond global measures of empathy-related responding if one is interested in positive development. Sympathy, but not personal distress, appears to be related to optimal emotional regulation (Eisenberg et al., 1994, 1996, 1998), and therefore is more likely to be linked to optimal social functioning, including general social competence in childhood (Eisenberg et al., 1996; Murphy et al., 1999), higher levels of moral reasoning (Carlo, Eisenberg, & Knight, 1992), and low hostility toward other people (Davis, 1994). Global empathy is probably most useful to study when one is interested in emotional arousability or young children's emotional responding to others, whereas sympathy and personal distress are probably more closely linked (positively and negatively, respectively) to positive social and emotional development and behavior.

Most measures of empathy-related responding measure either dispositional responding (e.g., other- and self-report questionnaires) or situational responding in experimental contexts in which study participants are exposed to empathy-inducing films or enactments. Because empathy-related responding may differ somewhat in real-life and experimental settings, more information on empathy-related reactions in everyday life is needed. Zahn-Waxler et al.'s (1992) approach of having parents report on young children's real-life reactions to others' distresses is very promising; similar techniques could be used to assess children's or adults' vicarious emotional responses. Perhaps daily diaries in which older children and adults report on their empathy-related experiences would be useful in learning more about how individuals process and respond to empathy-related emotional experiences. Data of this sort might also provide information on the factors in real-life situations that sometimes inhibit individuals from assisting others when they do experience empathy and sympathy.

In summary, because empathy-related responding is a process that occurs inside people, it is difficult to measure. A multimethod approach generally is recommended (especially when assessing situational empathy-related responding) because different measures may tap different aspects of empathy-related responding and have different strengths and weaknesses. In addition, there is a need for additional work on assessment tools and procedures, especially in regard to measures used to assess empathy, sympathy, and personal distress in children. Because empathy and its related responding plays a significant role in promoting positive behaviors such as helping and interpersonal understanding, as well as in inhibiting aggression and antisocial behaviors, improvements in the measurement of empathy will benefit the research on optimal functioning.

Appendix 17.1
Eisenberg et al. Child-Report Sympathy Scale

1. I feel sorry for other kids who don't have toys and clothes.
2. When I see someone being picked on, I feel kind of sorry for them.
3. I feel sorry for people who don't have the things that I have.
4. When I see another child who is hurt or upset, I feel sorry for them.
5. I often feel sorry for other children who are sad or in trouble.
6. I *don't* feel sorry for other children who are being teased or picked on.

Note. Directions for the measure are: "I'll read you some sentences, and you tell me if they are like you or not like you. There are no right or wrong answers. For example, 'I like to go to the movies.'" The child is first asked if the sentence is like him/her or not, and then if it is, if it is "really" (scored 1) or "sort of" like him/her (scored 2) ("not like" is scored 3). To make a 3 high for most items, reverse items.

Appendix 17.2
Parents' (or Teachers') Reports of Children's Sympathy/Empathy

	Really true	Sort of true				Sort of true	Really true
1.	____	____	My child often feels sorry for others who are less fortunate.	or	My child does not often feel sorry for those who are less fortunate.	____	____
2.	____	____	My child usually feels sympathy for others.	or	My child rarely feels sympathy for others.	____	____
3.	____	____	My child usually feels sorry for other children who are being teased.	or	My child rarely feels sorry for other children who are being teased.	____	____
4.	____	____	My child rarely feels sympathy for other children who are upset or sad.	or	My child usually feels sympathy for other children who are upset or sad.	____	____
5.	____	____	My child gets upset when she/he sees another child being hurt.	or	My child does not get upset when she/he sees another child being hurt.	____	____

Note. Directions read, "Please indicate what you feel to be your child's actual tendencies in response to each question, in your opinion. First decide what kind of child your child is like, the one described on the left or the one described on the right, and then indicate whether this is just 'sort of true' or 'really true' for your child. Thus, for each item, put a check in one of the four slots." Change wording from "my child" to "this child" for use with teachers. This scale was used in Eisenberg, Fabes, et al. (1998), where it also included a rating, "In general, to what degree does this child feel sympathetic?" (rated from 1 = very slightly or not at all to 5 = extremely). Items were standardized and combined after reversing items so they were all in the same direction.

References

Batson, C. D. (1991). *The altruism question: Toward a social-psychological answer.* Hillsdale, NJ: Erlbaum.

Bryant, B. (1982). An index of empathy for children and adolescents. *Child Development, 53,* 413–425.

Bryant, B. (1987). Critique of comparable questionnaire methods in use to assess empathy in children and adults. In N. Eisenberg & J. Strayer (Eds.), *Empathy and its development. Cambridge studies in social and emotional development* (pp. 361–373). New York: Cambridge University Press.

Buck, R. (1984). *The communication of emotion.* New York: Guilford Press.

Cacioppo, J. T., & Sandman, C. A. (1978). Physiological differentiation of sensory and cognitive tasks as a function of warning processing demands and reported unpleasantness. *Biological Psychology, 6,* 181–192.

Cacioppo, J. T., Uchino, B. N., Crites, S. L., Snydersmith, M. A., Smith, G., et al. (1992). Relationship between facial expressiveness and sympathetic activation in emotion: A critical review, with emphasis on modeling underlying mechanisms and individual differences. *Journal of Personality and Social Psychology, 62,* 110–128.

Carlo, G., Eisenberg, N., & Knight, G. P. (1992). An objective measure of adolescents' prosocial moral reasoning. *Journal of Research on Adolescence, 2,* 331–349.

Cole, P. M. (1986). Children's spontaneous control of facial expression. *Child Development, 57,* 1309–1321.

Davis, M. H. (1983). Measuring individual differences in empathy: Evidence for a multidimensional approach. *Journal of Personality and Social Psychology, 44,* 113–126.

Davis, M. H. (1994). *Empathy: A social psychological approach.* Madison, WI: Brown & Benchmark.

Davis, M. H., & Franzoi, S. L. (1991). Stability and change in adolescent self-consciousness and empathy. *Journal of Research in Personality, 25,* 70–87.

Eisenberg, N., Carlo, G., Murphy, B., & Van Court, P. (1995). Prosocial development in late adolescence: A longitudinal study. *Child Development, 66,* 911–936.

Eisenberg, N., & Fabes, R. (1990). Empathy: Conceptualization, assessment, and relation to prosocial behavior. *Motivation and Emotion, 14,* 131–149.

Eisenberg, N., & Fabes, R. (1998). Prosocial development. In W. Damon (Series Ed.) & N. Eisenberg (Vol. Ed.), *Handbook of Child Psychology: Vol. 3. Social, emotional, and personality development* (5th ed., pp. 701–778). New York: Wiley.

Eisenberg, N., Fabes, R. A., Bustamante, D., Mathy, R. M., Miller, P. A., et al. (1988). Differentiation of vicariously induced emotional reactions in children. *Developmental Psychology, 24,* 237–246.

Eisenberg, N., Fabes, R. A., Murphy, B., Karbon, M., Maszk, P., et al. (1994). The relations of emotionality and regulation to dispositional and situational empathy-related responding. *Journal of Personality and Social Psychology, 66,* 776–797.

Eisenberg, N., Fabes, R. A., Murphy, B., Karbon, M., Smith, M., et al. (1996). The relations of children's dispositional empathy-related responding to their emotionality, regulation, and social functioning. *Developmental Psychology, 32,* 195–209.

Eisenberg, N., Fabes, R. A., Schaller, M., Carlo, G., & Miller, R. A. (1991). The relations of parental characteristics and practices to children's vicarious emotional responding. *Child Development, 62,* 1393–1408.

Eisenberg, N., Fabes, R. A., Schaller, M., Miller, P. A., Carlo, G., et al. (1991). Personality and socialization correlates of vicarious emotional responding. *Journal of Personality and Social Psychology, 61,* 459–471.

Eisenberg, N., Fabes, R. A., Shepard, S. A., Murphy, B. C., Jones, J., et al. (1998). Contemporaneous and longitudinal prediction of children's sympathy from dispositional regulation and emotionality. *Developmental Psychology, 34,* 910–924.

Eisenberg, N., & Lennon, R. (1983). Sex differences in empathy and related capacities. *Psychological Bulletin, 94,* 100–131.

Eisenberg, N., & Miller, P. A. (1987). The relation of empathy to prosocial and related behaviors. *Psychological Bulletin, 101,* 91–119.

Eisenberg, N., Schaller, M., Fabes, R. A., Bustamante, D., Mathy, R., et al. (1988). The differentiation of personal distress and sympathy in children and adults. *Developmental Psychology, 24,* 766–775.

Eisenberg, N., Shea, C. L., Carlo, G., & Knight, G. (1991). Empathy-related responding and cognition: A "chicken and the egg" dilemma. In W. Kurtines & J. Gewirtz (Eds.), *Handbook of moral behavior and development. Vol. 2. Research* (pp. 63–88). Hillsdale, NJ: Erlbaum.

Eisenberg-Berg, N., & Lennon, R. (1980). Altruism and the assessment of empathy in the preschool years. *Child Development, 51,* 552–557.

Fabes, R. A., Eisenberg, N., & Eisenbud, L. (1993). Behavioral and physiological correlates of children's reactions to others in distress. *Developmental Psychology, 29,* 655–663.

Feshbach, N. D. (1978). Studies of empathic behavior in children. In B. A. Maher (Ed.), *Progress in experimental personality research* (Vol. 8, pp. 1–47). New York: Academic Press.

Gottman, J. M., Katz, L. F., & Hooven, C. (1997). *Meta-emotion: How families communicate emotionally.* Hillsdale, NJ: Erlbaum.

Hoffman, M. L. (1982). The measurement of empathy. In C. E. Izard (Ed.), *Measuring emotions in infants and children* (pp. 279–296). Cambridge: Cambridge University Press.

Hoffman, M. L. (2000). *Empathy and moral development.* Cambridge, UK: Cambridge University Press.

Holmgren, R. A., Eisenberg, N., & Fabes, R. A. (1998). The relations of children's situational empathy-related emotions to dispositional prosocial behavior. *International Journal of Behavioral Development, 22,* 169–193.

Iannotti, R. J. (1985). Naturalistic and structural assessments of prosocial behavior in preschool children: The influence of empathy and perspective taking. *Developmental Psychology, 21,* 46–55.

Kalliopuska, M. (1983). Verbal components of emotional empathy. *Perceptual and Motor Skills, 56,* 487–496.

Lacey, J. I., Kagan, J., Lacey, B. C., & Moss, H. A. (1963). The visceral level: Situational determinants and behavioral correlates of autonomic response patterns. In P. H. Knapp (Ed.), *Expression of the emotions in man* (pp. 161–196). New York: International Universities Press.

Lazarus, R. S. (1975). A cognitively oriented psychologist looks at biofeedback. *American Psychologist, 30,* 553–561.

Lennon, R., Eisenberg, N., & Carroll, J. (1983). The assessment of empathy in early childhood. *Journal of Applied Developmental Psychology, 4,* 295–302.

Losoya, S., & Eisenberg, N. (2001). Affective empathy. In J. A. Hall & F. J. Bernieri (Eds.), *Interpersonal sensitivity: Theory and measurement. The LEA series in personality and clinical psychology* (pp. 21–43). Mahwah, NJ: Erlbaum.

MacDowell, K. A., & Mandler, G. (1989). Constructions of emotion: Discrepancy, arousal, and mood. *Motivation and Emotion, 13,* 105–124.

Mehrabian, A., & Epstein, N. A. (1972). A measure of emotional empathy. *Journal of Personality, 40,* 523–543.

Miller, P. A., & Eisenberg, N. (1988). The relation of empathy to aggressive and externalizing/antisocial behavior. *Psychological Bulletin, 103,* 324–344.

Miller, P. A., Eisenberg, N., Fabes, R. A., & Shell, R. (1996). Relations of moral reasoning and vicarious emotion to young children's prosocial behavior toward peers and adults. *Developmental Psychology, 32,* 210–219.

Murphy, B. C., Shepard, S. A., Eisenberg, N., Fabes, R. A., & Guthrie, I. K. (1999). Contemporaneous and longitudinal relations of young adolescents' dispositional sympathy to their emotionality, regulation, and social functioning. *Journal of Early Adolescence, 19,* 66–97.

Saarni, C. (1990). Emotional competence: How emotions and relationships become integrated. In R. A. Thompson (Ed.), *Socioemotional development* (pp. 115–182). Lincoln: University of Nebraska Press.

Spinrad, T. L., Losoya, S. H., Eisenberg, N., Fabes, R. A., Shepard, S. A., et al. (1999). The relations of parental affect and encouragement to children's moral emotions and behavior. *Journal of Moral Education, 28,* 323–337.

Strayer, J. (1987). Picture-story indices of empathy. In N. Eisenberg & J. Strayer (Eds.), *Empathy and its development* (pp. 351–355). Cambridge: Cambridge University Press.

Strayer, J. (1993). Children's concordant emotions and cognitions in response to observed emotions. *Child Development, 64,* 188–201.

Strayer, J., & Schroeder, M. (1989). Children's helping strategies: Influences of emotion, empathy, and age. *New Directions for Child Development, 44,* 85–105.

Wallbott, H. G., & Scherer, K. R. (1991). Stress specificities: Differential effects of coping style, gender, and type of stressor on autonomic arousal, facial expression, and subjective feeling. *Journal of Personality and Social Psychology, 61,* 147–156.

Wilson, B. H., & Cantor, J. (1985). Developmental differences in empathy with a television protagonist's fear. *Journal of Experimental Child Psychology, 39,* 284–299.

Wood, J. V., Saltzberg, J. A., & Goldsamt, L. A. (1990). Does affect induce self-focused attention? *Journal of Personality and Social Psychology, 58,* 899–908.

Zahn-Waxler, C., Cole, P. M., Welsh, J. D., & Fox, N. A. (1995). Psychophysiological correlates of empathy and prosocial behaviors in preschool children with behavior problems. *Development and Psychopathology, 7,* 27–48.

Zahn-Waxler, C., Friedman, S. L., & Cummings, E. M. (1983). Children's emotions and behaviors in response to infants' cries. *Child Development, 54,* 1522–1528.

Zahn-Waxler, C., Radke-Yarrow, Wagner, E., & Chapman, M. (1992). Development of concern for others. *Developmental Psychology, 28,* 126–136.

18

The Assessment of Adult Attachment Security

Frederick G. Lopez

In the 1980s, research on adult attachment emerged as a prominent line of inquiry across several psychological disciplines, including social, developmental, clinical, and counseling psychology. Scores of studies using a variety of samples, measures, and methodologies have converged on a powerful conclusion: Relative to their insecurely attached peers, adults with secure attachment styles and orientations demonstrate more competent functioning across many performance and adjustment domains (Lopez & Brennan, 2000). Indeed, secure adults consistently exhibit more flexible cognitive processes, mature forms of affect regulation, and constructive relationship behaviors.

Given its strong associations with healthy and adaptive self-regulation in adulthood, attachment security arguably could serve as a key construct in the continued development of positive psychology (Seligman & Csikszentmihalyi, 2000; Snyder & Lopez, 2002). In light of this possibility, I pursue several objectives in this chapter. I begin by introducing the construct of attachment security, briefly exploring its theoretical origins, and tracing its evolving conceptualization. I then comment on two distinct traditions (i.e., interview-based vs. self-report) in the assessment of adult attachment security. Following this, I explore important issues and controversies in the assessment of attachment security, including questions regarding the stability, singularity, and the appropriate conceptualization and operationalization of the construct. Finally, I note new extensions of construct measurement and speculate on other potentially fruitful directions for future research.

To meet these multiple objectives within the page limits of this chapter, I must cover the topics in broad brush strokes and, wherever possible, refer the reader elsewhere to more detailed discussions. Furthermore, because literally dozens of attachment-related scales, questionnaires, and interview protocols exist, I restrict my review to several of the more prominent self-report and interview-based measures of adult attachment styles and orientations and exclude consideration of other measures of attachment-related perceptions, such as retrospective measures of early parental bonds or indexes of parent–adolescent relationship quality. Despite these limitations, my overarching goal is to provide an efficient presentation of key issues in the conceptualization and assessment of adult attachment security.

Origins and Evolution of the Construct of Adult Attachment Security

Contemporary research on adult attachment has its ideological roots in the seminal works of John Bowlby and Mary Ainsworth, the primary architects of attachment theory (Bretherton, 1992). Both Bretherton (1992) and Karen (1994), as well as Ainsworth and Bowlby (1991), provide excellent historical accounts of the origins and early development of attachment theory.

Drawing on his clinical observations of orphaned and delinquent children and ideas from ethology, systems theory, and cognitive science, Bowlby (1969/ 1982) proposed that important qualities of the infant–caregiver relationship were causally related to significant aspects of child behavior and emotional experience, as well as to the formation of healthy and unhealthy developmental trajectories. For Bowlby, the "attachment system" regulating the proximity-seeking behaviors linking infants and their caregivers represented a unique, evolutionarily based motivational system (i.e., independent of the gratification of libidinal needs and drives) whose primary function was providing protection and emotional security.

In particular, Bowlby argued that, within the first years of life, the infant would represent his or her early attachment-related experiences with primary caregivers in the form of cognitive schema, referred to as an internal working model (IWM) of self and other. The IWM presumably integrated the child's perceptions of his or her competence and lovability (self model) with expectations regarding the accessibility and responsiveness of attachment figures (other model). Infants who received warm, responsive, and nonintrusive care from their attachment figures were assumed to form a *secure* attachment model that, among other things, promoted exploration, environmental mastery, and progressively more competent and autonomous forms of self-regulation. By contrast, infants who experienced their caregivers as intrusive, inconsistently responsive, or as consistently rejecting were likely to form either an *anxious* or *avoidant* orientation wherein care- and proximity-seeking behaviors were either chronically activated or suppressed. These outcomes were further assumed to lead to observable deficits in affect regulation and social competencies. Ainsworth and her colleagues used the "strange situation" paradigm, which is an observational methodology for studying infant reactions to standardized episodes of maternal separation and reunion to explore infant–caregiver attachment behavior. This methodology provided preliminary empirical support for the existence of these distinct interpersonal orientations, or "attachment styles" that are presumed to reflect critical variations in the underlying IWM (Ainsworth, Blehar, Waters, & Wall, 1978).

Crucial to the eventual extension of the theory to adulthood was Bowlby's lifespan ("cradle to grave") perspective regarding the operation of the attachment system, as well as his specific hypotheses regarding the "working" nature of these cognitive schemas (Bowlby, 1979). Bowlby believed that, once formed, the IWM acquired relatively stable, self-validating properties because these models (a) organized internal appraisals and interpersonal behaviors along pathways that were adaptive in the person's earlier development, (b) were "carried forward" as a template for guiding perceptions and expectations in later relationships, and (c) thereby shaped the person's subsequent social experiences in schema-consistent ways.

Adult Attachment Security: The Emergence of Two Assessment Traditions

Empirical extensions of attachment theory to the study of adult functioning began in the mid-1980s and emanated from two independent sources: developmental psychology and social psychology. In developmental psychology, Mary Main (a student of Ainsworth's) and colleagues began by interviewing the maternal participants of strange situation studies about their own childhood experiences with parental figures. Interviews explored participants' recollections of their early relationships with parents around themes of distress, separation, and care. This work led to the construction and validation of the Adult Attachment Interview (AAI), which is now the most prominent interview-based methodology for assessing adult attachment security (George, Kaplan, & Main, 1985), as well as to a four-group taxonomy of adult attachment classification (Main & Goldwyn, 1984, 1998).

Around the same time, two social psychologists, Cindy Hazan and Phillip Shaver, applied attachment theory to the study of adult romantic relationships by fashioning a simple, three-item self-report measure patterned after Ainsworth et al.'s (1978) three-group taxonomy (Hazan & Shaver, 1987). Hazan and Shaver's preliminary study found support for several theory-derived hypotheses regarding relations between their three adult attachment styles and various indexes of relationship perceptions and functioning. Their seminal investigation also prompted other investigators (Bartholomew & Horowitz, 1991) to refine the three-group taxonomy by differentiating two types of avoidant styles (dismissive and fearful), thereby creating a classification system that roughly paralleled Main and Goldwyn's (1984) four groups. Table 18.1 contains summary descriptions of the classification systems.

Issues in the Assessment of Adult Attachment Security

As others already have noted (Bartholomew & Shaver, 1998; Simpson & Rholes, 1998), the developmental and social psychological research initiatives respectively (but not exclusively) promoted the growth of interview-based and self-report assessment traditions in the adult attachment literature. More important, these research traditions have now produced an array of measures that also differ with respect to domain (family vs. peer/intimate) and dimensionality (categorical vs. continuous scores; Bartholomew & Shaver, 1998). As might be expected, this diversity has generated several debates regarding the appropriate conceptualization and assessment of adult attachment security. In the

Table 18.1. Three Prominent Classification Systems of Adult Attachment Styles

Hazan and Shaver (1987)	Description
Secure	I find it relatively easy to get close to others and am comfortable depending on them and having them depend on me. I don't often worry about being abandoned or about someone getting too close to me.
Avoidant	I am somewhat uncomfortable being close to others; I find it difficult to trust them completely, difficult to allow myself to depend on them. I am nervous when anyone gets too close, and often love partners want me to be more intimate than I feel comfortable being.
Anxious	I find that others are reluctant to get as close as I would like. I often worry that my partner doesn't really love me or won't want to stay with me. I want to merge completely with another person, and this desire sometimes scares people away.

Bartholomew and Horowitz (1991)	Description
Secure	It is easy for me to become emotionally close to others. I am comfortable depending on others and having others depend on me. I don't worry about being alone or having others not accept me.
Dismissing	I am comfortable without close emotional relationships. It is very important for me to feel independent and self-sufficient, and I prefer not to depend on others or have others depend on me.
Preoccupied	I want to be completely emotionally intimate with others, but I often find that others are reluctant to get as close as I would like. I am uncomfortable being without close relationships, but I sometimes worry that others don't value me as much as I value them.
Fearful	I am uncomfortable getting close to others. I want emotionally close relationships, but I find it difficult to trust others completely or to depend on them. I worry that I will be hurt if I allow myself to become too close to others.

Main and Goldwyn (1984, 1998)[a]	Description
Secure/ autonomous	Interviewee demonstrates coherent, collaborative discourse. Interviewee values attachment, but seems objective regarding any particular event/relationship. Description and evaluation of attachment-related experiences are consistent, whether experiences are favorable or unfavorable. Discourse does not notably violate any of Grice's (1975) maxims.
Dismissing	Interview is not coherent and interviewee is dismissing of attachment-related experiences and relationships. Interviewee "normalizes" these experiences with generalized representations of history unsupported or actively contradicted by episodes recounted, thus violating Grice's maxim of quality. Transcripts also tend to be excessively brief, violating the maxim of quantity.

(continued)

Table 18.1. *(continued)*

Main and Goldwyn (1984, 1998)[a]	Description
Preoccupied	Interview is not coherent and interviewee is preoccupied with or by past attachment relationships/experiences. Interviewee appears angry, passive, or fearful and uses sentences that are often long, grammatically entangled, or filled with vague uses, thus violating Grice's maxims of manner and relevance. Transcripts are often excessively long, violating the maxim of quantity.
Unresolved/ disorganized	During discussions of loss or abuse, interviewee shows striking lapse in the monitoring of reasoning or discourse. For example, the person may briefly indicate a belief that a dead person is still alive in the physical sense or that this person was killed by a childhood thought. Interviewee may lapse into prolonged silence or eulogistic speech.

[a]Adapted from chapter by Hesse (1999). Copyright 1999 by Guilford Press. Reprinted with permission.

sections that follow, I consider these assessment issues in greater detail and, I hope, provide readers with sufficient information for making sound decisions regarding instrument selection and use.

A "State of Mind" or a "Mindful State?"

Interview and self-report measures of adult attachment security are largely premised on different assumptions about the conscious accessibility of the IWM. Interview methods generally assume that the adult IWM is not fully conscious and is also vulnerable to defensive distortion, thereby requiring sensitive inquiry and objective recording of participant responses, with final assessment classification based on discourse analysis by independent raters. For example, the AAI assesses adults' "state of mind with respect to attachment" by way of an audiotaped, 18-item, hour-long, semistructured interview probing the participant's past and present relationships with their parents and addressing early memories around themes of distress and separation. In his detailed and comprehensive discussion of the historical development and validation of the AAI, Hesse (1999) noted that, following the verbatim transcription of the interview, independent raters trained in using Main's classification system (Main & Goldwyn, 1984, 1998) classify participants into one of four groups (see Table 18.1) on the basis of the overall "coherence" of the narrative, reflected by the interviewee's ability to abide by the principles of rational, cooperative discourse (Grice, 1975). In short, the *manner* in which persons attempt to access and describe their early relationship experiences with parents is more critical to their ultimate attachment classification than is the specific *content* of their disclosures.

Persons classified as "secure/autonomous" demonstrate a clear capacity to respond thoughtfully, meaningfully, and coherently to the probing set of questions, regardless of the overall positivity or negativity of their reported early experiences. By contrast, persons classified as either "dismissive," "preoccupied," or "unresolved/disorganized" demonstrate characteristic memory retrieval difficulties, language dysfluencies, or other "lapses" in self-monitoring, thereby adversely affecting the overall coherence of their narratives. Although the standard AAI rating scales typically are used to produce categorical classifications, an alternative scoring system has been developed that uses a Q-sort methodology and that yields continuous scores on two independent dimensions (security/anxiety and hyperactivation/deactivation) assessing both the IWM and the organization of thought reflected in the interview transcripts (Kobak, Cole, Ferenz-Gillies, & Fleming, 1993). Kobak et al. (1993) reported a kappa of .65 (indicating adequate agreement) between attachment categorical classifications obtained using the two scoring systems.

By definition, self-report measures assume that the IWM can be consciously accessed and reliably reported by participants using standard checklists or rating scales to describe their typical relationship patterns with intimate peers. Hence, these methods conceptualize the IWM not as a partially unconscious "state of mind" but more as a conscious "mindful state" of generalized expectations and preferences regarding relationship intimacy that guide participants' information processing of relationship experiences as well as their behavioral response patterns. For example, respondents to Hazan and Shaver's (1987) preliminary three-item measure (see Table 18.1) simply select the paragraph that best describes their feelings about romantic relationships, thereby classifying themselves as either "secure," "anxious," or "avoidant." As mentioned, Bartholomew and Horowitz (1991) expanded the original 3-group classification system (see Table 18.1) to include two avoidant styles (i.e., "dismissive" and "fearful"), whereas others (Collins & Read, 1990; Simpson, Rholes, & Phillips, 1996) developed alternative self-report measures by unpacking these original paragraph descriptions into a set of items that could be continuously rated and scored. Research on the underlying dimensional structure of adult attachment has generally yielded support for a two-dimensional factor structure (Simpson & Rholes, 1998), with one dimension tapping comfort with interpersonal closeness and dependency (i.e., avoidance) and the other representing fear of interpersonal rejection or abandonment (i.e., anxiety). In addition, these scale developments facilitated the construction of newer, factor analytically derived measures of adult attachment that possess enhanced internal consistency (e.g., Experiences in Close Relationships [ECR] measure; Brennan, Clark, & Shaver, 1998).

How Stable Is Adult Attachment Security?

Interview and self-report measures of adult attachment take different positions regarding the conscious accessibility of the IWM, yet both assume (in keeping with Bowlby's assumption) that, once assessed, a person's "adult attachment style" or "adult attachment orientation" represents a relatively stable construct.

From a measurement perspective, the temporal stability of a construct can be indexed by test–retest associations between either classifications (using frequency analysis and kappa coefficients) or continuous scores (using correlations). Also, because retesting with interview methods such as the AAI often involves different interviewers, temporal stability also can be indexed by interrater correspondence over time (see Table 18.2 for reliability and validity information of several prominent adult attachment measures).

Evidence in support of the temporal stability of AAI classifications is moderate to strong. For example, in a study of AAI stability (over a three-month period) within a young adult Israeli sample, Sagi et al. (1994) found high interrater reliability across the two time points (range of 87%–95%), as well as moderately high AAI classification correspondence over the same interval (90%). Similar test–retest stability estimates were reported by Bakermans-Kranenburg and van IJzendoorn (1993), and both studies found that categorization could not be attributable to interviewer differences (see Hesse, 1999, for a more complete discussion). An extensive meta-analysis of AAI studies also has yielded strong support for the cross-generational continuity of attachment organization, indexed by correspondences between parents' AAI classification and their offspring's strange situation classification (van IJzendoorn, 1995). Elsewhere, Davila (2001) reported that interrater reliabilities for the four scales of the Family and Peer Attachment Interview (FPAI; Bartholomew, 1998), a protocol patterned after the AAI, ranged from .73 (preoccupied) to .89 (dismissing), and Scharfe and Bartholomew (1994) found moderate test–retest correlations of these interview-based prototype ratings over an eight-month period.

There also is evidence, albeit mixed, in support of the temporal stability of prominent self-report measures of adult attachment. Using the Relationship Questionnaire (RQ), Scharfe and Bartholomew (1994) reported that approximately 60% of their young adult sample demonstrated the same attachment style over an eight-month interval. In two independent studies using the Attachment Style Measure (ASM), Fuller and Fincham (1995) and Kirkpatrick and Hazan (1994) found attachment style correspondences of 65 to 70% over periods of two and four years, respectively, within samples of dating and married couples. More recently, Davila, Burge, and Hammen (1997) examined attachment-style stability (also assessed by the ASM) over a two-year period within a sample of late adolescent women; they also explored whether changes in attachment style appeared to reflect changes in current circumstances (i.e., as reflected by measures of chronic or episodic stress) or more stable individual differences. These investigators found that rates of attachment-style instability ranged from 28% (over six months) to 34% (over two years); they also concluded that this observed variability appeared to reflect individual differences in susceptibility to change.

There is surprisingly less stability information on the dimensional self-report measures of adult attachment. With regard to the three Adult Attachment scale (AAS) subscales, moderately high test–retest correlations (range of rs = .52 - .71) have been observed over periods of two months (Collins & Read, 1990) and eight months (range of rs = .64 - .73; Scharfe & Bartholomew, 1994). Citing unpublished data, Lopez, Melendez, and Rice (2000) reported moderate (two-month) test–retest correlations for each of the two Adult Attach-

Table 18.2. Characteristics of Adult Attachment Measures

Name of measure	Format	Number of items, questions	Subscales	Administration time (in min.)	Reliability			Construct validity
					Interrater	Internal consistency	Test–retest	
AAI	Interview	18	25	60	.87–.95[a]	.87–.91[b]	Strong	Excellent
FPAI	Interview	Variable	4	60	.73–.89	.85–.92	Moderate	Some support
ASM	Self-report	Single-item (3 categories)	N/A	2–3	N/A	N/A	Moderate	Good
RQ	Self-report	Single-item (4 categories)	N/A	2–3	N/A	N/A	moderate	Good
AAS	Self-report	18	3	3–5	N/A	.69–.75	Moderate	Good
AAQ	Self-report	17	2	3–5	N/A	.70–.76[c]	Moderate[d]	Good
ECR	Self-report	36[e]	2	6–8	N/A	.91–.94	Moderate	Good

[a] For individual AAI categories.
[b] For Q-sort dimensional rating scales.
[c] Based on current 17-item version.
[d] Based on earlier 13-item version.
[e] Short-form version.

Note. AAI = Adult Attachment Interview (George, Kaplan, & Main, 1985); FPAI = Family and Peer Attachment Interview (Bartholomew, 1998); ASM = Attachment Style Measure (Hazan & Shaver, 1987); RQ = Relationship Questionnaire (Bartholomew & Horowitz, 1991); AAS = Adult Attachment Scale (Collins & Read, 1990); AAQ = Adult Attachment Questionnaire (Simpson, Rholes, & Phillips, 1996); ECR = Experiences in Close Relationships (Brennan, Clark, & Shaver, 1998).

ment Questionnaire (AAQ) subscales (avoidance $r = .79$; anxiety $r = .64$). Lopez and Gormley (2002) found that ECR subscales assessing avoidance and anxiety demonstrated moderate stability over a six-month period ($rs = .71$ and $.68$, respectively) within a sample of college freshmen.

Are Interview and Self-Report Measures of Adult Attachment Security Measuring the Same Thing?

In light of their differential emphasis on familial and intimate peer relationships, it is not surprising that some early comparisons of the AAI with self-report measures found weak between-method correspondence at the level of typological categories. These findings have raised doubt about whether interview and self-report measures are assessing the same construct (Crowell et al., 1996). For some, these findings indicate that only interview methods are capable of sensitively assessing the internal working model whereas self-report measures can only assess one's "attachment style" in current intimate relationships (Dozier & Tyrell, 1998). Bartholomew and Shaver (1998), however, showed that measures in the same domain that use similar methods demonstrate greater correspondence and proposed that interview and self-report methods can be productively viewed from a "continuum" perspective of assessment. More recently, Shaver, Belsky, and Brennan (2000) administered the AAI and the AAS to a community sample of adult women and examined the correlations of specific AAI coding scales with AAS subscale scores. They found that AAI scales assessing "coherence of transcript" and "coherence of mind" were significantly correlated with each AAS subscale, and most prominently with the AAS Depend scale, which measures comfort with both care-seeking and care-giving. While cautioning that the AAI and the AAS may not be measuring the same construct and thus should not be substituted for one another (a general consensus among attachment scholars), these authors suggest that development of a functional self-report measure of "state of mind with respect to attachment" may indeed be possible.

Do Adult Attachment Characteristics Embody Taxonic or Dimensional Properties?

Recent studies by Fraley and his colleagues (Fraley & Waller, 1998; Fraley, Waller, & Brennan, 2000) lend further credence to the belief that more sensitive, reliable, and valid self-report measures of adult attachment can be developed. Using taxometric investigative methods, Fraley and Waller (1998) found no evidence that adult attachment styles represent discrete taxa, leading them to argue strongly in favor of dimensional conceptualizations and assessments of adult attachment security. Although their preliminary evidence and conclusions are persuasive, categorical and prototypical assessments of attachment styles are deeply rooted in the attachment literature, and their continued use has been supported by others (Klohnen & John, 1998).

Fraley et al. (2000) advanced efforts to improve the measurement sensitivity of self-report measures of adult attachment by conducting an item response analysis of several measures. Item response theory (IRT) and analysis are concerned with whether scale items have a high and evenly distributed degree of measurement precision. These researchers found that although the ECR scales had the best psychometric properties and "had test information functions that were clearly higher than those of the other attachment scales," (p. 357), this measure (along with the other selected measures) demonstrated relatively low or unevenly distributed test information curves, underscoring the need for better items. Even following some item readjustments, revised ECR scales assessed security with less precision than they assessed insecurity. This suggests that the self-report assessment of adult attachment can be strengthened by developing new items that assess the low ends of the avoidance and anxiety dimensions (i.e., items more reflective of security) with greater fidelity.

Adult Attachment Security: An Individual Differences Variable or Relationship Construct?

Another vexing issue common to both interview and self-report measures of adult attachment security is whether assessed variation is best conceptualized as an individual differences variable or relationship-specific construct (Kobak, 1994) and, relatedly, whether people possess singular or multiple attachment models (Collins & Read, 1994). An individual differences conceptualization is more dominant in the literature, although there is mounting evidence that adults may vary their attachment-related expectations and behavior across specific contexts and relationships. For example, Baldwin, Keelan, Fehr, Enns, and Koh-Rangarajoo (1996) found that most persons possess relational schemas reflecting a range of attachment orientations, that these schemas can be experimentally "primed," and that the relative availability and accessibility of this schematic knowledge affect cognitive processes regarding relationships. In addition, several studies assessing the attachment styles or orientations of both members in dating or married couples have found that the influence of one's own attachment style on relationship perceptions or behavior is to some extent moderated by the contribution of one's partner's attachment style or orientation (see Lopez & Brennan, 2000). Furthermore, there is evidence that within-person variability in attachment patterns across relationships has significant differential consequences on personal and relational adjustment outcomes (La-Guardia, Ryan, Couchman, & Deci, 2000). Of course, if people possess multiple attachment models, then it ultimately must be determined whether these models are organized in a hierarchical "network" fashion (Collins & Read, 1994) or in some other cognitive configuration.

Beyond the Controversies: What Can We Conclude (For Now) About Adult Attachment Security and Its Measurement?

In our review of much of the recent literature, Kelly Brennan and I concluded that adult attachment security incorporates a myriad set of competencies that may be essential to the development and maintenance of psychological health and effectiveness (Lopez & Brennan, 2000). Persons classified as "secure" or otherwise assessed as having low levels of interpersonal avoidance and anxiety demonstrate enhanced abilities to tolerate ambiguity and uncertainty, engage in collaborative problem-solving, form accurate perceptions of others, effectively manage their own emotional arousal, and display cognitive and appraisal processes that evince less distorted and more integrative, self-reflective operations. We also proposed that adult attachment security might be best conceptualized as a relatively enduring self-context relation, one that optimizes both favorable self-organization and reorganization processes by promoting continuing and creative engagements with others.

As noted previously, there is general consensus among adult attachment scholars that interview and self-report measures, although possibly tapping some common elements (see Shaver et al., 2000), are more likely assessing different aspects and indicators of adult attachment security. Interview methods such as the AAI are better suited for assessing how early memories, along with the lexical and affect regulation processes triggered by their attempted retrieval and description, may illuminate the underlying IWM. Possible drawbacks, however, are the costs involved in individual administration and in training raters.

Self-report measures are more appropriate for assessing conscious awareness of one's own attachment-related interpersonal characteristics, especially in the context of intimate peer relationships. These measures clearly are less expensive and more convenient to use, yet they also are more vulnerable to defensive distortion and response set biases. Relative to other self-report scales, the ECR demonstrates superior subscale reliabilities; although, similar to other self-report adult attachment scales, its items assess variability at the "secure" end of its subscales with less fidelity than at the insecure end. Whether new self-report measures can be developed to assess less conscious aspects of adult attachment styles and orientations is an open question that should be pursued.

New Directions and Developments in the Assessment of Adult Attachment Security

The construct of adult attachment security holds considerable promise for integrating and unifying many characteristics of persons and of close relationships typically associated with positive psychological health and effectiveness. Contemporary attachment theory also has demonstrated considerable versatility and generativity in the exploration of security-related processes and outcomes in nonfamilial/nonintimate relationship domains, such as work relationships (Hardy & Barkham, 1994; Schirmer & Lopez, 2001) and teacher–student relationships (Larose, Bernier, Soucy, & Duchesne, 1999; Lopez, 1997). Continued excursions into these territories seem both likely and desirable. Yet even more promising are efforts at extending construct-related assessment and research into the domain of therapeutic relationships (Slade, 1999). If, as Bowlby (1988) believed, insecure IWMs can be revised in the context of a positive therapeutic encounter, then the study of therapist–client attachment-related dynamics is a critical area for greater inquiry. One especially noteworthy measure of adult attachment security in this context is the Client Attachment to

Therapist Scale (CATS; Mallinckrodt, Gantt, & Coble, 1995). Developed and validated on a clinical sample, this 36-item self-report measure contains three factor-analytically derived subscales (i.e., secure, avoidant/fearful, and preoccupied/merger), each reflecting distinct client attachment orientations toward the therapist. Subsequent research by the developers of the CATS has linked both family-of-origin separation anxieties and alexithymia (i.e., reported difficulties in accessing and identifying affective states) with insecure orientations toward the therapist (Mallinckrodt, King, & Coble, 1998).

Another potential direction is in the cross-cultural study of adult attachment security. Although Bowlby emphasized the universality of attachment systems (and, by extrapolation, the cross-cultural validity of attachment theory), this assumption has been seriously challenged (Rothbaum, Weisz, Pott, Miyake, & Morelli, 2000). Though several studies of adult attachment have used non-U.S. samples (e.g., Israel, Australia), most have been "Western" societies, underscoring the particular need to extend adult attachment research to non-Western groups. This raises challenges for instrument development. Yet even within a U.S. sample, there is preliminary evidence that theoretically expected relationships between the quality of parental bonds and adult attachment security may vary as a function of race/ethnicity (Lopez et al., 2000).

Conclusion

The assessment of adult attachment security has evolved along two parallel tracks. These tracks typically (but not exclusively) use interview-based and self-report methodologies and place differential emphasis of familial and intimate peer relationships. These methodologies are largely premised on different assumptions about the conscious accessibility of the IWM of self and other that is presumed to underlie critical variations in adult attachment styles. Taken together, these approaches provide support for the views that adult attachment styles incorporate both conscious and unconscious features, that they assess relatively stable characteristics of persons (and more likely of relationships), and that they may be best conceptualized as dimensions and not as discrete taxa. Although interview methods, such as the AAI, may provide more sensitive assessments of the underlying IWM, it is possible that continuing development of self-report methods may approximate this capability. Recent assessment-related extensions to the study of nonfamilial (e.g., therapeutic) relationships, along with emergent cross-cultural studies of adult attachment, should further advance our understanding of how adult attachment security affects the course of psychological health and effectiveness in different contexts and across the lifespan.

References

Ainsworth, M. D. S., Blehar, M. C., Waters, E., & Wall, S. (1978). *Patterns of attachment: A psychological study of the Strange Situation.* Hillsdale, NJ: Erlbaum.

Ainsworth, M. D. S., & Bowlby, J. (1991). An ethological approach to personality development. *American Psychologist, 46,* 333–341.

Bakermans-Kranenburg, M. J., & van IJzendoorn, M. H. (1993). A psychometric study of the Adult Attachment Interview: Reliability and discriminant validity. *Developmental Psychology, 29,* 870–879.

Baldwin, M. W., Keelan, J. P. R., Fehr, B., Enns, V., & Koh-Rangarajoo, E. (1996). Social–cognitive conceptualization of attachment working models: Availability and accessibility effects. *Journal of Personality and Social Psychology, 71,* 94–109.

Bartholomew, K. (1998). *The Family and Peer Attachment Interview.* Unpublished manuscript, Simon Fraser University, Burnaby, British Columbia, Canada.

Bartholomew, K., & Horowitz, L. M. (1991). Attachment styles among young adults: A test of a four-category model. *Journal of Personality and Social Psychology, 61,* 226–244.

Bartholomew, K., & Shaver, P. R. (1998). Methods of assessing adult attachment: Do they converge? In J. A. Simpson & W. S. Rholes (Eds.), *Attachment theory and close relationships* (pp. 25–45). New York: Guilford Press.

Bowlby, J. (1979). *The making and breaking of affectional bonds.* London: Tavistock.

Bowlby, J. (1982). *Attachment and loss. Vol. I: Attachment.* London: Tavistock. (Original published 1969)

Bowlby, J. (1988). *A secure base: Parent-child attachment and healthy human development.* New York: Basic Books.

Brennan, K. A., Clark, C. L., & Shaver, P. R. (1998). Self-report measurement of adult attachment: An integrative overview. In J. A. Simpson & W. S. Rholes (Eds.), *Attachment theory and close relationships* (pp. 46–76). New York: Guilford Press.

Bretherton, I. (1992). The origins of attachment theory: John Bowlby and Mary Ainsworth. *Developmental Psychology, 28,* 759–775.

Collins, N., & Read, S. J. (1990). Adult attachment, working models, and relationship quality in dating couples. *Journal of Personality and Social Psychology, 58,* 644–663.

Collins, N., & Read, S. J. (1994). Cognitive representations of attachment: The structure and function of working models. In K. Bartholomew & D. Perlman (Eds.), *Attachment processes in adulthood* (pp. 53–90). London: Jessica Kingsley.

Crowell, J. A., Waters, E., Treboux, D., O'Connor, E., Colon-Downs, E., et al. (1996). Discriminant validity of the Adult Attachment Interview. *Child Development, 67,* 2585–2599.

Davila, J. (2001). Refining the association between excessive reassurance seeking and depressive symptoms: The role of related interpersonal constructs. *Journal of Social and Clinical Psychology, 20,* 538–559.

Davila, J., Burge, D., & Hammen, C. (1997). Why does attachment style change? *Journal of Personality and Social Psychology, 73,* 826–838.

Dozier, M., & Tyrell, C. (1998). The role of attachment in therapeutic relationships. In J. A. Simpson & W. S. Rholes (Eds.), *Attachment theory and close relationships* (pp. 221–248). New York: Guilford Press.

Fraley, R. C., & Waller, N. G. (1998). Adult attachment patterns: A test of the typological model. In J. A. Simpson & W. S. Rholes (Eds.), *Attachment theory and close relationships* (pp. 77–114). New York: Guilford Press.

Fraley, R. C., Waller, N. G., & Brennan, K. A. (2000). An item response theory analysis of self-report measures of adult attachment. *Journal of Personality and Social Psychology, 78,* 350–365.

Fuller, T. L., & Fincham, F. D. (1995). Attachment style in married couples: Relation to current marital functioning, stability over time, and method of assessment. *Personal Relationships, 2,* 17–34.

George, C., Kaplan, N., & Main, M. (1985). *The Adult Attachment Interview.* Unpublished protocol, Department of Psychology, University of California, Berkeley.

Grice, P. (1975). Logic and conversation. In P. Cole & J. L. Moran (Eds.), *Syntax and semantics: Vol. 3. Speech acts* (pp. 41–58). New York: Academic Press.

Hardy, G. E., & Barkham, M. (1994). The relationship between interpersonal attachment and work difficulties. *Human Relations, 47,* 430–445.

Hazan, C., & Shaver, P. (1987). Romantic love conceptualized as an attachment process. *Journal of Personality and Social Psychology, 52,* 511–524.

Hesse, E. (1999). The Adult Attachment Interview: Historical and current perspectives. In J. Cassidy & P. R. Shaver (Eds.), *Handbook of attachment: Theory, research, and clinical applications* (pp. 395–433). New York: Guilford Press.

Karen, R. (1994). *Becoming attached*. New York: Warner.

Kirkpatrick, L., & Hazan, C. (1994). Attachment styles and close relationships: A four-year prospective study. *Personal Relationships, 1*, 123–142.

Klohnen, E. C., & John, O. P. (1998). Working models of attachment: A theory-based prototype approach. In J. A. Simpson & W. S. Rholes (Eds.), *Attachment theory and close relationships* (pp. 115–140). New York: Guilford Press.

Kobak, R. (1994). Adult attachment: A personality or relationship construct? *Psychological Inquiry, 5*, 42–44.

Kobak, R. R., Cole, H. E., Ferenz-Gillies, R., & Fleming, W. S. (1993). Attachment and emotion regulation during mother-teen problem solving: A control theory analysis. *Child Development, 64*, 231–245.

LaGuardia, J. G., Ryan, R. M., Couchman, C. E., & Deci, E. L. (2000). Within-person variation in security of attachment: A self-determination theory perspective on attachment, need fulfillment, and well-being. *Journal of Personality and Social Psychology, 79*, 367–384.

Larose, S., Bernier, A., Soucy, N., & Duchesne, S. (1999). Attachment style dimensions, network orientations, and the process of seeking help from college teachers. *Journal of Social and Personal Relationships, 16*, 225–247.

Lopez, F. G. (1997). Student–professor relationships styles, childhood attachment bonds, and current academic orientations. *Journal of Social and Personal Relationships, 14*, 271–282.

Lopez, F. G., & Brennan, K. A. (2000). Dynamic processes underlying adult attachment organization: Toward an attachment-theoretical perspective on the healthy and effective self. *Journal of Counseling Psychology, 47*, 283–300.

Lopez, F. G., & Gormley, B. A. (2002). Stability and change in adult attachment style over the first-year college transition: Relations to self-confidence, coping, and distress patterns. *Journal of Counseling Psychology, 49*, 355–364.

Lopez, F. G., Melendez, M., & Rice, K. R. (2000). Parental divorce, parent-child bonds, and adult attachment orientations: A comparison of three racial/ethnic groups. *Journal of Counseling Psychology, 47*, 177–186.

Main, M., & Goldwyn, R. (1984). *Adult attachment scoring and classification system*. Unpublished manuscript, University of California, Berkeley.

Main, M., & Goldwyn, R. (1998). *Adult attachment scoring and classification system*. Unpublished manuscript, University of California, Berkeley.

Mallinckrodt, B., Gantt, D. L., & Coble, H. M. (1995). Attachment patterns in the psychotherapy relationship: Development of the Client Attachment to Therapist scale. *Journal of Counseling Psychology, 42*, 307–317.

Mallinckrodt, B., King, J. L., & Coble, H. M. (1998). Family dysfunction, alexithymia, and client attachment to therapist. *Journal of Counseling Psychology, 45*, 497–504.

Rothbaum, F., Weisz, J., Pott, M., Miyake, K., & Morelli, G. (2000). Attachment and culture: Security in the United States and Japan. *American Psychologist, 55*, 1093–1104.

Sagi, A., van IJzendoorn, M. H., Scharf, M., Koren-Karie, N., Joels, T., et al. (1994). Stability and discriminant validity of the Adult Attachment Interview: A psychometric study in young Israeli adults. *Developmental Psychology, 30*, 771–777.

Scharfe, E., & Bartholomew, K. (1994). Reliability and stability of adult attachment patterns. *Personal Relationships, 1*, 23–43.

Schirmer, L. L., & Lopez, F. G. (2001). Probing the social support and work strain relationship among adult workers: Contributions of adult attachment orientations. *Journal of Vocational Behavior, 59*, 17–33.

Seligman, M. E. P., & Csikszentmihalyi, M. (2000). Positive psychology: An introduction. *American Psychologist, 55*, 5–14.

Shaver, P. R., Belsky, J., & Brennan, K. A. (2000). The Adult Attachment Interview and self-reports of romantic attachment: Associations across domains and methods. *Personal Relationships, 7*, 25–43.

Simpson, J. A., & Rholes, W. S. (1998). Attachment in adulthood. In J. A. Simpson & W. S. Rholes (Eds.), *Attachment theory and close relationships* (pp. 3–21). New York: Guilford Press.

Simpson, J. A., Rholes, W. S., & Phillips, D. (1996). Conflict in close relationships: An attachment perspective. *Journal of Personality and Social Psychology, 71*, 899–914.

Slade, A. (1999). Attachment theory and research: Implications for the theory and practice of individual psychotherapy with adults. In J. Cassidy & P. R. Shaver (Eds.), *Handbook of attachment: Theory, research, and clinical applications* (pp. 575–594). New York: Guilford Press.

Snyder, C. R., & Lopez, S. J. (Eds.). (2002). *Handbook of positive psychology.* New York: Oxford University Press.

van IJzendoorn, M. H. (1995). Adult attachment representations, parental responsiveness, and infant attachment: A meta-analysis on the predictive validity of the Adult Attachment Interview. *Psychological Bulletin, 117,* 387–403.

19

Measuring Forgiveness

Laura Yamhure Thompson and C. R. Snyder

Once a quiet concept that captured the attention of few scholars, forgiveness now is being studied by a variety of researchers. As the exploration of forgiveness has grown, measures have been designed to assess forgiveness in several ways. Some measures assess nondispositional forgiveness such as the (a) forgiveness of another person for a specific transgression (e.g., McCullough et al., 1998; Subkoviak et al., 1995), (b) forgiveness of a specific person (e.g., Hargrave & Sells, 1997), or (c) perception of forgiveness within one's family (e.g., Pollard, Anderson, Anderson, & Jennings, 1998). Other measures assess dispositional forgiveness (e.g., Berry, Worthington, Parrott, O'Connor, & Wade, 2001; Hebl & Enright, 1993; Mauger et al., 1992; Mullet, Houdbine, Laumonier, & Girard, 1998; Tangney, Fee, Reinsmith, Boone, & Lee, 1999). Currently, the majority of forgiveness measures assess the granting of forgiveness, and only measures that tap the granting of forgiveness will be addressed in this chapter. It should be noted, however, that some measures do tap the seeking of forgiveness (e.g., Tangney et al., 1999).

Issues in Measuring Forgiveness

To measure a construct, one must first conceptualize it. There has been much debate about how forgiveness should be conceptualized (see McCullough, Pargament, & Thoresen, 2000b). Most agree, however, that forgiveness is adaptive (e.g., Mauger et al., 1992; McCullough, 2000; McCullough & Worthington, 1995). In this regard, research supports the assertion that forgiveness has been linked with physiological health and psychological well-being (e.g., Mauger et al., 1992; Strasser, 1984; Subkoviak et al., 1995; Witvliet, in press). Conversely, unforgiveness has correlated positively with psychopathology (Mauger et al., 1992).

Not all scholars, however, tout forgiveness as being beneficial. Some have suggested that forgiving may make the forgiver vulnerable to revictimization (Katz, Street, & Arias, 1997) and victim-blaming (Bass & Davis, 1994) in abusive relationships. These conflicting views appear to stem, in part, from differences in how forgiveness is defined. Most researchers include the renunciation of anger or resentment as a main tenet in their definition of forgiveness (e.g., McCullough, 2000; Worthington, Sandage, & Berry, 2000). However, some researchers propose that reconciliation is a component of the forgiveness process (e.g., Hargrave & Sells, 1997), whereas others view forgiveness and reconciliation as separate processes (e.g., McCullough, 2000).

Forgiveness Definitions and Scales Developed by Researchers

To highlight the distinctions between forgiveness measures, next we will examine differences and similarities between our conceptualization and measure of forgiveness and the forgiveness conceptualizations and measures developed by five other groups of researchers.

Snyder and Yamhure Thompson

We define forgiveness as the framing of a perceived transgression such that one's attachment to the transgressor, transgression, and sequelae of the transgression is transformed from negative to neutral or positive. The source of a transgression, and therefore the object of forgiveness, may be oneself, another person or persons, or a situation that one views as being beyond anyone's control (e.g., an illness, "fate," or a natural disaster) (Yamhure Thompson et al., 2002). In this definition of forgiveness, "negative attachment" refers to the negatively valenced thoughts, emotions, or behaviors that one (who is transgressed against) experiences in response to the transgressor, the transgression, and the negative outcomes associated with the transgression. Thus, this negative attachment also includes cognitions, memories, affect, or behaviors that arise when one is reminded of the event. One who forgives is freed from a negative attachment by (a) transforming the valence of the attachment from negative to either neutral or positive, or (b) a combination of transforming the valence and weakening the attachment. Weakening the attachment means that a person no longer perceives him- or herself as being as strongly connected to the transgressor or transgression as was previously the case. This does not mean forgetting what happened but rather that one no longer perceives an ongoing negative connection to that person or event.

In cases involving the forgiveness of another person, the forgiver's freedom from negative attachment may open him or her to the possibility of developing benevolent and positive feelings for the forgiven. This would represent a transformation of the valence conferred on the attachment from negative to positive. That transformation to a neutral attachment, however, suffices in our forgiveness definition. If positive feelings do develop, the forgiver may or may not pursue reconciliation with the forgiven, and we thus contend that reconciliation is not a necessary component of forgiveness. Our perspective differs from other theorists who argue that compassion or empathy for the transgressor are necessary for forgiveness (McCullough, 2000).

We also view forgiveness as *intra*personal, whether the target of forgiveness is the self, a situation, or another person. Such forgiveness does not exclude the option of pursuing justice through the legal systems or other available recourses, as long as the motivation underlying such behavior is not vengeful, such vengefulness reveals negative attachment and nonforgiveness.

Measure

The forgiveness measure that we developed (Yamhure Thompson et al., 2002) is called the Heartland Forgiveness scale (HFS). As shown in Appendix 19.1, the HFS is an 18-item measure that assesses dispositional forgiveness; it is composed of three, six-item subscales for the measurement of forgiveness of self, others, and situations. Half of the items on each subscale are positively worded (i.e., they assess forgiveness) and half are negatively worded (i.e., they assess unforgiveness). Items are endorsed using a 7-point scale. There are verbal anchors of almost always false of me = 1, more often false of me = 3, more often true of me = 5, and almost always true of me = 7. To score the HFS, the nine negatively worded items are reverse-scored, and the values for all 18 items are then summed. Scores on each HFS subscale are obtained by summing the values reported for all of the items on their respective subscales.

McCullough and Colleagues

McCullough et al. (McCullough, 2000; McCullough et al., 1998) proposed that forgiveness reflects prosocial changes in interpersonal motivations such that one experiences: (a) decreased motivation to avoid personal and psychological contact with the offender; (b) decreased motivation to seek revenge or see harm come to the offender; and (c) increased motivation toward benevolence. Differing from our model, their model (a) hinges on changes in motivation and does not require changes in cognition, affect, or behavior (McCullough et al., 2000b); and (b) includes benevolence, which we would conceptualize as the transformation of the valence of the attachment from negative to positive. To meet our criterion of forgiveness, a person need only transform the attachment from negative to neutral, or decrease the attachment. We agree that a distinction between forgiveness and reconciliation should be drawn. As we have theorized, forgiveness is an *intra*personal process, whereas reconciliation is an *inter*personal process.

McCullough and colleagues (1998) place motivation at the core of their definition, viewing it as prosocial changes in *inter*personal motivations (McCullough, 2000). This implies that forgiveness is an intrapersonal process regarding interpersonal relationships. We agree that forgiveness is an intrapersonal process; however, our definition of forgiveness includes forgiveness of self and situations. Therefore, forgiveness is applicable not only to relationships with others but also to the relationship with oneself and the impersonal world. To summarize, the three main distinctions between our definition of forgiveness and the one used by McCullough and his colleagues are that (a) our definition requires changes in cognition and affect, whereas McCullough et al.'s definition only requires changes in motivation; (b) our definition does not require benevolence toward the transgressor, whereas McCullough et al.'s does; and (c) our definition includes the self and situations as potential targets for forgiveness, whereas McCullough et al.'s definition appears to apply only to forgiveness of others (although this is not explicitly stated).

Measure

The forgiveness measure designed by McCullough et al. (1998) is called the Transgression-Related Interpersonal Motivations Inventory (TRIM). The TRIM consists of 12 items, with two subscales that measure (a) the motivation to avoid personal and psychological contact with the transgressor; and (b) the motivation to seek revenge or see harm come to the transgressor. Items are endorsed using a 5-point scale ranging from strongly disagree = 1 to strongly agree = 5. To use McCullough et al.'s (2000b) terminology, the TRIM can be viewed as a measure of transgression-specific forgiveness. In essence, it measures the motivations toward two components of their definition of forgiveness. It does not measure the motivation toward benevolence, a construct included in their definition of forgiveness. For the purposes of this chapter, the TRIM will be regarded as a transgression-specific measure of forgiveness.

Enright and Colleagues

Enright and his colleagues define forgiveness as "a willingness to abandon one's right to resentment, negative judgment, and indifferent behavior toward one who unjustly hurt us, while fostering the undeserved qualities of compassion, generosity, and even love toward him or her" (Enright, Freedman, & Rique, 1998, pp. 46–47). Similar to McCullough et al.'s definition (1998), and unlike our definition, Enright et al.'s conceptualization includes benevolence toward the offender as a necessary component of forgiveness. In fact, Enright et al. (1998; Enright, 2000) not only require benevolence, but also spontaneously self-given love on the part of the forgiver toward the forgiven. Enright and Zell (1989) emphasized this by writing that "even though the forgiveness transformations are primarily internal, the fruition of forgiveness is entering into loving community with others" (p. 99). Despite their differences, however, all three groups of researchers (the authors, McCullough and colleagues, and Enright and colleagues) exclude reconciliation as a necessary component of forgiveness.

Although their definition could be applied to forgiveness of self and forgiveness of others, Enright and Zell (1989) clearly excluded forgiveness of situations by stating, "Forgiveness is between people. One does not forgive tornadoes or floods. How could one, for instance, again join in loving community with a tornado?" (p. 53). We theorize that it is possible to feel transgressed against by the impersonal world and that, as such, it may be a target for forgiveness.

Measure

The first of two measures developed by Enright is the Enright Forgiveness Inventory (EFI; Subkoviak et al., 1995), which is a 60-item self-report instrument of forgiveness for a specific transgression. EFI items assess six forgiveness dimensions—positive affect, behavior, and cognitions and the lack of negative affect, behavior, and cognitions toward the offender. Items are endorsed using a 6-point Likert-type scale. Respondents are asked to think of the most recent interpersonal transgression and transgressor in their lives. The six subscales of the EFI can be summed to yield a forgiveness score. There is also a 5-item pseudo-forgiveness scale that is used to "correct" the forgiveness score.

The second measure is the Willingness to Forgive scale (WTF; Hebl & Enright, 1993), which is a 16-item, scenario scale that measures the dispositional willingness to use forgiveness as a problem-solving strategy. The WTF was developed to assess the effectiveness of a forgiveness intervention, and the first 15 items are hypothetical, whereas the last item refers to the transgression that was the focus of the intervention. Respondents can select 1 of 10 possible ways of responding to each scenario; only one response is forgiveness. Four scores can be generated. These scores reflect the number of times forgiveness is selected as a solution for how the person would (a) respond to the hypothetical scenarios; (b) prefer to respond to the hypothetical scenarios; (c) have responded to the real scenario; and (d) would have preferred to respond to the real scenario.

Mauger and Colleagues

Mauger et al. (1992) do not identify a definition of forgiveness that was used in the development of the Forgiveness of Self and Forgiveness of Others (FS and FO) scale; however, given that they have generated scales to measure forgiveness of self and others, it follows that they view forgiveness as applying to both targets. Also, Mauger et al. indicated that a subjective sense of the two classes of behavior assessed by the scales can be gleaned by reviewing content of the scale. They state that "items on the Forgiveness of Others scale relate to taking revenge, justifying retaliation and revenge, holding grudges, and seeing other people as apt to cause one hurt," whereas the "Forgiveness of Self items focus on feelings of guilt over past acts, seeing oneself a sinful, and having a variety of negative attitudes toward yourself" (p. 174). One may infer that the FS and FO measure unforgiveness instead of forgiveness. One item on the FO scale reads "I am able to make up pretty easily with friends who have hurt me in some way" (p. 172), suggesting that Mauger includes reconciliation in the conceptualization of forgiveness of others. There is no indication that benevolence is part of this implicit definition of forgiveness, nor is forgiveness of situations (i.e., forgiveness of the impersonal world) addressed.

Measure

The forgiveness measure developed by Mauger et al. (1992) is composed of the FS and FO scales, two measures of dispositional forgiveness. The FS and FO are part of a larger, 301-item inventory (the Behavioral Assessment System; BAS) that samples behaviors related to personality disorders. Each of the two forgiveness subscales consists of 15 items that people endorse as being either true or false.

Hargrave and Sells

Hargrave and Sells (1997) defined forgiveness as "effort in restoring love and trustworthiness to relationships so that victims and victimizers can put an end to destructive entitlement" (p. 43). They view forgiveness within the framework of an ongoing relationship with another person. Thus, the topics of self- and situation-oriented forgiveness are not addressed. Hargrave and Sells proposed a hierarchical model of the work of forgiveness with two broad divisions, which they call exonerating and forgiving. In turn, exonerating is composed of insight and understanding, and forgiving is composed of giving the opportunity for compensation and the overt act of forgiving. Thus, there are four stations of forgiveness in this model.

Giving the opportunity for compensation is defined as "the ability to engage in interactions and relationship with the former perpetrator in a way that is perceived by the victim as nonthreatening and builds emotional bonding" (p. 46). Thus, prudent reconciliation is included in their conceptualization. Overt forgiving is defined as "the perceived ability of a person to discuss past relational damage with the perpetrator and resolve issues of responsibility for specific violations to the point where the relationship can be secure and trustworthy" (p. 46). The content of the overt forgiving items indicates that their forgiveness is not purely an intrapersonal event; it must be communicated overtly in some manner. Furthermore, two other factors seem to be included in their overt act definition and items: trust on the part of the forgiver and taking responsibility on the part of the transgressor. Therefore, Hargrave and Sells's definition differs from ours in that it is defined only as it relates to forgiveness of other people, it includes the act of reconciliation (or at least reconciliation as a goal), and it includes trust.

Measure

The Hargrave and Sells (1997) measure is called the Interpersonal Relationship Resolution scale (IRRS). It measures forgiveness of a particular person who has caused the respondent to "hurt." Therefore, this measure is person-specific rather than transgression-specific. The IRRS consists of two scales (forgiveness and pain). The forgiveness scale has 22 items and four subscales (i.e., insight = five items, understanding = five items, giving the opportunity for compensation = seven items, and overt act of forgiving = five items).

Tangney and Colleagues

Tangney et al. (1999) have proposed the following working definition of forgiveness:

(1) a cognitive–affective transformation following a transgression in which (2) the victim makes a realistic assessment of the harm done and acknowledges the perpetrator's responsibility, but (3) freely chooses to "cancel the debt," giving up the need for revenge or deserved punishments and any quest for restitution. This "canceling of the debt" also involves (4) a "cancellation of negative emotions" directly related to the transgression. In particular, in forgiving, the victim overcomes his or her feelings of resentment and anger for the act. In short, by forgiving, the harmed individual (5) essentially removes him or herself from the victim role. (p. 2)

This definition is similar to ours in that it does not include feelings of love or compassion as a necessary component in the conceptualization of forgiveness. In Tangney et al.'s model, simply giving up the negative emotions is sufficient. It may appear that the two theories contrast on the issue of whether forgiveness and the pursuit of justice are mutually exclusive. Tangney and her colleagues state that the need for punishment or restitution is unforgiving in nature. Yet the use of the word "need" should be noted. This could be interpreted as meaning that it is the motivation of the person that is important, not the behavior. For example, a person could pursue justice to protect others from being harmed by the transgressor, rather than as a result of his or her need for revenge or restitution. In this latter interpretation of part three of their definition, such a criterion for forgiveness would not conflict with our assertion that one can forgive and still pursue justice, as long as the motivation is not vengeful. The wording of Tangney et al.'s definition could be applied to forgiveness of self and of others. It does not address explicitly, however, impersonal transgressors (i.e., situations) as targets of forgiveness.

Measure

Tangney et al. (1999) have developed an unpublished measure of dispositional forgiveness called the Multidimensional Forgiveness Inventory (MFI). This is a scenario-based measure that consists of 72 questions regarding 16 different transgression scenarios. There are nine subscales: propensity to forgive others; propensity to forgive self; propensity to ask for forgiveness; time to forgive others; time to forgive self; propensity to blame others; propensity to blame self; sensitivity to hurt feelings; and anger-proneness. Respondents use a 5-point Likert-type scale to indicate their response to each question regarding the scenarios.

Development and Validation of the Heartland Forgiveness Scale

Studies indicate that people's scores on measures of dispositional forgiveness tend to be related to their scores on measures of mental health and well-being, whereas scores on measures of forgiveness of specific transgressions tend not to be significantly related to mental health and well-being (see McCullough & Witvliet, in press). Thus, measures of dispositional forgiveness appear to be especially useful for assessing psychological correlates of forgiveness. Currently, the HFS is the most comprehensive measure of the disposition to grant forgiveness: It is the only measure that assesses dispositional forgiveness of self, others, and situations. Therefore, next we will present more detailed information about the psychometric characteristics of the HFS.

HFS Reliability Estimates

INTERNAL CONSISTENCY RELIABILITIES. Internal consistency reliabilities for the HFS have been calculated using five student and two nonstudent samples, with sample sizes ranging from 123 to 651. The alphas ranged from .84 to .87 for the HFS scale, and alphas for the self, other, and situation subscales ranged from .71 to .83.

TEST–RETEST RELIABILITY. In a student sample (N = 193) using a three-week follow-up, the test–retest reliability of the HFS was .83 and ranged from .72 to .77 for the subscales (all ps < .001). The test–retest reliability of the HFS in a nonstudent sample (N = 57) using a nine-month follow-up was .77, and ranged from .66 to .70 for the subscales (all ps < .001).

HFS Construct Validity

In two studies using student samples (Ns of 228 and 276), the HFS was positively correlated (ps < .005) with three other measures of dispositional forgiveness: the combination of the FS and FO scales (r = .62); the WTF scale (r = .20); and the MFI (r = .46). The HFS has correlated significantly and negatively with the Transgression-Related Interpersonal Motivations Inventory (TRIM; r = −.25, p < .005; McCullough et al., 1998). Given that the TRIM assesses forgiveness of a specific offense perpetrated by another person, it is understandable that the correlation coefficient for the relationship between the TRIM and the forgiveness of others subscale of the HFS (r = −.39, p < .005) was slightly higher than that of the full HFS and the TRIM. Similarly, the forgiveness of others subscale of the HFS was significantly correlated with another measure of forgiveness of a specific transgression, the Enright Forgiveness Inventory (EFI; r = .21, p < .005; Subkoviak et al., 1995). Finally, the HFS and its subscales were not significantly correlated with forgiveness of a specific person, as measured by the IRRS (Hargrave & Sells, 1997).

MEASURES WITH WHICH HFS IS POSITIVELY CORRELATED. In a series of four student studies and two nonstudent studies (Ns ranging from 48 to 281), the HFS was significantly positively correlated with three measures of related constructs, all with p < .005: (a) the Cognitive Flexibility scale (Martin & Rubin, 1995), with rs of .46 and .52; (b) the Dyadic Trust scale (Larzelere & Huston, 1980), with r equal to .37; and (c) the distraction subscale of the Response Style Questionnaire (Nolen-Hoeksema & Morrow, 1991), with r equal to .33.

MEASURES WITH WHICH THE HFS IS NEGATIVELY CORRELATED. In studies (with Ns ranging from 48 to 281), the HFS was significantly negatively correlated with six measures of related constructs, all with $p < .005$: (a) the Hostile Automatic Thoughts scale (Snyder, Crowson, Houston, Kurylo, & Poirier, 1997), with rs equal to $-.35$, $-.44$, and $-.45$; (b) the rumination subscale of the Response Style Questionnaire (Nolen-Hoeksema & Morrow, 1991), with an r of $-.34$; and (d) the Beck Depression Inventory (Beck & Steer, 1987), an r of $-.68$.

Predictive Power of HFS Forgiveness in Romantic Relationships

Adult men and women ($N = 128$) who were involved in romantic relationships completed measures of forgiveness (i.e., the HFS), trust, hostility, relationship satisfaction, and relationship duration. These self-report measures were completed at the beginning of the study and then again nine months later. Results indicated that forgiveness was a stronger predictor of relationship duration than hostility. Relationship satisfaction was significantly predicted from the participant's trust of his or her partner and the participant's perception of how trusting his or her partner was of the participant. The degree of closeness (between participant and partner) added incremental validity by accounting for variance in relationship satisfaction above and beyond that accounted for by participant and partner trust.

Overall, these studies indicate that the HFS is a short, reliable, and valid instrument for assessing the general disposition to grant forgiveness, as well as more specific tendencies to be forgiving of oneself, other people, and situations.

Conclusion

In this chapter, we explored the differences and similarities among seven self-report measures of forgiveness and the conceptualizations of forgiveness on which those measures are based. Although all of these measures assess a person's propensity to grant forgiveness, there are substantial differences among the measures and among the conceptualizations of forgiveness that these measures were designed to assess. Those interested in selecting a measure to assess forgiveness for clinical or research purposes can use this chapter to help identify the measure(s) that might best match their needs.

Appendix 19.1
Heartland Forgiveness Scale

Directions: In the course of our lives negative things may occur because of our own actions, the actions of others, or circumstances beyond our control. For some time after these events, we may have negative thoughts or feelings about ourselves, others, or the situation. Think about how you *typically* respond to such negative events. Next to each of the following items write the number (from the 7-point scale below) that best describes how you *typically* respond to the type of negative situation described. There are no right or wrong answers. Please be as open as possible in your answers.

1	2	3	4	5	6	7
Almost always false of me		More often false of me		More often true of me		Almost always true of me

___ 1. Although I feel badly at first when I mess up, over time I can give myself some slack.

___ 2. I hold grudges against myself for negative things I've done.

___ 3. Learning from bad things that I've done helps me get over them.

___ 4. It is really hard for me to accept myself once I've messed up.

___ 5. With time I am understanding of myself for mistakes I've made.

___ 6. I don't stop criticizing myself for negative things I've felt, thought, said, or done.

___ 7. I continue to punish a person who has done something that I think is wrong.

___ 8. With time I am understanding of others for the mistakes they've made.

___ 9. I continue to be hard on others who have hurt me.

___ 10. Although others have hurt me in the past, I have eventually been able to see them as good people.

___ 11. If others mistreat me, I continue to think badly of them.

___ 12. When someone disappoints me, I can eventually move past it.

___ 13. When things go wrong for reasons that can't be controlled, I get stuck in negative thoughts about it.

___ 14. With time I can be understanding of bad circumstances in my life.

___ 15. If I am disappointed by uncontrollable circumstances in my life, I continue to think negatively about them.

___ 16. I eventually make peace with bad situations in my life.

___ 17. It's really hard for me to accept negative situations that aren't anybody's fault.

___ 18. Eventually I let go of negative thoughts about bad circumstances that are beyond anyone's control.

Scoring Instructions:

To calculate the scores for the HFS and its three subscales, first reverse score items 2, 4, 6, 7, 9, 11, 13, 15, and 17. Then sum the values for the items that compose each scale (with appropriate items being reverse scored): HFS (items 1–18), self subscale (items 1–6), other subscale (items 7–12), situation subscale (items 13–18).

References

Bass, E., & Davis, L. (1994). *The courage to heal.* New York: Harper Perennial.

Beck, A. T., & Steer, R. A. (1987). *The Beck Depression Inventory.* San Antonio, TX: Psychological Corporation.

Berry, J. W., Worthington, E. L., Jr., Parrott, L., O'Connor, L., & Wade, N. G. (2001). Dispositional forgiveness: Development and construct validity of the Transgression Narrative Test of Forgiveness (TNTF). *Personality and Social Psychology Bulletin, 27,* 1277–1290.

Enright. R. D. (2000). *Helping clients forgive: An empirical guide for resolving anger and restoring hope.* Washington, DC: American Psychological Association.

Enright, R. D., Freedman, S., & Rique, J. (1998). The psychology of interpersonal forgiveness. In R. D. Enright & J. North (Eds.), *Exploring forgiveness* (pp. 46–62). Madison: University of Wisconsin Press.

Enright, R. D., & Zell, R. L. (1989). Problems encountered when we forgive another. *Journal of Psychology and Christianity, 8,* 52–60.

Hargrave, T. D., & Sells, J. N. (1997). The development of a forgiveness scale. *Journal of Marital and Family Therapy, 23,* 41–63.

Hebl, J. H., & Enright, R. D. (1993). Forgiveness as a psychotherapeutic goal with elderly females. *Psychotherapy, 30,* 658–667.

Katz, J., Street, A., & Arias, I. (1997). Individual differences in self-appraisals and responses to dating violence scenarios. *Violence and Victims, 12*(3), 265–276.

Larzelere, R. E., & Huston, T. L. (1980). The dyadic trust scale: Toward understanding interpersonal trust in close relationships. *Journal of Marriage and the Family, 42,* 595–604.

Martin, M. M., & Rubin, R. B. (1995). A new measure of cognitive flexibility. *Psychological Reports, 76,* 623–626.

Mauger, P. A., Perry, J. E., Freeman, T., Grove, D. C., McBride, A. G., et al. (1992). The measurement of forgiveness: Preliminary research. *Journal of Psychology and Christianity, 11,* 170–180.

McCullough, M. E. (2000). Forgiveness as human strength: Theory, measurement, and links to well-being. *Journal of Social and Clinical Psychology, 19,* 43–55.

McCullough, M. E., Pargament, K. I., & Thoresen, C. E. (Eds.). (2000a). *Forgiveness: Theory, research, and practice.* New York: Guilford Press.

McCullough, M. E., Pargament, K. I., & Thoresen, C. E. (Eds.). (2000b). The psychology of forgiveness: History, conceptual issues, and overview. In M. E. McCullough, K. I. Pargament, & C. E. Thoresen (Eds.), *Forgiveness: Theory, research, and practice* (pp. 1–14). New York: Guilford Press.

McCullough, M. E., Rachal, K. C., Sandage, S. J., Worthington, E. L., Jr., Brown, S. W., et al. (1998). Interpersonal forgiving in close relationships II: Theoretical elaboration and measurement. *Journal of Personality and Social Psychology, 75,* 1586–1603.

McCullough, M. E., & Witvliet, V. O. (in press). The psychology of forgiveness. In C. R. Snyder and S. J. Lopez (Eds.), *The handbook of positive psychology.* New York: Oxford University Press.

McCullough, M. E., & Worthington, E. L., Jr. (1995). Promoting forgiveness: A comparison of two brief psychoeducational group interventions with a waiting-list control. *Counseling and Values, 40,* 55–68.

Mullet, E., Houdbine, A., Laumonier, S., & Girard, M. (1998). "Forgiveness": Factor structure in a sample of young, middle-aged, and elderly adults. *European Psychologist, 3,* 289–297.

Nolen-Hoeksema, S., & Morrow, J. (1991). A prospective study of depression and distress following a natural disaster: The 1989 Loma Prieta earthquake. *Journal of Personality and Social Psychology, 61,* 105–121.

Pollard, M. W., Anderson, R. A., Anderson, W. T., & Jennings, G. (1998). The development of a family forgiveness scale. *Journal of Family Therapy, 20,* 95–109.

Snyder, C. R., Crowson, J. J., Jr., Houston, B. K., Kurylo, M., & Poirier, J. (1997). Assessing hostile automatic thoughts: Development and validation of the HAT Scale. *Cognitive Therapy and Research, 21,* 477–492.

Snyder, C. R., & Higgins, R. L. (1988). Excuses: Their effective role in the negotiation of reality. *Psychological Bulletin, 104,* 23–35.

Strasser, J. A. (1984). The relation of general forgiveness and forgiveness type to reported health in the elderly. *Dissertation Abstracts International, 45*(6), 1733B.

Subkoviak, M. J., Enright, R. D., Wu, C. R., Gassin, E. A., Freedman, S., Olson, L. M., et al. (1995). Measuring interpersonal forgiveness in late adolescence and middle adulthood. *Journal of Adolescence, 18,* 641–655.

Tangney, J., Fee, R., Reinsmith, C., Boone, A. L., & Lee, N. (1999, Aug.). *Assessing individual differences in the propensity to forgive.* Paper presented at the annual meeting of the American Psychological Association, Boston, MA.

Witvliet, C. V. O. (in press). Forgiveness and health: Review and reflections on a matter of faith, feelings, and physiology. *Journal of Psychology and Theology.*

Worthington, E. L., Jr., Sandage, S. J., & Berry, J. W. (2000). Group interventions to promote forgiveness. In M. E. McCullough, K. I. Pargament, & C. E. Thoreson (Eds.), *Forgiveness: Theory, research, and practice* (pp. 228–253). New York: Guilford Press.

Yamhure Thompson, L., Snyder, C. R., Hoffman, L., Michael, S. T., Rasmussen, H., et al. (2002). *Dispositional forgiveness of self, others, and situations.* Manuscript submitted for publication.

20

Sense of Humor

Rod Martin

In contemporary Western culture, a sense of humor is widely viewed as a desirable—even virtuous—personality characteristic. Individuals with a greater sense of humor are thought to be better able to cope with stress, to get along well with others, and to enjoy better mental and even physical health (e.g., Lefcourt, 2001a). Humor, however, has not always been viewed so positively. Indeed, the earliest theories of laughter, dating to Aristotle and Plato and continuing in some form to the present day (e.g., Gruner, 1997), view it as resulting from a sense of superiority derived from ridiculing others for their stupidity, weakness, or ugliness. This view holds little promise, however, for including humor as part of positive psychology. The existence of such conflicting perspectives may be understood by examining the ways in which the conceptualization of humor has evolved over several centuries.

Evolution of the Humor Concept

Ruch (1998a) has traced the etymology of "humor," which originated in the classical Greek theory of four humors or bodily fluids (blood, phlegm, black bile, and yellow bile) that were thought to influence all aspects of bodily and psychic function. Over time, humor came to refer to mood (a meaning still present when we speak of someone being in good or bad humor), and eventually it evolved into a connotation of wittiness, funniness, and laughableness, although not necessarily in a benevolent sense. Until the end of the 17th century, it was socially acceptable to laugh at individuals who were deformed or mentally ill, and the exchange of hostile witty remarks was a popular form of interaction in fashionable society. Under the influence of the humanistic movements of the 18th century, however, these aggressive forms of laughter began to be viewed as unrefined and vulgar.

Humanistic philosophers and moralists began to conceptualize forms of laughter and amusement that they considered more socially appropriate. To distinguish these acceptable expressions of laughter, they co-opted the term "humor" and gave it a restricted and specialized meaning. Distinct from other laughter-related phenomena (e.g., wit, comedy, sarcasm, irony, satire, ridicule), humor was used to refer exclusively to a sympathetic, tolerant, and benevolent amusement at the imperfections of the world and the foibles of human nature in general. Humor also acquired a connotation of not taking oneself too seriously, being able to poke fun at oneself, and maintaining a philosophical detachment in one's outlook. Thus, humor was distinguished from other sources of laughter, such as wit, which was viewed as more sarcastic, biting, and cruel. Individuals who expressed the benevolent, nonhostile, philosophical forms of amusement encompassed by this revised conception of humor were considered refined and noble, in contrast to those who engaged in coarse joking, witty repartee, and laughter at the expense of others. By the Victorian era, a sense of humor (in this restricted meaning) had become a virtue, along with common sense, tolerance, and compromise.

This distinction between humor and other sources of laughter was adopted by Freud (1928), who viewed humor (in this narrow sense) as one of the healthiest defense mechanisms, as distinct from wit or joking, which he viewed as a means of expressing unacceptable aggressive and sexual impulses. According to Freud, humor allows one to maintain a detached perspective in the face of misfortune and adversity, thus sparing oneself the depression, anxiety, and anger that might normally arise, while maintaining a realistic view of oneself and the world. Thus, Freud accepted the virtuous and humanitarian meanings of this restricted definition of humor and added a psychological connotation of mental health and well-being.

Subsequent psychological theorists, such as Maslow (1954) and Allport (1961), have echoed these themes, suggesting that a healthy or mature personality is characterized by a particular style of humor that is nonhostile, philosophical, and self-deprecating yet self-accepting. Notably, these authors viewed this healthy form of humor as relatively rare, in contrast with the majority of everyday joking and the type of comedy typically found in the media. In addition, they suggested that healthy forms of humor are more likely to be accompanied by a chuckle than by hearty laughter. These formulations suggest that psychological health relates not only to the presence of certain kinds of adaptive humor but also to the absence of more maladaptive forms of humor. Current views of humor as a component of positive psychology can be traced to these ideas.

Contemporary Meanings of Humor

The picture has become somewhat confused over the past century, however, because the term *humor,* as used both by the layperson and by psychological researchers, generally has lost its narrow focus and has evolved to become a broad umbrella term for all laughter-related phenomena. Humor now refers to all forms of laughter, including jokes, stand-up comedy, television sitcoms, political satire, and ridicule. In this sense, humor now can be aggressive and hostile, as well as benevolent and philosophical (Ruch, 1996). Much of the psychological humor research in the past few decades also has followed this trend, broadening the meaning of humor while retaining the view that it is conducive to psychological health. Thus, studies aimed at elucidating potential benefits of humor typically have used loose operational definitions that may include elements that would not have been considered healthy or desirable in past formulations. For example, the existing self-report measures of humor (to be described subsequently) generally do not assess the specific ways in which individuals use or express humor. Similarly, laboratory studies of effects of humor on aspects of physical health have tended to make use of comedy videotapes with little attention given to the content of the comedy or type of humor. As discussed subsequently, this failure to distinguish adaptive and maladaptive forms of humor may be one reason for the inconsistent findings in the research on the relationship between humor and physical and mental health.

In current psychological research, then, humor is a broad and multifaceted construct (Martin, 2000). It may refer to characteristics of a stimulus (jokes, cartoons, comedy films); to mental processes involved in creating, perceiving, understanding, and appreciating humor ("getting the joke"); or to the responses of the individual (amusement, exhilaration, smiling, laughter). Humor involves both cognitive and emotional elements. Although most humor occurs in interpersonal contexts, it also can be a purely intrapsychic phenomenon (amused outlook on life, not taking oneself too seriously). Humor may be a state (amusement, cheerfulness, exhilaration) or a trait (sense of humor).

The term "sense of humor" is used in contemporary psychology to refer to humor as an enduring personality trait (see Ruch, 1998b, for reviews of recent research on sense of humor in personality psychology). There is little consensus about how to define and measure sense of humor as a trait, however, and researchers use the term in many different ways (Martin, 1998). Thus, sense of humor may be conceptualized as a habitual behavior pattern (tendency to laugh frequently, to tell jokes and amuse others, to laugh at other people's jokes), an ability (to create humor, to amuse others, to "get the joke," to remember jokes), a temperamental trait (habitual cheerfulness), an aesthetic response (enjoyment of particular types of humorous material), an attitude (positive attitude toward humor and humorous people), a world view (bemused outlook on life), or a coping strategy (tendency to maintain a humorous perspective in the face of adversity). These various definitions of sense of humor may not be highly intercorrelated (indeed, some may even be inversely related), and not all are likely to be relevant to positive psychology. One of the challenges of research on humor in the context of positive psychology is to identify which aspects or components of the humor construct are most relevant to mental health and successful adaptation.

Humor as a Way of Coping and Enhancing Relationships

One conceptualization that seems particularly germane to positive psychology is the view of humor as a way of coping with stress. This is consistent with the Freudian notion of humor as a healthy defense mechanism. In this view, a humorous perspective mitigates the negative consequences of adversity. Based on Lazarus and Folkman's (1984) transactional model of stress, humor may be viewed as a form of cognitive appraisal that involves perceiving potentially stressful situations in a more benign, less threatening manner (Kuiper, Martin, & Olinger, 1993). According to incongruity theories of humor (e.g.,

Suls, 1972), which can be traced to the philosophical writings of Kant and Schopenhauer, humor involves the bringing together of two normally disparate ideas, concepts, or situations in a surprising or unexpected manner. The shifts in perspective accompanying humor have been seen by a number of writers as the basis for its hypothesized effectiveness as an appraisal-focused coping strategy (e.g., Dixon, 1980; O'Connell, 1976). Research evidence for humor as a coping mechanism is somewhat equivocal, however (for a review, see Lefcourt, 2001b). As discussed subsequently, this may be a result of inadequacies in the way humor has been conceptualized and measured.

Related to the view of humor as a coping mechanism is the idea that humor contributes to psychological health and resistance to stress by enhancing social support. Thus, individuals with a greater sense of humor are thought to be more socially competent (Bell, McGhee, & Duffey, 1986); in turn, it may be easier for such persons to attract and maintain friendships and develop a rich social support network, and consequently to obtain the mental and physical health benefits of social support (Cohen & Wills, 1985). However, there is currently only limited research examining the effects of humor on social support or other aspects of interpersonal relationships such as attraction, intimacy, or relationship satisfaction (e.g., Murstein & Brust, 1985; Ziv & Gadish, 1989). This appears to be a potentially fruitful avenue for additional research.

Measuring Sense of Humor

In view of the different ways of conceptualizing sense of humor, it is not surprising that researchers have developed a variety of approaches to measurement, including self-reports, humor appreciation measures, ability tests, and behavioral observation techniques. I will discuss the most widely used measures (see Ruch, 1998b, for a complete list of measures).

Self-Report Measures of Sense of Humor

In humor research over the past two decades, self-report measures have been the most widely used method for assessing sense of humor. In these tests, respondents are asked to rate their agreement with a series of self-descriptive statements relating to their tendency to laugh frequently, to tell jokes, to laugh at others' jokes, to appreciate humor, and so on.

COPING HUMOR SCALE. The Coping Humor scale (CHS; Martin & Lefcourt, 1983) was designed to assess the degree to which individuals report using humor to cope with stress. It contains seven items that are self-descriptive statements such as "I have often found that my problems have been greatly reduced when I tried to find something funny in them" and "I can usually find something to laugh or joke about even in trying situations." The CHS has Cronbach alphas in the .60 to .70 range and a test–retest reliability coefficient of .80 over a 12-week period (Martin, 1996). No sex differences usually are found. There is considerable construct validity support for the measure (summarized in Lefcourt & Martin, 1986; and Martin, 1996). For example, scores on the CHS have correlated significantly with peer ratings of individuals' tendency to (a) use humor to cope with stress ($r = .50$) and (b) not take themselves too seriously ($rs = .58$ to $.78$). In addition, the CHS was significantly correlated with the rated funniness of participants' humorous monologues created while watching a stressful film ($r = .50$). In a naturalistic study, dental patients with higher scores on the CHS were found to engage in significantly more joking and laughter before undergoing dental surgery (Trice & Price-Greathouse, 1986). The measure generally is uncorrelated with measures of social desirability, thereby lending discriminant validity support. The CHS has been used widely in research on humor as a coping mechanism (see review in Martin, 1996). The scale does have some psychometric limitations, however, including relatively low internal consistency resulting from low item-total correlations of some items.

SITUATIONAL HUMOR RESPONSE QUESTIONNAIRE. The Situational Humor Response Questionnaire (SHRQ; Martin & Lefcourt, 1984) defines sense of humor in terms of the frequency with which a person smiles and laughs in a wide variety of life situations. Thus, this measure is based on the assumption that overt expressions of smiling and laughter are valid indicators of the more private and elusive processes involved in perceiving, creating, and enjoying humor in daily life. The scale comprises 18 items that present participants with brief descriptions of situations (e.g., "if you were eating in a restaurant with some friends and the waiter accidentally spilled a drink on you"). These include both pleasant and unpleasant situations, ranging from specific and structured to general and unstructured, and from relatively common to relatively unusual. For each item, respondents are asked to rate the degree to which they would be likely to laugh in such a situation, using five Guttman-type response options ranging from "I would not have been particularly amused" to "I would have laughed heartily." In addition to the 18 situational items, the scale contains three self-descriptive items relating to the frequency with which the participant generally laughs and smiles in a wide range of situations.

The SHRQ has Cronbach alphas in the .70 to .85 range and test–retest correlations of around .70 (Lefcourt & Martin, 1986). Males and females typically do not differ. The validity support for the SHRQ is extensive (see Lefcourt & Martin, 1986; and Martin, 1996). For example, scores on the SHRQ correlated significantly with the frequency and duration of spontaneous laughter during unstructured interviews (rs ranging from .30 to .62). SHRQ scores also have correlated significantly with peer ratings of participants' frequency of laughter and tendency to use humor in coping with stress (rs ranging from .30 to .50). In addition, scores have correlated significantly with the rated funniness of monologues created by participants in the laboratory ($rs = .21$ to $.44$). Martin and Kuiper (1999) also found that individuals with higher scores on the SHRQ recorded a significantly higher frequency of laughter over a three-day period. That the measure is not significantly correlated with measures of social desirability lends discriminant validity. The SHRQ has been used extensively in research on humor, including studies of stress-moderating effects of humor (see Martin, 1996, for a review).

The SHRQ has been criticized for defining sense of humor purely in terms of laughter frequency (Thorson, 1990). Indeed, as Martin (1996) acknowledged, laughter can occur without humor, and there can be humor without laughter. Nonetheless, correlations between the SHRQ and various measures of personality and well-being are comparable to those found with other self-report humor measures such as the CHS. This similarity with other humor scales may result from the inclusion in the SHRQ of a number of items describing unpleasant or mildly stressful situations. Thus, more than just assessing the frequency of laughter per se, the SHRQ appears to address the tendency to maintain an amused outlook when faced with unpleasant or potentially embarrassing events. A potentially more serious shortcoming of this measure is that the situations described in the items are specific to university students' experiences and it is therefore less suitable for other populations. Furthermore, the situations described in the items have become somewhat dated over time and may be difficult for many people to relate to.

THE SENSE OF HUMOR QUESTIONNAIRE. The Sense of Humor Questionnaire (SHQ; Svebak, 1974) comprises three seven-item subscales corresponding to three dimensions hypothesized to be essential to a sense of humor: (a) metamessage sensitivity, or the ability to recognize humor in situations (e.g., "I can usually find something comical, witty, or humorous in most situations"); (b) liking of humor, or the enjoyment of humor and the humorous role (e.g., "It is my impression that those who try to be funny really do it to hide their lack of self-confidence"; this item is negatively keyed); and (c) emotional expressiveness, or the tendency to freely express one's emotions (e.g., "If I find a situation very comical, I find it very hard to keep a straight face even when nobody else seems to think it's funny").

Lefcourt and Martin (1986) reported alphas in the .60 to .75 range for the metamessage sensitivity and liking of humor subscales, but alphas less than .20 for emotional expressiveness. In their subsequent research, therefore, they used only the first two subscales. Test–retest reliabilities of these two subscales over one month have been .58 to .78. Support for the validity of the metamessage sensitivity and liking of humor subscales has been provided by significant correlations with peer ratings of humor, as well as with the SHRQ, CHS, and other self-report humor measures. The SHQ subscales have not correlated significantly with scores on the Marlowe-Crowne Social Desirability scale (Lefcourt & Martin, 1986). A short (six-item) version of the SHQ also has been developed (Svebak, 1996) for use in epidemiological surveys.

MULTIDIMENSIONAL SENSE OF HUMOR SCALE. The Multidimensional Sense of Humor scale (MSHS; Thorson & Powell, 1993) was designed as a broad measure of six hypothesized dimensions of humor (recognition of oneself as a humorous person, recognition of others' humor, appreciation of humor, laughing, humorous perspective-taking, and coping humor). Factor analyses of the 24-item scale have revealed a somewhat different structure from the one originally hypothesized, although four factors typically have been found: (a) humor production and social uses of humor (e.g., "I use humor to entertain my friends"), (b) coping humor (e.g., "Uses of humor or wit help me master difficult situations"), (c) negative attitudes toward humor (e.g., "People who tell jokes are a pain in the neck"), and (d) positive attitudes toward humor (e.g., "I like a good joke"). Several of the items typically load highly on more than one factor, and factor scores have an average intercorrelation of more than .45. The total scale has a Cronbach alpha of .90, but reliabilities for the factor scores have not been reported. Thus, although the measure is described as multidimensional, use of a single total score seems most appropriate. The scale is slanted toward attitudes or beliefs about humor (e.g., "Calling somebody a comedian is a real insult" and "Humor is a lousy coping mechanism"). The MSHS has been used in several studies on the relationship between sense of humor and various aspects of psychological health (for a review, see Thorson, Powell, Sarmany-Schuller, & Hampes, 1997).

Alternative Conceptualizations and Approaches to Measuring Sense of Humor

In addition to self-report measures, researchers have used several other approaches to assessing sense of humor. Each of these measurement approaches is based on a different conceptualization of sense of humor.

HUMOR APPRECIATION MEASURES. In the humor appreciation approach, participants are asked to rate their enjoyment or perceived funniness of a number of jokes, cartoons, and other humorous materials. These stimuli are typically grouped into various categories (e.g., innocent, aggressive, sexual) on the basis of either a priori judgments of the researchers or factor analytical procedures. Preferences for particular types of jokes have been assumed to relate to aspects of personality, such as aggressive tendencies. Most of the research on humor before the 1980s took this approach (see Martin, 1998). Some of the early researchers attempted to use this method to study relationships between humor appreciation and various aspects of mental health. For example, O'Connell (1960) created the Wit and Humor Appreciation Test (WHAT), which contained jokes that were judged by a panel of clinical psychologists to represent hostile wit, nonsense wit, and humor (in the Freudian sense). Although some evidence was found that well-adjusted individuals preferred jokes representing humor (as opposed to wit) more than did maladjusted individuals, subsequent investigations provided little corroboration of these findings (O'Connell, 1976).

A problem with this content-focused approach is revealed by more recent research showing that the *content* of humorous materials is generally less important than the *structure* in determining individuals' appreciation ratings. On this point, Ruch (1992; Ruch & Hehl, 1998) has conducted a series of factor analytical studies on a wide assortment of jokes and cartoons with samples of participants spanning a broad range of ages, occupations, and nationalities. Using ratings of both funniness and aversiveness of the humor stimuli, he consistently has found three stable factors of humor appreciation. The two largest factors relate to structural aspects of the jokes and cartoons (resolved versus unresolved incongruity), whereas a third factor relates to content (sexual themes). Ruch constructed the 3–WD (Witz–Dimensionen) humor test to assess the degree to which individuals appreciate jokes and cartoons in each of these domains and, in a number of studies, he has investigated personality correlates of these humor preference dimensions. A major finding has been that individuals with conservative social attitudes prefer humor in which the incongruity is resolved, whereas individuals high on sensation seeking prefer unresolved incongruity (nonsense humor). Research with the 3–WD and several self-report sense of humor scales has shown very little correlation between the two measurement approaches (Kohler & Ruch, 1996). Thus, humor appreciation measures and self-report scales appear to measure quite different constructs.

A MEASURE OF HUMOR AS CHEERFUL TEMPERAMENT. Another alternative approach to humor is represented by Ruch's temperament approach (Ruch & Kohler, 1998), in which dispositions to cheerfulness, seriousness, and bad mood are viewed as traits forming the temperamental basis of humor. Ruch, Kohler, and van Thriel (1996) developed the State-Trait Cheerfulness Inventory (STCI) to assess individual differences in these traits as well as related states. In a series of studies they have found that individuals with higher trait scores on this measure are more likely to maintain positive emotions in situations that are normally conducive to negative emotion. This may be a useful alternative approach to conceptualizing and measuring humor, because it relates to the traditional narrow definition of humor discussed previously. The state scale (with day, week, month instructions) also is well-suited for pre–post measures in intervention studies. As such, it is the only self-report humor measure that is sensitive to change.

Q-SORT TECHNIQUE FOR ASSESSING HUMOROUS BEHAVIOR. Based on an act-frequency approach to personality, Craik, Lampert, and Nelson (1996) developed the Humorous Behavior Q-sort deck as a method for observers to describe humor-related everyday behaviors of individuals. The 100-card deck contains statements describing a range of humorous conduct (e.g., "Uses good-natured jests to put others at ease," "Spoils jokes by laughing before finishing them"). Trained observers who are well-acquainted with an individual's behavior patterns sort the cards into nine piles ranging from least to most characteristic of the individual. Factor analyses of self-descriptive Q-sorts of university students have revealed five factors reflecting different styles of humorous conduct: socially warm versus cold, reflective versus boorish, competent versus inept, earthy versus repressed, and benign versus mean-spirited. Craik and Ware (1998) reported evidence for interrater reliability and validity of this assessment procedure. This approach holds promise for the study of individual differences in humor using an observational rather than a self-report methodology.

ABILITY TESTS OF HUMOR. Several researchers have developed methods of assessing humor as an ability comparable to creative ability or intelligence. Here the focus is on the evaluation of maximal rather than typical performance. For example, Lefcourt and Martin (1986) had participants create humorous monologues in the laboratory, which were then rated by trained judges of funniness (based on criteria relating to the presence of incongruity, novelty, surprise, etc.). Kohler and Ruch (1996) used a similar technique in a cartoon punch-line production test. Feingold and Mazzella (1991) developed several tests of aspects of "verbal humor ability," including humor information, joke knowledge, humor reasoning, and joke comprehension.

Humor Measurement Issues

Much of the psychological research on humor over the past two decades has been based on the assumption that a sense of humor is associated with psychological health and well-being. Individuals with a greater sense of humor are thought to be able to cope more effectively with stress, to experience less negative moods, to enjoy greater physical health, and to have more positive and healthy relationships with others. Despite these widely held views, however, the evidence from research using the various humor measures described previously has been surprisingly weak and inconsistent. For example, Kuiper and Martin (1998) presented a series of five studies examining relations between several self-report measures of humor (the CHS, SHRQ, and SHQ) and various measures relating to aspects of mental health and "positive personality" (e.g., dispositional optimism, psychological well-being, self-esteem, depression, anxiety, social avoidance). Based on their findings, they concluded that the humor scales are relatively weak indicators of mental health, in contrast with other measures associated with positive psychology such as dispositional optimism (Scheier & Carver, 1985). Furthermore, although some researchers reported stress-buffering effects of sense of humor as measured by self-report scales (e.g., Martin & Dobbin, 1988; Martin & Lefcourt, 1983), a number of others, often with larger sample sizes, have failed to replicate these findings (e.g., Anderson & Arnoult, 1989; Porterfield, 1987). In addition, in a review of research on humor, laughter, and physical health, Martin (2001) found no consistent evidence for relationships between sense of humor measures and such health indicators as immunity, pain tolerance, blood pressure, longevity, or illness symptoms. In sum, widely held assumptions about psychological and physical health benefits of a sense of humor are not strongly or consistently supported by research with the existing humor measures.

A possible explanation for these weak findings relates to the historical distinctions between potentially adaptive and maladaptive forms of humor discussed previously. Past theorists noted that healthy psychological functioning is associated with distinctive styles of humor (e.g., perspective-taking, self-deprecating, or affiliative humor) and that other forms of humor (e.g., sarcastic, disparaging, or defensively avoidant humor) actually may be deleterious to well-being (e.g., Allport, 1961; Freud, 1928; Maslow, 1954). Thus, in studying the relationship between humor and psychological health, it may be just as important to examine the kinds of humor that people do *not* typically express as to study the kinds of humor that they *do* express.

Unfortunately, this distinction between healthy and unhealthy forms of humor has been largely ignored in recent humor research. Although the existing measures are based on the assumption that humor is adaptive, beneficial for coping, and so forth, they do not generally ask respondents about the specific ways in which they express or use humor. For example, individuals who frequently engage in sarcastic "put-down" humor or who use humor as a form of defensive denial to avoid dealing constructively with their problems may be likely to endorse such typical humor scale items as "Uses of wit or humor help me master difficult situations" or "I can often crack people up with the things I say." Thus, high scores on these measures may not necessarily reflect the more adaptive or psychologically healthy forms of humor described by earlier psychologists such as Allport, Maslow, and Freud.

A related problem with the existing self-report humor measures is that they focus on only a narrow range of humor expression. Although researchers often assume that the various scales measure different aspects of humor, multitrait, multimethod, and factor analytical studies indicate that they have much overlap. For example, when scales are grouped according to whether they are purported to measure humor appreciation versus humor creation, the correlations between scales across the two categories are generally as high as those between scales within each category (Kohler & Ruch, 1996). Moreover, factor analyses of the most widely used self-report humor measures have found that most of the variance is accounted for by only one or two factors (Kohler & Ruch, 1996; Ruch, 1994). With regard to broader personality dimensions, these scales tap primarily into extraversion, and they have minimal loadings on other potentially important personality dimensions such as neuroticism (Kohler & Ruch, 1996; Ruch, 1994).

In summary, although the existing self-report humor measures generally show acceptable reliability and validity, they have some important limitations, especially with regard to their suitability for research in positive psychology. Most notably, they tap into only a limited range of potential humor dimensions. In particular, none of the current measures explicitly assess dimensions that involve potentially maladaptive styles or expressions of humor. Moreover, although the existing measures are assumed to assess healthy forms of humor, they do not appear to distinguish adequately between adaptive and maladaptive uses of humor. Limitations in the measures may account, at least in part, for the equivocal findings in the research on sense of humor and mental health. Accordingly, further work on humor as a component of positive psychology may require the development of refined theories, conceptualizations, and measures.

Recent Developments in Measurement of Sense of Humor

Although research using the existing measures of sense of humor has made valuable contributions to the understanding of various aspects of humor, additional efforts are needed in refining the conceptualization and measurement of sense of humor. As noted previously, humor has become an umbrella term, and more work is needed to determine what are the components, how they are interrelated, and how they relate to other personality dimensions and aspects of human functioning. As Ruch (1996) has suggested, it may be best to think of humor as a category label for a class of traits (similar to temperament, intelligence, or emotion). As such, only some of the components of this class are likely to be related to health and well-being.

Some efforts are currently underway to refine the measurement of humor, and particularly to develop measures that more clearly distinguish between adaptive and maladaptive dimensions of humor. For example, Martin and colleagues (Martin, Puhlik-Doris, Larsen, Gray, & Weir, in press) recently have developed a measure that attempts to distinguish between potentially beneficial and detrimental humor styles. Based on a review of past theoretical and research literature, they hypothesized four main dimensions of humor expression, two of which are considered relatively healthy or adaptive and two others as being relatively unhealthy. Cutting across the healthy and unhealthy dimension is another distinction regarding humor—that which is expressed interpersonally and that which is largely intrapsychic or self-directed. The resulting measure, called the Humor Styles Questionnaire (HSQ), contains four subscales: (a) affiliative humor (tendency to amuse others and engage in humor in a way that promotes social cohesiveness); (b) self-enhancing humor (perspective-taking humor, humor as coping); (c) aggressive humor (sarcasm, use of humor to ridicule and manipulate others); and (d) self-defeating humor.

Unlike most of the existing self-report humor scales, the HSQ was developed following a rigorous and systematic test construction process according to Jackson's (1970) construct-based approach. Beginning with a large pool of items assumed to tap the four hypothesized dimensions, over a series of studies with fairly large sample sizes, the items were selected and further refined on the basis of their contribution to the internal consistency of their intended scale, as well as low correlations with the other three scales. This procedure resulted in four stable factors relating to largely orthogonal dimensions.

Initial validity research has provided promising evidence for the construct validity of each scale, as well as discriminant validity among the four scales. For example, the two measures of "healthy" styles of humor are (a) generally positively related to indicators of psychological health and well-being such as self-esteem, positive emotions, social support, and intimacy; and (b) negatively related to negative moods such as depression and anxiety. In contrast, the two measures of "unhealthy" uses of humor are (a) positively correlated with measures of poor psychological functioning, including depression, anxiety, hostility, and psychiatric symptoms; and (b) negatively related with self-esteem, social support, and relationship satisfaction. Together, the four subscales account for considerably more of the variance in measures of mental health and well-being than do previous humor scales. In addition, the scales relate differentially with all five factors of the Five Factor Model of personality (John, 1990), indicating that they tap into a broad range of personality dimensions and are not simply indicators of extraversion as has been the case with previous humor measures. It is interesting to note that although there are no sex differences on the two detrimental humor scales, men obtain significantly higher scores than women on both the maladaptive scales. This finding suggests that the HSQ may be useful in exploring important sex differences in adaptive uses of humor that were largely obscured by previous measures and only hinted at in the literature (e.g., Lefcourt, 2001b).

Overall, the HSQ measures dimensions of humor that are not tapped by previous measures and, in particular, it is the first self-report measure to assess dimensions of humor that are less desirable and potentially detrimental to well-being. In addition, by carefully refining items that are unrelated to these maladaptive dimensions, the two other questionnaire scales may be purer measures of beneficial or "healthy" humor than are those that currently exist in the literature. Additional research is needed to explore ways in which these different styles of humor relate to interpersonal relationships and coping with stress.

Conclusion

In conclusion, a number of published measures of sense of humor with generally adequate reliability and validity currently are available. Although the various self-report measures purport to assess different components of humor, they predominantly tap into the same general dimensions, particularly extraversion. In addition, the existing measures have demonstrated only limited usefulness in the assessment of humor as a component of positive psychology, as indicated by inconsistent and generally weak correlations with measures of various components of mental and physical health and well-being. Although these measures were designed to assess healthy forms of humor, they may not adequately distinguish between adaptive and maladaptive humor styles, a distinction that has long been made by philosophers and earlier psychologists. There is a need for a new generation of measures that go beyond a simplistic approach that views most forms of humor as conducive to mental health and well-being. Recent initiatives in this direction have been noted. Potentially fruitful avenues for future research include more careful delineation of adaptive and maladaptive uses of humor in coping with stress, as well as examination of the ways in which humor may both facilitate and impair social relationships. Future research may show that the absence of maladaptive humor styles is at least as important to psychological well-being as is the presence of adaptive humor styles. Armed with more refined theories, conceptualizations, and measures of humor, it is hoped that researchers will be able to make more progress in understanding the role of humor as a component of positive psychology.

References

Allport, G. W. (1961). *Pattern and growth in personality*. New York: Holt, Rinehart & Winston.

Anderson, C. A., & Arnoult, L. H. (1989). An examination of perceived control, humor, irrational beliefs, and positive stress as moderators of the relation between negative stress and health. *Basic and Applied Social Psychology, 10,* 101–117.

Bell, N. J., McGhee, P. E., & Duffey, N. S. (1986). Interpersonal competence, social assertiveness and the development of humour. *British Journal of Developmental Psychology, 4,* 51–55.

Cohen, S., & Wills, T. A. (1985). Stress, social support, and the buffering hypothesis. *Psychological Bulletin, 98,* 310–357.

Craik, K. H., Lampert, M. D., & Nelson, A. J. (1996). Sense of humor and styles of everyday humorous conduct. *Humor, 9,* 273–302.

Craik, K. H., & Ware, A. P. (1998). Humor and personality in everyday life. In W. Ruch (Ed.), *The sense of humor: Explorations of a personality characteristic* (pp. 63–94). New York: Mouton de Gruyter.

Dixon, N. F. (1980). Humor: A cognitive alternative to stress? In I. G. Sarason & C. D. Spielberger (Eds.), *Stress and anxiety* (Vol. 7, pp. 281–289). Washington, DC: Hemisphere Publishing.

Feingold, A., & Mazzella, R. (1991). Psychometric intelligence and verbal humor ability. *Personality and Individual Differences, 12,* 427–435.

Freud, S. (1928) Humour. *International Journal of Psychoanalysis, 9,* 1–6.

Gruner, C. R. (1997). *The game of humor: A comprehensive theory of why we laugh.* New Brunswick, NJ: Transaction.

Jackson, D. N. (1970). A sequential system for personality scale development. In C. D. Spielberger (Ed.), *Current topics in clinical and community psychology* (Vol. 2, pp. 61–96). New York: Academic Press.

John, O. P. (1990). the "Big Five" factor taxonomy: Dimensions of personality in the natural language and in questionnaires. In L. A. Pervin (Ed.), *Handbook of personality: Theory and research* (pp. 66–100). New York: Guilford Press.

Kohler, G., & Ruch, W. (1996). Sources of variance in current sense of humor inventories: How much substance, how much method variance? *Humor, 9,* 363–397.

Kuiper, N. A., & Martin, R. A. (1998). Is sense of humor a positive personality characteristic? In W. Ruch (Ed.), *The sense of humor: Explorations of a personality characteristic* (pp. 159–178). New York: Mouton de Gruyter.

Kuiper, N. A., Martin, R. A., & Olinger, L. J. (1993). Coping humour, stress, and cognitive appraisals. *Canadian Journal of Behavioural Science, 25,* 81–96.

Lazarus, R. S., & Folkman, S. (1984). *Stress, appraisal, and coping.* New York: Springer.

Lefcourt, H. M. (2001a). *Humor: The psychology of living buoyantly.* New York: Kluwer Academic.

Lefcourt, H. M. (2001b). The humor solution. In C. R. Snyder (Ed.), *Coping and copers: Adaptive processes and people* (pp. 68–92). New York: Oxford University Press.

Lefcourt, H. M., & Martin, R. A. (1986). *Humor and life stress: Antidote to adversity.* New York: Springer-Verlag.

Martin, R. A. (1996). The Situational Humor Response Questionnaire (SHRQ) and Coping Humor scale (CHS): A decade of research findings. *Humor, 9,* 251–272.

Martin, R. A. (1998). Approaches to the sense of humor: A historical review. In W. Ruch (Ed.), *The sense of humor: Explorations of a personality characteristic* (pp. 15–62). New York: Mouton de Gruyter.

Martin, R. A. (2000). Humor. In A. E. Kazdin (Ed.), *Encyclopedia of psychology* (Vol. 4, pp. 202–204). Washington, DC: American Psychological Association.

Martin, R. A. (2001). Humor, laughter, and physical health: Methodological issues and research findings. *Psychological Bulletin, 127,* 504–519.

Martin, R. A., & Dobbin, J. P. (1988). Sense of humor, hassles, and immunoglobulin A: Evidence for a stress-moderating effect of humor. *International Journal of Psychiatry in Medicine, 18,* 93–105.

Martin, R. A., & Kuiper, N. A. (1999). Daily occurrence of laughter: Relationships with age, gender, and Type A personality. *Humor, 12,* 355–384.

Martin, R. A., & Lefcourt, H. M. (1983). Sense of humor as a moderator of the relation between stressors and moods. *Journal of Personality and Social Psychology, 45,* 1313–1324.

Martin, R. A., & Lefcourt, H. M. (1984). Situational Humor Response Questionnaire: Quantitative measure of sense of humor. *Journal of Personality and Social Psychology, 47,* 145–155.

Martin, R. A., Puhlik-Doris, P., Larsen, G., Gray, J., & Weir, K. (in press). Individual differences in uses of humor and their relation to psychological well-being: Development of the Humor Styles Questionnaire. *Journal of Research in Personality.*

Maslow, A. H. (1954). *Motivation and personality.* New York: Harper & Row.

Murstein, B. I., & Brust, R. G. (1985). Humor and interpersonal attraction. *Journal of Personality Assessment, 49,* 637–640.

O'Connell, W. E. (1960). The adaptive functions of wit and humor. *Journal of Abnormal and Social Psychology, 61,* 263–270.

O'Connell, W. E. (1976). Freudian humour: The eupsychia of everyday life. In A. J. Chapman & H. C. Foot (Eds.), *Humour and laughter: Theory, research, and applications* (pp. 313–329). London: Wiley.

Porterfield, A. L. (1987). Does sense of humor moderate the impact of life stress on psychological and physical well-being? *Journal of Research in Personality, 21,* 306–317.

Ruch, W. (1992). Assessment of appreciation of humor: Studies with the 3–WD humor test. In C. D. Spielberger & J. N. Butcher (Eds.), *Advances in personality assessment* (Vol. 9, pp. 27–75). Hillsdale, NJ: Erlbaum.

Ruch, W. (1994). Temperament, Eysenck's PEN system, and humor-related traits. *Humor, 7,* 209–244.

Ruch, W. (1996). Measurement approaches to the sense of humor: Introduction and overview. *Humor, 9,* 239–250.

Ruch, W. (1998a). Sense of humor: A new look at an old concept. In W. Ruch (Ed.), *The sense of humor: Explorations of a personality characteristic* (pp. 3–14). New York: Mouton de Gruyter.

Ruch, W. (Ed.). (1998b). *The sense of humor: Explorations of a personality characteristic.* New York: Mouton de Gruyter.

Ruch, W., & Hehl, F. J. (1998). A two-mode model of humor appreciation: Its relation to aesthetic appreciation and simplicity-complexity of personality. In W. Ruch (Ed.), *The sense of humor: Explorations of a personality characteristic* (pp. 109–142). New York: Mouton de Gruyter.

Ruch, W., & Kohler, G. (1998). A temperament approach to humor. In W. Ruch (Ed.), *The sense of humor: Explorations of a personality characteristic* (pp. 203–230). New York: Mouton de Gruyter.

Ruch, W., Kohler, G., & van Thriel, C. (1996). Assessing the "humorous temperament": Construction of the facet and standard trait forms of the State-Trait-Cheerfulness Inventory—STCI. *Humor, 9,* 303–340.

Scheier, M. F., & Carver, C. S. (1985). Optimism, coping, and health: Assessment and implications of generalized outcome expectancies. *Health Psychology, 4,* 219–247.

Suls, J. M. (1972). A two-stage model for the appreciation of jokes and cartoons. In J. H. Goldstein & P. E. McGhee (Eds.), *The psychology of humor: Theoretical perspectives and empirical issues* (pp. 81–100). New York: Academic Press.

Svebak, S. (1974). Revised questionnaire on the sense of humor. *Scandinavian Journal of Psychology, 15,* 328–331.

Svebak, S. (1996). The development of the Sense of Humor Questionnaire: From SHQ to SHQ–6. *Humor, 9,* 341–361.

Thorson, J. A. (1990). Is propensity to laugh equivalent to sense of humor? *Psychological Reports, 66,* 737–738.

Thorson, J. A., & Powell, F. C. (1993). Development and validation of a Multidimensional Sense of Humor scale. *Journal of Clinical Psychology, 48,* 13–23.

Thorson, J. A., Powell, F. C., Sarmany-Schuller, I., & Hampes, W. P. (1997). Psychological health and sense of humor. *Journal of Clinical Psychology, 53,* 605–619.

Trice, A. D., & Price-Greathouse, J. (1986). Joking under the drill: A validity study of the Coping Humor scale. *Journal of Social Behavior and Personality, 2,* 265–266.

Ziv, A., & Gadish, O. (1989). Humor and marital satisfaction. *Journal of Social Psychology, 129,* 759–768.

21

The Assessment of Gratitude

Robert A. Emmons, Michael E. McCullough, and Jo-Ann Tsang

In ordinary life we hardly realize that we receive a great deal more than we give, and that it is only with gratitude that life becomes rich.
—Dietrich Bonhoeffer

Gratitude defies easy classification. It has been conceptualized as an emotion, an attitude, a moral virtue, a habit, a personality trait, and a coping response. The word *gratitude* is derived from the Latin *gratia*, meaning grace, graciousness, or gratefulness. All derivatives from this Latin root "have to do with kindness, generousness, gifts, the beauty of giving and receiving, or getting something for nothing" (Pruyser, 1976, p. 69). Subjectively, gratitude is a felt sense of wonder, thankfulness, and appreciation for benefits received. It can be given interpersonally or transpersonally (to God, nature, the cosmos). It cannot, however, be directed toward the self. Although a variety of life experiences can elicit feelings of gratitude, gratitude normally stems from the perception that one has received a gift or benefit from another person. People feel grateful when they perceive that others have intentionally provided a benefit. Fitzgerald (1998) identified three components of gratitude: (a) a warm sense of appreciation for somebody or something; (b) a sense of good will toward that person or thing; and (c) a disposition to act positively that flows from appreciation and goodwill. A grateful person recognizes the receipt of someone else's generosity.

We have argued that gratitude is a human strength (Emmons & Crumpler, 2000; Emmons & Shelton, 2002) in that it enhances one's personal and relational well-being and is quite possibly beneficial for society as a whole. In this chapter, we synthesize classical and contemporary perspectives on gratitude and describe how gratitude has been conceptualized and measured in contemporary research. We offer suggestions for assessing gratitude in ways that might enable researchers and practitioners to benefit from the growing science of gratitude research.

Preparation of this chapter was supported by a generous grant from the John Templeton Foundation.

Theoretical Background

Historically, gratitude has been considered a virtue that can contribute to living well. Classical writers focused on the good life and emphasized the cultivation and expression of gratitude for the health and vitality of both citizenery and society. Across cultures and time, experiences and expressions of gratitude have been treated as both basic and desirable aspects of human personality and social life. For example, gratitude is a highly prized human disposition in Jewish, Christian, Muslim, Buddhist, and Hindu thought. Ancient Roman philosophers such as Seneca and Cicero held that gratitude is a supremely valued human virtue. Conversely, expressions of ingratitude have been harshly viewed as forms of moral degeneracy. The philosopher David Hume is quoted as saying that ingratitude is "the most horrible and unnatural of all crimes that humans are capable of committing" (Hume, 1888, p. 466). Indeed, the consensus among the world's religious and ethical writers is that people are obligated to feel and express gratitude in response to received benefits. Writers within the virtue ethics tradition generally placed greater importance on its obligatory nature than on its emotional aspects, with the exception of Spinoza (1677/1981), who viewed gratitude as the reciprocation of love with love.

On the basis of the historical views, one can infer that the response of grateful people benefit not only themselves but the wider community as well. Thomas Aquinas (1981) understood gratitude as a secondary virtue associated with the primary virtue of justice (rendering to others their right or due, and in accord with some measure of basic equality). Gratitude is a motivator of altruistic action, according to Aquinas, because it entails thanking one's benefactors and generating a fitting and appropriate response. One dissenting voice, however, was that of Aristotle (1962), who viewed gratitude as incompatible with magnanimity and therefore did not include it on his list of virtues. Magnanimous people, according to Aristotle, insist on their self-sufficiency and therefore find it demeaning to be indebted and thus grateful to others.

Throughout history, gratitude has been portrayed as a vital civic virtue. In all likelihood, the first influential theoretical treatment of gratitude from a broad communal perspective was Adam Smith's (1790/1976) volume, *The Theory of Moral Sentiments*. Smith proposed gratitude as an essential social emotion—on par with emotions such as resentment and affection. According to Smith, gratitude is one of the primary motivators of benevolent behavior toward a benefactor. To this point, Smith wrote, "The sentiment which most immediately and directly prompts us to reward, is gratitude" (p. 68). Smith observed that society can function purely on utilitarian grounds or on the basis of gratitude, but he clearly believed that societies of gratitude were more attractive in large part because they provide an important emotional resource for promoting social stability. Following Smith's line of thought, the sociologist Georg Simmel (1950) argued that gratitude was a cognitive–emotional supplement to sustain one's reciprocal obligations. Because formal social structures such as the law and social contracts are insufficient to regulate and ensure reciprocity in human interaction, gratitude serves to remind people of their need to reciprocate.

During exchange of benefits, gratitude prompts one person (a beneficiary) to be bound to another (a benefactor) during exchange of benefits, thereby reminding beneficiaries of their reciprocity obligations. He referred to gratitude as "the moral memory of mankind . . . if every grateful action . . . were suddenly eliminated, society (at least as we know it) would break apart" (1950, p. 388). From this sociological exchange perspective, gratitude serves the utilitarian function of social cohesion, in contrast to a psychological perspective that would emphasize gratitude as a valuable inner state to cultivate for its own sake (Emmons & Shelton, 2002).

Contemporary Approaches

Until recently, psychologists have had less to say about gratitude than have moral philosophers and sociologists. Even those psychologists specializing in the study of emotion have, by and large, failed to explore its contours (Emmons & Shelton, 2002), an observation that we make in a recently published review of the literature on gratitude (McCullough, Kilpatrick, Emmons, & Larson, 2001). Building on the work of Smith, Simmel, and others, we theorized that gratitude is a moral affect—that is, one with moral precursors and consequences. They hypothesized that by experiencing gratitude, a person is motivated to carry out prosocial behavior, is energized to sustain moral behaviors, and is inhibited from committing destructive interpersonal behaviors. Because of its specialized functions in the moral domain, they likened gratitude to empathy, sympathy, guilt, and shame. Gratitude has a special place in the grammar of moral life. Whereas empathy and sympathy operate when people have the opportunity to respond to the plight of another person and guilt and shame operate when people have failed to meet moral standards or obligations, gratitude operates typically when people acknowledge that they are the recipients of prosocial behavior. Specifically, we posited that gratitude serves as a *moral barometer,* providing individuals with an affective readout that accompanies the perception that another person has treated them prosocially. Second, we posited that gratitude serves as a *moral motive,* stimulating people to behave prosocially after they have been the beneficiaries of other people's prosocial behavior. Third, we posited that gratitude serves as a *moral reinforcer,* encouraging prosocial behavior by reinforcing people for their previous prosocial behavior.

McCullough et al. (2001) adduced evidence from a wide variety of studies in personality, social, developmental, and evolutionary psychology to support this conceptualization. For example, Trivers (1971) viewed gratitude as an evolutionary adaptation that regulates people's responses to altruistic acts. In this sense, gratitude could be a key element in the emotional system underlying reciprocal altruism. Recent research does indeed indicate that gratitude may be a psychological mechanism underlying reciprocal exchange in human and nonhuman primates (de Waal & Berger, 2000). Certainly, however, this does not mean that gratitude serves merely this function or can be reduced to an exchange mechanism in a social economy, but this is how gratitude has been portrayed in the sociological literature. In addition to the moral and prosocial contours of gratitude, there are reasons to believe that experiences of gratitude might be associated—perhaps even in a causal fashion—with indexes of happiness and well-being, a point that we will subsequently address.

To summarize the theoretical perspectives described thus far, existing gratitude theory and research demonstrate a high degree of consensus on a variety of points. First, the existing treatments agree that gratitude is part of a highly functional psychological apparatus that helps people to maintain their obligations to one another. Second, most existing theoretical treatments concur that gratitude is present under a specific set of attributions: (a) when a benefit is evaluated positively; (b) when the benefit that one has encountered is not attributed to one's own effort; and (c) when the benefit was rendered intentionally by the benefactor. Finally, existing research suggests that gratitude is a typically pleasant experience that is linked to contentment, happiness, and hope.

Our theory is contrary to the social–scientific conceptualizations of gratitude that have arisen in the past 50 years where the assumption has been that gratitude is a monolithic, unidimensional construct. Implicitly, the existing conceptualizations of gratitude would suggest that individual experiences of gratitude differ along a single dimension that might best be referred to as "intensity"; that is to say, people are only "more grateful" or "less grateful"; no other distinctions need be made to understand the gratitude experience. On closer examination, however, there appears to be several other meaningful distinctions that might be made concerning various aspects of gratitude.

Four Perspectives From Which Gratitude Can Be Observed

Our expanded conceptualization of gratitude explicitly posits at least four different perspectives from which (and from these perspectives, four dimensions along which) experiences of gratitude might be understood. The four perspectives from which gratitude might be observed are the (a) dispositional perspective; (b) benefit perspective; (c) benefactor perspective; and (d) benefit × benefactor perspective. The dispositional perspective is the most general perspective from which we might refer to a person as being "grateful" or "ungrateful," labels that ostensibly refer to a person's tendencies to experience gratitude over time and across situations. From the benefit perspective, gratitude is understood by observing peoples' degree of gratitude in response to a particular benefit that they have received. The question about gratitude, from a benefit perspective, is whether we are grateful *for something*. From a benefactor perspective, gratitude is understood by observing people's degree of gratitude for a particular person who has conferred benefits to them in the past. Children typically are expected to be grateful to their parents without having to produce an exhaustive tally of the benefits that their parents have conferred. The exact nature of the benefits received in the past is not the main focus. Rather, from a benefactor perspective, the main question is whether a person feels grateful *to someone*. The benefit × benefactor perspective is a marriage of the benefit perspective and the benefactor-centered perspective. From this final perspective, we are interested in the degree of gratitude that a person feels for a particular benefit (e.g., paying one's college tuition, allowing one to merge into traffic, taking out the trash) that a particular benefactor (e.g., a father, a stranger on the highway, a roommate) has bestowed. Thus, the question from the benefit × benefactor perspective is whether a person is grateful *to someone for something*. Here the emphasis is on both the gift and the giver.

Facets of the Grateful Disposition

Rosenberg (1998) noted that a key characteristic of affective traits such as hostility and anxiety is that they lower the threshold for experiencing certain emotional states. Elevated hostility, for example, lowers the threshold for experiencing anger. Insofar as the grateful disposition is an affective tendency toward recognizing and responding to the role of other moral agents' benevolence in one's positive outcomes, this disposition might possess several particular facets that manifest themselves in discrete emotional experience (i.e., in day-to-day experiences of gratitude). We use the term "facets" to refer to the elements of the grateful disposition, rather than the term "dimensions," because we do not assume that the following elements of people's psychological and interpersonal experiences of gratitude are necessarily distinct or independent. Instead, we believe that they are all features of dispositionally grateful people's discrete experiences of gratitude.

The first facet of the grateful disposition might be called gratitude *intensity*. In experiencing a positive event, a person with a strong grateful disposition might feel more intensely grateful than would someone less disposed toward gratitude. A second facet of the grateful disposition is gratitude *frequency*. Someone with a strong grateful disposition might report feeling grateful several times per day, and gratitude might be elicited by even the simplest favor or act of politeness. Conversely, for someone less disposed toward gratitude, such a favor or act of politeness might be insufficient to elicit gratitude now and in the future. As a result, the person with a weaker grateful disposition might experience less gratitude within a specified time period (e.g., hours, days, weeks, etc.). A third facet of the grateful disposition is gratitude *span*. Gratitude span refers to the number of life circumstances for which a person feels grateful at a given time. Someone with a strong grateful disposition might be expected to feel grateful for their families, their jobs, their health, and life itself, along with a wide variety of other benefits. Someone less disposed toward gratitude, however, might be aware of experiencing gratitude for fewer aspects of their lives. A fourth facet of the grateful disposition is gratitude *density*. Gratitude density refers to the number of persons to whom one feels grateful for a single positive outcome or life circumstance. When asked to whom one feels grateful for a certain outcome, say, obtaining a good job, someone with a strong grateful disposition might list a large number of others, including parents, elementary school teachers, tutors, mentors, fellow students, and God or a higher power. Someone less disposed toward gratitude might feel grateful to fewer people for such a benefit.

Links Between Dimensions and Facets of Gratitude

The four dimensions of gratitude are not equally applicable to all four perspectives from which gratitude can be observed. From the dispositional perspective (where someone's general, trait-like tendencies to be grateful across a wide variety of life circumstances is the focus), we would be interested in assessing people's gratitude along all four dimensions (intensity, frequency, span, and density). On the other hand, from the benefit perspective (where people's gratitude for a single, isolated benefit is the focus), we would be interested in gratitude intensity, frequency, and density, but not gratitude span. From the benefactor perspective (in which people's gratitude to a single person for an unspecified benefit or series of benefits is the focus), we are interested in intensity, gratitude frequency, and gratitude span, but not gratitude density. From the benefit × benefactor perspective (where a person's gratitude to a particular benefactor for a specific benefit is the focus), we would be interested in gratitude intensity and gratitude frequency but not gratitude span or gratitude density.

Review of Research on Gratitude and Its Assessment

Until only quite recently, no standardized, agreed on means of measuring any of the various aspects of gratitude was available. Instead, gratitude has been measured in a multitude of different ways and forms. These previous measures of gratitude can be subsumed under the four categories of free-response, ratings, attributions, and behavioral measures. In some studies, gratitude has been assessed as a dependent variable, a state whose intensity is influenced by other variables, whereas in other studies, gratitude has been treated as an independent variable that can influence various behavioral or cognitive–affective outcomes.

Free Response

This category refers to research consisting of interviews or free response answers to questions about gratitude. For example, Teigen (1997) had participants write about two instances in which they felt grateful: one when they were grateful to someone specifically and another where they were generally grateful, for instance, "grateful to life." Russell and Paris (1994) asked children to tell stories about protagonists who were feeling different emotions, including one story where the person felt "very grateful."

Gratitude frequency is one facet that is amenable to free responses. Okamoto and Robinson (1997) presented their participants with helping vignettes and asked them to write down what they would say or do in response to someone helping them. The frequency of participants writing that they would say "thank you" depended on characteristics of the helper and the nature of the help. Sommers and Kosmitzki (1988) gave participants a list of emotions and asked them a number of questions using that list, including which emotions they experienced regularly and which emotions they thought were most construc-tive. Individuals often listed gratitude as one of the responses to these two questions. In addition, a variant of gratitude span has been measured by the Gallup poll (1996), where researchers asked telephone interviewees to list two or three things for which they felt grateful. Although participants were not asked to list all the things they felt grateful for, this question tapped into the different types of benefits that people might feel grateful about (e.g. health, job/career, children, just being alive).

Along with these gratitude-specific measures, researchers also have coded gratitude themes in free responses to questions that were not specifically geared toward gratitude. For example, Barusch (1999) found in her interviews of women's life stories that gratitude was a common theme among elderly women living in poverty. Walker and Pitts (1998) asked participants to list the charac-teristics of a highly moral person, religious person, and spiritual person, and found that "thankful" was a moderately prototypical aspect of a spiritual person. Likewise, Bernstein and Simmons (1974) interviewed adolescent kidney donors and found that donors frequently mentioned gratitude from the organ recipient as a rewarding response. Coffman (1996) found that parents who survived Hurricane Andrew also frequently mentioned being grateful that they and their families made it through the disaster alive. Reibstein (1997) coded inter-views with committed romantic couples for grateful verbal and physical behav-ior. In this way, techniques such as interviews and free-response questions can be used to explore the nature and depth of gratitude.

Rating Scales

By far the most frequently used measure of gratitude is the rating scale. Some studies using rating scales explore the grateful disposition. For example, Saucier and Goldberg (1998) had participants and their peers rate the partici-pant on thankfulness, as well as other possible traits that might be independent of the Big Five Inventory, and found that a two-item personality measure consisting of the adjectives "grateful" and "thankful" was correlated $r = .31$ with the agreeableness factor of the Big Five. In addition, the 1998 Gallup poll asked individuals if they knew many people who seemed grateful for no clear reason. Regarding an aspect of gratitude density, individuals have rated their gratitude toward God (Gallup, 1998), friends (Parker & de Vries, 1993), a professor who administered an exam (Overwalle, Mervielde, & De Schuyter, 1995), and simply "others" (i.e., Gallup, 1998). Some studies examined gratitude frequency. For example, a 1998 Gallup poll asked individuals how often they gave thanks to God and to other people. Eighty-nine percent of the adults and 78% of the teenagers surveyed said they express gratitude to God at least some of the time, whereas 97% of the adults and 96% of the teens said they expressed thanks to others at least some of the time. Weiner, Russell, and Lerman (1979) asked students to remember a successful test and write down three emotions that they felt after learning of their success. A response of gratitude could indicate a higher gratitude frequency. Other studies ask participants to rate the intensity of their felt gratitude, along with other emotions (Hegtvedt, 1990;

Overwalle et al., 1995; Veisson, 1999). In many of these studies, participants read scenarios and were asked to rate the gratitude they would feel if those events happened to them or to rate how the protagonist of the vignette would feel (Lane & Anderson, 1976; Rodrigues, 1995; Tesser, Gatewood, & Driver, 1968).

Despite the many ways in which gratitude has been rated in studies, there has been little work done on developing an actual gratitude scale. In all of the aforementioned studies, gratitude measurements have consisted of at most three items, and many studies include only a single measure of gratitude. In some cases, gratitude is a subscale within a scale. For instance, Ventura found a "religious, thankful, content" factor in her use of the Family Coping Inventory (Ventura, 1986; Ventura & Boss, 1983). Still, this factor does not exclusively measure gratitude. Clearly, a reliable gratitude scale is needed that taps into all the many facets of gratitude.

Attributional Measures

Along with more direct measures of interviews and self-report scales, gratitude also has been measured indirectly through attributions and behaviors. In a study examining self-enhancing attributions, Farwell and Wohlwend-Lloyd (1998) measured participants' attributions of success to either their own ability and effort or their task partner's ability and effort. Participants indicated their degree of liking and gratitude toward the partner. Attributing success to oneself was associated with less gratitude toward the partner. It can be inferred that attributing one's own success to another person measures gratitude in a certain sense, as gratitude is the emotion felt when success is attributed to other people (Weiner et al., 1979). Baumeister and Ilko (1995) also measured gratitude within an attributional paradigm. They asked participants to write about a major success experience. In nearly half of the accounts, people acknowledged receiving help from others for their success. Essays were subsequently coded for the frequency with which others were thanked for the help they provided. Participants were more likely to express gratitude when they were led to believe the essays would be read in public as compared to when they believed the essays were to remain private, suggesting that impression-management concerns influence expressed gratitude.

Behavioral Measures

A small number of studies have looked at grateful behavior. Becker and Smenner (1986) observed whether young children said "thank you" during trick-or-treating without being prompted by their parents. Other research on college students looked at people's reactions after having the door held open for them. Saying "thank you" or smiling was taken as a grateful response (Okamoto & Robinson, 1997; Ventimiglia, 1982). Taking a more sociological slant, Goldsmith and Fitch (1997) used field notes and ethnographic interviews to study advice giving and receiving. They found that individuals often accepted the advice of someone they respected as a sign of gratitude for help received by the advice-giver. Stein (1989) observed grateful and ungrateful responses while working in soup kitchens and pantries. Behavioral observations such as these have an advantage over self-report measures in that they lessen social desirability concerns; however, it is often difficult for researchers to know whether they are actually measuring gratitude or a form of politeness or some other construct. Therefore, a combination of behavioral measures and self-report measures of gratitude might be the most useful for researchers studying gratitude.

Dispositional Measures of Gratitude

Although gratitude conceivably could exist as an affective trait, a mood, and an emotion, measurement advances recently have been made at the level of gratitude as an affective trait (McCullough, Emmons, & Tsang, 2002). McCullough and colleagues defined the grateful disposition as a generalized tendency to recognize and respond with positive emotions (appreciation, thankfulness) to the role of other moral agents' benevolence in the positive experiences and outcomes that one obtains. Two self-report measures of gratitude as a personality disposition have been constructed: the GRAT (Watkins, Grimm, & Hailu, 1998) and the Gratitude Questionnaire (GQ; McCullough et al., 2002). These individual difference measures emphasize the emotional component of gratitude more so than the moral component of reciprocity described previously.

Watkins et al. (1998) reported three factors in their 44-item GRAT scale: resentment (bitterness, sense of entitlement); simple appreciation (for common pleasures); and social appreciation (for others and the importance of expressing thanks). Some example items include

- I basically feel like life has ripped me off.
- Sometimes I find myself overwhelmed by the beauty of a musical piece.
- I feel deeply appreciative for the things that others have done for me in my life.

Scores on the GRAT correlate positively and moderately with positive states and traits such as internal locus of control, intrinsic religiosity, and life satisfaction; moreover, scores correlate negatively and moderately with negative states and traits such as depression, extrinsic religiosity, narcissism, and hostility (Watkins et al., 1998). In one experiment, high scorers on the GRAT showed a positive memory bias: they recalled a greater number of positive memories when instructed to do so and even rated their memories of unpleasant experiences more positively over time relative to the initial emotional impact of these negative events.

The other dispositional measure that has been developed is the GQ–6 (McCullough et al., 2002). We originally developed 39 positively and negatively worded items that assess experiences and expressions of gratefulness and appreciation in daily life, as well as feelings about receiving from others. Items reflected the gratitude intensity facet (e.g., "I feel thankful for what I have received in life"), the gratitude frequency facet (e.g., "Long amounts of time can go by before I feel grateful to something or someone"), the gratitude span facet (e.g., "I sometimes feel grateful for the smallest things"), and the gratitude density facet (e.g., "I am grateful to a wide variety of people"). Respondents endorsed each item on a 7-point Likert-type scale (where 1 = strongly disagree and 7 = strongly agree). The following six items appear in the final version of the scale (the GQ–6):

- I have so much in life to be thankful for.
- If I had to list everything that I felt grateful for, it would be a very long list.
- When I look at the world, I don't see much to be grateful for (reverse-scored).
- I am grateful to a wide variety of people.
- As I get older I find myself more able to appreciate the people, events, and situations have been part of my life history.
- Long amounts of time can go by before I feel grateful to something or someone (reverse-scored).

The GQ-6 has an alpha of .82 and is unidimensional. McCullough et al. (in press) examined the validity of a one-factor solution for the six items via structural equation models with maximum likelihood estimation. Using three different fit indexes, the one-factor model provided an adequate fit to the data. Evidence for the validity of the GQ is beginning to accrue. High scorers on the GQ report more frequent positive emotions, life satisfaction, vitality, optimism, and lower levels of depression and stress (McCullough et al., 2002). Those who regularly attend religious services and engage in religious activities such as prayer and the reading of religious material are more likely to score high on the GQ. Grateful, relative to less grateful people, are more likely to score high on measures of spirituality that tap a belief in the interconnectedness of all life and a commitment to and responsibility to others. Grateful individuals place less importance on material goods; they are less likely to judge their own and others success in terms of possessions accumulated; they are less envious of wealthy persons; and are more likely to share their possessions with others relative to less grateful persons. In terms of basic personality dispositions, grateful people are more open to experience, conscientious, extraverted, and agreeable and are less neurotic than are less grateful counterparts.

Data from informants who know grateful people also indicate that the grateful disposition is associated with positive correlates. The informants of people with strong dispositions toward gratitude reported that these grateful friends engaged in more prosocial behaviors (e.g., loaning money, providing compassion, sympathy, and emotional support) in the previous month (and in general) than did the informants of less grateful individuals (McCullough et al., 2002).

Experimental Inductions of Gratitude

Schweitzer (1969) referred to gratitude as "the secret of life" (p. 36). He went on to say that the greatest thing in life is to "give thanks for everything. He who has learned this knows what it means to live" (1969, p. 41). Psychological research similarly suggests that a grateful response to life circumstances may be an adaptive psychological strategy and an important process by which people positively interpret everyday experiences. The ability to notice, appreciate, and savor the elements of one's life has been viewed as a crucial determinant of well-being (Bryant, 1989; Janoff-Bulman & Berger, 2000; Langston, 1994). We have been conducting research (Emmons & McCullough, in press) to determine if there are measurable benefits to regularly focusing on one's blessings, and if an effective way to make one aware of benefits received is to engage in a self-guided gratitude-thought listing procedure. In particular, we have been interested in the effect of this reflective process on psychological well-being, social relationships, and perceptions of physical health. Bold claims, such as those made by Schweitzer, have been made concerning the power of gratitude to bring about positive emotional transformations in people's lives (Emmons & Shelton, 2002); we have been attempting to put these claims to empirical test.

In one study, undergraduate participants were asked to keep gratitude journals where they wrote up to five things for which they were grateful or thankful. Those who kept gratitude journals on a *weekly* basis exercised more regularly, reported fewer physical symptoms, felt better about their lives as a whole, and were more optimistic about the upcoming week compared to those who recorded hassles or neutral life events (Emmons & Crumpler, 2000). In a second experiment, we had students keep *daily* gratitude journals (Emmons & McCullough, in press). The gratitude condition resulted in higher reported levels of the positive states of alertness, enthusiasm, determination, attentiveness, and energy compared to a focus on hassles or a downward social comparison (ways in which participants thought they were better off than others). There was no difference in levels of unpleasant emotions reported in the three groups. Participants in the daily gratitude condition were more likely to report having helped someone with a personal problem or having offered emotional support to another, relative to the hassles or social comparison conditions. This indicates that, relative to a focus on complaints, an effective strategy for producing reliably higher levels of pleasant affect is to lead people to reflect, on a daily basis, and to write about those aspects of their lives for which they are grateful. We do not know how long these effects last and whether they can be sustained over time. Additional studies are needed to examine the long-term affective and interpersonal consequences of experimentally induced gratitude and to examine the effect of gratitude manipulations compared to other positive emotional inductions.

Future Directions

Beyond what we have reviewed in this chapter, a range of additional methodologies may be useful in exploring the contours of gratitude. Narrative accounts of autobiographical incidents are a powerful methodology for studying the phenomenology of emotional experience (Leith & Baumeister, 1998). First-person, open-ended accounts of emotional experiences can yield insights into the meaning and experience of profoundly felt emotions. They provide valuable information that cannot be acquired through more restrictive (e.g., question-naire or laboratory) procedures. It is important to note that such qualitative assessment is also not subject to response-scale biases (Diener, 1994). We have experimented with this approach in collecting narrative accounts of gratitude. In a study of subjective well-being in 130 persons with neuromuscular disorders (Emmons & Krause, in press), we asked participants to write about a time in which they felt a deep sense of appreciation or gratitude to someone. The following sample narrative illustrates the range and intensity of feeling ex-pressed in these stories:

> All of my life, people have been involved to assist me in getting dressed, showered, to work/school, etcetera. It was my hope that one day I would be able to do something really significant for someone else. I met a man who was married and very unhappy. He and his wife had a little boy born to them and then die at 7 months of age. For ten years they remained married, trying to have another baby. They were never able to have a child again. They divorced and he became my friend and lover. He told me of his life's dream of having another child. I got pregnant from him and had a miscar-riage. I got pregnant again and had an ectopic pregnancy (no loss of my tube, thank God!) A shot took care of the problem. I got pregnant a 3rd time; our beautiful son was born on December 20th, 1998. I have never felt as grateful for anything in my life. I was actually able to give something back to someone. And I was supposed to die before I was 2 years old.

We have been struck by the profound depth of feeling that is conveyed within these essays. It is doubtful that these powerful expressions and personal meanings of gratitude would have revealed themselves as directly to us through structured self-report questionnaires, reports from informants, or even through experimental inductions of gratitude.

A priority for future research on gratitude (and for human strengths and virtues in general) should be the development of non–self-report measures. McCullough et al. (2002) had considerable success in measuring dispositional gratefulness by aggregating the ratings of knowledgeable informants. In fact, these ratings by peers show a considerable degree of convergence with self-report and have fairly high generalizability coefficients (interrater reliabilities were approximately IRR = .65). Although dispositional measures such as the GQ–6 are psychometrically adequate, there is reason to believe that global, single-session reports have limitations. Using latent variables that rely on multiple indicators of a construct represents an advance over single measures. To advance a science of gratitude, it will be important to combine multiple sources of data in addition to self-reports to better understand cognitive and emotional processes involved in experiences and expressions of gratefulness. Heteromethod assessment enables researchers to measure systematic biases that might distort the accuracy of responses and to statistically control for these. Piedmont, McCrae, Riemann, and Angleitner (2000) argued that compar-ing self-reports with rating data from knowledgeable informants improves the quality of personality assessment, and Diener (1994) reviewed a number of nontraditional methods for assessing subjective well-being, many of which might be used fruitfully in the study of gratitude.

Although self-reports are and probably will continue to be the most common means of measuring emotional states and dispositions such as gratitude, multi-method assessment will become more important if substantial progress is to occur in the scientific study of gratitude. Priming techniques (e.g., Mikulincer, Birnbaum, Woddis, & Nachmias, 2000) might be effective in activating grateful cognitions and examining their effects on prosocial behaviors. Demonstrating that heightened accessibility to grateful thoughts and feelings is associated with prosocial actions is a potentially powerful way to evaluate the hypothesis that gratitude is a moral motive (McCullough et al., 2001). In addition, assessment of facial expressions and physiology during intense episodes of gratitude might be useful for exploring the extent to which gratitude is a unique emotion (McCullough et al., 2002). To the extent that the phenomenological experience of gratitude does indeed manifest itself through physiological channels in a distinctive way, psychophysiological methods could become valuable for assessing gratitude as well.

Conclusion

Does gratitude make people happier than they would be otherwise? Some evidence suggests that it does. Does gratitude literally fuel prosocial behavior? Some research and theory suggests that this is a possibility. Do relationships and societies characterized by gratitude lead to better joint and individual outcomes for the people involved? It is conceivable. However, despite how intriguing such questions might seem to eager positive psychologists, the lack of valid and reliable measures of gratitude has made it difficult to answer these questions decisively. Recent development in the measurement of gratitude-related constructs should help to make such studies possible. As these measures are refined and new ones are developed to measure gratitude in different ways, it will become possible for us to learn even more about the role that gratitude might play in personal and social well-being.

References

Aquinas, T. (1981). *Summa theologica*. Westminster, MD: Christian Classics.

Aristotle. (1962). *Nichomachean ethics* (M. Ostwald, Trans.). Indianapolis, IN: Bobbs-Merrill.

Barusch, A. S. (1999). Religion, adversity, and age: Religious experiences of low-income elderly women. *Journal of Sociology and Social Welfare, 26,* 125–142.

Baumeister, R. F., & Ilko, S. A. (1995). Shallow gratitude: Public and private acknowledgement of external help in accounts of success. *Basic and Applied Social Psychology, 16,* 191–209.

Becker, J. A., & Smenner, P. C. (1986). The spontaneous use of *thank you* by preschoolers as a function of sex, socioeconomic status, and listener status. *Language in Society, 15,* 537–546.

Bernstein, D. M., & Simmons, R. G. (1974). The adolescent kidney donor: The right to give. *American Journal of Psychiatry, 131,* 1338–1343.

Bryant, F. B. (1989). A four-factor model of perceived control: Avoiding, coping, obtaining, and savoring. *Journal of Personality, 57,* 773–797.

Coffman, S. (1996). Parents' struggles to rebuild family life after Hurricane Andrew. *Issues in Mental Health Nursing, 17,* 353–367.

Diener, E. (1994). Assessing subjective well-being: Progress and opportunities. *Social Indicators Research, 31,* 103–157.

Emmons, R. A., & Crumpler, C. A. (2000). Gratitude as a human strength: Appraising the evidence. *Journal of Social and Clinical Psychology, 19,* 56–69.

Emmons, R. A., & Krause, L. R. (in press). *Voices from the heart: Narratives of gratitude and thankfulness in persons with neuromuscular diseases.* Unpublished manuscript, University of California, Davis.

Emmons, R. A., & McCullough, M. E. (in press). Counting blessings versus burdens: An experimental investigation of gratitude and subjective well-being in daily life. *Journal of Personality and Social Psychology.*

Emmons, R. A., & Shelton, C. S. (2002). Gratitude and the science of positive psychology. In C. R. Snyder & S. J. Lopez (Eds.), *Handbook of positive psychology* (pp. 459–471). New York: Oxford University Press.

Farwell, L., & Wohlwend-Lloyd, R. (1998). Narcissistic processes: Optimistic expectations, favorable self-evaluations, and self-enhancing attributions. *Journal of Personality, 66,* 65–83.

Fitzgerald, P. (1998). Gratitude and justice. *Ethics, 109,* 119–153.

Gallup G. H., Jr. (1998, May). *Thankfulness: America's saving grace.* Paper presented at the National Day of Prayer Breakfast, Thanks-Giving Square, Dallas.

Gallup Poll Monthly. (1996, Nov.). Princeton, NJ: Gallup Organization.

Goldsmith, D. J., & Fitch, K. (1997). The normative context of advice as social support. *Human Communication Research, 23,* 454–476.

Hegtvedt, K. A. (1990). The effect of relationship structure on emotional responses to inequity. *Social Psychology Quarterly, 53,* 214–228.

Hume, D. (1888). *A treatise of human nature.* Oxford: Clarendon.

Janoff-Bulman, R., & Berger, A. R. (2000). The other side of trauma: Towards a psychology of appreciation. In J. H. Harvey & E. D. Miller (Eds.), *Loss and trauma: General and close relationship perspectives* (pp. 29–44). Philadelphia, PA: Brunner-Routledge.

Lane, J., & Anderson, N. H. (1976). Integration of intention and outcome in moral judgment. *Memory and Cognition, 4,* 1–5.

Langston, C. A. (1994). Capitalizing on and coping with daily-life events: Expressive responses to positive events. *Journal of Personality and Social Psychology, 67,* 1112–1125.

Leith, K. P., & Baumeister, R. F. (1998). Empathy, shame, guilt, and narratives of interpersonal conflicts: Guilt-prone people are better at perspective taking. *Journal of Personality, 66,* 13–35.

McCullough, M. E., Emmons, R. A., & Tsang, J. (2002). The grateful disposition: A conceptual and empirical topography. *Journal of Personality and Social Psychology, 82,* 112–127.

McCullough, M. E., Kirkpatrick, S., Emmons, R. A., & Larson, D. (2001). Is gratitude a moral affect? *Psychological Bulletin, 127,* 249–266.

Mikulincer, M., Birnbaum, G., Woddis, D., & Nachmias, O. (2000). Stress and accessibility of proximity-related thoughts: Exploring the normative and intraindividual components of attachment theory. *Journal of Personality and Social Psychology, 78,* 509–523.

Okamoto, S., & Robinson, W. P. (1997). Determinants of gratitude expressions in England. *Journal of Language and Social Psychology, 16,* 411–433.

Overwalle, F. V., Mervielde, I., & De Schuyter, J. (1995). Structural modeling of the relationships between attributional dimensions, emotions, and performance of college freshmen. *Cognition and Emotion, 9,* 59–85.

Parker, S., & de Vries, B. (1993). Patterns of friendship for women and men in same and cross-sex relationships. *Journal of Social and Personal Relationships, 10,* 617–626.

Piedmont, R. L., McCrae, R. R., Riemann, R., & Angleitner, A. (2000). On the invalidity of validity scales: Evidence from self-reports and observer ratings in volunteer samples. *Journal of Personality and Social Psychology, 78,* 582–593.

Pruyser, P. W. (1976). *The minister as diagnostician: Personal problems in pastoral perspective.* Philadelphia, PA: Westminster Press.

Reibstein, J. (1997). Rethinking marital love: Defining and strengthening key factors in successful partnerships. *Sexual and Marital Therapy, 12,* 237–247.

Roberts, R. C. (1998). Character ethics and moral wisdom. *Faith and Philosophy, 15,* 478–499.

Rodrigues, A. (1995). Attribution and social influence. *Journal of Applied Social Psychology, 25,* 1567–1577.

Rosenberg, E. L. (1998). Levels of analysis and the organization of affect. *Review of General Psychology, 2,* 247–270.

Russell, J. A., & Paris, F. A. (1994). Do children acquire the concepts for complex emotions abruptly? *International Journal of Behavioral Development, 17,* 349–365.

Saucier, G., & Goldberg, L. R. (1998). What is beyond the Big Five? *Journal of Personality, 66,* 495–523.

Schweitzer, A. (1969). *Reverence for life* (R. H. Fuller, trans.). New York: Harper & Row.

Simmel, G. (1950). *The sociology of Georg Simmel.* Glencoe, IL: Free Press.

Smith, A. (1976). *The theory of moral sentiments* (6th ed.). Oxford: Clarendon Press. (Original published 1790)

Sommers, S., & Kosmitzki, C. (1988). Emotion and social context: An American–German comparison. *British Journal of Social Psychology, 27,* 35–49.

Spinoza, B. (1981). *Ethics* (G. Eliot, Trans.). Salzburg, Austria: University of Salzburg. (Original published 1677)

Stein, M. (1989). Gratitude and attitude: A note on emotional welfare. *Social Psychology Quarterly, 52,* 242–248.

Teigen, K. H. (1997). Luck, envy, and gratitude: It could have been different. *Scandinavian Journal of Psychology, 38,* 313–323.

Tesser, A., Gatewood, R., & Driver, M. (1968). Some determinants of gratitude. *Journal of Personality and Social Psychology, 9,* 233–236.

Trivers, R. L. (1971). The evolution of reciprocoal altruism. *Quarterly Review of Biology, 46,* 35–57.

Veisson, M. (1999). Depressive symptoms and emotional states in parents of disabled and non-disabled children. *Social Behavior and Personality, 27,* 87–98.

Ventimiglia, J. C. (1982). Sex roles and chivalry: Some conditions of gratitude to altruism. *Sex Roles, 8,* 1107–1122.

Ventura, J. N. (1986). Parent coping, a replication. *Nursing Research, 35,* 77–80.

Ventura, J. N., & Boss, P. G. (1983). The Family Coping Inventory applied to parents with new babies. *Journal of Marriage and the Family, 45,* 867–875.

de Waal, F. B. M., & Berger, M. L. (2000). Payment for labour in monkeys. *Nature, 404,* 563.

Walker, L. J., & Pitts, R. C. (1998). Naturalistic concepts of moral maturity. *Developmental Psychology, 34,* 403–419.

Watkins, P. C., Grimm, D. L., & Hailu, L. (1998, June). *Counting your blessings: Grateful individuals recall more positive memories.* Presented at the 11th Annual Convention of the American Psychological Society, Denver, CO.

Weiner, B., Russell, D., & Lerman, D. (1979). The cognition–emotion process in achievement-related contexts. *Journal of Personality and Social Psychology, 37,* 1211–1220.

Part V

Religious and Philosophical Models and Measures

22

Measuring Religious Constructs: A Hierarchical Approach to Construct Organization and Scale Selection

Jo-Ann Tsang and Michael E. McCullough

Although religion deals with humankind's ultimate concerns, such as universal compassion or the quest for divine peace and perfection, to some people the psychological study of religion and spirituality may seem only marginally relevant to positive psychology. In part, this could be because of the negative stances that many theorists have taken toward religion. For instance, Freud (1927/1953) compared religion to an infantile stage of development, calling it the "universal obsessional neurosis of humanity" (pp. 77–78). He believed that religion restricts people's impulses, filling their need for an omnipotent father who will protect them from the powerfulness of nature and rectifying the shortcomings and sufferings they experience in this life. Although Freud thought that religion effectively helped individuals allay anxiety, he also posited that reliance on religion prevented humankind from facing reality and growing past their fears and that it was a societal barrier to the progress of science and reason.

Other theorists and scholars have associated religiousness with mental weakness and deficiency (e.g., Dittes, 1969; Ellis, 1960). A number of empirical studies have shown that religious involvement is negatively related to personal competence and control, self-acceptance and self-actualization, and open-mindedness and flexibility (see Batson, Schoenrade, & Ventis, 1993, for a review). In addition, several studies in the mid-20th century linked religious involvement with prejudice and negative social attitudes (e.g., Adorno, Frenkel-Brunswik, Levinson, & Sanford, 1950). In light of these theories and findings, it is easy to justify ambivalence about the place of religion in a psychology of "strength" and "virtue."

Yet other psychologists have concluded that religion promotes growth and mental health. For example, Allport (1937, 1950) believed that mature religion unifies an individual's personality. Although he thought that religion was not the only possible unifying philosophy of life that could develop and maintain a mature personality, Allport believed it to be superior to other philosophies in that "religion is the search for value underlying *all* things" (1937, p. 226).

This comprehensiveness of religion allows it to organize the rest of the person's life in an integrated way. Allport was not alone in believing that religion promotes psychological growth. Other theorists have posited that religion encourages self-realization and enlightenment (Bertocci, 1958; James, 1902/1990; Johnson, 1959) as well as cognitive growth (Elkind, 1970).

Recent research has uncovered positive relationships between religion and particular indexes of physical and mental health (e.g., Koenig, McCullough, & Larson, 2001). Certain forms of religiousness are associated with lower levels of depressive symptoms (e.g., McCullough & Larson, 1999), higher subjective well-being (e.g., Koenig et al., 2001), and even longer life (e.g., McCullough, Hoyt, Larson, Koenig, & Thoresen, 2000). In addition, specific dimensions of religion appear to be related to positive social attitudes such as tolerance toward others (see Batson et al., 1993, for a review). Therefore, although religion is not exclusively a force for good, it may encourage individual health and social harmony in some contexts. Because of this potential, it may be worthwhile for researchers and practitioners to measure different aspects of religiousness. In this chapter, we discuss many important issues in the measurement of religion and spirituality and present a hierarchical model for conceptualizing the various aspects of religiousness that might be measured empirically.

Religion Versus Spirituality: Definitions

We begin by briefly distinguishing between religion and spirituality. This is a formidable task, because many psychologists have presented multiple definitions of their own (see Pargament, 1997, for a review). One definition of religion that encompasses diverse perspectives and can be applied to many different types of religiousness is presented by Hill et al. (2000):

> A. The feelings, thoughts, experiences, and behaviors that arise from a search for the sacred. . .
> AND/OR
> B. A search for non-sacred goals (such as identity, belongingness, meaning, health, or wellness) in a context that has as its primary goal the facilitation of (A);
> AND:
> C. The means and methods (e.g., rituals or prescribed behaviors) of the search that receive validation and support from within an identifiable group of people. (p. 66)

Using this definition, religion is set apart from other concepts by its relation to the sacred, which according to Hill et al. (2000) can include "a divine being, divine object, Ultimate Reality, or Ultimate Truth as perceived by the individual" (p. 66). Though nonreligious philosophies can, similar to religion, give individuals meaning and purpose in their lives, religion provides meaning and purpose in relation to the sacred (as defined by the individual). This definition incorporates many different aspects of religion, including religious belief, religious sentiment, mystical experiences, and religious behavior. It also acknowledges that religion serves other nonsacred ends for many people and that it occurs in the context of a religious community.

Hill et al. (2000) also outlined the history of the relationship between religion and spirituality, noting that in the past the two terms have been closely linked but that a distinction between being religious and being spiritual recently has emerged. The differentiation between the terms has become important as increasing numbers of individuals have begun to identify themselves as "spiritual but not religious" (Zinnbauer et al., 1997). More and more, the term "spiritual" is used for individual religious experiences, whereas the term "religious" is used for institutionalized religion. In the minds of many people in the general population, spirituality is seen as more positive, experiential, and genuine, whereas religion connotes stale, ritualistic, empty observances (Hill et al., 2000). Yet defining spirituality and religion dichotomously in terms of good–bad or individual–institutional is simplistic, and does not capture the considerable overlap between the two. For example, nearly three quarters of the participants in Zinnbauer et al.'s (1997) study identified themselves as being both spiritual and religious. Moreover, many of the field's pioneers (e.g., James, 1902/1990; Pratt, 1930) emphasized that transcendent and relational components were intrinsic to religion per se.

In distinguishing between religion and spirituality, Hill et al. (2000) defined spirituality separately from religion yet maintained that spirituality could be an integral part of a person's religiousness. They defined spirituality as "the feelings, thoughts, and behaviors that arise from a search for the sacred" (p. 66), without the added components of nonsacred goals and religious community. With this definition, it is possible for individuals to be both spiritual and religious if they endorse the first criterion of religion (i.e., the search for the sacred). However, it is also possible to be spiritual without religion (searching for the sacred outside of a religious community) or to be religious without being spiritual (pursuing nonsacred goals in a religious context). In addition, this definition of spirituality preserves the individual–institutional distinction between spirituality and religion, but it acknowledges that religion contains both individual and institutional components.

Because many individuals may identify themselves as religious but not spiritual, it is important to use measures that examine not only religiousness but spirituality as well. It also is necessary for psychologists to consider tools that acknowledge the overlap between religiousness and spirituality while also observing their distinctiveness.[1]

General Measurement Issues

Gorsuch (1984) noted that measurement was both a bone and a boon to the psychology of religion. Specifically, the psychology of religion suffers from an abundance of scales and a lack of alternatives to self-report measures.

---

[1]Despite Hill et al.'s (2000) comprehensive definitions of religiousness and spirituality, the majority of measures of religiousness and spirituality tend to be in the area of Western rather

An Abundance of Scales

In psychology of religion, there often exist multiple scales measuring similar constructs, and psychometrically sound scales in similar content areas of religion tend to produce similar results. Indeed, because so many scales already exist for measuring religion dependably, Gorsuch argued that psychologists should refrain from constructing new scales without first doing a thorough literature review to guarantee that an adequate scale did not already exist. He also stated that if a new scale is developed, psychologists should show that it adds new information to existing scales. In addition, Gorsuch maintained that psychologists should shift their emphasis away from designing new measures and toward exploring the relationships between the existing measures and other psychological constructs.

Regrettably, Gorsuch's words of wisdom have gone largely unheeded by many psychologists in the past 15 years. The development of new assessment tools for measuring religiousness accelerates at an extremely fast rate—at least 40 new measures of religiousness were published between 1985 and 1999 (Hill & Hood, 1999)—often resulting in near duplication of one of the approximately 200 published measures of religion. We think that such well-intentioned efforts at scale development and revision will fail to yield new fundamental insights, wasting resources that could be directed toward weightier issues in the study of religion. Rather than constructing new scales, psychologists would fare better to choose among the many pre-existing tools for assessing religiousness. These measures have been reviewed repeatedly (e.g., Hill & Hood, 1999), so their psychometric properties and applications can be considered.

Is Self-Report the Only Answer?

Unfortunately, the success psychologists have experienced in designing measures of religion has been one-sided. The measurement design of choice overwhelmingly has been close-ended, self-report questionnaires, at the expense of other forms of measurement (Gorsuch, 1984). The preference for self-report, close-ended questionnaires stems in part from their ease of administration and scoring. Interview measures of religion have existed—for example, Allen and Spilka (1967) originally used interviews to assess their committed and consensual dimensions of religion—but these measures often give way to less cumbersome self-report questionnaires (e.g., Spilka, Stout, Minton, & Sizemore, 1977). The use of alternative measurement techniques is necessary, however, for accurate study and assessment of religiousness. For example, theories of religious motivation such as Allport's widely cited dimensions of intrinsic and extrinsic religious orientation (Allport & Ross, 1967) would greatly benefit from non–self-report measures of motivations for being religious. The use of self-report measures to the exclusion of alternative measures in studies of religious

---

than Eastern religion. Very few scales exist that assess spirituality from an Eastern point of view, and the construction and validation of these types of scales are sorely needed.

motivation (as well as many other areas) is suboptimal because it is not clear that individuals always have conscious access to their motivations (e.g., Nisbett & Wilson, 1977).

Self-report measures also may suffer from social desirability biases. For example, the relationship between intrinsic religious orientation and racial tolerance has been thrown into question because of the link between intrinsic religiousness and social desirability (Batson, Naifeh, & Pate, 1978; see Trimble, 1997, for a review). It is therefore important to use methods of assessment beyond self-report measures. One possible alternative is to use peer reports of target individuals' religiousness (i.e., Piedmont, 1999). In addition, psychologists might construct behavioral measures of religiousness that complement existing self-report measures. Supplementing self-report measures of religiousness with other avenues of measurement will help psychologists attain a clearer picture of the character and consequences of religiousness.

Strategies for Selecting Measures

Because of the multifaceted nature of religion and religious experience, there is not one best measure of religiousness. Measures exist for assessing religious belief, religious commitment, religious affiliation, religious development, religious maturity, and so on. Given this staggering set of options, we think the selection of religious measures should be based on theoretical principles rather than on personal tastes or convenience. One important principle to consider is whether religion consists of one general factor or many different factors. Gorsuch (1984) suggested that religion is a general factor that can be subdivided into other religious dimensions. He proposed that it would be appropriate to measure the general religious factor when it was being used to predict many other variables, whereas subdimensions should be used to predict the exceptions to the general rule. For example, when looking at the relationship between religion and broad variables such as age differences in religiousness, the use of a general religious factor is appropriate. When predicting a more specific variable such as prejudice, however, it becomes necessary to use subdimensions of religion to see the complete relationship.

A Hierarchical Model

Gorsuch's insights can be formalized by viewing religiousness and spirituality as a hierarchically structured psychological domain. Higher levels of organization reflect broad individual differences among persons in highly abstracted, trait-like qualities. At this higher, trait-like level (we shall call it Level I), the goal of measurement is to assess broad dispositional differences in religious tendencies or traits so that one might draw conclusions about how "religious" a person is. We label this the *dispositional* level of organization.

Beyond individual differences in the disposition toward religiousness, people manifest tremendous diversity in how they experience religious (and spiritual) realities, their motivations for being religious, and their deployment of their religion to solve problems in the world. We call this second level (Level II) the *operational* level of organization.

Insights about the general nature and operation of religiousness and spirituality are complex because constructs at these two levels of organization do not function independently. Operational-level measures frequently contain variance that can be attributed to dispositional constructs. For instance, people who are inclined to use religion to cope with stress (an operational, Level II concept) are probably more disposed toward being religious in general (a dispositional, Level I concept; Pargament, 1997). This overlap can be controlled in multivariate research. We would propose that before psychologists conclude that any particular Level II religiousness factor significantly affects the psychological lives of individuals, it is necessary to control for Level I religious variables. Otherwise, psychologists cannot know if their effects are a result of an operational religious variable rather than to general religiousness.

Pargament (1997) provides good examples of the application of a hierarchical model to the relationships among religious constructs, although he has not explicitly described the formal hierarchical structure that we propose. In their studies of religious coping (religion at the operational level of organization), Pargament and colleagues typically use measures of general religiousness (e.g., single-item measures of frequency of prayer and religious attendance) to control for individual differences at the dispositional level of organization. This measurement strategy has allowed these investigators to make substantive conclusions about specific religious operations (particular religious strategies for coping with stress) while being careful not to confound such observations with the effects of general, dispositional differences in religiousness.

In the remainder of this chapter, we use this hierarchical model for organizing religiousness and spirituality to review some of the more promising scales for assessing religiousness at both the dispositional and operational levels.

Measuring Religiousness at the Dispositional Level

At the dispositional level (Level I), we are interested in assessing broad individual differences in people's religiousness or spirituality. We postulate that there exists a personality trait with moderate independence from the Big Five personality dimensions (John & Srivastava, 1999) that predisposes people to an interest in religious pursuits. This idea receives indirect support from three sources.

First, within relatively homogenous cultural groups, many indicators of seemingly distinct aspects of religiousness—frequency of involvement in religious activities, self-reported importance of religion, or engagement in private religious practices—are correlated at nontrivial levels. On average, people who are prone to attend a religious congregation are more likely to pray, say that religion is a guiding force in their lives, and so forth. Measures of ostensibly separate aspects of religiousness frequently correlate as highly as .60 to .80 (Gorsuch, 1984; McCullough, Worthington, Maxey, & Rachal, 1997). Second, even when multiple-item measures of religion are factor-analyzed, the factors that emerge tend to be intercorrelated, suggesting the existence of a higher order dimension. Third, recent evidence from behavioral genetics suggests that

Table 22.1. Suggested Measures for Assessment of Dispositional Aspects of Religion and Spirituality

Reference	Scale name
Burris and Tarpley (1998)	Immanence
Cloninger et al. (1993)	Self-transcendence subscale of the Temperament and Character Inventory
Hatch, Burg, Naberhaus, and Hellmich (1998)	Spiritual Involvement and Beliefs scale
Hood (1975)	Mysticism scale
Paloutzian and Ellison (1982)	Spiritual Well-Being scale
Piedmont (1999)	Spiritual Transcendence scale
Plante and Boccaccini (1997)	Santa Clara Strength of Religious Faith Questionnaire
Rohrbaugh and Jessor (1975)	Religiosity Measure
Worthington et al. (1998)	Religious Commitment Inventory (RCI–10)

religious inclinations are partially heritable (for review see D'Onofrio, Eaves, Murrelle, Maes, & Spilka, 1999).

Individual differences in Level I religiousness can be assessed easily by examining the common variance in a few items or behavior samples. For example, Rohrbaugh and Jessor's (1975) scale of general religiousness yielded a highly reliable and consistent unidimensional measure of general religiousness with only eight questions. Their items measure frequency of church attendance, prayer, the amount of religious influence in participants' lives, certainty of religious doctrine, experiences of religious reverence, and feelings of comfort and security from religion. These items of general religiousness were highly correlated with a separate item of self-reported religiousness ($rs = .78$ to $.84$). The common variance in the small number of questions used by Pargament (1997) to assess general religiousness also assess Level I adequately. In addition, the Santa Clara Strength of Religious Faith Questionnaire (SCSORF) is a useful measure of strength of religious faith. Plante and Boccaccini (1997), noting that the majority of religiousness scales were designed for use with individuals who were self-categorized as religious, constructed the 10-item SCSORF as a more broad measure of faith for use in the general population.

In addition, there exist a number of scales that assess dispositional levels of spirituality. MacDonald, LeClair, Holland, Alter, and Friedman (1995) provided a good review of the properties and applications of 20 measures of spirituality, mysticism, and transpersonal experiences. They purposefully selected many of their scales for their independence from traditional measures of religiousness. (See Table 22.1 for references to these and several other measures of dispositional religiousness and spirituality.)

The measurement of Level I religiousness has been fruitful for studying the relationship of religion to physical and psychological health. For example, McCullough and Larson (1999) concluded that general measures of religious involvement tended to be negatively related to depression. Furthermore,

Table 22.2. Suggested Measures for Assessment of Operational Aspects of Religion and Spirituality

Reference	Scale name
Religious orientation	
Allport and Ross (1967)	Religious Orientation Scales: Intrinsic and Extrinsic
Batson and Schoenrade (1991a, 1991b)	Quest Religious Orientation
Hoge (1972)	Intrinsic Religious Motivation Scale
Coping	
Pargament et al. (1990)	Religious Coping Activities Scale
Pargament et al. (1988)	Religious Problem-Solving Scales
Pargament, Koenig, and Perez (1998)	RCOPE
Prayer	
Bade and Cook (1997)	Prayer Functions Scale
Luckow, McIntosh, Spilka, and Ladd (2000)	No name given
Poloma and Pendleton (1989)	Types of prayer
Richards (1991)	Types of prayer

religious involvement also predicts lower use of alcohol, tobacco, and illicit drugs, along with fewer substance abuse problems. In addition, people who are higher in dispositional religiousness tend to have greater happiness and satisfaction with life (Myers & Diener, 1995). However, many other relationships between religiousness and health may surface through the examination of Level II religious constructs.

Measuring Religiousness at the Operational Level

The content of people's religiousness theoretically can be distinguished from the functions of religion in their lives (Gorsuch, 1984). In a similar way, we suggest that the higher order, dispositional aspect of religion exists independently of the operational aspects of religion (at which we might assess such differences in the *functions* or *experiences* of a person's religious life). Two people who are equally disposed toward being religious—in other words, they have identical Level I religiousness—may have very different ways of experiencing, expressing, and deploying their religiousness to solve life's problems.

Religious operations (what we call Level II religiousness) are manifold. It would be impossible to describe them all in this chapter. Therefore, we focus on a few exemplars. They include the motivations behind a person's religiousness, the ways an individual might use his or her religion in coping, and prayer. To complement our discussion, in Table 22.2 we recommend some published scales for assessing these and similar Level II constructs.

Religious Orientation

Allport and Ross's (1967) distinction between intrinsic and extrinsic religious orientation is one of the most established Level II concepts in the psychology of religion. The extrinsically religious person uses religion as a means to another end, whereas the intrinsically religious person holds religion as an ultimate goal.

Extrinsic Orientation

Persons with this orientation are disposed to use religion for their own ends. The term is borrowed from axiology, to designate an interest that is held because it serves other, more ultimate interests. Extrinsic values are always instrumental and utilitarian. Persons with this orientation may find religion useful in a variety of ways—to provide security and solace, sociability and distraction, status and self-justification. The embraced creed is held lightly or else selectively shaped to fit more primary needs. In theological terms the extrinsic type turns to God, but without turning away from the self.

Intrinsic Orientation

Persons with this orientation find their master motive in religion. Other needs, strong as they may be, are regarded as of less ultimate significance, and they are, so far as possible, brought into harmony with the religious beliefs and prescriptions. Having embraced a creed the individual endeavors to internalize it and follow it fully. It is in this sense that he lives his religion. (Allport & Ross, 1967, p. 434)

Allport (1950) believed that extrinsically religious individuals used religion to buffer anxiety but did not take religion's lessons to heart. Therefore, extrinsic religion was responsible for the relationships between religion and undesirable traits such as prejudice. In contrast, the more mature intrinsically religious individuals, though rarer than the extrinsically religious, represented the positive end toward which religion was striving: these individuals should be more helpful, more loving, and less prejudiced, according to this definition (e.g., Allport & Ross, 1967).

Reliabilities for Allport and Ross's (1967) Religious Orientation scale (ROS) have ranged from .73 to .82 for the intrinsic scale, and .35 to .70 for the extrinsic scale (Trimble, 1997). Hoge's (1972) version of the intrinsic religiousness scale shows higher reliability (.90). Trimble (1997) also points out that Hoge's (1972) scale is more theoretically succinct, measuring only religious motivation and leaving out behavior, cognitions, and perceptions. Yet, despite the superior psychometric and theoretical properties of Hoge's scale, Allport and Ross's (1967) ROS remains the most widely used measure of religious orientation.

Allport and Ross's (1967) measurement of intrinsic and extrinsic religious orientation has been challenged. Perhaps one of the greatest criticisms came from Batson and his colleagues. Stating that the ROS excluded the critical, open-minded component in Allport's original concept of intrinsic religious orientation, Batson added an additional dimension of religious orientation: religion as quest (e.g., Batson & Schoenrade, 1991a, 1991b). Quest was defined as an approach that involves honestly facing existential questions in all their complexity, while at the same time resisting clear-cut, pat answers. An individual who approaches religion in this way recognizes that he or she does not know, and probably will never know, the final truth about such matters. Still, the questions are deemed important, and however tentative and subject to change, answers are sought. (Batson et al., 1993, p. 166)

Batson et al. (1993) constructed a 12-item Quest religious orientation scale to measure this questioning, reflective component to the mature religious sentiment.

EMPIRICAL DIFFERENCES AMONG EXTRINSIC, INTRINSIC, AND QUEST RELIGIOUS ORIENTATIONS. The necessity of adding a quest dimension to the concept of religious orientation becomes apparent when one observes the growing empirical evidence for differences between extrinsic, intrinsic, and quest religiousness. As Allport and Ross (1967) predicted, extrinsic religious orientation continues to be associated with prejudice against a plethora of different minority groups. However, scores on intrinsic religious orientation scales are related to decreased prejudice only on self-reports and when prejudice is condemned by the individual's religious community. Many studies using behavioral measures of prejudice (e.g., Batson, Flink, Schoenrade, Fultz, & Pych, 1986; Batson et al., 1978), or looking at prejudice that is not strictly prohibited by the church, such as prejudice against lesbians and gay men or Communists (e.g., Herek, 1987; McFarland, 1989), show intrinsic religion to be related to *increased* prejudice. Quest is the only religious orientation consistently related to decreased prejudice (Batson et al., 1993).

The three different religious orientations also relate in different ways to helping behavior. Specifically, high scores on the extrinsic religion scale often are unrelated to helping, or are related to decreased helping. High scores on intrinsic religion measures are related to the appearance of helpfulness, but often this help seems to serve the individual's need to appear helpful, rather than addressing the specific situation of the person in need. In contrast, although high scores on the quest scale are not related to an increase in helping in general, they are related to helping that is sensitive to the need of the other person (see Batson et al., 1993, for a review). Looking at the intersection between helping behavior and prejudice, Batson, Floyd, Meyer, and Winner (1999) found that individuals scoring high on intrinsic religion were less likely to help a gay person than a nongay person, regardless of whether the helping opportunity would or would not promote homosexuality. In contrast, Batson, Eidelman, Higley, and Russell (2001) found that those scoring higher in quest religion were less likely to help an antigay individual, but only if helping that individual would promote antigay behavior. In this way, knowledge of people's religious orientation can predict whether, and whom, someone will help.

In summary, the issue of religious orientation has shown that, in certain areas of psychology, differentiation among multiple religious dimensions is useful and necessary. In fact, an inaccurate picture is portrayed of the relationship between religion and other psychological concepts such as prejudice if Level II measurements such as orientation are not considered.

Religion and Coping

People often turn to the sacred in times of stress, particularly in extreme situations of turmoil and threat. Just as there are different types of religious orientation, there are different ways that people might use religion to cope with individual life stressors. Just as much of religion's association with such negative concepts as prejudice can be explained by differences in religious orientation, the relationship between religion and well-being can be greatly clarified by examining the ways people use their religion to cope.

Although religion is not universally used as an aid in coping, it is clear that in certain stressful circumstances, many people will turn to religion as a way to cope (Pargament, 1997). Psychologists have developed measures for assessing both (a) general religious styles for coping with problems and (b) particular religious strategies for coping with specific stressors. Pargament et al. (1988) described (a) a *collaborative* religious problem-solving style, which involves an active, relational interchange with God in solving problems; (b) a *deferring* religious problem-solving style, which involves relinquishing problems to God that the individual is unable or unwilling to resolve personally; and (c) a *self-directing* style that reflects the fact that God gives people the liberty to direct their own lives. The Religious Problem-Solving scales (Pargament et al., 1988) assess these three religious problem-solving styles with 12 self-report items each (six-item short forms also are described). These subscales have theoretically expected correlations with measures of Level I religiousness, locus of control, religious orientation, and self-esteem.

Pargament and colleagues also have developed a comprehensive measure of the many ways that people might use their religiousness to cope with specific stressors. The most recent culminations of this effort are the religious coping scale (RCOPE; Pargament, Koenig, & Perez, 1998) and the Brief RCOPE (Pargament, Smith, Koenig, & Perez, 1998). The RCOPE consists of 21 subscales that assess the extent to which the individual uses each of 21 religious coping strategies (e.g., benevolent religious reappraisal, punishing God reappraisal, active religious surrender, passive religious deferral, seeking spiritual support, religious helping, etc.). Although these subscales appear to be useful in their own right, there is evidence that their structure can be simplified into a two-factor structure consisting of positive (adaptive) and negative (maladaptive) religious coping strategies. Pargament et al. (1998) developed the 14-item brief RCOPE to assess these two global religious coping factors. They provided some evidence that the use of positive religious coping was positively related to mental health and physical health, whereas the opposite was generally true for negative religious coping. More recently, Pargament, Koenig, Tarakeshwar, and Hahn (in press) demonstrated that negative religious coping (therein renamed *religious struggle*) is related to mortality among medically ill older adults. These measures of religious coping could have a variety of applications to the study of health and well-being, particularly within a classical stress-and-coping framework.

Prayer

Prayer is one of the fundamental aspects of religious life (Heiler, 1958; McCullough & Larson, 1999). As such, the study of prayer as a Level II or operational form of religiousness may provide unique insight into the ways that people "do religion" in their daily life. Until recently, acknowledgment of the fact that prayer occurs in a variety of forms and styles was all but neglected in empirical psychology. This was due in part to the lack of self-report measures for assessing these various aspects of prayer.

Poloma and Pendleton (1989) were among the first social scientists to study prayer as a multidimensional experience. To do so, they developed multi-item scales for assessing the four types of prayer described by Heiler (1958) and Pratt (1930): meditative prayer (i.e., thinking about or reflecting on God); ritual prayer (reading prayers or reciting them from memory); colloquial prayer (communicating with God in a conversational style); and petitionary prayer (requesting that God meet the specific needs of oneself or others). Poloma and Pendleton also created a measure to assess the frequency with which prayer led to strong spiritual or religious experience. These five scales demonstrated adequate internal consistency and were related to several measures of life satisfaction. It also is worth noting that Poloma and Pendleton controlled for Level I religiousness with a single prayer frequency item before making inferences about the relationships of the specific types of prayer with measures of life satisfaction.

Several other researchers have developed measures of prayer. Luckow, McIntosh, Spilka, and Ladd's (2000) factor analysis of the items from several previous measures of types of prayer led to the identification of seven different types of prayer: intercessory–thanksgiving; ritualistic; material petition; habit; meditation–awareness; confession–closeness; and egocentric petition. Laird, Snyder, Rapoff, and Green (2001) specifically identified and validated different types of private prayer: adoration; confession; thanksgiving; supplication; and reception. In a different vein, Bade and Cook (1997) developed a functional measure of prayer that attempts to assess the specific ways that individuals might use prayer to cope. This 58-item checklist consists of four coping functions that prayer can serve: (a) providing acceptance; (b) providing calm and focus; (c) deferring and avoiding; and (d) providing assistance. Cook and Bade (1998) reported that these various scales had patterns of correlations with locus of control, religious problem-solving style, and the use of religious coping strategies. Moreover, Schoneman and Harris (1999) found correlational evidence consistent with the idea that some of these functions of prayer may be related positively to anxiety (using prayer to defer or avoid coping), whereas others are related negatively to anxiety (providing assistance).

The existing self-report questionnaires for measuring prayer may be useful, both for assessing the types of prayer that people use and the functions that prayer might serve in their coping efforts. It also is worth noting—in the spirit of our desire to point out alternatives to cross-sectional questionnaire assessment of religious variables—that prayer can be measured using other methods as well. For example, McKinney and McKinney (1999) demonstrated that use of prayer could be assessed using a daily diary method. These measures, along with self-reports of prayer, would allow researchers to tap into this important Level II religious variable.

Conclusion

As Gorsuch (1984) noted nearly two decades ago, measurement is the boon of the psychology of religion. That is still the case today. The abundance of scales benefits not only psychologists of religion, but any psychologist interested in looking at the associations of religiousness with other aspects of people's lives. From the perspective of positive psychology, certain forms of religiousness show promising associations with physical and mental health, the promotion of tolerance and prosocial behavior, and positive interpersonal relationships, to name a few. Because of the potential for religiousness to influence individual lives in a positive way, and the pervasiveness of religiousness and spirituality around the world, positive psychology would do well to integrate religious and spiritual concepts into its perspective.

The availability of so many measures of religiousness also can pose challenges to individuals who are unfamiliar with the psychology of religion. We have attempted to simplify the process by classifying religious and spiritual psychological concepts into a two-level hierarchical structure. At the superordinate level are dispositional measures of general religiousness, which assess religiousness as broad individual differences among persons in the tendency toward religious interests and sentiments. At a subordinate level of organization are operational measures of religiousness, which assess how particular aspects of religion function. Examples of operational measures include religious orientation, religious coping, and prayer.

The specific religious concept that a psychologist chooses to measure must be driven by theory. In addition, psychologists interested in Level II religious operations should concurrently assess Level I religiousness. Without Level I measures, a researcher mistakenly could conclude that operational variables are producing effects when, in reality, the effects could be accounted for by general religiousness.

We urge researchers and practitioners to eschew the practice of measuring religious constructs with single-item measures (see also McCullough & Larson, 1999). Although single-item measures of frequency of prayer, attendance at religious services, or self-rated religiousness have much to offer in terms of face validity, their dependability is limited by the psychometric weaknesses that plague all single-item measures of psychological constructs. Assuming that the internal consistency of a single-item measure is .50 (which may be generous), then the associations with such a measure of religiousness with another construct would be attenuated by 29% relative to the true relation among the constructs in the population (Hunter & Schmidt, 1990). This level of attenuation is too high and completely unnecessary given the fact that highly reliable multi-item measures of religious constructs are widely available.

Similar to others before us, we also recommend the use of alternative measurement techniques to supplement self-report questionnaires of religiousness and spirituality. Many of the relationships between religiousness and other concepts are subject to socially desirable responding, or may be of limited validity in some applications. Use of peer reports, interviews, behavioral measures, and other alternatives to self-report questionnaires can provide us with a richer notion of religiousness and spirituality and a broader understanding of its associations with other domains of human functioning.

References

Adorno, T. W., Frenkel-Brunswik, E., Levinson, D. J., & Sanford, R. N. (1950). *The authoritarian personality.* New York: Harper.

Allen, R. O., & Spilka, B. (1967). Committed and consensual religion: A specification of religion–prejudice relationships. *Journal for the Scientific Study of Religion, 6,* 191–206.

Allport, G. W. (1937). *Personality: A psychological interpretation.* New York: Henry Holt.

Allport, G. W. (1950). *The individual and his religion: A psychological interpretation.* New York: Macmillan.

Allport, G. W., & Ross, J. M. (1967). Personal religious orientation and prejudice. *Journal of Personality and Social Psychology, 5,* 432–443.

Bade, M. B., & Cook, S. W. (1997, Aug.). *Functions and perceived effectiveness of prayer in the coping process.* Paper presented at the 1997 meeting of the American Psychological Association, Chicago.

Batson, C. D., Eidelman, S. H., Higley, S. L., & Russell, S. A. (2001). "And who is my neighbor?" II: Quest religion as a source of universal compassion. *Journal for the Scientific Study of Religion, 40,* 39–50.

Batson, C. D., Flink, C. H., Schoenrade, P. A., Fultz, J., & Pych, V. (1986). Religious orientation and overt versus covert racial prejudice. *Journal of Personality and Social Psychology, 50,* 175–181.

Batson, C. D., Floyd, R. B., Meyer, J. M., & Winner, A. L. (1999). "And who is my neighbor?:" Intrinsic religion as a source of universal compassion. *Journal for the Scientific Study of Religion, 38,* 445–457.

Batson, C. D., Naifeh, S. J., & Pate, S. (1978). Social desirability, religious orientation, and racial prejudice. *Journal for the Scientific Study of Religion, 17,* 31–41.

Batson, C. D., & Schoenrade, P. A. (1991a). Measuring religion as quest: 1. Validity concerns. *Journal for the Scientific Study of Religion, 30,* 416–429.

Batson, C. D., & Schoenrade, P. A. (1991b). Measuring religion as quest: 2. Reliability concerns. *Journal for the Scientific Study of Religion, 30,* 430–447.

Batson, C. D., Schoenrade, P. A., & Ventis, W. L. (1993). *Religion and the individual.* New York/Oxford: Oxford University Press.

Bertocci, P. A. (1958). *Religion as creative insecurity.* New York: Association Press.

Burris, C. T., & Tarpley, W. R. (1998). Religion as being: Preliminary validation of the Immanence scale. *Journal of Research in Personality, 32,* 55–79.

Cloninger, C. R., Svrakic, D. M., & Przybeck, T. R. (1993). A psychobiological model of temperament and character. *Archives of General Psychiatry, 50,* 975–990.

Cook, S. W., & Bade, M. K. (1998, Aug.). *Reliability and validity information for the prayer functions scale.* Paper presented at the 1998 meeting of the American Psychological Association, San Francisco.

Dittes, J. E. (1969). Psychology of religion. In G. Lindzey & E. Aronson (Eds.), *The handbook of social psychology* (Vol. 5, pp. 602–659). Reading, MA: Addison-Wesley.

D'Onofrio, B. M., Eaves, L. J., Murrelle, L., Maes, H. H., & Spilka, B. (1999). Understanding biological and social influences on religious affiliation, attitudes, and behaviors: A behavior genetic perspective. *Journal of Personality, 67,* 953–984.

Elkind, D. (1970). The origins of religion in the child. *Review of Religious Research, 12,* 35–42.

Ellis, A. (1960). There is no place for the concept of sin in psychotherapy. *Journal of Counseling Psychology, 7,* 188–192.

Freud, S. (1953). *The future of an illusion* (Trans. W. D. Robson-Scott). Garden City, NY: Doubleday Anchor Books. (Original published 1927)

Gorsuch, R. L. (1984). The boon and bane of investigating religion. *American Psychologist, 39,* 228–236.

Hatch, R. L., Burg, M. A., Naberhaus, D. S., & Hellmich, L. K. (1998). The Spiritual Involvement and Beliefs scale: Development and testing of a new instrument. *The Journal of Family Practice, 46,* 476–486.

Heiler, F. (1958). *Prayer* (Trans. and Ed. S. McComb). New York: Galaxy Books/Oxford University Press. (Original published 1932)

Herek, G. M. (1987). Religious orientation and prejudice: A comparison of racial and sexual attitudes. *Personality and Social Psychology Bulletin, 13,* 34–44.

Hill, P. C., & Hood, Jr., R. W. (Eds.). (1999). *Measures of religiosity.* Birmingham, AL: Religious Education Press.

Hill, P. C., Pargament, K. I., Hood, Jr., R. W., McCullough, M. E., Swyers, J. P., et al. (2000). Conceptualizing religion and spirituality: Points of communality, points of departure. *Journal for the Theory of Social Behavior, 30,* 51–77.

Hoge, D. R. (1972). A validated intrinsic religious motivation scale. *Journal for the Scientific Study of Religion, 11,* 369–376.

Hood, R. W., Jr. (1975). The construction and preliminary validation of a measure of reported mystical experience. *Journal for the Scientific Study of Religion, 16,* 155–163.

Hunter, J. E., & Schmidt, F. L. (1990). *Methods of meta-analysis: Correcting error and bias in research findings.* Thousand Oaks, CA: Sage.

James, W. (1990). *The varieties of religious experience.* New York: Vintage Books/The Library of America. (Original published 1902)

John, O., & Srivastava, S. (1999). The Big Five Trait taxonomy: History, measurement, and theoretical perspectives. In L. A. Pervin & O. P. John (Eds.), *Handbook of personality: Theory and research* (2nd ed., pp. 102–138). New York: Guilford Press.

Johnson, P. E. (1959). *Psychology of religion* (Rev. ed.). New York: Abingdon.

Koenig, H. G., McCullough, M. E., & Larson, D. B. (2001). *Handbook of religion and health.* New York: Oxford University Press.

Laird, S. P., Snyder, C. R., Rapoff, M. A., & Green, S. (2001). *Measuring private prayer: The development and validation of the Multidimensional Prayer Inventory.* Unpublished manuscript, University of Kansas, Lawrence.

Luckow, A. E., McIntosh, D. N., Spilka, B., & Ladd, K. L. (2000, Feb.). *The multidimensionality of prayer.* Paper presented at the annual convention of the Society for Personality and Social Psychology, Nashville, TN.

MacDonald, D. A., LeClair, L., Holland, C. J., Alter, A., & Friedman, H. L. (1995). A survey of measures of transpersonal constructs. *Journal of Transpersonal Psychology, 27,* 171–235.

McCullough, M. E., Hoyt, W. T., Larson, D. B., Koenig, H. G., & Thoresen, C. E. (2000). Religious involvement and mortality: A meta-analytic review. *Health Psychology, 19,* 211–222.

McCullough, M. E., & Larson, D. B. (1999). Religion and depression: A review of the literature. *Twin Research, 2,* 126–136.

McCullough, M. E., Worthington, E. L., Jr., Maxey, J., & Rachal, K. C. (1997). Gender in the context of supportive and challenging religious interventions. *Journal of Counseling Psychology, 44,* 80–88.

McFarland, S. G. (1989). Religious orientations and the targets of discrimination. *Journal for the Scientific Study of Religion, 28,* 324–336.

McKinney, J. P., & McKinney, K. G. (1999). Prayer in the lives of adolescents. *Journal of Adolescence, 22,* 279–290.

Myers, D. G., & Diener, E. (1995). Who is happy? *Psychological Science, 6,* 10–19.

Nisbett, R. E., & Wilson, T. D. (1977). Telling more than we can know: Verbal reports on mental processes. *Psychological Review, 84,* 231–259.

Paloutzian, R. F., & Ellison, C. W. (1982). Loneliness, spiritual well-being, and the quality of life. In L. Peplau & D. Perlman (Eds.), *Loneliness: A sourcebook of current theory, research and therapy* (pp. 224–237). New York: John Wiley.

Pargament, K. I. (1997). *The psychology of religion and coping: Theory, research, practice.* New York: Guilford Press.

Pargament, K. I., Ensing, D. S., Falgout, K., Olsen, H., Reilly, B., et al. (1990). God help me: (I): Religious coping efforts as predictors of the outcomes to significant negative life events. *American Journal of Community Psychology, 18,* 793–824.

Pargament, K. I., Kennell, J., Hathaway, W., Grevengoed, N., Newman, J., et al. (1988). Religion and the problem-solving process: Three styles of coping. *Journal for the Scientific Study of Religion, 27,* 90–104.

Pargament, K. I., Koenig, H. G., & Perez, L. M. (1998, Aug.). *The many methods of religious coping: Development and initial validation of the RCOPE.* Paper presented at the annual meeting of the American Psychological Association, San Francisco.

Pargament, K. I., Koenig, H. G., Tarakeshwar, N., & Hahn, J. (in press). Religious struggle as a predictor of mortality among medically ill elderly patients: A two-year longitudinal study. *Archives of Family Medicine.*

Pargament, K. I., Smith, B. W., Koenig, H. G., & Perez, L. (1998). Patterns of positive and negative religious coping with major life stressors. *Journal for the Scientific Study of Religion, 37,* 710–724.

Piedmont, R. L. (1999). Does spirituality represent the sixth factor of personality? Spiritual transcendence and the Five-Factor Model. *Journal of Personality, 67,* 985–1013.

Plante, T. G., & Boccaccini, M. T. (1997). The Santa Clara Strength of Religious Faith Questionnaire. *Pastoral Psychology, 45,* 375–387.

Poloma, M. M., & Pendleton, B. F. (1989). Exploring types of prayer and quality of life: A research note. *Review of Religious Research, 31,* 46–53.

Pratt, J. B. (1930). *The religious consciousness.* New York: MacMillan.

Richards, D. G. (1991). The phenomenology and psychological correlates of verbal prayer. *Journal of Psychology and Theology, 19,* 354–363.

Rohrbaugh, J., & Jessor, R. (1975). Religiosity in youth: A personal control against deviant behavior. *Journal of Personality, 43,* 136–155.

Schoneman, S. W., & Harris, J. I. (1999, Aug.). *Preferred prayer styles and anxiety control.* Paper presented at the convention of the American Psychological Association, Boston.

Spilka, B., Stout, L., Minton, B., & Sizemore, D. (1977). Death and personal faith: A psychometric investigation. *Journal for the Scientific Study of Religion, 16,* 169–178.

Trimble, D. E. (1997). The Religious Orientation Scale: Review and meta-analysis of social desirability effects. *Educational and Psychological Measurement, 57,* 970–986.

Worthington, E. L., Jr., Hight, T. L., McCullough, M. E., Schmitt, M. M., Berry, J. T., et al. (1998). *The Religious Commitment Inventory-10: Development, refinement, and validation of a brief scale for counseling and research.* Unpublished manuscript, Virginia Commonwealth University, Richmond.

Zinnbauer, G. J., Pargament, K. I., Cole, B. C., Rye, M. S., Butter, E. M., et al. (1997). Religion and spirituality: Unfuzzying the fuzzy. *Journal for the Scientific Study of Religion, 36,* 549–564.

23

Moral Judgment Maturity: From Clinical to Standard Measures

John C. Gibbs, Karen S. Basinger, and Rebecca L. Grime

Moral maturity is an integral aspect of positive individual and collective human life. In human development, the morally mature person evidences not only the courage to do what is right (see chapter 12, this volume) and an empathic "connection" with others (see chapters 15–19, this volume), but also a clear grasp of the bases for interpersonal and societal norms of life, affiliation, contract or truth, property, law, and legal justice. "Clarity" can be interpreted as a profound discernment of that which is intrinsically moral, unconfounded with extraneous considerations. Furthermore, most researchers posit that moral judgment maturity is "constructed," a cognitive process of mental coordination that is distinguishable from traditional identification or internalization notions of moral development (see Gibbs, in press; cf. Schulman, in press). This chapter focuses on the history and construct validity pertaining to instruments measuring moral judgment maturity.

History: From Clinical to Standard Measures

Measures of moral judgment maturity generally have derived from cognitive developmental theory, and have evolved from clinical interviews into more standard measures of production and evaluation. Researchers who have developed measures of moral judgment maturity using the cognitive developmental approach have conceptualized moral judgment in terms of a basic, cross-culturally discernible sequence of stages (Gibbs, 1995, in press).

Piaget: The Methode Clinique

Drawing from earlier work by James Mark Baldwin and others, Jean Piaget (1965/1932) innovated what became known as cognitive developmental theory in his classic work *The Moral Judgment of the Child.* In this exploratory work with children ages 6 through 13, Piaget viewed his young participants as active structurers of their experience. To identify basic age-typical cognitive structures, Piaget used task stimuli appropriate to children (e.g., pairs of simple stories describing a child's or parent's acts in a familiar situation) and asked the children to explain their responses using the *methode clinique*. The clinical method is similar to diagnostic or therapeutic interviews, projective testing, and "the kind of informal exploration often used in pilot research throughout the behavioral sciences" (Flavell, 1963, p. 28). The trained clinical interviewer achieves "a middle course between systematization due to preconceived ideas and incoherence due to the absence of any directing hypothesis" (Piaget, 1973/1929, p. 20).

Through such exploratory interviews, Piaget (1965/1932) found that children's moral judgment develops from generally superficial or concrete impressions to a deeper understanding of the bases for moral decisions and values in interpersonal relationships. His interviews pertained to moral areas such as stealing, lying, retributive justice, "immanent" (naturally embedded) justice, distributive justice, reciprocity, and authority. For example, in the stealing area, he presented children with paired stories of transgressions, asking which story depicted the "naughtier" act and why. In one story pair, a story depicted a protagonist who accidentally breaks 15 cups on his (or, for female interviewees, her) way to dinner, whereas the other story depicted a protagonist who breaks one cup as he tries to sneak a treat out of the cupboard. The younger (6- and 7-year-old) participants were impressed by the "external, tangible" (p. 166) event of so many broken cups, and often judged the coming-to-dinner child to be naughtier—even though that child was not the one with mischievous intentions.

Piaget's research design was criticized in subsequent literature (e.g., Miller, 1998) for its confounding of the intentionality variable and degree-of-damage variables. In fairness, however, the "confounding" was quite deliberate; Piaget's aim was not to investigate whether young children understand intentions (his research had established that they do), but rather to study whether and how children at different ages coordinate intentionality with external consequence. Given this aim, Piaget's juxtaposition of these variables was appropriate and indeed successful in documenting children's vulnerability to superficial (concrete, external, tangible) moral judgment.

Damon and Enright: Distributive Justice

Since Piaget's innovative work, many cognitive developmentalists have used the clinical method to study both moral development in a broad sense (e.g., Kohlberg, discussed later in the chapter) and children's conceptual development in particular areas relevant to moral judgment development and maturity. These include not only the areas explored by Piaget (1965/1932), but also the topics of friendship (Selman, 1980; Youniss, 1980), interpersonal negotiation strategy (Selman & Shultz, 1990), prosocial behavior or altruism (Eisenberg, 1982; chapter 17, this volume), and society or social institutions (Adelson, Green, & O'Neil, 1969; Furth, 1980). Among the areas originally studied by Piaget was distributive justice (i.e., the fair sharing of goods); this area was examined more extensively by William Damon (1977), who used the clinical method to probe children's decisions concerning real-life as well as hypothetical distributive-justice problems.

In the distributive justice area of moral development, measurement techniques have evolved from the clinical method to more standard instrumentation (Enright, Franklin, & Manheim, 1980). In the clinical method,

> once a child generates a decision, other alternatives are presented to see whether the child continues to hold the original belief when faced with new possibilities. . . . The interviewer is in effect presenting a paired-item test, the pair at any time being the child's current distributive belief and the interviewer's probe. Since an interview does not follow a fixed format, not all alternatives representing each stage may be presented to any given child. (p. 194)

Although skilled use of the clinical method permits developmental comparisons across interviewees (Damon, 1977), Robert Enright and colleagues (1980) noted that systematic use of the paired-item procedure in a fixed format would promote standardization of the assessment. Accordingly, Enright et al. developed the Distributive Justice scale (DJS), which presents all possible paired comparisons to all participants; the DJS thereby not only promotes valid comparisons across participants, but it also makes possible "objective" or noninferential scoring. The DJS may be termed an "evaluation" (rating, recognition, objective) measure insofar as participants need only evaluate an item as preferred. Evaluation measures may be distinguished from "production" measures, such as Piaget's or Damon's, in which participants must produce reasons or justifications for their decisions or evaluations.

The DJS consists essentially of two distributive justice dilemma stories (represented in drawings), and a standardized forced-choice procedure for assessing respondents' stage level. One story depicts children who have made pictures at a summer camp. The pictures are sold and paid for with a lot of nickels. How many nickels should each child get? Each drawing of a possible distribution depicts four children: one bigger, one poor, one having made the most number of pictures, and one who simply wants more of the nickels. The drawing for an immature stage shows, for example, the most nickels going to a child who simply wanted to get the most. Representing a somewhat more advanced level is a drawing showing all the children getting the exact same number of nickels. Still more mature is a drawing depicting a compromise distribution (more nickels going to the more meritorious *and* more needy children). The DJS is exhaustive in that each stage-drawing is paired with every other stage-drawing.

Characteristics of the DJS are summarized in Table 23.1, along with the psychometric properties of other measures. Of particular note is the strength of the DJS's construct validity. The DJS evidenced good discriminant validity in that it correlated positively with age more than with verbal ability; correlated positively with logical reciprocity (conservation) judgments; and evidenced a similar age trend in a non-Western culture (Enright et al., 1980). DJS maturity correlated with social class and a behavioral measure of popularity (see Lapsley, 1996).

Table 23.1. Types and Characteristics of Moral Judgment Measures

Type and name of measure	Target age (years)	Number of items	Administration time (minutes)	Internal reliability	Construct validation
Production					
Moral Judgment Interview (MJI) (Colby & Kohlberg, 1987)	10–100	15–33 (Form A)	30–60	.92–.96	Strong
Sociomoral Reflection Measure–Short Form (SRM-SF) (Gibbs et al., 1992)	9–100	11	20	.92	Excellent
Evaluation					
Distribution Justice Scale (DJS) (Enright et al., 1980)	5–11	20	12–15	.61–.77	Excellent
Defining Issues Test (DIT) (Rest et al., 1999)	15–100	72	50	.76–.78 (P index)	Strong
Sociomoral Reflection Objective Measure (SROM) (Gibbs et al., 1984)	14–100	16	45	.77–.87	Some support
Sociomoral Reflection Objective Measure–Short Form (SROM-SF) (Basinger & Gibbs, 1987)	16–100	12	20	.77–.75	Some support

Kohlberg: The Moral Judgment Interview

The distributive justice research of Damon, Enright, and others represents an area in which assessment evolved from Piaget's clinical method to standard instrumentation. Although the distributive justice work has had some impact, by far the most influential methodological and theoretical evolution from Piaget's seminal work has been initiated by Lawrence Kohlberg (1958). Kohlberg (1984) retained Piaget's relatively broad scope, or molar scale, of moral judgment—indeed, he described moral stages that cut across moral value areas—as well as Piaget's clinical method of interviewing. For the interview stimulus, however, Kohlberg replaced Piaget's story pairs with dilemmas, asking after each dilemma what the protagonist should do and why. The resulting format he called the Moral Judgment Interview (MJI). Kohlberg's scoring system for MJI responses underwent refinement, culminating in the fixed format of Standard Issue Scoring (Colby et al., 1987). As described by Colby and Kohlberg (1987):

> The Standard Issue Moral Judgment Interview [MJI] consists of three parallel forms. Each form comprises three hypothetical moral dilemmas . . . [that] focus on the two moral issues that were chosen to represent the central value conflict in that dilemma. For example, the familiar Heinz dilemma ["Should Heinz steal a drug to save his dying wife if the only druggist able to provide the drug insists on a high price that Heinz cannot afford to pay?"] is represented in Standard Scoring as a conflict between the value of preserving life and the value of upholding the law. (p. 41)

In addition to justifying their moral decisions in the hypothetical dilemmas, participants are asked to evaluate and justify the "issues" or values that have been "predefined" (p. 41) per dilemma. Thus, on the Heinz dilemma, participants produce reasons for the importance of saving a life and obeying the law, respectively. Many of the stage-scorable justifications of participants are prompted by these moral evaluation questions (Gibbs, Basinger, & Fuller, 1992).

The Standard Issue MJI was a mixed success (see Table 23.1). On one hand, the instrument evidenced good test–retest and interrater reliability, and good theoretical construct validity (although the construct validity results were controversial; see discussion later in this chapter; Colby, Kohlberg, Gibbs, & Lieberman, 1983). On the other hand, the Standard Issue scoring system was so demandingly intricate that Miller (1998) suggested "it may be *the* most complex scoring system in the psychological literature" (p. 235). Although good interrater reliability is possible, its attainment requires very extensive training. Furthermore, optimal use of the MJI requires (especially for younger participants) time-consuming individual interviewing.

Production and Evaluation Alternatives to the MJI

Two "main alternatives" to the MJI—one a production measure and the other an evaluation measure—represent additional contributions to the development of standard ways to measure moral judgment maturity (Miller, 1998, p. 235). Both are less complex than the MJI.

THE SOCIOMORAL REFLECTION MEASURE—SHORT FORM. The production measure is the Sociomoral Reflection Measure—Short Form (SRM–SF; Gibbs et al., 1992). As does the MJI, the SRM–SF elicits reasoning concerning moral values that are representative of the moral domain (life, law, affiliation, contract, etc.). Whereas the MJI uses moral dilemmas to stimulate this elicitation, the SRM–SF uses 11 brief, lead-in statements (e.g., "Let's say a friend of yours needs help and may even die, and you're the only person who can save him or her"; or, "Think about when you've made a promise to a friend of yours"). The lead-in statements are followed by evaluation questions—for example, "How important is it for a person (without losing his or her own life) to save the life of a friend? Circle one: very important/important/not important." The SRM–SF uses such evaluation questions for all of the moral values tapped by the measure (rather than only a few of the moral values, as on the MJI). The omission of dilemmas permits a streamlined format and obviates methodological criticism (e.g., Boyes & Walker, 1988).

The SRM–SF has excellent psychometric properties and several practical advantages. The SRM–SF evidences acceptable levels of reliability (interrater, test–retest, internal consistency) and validity (criterion-related, construct). For example, the SRM–SF demonstrated good concurrent validity ($r = .69$) with the MJI (Basinger, Gibbs, & Fuller, 1995) and comparable age trends in samples from Italy (Gielen, Comunian, & Antoni, 1994), Northern Ireland (Ferguson, McLernon, & Cairns, 1994), and Sweden (using Gibbs, Widaman, & Colby's [1982] previous long-form version; Nilsson, Crafoord, Hedengren, & Ekehammar, 1991). The measure correlates with theoretically relevant variables such as social perspective-taking (Mason & Gibbs, 1993a, 1993b) and prosocial behavior (Comunian & Gielen, 1995, 2000), but not with social desirability (Basinger et al., 1995). Its discriminant validity is supported by its consistent identification of delinquent samples as developmentally delayed in moral judgment (e.g., Barriga, Morrison, Liau, & Gibbs, in press; Gavaghan, Arnold, & Gibbs, 1983; Gregg, Gibbs, & Basinger, 1994). Relative to the MJI, the SRM–SF is group-administrable, takes less time to complete (see Table 23.1), requires less inferential scoring time (25 to 30 minutes versus 30 to 60 minutes to score a transcribed MJI protocol), and is accompanied by adequate self-training materials. In her review of the SRM–SF, Laura Berk (2000) concluded, "Apparently, moral judgment can be measured without using dilemmas—a discovery that is likely to ease the task of conducting moral developmental research" (p. 492).

THE DEFINING ISSUES TEST. The other main alternative to the MJI is an evaluation measure: the Defining Issues Test (DIT; Rest, 1979; Rest, Narvaez, Bebeau, & Thoma, 1999). As does the MJI, the DIT uses moral dilemmas to elicit moral evaluations. The DIT requires participants to evaluate (rate and rank) the importance of stage-significant statements of moral reasoning (derived from an early MJI scoring manual) in the context of a set of six moral dilemmas. In connection with the Heinz dilemma,[1] for example, participants evaluate the importance of moral reasoning appeals such as, "Isn't it only natural for a loving husband to care so much for his wife that he'd steal?" (indicative of Stage 3 moral judgment). Such evaluations identify the moral judgment "issues" that the participant sees as most relevant or definitive of the dilemma (hence the name "Defining Issues Test"). Differential patterns of evaluation permit developmentally relevant distinctions among performances. A participant who evaluates higher stage statements as "most important" presumably evidences greater moral judgment maturity than does a participant whose highest evaluations go to lower stage statements.

The DIT generally has "strong psychometric properties" and practical advantages (Lapsley, 1996, p. 100) relative to the MJI. The DIT's concurrent validity with the MJI is in the .60s or .70s. The DIT can be group-administered, requires less administration time, and is objectively or noninferentially scored. It has good test–retest and internal consistency reliability. The measure detects longitudinal development in moral judgment, is not contaminated with cohort or generational effects, and has good discriminant validity with regard to IQ, personality attributes, social attitudes, and other measures of cognitive development (see Rest, 1979; Rest et al., 1999). On the other hand, the DIT is of limited value for use with participant populations where reading competence is limited, such as children and delinquent youth (Gibbs et al., 1992). Other evaluation measures (such as the Sociomoral Reflection Objective Measure [SROM] and the Sociomoral Reflection Objective Measure–Short Form [SROM–SF]; Basinger & Gibbs, 1987; Gibbs et al., 1984; see also Lind, 1986), although less complex than the DIT in certain respects, also are of limited value with younger or marginally literate participants.

Construct Validity Issues

As noted previously, most of the work on assessing moral judgment maturity has derived from cognitive developmental theory. Within that theoretical approach, most researchers have followed Colby and Kohlberg's (1987) argument that construct validity issues should be examined mainly in terms of whether a given measure "fits" or yields data consistent with the predictions or expectations entailed in the cognitive developmental theory. Two primary theoretical expectations follow from the claim that the basic age trend in moral judgment is best conceptualized as "an organization passing through an invariant developmental sequence" (p. 69) of stages (see also Miller, 1998): stage consistency and invariant sequence. Evaluation of research support for these expectations requires scrutiny of the pertinent research methods.

---

[1]The Heinz dilemma is not included in a new, streamlined and shorter version of the DIT in preparation (Rest et al., 1999, p. 8).

Stage Consistency

The stage consistency expectation follows from the cognitive developmental approach: "If it makes sense to say that children are 'in' a particular stage, then their reasoning should consistently fall within this stage" (Miller, 1998, p. 236). Cognitive developmental stage work in relatively molecular areas such as distributive justice do appear to evidence adequate stage consistency. Enright et al. (1980) found per-stage internal consistencies to average in the .60s (and in the .60s to .70s for general internal consistency; see Table 23.1), but to be only .35 for a transitional immature stage. Damon (1977) found similar average correlations between distributive justice stage and related social cognitive concepts.

The internal consistency of more broadly defined moral judgment stages is more problematic. As Lapsley (1996, pp. 95–97) indicated,

> Critics charge that Standard Issue Scoring rules tend to homogenize stage responding, with the effect that stage heterogeneity is unreported or underestimated, and that stage consistency is thereby overestimated. . . . There is . . . clear evidence of stage fluctuation within, and stage inconsistency across, dilemmas, indicating that moral structures are quite flexible and that adults base their moral judgments on *several* stage structures, depending on dilemma type.

Such a conclusion is consistent with Piaget's (1932/1965) view of moral judgment "stages." Piaget noted flexibility in stage usage, even in the course of a single interview (pp. 125–126).

Controversy also has surrounded some of the longitudinal studies that have evaluated the construct validity expectation that the stages should appear in a standard, consecutive order (invariant sequence). The stage consistency and invariant sequence issues are related. Mainly because of variability in stage use, Piaget suggested that immature and mature moral judgment, although "distinct" (p. 124), be understood not as "stages" (p. 126) but rather as "phases" (p. 317) that partially overlap. Similarly, on the basis of a two-year longitudinal study of development in distributive justice (and conceptions of adult authority), Damon concluded, "Although stages of social cognition express important qualitative differences among various social reasoning patterns appearing successively throughout childhood, actual day-to-day development is gradual, mixed, and often uneven" (Damon, 1980, p. 1017).

In contrast to Damon's longitudinal study, Kohlberg's longitudinal study of moral judgment lasted more than 20 years, involving periodic assessment every three to four years. The results were largely consistent with the expectations of invariant, progressive sequence (no stage skipping; negligible stage regression, etc.; see Colby et al., 1983; cf. Boom, Brugman, & van der Heijden, 2001; cf. Walker, 1989). Miller (1998), however, cautioned:

> It should be noted . . . that apparent regressions in earlier longitudinal data served as one basis for revising the scoring system; that is, the regression was removed by changing the scoring to place the apparently immature response at a higher level. Although this approach is defensible (Colby et

al., 1983), it does raise doubts in a skeptic's mind about just how empirically testable the claim of invariant sequence is. (Miller, 1998, pp. 236–237)

Overall, the construct validity of cognitive developmental measures of moral judgment stage maturity is problematic in terms of Kohlberg's strong claims for stage consistency and invariant sequence, but reasonably good if one adopts the original Piagetian overlapping-phases model of moral judgment development. Piaget's model can be discerned in more recent revisionist renditions of the nature of moral judgment stage development (e.g., Damon, 1980; Fischer, 1983). In fairness, Colby et al. (1983) themselves depicted the overlapping prevalence "curves" of stage development, "with earlier stages dropping out as later stages enter, such that the subject seems to be always in transition from one stage to the next" (p. 49).

The Moral Domain

Another construct validity issue is whether Kohlbergian cognitive–developmental measures of moral judgment adequately represent the domain of morality. Elliott Turiel (1998) argued that morality in the Kohlbergian model is confounded with social conventional knowledge, and accordingly should be reconceptualized to focus on justice in the strict sense. In contrast, Carol Gilligan (1982; Gilligan & Attanuci, 1988) argued that the Kohlbergian model needs expansion to include care-related concerns associated with the feminine "voice" in morality. In response to Turiel's works, Colby and Kohlberg (1987) argued that morality and social convention are not after all "completely independent" (p. 15); and in response to Gilligan, they pointed out that their Platonic conceptualization of justice includes "many or most moral concerns of care" (p. 24). In support of the Colby and Kohlberg defense are factor analytical results indicating that the moral domain as defined and sampled in Kohlberg production measures is a unitary factor (Basinger et al., 1995; Colby et al., 1983). Within that domain, female participants—although not prejudicially scored lower in stage assessment—do make more care-related appeals (Garmon, Basinger, Gregg, & Gibbs, 1996; cf. Walker, 1995).

The domain issues literature has not yielded new standard measures of moral judgment maturity. To illustrate his conception of judgment development in the moral domain, Turiel (1998) pointed mainly to distributive justice (the DJS measure described previously). Gilligan (1982; Gilligan & Belenky, 1980) posited from interview data three broad levels in "the feminine ethic," but the psychometric status of this typology "is unclear, since no scoring system has yet been developed to assess such [levels] and they have been omitted from her more recent presentations of the theory" (Walker, 1995, p. 86).

Conclusion

Various instruments have been developed for measuring moral judgment maturity. These instruments can be classified in various ways: clinical or standard; area-specific (mainly, distributive justice) or broad; and production or evaluation. For example, the DJS can be classified as area-specific, evaluation, and standard, whereas the MJI can be classified as broad, production, and evolving from clinical to standard (standard issue scoring). The SRM–SF and DIT (as well as the SROM and SROM–SF) also are broad standard measures, but the former targets production responses whereas the latter targets exclusively evaluation responses.

These measures share the cognitive developmental view of moral judgment maturity as a profound moral understanding differentiated from extraneous considerations—that is, a grasp of that which is intrinsically moral (Gibbs, in press). The extraneous considerations may be salient situational features including impressive consequences or powerful authority figures (as in Piaget's clinical method of assessment); pragmatic or egocentric criteria (as in Damon's assessment work, Enright et al.'s DJS, or Gibbs et al.'s SRM–SF); or the social conventions of a group (as in Kohlberg's MJI, Rest et al.'s DIT, or Gibbs et al.'s SRM–SF in terms of "Moral Type B," or moral ideality). Some of the measures are age-targeted: the DJS may be optimal for an assessment of moral judgment development in the childhood years, whereas the DIT yields a range of moral judgment maturity scores for the adult years. The SRM–SF is the most broadly targeted, suitable from the late childhood through the adolescent and adult years. Measures of moral judgment maturity should be used with other measures of positive moral functioning, such as moral identity (see Barriga et al., in press), moral courage (Gibbs et al., 1986; also chapter 12, this volume), and empathy or related social variables (chapters 13–21, this volume). In other words—as in Ann Colby and William Damon's (1992) study of moral exemplars—researchers should study and assess moral judgment maturity in the larger context of positive individual and collective social life.

Appendix 23.1
SRM–SF

1. Think about when you've made a promise to a friend of yours. How important is it for people to keep promises, if they can, to friends? Circle one:

   very important   important   not important

WHY IS THAT VERY IMPORTANT / IMPORTANT / NOT IMPORTANT (WHICHEVER ONE YOU CIRCLED)? (This format is also used for the remaining questions.)

2. What about keeping a promise to anyone? How important is it for people to keep promises, if they can, even to someone they hardly know?
3. What about keeping a promise to a child? How important is it for parents to keep their promises to their children?
4. In general, how important is it for people to tell the truth?
5. Think about when you've helped your mother or father. How important is it for children to help their parents?
6. Let's say a friend of yours needs help and may even die, and you're the only person who can save him or her. How important is it for a person to save the life of a friend?
7. What about saving the life of anyone? How important is it for a person (without losing his or her own life) to save the life of a stranger?
8. How important is it for a person to live even if that person doesn't want to?
9. How important is it for people not to take things that belong to other people?
10. How important is it for people to obey the law?
11. How important is it for judges to send people who break the law to jail?

References

Adelson, J., Green, B., & O'Neil, R. (1969). Growth of the idea of law in adolescence. *Developmental Psychology, 1,* 327–332.

Barriga, A. K., Morrison, E. M., Liau, A. K., & Gibbs, J. C. (in press). Moral cognition: Explaining the gender difference in antisocial behavior. *Merrill-Palmer Quarterly.*

Basinger, K. S., & Gibbs, J. C. (1987). Validation of the Sociomoral Reflection Objective Measure–Short Form. *Psychological Reports, 61,* 139–146.

Basinger, K. S., Gibbs, J. C., & Fuller, D. (1995). Context and the measurement of moral judgment. *International Journal of Behavioral Development, 18,* 537–556.

Berk, L. E. (2000). *Child development* (5th ed.). Boston: Allyn & Bacon.

Boom, J., Brugman, D., & van der Heijden, P. G. M. (2001). Hierarchical structure of moral stages assessed by a sorting task. *Child Development, 72,* 535–548.

Boyes, M. C., & Walker, L. J. (1988). Implications of cultural diversity for the universality claims of Kohlberg's theory of moral reasoning. *Human Development, 31,* 44–59.

Colby, A., & Damon, W. (1992). *Some do care: Contemporary lives of moral commitment.* New York: Free Press.

Colby, A., & Kohlberg, L. (1987). *The measurement of moral judgment: Theoretical foundations and research validation* (Vol. 1). Cambridge: Cambridge University Press.

Colby, A., Kohlberg, L., Gibbs, J. C., & Lieberman, M. (1983). A longitudinal study of moral judgment. *Monographs of the Society for Research in Child Development, 48* (1–2, Serial No. 200).

Colby, A., Kohlberg, L., Speicher, B., Hewer, A., Candee, D., et al. (1987). *The measurement of moral judgment* (Vol. 2). Cambridge: Cambridge University Press.

Comunian, L., & Gielen, U. P. (1995). A study of moral reasoning and prosocial action in Italian culture. *Journal of Social Psychology, 135,* 699–706.

Comunian, L., & Gielen, U. P. (2000). Sociomoral reflection and prosocial and antisocial behavior: Two Italian studies. *Psychological Reports, 87,* 161–175.

Damon, W. (1977). *The social world of the child.* San Francisco: Jossey-Bass.

Damon, W. (1980). Patterns of change in children's social reasoning: A two-year longitudinal study. *Child Development, 51,* 1010–1017.

Eisenberg, N. (1982). The development of reasoning regarding prosocial behavior. In N. Eisenberg (Ed.), *The development of prosocial behavior* (pp. 219–249). New York: Academic Press.

Enright, R., Franklin, C. C., & Manheim, L. A. (1980). Children's distributive justice reasoning: A standardized and objective scale. *Developmental Psychology, 16,* 193–202.

Ferguson, N., McLernon, F., & Cairns, E. (1994). The Sociomoral Reflection Measure–Short Form: An examination of its reliability and validity in a northern Irish setting. *British Journal of Educational Psychology, 64,* 483–489.

Fischer, K. (1983). Illuminating the processes of moral development. In A. Colby, L. Kohlberg, J. Gibbs, & M. Lieberman (Eds.), *A longitudinal study of moral judgment. Monographs of the Society for Research in Child Development, 48* (Serial No. 200), pp. 97–106.

Flavell, J. H. (1963). *The developmental psychology of Jean Piaget.* Princeton, NJ: D. Van Nostrand.

Furth, H. G. (1980). *The world of grown-ups: Children's conceptions of society.* New York: Elsevier.

Garmon, L. C., Basinger, K. S., Gregg, V. R., & Gibbs, J. C. (1996). Gender differences in stage and expression of moral judgment. *Merrill-Palmer Quarterly, 42,* 418–437.

Gavaghan, M. P., Arnold, K. D., & Gibbs, J. C. (1983). Moral judgment in delinquents and non-delinquents: Recognition versus production measures. *Journal of Psychology, 114,* 267–274.

Gibbs, J. C. (1995). The cognitive–developmental perspective. In W. M. Kurtines & J. L. Gewirtz (Eds.), *Moral development: An introduction* (pp. 27–48). Boston: Allyn & Bacon.

Gibbs, J. C. (in press). *Moral development and reality: Beyond the theories of Kohlberg and Hoffman.* Thousand Oaks, CA: Sage.

Gibbs, J. C., Arnold, K. D., Morgan, R. L., Schwartz, E. S., Gavaghan, M. P., et al. (1984). Construction and validation of a multiple-choice measure of moral reasoning. *Child Development, 55,* 527–536.

Gibbs, J. C., Basinger, K. S., & Fuller, D. (1992). *Moral maturity: Measuring the development of sociomoral reflection.* Hillsdale, NJ: Erlbaum.

Gibbs, J. C., Clark, P. M., Joseph, J. A., Green, J. L., Goodrick, T. S., et al. (1986). Relations between moral judgment, moral courage, and field independence. *Child Development, 57,* 185–193.

Gibbs, J. C., Widaman, K. F., & Colby, A. (1982). Construction and validation of a simplified, group-administrable equivalent to the Moral Judgment Interview. *Child Development, 53,* 895–910.

Gielen, U. P., Comunian, A. L., & Antoni, G. (1994). An Italian cross-sectional study of Gibbs' Sociomoral Reflection Measure—Short Form. In A. L. Comunian & U. P. Gielen (Eds.), *Advancing psychology and its applications: International perspectives* (pp. 125–134). Milan: Franco-Angeli.

Gilligan, C. (1982). *In a different voice: Psychological theory and women's development.* Cambridge, MA: Harvard University Press.

Gilligan, C., & Attanuci, J. (1988). Two moral orientations: Gender differences and similarities. *Merrill-Palmer Quarterly, 34,* 223–237.

Gilligan, C., & Belenky, M. F. (1980). A naturalistic study of abortion decisions. In R. Selman & R. Yandow (Eds.), *Clinical-developmental psychology* (pp. 69–90). San Francisco: Jossey-Bass.

Gregg, V. R., Gibbs, J. C., & Basinger, K. S. (1994). Patterns of developmental delay in moral judgment by male and female delinquents. *Merrill-Palmer Quarterly, 40,* 538–553.

Kohlberg, L. (1958). *The development of modes of thinking and choices in the years from 10 to 16.* Unpublished doctoral dissertation, University of Chicago.

Kohlberg, L. (1984). *The psychology of moral development: Essays on moral development* (Vol. 2). San Francisco: Harper & Row.

Lapsley, D. K. (1996). *Moral psychology.* New York: HarperCollins.

Lind, G. (1986). Cultural differences in moral judgment? A study of West and East European University Students. *Behavioral Science Research, 20,* 208–225.

Mason, M. G., & Gibbs, J. C. (1993a). Social perspective-taking and moral judgment among college students. *Journal of Adolescent Research, 8,* 109–123.

Mason, M. G., & Gibbs, J. C. (1993b). Role-taking opportunities and the transition to advanced moral judgment. *Moral Education Forum, 18,* 1–12.

Miller, S. A. (1998). *Developmental research methods* (2nd ed.). Upper Saddle River, NJ: Prentice-Hall.

Nilsson, I., Crafoord, J., Hedengren, M., & Ekehammar, B. (1991). The sociomoral reflection measure: Applicability to Swedish children and adolescents. *Scandinavian Journal of Psychology, 32,* 48–56.

Piaget, J. (1965). *The moral judgment of the child* (Trans. M. Gabain). New York: Free Press. (Original published 1932)

Piaget, J. (1973). *The child's conception of the world* (Trans. J. Tomlinson & A. Tomlinson). London: Paladin. (Original published 1929)

Rest, J. R. (1979). *Development in judging moral issues.* Minneapolis: University of Minnesota Press.

Rest, J. R., Narvaez, D., Bedeau, M. J., & Thoma, S. J. (1999). *Postconventional moral thinking: A neo-Kohlbergian approach.* Mahwah, NJ: Erlbaum.

Schulman, M. (in press). How we become moral: The sources of moral motivation. In C. R. Snyder & S. J. Lopez (Eds.), *Handbook of positive psychology.* New York: Oxford University Press.

Selman, R. L. (1980). *The growth of interpersonal understanding: Developmental and clinical studies.* New York: Academic Press.

Selman, R. L., & Shultz, L. H. (1990). *Making a friend in youth: Developmental theory and pair therapy.* Chicago: University of Chicago Press.

Turiel, E. (1998). The development of morality. In N. Eisenberg (Ed.), *Handbook of child psychology: Vol. 3. Social, emotional, and personality development* (pp. 863–932). New York: Wiley.

Walker, L. J. (1989). A longitudinal study of moral reasoning. *Child Development, 60,* 157–166.

Walker, L. J. (1995). Sexism in Kohlberg's moral psychology? In W. M. Kurtines & J. L. Gewirtz (Eds.), *Moral development: An introduction* (pp. 83–108). Boston: Allyn & Bacon.

Youniss, J. (1980). *Parents and peers in social development: A Sullivan–Piaget perspective.* Chicago: University of Chicago Press.

Part VI

Models and Measures of Positive Processes, Outcomes, and Environments

24

Vocational Psychology Assessment: Positive Human Characteristics Leading to Positive Work Outcomes

Christine Robitschek

Work can play many roles in a person's life: It can be a way of earning money to support a chosen lifestyle, a pathway on which a person progresses (e.g., earns promotions and recognition), or a mechanism by which one expresses purpose in life and self-concept (Super, 1963; Wrzesniewski, McCauley, Rozin, & Schwartz, 1997). Work provides benefits to both the individual engaging in the work and to society (e.g., Gerstel & Gross, 1987), which reflects positive psychology's shared emphases on personal and societal well-being (M. E. P. Seligman & Csikszentmihalyi, 2000). If workers are to strive for positive outcomes for themselves and society, however, they must possess or develop positive human characteristics and behaviors. This chapter addresses these characteristics, behaviors, and outcomes. The first section introduces the domain of vocational assessment and provides a brief history. The second section briefly presents several theories and identifies important constructs drawn from these theories. The third section specifies instruments that measure these constructs. The fourth section identifies areas for future assessment efforts.

There are many social scientists and practitioners, each with their own theories, techniques, constructs, and assessment tools, who study the work environment. For example, vocational psychologists are interested in understanding, measuring, and predicting people's career development, occupational choices, and work adjustment. Also, industrial–organizational psychologists seek to understand and improve the workplace and the worker's role in the workplace. Career counselors focus on helping people to make informed career choices and to develop a healthy balance between work and other life roles. Despite differing perspectives, what these professionals share is a focus on positive aspects of human functioning. They ask questions such as how we can help people to make suitable and satisfying career choices (e.g., Dawis & Lofquist, 1984) and to expand their interests and capabilities (e.g., Mitchell & Krumboltz, 1996). Because of space limitations, this chapter will not identify every positive construct in the work domain, nor will it cover the entire breadth of perspectives on work. A few examples of relevant topics that the reader may find interesting but will not be covered in this chapter are Savickas's (2000) taxonomy of human strengths, which is derived from vocational theory and can be applied across life domains; Wrzesniewski and colleagues' (Wrzesniewski et al., 1997) assessment of work as job, career, or calling; and Sympson's (1999) operationalization of hope in the work domain. Given the expertise of the author, the chapter focuses on several theories, constructs, and assessment tools that can be found in the vocational psychology literature.

Modern vocational psychology and assessment began when Frank Parsons (1909) advanced the first clear theory of vocational choices, although efforts to help people find meaningful careers can be traced back several centuries. Parsons reasoned that good choices involved understanding one's self and the world of work, along with identifying a good match between one's self and the world of work. Much of our current vocational assessment still follows Parsons's theory—in particular, identifying positive characteristics of the self (including positive processes such as career decision making) and the world of work.

I will focus on two areas within vocational assessment that are particularly relevant to positive psychology. The first area specifies some of the positive characteristics and skills that a person needs to make satisfying, productive career decisions. The second area explores how positive the work arena is in a person's life. In following sections, I address each of these areas in terms of relevant vocational theory, psychological constructs, and assessment tools. I have selected three of the most influential theories and discuss assessment of positive characteristics and skills and outcomes of positive work in the context of these theories. These theories cannot be discussed in their entirety, however, and I would refer the reader to reviews (e.g., Brown & Brooks, 1996). Aspects of the theories are discussed in sufficient detail for the reader to grasp their relevance to positive psychological assessment.

Theoretical Background

In this section I describe aspects of three vocational theories: John Holland's (1959, 1985a) vocational theory, the Theory of Work Adjustment (Dawis & Lofquist, 1984), and Donald Super's (1980) theory.

John Holland's Theory

John Holland's vocational theory probably is the most influential theory in vocational assessment (Spokane, 1996). Holland explored interests, identity, and congruence. Chief among the positive person characteristics focused on by Holland, is "interests," which are activities or tasks that arouse our curiosity, attention, and enjoyment. This definition encompasses Ryan and Deci's (2000) concept of intrinsic motivation but also includes activities and tasks that are congruent with our self-concepts, that are important to us, and that allow us to express our values and fulfill our needs (aspects of Ryan and Deci's extrinsic motivation). Interests can be an indicator of a person's vocational strengths— that is, areas in which the person is likely to be motivated to learn and perform at a high level. Buckingham and Clifton (2001) have suggested that people have their greatest room for improvement and excellence in areas of strength. Thus, if we can identify people's vocational interests (i.e., vocational strengths), this should help in identifying how people can maximize their vocational potentials.

Holland (1959) posited a hexagonal model of interests, which he viewed as personality types. These six types (with examples of typical interests) are (a) realistic (e.g., mechanics, agriculture, and sports); (b) investigative (e.g., science and scholarly pursuits); (c) artistic (e.g., visual and culinary arts, creative writing, and drama); (d) social (e.g., teaching, counseling, and other helping professions); (e) enterprising (e.g., selling products, services, or ideas); and (f) conventional (e.g., typing, filing, and accounting). A person's profile of interests can be expressed by scores on relatively independent scales measuring these six types. Profiles that consist of the three highest scores among these six types are typical, although some people can best be described in fewer or greater numbers of types. For example, a renaissance person, with diverse interests, might be described in terms of all six types, and a person with highly focused interests might be described in terms of just one type.

A second positive construct discussed by Holland is "identity," which is defined as "possession of a clear and stable picture of . . . goals, interests, and talents" (Holland, Johnston, & Asama, 1993, p. 1). Identity reflects the extent to which people believe that they know themselves. This may or may not be grounded in an accurate assessment of oneself. But irrespective of the accuracy, vocational identity strongly affects vocational choices. For example, if I believe that I have the talent and interest to be a professional tri-athlete and I want to achieve this goal, it likely will influence my behavior and the extent to which I pursue this goal. Thus, I should work harder and be more focused in this area in comparison to an area that is not part of my identity. My vocational identity may change if I discover that my initial identity was based on inaccurate information (e.g., I do not have the skills to be a professional tri-athlete). But the strength of my identity continues to influence my decision making. For adults in midlife transitions, a changing vocational identity may be construed as a generative and positive process rather than a negative or pathological process. As people redefine their vocational identity, they may discover that their goals, interests, or talents have changed, or their previous vocational identity was based on inaccurate information. Thus, they create a new vocational identity.

A third construct is Holland's (1985a) "congruence," which is defined as the level of similarity between a person's Holland code and the code for the work environment in which the individual is anticipating working or currently working. Congruence is relevant to positive psychology because research has shown that higher levels of congruence are related to higher levels of job satisfaction (e.g., Gottfredson & Holland, 1990).

Theory of Work Adjustment

The Theory of Work Adjustment (TWA; Dawis & Lofquist, 1984) also addresses congruence, but with a different definition than Holland uses. Whereas Holland addressed congruence in terms of interests, in TWA congruence (which is called "correspondence" in TWA) is defined in two different ways. First, correspondence is the extent to which the supports provided by a work environment match with the needs of the worker. Thus, correspondence refers to work values or needs (i.e., what the individual wants to get out of a job, what is important to the worker), rather than interests. TWA posits that the greater the degree of correspondence between the worker's needs and the pattern of reinforcers in the work environment, the greater the degree of job satisfaction. Second, correspondence refers to the extent to which the worker's abilities match the abilities required by the job. The greater the correspondence between the worker's skills and the skills required by the job, the greater the degree of satisfactoriness in the worker's perfor- mance on the job. In sum, TWA theorists assert that greater correspondence relates to higher work satisfaction and productivity. In this chapter I focus on work values and work environment reinforcers. The reader is directed to Dawis and Lofquist for information about worker abilities, ability require- ments of occupations, and correspondence between abilities and ability requirements, leading to satisfactoriness.

There are several other person variables within TWA that relate directly to the "adjustment" aspects of the theory. In describing TWA, Dawis (1996) suggests that workers respond differently to perceptions of discorrespondence between their needs and the work environment reinforcers. Specifically, work- ers' response styles can be described in terms of celerity (how quickly a worker tries to change the discorrespondence), pace (how much effort is expended in this process), rhythm (the pattern of this process, e.g., cyclical or steady), and endurance (how long the worker engages in this process). TWA theorists also address the level of flexibility the worker has—that is, the extent to which workers can tolerate discorrespondence (Dawis). When workers reach their limits of flexibility, modes of adjustment become salient. In this regard, an active mode involves the worker trying to change the work environment (e.g., trying to improve employer-provided health care benefits). A reactive mode involves the worker trying to change the self (e.g., reconsidering the relative importance of particular needs that are not being met sufficiently by the em- ployer). These response styles have considerable relevance not only for TWA but also for all domains of a person's life. The response styles speak to how people adjust or adapt to new environments or changes in their current environ- ments, whether those environments are in the workplace, among close relation- ships, or in the larger community.

Life-Span, Life-Space Theory of Career Development

Similar to Holland's theory and TWA, Super's life-span, life-space theory (Su- per, 1980) follows Parson's hypothesis that a good fit between one's self and the world of work will contribute to a satisfying work life. But Super went beyond this and took a developmental approach to understanding career devel- opment across the lifespan. Of specific interest to positive psychologists are concepts of career exploration, career maturity and adaptability, self-concept development, role salience, and the balance of life roles (Super, Savickas, & Super, 1996).

Super (1980) believed that career exploration is needed in two distinct areas—the self and the world of work. He focused on exploration of the self, with the purpose of developing and identifying occupational self-concepts. Occupational self-concepts (Super, 1963) were defined as an individual's subjective perceptions of the self as they relate to work environments. "Occupational self-concepts" is plural to signify Super's belief that people have multiple occupational self-concepts rather than one "vocational identity." Some occupational self-concepts are specific to a particular type of occupation (e.g., "I see myself as good at accounting"). Other occupational self-concepts are applicable across a wide range of occupations (e.g., "I see myself as a hard worker"). When we make career decisions, we thus are trying to implement our occupational self-concepts. In addition, the extent to which we are implementing our occupational self-concepts in a particular job should influence our satisfaction with work and life (e.g., Super, 1982, as cited in Super et al., 1996).

Similar to TWA, Super (1983) responded to the potential for unstable career paths. Super described this process as "adaptability," and stated that this was the hallmark of a person with "career maturity." Career maturity is defined as the extent to which a person is ready to cope with the changing demands of life in the vocational realm, including both developmental or expected changes and unanticipated changes (Savickas, 1984). For example, the college student who is ready to make an occupational choice would be considered as being career-mature. Similarly, the laid-off mid-life adult who is ready to explore new vocational possibilities is considered career-mature.

Another important aspect of Super's theory is "role salience," which is the absolute and relative importance of a particular life role (e.g., the worker role in relation to other life roles). Super (1980) emphasized that the worker role will have differing levels of importance for people, and that part of these differences will be accounted for by the other roles in the person's life. Therefore, for people to make good vocational choices, they first must be aware of the role of work in their lives and how work relates to their other life roles. These life roles can include both personal roles, such as leisurite, and socially integrated roles, such as citizen and life partner. Full awareness of the importance of and interactions among various life roles can help people to lead full and productive lives across multiple life domains.

Summary of Vocational Theories

The primary focus of these theories is human strength. In particular, these strengths are skills and characteristics that help people to make good career decisions. When people make good career decisions, they are more satisfied with their lives and they contribute more fully to society. Thus, both the individual and society reap the benefits, which is a hallmark of positive psychology (M. E. P. Seligman & Csikszentmihalyi, 2000).

Construct Measurement

In the remaining sections of this chapter, I will describe positive, vocational assessment tools of career exploration, vocational interests, identity and self-concept, work values, congruence and correspondence, work satisfaction, role salience and balance, and career maturity and adaptability. Only instruments with good evidence for reliability and validity are presented. Although 14 assessment instruments and 1 index are described, many more remain unmentioned. The reader is directed to Kapes, Mastie, and Whitfield (1994), L. Seligman (1994), and Levinson, Ohler, Caswell, and Kiewra (1998) for descriptions of many other measures.

Career Exploration

Based on Parson's (1909) theory of vocational choice, most current theories of career development and choice highlight the importance of career exploration. In this section, I present two instruments that measure this construct.

CAREER EXPLORATION SURVEY. The Career Exploration Survey (CES; Stumpf, Colarelli, & Hartman, 1983) is a 59-item instrument that is administered and scored by the researcher or practitioner. Test takers respond to each item on a 5-point Likert scale, with anchors that vary to match item content. For example, 1 = "little" or "not satisfied" and 5 = "A great deal" or "very satisfied." The instructions ask test takers to answer items in the context of the three months before taking the CES. Results yield scores on 16 dimensions of career exploration. Several dimensions are aspects of the exploration process: environmental exploration, self-exploration, number of occupations considered, intended-systematic exploration, frequency (of exploratory behavior), amount of information, and focus. Three dimensions are aspects of reactions to exploration: satisfaction with information, explorational stress, and decisional stress. Six dimensions are aspects of beliefs: employment outlook, certainty of career exploration outcome, external search instrumentality, internal search instrumentality, method instrumentality, and importance of obtaining preferred position. The CES provides a multidimensional perspective on exploration. (See Stumpf et al., 1983, for psychometric information.)

CAREER EXPLORATION SCALE. The Career Exploration Scale (CE) of the Career Development Inventory (Super, Thompson, Lindeman, Jordaan, & Myers, 1988) is a 20-item multiple-choice scale that is administered by the researcher or practitioner and scored by the inventory publisher (Consulting Psychologists Press). The CE measures career exploration as a unitary construct. Reliability and validity information is available in Super, Thompson, Lindeman, et al. (1988).

Researchers and practitioners should use the CE if they are interested in career exploration as a unitary construct (e.g., in a research study with many other variables) and use the CES if they are interested in career exploration as a multidimensional construct. Other considerations include the convenience of the CES, because of scoring by the researcher or practitioner, and being in the public domain, and the developmental perspective of the CE (i.e., the CE assesses exploration as a developmental stage and the CES assesses exploration as a behavior, including attitudes toward and reactions to that behavior).

Vocational Interests

Again, drawing on Parson's (1909) theory of career choice, many current vocational theories emphasize the importance of vocational interests. In this section, I present three widely used measures of vocational interests.

SELF-DIRECTED SEARCH. The Self-Directed Search (SDS; Holland, Fritzche, & Powell, 1994) is a 228-item instrument that is administered and scored by the test taker. Materials are available from Psychological Assessment Resources. Results yield Holland codes for "activities" (things the test taker would like to do), "competencies" (things the test taker already can do well), "occupations" (things for which the test taker has interest or finds appealing), and "self-estimates" (self-ratings of abilities compared with other people). The test taker calculates a composite Holland code, which includes all of these areas. There are several forms of the SDS (Holland, Powell, & Fritzche, 1997): (a) Form R is the most commonly used form and is appropriate for high school and college students and adults; (b) Form E is written at a fourth-grade level for people with limited reading skills; (c) Form CP is designed for adult workers who are professionals or in transition; and (d) Career Explorer is for junior high school and middle school students. Other forms are available in several languages. The SDS is used in conjunction with the *Occupations Finder,* a booklet with a wide variety of occupations, listed by Holland code, as a means for test takers to compare their codes with the codes of occupations, and the *Educational Opportunities Finder* and *Leisure Finder,* which are used in similar ways. Reliability and validity information is available in Holland et al. (1994).

VOCATIONAL PREFERENCE INVENTORY. The Vocational Preference Inventory (VPI; Holland, 1985b) is a 160-item instrument that is administered and scored by the researcher or practitioner. The VPI also can be scored by the test taker. Materials are available from Psychological Assessment Resources. Test takers indicate their interest in specific occupations by marking "yes," "no," or "undecided." Results yield scores on each of the six Holland types. Four additional scales measure aspects of personality: self-control, masculinity–femininity, status, and acquiescence. An additional scale is called infrequency, and serves as a validity check. The VPI does not provide a direct means for linking the test taker's Holland code with the codes for specific occupations. Reliability and validity information is available in Holland (1985b).

STRONG INTEREST INVENTORY. The Strong Interest Inventory (SII; Harmon, Hansen, Borgen, & Hammer, 1994) is a 317-item instrument that is administered by the researcher or practitioner and scored by the publisher, Consulting Psychologists Press. Test takers mark if they "like," are "indifferent" to, or "dislike" items in five areas, including occupations, school subjects, activities, leisure activities, and types of people. In addition, test takers mark their preference between two activities, identify their characteristics, and mark their preferences in the world of work. Three sets of scores, related to Holland types, are provided in the results. The general occupational themes are composite Holland codes. The basic interest scales are subscales of the Holland codes. The occupational scales compare the test taker's profile with the profiles of people who are successfully employed in specific occupations.

The SII also yields scores on four bipolar Personal Style scales, which describe aspects of how the test taker prefers to interact with the world around him or her (Harmon et al., 1994). The scales are work style, learning environment, leadership style, and risk taking/adventure. Readers are directed to Harmon et al. (1994) for reliability and validity information for the SII.

These three measures of vocational interests have different strengths. First, the SDS is useful in examining discrepancies between an individual's Holland codes as indicated by the different areas measured by the SDS. For example, a person might have had a high level of interest and involvement in the performing arts before becoming a full-time homemaker. But now, however, that person might have only a moderate or even low artistic score in the composite code because of little recent opportunity to express this interest. In contrast, this person might have a relatively high enterprising score in the composite because of successfully chairing a daughter's Girl Scout cookie drives and a son's Boy Scout popcorn sales events (these things are reflected in the activities and competencies areas of the SDS).

Second, the SII is particularly useful with clients because it divides the client's Holland codes into the basic interest scales. For example, a client might be surprised by a moderately high enterprising code, saying "I hate sales!" On further reflection, the client reports enjoying persuading others to change their opinions (i.e., the client enjoys selling ideas). This distinction should be evident in the basic interest scales. Also, the SII gives clients direct comparisons of their profiles with people in a wide range of occupations. In contrast, *Occupations Finder* of the SDS relates clients' Holland codes with the codes of occupations.

Finally, the VPI is particularly useful in research. A shortened version, which yields only Holland codes, can be purchased from the inventory publisher for a reduced fee, yielding a measure of interest codes that is not confounded by the test taker's abilities, as is the SDS.

Identity and Self-Concept

The Vocational Identity Scale (VI) of My Vocational Situation (Holland, Gottfredson, & Power, 1980) measures vocational identity, which is defined as "the possession of a clear and stable picture of one's goals, interests, personality, and talents" (Holland, Daiger, & Power, 1980, p. 1). The VI is available from Consulting Psychologists Press. The VI scale consists of 18 true–false items and is administered and scored by the researcher or practitioner. Psychometric information is available in Holland et al. (1993).

Work Values

In Super's (1980) theory and in the Theory of Work Adjustment (Dawis & Lofquist, 1984), work values play a central role in understanding a person's career development and satisfaction. In this section, I describe an assessment tool from each of these theories.

MINNESOTA IMPORTANCE QUESTIONNAIRE. The Minnesota Importance Questionnaire (MIQ; Rounds, Henly, Dawis, Lofquist, & Weiss, 1981) has two parallel forms: a 190-item paired form, in which the test taker identifies which statement in each pair is more important to him or her; and a 21-item ranked form, in which the test taker rank-orders the items in each set of five statements. Twenty additional items on the paired form (21 on the ranked form) assess the absolute importance of each need. The MIQ yields scores on six values scales: achievement, comfort, status, altruism, safety, and autonomy, and multiple subscales (20 for the paired form, 21 for the ranked form) that measure more basic work needs. Both forms must be scored by the questionnaire publisher (i.e., Vocational Psychology Research, University of Minnesota–Minneapolis). Results are returned to the researcher or practitioner with a profile of scores on each of the needs and values and a list of correspondence scores comparing the test taker's values profile with the reinforcer patterns for a wide variety of occupations. A validity score, called the LCT score (i.e., logically consistent triads), also is given. The LCT score indicates the extent to which the test taker was consistent in reporting the relative importance of the work needs. Reliability and validity information is available in Rounds et al. (1981).

VALUES SCALE. The Values scale (VS; Nevill & Super, 1986b) is a 106-item instrument that is administered and scored by the researcher or practitioner. It also can be scored by the scale publisher (Consulting Psychologists Press). Test takers indicate the level of importance for each item on a 4-point Likert scale ranging from "of little or no importance" to "very important." Results yield scores on 21 scales (e.g., economic rewards, life style, and cultural identity). Each contains a blend of items referring to general values as well as values specific to work. Some but not all of the scales on the VS have names that are very similar to the needs scales of the MIQ. Reliability and validity information is available in Nevill and Super (1986b).

The MIQ is particularly helpful when working with clients who want to understand how their values can manifest in the work domain. The VS is particularly useful with clients exploring values in life domains. These two instruments are equally useful for researchers.

Congruence–Correspondence

Each of these words refers to the degree of similarity between some aspect of an individual and related aspects of his or her environment. Congruence specifically refers to the degree of similarity between a person's interests and the extent to which these interests can be expressed in a specific work environment (Holland, 1985a). Correspondence specifically refers to the degree of similarity between a person's work values and the level of reinforcers for these values in a specific work environment (Dawis & Lofquist, 1984).

C–INDEX. Many indexes of congruence have been developed. Brown and Gore (1994) evaluated these various indexes, identifying problems with each. They put forth the most psychometrically sound index to date, called the C–Index. The C–Index easily is calculated by hand and consists of summing weighted measures of each pairing of letters in the individual's Holland code and the code of the occupation. The main advantages of this index over others is that it allows for greater discrimination among individuals with similar but not identical Holland codes, and the congruence scores are normally distributed.

CORRESPONDENCE. Although correspondence between a worker's needs and the reinforcers provided by a work environment is an important construct in TWA, quantifying correspondence continues to be difficult (Dawis, 1996). Similar to the processes of assessing congruence in the Holland system, results vary depending on which method is used (Rounds, Dawis, & Lofquist, 1987). In contrast to the Holland system (see Brown & Gore, 1994), however, no one method of measuring correspondence has emerged. This remains an area for further research.

Work Satisfaction

Although work satisfaction is a part of most vocational theories, the extent to which work satisfaction is an explicit theoretical aspect differs greatly among theories. The concept is most explicit in the Theory of Work Adjustment (Dawis & Lofquist, 1984). In this section, I present two measures of work satisfaction, one derived from the Theory of Work Adjustment and the other derived separately from the theories discussed in this chapter.

MINNESOTA SATISFACTION QUESTIONNAIRE. The Minnesota Satisfaction Questionnaire (MSQ; Weiss, Dawis, England, & Lofquist, 1967) is administered and scored by the researcher or practitioner, or can be scored by the publisher (Vocational Psychology Research, University of Minnesota). Two forms are available: the 100-item long form and the 20-item short form. The MSQ measures the degree to which test takers are satisfied with aspects of their current job that relate to the 20 vocational needs identified in the Minnesota Importance Questionnaire (paired form). Test takers respond to each item on a 5-point Likert scale ranging from "very satisfied" to "very dissatisfied." Reliability and validity information is available in Weiss et al. (1967).

JOB IN GENERAL. A more recent measure of job satisfaction is the Job in General (JIG; Ironson, Smith, Brannick, Gibson, & Paul, 1989), which provides a global measure of job satisfaction. The JIG has 18 items (phrases) that are

positive and negative, global, evaluative descriptors of jobs. Tests takers identify if each phrase describes their current job by marking "yes," "no," or "?" (if
not sure). The JIG is administered and scored by the researcher or practitioner.
Reliability and validity information is available in Ironson et al. (1989).

Researchers and practitioners should use the JIG if they are interested
in work satisfaction as a unitary construct. Users should consider the MSQ if
they are interested in multidimensional work satisfaction, particularly as work
satisfaction relates to the satisfaction of work values.

Role Salience and Balance

Super (1980) put forth these constructs from a vocational perspective. *Role
salience* refers to the absolute and relative importance of various life roles.
Role balance refers to the extent to which a person is comfortable with the
amount of time and energy put into each role in relation to other life roles.

SALIENCE INVENTORY. The Salience Inventory (SI; Nevill & Super, 1986a)
is a 170-item instrument that is administered and scored by the researcher or
practitioner. The SI also can be scored by the publisher, Consulting Psychologists Press. Test takers rate each item on a 4-point scale from "never or rarely/
little or none" to "almost always or always/a great deal." Results yield scores
for five life roles: student, worker, homemaker (including parenting and partner
roles), leisurite, and citizen. Within each of these life roles, three aspects of
salience are tapped (yielding a total of 15 subscale scores: 3 aspects of salience
× 5 life roles). These three aspects or salience are participation (i.e., what the
test taker actually does in this life role), commitment (i.e., attitudinal and
affective importance of the life role), and value expectations (i.e., the degree
to which the life role is expected to fulfill the test taker's values and needs).
Thus, the SI informs us not only about which roles are most important but
also the extent to which test takers actually are engaged in activities (participation) that are important (commitment) and meet their needs (values expectations). Reliability and validity information is available in Nevill and Super
(1986a).

LIFE-CAREER RAINBOW. The Life-Career Rainbow (Super, 1980) is a qualitative way to assess role salience, among other constructs. Construction of the
Rainbow can be completed by the individual being assessed, after thorough
instructions are given, or by this individual in conjunction with the researcher
or practitioner. The life-span is represented by the length of the Rainbow, with
the left and right ends representing birth and death, respectively. Each band
of the Rainbow represents a different life role. The width of each band at any
given point in the life-span represents the salience of that life role at that point
in time. For example, the "worker" band of the Rainbow likely would be empty
for most people until sometime in the teenage years, at which point it might
be fairly narrow (compared with other bands) if the worker role has minimal
salience. In the adult years, the worker band might be wide, if, for example,
the individual is employed full-time, outside the home, in a job that has meaning

and purpose for the worker. This band is likely to narrow again, or end completely after retirement, depending on whether the person quits work altogether or continues to work in some part-time capacity after formally retiring. A cross-section of the Rainbow at any point across the life-span provides a picture of the life-space (i.e., a comprehensive view of the multiple life roles a person plays at any one time).

Although the Life-Career Rainbow might be of limited utility to researchers, particularly those involved in quantitative research, it is very useful to practitioners and their clients. Similar to the Salience Inventory, the Rainbow can help clients to understand the relative importance of various life roles and how these roles might interact. In contrast to the Salience Inventory, however, the Rainbow adds the life-span dimension, which allows people to explore how the importance of these roles, and even the presence or absence of each role, has changed over time. Furthermore, the Rainbow allows people to be planful about how they will structure their life space and balance their life roles in the future.

Career Maturity and Adaptability

Super (1980) also put forth these constructs. *Career maturity* originally referred to an individual's readiness to take predictable steps in the career development process. *Career adaptability* refers to an individual's readiness to handle all types of changes in the worker role, including predictable and unexpected changes.

CAREER DEVELOPMENT INVENTORY. The Career Development Inventory (CDI; Super, Thompson, Lindeman, et al., 1988) is a 120-item multiple-choice instrument that is administered by the researcher or practitioner and scored by the publisher (Consulting Psychologists Press). The CDI assesses readiness to make educational and vocational decisions. Two forms are available, one for junior and senior high school students and one for college students. Results yield scores on eight scales: career planning, career exploration, decision making, world of work, knowledge of preferred occupational group, career development attitudes, career development knowledge and skills, and career orientation (which is a global measure of career maturity). Reliability and validity information is available in Super, Thompson, Lindeman, et al. (1988) and Punch and Sheridan (1985).

ADULT CAREER CONCERNS INVENTORY. The Adult Career Concerns Inventory (ACCI; Super, Thompson, & Lindeman, 1988) is a 61-item instrument that is administered by the researcher or practitioner and typically scored by the publisher (Consulting Psychologists Press). It measures adults' readiness to adapt to changes in the worker role; however, it also can be used with adolescents approaching entering the work force. Test takers respond to each item on a 5-point Likert scale ranging from "no concern" to "great concern." Results yield scores on five major stages of career development and three substages within each major stage. Although the ACCI deals explicitly with "concerns" rather than strengths, it can be used to identify areas of relative strength in this process—that is, areas of development that are of little concern because they have been mastered. Reliability and validity information for the ACCI is available from Super, Thompson, and Lindeman (1988) and Super, Thompson, Lindeman, et al. (1988).

The primary difference between these two instruments is the developmental stages on which they focus. The CDI is for adolescent and young adults who are still making early career decisions. The ACCI can be used across the lifespan, although it was developed for use with adults who are contemplating or in the midst of career transitions.

Measurement Issues and Future Developments

There is considerable evidence to indicate solid reliability and validity for all of the instruments discussed in this chapter. Readers are directed to the references mentioned throughout for test-specific measurement issues. There are several themes, however, that have emerged in recent years. First, growing awareness of multicultural issues, in general, has raised questions about whether our current vocational assessments are valid for use with diverse populations (Subich & Billingsley, 1995). For example, when working with women or studying their career development, Betz (1993) cautioned that the results of vocational interest inventories might reflect gender role socialization processes rather than intrinsically motivated preferences. Thus, traditional use of interest inventories will act to maintain the status quo, rather than encouraging women to explore nontraditional interests and occupations. Also, Fouad (1993) stated that many vocational assessment instruments do not have norms for members of racial and ethnic minorities, nor is it known if many of these instruments are reliable and valid for these groups of people. We need to devote considerable effort and resources to addressing the applicability of the measures across diverse groups and cultures.

A second theme involves the changing world of work. In the early years of vocational psychology, the field was responding to the industrial revolution, which required developing ways to match potential workers with specific occupations (Krumboltz & Coon, 1995). Many reliable and valid instruments were developed to measure characteristics of the worker and the work environment to aid in the matching process, including many of the instruments presented in this chapter. As the world of work has changed, however, vocational assessment has failed to keep pace. For example, the structure of the workplace is changing from hierarchical to a team structure; job descriptions are more fluid and less rigid; and workers have ongoing needs to acquire new skills, even within the tenure of one job (Krumboltz & Coon, 1995). Vocational assessment devices need to respond to these changes in the world of work by reconsidering the theories that underlie the constructs currently measured. In other words, the validity of the constructs themselves needs to be questioned. Given the dramatic changes in the world of work, do each of these constructs still have meaning for career development?

Finally, future developments in vocational assessment need to address the distinction between "what is" and "what might be" in a person's work life. As Krumboltz (e.g., Mitchell & Krumboltz, 1996) has pointed out, we do a disservice to people if vocational assessment limits their choices to options to which they already have been exposed. Vocational assessment, particularly in the context of positive psychology, should open doors and increase the range of options that people perceive in the world of work. Current vocational assessment tools do an excellent job of assessing "what is." We now need to add to these tools to include "measures of the possible."

References

Betz, N. E. (1993). Issues in the use of ability and interest measures with women. *Journal of Career Assessment, 1,* 217–232.

Brown, D., & Brooks, L. (1996). *Career choice and development* (3rd ed.). San Francisco: Jossey-Bass.

Brown, S. D., & Gore, P. A. (1994). An evaluation of interest congruence indices: Distribution characteristics and measurement properties. *Journal of Vocational Behavior, 45,* 310–327.

Buckingham, M., & Clifton, D. O. (2001). *Now, discover your strengths.* New York: Free Press.

Dawis, R. V. (1996). The theory of work adjustment and person–environment–correspondence counseling. In D. Brown & L. Brooks (Eds.), *Career choice and development* (3rd ed., pp. 75–120). San Francisco: Jossey-Bass.

Dawis, R. V., & Lofquist, L. H. (1984). *A psychological theory of work adjustment.* Minneapolis: University of Minnesota Press.

Fouad, N. A. (1993). Cross-cultural vocational assessment. *Career Development Quarterly, 42,* 4–13.

Gerstel, N., & Gross, H. E. (Eds.). (1987). *Families and work.* Philadelphia: Temple University Press.

Gottfredson, G. D., & Holland, J. L. (1990). A longitudinal test of the influence of congruence: Job satisfaction, competency utilization, and counterproductive behavior. *Journal of Counseling Psychology, 37,* 389–398.

Harmon, L. W., Hansen, J. C., Borgen, F. H., & Hammer, A. L. (1994). *Strong Interest Inventory: Applications and technical guide.* Palo Alto, CA: Consulting Psychologists Press.

Holland, J. L. (1959). A theory of vocational choice. *Journal of Counseling Psychology, 6,* 35–45.

Holland, J. L. (1985a). *Making vocational choices* (2nd ed.). Englewood Cliffs, NJ: Prentice Hall.

Holland, J. L. (1985b). *Manual for the Vocational Preference Inventory.* Odessa, FL: Psychological Assessment Resources.

Holland, J. L., Daiger, D. C., & Power, P. G. (1980). *My Vocational Situation: Description of an experimental diagnostic form for the selection of vocational assistance.* Palo Alto, CA: Consulting Psychologist Press.

Holland, J. L., Fritzche, B. A., & Powell, A. B. (1994). *Technical manual for the Self-Directed Search.* Odessa, FL: Psychological Assessment Resources.

Holland, J. L., Gottfredson, D. C., & Power, P. G. (1980). Some diagnostic scales for research in decision making and personality: Identity, information, and barriers. *Journal of Personality and Social Psychology, 39,* 1191–1200.

Holland, J. L., Johnston, J. A., & Asama, N. F. (1993). The Vocational Identity Scale: A diagnostic and treatment tool. *Journal of Career Assessment, 1,* 1–12.

Holland, J. L., Powell, A. B., & Fritzche, B. A. (1997). *Self-Directed Search: Professional user's guide.* Odessa, FL: Psychological Assessment Resources.

Ironson, G. H., Smith, P. C., Brannick, M. T., Gibson, W. M., & Paul, K. B. (1989). Construction of a Job in General scale: A comparison of global, composite, and specific measures. *Journal of Applied Psychology, 74,* 193–200.

Kapes, J. T., Mastie, M. M., & Whitfield, E. A. (Eds.). (1994). *A counselor's guide to career assessment instruments* (3rd ed.). Alexandria, VA: National Career Development Association.

Krumboltz, J. D., & Coon, D. W. (1995). Current professional issues in vocational psychology. In W. B. Walsh & S. H. Osipow (Eds.), *Handbook of vocational psychology: Theory, research, and practice* (2nd ed., pp. 391–426). Mahwah, NJ: Erlbaum.

Levinson, E. M., Ohler, D. L., Caswell, S., & Kiewra, K. (1998). Six approaches to the assessment of career maturity. *Journal of Counseling and Development, 76,* 475–482.

Mitchell, L. K., & Krumboltz, J. D. (1996). Krumboltz's learning theory of career choice and counseling. In D. Brown & L. Brooks (Eds.), *Career choice and development* (3rd ed., pp. 233–280). San Francisco: Jossey-Bass.

Nevill, D. D., & Super, D. E. (1986a). *The Salience Inventory: Theory, application and research.* Palo Alto, CA: Consulting Psychologists Press.

Nevill, D. D., & Super, D. E. (1986b). *The Values scale.* Palo Alto, CA: Consulting Psychologists Press.

Parsons, F. (1909). *Choosing a vocation.* Boston: Houghton-Mifflin.

Punch, K. F., & Sheridan, B. E. (1985). Some measurement characteristics of the Career Development Inventory. *Measurement and Evaluation in Counseling and Development, 18,* 196–202.

Rounds, J. B., Dawis, R. V., & Lofquist, L. H. (1987). Measurement of person–environment fit and prediction of satisfaction in the theory of work adjustment. *Journal of Vocational Behavior, 31,* 297–318.

Rounds, J. B., Henly, G. A., Dawis, R. V., Lofquist, L. H., & Weiss, D. J. (1981). *Manual for the Minnesota Importance Questionnaire: A measure of vocational needs and values.* Minneapolis: University of Minnesota.

Ryan, R. M., & Deci, E. L. (2000). Self-determination theory and the facilitation of intrinsic motivation, social development, and well-being. *American Psychologist, 55,* 68–78.

Savickas, M. L. (1984). Career maturity: The construct and its measurement. *Vocational Guidance Quarterly, 32,* 222–231.

Savickas, M. L. (2000, Aug.). Building human strength: Career counseling's contribution to a taxonomy of positive psychology. In W. B. Walsh (Chair), *Fostering human strength: A counseling psychology perspective.* Symposium presented at the annual meeting of the American Psychological Association, Washington, DC.

Seligman, L. (1994). *Developmental career counseling and assessment* (2nd ed.). Thousand Oaks, CA: Sage.

Seligman, M. E. P., & Csikszentmihalyi, M. (2000). Positive psychology: An introduction. *American Psychologist, 55,* 5–14.

Spokane, A. R. (1996). Holland's theory. In D. Brown & L. Brooks (Eds.), *Career choice and development* (3rd ed.). San Francisco: Jossey-Bass.

Stumpf, S. A., Colarelli, S. M., & Hartman, K. (1983). Development of the Career Exploration Survey (CES). *Journal of Vocational Behavior, 22,* 191–226.

Subich, L. M., & Billingsley, K. D. (1995). Integrating career assessment into counseling. In W. B. Walsh & S. H. Osipow (Eds.), *Handbook of vocational psychology: Theory, research, and practice* (2nd ed., pp. 261–294). Mahwah, NJ: Erlbaum.

Super, D. E. (1963). Self-concepts in vocational development. In D. E. Super, R. Starshevsky, N. Matlin, & J. P. Jordaan (Eds.), *Career development: Self-concept theory* (pp. 17–32). New York: College Entrance Examination Board.

Super, D. E. (1980). A life-span, life-space approach to career development. *Journal of Vocational Behavior, 13,* 282–298.

Super, D. E. (1983). Assessment in career guidance: Toward truly developmental counseling. *Personnel and Guidance Journal, 61,* 555–562.

Super, D. E., Savickas, M. L., & Super, C. M. (1996). The life-span, life-space approach to careers. In D. Brown & L. Brooks (Eds.), *Career choice and development* (3rd ed., pp. 121–178). San Francisco: Jossey-Bass.

Super, D. E., Thompson, A. S., & Lindeman, R. H. (1988). *Adult Career Concerns Inventory: Manual for research and exploratory use in counseling.* Palo Alto, CA: Consulting Psychologists Press.

Super, D. E., Thompson, A. S., Lindeman, R. H., Jordaan, J. P., & Myers, R. A. (1988). *Manual for the Adult Career Concerns Inventory and the Career Development Inventory.* Palo Alto, CA: Consulting Psychologists Press.

Sympson, S. (1999). *Validation of the Domain Specific Hope scale: Exploring hope in life domains.* Unpublished doctoral dissertation, University of Kansas, Lawrence.

Weiss, D. J., Dawis, R. V., England, G. W., & Lofquist, L. H. (1967). Manual for the Minnesota Satisfaction Questionnaire. *Minnesota Studies in Vocational Rehabilitation, XXI.* Minneapolis: University of Minnesota.

Wrzesniewski, A., McCauley, C., Rozin, P., & Schwartz, B. (1997). Jobs, career, and callings: People's relations to their work. *Journal of Research in Personality, 31,* 21–33.

25

Positive Coping: Mastering Demands and Searching for Meaning

Ralf Schwarzer and Nina Knoll

Coping can be defined as an effort to manage and overcome demands and critical events that pose a challenge, threat, harm, loss, or benefit to a person (Lazarus, 1991). The term *coping* often has been used in a more narrow sense as a response required of an organism to adapt to adverse circumstances. In the context of a recent positive psychology movement, however, the conceptualization of coping is broadening and now includes self-regulated goal attainment strategies and personal growth as well (for reviews see Snyder, 1999; Snyder & Lopez, 2002).

Coping can occur as a response to an event or in anticipation of upcoming demands, but it also can involve a proactive approach to self-imposed goals and challenges. Many attempts have been made to reduce the universe of possible coping behaviors to a more parsimonious set of coping dimensions. Researchers have come up with two basic distinctions, such as (a) instrumental, attentive, vigilant, or confrontative coping on the one hand; as opposed to (b) avoidant, palliative, and emotional coping on the other (for an overview, see Schwarzer & Schwarzer, 1996). A well-known approach has been put forward by Lazarus (1991), who separates *problem-focused* from *emotion-focused* coping. Another conceptual distinction is between *assimilative* and *accommodative* coping, whereby the former aims at modifying the environment and the latter at modifying oneself (Brandtstädter, 1992). Assimilative coping implies tenacious goal pursuit, and accommodative coping flexible goal adjustment. Similarly, the terms *primary control* versus *secondary control* (Rothbaum, Weisz, & Snyder, 1982) or *mastery* versus *meaning* (Taylor, 1983) have been defined.

This chapter is organized into two parts, using the terms *mastery* and *meaning* as proxies for the two broad processes of coping described previously. *Mastery* pertains to problem-focused or assimilative coping with demands, whereas *meaning* refers to accommodative coping. These coping processes need not be applied exclusively. They may occur more or less simultaneously, or in a certain time order, for example, when individuals first try to alter the demands that are at stake and, after failing, turn inward to reinterpret their plights and find subjective meaning in them. We will not discuss the abundance of possible thoughts and behaviors but will focus on an innovative

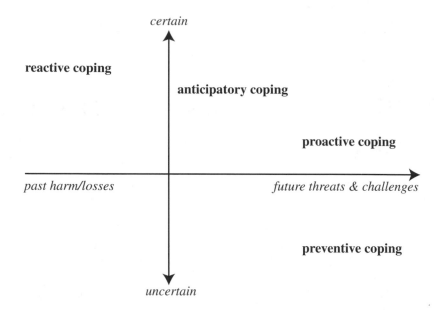

Figure 25.1.   Four perspectives of coping in terms of timing and certainty.

theoretical perspective that emphasizes positive coping and expands on previous approaches. The following section will distinguish between four kinds of adaptation, with proactive coping being the prototype of positive coping (Schwarzer, 2000).

Mastering Challenging Demands: Proactive Coping Theory

Stressful demands (e.g., earlier loss, ongoing harmful encounter, or events in the future) seem threatening to someone who feels incapable of matching the upcoming tasks with available resources. In light of the complexity of stressful episodes in social contexts, human coping cannot be reduced to primitive forms, such as fight-and-flight responses or relaxation. Coping depends on the time perspective of the demands and the subjective certainty of the events.

To introduce a new perspective, we distinguish between reactive, anticipatory, preventive, and proactive coping, and how each type of coping helps us grapple with events of the past, present, and future. Reactive coping alludes to harm or loss experienced in the past, whereas anticipatory coping pertains to imminent threat in the near future. Preventive coping foreshadows an uncertain threat potential in the distant future, and proactive coping involves upcoming challenges that are potentially self-promoting (see Figure 25.1).

Reactive coping can be defined as an effort to deal with a past or present stressful encounter or to compensate for or accept harm or loss. Examples of harm or loss are marital dissolution, losing one's job, doing poorly at a job interview, having an accident, and being criticized by parents or friends. All of these events have happened in the *past*; thus, the individual who needs to cope either has to compensate for the loss or alleviate the harm. Another option is to readjust goals, find benefit, or search for meaning. Reactive coping may be problem-focused, emotion-focused, or social-relation-focused. For coping with loss or harm, individuals need to be resilient. Because they aim at compensation or recovery, they need "recovery self-efficacy," a particular optimistic belief in their capability to overcome setbacks (Schwarzer, 1999).

Anticipatory coping is fundamentally different from reactive coping because the critical event has not yet occurred. It can be regarded as an effort to deal with pending threat. In anticipatory coping, individuals face a critical event that is certain or fairly certain to occur in the near future. Examples are holding a scheduled public speech, a dentist appointment, a job interview, adapting to parenthood, increased workload, an exam, promotion, retirement, company downsizing, and so forth. There is a risk that the upcoming event subsequently may cause harm or loss, and the person has to manage this perceived risk. The situation is appraised as either threatening, challenging, or benefiting, or some of each. The function of coping may lie in solving the actual problem, such as increasing effort, enlisting help, or investing other resources. Another function may lie in feeling good in spite of the risk, for example by redefining the situation as less threatening, by distraction, or by gaining reassurance from others. Thus, anticipatory coping can be understood as the management of known risks, which includes investing one's resources to prevent or combat the stressor or to maximize an anticipated benefit. One of the personal resource factors is situation-specific "coping self-efficacy" (Schwarzer & Renner, 2000), an optimistic self-belief of being able to cope successfully with the particular situation.

Although anticipatory coping is considered to be a short-term engagement with high-certainty events, *preventive coping* is an effort to prepare for uncertain events in the long run. The aim is to build up general resistance resources that result in less strain in the future by minimizing the severity of the impact. Thus, the consequences of stressful events, should they occur, would be less severe. In preventive coping, individuals consider a critical event that may or may not occur in the distant future. Examples of such events are job loss, forced retirement, crime, illness, physical impairment, disaster, or poverty. When people carry a spare key, double-lock their doors, have good health insurance, save money, or maintain social bonds, they cope in a preventive way and build up protection without knowing whether they will ever need it.

The perception of ambiguity need not be limited to single events. There can be a vague wariness that "something" might happen, which motivates a person to be prepared for "anything." The individual prepares for the occurrence of nonnormative life events that are appraised as more or less threatening. Coping is a kind of risk management because one has to prepare for various unknown risks in the distant future. The perceived ambiguity stimulates a broad range of coping behaviors. Because all kinds of harm or loss could materialize one day, people build up general resistance resources by accentuating their psychological strengths and accumulating wealth, social bonds, and skills—"just in case." Skill development, for example, is a coping process that may help to prevent possible trouble. Preventive coping is not born out of an acute stress situation. It is not sparked by state anxiety, but rather by some level of trait worry, or at least reasonable concern about the dangers of life. General "coping self-efficacy" seems to be a good personal prerequisite to plan and initiate successfully multifarious preventive actions that help build up resilience against threatening nonnormative life events in the distant future.

The prototype of positive coping is *proactive coping* because it does not require any negative appraisals, such as harm, loss, or threat. Proactive coping reflects efforts to build up resources that facilitate promotion toward challenging goals and personal growth. In proactive coping, people hold a vision. They see risks, demands, and opportunities in the distant future, but they do not appraise them as potential threat, harm, or loss. Rather, they perceive demanding situations as personal challenges. *Coping becomes goal management instead of risk management.* Individuals are not reactive but proactive in the sense that they initiate a constructive path of action and create opportunities for growth. The proactive individual strives for life improvement and builds up resources that ensure progress and quality of functioning. Proactively creating better living conditions and higher performance levels is experienced as an opportunity to render life meaningful. Stress is interpreted as "eustress"—that is, productive arousal and vital energy (Selye, 1974).

Preventive and proactive coping are partly manifested in the same kinds of overt behaviors, such as skill development, resource accumulation, and long-term planning. It makes a difference, however, if the motivation emanates from threat or challenge appraisals because worry levels are higher in the former and lower in the latter. Proactive individuals are motivated to meet challenges, and they commit themselves to their own personal high-quality standards.

Self-regulatory goal management includes ambitious goal setting and tenacious goal pursuit. Goal pursuit requires "action self-efficacy," an optimistic belief that one is capable of initiating and maintaining difficult courses of action. This is similar to the "agency" component of the *hope* construct proposed by Snyder (1994). The role of beliefs in self-regulatory goal attainment has been spelled out in more detail in a different theory that was designed to explain health behavior change, the Health Action Process Approach (Schwarzer, 1992, 1999, 2001; Schwarzer & Renner, 2000). The distinction between these four perspectives of coping is advantageous because it moves the focus away from mere responses to negative events toward a broader range of risk and goal management that includes the active creation of opportunities and the positive experience of stress. Aspinwall and Taylor (1997) have described a proactive coping theory that is similar, but not identical, to the present one. What they call proactive coping is mainly covered by the term preventive coping in this approach (see Greenglass, Schwarzer, & Taubert, 1999). Before we proceed with operational definitions, it is necessary to address the other area of positive coping.

Searching for Meaning

This section will deal with conceptualizations of "meaning" and its role in the coping process. Meaning has been one focus in a number of prominent stress and coping theories concerned with adaptation to a variety of stressful encounters (Lazarus, 1991). Authors vary in the roles they ascribe to the search for meaning in the coping process: They conceptualize it as distinct from coping (Affleck & Tennen, 1996), intertwined with coping (Folkman & Moskowitz, 2000), or being a factor that shapes coping in the process (i.e., appraisals; Lazarus, 1991).

Researchers also scrutinize different levels of meaning in the coping process. For example, Folkman and Moskowitz (2000) differentiate situational and global meaning. *Situational meaning* refers to appraisals of stress where it helps determine the degree of personal significance of the encounter in relation to a person's beliefs, goals, or values. *Global meaning,* on the other hand, is more concerned with abstract, generalized meaning that is related to people's more existential assumptions or "assumptive worlds" (Janoff-Bulman, 1992).[1]

Most researchers concerned with the issue of finding meaning in adversity conceptualize it as a powerful human strength commonly associated with the minimization of harm to an individual's physical (e.g., Affleck, Tennen, Croog, & Levine, 1987) and psychological health (e.g., Davis, Nolen-Hoeksema, & Larson, 1998). First, a more situational approach to meaning as emphasized by Lazarus (1991) and Folkman and Moskowitz (2000) is described. Following this, more global conceptualizations of meaning emerging primarily from trauma literature are reported.

Situational Approach

Lazarus (1991) asserted that an emotional meaning of a person–environment relationship is constructed by the process of appraisal. Whether a situation is relevant to one's goals, beliefs, or values is determined by a number of automatic decisions concerning a particular encounter. In terms of Lazarus's theory, a situation would be appraised as or given meaning as being relevant or nonrelevant, posing a threat, harm–loss, or challenge (Lazarus & Folkman, 1984). Creating meaning in terms of appraisal is suggested to determine the significance of an adaptational encounter.

Folkman and Moskowitz (2000) argue that the construal of meaning not only serves to estimate the relevance of a situation and choice of coping, but also plays a vital role for coping behavior itself, especially coping that supports *positive affect.* In an effort to shed light on the "other side of coping," the authors identify three meaning-related coping strategies that foster positive emotions in the context of prolonged stress: positive reappraisal, problem-focused coping, and infusing ordinary events with positive meaning.

In a longitudinal study of AIDS caregivers covering a period of eight months surrounding the death of their partners (Moskowitz, Folkman, Collette, & Vittinghoff, 1996), the authors found positive reappraisal independently

---

[1] Because this chapter is primarily concerned with meaning observed and studied in the stress and coping process, more general accounts of seeking meaning in life will not be discussed further. Suggested readings on this fascinating and well-studied topic include works by Antonovsky (1993), Ryff and Singer (1998), and Wong and Fry (1998).

related with increases in positive affect, pointing to caregivers' reappraisal of a painful experience as worthwhile. Similarly, caregivers reported an increased effort at problem-focused coping before the partner's death. Likewise, a strong association with positive affect during this period was found. Folkman and Moskowitz (2000) proposed that problem-focused coping may relate to finding meaning in that it supports feelings of efficacy and situational mastery. They emphasize that almost all caregivers were readily able to report positive events in the midst of their ongoing stress. Most of these events were actually ordinary (see Table 25.1), but they were nevertheless reported as positive. It is suggested that during the course of a chronically stressful situation (such as long-term care-giving), ordinary experiences are infused with positive meaning and serve as breathers that contribute to positive affect.

In her recent theory on the Broaden and Build Model of Positive Emotions, Fredrickson (2002) emphasized the importance of positive emotions for health and well-being. Fredrickson has claimed that negative emotional states are associated with narrow and fixated thinking and action. Positive emotions, on the other hand, broaden an individual's thought and action repertoire and thereby build the individual's enduring personal resources. Fredrickson proposed that by this mechanism, positive emotions have a lasting undoing effect on negative emotions. Accordingly, strategies that cultivate positive emotions, for example relaxation and finding positive meaning, should be suitable for preventing and treating problems such as anxiety, depression, or aggression.

Global Approach

Appraised situational meaning contrasts with global meaning. The global approach refers to a more abstract, generalized understanding of meaning that is connected with individuals' fundamental assumptions, beliefs, or expectations about the world and the self in the world (e.g., Wortman, Silver, & Kessler, 1993). The manner with which persons search for meaning while coping with an adverse event is thought of as an attempt to reconstruct existential beliefs and distal goals that define one's identity (assumptive world; Janoff-Bulman, 1992).

One prominent theory that incorporates meaning finding as a cornerstone is Taylor's (1983) theory of cognitive adaptation to threatening events. The theory proposes three main dimensions of adaptation: search for meaning, sense of mastery, and self-enhancement. The three dimensions are not orthogonal. Instead, it is assumed that one process may serve different functions. For example, a causal explanation can provide meaning as well as increase one's sense of mastery at the same time. Taylor has suggested that meaning "invokes a need to understand why a crisis occurred and what its impact has been" (1983, p. 112). By understanding the cause of an event, one may appraise its significance and what it symbolizes about one's life, often leading to existential reappraisals of life and one's appreciation for it. In a study with breast cancer patients, Taylor found that the majority of women reported positive changes since their recent bout with cancer. Ninety-five percent of patients had a personal explanation for why they developed cancer.

Table 25.1. Studies Using Qualitative Assessment of "Meaning"

Authors/ study population	"Meaning" in the coping process	Strategies	Measures/ qualitative assessment	Coding/categories (examples)
Folkman & Moskowitz (2000) AIDS caregivers	Appraised situational meaning influences choice of coping strategy Meaning is integral to coping that supports positive affect	Positive reappraisal Problem-focused coping Infusing ordinary events with positive meaning (qualitative)	*Positive reappraisal, problem-focused coping:* Ways of Coping Questionnaire (Folkman & Lazarus, 1988) *Infusing events with positive meaning:* Describe "something that you did or something that happened to you that made you feel good and that was meaningful to you and helped you through the day" (Folkman & Moskowitz, 2000; p. 651)	Events infused with positive meaning Planned: Preparing a meal, meeting friends Unplanned: Seeing a beautiful flower, receiving a compliment for something minor
Taylor (1983); Taylor, Lichtman, & Wood (1984) Breast cancer patients	Finding meaning as a causal analysis that provides an answer to the question of why something bad happened, a rethinking of one's priorities to restructure life along more satisfying lines Finding meaning may be intertwined with a sense of mastery	Understanding of the origin and impact of the crisis as well as its personal significance By finding meaning, chance for regaining a sense of control over crisis and its side effects	*Meaning:* Patients were asked if they had any hunches about the origin of their cancer, who they thought was responsible for their cancer, and what were the implications of the cancer for the patient's life.	Narrative accounts of patients coded along the following lines: *Meaning/origin of crisis:* stress, specific carcinogen, heredity, diet, blow to breast, other *Meaning/responsibility:* oneself, someone else, environment, chance *Meaning/implications:* reappraisal of life, new attitude toward life, self-knowledge, self-change, reordering priorities, construe positive meaning

(continued)

Table 25.1. (continued)

Authors/ study population	"Meaning" in the coping process	Strategies	Measures/ qualitative assessment	Coding/Categories (Examples)
Davis, Nolen-Hoeksema, & Larson (1998) Bereaved family members	Finding meaning as a catalyst for the review of one's priorities connected with a shift of focus from the event itself to understanding the self in the context of adversity Deriving benefit from loss as a key means of assigning positive value to the event for one's own life	*Sense-making:* Developing an explanation for the loss within existing fundamental worldviews *Benefit-finding:* Pursuit for the silver lining of adversity	*Sense-making:* "Do you feel that you have been able to make sense of the death?" (Davis et al. 1998, p. 565) *Benefit-finding:* "Sometimes people who lose a loved one find some positive aspect in the experience. For example, some people feel they learn something about themselves or others. Have you found anything positive in the experience?" (Davis et al. 1998, p. 565)	*Sense-making:* Predictability, acceptance/Part of life cycle, God, patient accepted death, just happens, expected it, experienced growth, other *Benefit-finding:* Growth in character, gained perspective, brought family together, positive support from others, others benefit, better it is over
Affleck & Tennen (1996) Fibromyalgia patients Affleck, Tennen, Croog, & Levine (1987) Heart-attack survivors	Authors distinguish between meaning-associated beliefs about benefit-finding and benefit-reminding as a coping strategy	*Benefit-finding:* Search for uplifting meaning from a threatening experience *Benefit-reminding:* More or less frequent use of benefit cognitions to alleviate impact of a stressful situation	*Benefit-finding:* "[. . .] do you see any positive benefits, gains, or advantages in the experience? If so what are they?" (Affleck et al., 1987, p. 31) *Benefit-reminding:* Participants rate how much they "reminded [themselves] of some of the benefits that come from living with their chronic pain" (Affleck & Tennen, 1996, p. 915)	*Benefit-finding* (Affleck et al., 1987): Change in philosophy of life/values/religious views, change in family life and family relationships, insight into need for avoiding stress and conflict, change in mode of life to increase enjoyment, learn value of health behavior, increased longevity

In a newer study, Bower, Kemeny, Taylor, and Fahey (1998) identified 40 HIV seropositive men who recently had experienced the loss of a close friend or partner to AIDS. Finding meaning was assessed qualitatively in an extensive interview procedure. The authors state that individuals who reported having found meaning in the loss of a friend or loved one were maintaining relatively high levels of CD4 T helper cells (indicators of immune functioning) and were less likely to die over the follow-up period (Bower et al., 1998).

Evidence suggests that reintegrating the understanding of the event into a broader framework may in few instances either take very long, or it will not be achieved at all. In a study with bereaved persons having lost a spouse or child to violent death, Lehman, Wortman, and Williams (1987) found evidence for failed assimilation efforts even after four to seven years post-loss. They report that even many years after the traumatic loss, families struggled with reoccurring memories, thoughts, or mental pictures of the deceased. Also, the majority of families had by this time not found meaning in what had happened, a finding that points to the possibility that closure through integration of an event into a meaningful framework had not been achieved.

The number of findings leading to contradictory evidence concerning the adaptational value of finding meaning in a stressful incident inspired researchers to subdivide the construct further (Affleck & Tennen, 1996; Davis et al., 1998). In a prospective study with relatives of terminally ill patients, Davis et al. (1998) found evidence pointing to a two-dimensional construal of meaning as "sense-making" and "benefit-finding"(see Table 25.1). Sense-making relates to finding an explanation for what happened, for instance in the case of a major illness, integrating it into existing schemata (or adjusting schemata), such as religion, knowledge about health, or antecedents–consequences of illness. Benefit–finding, on the other hand, is connected with finding meaning by taking into account positive implications of a negative event or the pursuit for the silver lining of adversity.

Affleck and Tennen (1996; Tennen & Affleck, 2002) emphasize the benefit-finding perspective in the search for meaning in the context of severe medical problems. In a study with heart attack survivors (Affleck et al., 1987), the authors found that eight years after the incident, initial benefit-finders were in significantly better cardiac health and were less likely to have suffered a subsequent heart attack. Also, they made an effort to distinguish between the belief about finding benefit following a crisis (benefit-finding) and a coping strategy as an intentional cognition or a behavioral attempt to manage a stressful encounter (benefit-reminding; Tennen & Affleck, 2002). Benefit-reminding as a coping strategy is conceptualized as an effortful, more or less frequent use of benefit cognitions to ease the stressful impact of a situation. In a study with fibromyalgia patients, an extensive self-monitoring method was used to assess patients' use of benefit-reminding as well as their symptoms and experiences. The data revealed significant individual differences in the use of benefit-reminding and its relation to reports of having found benefits in the experience. Also, within-subject analyses suggested that on benefit-reminding days, individuals were more likely to experience pleasurable mood, regardless of reported pain intensity.

Searching for meaning, thus, can be considered a broad category of positive coping, including situational and global meaning, benefit-finding, and benefit-reminding, among others. Empirical evidence attests to the fact that meaning and positive emotions help to restore an individual's world view and may build additional personal resources.

Assessment of Positive Coping

Coping has been measured mainly by the use of questionnaires, such as checklists or psychometric scales. In a review, Schwarzer and Schwarzer (1996) described 13 conventional inventories that were designed to assess numerous aspects of coping. These measures include various subscales to cover a broad area of coping behaviors, such as problem-solving, avoidance, seeking social support or information, denial, reappraisal, and others. One of the conclusions is that it is very difficult to measure coping in a satisfactory manner. Coping is extremely idiosyncratic and is multiply determined by situation and personality factors. Theory-based psychometric scales can only assess part of it. Experimental measurement approaches, in contrast, often remain at an individual and descriptive level, not allowing generalized conclusions for groups of individuals. We will address some basic measurement issues in the next section, but first we will give examples for the assessment of constructs described previously.

Approaches that try to tap innovative aspects of positive coping are (a) the mastery of future threats and challenges, as reflected by preventive or proactive coping, and (b) the search for meaning. *Preventive coping* aims at uncertain threatening events that may loom in the distant future. People accumulate resources and take general precautions to be protected against a variety of threats. A 10-item preventive coping subscale is included in the Proactive Coping Inventory (PCI; Greenglass et al., 1999). Typical items include, "I plan for future eventualities," "Before disaster strikes I am well-prepared for its consequences," and "I prepare for adverse events." Encouraging empirical evidence is available for the PCI (Greenglass, in press). It may be of advantage, however, to select more situation-specific items, such as, "I plan my day by making a to-do list," "My car does not run out of gas because I fill up earlier than necessary," "I set aside money for use in case of an emergency," or "I practice regular physical exercise to prevent ill health." These examples document that preventive coping is a common daily behavior for most people. However, whether an individual can be characterized as a typical "preventive coper" is a matter of degree. There also is a strong overlap with proactive coping, and often it is not immediately clear whether a particular behavior would count as being preventive or proactive. A final conclusion can be made only after determining whether the underlying appraisal has been a threat (preventive) or a challenge (proactive).

Proactive coping aims at uncertain challenging goals, and people accumulate resources and develop skills and strategies in their pursuit. The PCI includes the Proactive Coping subscale (see Appendix 25.1) that has been tested in various samples and is available in several languages. There are 14 items that form a unidimensional scale (see Appendix 25.1). It has satisfactory psychometric properties, and evidence for its validity is emerging. In several studies in Canada, Poland, and Germany, it has been found that proactive coping

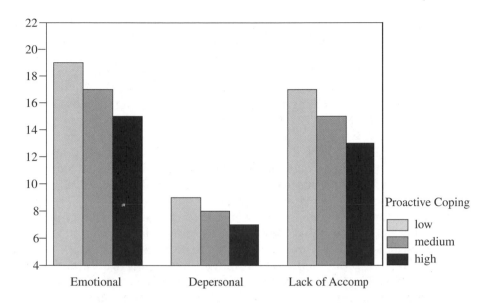

Figure 25.2. Relationship between proactive coping and burnout.

is positively correlated with perceived self-efficacy and negatively with job burnout in different professions (Greenglass, in press). In 316 German teachers, for example, its internal consistency was alpha = .86 (unpublished data). Correlations were r = .61 with perceived self-efficacy, r = .50 with self-regulation, and r = −.40 with procrastination. Job burnout was defined three-dimensionally in terms of emotional exhaustion, depersonalization, and lack of accomplishment (Maslach, Jackson, & Leiter, 1996). Burnout is a relevant construct for the validation because it should not be compatible with proactive coping. To illustrate the relationships, the sample was subdivided into low, medium, and high proactive teachers who were plotted against the three dimensions of burnout. Figure 25.2 displays a pattern of decreasing burnout with increasing levels of proactive coping.

Assessment of *meaning* in the coping process relies on qualitative approaches. Some of the reviewed theories and studies are summarized and presented together with applied qualitative operationalizations in Table 25.1. Additional measurement issues concerning the handling and quantification of narrative accounts will be briefly discussed in the following section.

Measurement Issues

Coping measurement is complicated by a number of conceptual issues, some of which pertain to the stability, generality, and dimensionality of coping (Perrez, 2001; Schwarzer & Schwarzer, 1996). Difficulties occur necessarily when an attempt is made to measure coping. The assessment of coping does not equal the assessment of most other constructs in psychology, in particular not the way personality is typically measured. Coping is highly situation-dependent, and it changes rapidly and unforeseeably as the stressful life encounter unfolds.

The assessment of coping can represent a detailed description of cognitions and behaviors of an individual dealing with a stressful encounter. This method does justice to the fact that coping is a process, and it allows the identification of contingencies between changing situations and changing actions, be it by time sampling or event sampling. For example, one can assess whether a person always applies and reapplies the same set of strategies or uses a broad range of tactics that are well-adapted to changing encounters. This idiographic approach is suitable for single cases in clinical settings, but it is not common in field research. Rather, the focus in empirical studies is on individual differences. Stability then refers to the pattern similarity of interindividual differences at multiple points in time. If, for example, some persons cope in a mastery-oriented manner, whereas others do so in a more meaning-oriented manner, and if this reoccurs at later observations, one is inclined to attribute stable coping preferences to these individuals. When we measure coping with standardized instruments, we therefore imply that people can be characterized by some preferred ways of coping with adversity and that they continue to apply the same kind of strategies over time. This dispositional implication helps to reduce the complexity of coping assessment, but it does so at a high price: It assumes that the uniqueness of a situation-specific coping response represents a negligible aspect.

Closely related to stability is another problem, namely the consistency of coping responses across different situations (generality). Do people apply the same strategy when they face an exam, the bereavement of a loved one, or an argument with their spouse? They may not show the *same* responses, but they may be characterized by a general tendency to select appropriate behaviors either from the class of avoidance or from the class of confrontation strategies. If all responses could be explained by the challenging events, this would reflect a pure situation determinism. In contrast, the person–situation interaction would suggest joint influences from person characteristics and situation characteristics. A moderate amount of generality implies that people construct a series of person-dependent strategies for a class of situations. The measurement of coping only can be fruitful under the assumptions that individuals generalize across situations and evoke a limited set of strategies that they reapply in different situations.

The debate about dispositional versus situational coping assessment was sparked by Stone and Neale (1984), who attempted to develop an instrument to assess daily coping for use in longitudinal studies. In a pilot study, individuals were asked how to handle a recent problem by responding to 87 coping items. Eight categories were established: (a) distraction, (b) situation redefinition, (c) direct action, (d) catharsis, (e) acceptance, (f) social support, (g) relaxation, and (h) religion. Because the psychometric properties repeatedly turned out to be unsatisfactory, the authors abandoned their intention to construct psychometric rating scales with multiple items and decided to apply the eight categories directly with an open-ended response format. Participants checked the appropriate categories and wrote down descriptions of their coping behaviors where applicable. The authors claim content validity for this measure and argue that this approach has advantages over traditional ones. In particular, they question the usefulness of internal consistency in coping measurement, of retrospective assessment, and of representing coping processes by a sum score. That Stone and Neale did not develop reliable and valid psychometric coping scales and that they resorted to a written structured interview can be considered as a blessing today because their article has sparked an ongoing debate about the merits of situation-oriented coping assessment (Tennen, Affleck, Armeli, & Carney, 2000).

The *meaning* construct in the context of stressful or traumatic life events has largely been assessed qualitatively (see Table 25.1). The interview approach seems more than appropriate given the challenges associated with assessing the search for meaning in very different life-event situations. Sommer and Baumeister (1998) suggest a list of guidelines derived from their own work that proved useful in this context. They suggest, first, careful consideration of at least one clear independent variable, for example by collecting first-person accounts from two study groups. Second, dichotomous yes–no coding schemes prove more reliable (higher interrater agreement) than continuous scales. Third, codings should follow clear guidelines (e.g., accounting for present as well as absent statement content in narratives). Fourth, they suggest that there should be a sufficient number of stories to code in each type (study group) to enhance statistical power. They recommend a minimum of 60 narratives in each group. Also, with shorter accounts, larger samples prove beneficial because lack of detail in narratives is associated with greater baseline rates of "no" codings. Fifth, it is often the case that a priori determined codings and hypotheses have to be supplemented with new coding categories derived from initial coding or reading of the narrative accounts. To avoid capitalizing on chance, Sommer and Baumeister recommended that findings based on ideas that emerged during the coding process be replicated. Sixth, authors suggest that one method of increasing the available sample is to ask participants to adopt two perspectives of an encounter, despite statistical problems associated with this method.

Future Developments

The field of coping is one of the most complex in psychology. Measurement cannot be better than the constructs that are supposed to be measured. The additional elaboration and differentiation of concepts need to precede any attempt at proper assessment. As an example for such a differentiation of concepts, we have chosen proactive coping theory (Aspinwall & Taylor, 1997; Schwarzer, 2000). The measurement of proactive behaviors, personal growth, positive reappraisals, and positive emotions in the context of stress adaptation should not remain at the level of psychometric scales, but it should account for changes within a particular coping episode.

Coping can be understood only when it is regarded as a process (Lazarus, 1991), which implies a longitudinal approach of measurement. However, it is not sufficient simply to select several points in time because the researcher cannot be certain about the optimal time window when significant changes take place. Therefore, a more continuous measurement is recommended. The closest to this suggestion is the daily process approach to measuring coping, commonly referred to as Experience Sampling Method (Tennen et al., 2000), where participants respond at least once a day when prompted by an ambulatory device. The main disadvantage of this method is its reactivity, which means that coping responses are artificially constructed because of the demands of a study design. But the overall approach appears promising. In the future, we can expect advances in the computerized simultaneous assessment under real-life conditions.

Appendix 25.1
Proactive Coping Scale

The following statements deal with reactions you may have to various situations. Indicate how true each of these statements is depending on how you feel about the situation. Do this by checking the most appropriate box.

In scoring responses, 1 is assigned to "not at all true," 2 to "barely true," 3 to "somewhat true," and 4 to "completely true."

1. I am a "take charge" person.
2. I try to let things work out on their own. (-)
3. After attaining a goal, I look for another, more challenging one.
4. I like challenges and beating the odds.
5. I visualize my dreams and try to achieve them.
6. Despite numerous setbacks, I usually succeed in getting what I want.
7. I try to pinpoint what I need to succeed.
8. I always try to find a way to work around obstacles; nothing really stops me.
9. I often see myself failing so I don't get my hopes up too high. (-)
10. When I apply for a position, I imagine myself filling it.
11. I turn obstacles into positive experiences.
12. If someone tells me I can't do something, you can be sure I will do it.
13. When I experience a problem, I take the initiative in resolving it.
14. When I have a problem, I usually see myself in a no-win situation. (-)

Note. (-) indicates reverse-item scoring. From the Proactive Coping Inventory (PCI; Greenglass et al., 1999)

References

Affleck, G., & Tennen, H. (1996). Construing benefits from adversity: Adaptational significance and dispositional underpinnings. *Journal of Personality, 64,* 899–922.

Affleck, G., Tennen, H., Croog, S., & Levine, S. (1987). Causal attribution, perceived benefits, and morbidity following a heart attack: An eight-year study. *Journal of Consulting and Clinical Psychology, 55,* 29–35.

Antonovsky, A. (1993). The structure and properties of the sense of coherence scale. *Social Sciences and Medicine, 36,* 725–733.

Aspinwall, L. G., & Taylor, S. E. (1997). A stitch in time: Self-regulation and proactive coping. *Psychological Bulletin, 121,* 417–436.

Bower, J. E., Kemeny, M. E., Taylor, S. E., & Fahey, J. L. (1998). Cognitive processing, discovery of meaning, CD4 decline, and AIDS-related mortality among bereaved HIV-seropositive men. *Journal of Consulting and Clinical Psychology, 66,* 979–986.

Brandtstädter, J. (1992). Personal control over development: Implications of self-efficacy. In R. Schwarzer (Ed.), *Self-efficacy: Thought control of action* (pp. 127–145). Washington, DC: Hemisphere.

Davis, C., Nolen-Hoeksema, S., & Larson, J. (1998). Making sense of loss and benefiting from the experience: Two construals of meaning. *Journal of Personality and Social Psychology, 75,* 561–574.

Folkman, S., & Lazarus, R. S. (1988). *Ways of Coping Questionnaire. Manual.* Palo Alto, CA: Consulting Psychologists Press.

Folkman, S., & Moskowitz, J. (2000). Positive affect and the other side of coping. *American Psychologist, 55,* 647–654.

Fredrickson, B. L. (2002). Positive emotions. In C. R. Snyder & S. J. Lopez (Eds.), *The handbook of positive psychology* (pp. 120–134). New York: Oxford University Press.

Greenglass, E. R. (in press). Proactive coping. In E. Frydenberg (Ed.), *Beyond coping: Meeting goals, visions and challenges.* Oxford: Oxford University Press.

Greenglass, E. R., Schwarzer, R., & Taubert, S. (1999). *The Proactive Coping Inventory (PCI): A multidimensional research instrument* [On-line publication]. Available at http://userpage.fu-berlin.de/ˌhealth/greenpci.htm

Janoff-Bulman, R. (1992). *Shattered assumptions: Toward a new psychology of trauma.* New York: Free Press.

Lazarus, R. S. (1991). *Emotion and adaptation.* New York: Oxford University Press.

Lazarus, R. S., & Folkman, S. (1984). *Stress, appraisal, and coping.* New York: Springer.

Lehman, D. R., Wortman, C. B., & Williams, A. F. (1987). Long-term effects of losing a spouse or child in a motor vehicle crash. *Journal of Personality and Social Psychology, 52,* 218–231.

Maslach, C., Jackson, S. E., & Leiter, M. P. (1996). *Maslach Burnout Inventory Manual* (3rd ed.). Palo Alto, CA: Consulting Psychologists Press.

Moskowitz, J. T., Folkman, S., Collette, L., & Vittinghoff, E. (1996). Coping and mood during AIDS-related caregiving and bereavement. *Annals of Behavioral Medicine, 18,* 49–57.

Perrez, M. (2001). Coping assessment. In N. J. Smelser & P. B. Baltes (Eds.), *The international encyclopedia of the social and behavioral sciences* (pp. 2766–2770). Oxford: Elsevier.

Rothbaum, F., Weisz, J. R., & Snyder, S. (1982). Changing the world and changing the self: A two-process model of perceived control. *Journal of Personality and Social Psychology, 42,* 5–37.

Ryff, C. D., & Singer, B. (1998). The role of purpose in life and personal growth in positive human health. In P. T. Wong & P. Fry (Eds.), *The human quest for meaning* (pp. 213–235). Mahwah, NJ: Erlbaum.

Schwarzer, R. (Ed.). (1992). *Self-efficacy: Thought control of action.* Washington, DC: Hemisphere.

Schwarzer, R. (1999). Self-regulatory processes in the adoption and maintenance of health behaviors. The role of optimism, goals, and threats. *Journal of Health Psychology, 4,* 115–127.

Schwarzer, R. (2000). Manage stress at work through preventive and proactive coping. In E. A. Locke (Ed.), *The Blackwell handbook of principles of organizational behavior* (pp. 342–355). Oxford: Blackwell.

Schwarzer, R. (2001). Social-cognitive factors in changing health-related behavior. *Current Directions in Psychological Science, 10,* 47–51.

Schwarzer, R., & Renner, B. (2000). Social-cognitive predictors of health behavior: Action self-efficacy and coping self-efficacy. *Health Psychology, 19,* 487–495.

Schwarzer, R., & Schwarzer, C. (1996). A critical survey of coping instruments. In M. Zeidner & N. S. Endler (Eds.), *Handbook of coping: Theory, research and applications* (pp. 107–132). New York: Wiley.

Selye, H. (1974). *Stress without distress.* New York: J. B. Lippincott.

Snyder, C. R. (1994). *The psychology of hope. You can get there from here.* New York: Free Press.

Snyder, C. R. (Ed.). (1999). *Coping: The psychology of what works.* New York: Oxford University Press.

Snyder, C. R., & Lopez, S. J. (Eds.). (2002). *The handbook of positive psychology.* New York: Oxford University Press.

Sommer, K. L., & Baumeister, R. F. (1998). The construction of meaning from life events: Empirical studies of personal narratives. In P. T. Wong & P. Fry (Eds.), *The human quest for meaning* (pp. 143–161). Mahwah, NJ: Erlbaum.

Stone, A. A., & Neale, J. M. (1984). New measure of daily coping: Development and preliminary results. *Journal of Personality and Social Psychology, 46,* 892–906.

Taylor, S. E. (1983). Adjustment to threatening events: A theory of cognitive adaptation. *American Psychologist, 38,* 1161–1173.

Tennen, H., & Affleck, G. (2002). Benefit-finding and benefit-reminding. In C. R. Snyder & S. J. Lopez (Eds.), *The handbook of positive psychology* (pp. 584–597). New York: Oxford University Press.

Tennen, H., Affleck, G., Armeli, S., & Carney, M. A. (2000). A daily process approach to coping. *American Psychologist, 55,* 626–636.

Wong, P. T., & Fry, P. (Eds.). (1998). *The human quest for meaning.* Mahwah, NJ: Erlbaum.

Wortman, C. B., Silver, R. C., & Kessler, R. C. (1993). The meaning of loss and adjustment to bereavement. In M. S. Stroebe, W. Stroebe, & R. O. Hansson (Eds.), *Bereavement: A source book of research and intervention* (pp. 349–366). London: Cambridge University Press.

26

The Measurement and Utility of Adult Subjective Well-Being

Corey L. M. Keyes and Jeana L. Magyar-Moe

> It is not enough to know how man reacts: we must know how he feels, how he sees his world, . . . why he lives, what he fears, for what he would be willing to die. Such questions of existence must be put to man directly.— Gordon Allport (quoted in Severin, 1965, p. 42).

Social scientists have devised many tools to tap people's perceptions of their existence—their subjective view of their life experience. From this, two general lines of well-being research have evolved. Evaluations of the degree of positive feelings (e.g., happiness) experienced and of perceptions (e.g., satisfaction) of one's life overall constitute the first line of research, the examination of *emotional well-being* (Diener, Suh, Lucas, & Smith, 1999; Gurin, Veroff, & Feld, 1960). The second stream of well-being research specifies dimensions of *positive functioning* in terms of psychological well-being (Jahoda, 1958; Keyes, 1998; Ryff, 1989b; Ryff & Keyes, 1995) and social well-being (Keyes, 1998). Overall, then, subjective well-being consists of two broad domains: emotional well-being and positive functioning (cf. Ryan & Deci, 2001; Waterman, 1993). These two domains and the quality of their measures will be reviewed in this chapter. Because most research on subjective well-being focuses on individuals aged 18 or older, this chapter focuses on well-being in adults.[1] Moreover, this chapter examines the nature of the "utility" of subjective well-being in terms of its association with workplace productivity and health outcomes.

Emotional Well-Being

Emotional well-being is a specific dimension of subjective well-being that consists of perceptions of avowed happiness and satisfaction with life and the

---

[1] Scales of emotional well-being and life satisfaction (see, e.g., Bender, 1997; McCullough, Huebner, & Laughlin, 2000) have been adapted for use in children and adolescents. To date, there

balance of positive to negative affects. Whereas happiness is based on spontaneous reflections of pleasant and unpleasant feelings in one's immediate experience, life satisfaction represents a long-term assessment of one's life.

The threefold structure of emotional well-being, consisting of life satisfaction, positive affect, and negative affect, has been confirmed in numerous studies (e.g., Bryant & Veroff, 1982; Lucas, Diener, & Suh, 1996; Shmotkin, 1998). The debate over the structure of positive and negative affect, however, continues to this day and creates some confusion around the emotional well-being construct (see Green & Salovey, 1999; Russell & Carroll, 1999; Tellegen, Watson, & Clark, 1999a, 1999b; and Watson & Tellegen, 1999, for several recent scholarly debates on this topic). Are positive and negative affect opposite ends of a single continuum (i.e., highly correlated), or are these feelings relatively independent (i.e., modestly correlated) dimensions of well-being? Evidence supports both the unidimensional (Feldman-Barrett & Russell, 1998; Russell & Carroll, 1999) *and* the bidimensional (Diener & Emmons, 1985) models.[2] Nevertheless, the coupling of satisfaction and affect serves as a meaningful and measurable conceptualization of well-being.

Measures

Available single-item measures of life satisfaction are adaptations of Cantril's (1965) Self-Anchoring scale, which asks respondents to "rate their life overall

---

has been no research on the adaptation of measures of positive functioning for use with children and youth.

[2] Regarding the inconclusiveness of positive and negative affect dimensionality findings, contact the first author of this chapter for a detailed discussion of orthogonality. Some of these findings regarding the dimensionality of positive and negative affect also may be explained according to the context-dependence theory of affects (Zautra, Potter, & Reich, 1997). When individuals are experiencing high levels of demands or are distressed, affective states should correlate strongly and negatively such that one who feels high negative affect concurrently feels little to no positive affect. As such, the structure of emotions becomes unidimensional. When not stressed, or when in a state of equilibrium, individuals' affective states tend to correlate modestly such that one who feels high levels of positive affect also may report feelings of negative affect of varying intensity at the same time. Thus, the structure of emotions becomes bidimensional. Indeed, Zautra and colleagues (1997) found a significantly larger negative correlation of positive and negative affect among individuals who had experienced a high number of life events in the past week compared with those who had experienced few life events in the past week. In addition, the self-theory of subjective change and mental health (Keyes & Ryff, 2000) suggests that perceived personal changes are distressing, whereas the perception of remaining the same person is conducive to mental health.

The self-theory of subjective change and mental health (Keyes & Ryff, 2000) also provides a plausible explanation regarding the dimensionality of positive and negative affect. According to this theory, evidence for unidimensional and bidimensional models of affect depends on individuals' perceived levels of personal change. More specifically, the crux of this self-theory is that people evaluate perceived personal change against their self-standards to decide whether the information is good, bad, or a mixture of both. The perception of remaining the same should be most desirable because it coincides with the desire for self-consistency and satisfies the organismic desire for equilibrium. The perception of decline should be least desirable because it signals inconsistency over time, and this information is also unflattering, thereby violating both the self-consistency and self-enhancement standards of this model. Finally, perceived improvement should be evaluated

these days" on a scale from 0 to 10, where 0 = "worst possible life overall" and 10 = "the best possible life overall." Variants of Cantril's measure have been used extensively and have been applied to the measurement of avowed happiness with life (Andrews & Withey, 1976). Multi-item scales of life satisfaction and happiness also have been developed and used extensively (see Diener, 1984, p. 546; see also chapter 13, this volume, for a list of measures of positive affect and emotional well-being).

Most positive and negative affect measures tap the frequency with which a respondent reports experiencing the symptoms of these affects. For example, individuals often are asked to indicate how much of the time during the past 30 days they have felt six types of negative and six types of positive indicators of affect: "all," "most," "some," "a little," or "none of the time." Symptoms of negative affect usually include feeling (a) so sad nothing could cheer you up; (b) nervous; (c) restless or fidgety; (d) hopeless; (e) that everything was an effort; and (f) worthless. Symptoms of positive affect usually involve feeling (a) cheerful; (b) in good spirits; (c) extremely happy; (d) calm and peaceful; (e) satisfied; and (f) full of life.

Estimates of internal reliability of the multi-item scales of life satisfaction (Diener, 1993; Diener, Emmons, Larsen, & Griffin, 1985; Pavot & Diener, 1993) and positive and negative affect (see, e.g., Mroczek & Kolarz, 1998) usually exceed .80; single-item indicators of well-being are less reliable. In addition, researchers have found that social desirability is not a major confound in the well-being literature and that ratings of life satisfaction tend to be more stable than reports of positive and negative affect (Diener, 1984; Larsen, Diener, & Emmons, 1985).

Positive Functioning

Positive functioning consists of the multidimensional constructs of psychological well-being and social well-being (Keyes, 1998; Ryff, 1989a). Like emotional well-being, the focus of psychological well-being remains at the individual level, whereas relations with others and the environment are the primary aims of social well-being. Ryff's (1989a) model of psychological well-being and Keyes's (1998) model of social well-being are delineated in the following sections.

Psychological Well-Being

A variety of concepts from personality, developmental, and clinical psychology has been synthesized as criteria of mental health (Jahoda, 1958) and psychological well-being (Ryff, 1989a). Elements of psychological well-being are descended from the Aristotelian theme of *eudaimonia,* which suggests that the highest of all goods achievable by human action is happiness derived from lifelong conduct aimed at self-development (Waterman, 1993). Thus, many aspects of

---

as both good and bad because the information is personally flattering and self-enhancing; however, the feeling of improvement violates the self-consistency standard.

psychological well-being are personified in concepts of self-actualization (Maslow, 1968), full functioning (Rogers, 1961), individuation (Jung, 1933; Von Franz, 1964), maturity (Allport, 1961), and successful resolution of adult developmental stages and tasks (Erikson, 1959; Neugarten, 1973).

Ryff (1989a) has purported that the preceding positive psychological perspectives can be integrated into a multidimensional model of psychological well-being. Each of the six dimensions of psychological well-being indicates the challenges that individuals encounter as they strive to function fully and realize their unique talents (see Keyes & Ryff, 1999; Ryff, 1989a, 1989b; Ryff & Keyes, 1995). Taken together, the six dimensions encompass a breadth of wellness that includes positive evaluation of oneself and one's past life, a sense of continued growth and development as a person, the belief that one's life is purposeful and meaningful, the possession of quality relations with others, the capacity to manage effectively one's life and surrounding world, and a sense of self-determination (Ryff & Keyes, 1995). (See Table 26.1 for detailed definitions of the distinct wellness dimensions of Ryff's (1989a) psychological well-being model.

Social Well-Being

Whereas psychological well-being is conceptualized as a primarily private phenomenon that is focused on the challenges encountered by adults in their private lives, social well-being represents a primarily public phenomenon focused on the social tasks encountered by adults in their social structures and communities. Social well-being consists of five elements that, together, indicate whether and to what degree individuals are functioning well in their social world (e.g., as neighbors, as coworkers, and as citizens; Keyes, 1998; Keyes & Shapiro, in press).

Social wellness originates in the classic themes of anomie and alienation (Mirowsky & Ross, 1989; Seeman, 1959). The issue of solidarity is carried forward from classic sociology to queries about the unity and sympathies of individuals with society. Drawing on these theoretical roots, Keyes (1998) developed multiple operational dimensions of social well-being that are defined in Table 26.1. Each dimension of social wellness represents challenges that people face as social beings.

The Structure and Measurement of Subjective Well-Being

Taken together, *emotional well-being* and *positive functioning* converge to create a comprehensive model of *subjective well-being* that takes into consideration multiple aspects of both the individual and his or her functioning in society. In total, subjective well-being includes elements of perceived happiness and life satisfaction, the balance of positive to negative affects, psychological well-being, and social well-being.

Table 26.2 contains the major domains of subjective well-being and examples of scale items used in the 1995 MacArthur Foundation national study of

Table 26.1.   Dimensions of Psychological and Social Well-Being Models

Dimensions of Ryff's Psychological Well-Being Model	Dimensions of Keyes's Social Well-Being Model
Self-acceptance: The criterion toward which adults must strive in order to feel good about themselves. Such self-acceptance is characterized by a positive attitude toward the self and acknowledging and accepting multiple aspects of self, including unpleasant personal aspects. In addition, self-acceptance includes positive feelings about past life.	*Social integration:* The evaluation of the quality of one's relationship to society and community. Integration is therefore the extent to which people feel they have something in common with others who constitute their social reality (e.g., their neighborhood), as well as the degree to which they feel that they belong to their communities and society.
Positive relations with others: Consists of the ability to cultivate and the presence of warm, trusting, intimate relationships with others. Concern for the welfare of others, and the ability to empathize, cooperate, and compromise all are aspects of this wellness dimension.	*Social contribution:* The evaluation of one's value to society. It includes the belief that one is a vital member of society, with something of value to give to the world.
Autonomy: Reflects the seeking of self-determination and personal authority or independence in a society that sometimes compels obedience and compliance. The abilities to resist social pressures so as to think or behave in certain ways, and to guide and evaluate behavior based on internalized standards and values, are crucial in this domain.	*Social coherence:* The perception of the quality, organization, and operation of the social world, and it includes a concern for knowing about the world. Social coherence is analogous to meaningfulness in life (Mirowsky & Ross 1989; Seeman 1959), and involves appraisals that society is discernible, sensible, and predictable.
Environmental mastery: Includes the ability to manage everyday affairs, to control a complex array of external activities, to make effective use of surrounding opportunities, and to choose or create contexts suitable to personal needs. A sense of mastery results when individuals recognize personal needs and desires and also feel capable of and permitted to take an active role in getting what they need from their environments.	*Social acceptance:* The construal of society through the character and qualities of other people as a generalized category. Individuals must function in a public arena that consists primarily of strangers. Individuals who illustrate social acceptance trust others, think that others are capable of kindness, and believe that people can be industrious. Socially accepting people hold favorable views of human nature and feel comfortable with others.
Purpose in life: Consists of one's aims and objectives for living, including the presence of life goals and a sense of directedness. Those with high purpose in life see their daily lives as fulfilling a direction and purpose and therefore view their present and past life as meaningful.	*Social actualization:* The evaluation of the potential and the trajectory of society. This is the belief in the evolution of society and the sense that society has potential that is being realized through its institutions and citizens.
Personal growth: Reflects the continuous pursuit of existing skills, talents, and opportunities for personal development and for realizing one's potential. In addition, personal growth includes the capacity to remain open to experience and to identify challenges in a variety of circumstances.	

successful midlife (MIDUS; see Keyes, 1998, and Mroczek & Kolarz, 1998, for descriptions of the sample and well-being measures). The MIDUS, as well as its measures, is exemplary because it is the only national study to have measured all facets of subjective well-being—namely emotional, psychological, and social well-being. It therefore is a model for research in this field and provides a comprehensive source for current and future studies of subjective well-being.

Three-item scales of psychological well-being and social well-being (see Ryff, 1989b, for the full 20-item scales of psychological well-being and Keyes, 1998, for the full 10-item scales of social well-being) are used in large national studies that often include an extensive assessment schedule (Ryff & Keyes, 1995). These reduced-item scales possess moderate internal reliabilities that range from .40 to .70. When the scales are summed to form scales of overall psychological well-being and overall social well-being, the internal reliabilities are very good (.80 or higher; see Keyes & Ryff, 1998).

Several studies using community and nationally representative samples have supported the theories of the factor structure of social and psychological well-being. Confirmatory factor models have revealed that the proposed five-factor conceptualization of social well-being is the best fitting model (Keyes, 1998), and the proposed six-factor theory of psychological well-being is the best fitting model (Ryff & Keyes, 1995). Moreover, elements of positive functioning (i.e., social and psychological well-being) are empirically distinct. The scales of social and psychological well-being correlated as high as .44, and exploratory factor analysis revealed two correlated ($r = .34$) factors with the scales of social well-being loading on a separate factor from the items measuring happiness, satisfaction, and the overall scale of psychological well-being (Keyes, 1996).

Measures of social well-being also are factorially distinct from traditional measures (happiness and satisfaction) of emotional well-being (Keyes, 1996). In addition, measures of emotional well-being (positive and negative affect, life satisfaction) are factorially distinct from measures of psychological well-being (Keyes, Shmotkin, & Ryff, 2002). In fact, McGregor and Little's (1998) factor analysis yielded two distinct factors that reveal an underlying emotional factor (including depression, positive affect, and life satisfaction) and an underlying psychological functioning factor (including four of the psychological well-being scales: personal growth, purpose in life, positive relations with others, and autonomy).

The scales of social well-being correlated around −.30 with a measure of dysphoric symptoms (Keyes, 1998). Keyes and Lopez's (2002) review also reported an average correlation of the scales of psychological well-being with standard measures of depression (i.e., the Center for Epidemiologic Studies–Depressed Mood scale [CES–D; Radloff, 1977] and the Zung [1965] Self-Rating Depression scale) around −.50, whereas measures of life satisfaction and quality of life correlated on average around −.40 with these depression scales. Confirmatory factor analyses of the CES–D subscales and the psychological well-being scales in the United States (as well as South Korea) have shown that a two-factor model consisting of a mental illness and a mental health latent factor provided the best fit to the data (Keyes, Ryff, & Lee, 2002). In that same study, the overall CES–D and psychological well-being scales correlated −.68 in the United States.

Table 26.2. Conception and Operationalization of Elements of Psychological, Social, and Emotional Well-Being From the MacArthur Foundation's Successful Midlife (MIDUS) National Study Conducted in 1995

Psychological well-being	Social well-being	Emotional well-being
Self-acceptance: Possess positive attitude toward the self; acknowledge and accept multiple aspects of self; feel positive about past life. • *In many ways, I feel disappointed about my achievements in life* (-)	**Social acceptance:** Have positive attitudes toward people; acknowledge others and generally accept people, despite others' sometimes complex and perplexing behavior. • *People who do a favor expect nothing in return.*	**Positive affect:** Experience symptoms that suggest enthusiasm, joy, and happiness for life. • *During the last 30 days, how much of the time did you feel cheerful; in good spirits; extremely happy; calm and peaceful; satisfied; and full of life?*[a]
Personal growth: Have feelings of continued development and potential and are open to new experience; feel increasingly knowledgeable and effective. • *I think it is important to have new experiences that challenge how I think about myself and the world.*	**Social actualization:** Care about and believe society is evolving positively; think society has potential to grow positively; think self-society is realizing potential. • *The world is becoming a better place for everyone.*	**Negative affect:** Absence of symptoms that suggest that life is undesirable and unpleasant. • *During the last 30 days, how much of the time did you feel so sad nothing could cheer you up; nervous; restless or fidgety; hopeless; that everything was an effort; worthless?*[a]
Purpose in life: Have goals and a sense of direction in life; past life is meaningful; hold beliefs that give purpose to life. • *I live life one day at a time and don't really think about the future.* (-)	**Social contribution:** Feel they have something valuable to give to society and to society; think their daily activities are valued by their community. • *I have something valuable to give to the world.*	**Life satisfaction:** Is a sense of contentment, peace, and satisfaction from small discrepancies between wants and needs with accomplishments and attainments. • *During the past 30 days, how much of the time did you feel satisfied; full of life?*[a] • *Overall these days, how satisfied are you with your life? (0–10, where 0 = terrible and 10 = delighted)* • *Satisfaction may be measured in life domains such as work, home, neighborhood, health, intimacy, finances, and parenting or it is measured globally (see the Satisfaction with Life scale, Diener et al., 1985).*

(continued)

Table 26.2. (continued)

Psychological well-being	Social well-being	Emotional well-being
Environmental mastery: Feel competent and able to manage a complex environment; choose or create personally-suitable community. • *The demands of everyday life often get me down.* (-)	**Social coherence:** See a social world that is intelligible, logical, and predictable; care about and are interested in society and contexts. • *I cannot make sense of what's going on in the world.* (-)	**Happiness:** Having a general feeling and experience of pleasure, contentment, and joy. • *Overall these days how happy are you with your life*[b] • *How frequently have you felt (joy, pleasure, happiness) in the past week, month, or year?*
Autonomy: Are self-determining, independent, and regulate internally; resist social pressures to think and act in certain ways; evaluate self by personal standards. • *I have confidence in my own opinions, even if they are different from the way most other people think.*	**Social integration:** Feel part of community; think they belong, feel supported, and share commonalities with community. • *I don't feel I belong to anything I'd call a community.* (-)	
Positive relations with others: Have warm, satisfying, trusting relationships; are concerned about others' welfare; capable of strong empathy, affection, and intimacy; understand give-and-take of human relationships. • *Maintaining close relationships has been difficult and frustrating for me.* (-)		

[a]Indicates response range from all the time (1), most the time (2), some of the time (3), a little of the time (4), none of the time (5).
[b]Indicates response range from worst possible situation (0) to best possible situation (10).

Note. A negative sign in parenthesis indicates that the item is reverse scored. Response options range from strongly disagree (1), moderately disagree (2), or slightly disagree (3), to neither agree nor disagree (4), slightly agree (5), moderately agree (6), or strongly agree (7).

The Utility of Subjective Well-Being

Since Aristotle, well-being—particularly happiness—has been deemed a *summum bonum* of life. In other words, as one of life's highest goods, well-being is an end rather than a means in life, because its consummation could quench desire and motivation and its accomplishment could render individuals complacent and unproductive. From this perspective, the utility of well-being is that it is the proverbial carrot at the end of life's stick that maintains individuals' motivations to be productive and ethical citizens. Alternatively, well-being may be conceptualized as a means rather than solely an end in life. If the objective of life is the process of living a healthy and productive life, then well-being may unleash human potential in terms of creativity, productivity, and community involvement.

Regarding the status of well-being, social scientific evidence suggests that well-being is a means to a better and more productive life. The elements of subjective well-being may contribute to quality adjusted life years (QALYs).[3] The utility of subjective well-being and reasons to work toward the enhancement of this positive state of functioning across some of life's domains follows. Specifically, the role of subjective well-being in relation to work productivity and physical and mental health status is addressed.

Work

A small but growing body of research suggests that facets of well-being are associated with a host of positive business unit outcomes. Employees who report more satisfaction with life and their jobs are more cooperative and more helpful to their colleagues, are more punctual and time efficient, show up for more days of work, and stay with a company longer than dissatisfied employees (Spector, 1997). Investigation of the happy–productive worker clearly links emotional well-being with management evaluations of work performance. Employees who report experiencing a greater balance of positive emotional symptoms over negative emotional symptoms received higher performance ratings from supervisors than employees who report feeling more negative than positive symptoms of emotion (Wright & Bonett, 1997; Wright & Cropanzano, 2000).

Meta-analyses of the relations between employee satisfaction with their workplace and their perceptions of personal development at and through work (i.e., whether they have close friendships at work) are reliably correlated with positive business-level outcomes. That is, businesses with more employees who have high levels of employee well-being also tend to report greater customer

---

[3] In the Global Burden of Disease study (Murray & Lopez, 1996) unipolar depression ranked second only to ischemic heart disease as the most potent cause of reduced healthy years of life for adults of all ages. Furthermore, unipolar depression was the leading cause of disability life years among adults under the ages of 44 in developed and developing countries. Depression reduces productivity in society, amounting to billions in costs through health care and employment absence (Keyes & Lopez, 2002). Moreover, mood disorders are associated with nearly a third of all suicides (Rebellon, Brown, & Keyes, 2000; U.S. Department of Health and Human Services, 1998).

satisfaction and loyalty, greater profitability, more productivity, and lower rates of turnover (Harter & Schmidt, 2000; Harter, Schmidt, & Keyes, in press; Keyes, Hysom, & Lupo, 2000). Utility analyses conservatively estimate that companies with the most employees with high levels of well-being report dramatically higher monetary returns than companies in the lowest quartile of employee well-being (Harter & Schmidt, 2000; Harter et al., in press). Companies such as the Gallup Organization are developing techniques for promoting well-being in the workplace—for example, through the design and implementation of a strengths-based approach to business and management (see Buckingham & Clifton, 2001; Buckingham & Coffman, 1999; Clifton & Nelson, 1996), suggesting the potential for productive collaborations between employers and employees.

Health

Subjective well-being also may be a protective factor against physical illness in older adults (Ostir, Markides, Black, & Goodwin, 2000; see also Penninx et al., 1998). In a sample of Hispanic adults between the ages of 65 and 99 who had no limitations of daily life at the start of the study, Ostir and colleagues (2000) found that adults with high emotional well-being were half as likely as adults with low emotional well-being to have died or to have acquired limitations of activities of daily life two years later. These results were found even when controlling for sociodemographic variables, functional physical status, lifestyle indicators (i.e., smoking and drinking), and negative affect scores at baseline.

The incidence of mood disorders (Lewinsohn, Redner, & Seeley, 1991), and thereby the sequelae of depression such as suicide (Rebellon, Brown, & Keyes, 2000), may be reduced by the presence of subjective well-being. Because symptoms of depression (e.g., CES–D scale) and measures of subjective well-being are correlated but lie along independent axes (Keyes & Lopez, 2002), the absence of elements of well-being may be a risk factor for mental illness.

Low levels of subjective well-being could increase the risk for suicide. Weerasinnghe and Tepperman (1994) stated they could not locate a single study that had directly investigated the relationship of perceived happiness with suicide. The same authors were able to identify, however, several factors (marriage, religion, and employment) that promote happiness as well as to reduce the risk of suicide. Thus, as a potential risk factor for mood disorders, low-level well-being also may be an indirect risk factor for suicide. Low levels of social well-being, such as low social integration and low social contribution, also may prove to be direct risk factors for suicide (see Rebellon et al., 2000). A longitudinal study of a cohort of twins in Finland revealed that low life satisfaction was a causal predictor of suicide over a 20-year period (Koivumaa-Honkanen et al., 2001). Life satisfaction was measured as a composite of the following items: perceived interest in life, happiness with life, ease of living, and feelings of loneliness. After controling for sociodemographic variables, health status, health habits, and physical activity, the authors found that low levels of life satisfaction place men at a very high risk of suicide, relative to men who had higher levels of satisfaction with their lives.

Because low levels of well-being have been linked with negative health outcomes, it seems likely that the promotion of well-being may increase positive health outcomes and prevent the rapidity and prevalence of depression relapse following treatment (Keyes & Lopez, 2002). Unfortunately, as many as 70% of patients with unipolar depression relapse within six months of symptom remission (Ramana et al., 1995), and reduction of the rate of relapse only has partially been achieved via a continuation phase of therapy, during which patients are treated for a period of months following the initial remission of symptoms (U.S. Department of Health and Human Services, 1999). Alternatively, recent research by Fava suggests that use of well-being therapy (based on Ryff's [1989a] psychological well-being model), which seeks to promote psychological well-being during the residual phase of depression remission, may significantly reduce the relapse rate (Fava, 1999; Fava, Rafanelli, Grandi, Conti, & Belluardo, 1999).

Conclusion

One way to identify whether individuals are living well is to ask them. Subjective well-being is individuals' assessment of their lives. Research suggests that subjective well-being is multifactorial and multidimensional. It entails individuals' emotional assessments and reactions to their lives, as well as their cognitive assessments of their functioning in life.

Emotional well-being has been measured as the balance of positive to negative affect, avowed life satisfaction, and avowed happiness with life. *Positive functioning* has been measured as psychological well-being and social well-being. The dimensions of personal growth, purpose in life, positive relations with others, self-acceptance, environmental mastery, and autonomy constitute psychological well-being and social integration, social coherence, social acceptance, social actualization, and social contribution are the components of social well-being.

The evidence reviewed in this chapter indicated that there are internally reliable and accurate measures of emotional well-being, of psychological well-being, and of social well-being. Although research documents a consistent dimensional structure within each domain of subjective well-being, there has been very little research on the overall measurement structure of subjective well-being.

A proposal in this chapter is that subjective well-being may possess social utility. Measures of business profitability, productivity, and employee retention have increased as the level of employee well-being increased (Harter et al., in press). Levels of emotional well-being in older adults also have been shown to protect against mortality and the onset of physical disability (Ostir et al., 2000). Subjective well-being in its trait-like form may be implicated in the expression and experience of emotional states that facilitate and improve cognition and immune system function (Fredrickson, 1998; Salovey, Rothman, Detweiler, & Steward, 2000). There also is some evidence that low levels of subjective well-being may put individuals at risk for depression (Lewinsohn et al., 1991) and indirect evidence that low well-being places people at risk for suicide (Weera-sinnghe & Tepperman, 1994).

Studies show that subjective well-being also is associated with civic responsibility, the provision of emotional and material supports to more people, higher levels of generativity (i.e., intergenerational transmission of skills and resources), and local community involvement and volunteering (Keyes, 1996; Keyes & Ryff, 1998). As a consequence, well-being may be a result of, or a cause of, the feelings (i.e., social responsibility) and behaviors (volunteering) that generate social capital. Social capital consists of normative social obligations, feelings of trust, and social relationships bound by reciprocity. The ingredients of social capital help communities and organizations to arrive at shared objectives and then implement and achieve those objectives (see Coleman, 1988).

Although it is clear that subjective well-being can be measured reliably and accurately, the social utility of positive assessment remains blurred. Future research on the measurement of subjective well-being must take seriously the assessment of its social and economic utility among this nation's adults as well as its youth.

References

Allport, G. W. (1961). *Pattern and growth in personality*. New York: Holt, Rinehart & Winston.

Andrews, F. M., & Withey, S. B. (1976). *Social indicators of well-being: Americans' perceptions of life quality*. New York: Plenum Press.

Bender, T. A. (1997). Assessment of subjective well-being during childhood and adolescence. In G. D. Phye (Ed.), *Handbook of classroom assessment*. San Diego, CA: Academic Press.

Bryant, F. B., & Veroff, J. (1982). The structure of psychological well-being: A sociohistorical analysis. *Journal of Personality and Social Psychology, 43,* 653–673.

Buckingham, M., & Clifton, D. O. (2001). *Now, discover your strengths*. New York: The Free Press.

Buckingham, M., & Coffman, C. (1999). *First, break all the rules*. New York: Simon & Schuster.

Cantril, H. (1965). *The pattern of human concerns*. New Brunswick, NJ: Rutgers University Press.

Clifton, D. O., & Nelson, P. (1996). *Soar with your strengths*. New York: Dell.

Coleman, J. (1988). Social capital in the creation of human capital. *American Journal of Sociology, 94,* 95–120.

Diener, E. (1984). Subjective well-being. *Psychological Bulletin, 95,* 542–575.

Diener, E. (1993). Assessing subjective well-being: Progress and opportunities. *Social Indicators Research, 31,* 103–157.

Diener, E., & Emmons, R. A. (1985). The independence of positive and negative affect. *Journal of Personality and Social Psychology, 47,* 1105–1117.

Diener, E., Emmons, R. A., Larsen, R. J., & Griffin, S. (1985). The satisfaction with life scale. *Journal of Personality Assessment, 49,* 71–75.

Diener, E., Suh, E. M., Lucas, R. E., & Smith, H. L. (1999). Subjective well-being: Three decades of progress. *Psychological Bulletin, 125,* 276–302.

Erikson, E. (1959). Identity and the life cycle. *Psychological Issues, 1,* 18–164.

Fava, G. A. (1999). Well-being therapy: Conceptual and technical issues. *Psychotherapy and Psychosomatics, 68,* 171–179.

Fava, G. A., Rafanelli, C., Grandi, S., Conti, S., & Belluardo, P. (1999). Prevention of recurrent depression with cognitive behavioral therapy. *Archives of General Psychiatry, 56*(5), 479–480.

Feldman-Barrett, L., & Russell, J. A. (1998). Independence and bipolarity in the structure of current affect. *Journal of Personality and Social Psychology, 74,* 967–984.

Green, D. P., & Salovey, P. (1999). In what sense are positive and negative affect independent? A reply to Tellegen, Watson, and Clark. *Psychological Science, 10,* 304–306.

Gurin, G., Veroff, J., & Feld, S. (1960). *Americans view their mental health.* New York: Basic Books.

Harter, J. K., & Schmidt, F. L. (2000). Validation of a performance-related and actionable management tool: A meta-analysis and utility analysis. *Gallup Technical Report.* Lincoln, NE: Gallup Organization.

Harter, J. K., Schmidt, F. L., & Keyes, C. L. M. (2002). Well-being in the workplace and its relationship to business outcomes: A review of the Gallup studies. In C. L. M. Keyes & J. Haidt (Eds.), *Flourishing: positive psychology and the life well-lived.* Washington, DC: American Psychological Association.

Jahoda, M. (1958). *Current concepts of positive mental health.* New York: Basic Books.

Jung, C. G. (1933). *Modern man in search of a soul* (Trans. W. S. Dell & C. F. Baynes). New York: Harcourt, Brace & World.

Keyes, C. L. M. (1996). Social functioning and social well-being: Studies of the social nature of personal wellness. *Dissertation Abstracts International: Section B: the Sciences & Engineering. Vol 56*(12-B).

Keyes, C. L. M. (1998). Social well-being. *Social Psychology Quarterly, 61,* 121–140.

Keyes, C. L. M., Hysom, S. J., & Lupo, K. (2002). The positive organization: Leadership legitimacy, employee well-being, and the bottom line. *Psychologist Manager Journal, 4,* 142–153.

Keyes, C. L. M., & Lopez, S. J. (2002). Toward a science of mental health: Positive directions in diagnosis and intervention. In C. R. Snyder & S. J. Lopez (Eds.), *Handbook of positive psychology* (pp. 26–44). New York: Oxford University Press.

Keyes, C. L. M., & Ryff, C. D. (1998). Generativity in adult lives: Social structural contours and quality of life consequences. In D. McAdams & E. de St. Aubin (Eds.), *Generativity and adult development: Perspectives on caring for and contributing to the next generation* (pp. 227–263). Washington, DC: American Psychological Association.

Keyes, C. L. M., & Ryff, C. D. (1999). Psychological well-being in midlife. In S. L. Willis & J. D. Reid (Eds.), *Middle aging: Development in the third quarter of life* (pp. 161–180). Orlando, FL: Academic Press.

Keyes, C. L. M., & Ryff, C. D. (2000). Subjective change and mental health: A self concept theory. *Social Psychology Quarterly, 63,* 264–279.

Keyes, C. L. M., Ryff, C. D., & Lee, S-J. (2002). *Somatization and mental health: A comparative study of the idiom of distress hypothesis.* Paper submitted for publication.

Keyes, C. L. M., & Shapiro, A. (in press). Social well-being in the United States: A descriptive epidemiology. In C. D. Ryff, R. C. Kessler, & O. G. Brim, Jr. (Eds.), *A portrait of midlife in the United States.* Chicago: University of Chicago Press.

Keyes, C. L. M., Shmotkin, D., & Ryff, C. D. (2002). *Optimizing well-being: The empirical encounter of two traditions.* Paper submitted for publication.

Koivumaa-Honkanen, H., Honkanen, R., Viinamäki, H., Heikkilä, K., Kaprio, J., et al. (2001). Life satisfaction and suicide: A 20-year follow-up study. *American Journal of Psychiatry, 158,* 433–439.

Larsen, R. J., Diener, E., & Emmons, R. A. (1985). An evaluation of subjective well-being measures. *Social Indicators Research, 17,* 1–18.

Lewinsohn, P. M., Redner, J. E., & Seeley, J. R. (1991), The relationship between life satisfaction and psychosocial variables: New perspectives. In F. Strack & M. Argyle (Eds.), *Subjective well-being: An interdisciplinary perspective. International series in experimental social psychology, Vol. 21* (pp. 141–169). Chatham, UK: Pergamon Press.

Lucas, R. E., Diener, E., & Suh, E. (1996). Discriminant validity of well-being measures. *Journal of Personality and Social Psychology, 71,* 616–628.

Maslow, A. (1968). *Toward a psychology of being* (2nd ed.). New York: Van Nostrand.

McCullough, G., Huebner, S., & Laughlin, J. E. (2000). Life events, self-concept, and adolescent's positive subjective well-being. *Psychology in the Schools, 37,* 281–290.

McGregor, I., & Little, B. R. (1998). Personal projects, happiness, and meaning: On doing well and being yourself. *Journal of Personality and Social Psychology, 74,* 494–512.

Mirowsky, J., & Ross, C. E. (1989). *Social causes of psychological distress.* New York: Aldine.

Mroczek, D. K., & Kolarz, C. M. (1998). The effect of age on positive and negative affect: A developmental perspective on happiness. *Journal of Personality and Social Psychology, 75,* 1333–1349.

Murray, C. J. L., & Lopez, A. D. (Eds.). (1996). *The global burden of disease: A comprehensive assessment of mortality and disability from diseases, injuries, and risk factors in 1990 and projected to 2020.* Cambridge, MA: Harvard School of Public Health.

Neugarten, B. L. (1973). Personality change in late life: A developmental perspective. In C. Eisdorfer & M. P. Lawton (Eds.), *The psychology of adult development and aging* (pp. 311–335). Washington, DC: American Psychological Association.

Ostir, G. V., Markides, K. S., Black, S. A., & Goodwin, J. S. (2000). Emotional well-being predicts subsequent functional independence and survival. *Journal of the American Geriatrics Society, 48,* 473–478.

Pavot, W., & Diener, E. (1993). Review of the satisfaction with life scale. *Psychological Assessment, 5,* 164–172.

Penninx, B. W. J. H., Guralnik, J. M., Simonsick, E. M., Kasper, J. D., Ferrucci, L., et al. (1998). Emotional vitality among disabled older women: The Women's Health and Aging Study. *Journal of the American Geriatrics Society, 46,* 807–815.

Radloff, L. S. (1977). The CES–D scale: A self-report depression scale for research in the general population. *Applied Psychological Measurement, 1,* 385–401.

Ramana, R., Paykel, E. S., Cooper, Z., Hayhurst, H., Saxty, M., et al. (1995). Remission and relapse in major depression: A two-year prospective follow-up study. *Psychological Medicine, 25,* 1161–1170.

Rebellon, C., Brown, J., & Keyes, C. L. M. (2000). Mental illness and suicide. In C. E. Faupel & P. M. Roman (Eds.), *The encyclopedia of criminology and deviant behavior, volume four: Self destructive behavior and disvalued identity* (pp. 426–429). London: Taylor & Francis.

Rogers, C. R. (1961). *On becoming a person.* Boston: Houghton Mifflin.

Russell, J. A., & Carroll, J. M. (1999). On the bipolarity of positive and negative affect. *Psychological Bulletin, 125,* 3–30.

Ryan, R. M., & Deci, E. L. (2001). On happiness and human potentials: A review of research on hedonic and eudaimonic well-being. *Annual Review of Psychology, 52,* 141–166.

Ryff, C. D. (1989a). Beyond Ponce de Leon and life satisfaction: New directions in quest of successful ageing. *International Journal of Behavioral Development, 12,* 35–55.

Ryff, C. D. (1989b). Happiness is everything, or is it? Explorations on the meaning of psychological well-being. *Journal of Personality and Social Psychology, 57,* 1069–1081.

Ryff, C. D., & Keyes, C. L. M. (1995). The structure of psychological well-being revisited. *Journal of Personality and Social Psychology, 69,* 719–727.

Salovey, P., Rothman, A. J., Detweiler, J. B., & Steward, W. T. (2000). Emotional states and physical health. *American Psychologist, 55,* 110–121.

Seeman, M. (1959). On the meaning of alienation. *American Sociological Review, 24,* 783–791.

Severin, F. T. (1965). *Humanistic viewpoints in psychology.* New York: McGraw-Hill.

Shmotkin, D. (1998). Declarative and differential aspects of subjective well-being and implications for mental health in later life. In J. Lomranz (Ed.), *Handbook of aging and mental health: An integrative approach* (pp. 15–43). New York: Plenum Press.

Spector, P. E. (1997). *Job satisfaction: Application, assessment, cause, and consequences.* Thousand Oaks, CA: Sage.

Tellegen, A., Watson, D., & Clark, L. A. (1999a). On the dimensional and hierarchical structure of affect. *Psychological Science, 10,* 297–303.

Tellegen, A., Watson, D., & Clark, L. A. (1999b). Further support for a hierarchical model of affect: Reply to Green and Salovey. *Psychological Science, 10,* 307–309.

U.S. Department of Health and Human Services. (1998). *Suicide: A report of the Surgeon General.* Rockville, MD: Author.

U.S. Department of Health and Human Services. (1999). *Mental health: A report of the Surgeon General.* Rockville, MD: Author.

Von Franz, M. L. (1964). The process of individuation. In C. G. Jung (Ed.), *Man and his symbols* (pp. 158–229). New York: Doubleday.

Waterman, A. S. (1993). Two conceptions of happiness: Contrasts of personal expressiveness (eudaimonia) and hedonic enjoyment. *Journal of Personality and Social Psychology, 64,* 678–691.

Watson, D., & Tellegen, A. (1999). Issues in dimensional structure of affect—Effects of descriptors, measurement error, and response formats: Comment on Russell and Carroll (1999). *Psychological Bulletin, 125,* 601–610.

Weerasinnghe, J., & Tepperman, L. (1994). Suicide and happiness: Seven tests of the connection. *Social Indicators Research, 32,* 199–233.

Wright, T. A., & Bonett, D. G. (1997). The role of pleasantness and activation-based well-being in performance prediction. *Journal of Occupational Health Psychology, 2,* 212–219.

Wright, T. A., & Cropanzano, R. (2000). Psychological well-being and job satisfaction as predictors of job performance. *Journal of Occupational Health Psychology, 5,* 84–94.

Zautra, A. J., Potter, P. T., & Reich, J. W. (1997). The independence of affects is context-dependent: An integrative model of the relationship of positive and negative affect. In K. W. Schaie & M. P. Lawton (Eds.), *Annual review of gerontology and geriatrics* (Vol. 17, pp. 75–103). New York: Springer.

Zung, W. K. (1965). A self-rating depression scale. *Archives of General Psychiatry, 12,* 63–70.

27

Quality of Life

M. J. Power

The quality of life issue has captured the interests of early philosophers to modern social scientists. The latter have addressed the issue of quality of life in terms of social indicators and societal resources (e.g., gross national product, infant mortality, social mobility, etc.). The quality of life concept was introduced into medicine at a time when the traditional medical outcomes such as mortality and morbidity were being criticized for being too narrow in their foci; thus, these indicators fail to represent a wide range of other potential outcomes that also are relevant even in medicine. For example, in the treatment of cancer it was recognized that the treatment effects themselves could cause considerable impairment. Therefore, with such uncertain long-term treatment, an individual might opt to have a higher quality of life for a shorter period of time instead of a lower quality of life for a longer time.

This issue of the trade-off between life per se and quality of life was highlighted initially with the problems arising from the development of aggressive treatments for cancer. One of the first scales that was produced to assess functioning in cancer was the Karnofsky Performance Status scale (Karnofsky & Burchenal, 1949). The scale combined into a single value both an assessment of illness status (varying from normal fully recovered to death from the disease) and the self-care and social functioning status for the individual. This single rating scale, and more recent similar variants, have been developed widely in medicine because of the quick and easy way in which they can be used. A widely used example is the Global Assessment of Functioning (GAF) scale, which forms Axis V of the American Psychiatric Association's *Diagnostic and Statistical Manual (DSM-IV;* 1994). Again, the GAF uses a 0 to 100 rating scale and, as with the Karnofsky scale, requires the user to make a general rating of social functioning while also including a rating of symptom levels. The fact that these scales attempt to combine a complex multidimensional concept into a single rating leads to problems with reliability and validity (e.g., Clark & Fallowfield, 1986), although these problems do not seem to have stopped their widespread use.

An approach that also is based on the idea of a single scale or index has become widely used in health economics. This approach is best exemplified by the so-called Quality Adjusted Life Year (QALY) and the related Disability Adjusted Life Year (DALY) (a measure of the number of years of life that are lost by disability resulting from a specific illness; e.g., Torrance, 1996). The basic idea underlying the QALY is the use of a single score from 0 = dead to 1 = perfect health, with different levels of disability receiving intermediate classifications. For example, a person who lived for 10 years with a disability rating of 0.5 would, by this measure have $10 \times 0.5 = 5$ QALYs. In this manner, health economists compare the relative benefits of different treatments through the calculation of QALYs.

From a psychological perspective, the same problems arise with these health utility indexes as with the global rating scales of functioning (such as the GAF mentioned previously). That is, there is now considerable evidence (e.g., Power, Bullinger, Harper, & WHOQOL Group, 1999) that quality of life is a multidimensional construct that is best conceptualized by a number of separate domains and facets of domains and measured by more complex instruments. In this chapter, the evidence for the multidimensional nature of quality of life will be reviewed and instruments designed to measure the contours of quality will be discussed.

Multidimensional Approaches to Quality of Life

The "quality of life" phrase is used in many different ways, and a major issue is how the term should be defined and conceptualized. A key distinction is between health-related and non–health-related quality of life (e.g., Spilker, 1996). In this regard, the starting point for a number of the health-related definitions has been the well-known World Health Organization (1948) definition of health as "a state of complete physical, mental and social well-being and not merely the absence of disease or infirmity" (p. 28). The inclusion of the phrase "well-being" in the WHO definition has led some researchers to focus too narrowly on self-reported psychological well-being as being the only aspect of quality of life of importance (e.g., Dupuy, 1984). However, "well-being" has to be seen as the narrower term that is an important aspect of quality of life but that is not the only aspect that needs to be considered. The challenge has been to specify the range of health-related and non–health-related aspects of quality of life that also should be included, such that "quality of life" is not simply another term for "well-being."

The WHO definition of health has provided a clear starting point for defining quality of life (e.g., WHOQOL Group, 1995), but it leaves two key questions unaddressed. First, what other areas should be included in addition to the physical, mental, and social? Second, should the conceptualization include objective characteristics of the individual in addition to the individual's subjective evaluation? The existing definitions and measures take many varied approaches to these two questions, as will be illustrated subsequently when three of the most widely used measures are described. Nevertheless, there now may be an emerging consensus on both of these key issues. In addition to the physical, mental, and social aspects there now is a recognition that spiritual and religious aspects need to be included in health-related quality of life (e.g., Power et al., 1999; Spilker, 1996; WHOQOL Group, 1995), and that a range of aspects of the individual's physical environment needs to be included in non–health-related quality of life.

In relation to the second issue of the objective and the subjective evaluations, although many of the earlier measures included both objective characteristics (e.g., being able to run for a bus or walk up a flight of stairs) and subjective characteristics (e.g., rating satisfaction–dissatisfaction with level of physical mobility), most recent measures have focused solely on the subjective (WHO-QOL Group, 1998a). It makes sense that subjective and objective indicators must be kept separate. Indeed, how can an individual living in poverty in a village in India report a higher level of happiness and quality of life than a multimillionaire in Wall Street? This problem has led economists such as the Nobel prize-winning Amartya Sen (e.g., Sen, 2001) to reject subjective indicators because of their discordance with objective economic indicators. As a positive psychologist, however, I believe that the discordance between the objective and the subjective illustrates how the human spirit can overcome and even flourish under adversity.

Measures of Quality of Life

As mentioned previously, the quality of life concept was construed initially as a useful adjunct to traditional concepts of health and functional status. An overall health assessment, therefore, would have included a single measure of the person's physical health, a measure of functioning, and a measure of quality of life. Early attempts at assessments that went beyond physical health status sometimes took the form of a rating on a single scale, but, as stated, these scales unfortunately condensed a complex multidimensional concept into one dimension. To devise a reliable and valid quality of life measure, a broad range of independent domains covering all important aspects of quality of life is necessary. Furthermore, to devise a measure that is reliable and valid *cross-culturally* requires a different approach to instrument development (e.g., Bullinger, Power, Aaronson, Cella, & Anderson, 1996).

In this chapter I highlight two ground-breaking approaches to quality of life, the SF–36 and the EUROQOL group of instruments. (In this regard, I would note that a review of all existing generic measures of quality of life is beyond the scope of this chapter.) These two instruments have advanced the conceptualization and measurement of quality of life. They are not without their own limitations, however, and consideration will then be given to the WHOQOL instruments that have attempted to overcome some of the limitations of the SF–36 and the EUROQOL. These three instruments will be described in the subsequent sections.

The SF–36

The Medical Outcomes Survey Short Form 36, known now as the SF–36, is the most widely used generic measure of quality of life. It was developed by

John Ware and his colleagues (Ware & Sherbourne, 1992) and it comprises eight scales. Four of these scales summarize physical health (the physical functioning, role-physical, bodily pain, and general health subscales) and four summarize mental health (the vitality, social functioning, role-emotional, and mental health subscales). The SF–36 has acceptable psychometric properties, it has been translated into a wide variety of languages, and population norms exist for many countries (Ware, 1996).

On the downside, the SF–36 has manifested floor and ceiling effects, and it therefore is poor at measuring the extremes of high and low levels of quality of life (e.g., Ware, 1996). Another problem is that the SF–36 combines both subjective (e.g., "Have you felt downhearted and blue?") and objective items (e.g., "Can you climb several flights of stairs?"). Conceptually, these are very different questions. Indeed, although it is objectively possible to be restricted in an activity such as climbing stairs, one subjectively could be very unhappy or happy about the situation, as well as indifferent to it. As stated previously, the latest conclusion is that subjective and objective states should be measured separately rather than included in the same measure (e.g., WHOQOL Group, 1998a).

The EuroQOL

The second major approach to quality of life measurement is that of the Euro-QOL (EuroQOL Group, 1990). The EuroQOL includes a small number of dimensions of health status that are rated on three-point scales from 1 = no problem to 3 = extreme problems. The five dimensions assessed are mobility, self-care, usual activities, pain and discomfort, and anxiety and depression. The scale also includes a "health thermometer" that, similar to the global scales considered previously, asks respondents to rate their overall health on a 0 to 100 scale. The advantages of the scale are that it is brief, easy to use, and available in a wide range of languages. One major disadvantage, however, is that there is no "positive" end to the five dimensions, because well-being on the EuroQOL is defined by the *absence of problems* on the dimension rather than the presence of a positive view of that dimension. Consistent with the positive psychology tenets about examining human strengths (e.g., Snyder & Lopez, 2002), a valid measure of quality of life must assess the positive side of life, not just the absence of the negative. In addition, because of its brevity, the EuroQOL does not cover several areas or domains. The focus of the scale is explicitly on health-related quality of life, but, as discussed previously, the general concept goes beyond health and includes non–health-related domains such as the personal environment and spirituality. Even in regard to health, however, the dimensions are very limited and should be supplemented whenever possible with an illness-specific measure of quality of life.

The WHOQOL

The World Health Organization (WHO) definition noted previously of health as "a state of complete physical, mental and social well-being, not merely the absence of disease" (1948, p. 28) captures the starting point for an holistic view of health. Moreover, this definition provides strong clues about what domains should be considered in the measurement of health, well-being, and the broader concept of quality of life. The rationale and conceptual background for the development of the WHO's own measure of quality of life, the WHOQOL, has been described in detail in several recent publications (e.g., WHOQOL Group, 1998a). There were a number of key steps in the WHOQOL's development, which are summarized subsequently.

The first step involved an international collaborative review to establish a definition of quality of life and an approach to its assessment. This definition of quality of life provided the starting point:

> individuals' perception of their position in life in the context of the culture and value systems in which they live and in relation to their goals, expectations, standards and concerns. It is a broad ranging concept affected in a complex way by the persons' physical health, psychological state, level of independence, social relationships and their relationship to salient features of their environment. (WHOQOL Group, 1995, p. 1404)

A second step involved (a) breaking the definition of quality of life into those aspects of life (facets) considered necessary for comprehensive coverage; (b) defining these facets; and (c) generating a global question pool from which the WHOQOL questions would be derived. This work was carried out simultaneously in different cultural settings around the world to provide a cross-cultural base for the measure.

The WHOQOL Facets

Focus groups in each cultural setting generated suggestions regarding appropriate aspects of quality of life. The range and definition of facets were developed iteratively, such that each setting (or center) involved in the project considered and reconsidered the proposals from their own center, from other centers, and from the coordinating team. The list of facets used in the pilot WHOQOL is presented in Exhibit 27.1; the exhibit also shows the grouping of the facets into a set of six domains that includes the physical, psychological, independence, social relationships, environment, and spirituality. Next, 236 questions addressing these 29 facets of quality of life were constructed in readiness for translation (when not already in the local language) and field testing (see WHOQOL Group, 1998a). The piloting and subsequent psychometric evaluation had several purposes: (a) to examine the construct validity of the WHOQOL domain and facet structure, and refine and reduce it accordingly; (b) to select the optimum questions for each facet with the aim of producing a version of the WHOQOL for use in the field trials; and (c) to establish the WHOQOL's psychometric properties.

A standardized administration of the WHOQOL was given to participants in 15 different centers worldwide (Bangkok, Barcelona, Bath, Beer Sheva,

Exhibit 27.1.   Pilot WHOQOL Domains and Facets

Domain I: Physical
  1. Pain and discomfort
  2. Energy and fatigue
  3. Sexual activity
  4. Sleep and rest
  5. Sensory functions

Domain II: Psychological
  6. Positive feelings
  7. Thinking, learning, memory and concentration
  8. Self-esteem
  9. Bodily image and appearance
 10. Negative feelings

Domain III: Level of independence
 11. Mobility
 12. Activities of daily living
 13. Dependence on medicinal substances and medical aids
 14. Dependence on nonmedicinal substances (alcohol, tobacco, drugs)
 15. Communication capacity
 16. Work capacity

Domain IV: Social relationships
 17. Personal relationships
 18. Practical social support
 19. Activities as provider/supporter

Domain V: Environment
 20. Freedom, physical safety and security
 21. Home environment
 22. Work satisfaction
 23. Financial resources
 24. Health and social care: accessibility and quality
 25. Opportunities for acquiring new information and skills
 26. Participation in and opportunities for recreation/leisure activities
 27. Physical environment (pollution/noise/traffic/climate)
 28. Transport

Domain VI: Spirituality/religion/personal beliefs

Overall quality of life and general health perceptions

Harare, Madras, Melbourne, New Delhi, Panama City, Paris, Seattle, St. Petersburg, Tilburg, Tokyo, Zagreb). The details of the WHOQOL development and its psychometric properties have been presented elsewhere (WHOQOL Group, 1998a, 1998b), so only a selection of relevant issues will be addressed in this chapter. Considerable care was taken in considering cross-culturally comparable response scales. There was no problem in translating the labels for the extreme end points of the scales, but the labels for the 25%, 50%, and

75% points were derived by means of a scaling procedure to ensure similar meanings (see Szabo, 1996).

One of the opportunities that data collected in this way offered was the possibility to examine the actual structure and content of quality of life. Perhaps inspired by Maslow's (1970) original hierarchy of needs and work in personality theory, a number of influential approaches have conceptualized quality of life as a hierarchical structure or pyramid with overall well-being at the top, broad domains (such as physical, psychological, and social) at the intermediate level, and then specific facets or components of each domain at the bottom (e.g., Spilker, 1990). This overall hierarchical approach was adopted by the WHO-QOL Group. As a preliminary test of this predicted hierarchy, a table of facet and domain intercorrelations was produced. The most notable finding was that, whereas the experts had relegated sexual activity to the physical domain (facet-to-corrected-domain $r = .16$), the data showed that respondents considered sex to be part of the social relationships domain ($r = .41$), to which it was moved. The difference may of course tell us something about experts versus real people!

On a variety of psychometric criteria (see WHOQOL Group, 1998a), five of the facets (sensory functions, dependence on nonmedicinal substances, communication capacity, work satisfaction, and activities as a provider–supporter) were dropped from the generic measure. (It was noted, however, that some of these might need to be included in subsequent illness-specific or group-specific modules.) With these deletions, there were now 24 specific facets and several items measuring overall quality of life. In deciding on the number of items to choose for each retained facet, the decision was made to select four items per facet (four is the minimum number required for the scale reliability analyses that will be carried out in additional psychometric testing of the instrument). These decisions led to the selection of $25 \times 4 = 100$ items (including the four general items); thus, the revised field trial WHOQOL became known as the WHOQOL–100 (WHOQOL Group, 1998a).

The Cronbach alphas from this data set demonstrated good internal consistency for the facets with a range of .65 to .93. All facet scores range from 4 to 20, with higher scores denoting higher quality of life, except for the reverse scored facets pain and discomfort, negative feelings, and dependence on medication.

As noted in previous publications on the development of the WHOQOL (e.g., WHOQOL Group, 1995), it was possible that because of cultural diversity, each center could have required the development of its own unique version of the WHOQOL. The data presented so far suggest the opposite conclusion, however, in that it *has* been possible to identify a common item, facet, and domain structure to be used for the field trial WHOQOL–100. The data analyses showed that it was possible to develop a multicultural WHOQOL–100 that has acceptable psychometric properties for all the 15 pilot centers. Of course, there are a number of additional ways in which a universal core concept of quality of life can be tested within the present data set. One way is to test the universal versus culture-specific aspects of the WHOQOL with sophisticated multivariate analyses and compare the potential structures and loadings across the different centers. Although these analyses have been presented elsewhere in more detail (Power et al., 1999), some preliminary findings regarding the structure of the WHOQOL–100 will be shared.

Principal components factor analysis with varimax rotation was carried out on a random half of the pooled dataset (n = 2056) to establish possible alternative models to the six-domain structure. The analysis yielded four factors with eigenvalues greater than 1, and together they explained 58% of the variance. The scree plot of factors suggested this solution to be appropriate. The principal component extracted explained 37.9% of the observed variance, reflecting the strong relationships among many of the facets. The first factor included facets relating to the physical and level of independence domains, which may reflect a conjoint physical capacity domain. The second factor comprised all facets relating to the environment domain. The third factor comprised three of the facets relating to the psychological domain and the facet relating to spirituality. The fourth factor comprised all facets relating to the social relationships domain together with the facet relating to body image from the psychological domain. Overall, quality of life was found to load on all factors.

The conceptual model that had been generated for the WHOQOL before the data collection suggested a six-domain structure, as shown in Table 27.1. Therefore, in a series of confirmatory factor analyses, this structure was compared to a single-domain structure, and to the four-domain structure suggested by principal components analysis of the split-half sample. (Both negative feelings and bodily image facets were retained within the psychological domain, despite their loadings on the physical health and social relationships domains shown in the analysis.) The six-domain structure fell below 0.9 on the comparative fit index (which ranges in value from 0 to 1 and for which a value of 0.9 or greater is considered as a good degree of "fit" for the model in question) for the total sample population, for both ill and well participants when considered separately. Although the fit was substantially better than null models that assumed either that there was only a single domain or in which all facets were assumed to be independent of each other, the four-factor solution represented an improved model, as shown by the better fit indexes. Moreover, this structure was shown to be the best fit for both the ill and well samples. This four-domain model can be improved further, for example, by allowing certain facet-error terms to covary; details of these additional analyses are beyond the scope of this chapter and have been presented elsewhere (WHOQOL Group, 1998a, 1998b). The net effect of these analyses has been that the four-domain approach is used frequently, especially with the short form of the WHOQOL (see next discussion), although the six-domain approach can be used when a more detailed domain profile is of use.

The WHOQOL–BREF

The WHOQOL–100 allows detailed assessment of each individual facet relating to quality of life. In certain instances, however, the WHOQOL–100 may be too lengthy for practical use. The WHOQOL–BREF field trial version has been developed to provide a short form quality of life assessment that renders sum-

Table 27.1. WHOQOL-BREF Domains and Facets of Quality of Life Showing the Four-Domain Solution

Domain	Facets incorporated within domains Overall quality of life and general health
I. Physical health	Pain and discomfort Sleep and rest Energy and fatigue Mobility Activities of daily living Dependence on medicinal substances and medical aids Work capacity
II. Psychological	Positive feelings Thinking, learning, memory, and concentration Self-esteem Bodily image and appearance Negative feelings Spirituality/religion/personal beliefs
III. Social relationships	Personal relationships Social support Sexual activity
IV. Environment	Freedom, physical safety, and security Home environment Financial resources Health and social care: accessibility and quality Opportunities for acquiring new information and skills Participation in and opportunities for recreation/leisure activity Physical environment (pollution/noise/traffic/climate) Transport

mary scores for four domains rather than detailed scores at the facet level (WHOQOL Group, 1998b).

The WHOQOL–BREF contains a total of 26 questions (see Appendix 27.1). To provide a broad and comprehensive assessment, one item from each of the 24 facets contained in the WHOQOL–100 was included. In addition, two items from the overall quality of life and general health facet were included. At a conceptual level, it was agreed by the WHOQOL Group that comprehensiveness ought to be maintained in any abbreviated version of the WHOQOL–100 by selecting at least one question from each of the 24 facets relating to quality of life. The most general question from each facet (i.e., the item that correlated most highly with the total score, calculated as the mean of all facets) was chosen for inclusion in the WHOQOL–BREF. Individual items selected by this method were then examined by a panel to establish whether the putative items reflected the conceptually derived operationalizations of facets of quality of life. That is to say, they constituted a cohesive and interpretable domain, with good construct validity.

Confirmatory Factor Analysis WHOQOL–BREF Structure

The hypothetical structure of the WHOQOL–BREF is based on that shown in Table 27.2, with the addition of a higher order factor on which all four domains load. In both the data set relating to the original pilot and the data set relating to the field trial of the WHOQOL–100, an acceptable comparative fit index (CFI) was achieved when the data were applied to the four-domain structure using confirmatory factor analysis (CFI = .906 and .903, respectively). In the field trial data set the initial CFI was .870, suggesting that alterations to the model were necessary. When three pairs of error variances were allowed to covary (i.e., pain and dependence on medication, pain and negative feelings, home and physical environment) and two items were allowed to cross-load on other domains (i.e., safety allowed to load on the global domain and medication allowed to load negatively on the environment domain), the comparative fit index increased to .901. This suggests that all data sets fit the hypothetical structure well.

Comparison Between WHOQOL–100 and WHOQOL–BREF Scores

There were high correlations between domain scores based on the WHOQOL–100 and domain scores calculated using items included in the WHOQOL–BREF. These correlations ranged from .89 (for domain 3) to .95 (for domain 1).

Internal Consistency

Cronbach alpha values for each of the four domain scores ranged from .66 (for domain 3) to .84 (for domain 1), demonstrating acceptable internal consistency (see Table 27.2). Cronbach alpha values for domain 3 should be viewed with caution, however, because they were based on three scores (i.e., the personal relationships, social support, and sexual activity facets), rather than the minimum of four generally recommended for assessing reliability.

Discussion

The analyses presented in this chapter suggest that it has been possible to develop measures of quality of life that are reliable and valid for use in a range of cultures. The initial development of the pilot WHOQOL pooled input both at a conceptual level and in relation to specific items from culturally diverse centers. A general instrument was developed through an iterative process that included an agreed definition of quality of life, agreed definitions of the facets, the generation of a large item pool reflecting those definitions, and an agreed set of items for the pilot WHOQOL.

The first-phase analyses of the item response distributions, item-facet reliability analyses, and examination of item correlations with other facets showed that some items (as is usual) had to be eliminated based on psychomet-

Table 27.2. Internal Consistency of the WHOQOL-BREF Domains

	Cronbach alpha		
	Original data (n = 4802)	Field data (n = 3882)	New data (n = 2369)
Physical health	.82	.84	.80
Psychological	.75	.77	.76
Social relationships[a]	.66	.69	.66
Environment	.80	.80	.80

[a] = Only three items, therefore Cronbach alphas may not be reliable.

ric criteria from the item pool. In addition, the item analyses suggested that some facets should not be retained in the field trial instrument either because responses were, for example, too skewed, or, in the case of the activities as a provider–supporter and work satisfaction facets, because the facet demonstrated poor reliability and validity across cultures. It must be noted that, although facets related to sensory functioning, communication, and burden of care for others have been dropped from the core WHOQOL–100, it would be possible to develop add-on modules designed for either specific populations (e.g., those with sensory or communication dysfunctions) or for specific cultures in which these items could be included, as long as they met criteria specified by the WHOQOL Group. The development of the core WHOQOL–100 provides a first step in defining the core set of items needed to assess quality of life, but it is not intended to suggest that other aspects of quality of life should be excluded. For example, in some clinical studies it will be worthwhile to consider the addition of a disease-specific or treatment-specific WHOQOL or national questions if these are culturally relevant.

Future Directions

The analyses presented in this chapter represent an intermediate stage in the development of the WHOQOL measures. The WHOQOL–100 has been found to be a reliable and valid instrument measuring a broad range of domains of quality of life that can be used in a diverse range of cultures. There are, however, a significant number of questions yet to be addressed, which were not part of the pilot testing of the instrument. One of the main limitations of the data presented is that they are cross-sectional. Longitudinal data are now necessary to investigate the test–retest reliability of the instrument in populations that have not experienced significant life changes. In addition, it is necessary to collect longitudinal data from populations that have experienced significant life change and thereby assess the sensitivity or responsiveness of the instrument to change. Such studies are well under way in several centers with a variety of populations, but final published data are not yet available. Given the anticipated widespread use of the WHOQOL, it will be necessary to examine how a range of physical, psychological, and social interventions affect both general and specific aspects of quality of life. In addition, it is now necessary to test the WHOQOL–100 and the WHOQOL–BREF as instruments in their own right, as opposed to as "extracted" ones, as well as in a range of cultures that were not represented in the first sets of centers.

Conclusion

The chapter began with a look at the range of generic measures of quality of life that currently are available and that are in widespread use. Such measures include the long-established global scales such as the Karnofsky Performance Status scale and more recent derivatives such as the *DSM-IV* Global Assessment of Functioning (GAF) scale (APA, 1994). These single-measure global scales continue to be used in clinical audit and outcome studies because of their brevity and ease of application. They have questionable reliability and validity because they attempt to squeeze a multidimensional construct into a single dimension. A similar problem arises with the utility indexes used by health economists such as the QALY and the DALY. In addition, these measures require the identification of a disability value on a scale between 0 and 1 that is associated with different illnesses. There is no reason, however, why such values should be consistent across individuals with the same illness, across the same individual over time, and across different subgroups within the population.

A significant advance over single-index measures has been the more recent development of multidimensional approaches to quality of life assessment. Although even multidimensional scales can be used to produce single scales, their preferred use is in the form of profiles of scores across a limited number of dimensions or domains. Two of the most widely used of these measures are the SF–36 and the EuroQOL groups of instruments. The extensive use of these measures has led to the collection of rich data sets, including population norms for many cultures. There are limitations, however, with each measure. For example, the SF–36 is best used as a midrange assessment because it has been shown to have significant floor and ceiling effects. In addition, the measure mixes together so-called objective and subjective items that, it can be argued reasonably, go together like oil and water. The limitations of the EuroQOL include the fact that within the scale health is defined as the absence of problems rather than being construed in a more positive sense. The curtailment of the positive end of the scale in the EuroQOL makes it problematic for general population use because responses tend to have a very skewed distribution toward the "no problem" end of the scale.

A major part of this chapter focused on the development of a new group of quality of life scales, the WHOQOL measures. The WHOQOL took as its starting point the classic World Health Organization definition of health. Based on a number of influential conceptualizations of quality of life and related areas, an overall hierarchical structure was proposed that included overall quality of life, a set of specific domains, and specific facets that reflect aspects of each of those domains. The empirical work to date provides good support for such a structure, with confirmatory factor analyses offering good support for both the four-domain and the six-domain hierarchical solutions. The important point, however, is that these analyses strongly support the hierarchical approach to quality of life; they also show that a scoring system based on domain-level summary scores can provide a useful profile of scores—for example, in individual clinical use of the scales—but it may also be useful to produce an overall summative index from the scale. It is important to note that although the analyses show that the scale should not simply be used to provide an overall score, domain-level scores are also important. Other analyses of the WHOQOL have led to the generation of a short form of the measure, the WHOQOL–BREF.

Finally, the collection of data from a large number of different cultures has prompted the question of whether there is something universal about the aspects of our lives that contribute to our overall quality of life, across cultures. Although the term "quality of life" itself does not translate well into all languages, our analyses across a wide variety of cultures suggest that there are universal aspects of this concept that may well be linked to other universals in areas such as language, emotion, and social relationships (Power & Dalgleish, 1997).

Appendix 27.1
The WHOQOL–BREF Questions

1. How would you rate your quality of life?
2. How satisfied are you with your health?
3. To what extent do you feel that (physical) pain prevents you from doing what you need to do?
4. How much do you need any medical treatment to function in your daily life?
5. How much do you enjoy life?
6. To what extent do you feel your life to be meaningful?
7. How well are you able to concentrate?
8. How safe do you feel in your daily life?
9. How healthy is your physical environment?
10. Do you have enough energy for everyday life?
11. Are you able to accept your bodily appearance?
12. Have you enough money to meet your needs?
13. How available to you is the information that you need in your day-to-day life?
14. To what extent do you have the opportunity for leisure activities?
15. How well are you able to get around?
16. How satisfied are you with your sleep?
17. How satisfied are you with your ability to perform your daily living activities?
18. How satisfied are you with your capacity for work?
19. How satisfied are you with yourself?
20. How satisfied are you with your personal relationships?
21. How satisfied are you with your sex life?
22. How satisfied are you with the support you get from your friends?
23. How satisfied are you with the conditions of your living place?
24. How satisfied are you with your access to health services?
25. How satisfied are you with your transport?
26. How often do you have negative feelings such as blue mood, despair, anxiety, depression?

Note. From WHOQOL Group (1998b).

References

American Psychiatric Association. (1994). *Diagnostic and statistical manual of mental disorders* (4th ed.). Washington, DC: Author.

Bullinger, M., Power, M. J., Aaronson, N. K., Cella, D. F., & Anderson, R. T. (1996). Creating and evaluating cross-cultural instruments. In B. Spilker (Ed.), *Quality of life and pharmacoeconomics in clinical trials* (2nd ed.). Hagerstown, MD: Lippincott-Raven.

Clark, A., & Fallowfield, L. J. (1986). Quality of life measurements in patients with malignant disease: A review. *Journal of the Royal Society of Medicine, 79,* 165.

Dupuy, H. J. (1984). The Psychological General Well-Being (PGWB) Index. In N. K. Wenger, M. E. Mattson, C. D. Furberg, & J. Elinson (Eds.), *Assessment of quality of life in clinical trials of cardiovascular therapies* (pp. 170–183). New York: Le Jacq.

EuroQOL Group. (1990). EuroQOL—A new facility for the measurement of health-related quality of life. *Health Policy, 16,* 199–208.

Karnofsky, D., & Burchenal, J. (1949). *The clinical evaluation of chemotherapeutic agents in cancer.* New York: Columbia University Press.

Maslow, A. H. (1970). *Motivation and personality* (2nd ed.). New York: Harper and Row.

Power, M. J., Bullinger, M., Harper, A., & WHOQOL Group (1999). The World Health Organization WHOQOL-100: Tests of the universality of quality of life in 15 different cultural groups worldwide. *Health Psychology, 18,* 495–505.

Power, M. J., & Dalgleish, T. (1997). *Cognition and emotion: From order to disorder.* Hove, UK: Psychology Press.

Sen, A. (2001). Economic progress and health. In D. A. Leon & G. Watt (Eds.), *Poverty, inequality, and health: An international perspective* (pp. 333–345). Oxford: Oxford University Press.

Snyder, C. R., & Lopez, S. J. (2002). *Handbook of positive psychology.* New York: Oxford University Press.

Spilker, B. (1990). Introduction. In B. Spilker (Ed.), *Quality of life assessments in clinical trials* (pp. 1–10). New York: Raven Press.

Spilker, B. (Ed.). (1996). *Quality of life and pharmoeconomics in clinical trials* (2nd ed.). Hagerstown, MD: Lippincott-Raven.

Szabo, S. (1996). The World Health Organisation Quality of Life (WHOQOL) Assessment Instrument. In B. Spilker (Ed.), *Quality of life and pharmacoeconomics in clinical trials* (2nd ed., pp. 335–362). Hagerstown, MD: Lippincott-Raven.

Torrance, G. W. (1996). Designing and conducting cost-utility analyses. In B. Spilker (ed.), *Quality of life and pharmacoeconomics in clinical trials* (2nd ed., pp. 1105–1111). Hagerstown, MD: Lippincott-Raven.

Ware, J. E. (1996). The SF–36 health survey. In B. Spilker (Ed.), *Quality of life and pharmacoeconomics in clinical trials* (2nd ed., pp. 337–345). Hagerstown, MD: Lippincott-Raven.

Ware, J. E., & Sherbourne, C. D. (1992). The MOS 36-item short-form health status survey (SF–36): 1. Conceptual framework and item selection. *Medical Care, 30,* 473–483.

WHOQOL Group. (1995). The World Health Organization Quality of Life assessment (WHOQOL): Position paper from the World Health Organization. *Social Science and Medicine, 41,* 1403–1409.

WHOQOL Group. (1998a). The World Health Organization Quality of Life Assessment (WHOQOL): Development and general psychometric properties. *Social Science and Medicine, 46,* 1569–1585.

WHOQOL Group. (1998b). Development of the World Health Organization WHOQOL-BREF Quality of Life Assessment. *Psychological Medicine, 28,* 551–558.

World Health Organization. (1948). World Health Organization constitution. In *Basic documents.* Geneva, Switzerland: Author.

28

Environmental Assessment: Examining Influences on Optimal Human Functioning

*Heather N. Rasmussen, Jason E. Neufeld,
Jennifer C. Bouwkamp, Lisa M. Edwards, Alicia Ito,
Jeana L. Magyar-Moe, Jamie A. Ryder,
and Shane J. Lopez*

The idea that environmental factors influence how an individual functions is well accepted in psychology. In the early 1900s, this notion was popularized by behaviorists who argued that individual behavior could be explained, predicted, and modified if the mechanisms underlying environmental influences were understood (Conyne & Clack, 1981). In their efforts, behaviorists discovered principles by which the environment can affect behavior (e.g., punishment and reinforcement). These principles have proven so powerful that they have been adopted implicitly and explicitly in current conceptualizations of the environment (Walsh, Craik, & Price, 2000). Yet, despite knowledge of the principles by which the environment can shape the individual, there is a dearth of scholarship devoted to identifying the specific environmental variables that do the shaping. One reason for this scholarly lacunae is that environmental contexts are difficult to operationalize. A second reason could be the ideology of individualism that focuses on the person as the responsible agent of behaviors. A third reason is that the assessment of the environment may seem fruitless to some because the context may be perceived as fixed or too difficult to change.

To advance our understanding of human functioning, we must find a way to reliably operationalize environmental variables. Also, attention should be paid to discovering aspects of environments that promote healthy functioning and growth of individuals. Fortunately, work is being done to establish a scientific foundation that includes positive environmental characteristics (see Friedman & Wachs, 1999; Moos, 1991; Walsh & Betz, 1995). Researchers seek to understand and describe growth-promoting variables in the environment by defining positive constructs precisely and investigating them empirically. Such rigorous scientific investigation of positive environmental constructs may unleash a heretofore untapped force for change (Conyne & Clack, 1981). As the sophistication of environmental assessment increases, clinicians, as well as researchers, increasingly should consider the contexts in which individuals function.

The purpose of this chapter is twofold. First, we review the current environmental assessments in terms of history, key concepts, and models. We examine three environmental contexts—home, school, and work. We try to critically evaluate the literature in a manner that highlights the measurement of individuals' qualities and aspects of their environments with an emphasis on positive environmental elements that promote the growth and healthy functioning of individuals. Second, we expand the view of the environment by describing constructs and processes that are context-dependent and may be active ingredients of human growth. Accordingly, the reader is encouraged to include environmental elements when considering the functioning of those with whom they work and also to focus on the healthy and adaptive aspects of the contexts in which people live.

The Changing Foci of Environmental Assessment

The phrase *environmental psychology* has been applied to wide-ranging topics involving the role of the environment in the field of psychology (Anastasi, 1988). One conceptualization of environmental psychology has its roots in engineering psychology with its focus on the instantaneous effects of the environment on a person's performance and general well-being (Moos, 1976). Since the 1960s, a major focus within the field of environmental psychology has been on the cumulative effects of an environment on shaping human psychological development in all domains (Anastasi, 1988). Such a focus is exemplified in the writings of Lewis Mumford (1968), who purported that positive human and social qualities are vital to desirable environments and that a conceptual understanding of how to achieve these qualities would allow for the design of optimal environments.

Several approaches to environmental assessment have since evolved. Depending on the purpose of the assessment, the environment has been evaluated on a number of different levels. A description of the levels of analysis and foci of environmental assessment follows.

Levels of Analysis

A major distinction can be made about whether a conceptualization of the environment focuses on aspects of the *objective outer world* as they influence individuals or whether the conceptualization is aimed toward examining the *subjective world as the individual perceives and reacts to it* (Endler & Magnusson, 1976). The objective outer-world environment reflects elements such as physical and social factors, and the subjective world taps "the psychological significance of the environment to the individual" (Walsh & Betz, 1995, p. 312). Research providing a glimpse of how individuals interpret, perceive, and react to their environments would facilitate the understanding and prediction of individuals' behaviors in similar situations.

The most often examined level of analysis has been the global, composite indexes of socioeconomic level (Anastasi, 1988). These traditional global indexes are limited significantly, however, by their classification along a *single* continuum from good to bad or from high to low when, in fact, environments differ in the particular aspects of behavior they reinforce. For example, Anastasi pointed out that optimal environments for the development of athletic skills, academic achievement, and social functioning may be very dissimilar, thus "subenvironment scales" designed for measuring specific behavior domains may be more relevant and more representative of the environments under study.

Models and Approaches to Environmental Assessment

There are several models of environmental assessment that one can use to evaluate both the limitations and resources provided in a given setting. Three approaches pay adequate attention to environmental aspects that will help identify variables related to optimal human functioning.

Socioecological Model of Human Adaptation

Rudolph Moos (1991) developed an integrated conceptual framework and related assessment procedures for understanding the dynamic features of environments. His five-panel, socioecological model of human adaptation is shown in Figure 28.1. From this perspective, the environmental system (panel I) is made up of continuous life stressors and social resources in various life areas, including school, family, and work. The personal system (panel II) is composed of a person's demographic characteristics and personal resources such as self-esteem, cognitive ability, problem-solving skills, and needs and value orientations. Life crises and transitions (panel III) and the environmental and personal factors (panels I and II) that come before them can affect cognitive appraisal and coping responses (panel IV) and their effectiveness (panel V). The model is bidirectional, with reciprocal feedback potentially occurring at each stage (Moos, 1991).

Moos's (1991) model consists of three related dimensions (relationship dimension, the personal growth or goal orientation dimension, and the system maintenance and change dimension) of the environment that can be used in assessing the social climate of various settings. All three categories of evaluation are strengths-focused—highlighting what is working well for a person within a given setting. This framework is recommended strongly when looking to optimize human functioning from an environmental perspective.

Walsh and Betz's Five Foci of Environmental Assessment

Walsh and Betz (1995) have supported the idea that the assessment of an individual is incomplete if it does not include environmental components. Their

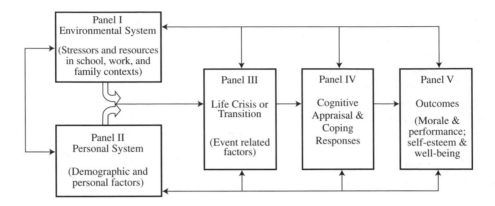

Figure 28.1. A conceptual model of the links between environmental and personal factors and school and nonschool outcomes (Moos, 1991).

recommended approach to environmental assessment assumes that a person and his or her environment are constantly influencing each other and that it is impossible to separate the two. Thus, assessing an individual's perception of his or her environment is just as crucial as evaluating the actual physical and social environment. In their work, Walsh and Betz discuss five foci. The first focus is on how the physical and spatial properties of a place may affect behavior. A second focus is on the organization of material artifacts in places. Third, they discuss centering on the traits of environments as perceived by human observers. The fourth focus in environmental assessment assesses the behavioral attributes of situations, and the fifth element is the institutional attributes of environments. This five-foci model of environmental assessment increases the likelihood of discovering both the limitations and resources of an environment and the effects of those on individuals' functioning.

The Four-Front Approach: Attending to Environmental Resources

Wright and Lopez (2002) posited that "at best, the environment remains as a vague background against which the person is featured . . . [it] overwhelmingly remains hidden in our thinking about and evaluation of a person" (p. 32). In response to this perceived deficiency in assessment, they have proposed a four-front approach (see chapter 1, this volume, for discussion of the four-front approach) to highlight the environment in individual appraisal. They assert that clinicians must be committed to examining the person's strengths and weaknesses as well as the resources and stressors present in the environment.

In practice, this is difficult because the developers of the *Diagnostic and Statistical Manual of Mental Disorders–IV (DSM–IV;* American Psychiatric Association, 1994) gave weight to environmental considerations through its Axis IV, which is concerned with psychosocial and environmental *problems.* Once again, assets and resources have been neglected in favor of pathology, weaknesses, and stressors, and currently there is no axis devoted to environmental supports (see chapter 2, this volume).

In congruence with the approach put forth by Wright and Lopez (2002), we believe that assessing environmental resources and stressors is critical to the conceptualization of any individual. As a result of this belief, all instruments examined in the forthcoming sections about environmental assessment in the home, at work, and at school are selected because of their potential for detecting, measuring, or highlighting the positive aspects of the particular environment that it was designed to assess.

Assessment of the Home Environment

As the primary setting of human development and social interaction, the home and family environment is the primary domain for assessment and change. Research has linked various aspects of the home environment and family functioning to children's cognitive and social development (Moos, 1991) and has shown its influence on the school (Felner, Aber, Primavera, & Cauce, 1985) and work (Repetti, 1986).

Assessment of the home–family environment began with measures of socioeconomic status such as the Home Index (Gough, 1954) and the American Home scale (Kerr, 1942). More complex conceptualizations have many different foci but there is not a comprehensive, universally accepted conceptualization of the home environment (although a few have produced useful assessment tools).

Scales Associated With the Circumplex Model of Home Environments

The Circumplex Model, developed by Olson, Russell, and Sprenkle (1989) to integrate therapy, research, and family system theory, presents a general view of family functioning. The three dimensions of the model—cohesion, flexibility, and communication—are shared with many other theoretical models in the field of marriage and family counseling and are assumed to be the major components of the family system. Family cohesion, the level of emotional bond that members have with one another, and family flexibility, the amount of change in leadership, roles, and relationship rules (Olson, 1992), have a curvilinear relationship with family functioning (Walsh & Olson, 1988). In other words, levels that are too high or too low are problematic. Each of these dimensions has four levels, creating 16 types of marital and family systems (illustrated in Figure 28.2). Family communication is a facilitating dimension that helps families to make changes on the cohesion and flexibility dimensions (Olson, 1992).

The Circumplex Model was chosen for highlight because it has been extensively researched, it shares many of the dimensions of other models, and it is associated with a group of highly researched assessment tools. One measure associated with the Circumplex Model is the Family Adaptability and Cohesion Evaluation Scales (FACES) II (Olson, Portner, & Bell, 1982). FACES II is designed for use in family therapy and may be used in treatment planning to describe the family's initial status, determine appropriate interventions, and for outcome evaluation (Olson, 2000). FACES II is a 30-item self-

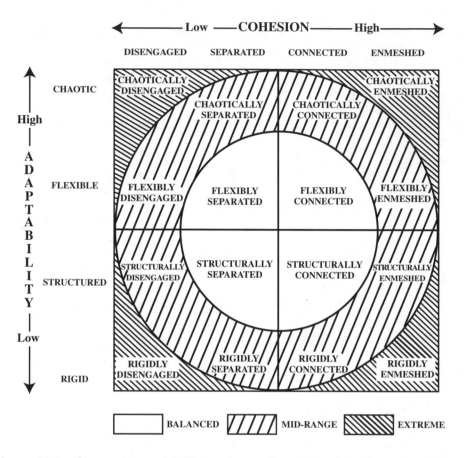

Figure 28.2. Circumplex model: Sixteen types of marital and family systems (Olson, Bell, & Portner, 1992). Reprinted with permission.

report instrument, and individuals are instructed to rate items based on a 5-point Likert-type scale with values ranging from "almost never" to "almost always." Each member of the family should complete the inventory separately because individuals do not see their family system in the same way (Olson, 1992). FACES II has good reliability and validity (see Table 28.1 for information about FACES II, as well as other measures discussed in this chapter). Internal consistency for cohesion ($r = .87$), adaptability ($r = .78$), and total scale ($r = .90$) are very good. Test–retest statistics at four to five weeks are .83 for cohesion and .80 for adaptability. Correlations between scales range from $r = .25$ to .65 (Olson, 1992).

The Home Observation for Measurement of the Environment

Possibly the most widely used home environment measure, the Home Observation for Measurement of the Environment (HOME) Inventory (Caldwell & Bradley, 1984), assesses the amount and quality of stimulation and support a child receives in the home environment (*Home Observation*, 2000). The HOME

Table 28.1. Scales for Environmental Assessment

Assessments	Purpose	Population	Administration	Psychometric properties
Home				
Family Adaptability and Cohesion Evaluation Scales II (FACES II; Olson, Portner, & Bell, 1982)	Measure family cohesion and adaptability	Family	40 items, self-report	Alpha coefficient for total scale is .90
Family Functioning Style Scale (FFSS; Deal, Trivette, & Dunst, 1988)	Measure family's strengths	Family	26 items, self-report or family-report	Alpha coefficient for total is .92
Home Observation for Measurement of the Environment (HOME; Caldwell & Bradley, 1984)	Measure quality and quantity of stimulation and support in home	Birth–3 years 3–6 years 6–10 years 10–15 years	45 items 55 items 59 items 60 items	Alpha coefficients for total scores are all above .90; inter-observer agreement is 90% or higher.
Work				
Organization Climate Index (Stern, 1970)	To measure formal administrative settings	Adults	300 true/false items	Is reliable and has been validated in its ability to distinguish between various organizational environments
Gallup StrengthsFinder (Gallup Organization, 2000)	Helps individuals to identify areas in their lives where they are likely to excel in various situations	Adults	180 self-report items	(See Buckingham & Clifton, 2001, for psychometric data.)
School				
Code for Instructional Structure and Student Academic Response (CISSAR; Greenwood, Delquadri, & Hall, 1978)	Ecobehavioral assessment system	Special needs students. (MS-CISSAR exists for mainstream environments and ESCAPE exists for preschool environments)	Is available in software program (EBASS); data are gathered through observation	Interobserver reliability: $r = .77$; test–retest reliability mean: $r = .88$
The Instructional Environment Scale–II (TIES–II, Ysseldyke & Christenson, 1993)	Ecobehavioral assessment system	Students, teachers, and parents	Interviews, checklists, and observation	Component interrater reliabilities .83 to .96; moderate content validity with achievement test subtests

is used to identify potential sources of risk in the environment so that appropriate remedial interventions may be provided (Boehm, 1985). The inventory is completed during a home visit with the child and primary caregiver through a combination interview–observation and scored using a yes–no format. Four forms of the inventory exist, each for use with a different age group. The Infant/Toddler (IT) HOME is for use with children from birth to age 3, the Early Childhood (EC) HOME should be used for children between the ages of 3 and 6, the Middle Childhood (MC) HOME is designed for children ages 6–10, and the Early Adolescent (EA) HOME is for ages 10–15 (*Home Observation*, 2000). The forms contain between 45 and 60 items that are clustered into multiple subscales. Each instrument assesses parental responsivity, parental acceptance, and availability of learning materials as well as dimensions unique to the age group, such as language stimulation in early childhood and encouragement of maturity in middle childhood (*Home Observation*, 2000). Scores on the Infant/Toddler HOME, the earliest and most researched version of the inventory, are significantly related to Binet IQ scores ($r = .72$; Boehm, 1985). See Table 28.1 for additional psychometric information.

Family Functioning Style Scale

One of the few assessments specifically designed to measure environmental strengths, the Family Functioning Style Scale (FFSS; Deal, Trivette, & Dunst, 1988) assesses the 12 qualities of strong families (e.g., commitment, coping strategies, flexibility, and communication) by asking family members the extent to which they believe their family possesses different strengths and capabilities. The FFSS was developed for use in family interventions to promote discussion about the ways that particular characteristics function as resources for meeting the family's needs (Deal et al., 1988). By identifying family strengths and resources, clinicians can mobilize these qualities to help the family acquire new competencies and build on existing capabilities (Trivette, Dunst, Deal, Hamer, & Propst, 1990). The scale contains 26 self-report items, measured on a 5-point likert-type scale, with values ranging from "not at all like my family" to "almost always like my family." The instrument may be completed individually or by two or more family members together (Deal et al., 1988). Preliminary data indicate that the FFSS has good reliability and validity. Factor analysis yielded a 5-factor solution accounting for 60% of the variance. Alpha coefficients are .92 for the total scale and .77 to .85 for the factors.

Issues to Consider in Home Assessment

The home environment comprises a multitude of complex factors; thus, researchers and clinicians may need to use more than one instrument, depending on the breadth and depth of environmental understanding desired. Whether one is using a short, self-report measure or a detailed, in-home observer rating scale, the four-front approach may be used. Although most instruments are not created to detect strengths and resources, they often reveal areas in which the home environment or family system is not deficient. These "adequacies" may be considered as potential strengths and resources and further explored as bases for development. This strategy is recommended for assessment in its present state; however, it is essential that instruments be developed that capture both the environment's strengths and weaknesses. By understanding strengths, clinicians will have a more complete view of their clients and be in a position to encourage growth.

Assessment of Workplace Environments

Researchers, in conjunction with personnel managers, began assessing work environments to determine which types of environmental workplace conditions were most conducive and detrimental to productivity and employee satisfaction. Schooler (1999) indicated that self-report questionnaires, observations by trained individuals, in-depth interviews, and reviews of records have all been used as a means to assess workplace environments. He has proposed that an accurate analysis of the workplace environment must be based on the way each individual perceives and reacts to their surroundings. Also important, he contended, is recognizing individual differences when designing environmental measures to take into consideration each individual's attempt to alter the environment to meet personal needs.

Measures of Work Environment Based on Holland's Theory

Holland (1987) asserted the importance of the workplace environment in his theory of career development. He emphasized the congruence of each individual's personality with various vocational environments. He identified six personality types—realistic, investigative, artistic, social, enterprising, and conventional—that indicate an individual's interests, preferences, and strengths. He researched how these personality types fit with different work environments. Instruments developed to measure interests and personality types based on his theory include the Vocational Preference Inventory (Holland, 1985), the Self-directed Search (Holland, 1994), and the Strong Interest Inventory (Holland, Hansen, Borgen, & Hammer, 1994). All have been shown to have adequate reliability and validity and are used in a variety of settings. Holland (1987) argued that congruence between personality and work environment leads to greater productivity and a larger sense of satisfaction. These observations have been further supported. Walsh, Craik, and Price (2000) examined the role of person–environment interaction in a variety of settings. Their findings support the assertion that individuals and their environments play a reciprocal role and the importance of positive person–environment interaction.

The Gallup StrengthsFinder

Buckingham and Coffman (1999) posed an important question: "What does a strong, vibrant workplace look like?" (p. 25). Their conceptualization of a positive work environment is the result of the Gallup's interviews of more than two million individuals working in a broad spectrum of jobs. After analysis of the responses, a limited number of indicators were found to measure the strength of the work environment. They found that pay, benefits, and organizational structure do not significantly affect the way that individuals rate their environment; rather, having the opportunity to grow and learn or being given the chance to do what one does best, helps create a positive workplace environment.

The Gallup StrengthsFinder (Gallup Organization, 2000) represents one of the few instruments available to assess positive work environments. Researchers were able to identify 34 reoccurring patterns or "themes" that are the substance behind an individual's success. Individuals discover which themes exist most strongly in their lives and learn to build on them. The Gallup StrengthsFinder consists of 180 pairs of descriptors that the individual is instructed to choose between. Based on their response patterns, an individual's five strongest theme areas are determined. Currently the Gallup Strengths-Finder is being used in a variety of workplace environments to increase employee productivity and satisfaction (Buckingham & Clifton, 2001).

Issues to Consider in Workplace Assessment

There are different methods to assess the workplace environment. Not all methods highlight the importance of looking at strengths within the environments, and instead may solely focus on deficits. Measures such as the Gallup StrengthsFinder (Gallup Organization, 2000) can increase understanding of the positive aspects that individuals can draw from and contribute to their various work settings. Based on an analysis of these variables, researchers and clinicians can help to increase organizational productivity and promote overall job satisfaction.

Assessment of the School Environment

Traditionally, professionals have relied on methods such as observation, teacher interviews, checklists, task analysis, parent interviews, and social histories to assess the school environment (Ysseldyke & Elliott, 1999). Developers of measures of classroom and school climate also have attempted to identify the climate or ambiance and the effect that it has on the learner. More current, formalized evaluations of school environments have been limited by their focus on within-student variables (Goh, Teslow, & Fuller, 1981), and their neglect of environmental factors that may play a role in outcomes. Although these formalized methods have attempted to enrich our understanding of the student and his or her performance in the classroom, these methods are limited in that they assess only the internal characteristics of students.

A Traditional Scale Associated With an Ecological Model of School Environments

Current approaches to exploring educational environments emphasize the importance of an ecological view of the school context, or "the interface between proximal processes in classrooms and schools and higher level school contexts" (Talbert & McLaughlin, 1999, p. 198). The tenets of instructional ecology suggest that learning does not only reside in the learner but rather "is functionally related to the setting in which takes place" (Ysseldyke & Elliott, 1999, p. 500).

With the recognition that individuals are affected by the complex environments in which they live, Moos (1991) acknowledged the connections between school, work, and family settings. According to Moos,

> our task is to formulate an integrated conceptual framework and develop assessment procedures that reflect the complex interplay of real-life processes. Thus, we must place learning environments in context and consider how the characteristics and influences of schools and classrooms are altered by other factors in the lives of students and educators, such as aspect of their family and work settings. (p. 29)

To this end, Moos has developed Social Climate scales for three settings: the classroom, the work environment, and the family (see the previous description of Moos's research).

Research on the learning environment with the Social Climate scales (Moos, 1991) has consistently demonstrated that at the elementary-school level, cohesive, task-oriented, and structured classes tend to improve more in reading and mathematics, and have equal levels of self-confidence and creativity in comparison to classes that are more flexible and engaging. Apparently, ideal programs are found in those basic skills schools in which students receive support as well as expected structure and in alternative schools in which flexibility is balanced with more task focus. At the middle- and high-school levels, research suggests that the promotion of student morale, interest in subject matter, and academic self-efficacy is facilitated by a classroom balance between task performance and organization on one hand and support and warmth on the other.

Innovative Scales Associated With the Ecological Model of School Environments: Measuring Instructional Environments

Instructional environments include school contexts as well as home and other contexts in which learning takes place (Ysseldyke & Elliott, 1999). For school psychologists and other mental health professionals, assessment of the academic environment can include "an evaluation of those variables that may have an impact upon student academic performance . . . behaviors that relate to academic engaged time, teacher instructional procedures, competing contingencies, and teacher–student monitoring procedures and expectations" (Shapiro, 1989, p. 33). Indeed, a thorough evaluation of student performance must include factors that contribute to school, including instruction, school organization, and the classroom itself (Ysseldyke & Elliott, 1999).

Ysseldyke and Elliott (1999) suggested that to provide the most appropriate planning and intervention services for students, assessments of educational environments should use an ecological perspective in exploring factors that affect student outcomes. Accordingly, ecobehavioral analysis is gaining popularity as a method of observing the relationships between students' and teachers' behaviors and their ecological contexts, and several instruments have been developed for the purpose of this kind of assessment. Two methods of ecobehavioral analysis commonly used in school settings include the Code for Instructional Structure and Student Academic Response (CISSAR; Greenwood, Delquadri, & Hall, 1978) and the Instructional Environment Scale–II (TIES–II; Ysseldyke & Christenson, 1993).

The CISSAR (Greenwood et al., 1978) was developed as one of the first forms of ecobehavioral assessment and is designed to allow for categorization of student and teacher behaviors (including academic responses, task management, competing responses, teacher position, and teacher behavior), as well as ecology of the classroom (including activity, task, and structure). The CISSAR has been combined with two other forms of ecobehavioral assessment, the Ecobehavioral System for Complex Assessments of Preschool Environments (ESCAPE) and the Mainstream CISSAR (MS–CISSAR), into one software program known as Ecobehavioral Assessment System Software (EBASS; Greenwood, Carta, Kamps, & Delquadri, 1992). This software can be used by school psychologists and other personnel to conduct observations with hand-held computers or laptops (Ysseldyke & Elliott, 1999). See Table 28.1 for details.

The TIES–II (Ysseldyke & Christenson, 1993) was developed to "assist education professionals in a systematic analysis of a target students' instructional environment, which includes both school and home contexts" (p. i). The TIES–II system is designed to assess learning, rather than the learner, and to consider the "total learning environment" (p. 4). To this end, the TIES–II uses multiple methods of assessment, including observation, interviewing, and analysis of permanent products from multiple sources (parents, teachers, and students). Information gathered from all sources and methods is organized into 12 instructional components and five home support for learning components that make up the TIES–II system, and it is frequently used for collaborative planning and designing of interventions to address school-related concerns. See Table 28.1 for psychometric properties of the TIES–II.

Issues to Consider in Assessment of the School Environment

As awareness of the value of identifying student strengths and ecology increases, along with a parallel growth in positive psychology, it is likely that instructional assessments such as the CISSAR and TIES–II will be used more frequently. The incorporation of more ecologically based assessments inevitably requires a larger time investment on the part of those conducting evaluations of students. Furthermore, it is possible that with high stakes decisions to be made, assessments will be perceived as either threatening or inefficient.

As school personnel work collaboratively to understand students' environments and to address students' needs, more complex assessment systems will continue to be used by professionals. Through the use of such systems, it is our hope that psychologists, social workers, and other professionals involved with children and adolescents can identify, recognize, and help students use their strengths and the strengths of the school environments.

Examining the Forces of the Environment

We have emphasized how essential environmental variables are for the complete understanding of human nature. Despite this long-standing recognition, however, we realize the power of the status quo to remain focused primarily on the individual. Some may refrain from examining environmental factors because of the perception that such external variables are largely immutable. Others may concede the malleability of external variables but believe that the individual represents the most feasible point of intervention. Despite these and other reasons for the relative lack of attention given to external factors, we hold that a comprehensive understanding of environmental variables has the potential to greatly enhance the understanding of human functioning, thereby allowing for greater sensitivity in research designs and interventions. Fortunately, several promising developments may revolutionize the way environmental factors are conceptualized and used by scientists and practitioners.

Positive Environments

The work of most behavioral scientists and practitioners is centered on discovering ways in which individuals can be helped to develop and change in positive ways. Most current conceptualizations of environmental factors, however, are not specifically focused on positive constructs. But recently, identifying situational factors that promote the positive development of the individual has been acknowledged as an essential goal of the field (Peterson & Seligman, 2001). It is recognized that the identification and incorporation of these enabling conditions is necessary to provide scientists and practitioners with guidance for helping individuals to develop assets (see the Search Institute [2000] for a strengths-based approach to healthy development).

Integrating Our Knowledge of Environmental Variables

Another shift in the conceptualization of environmental factors involves the increased recognition of the dynamic interaction that takes place between situational variables. Much of the available research on environmental factors, however, has focused on isolated variables, leaving theoretical models somewhat disconnected.

For many years, Moos (1984) has advocated the systems perspective of environmental variables. Moos has emphasized that not only do these variables interact with each other but so too do the distinct environments themselves. It is easy to envision how, for adolescents, the home environment will interact with the school environment. Moos proposed an open system of relational dynamics in acknowledgment of the interactivity of the variables and the environments to which they belong. It is posited that the use of a systems framework will allow much more powerful inquiries and interventions relating to environmental factors.

Diversity and Individuality

As conceptualizations of the environment become increasingly comprehensive in accounting for interaction among key variables, it is important not to lose sight of what the individual brings to the equation. Moos (1984) acknowledged that the personal characteristics of the individual must be considered within a conceptual framework of the environment. Indeed, Moos, as well as others (e.g., Holland, 1985), has incorporated personal preference into models of the environment. Beyond attention to personal preference, rather, a movement has begun within the behavioral sciences to fully acknowledge the inherent diversity and individuality.

Related to this latter topic, Claude Steele (2000) has conducted pioneering work to identify the contextual variables that affect ethnic minorities. He has found that the mere prospect of being negatively evaluated, as in the existence of a stereotype, may *cause* decreased performance. Specifically, evidence suggests that this decreased performance is not a result of lack of effort but rather high levels of effort directly are disrupted by the potential of a negative stereotype. Thus, Steele (2000) advocated the design of environments for "identity safety"; specific guidelines can be developed to ensure that diversity is appropriately respected across environments, and all individuals can be given the opportunity to thrive.

Conclusion

It is exciting to look toward the not so distant horizon where models of the environment will focus on positive variables, become increasingly systemic, and incorporate diversity. One goal is that these fresh conceptualizations of the environment will not only be more applicable in the pursuit of fostering human strengths but that they will act to inspire researchers and practitioners alike. Ultimately, the individual scientists and practitioners are responsible for incorporating environmental variables into their research and interventions. It seems obvious that because individuals draw meaning from their environments, consideration of contextual factors will allow the identification of variables from which individuals draw strength.

References

American Psychiatric Association. (1994). *Diagnostic and statistical manual of mental disorders* (4th ed.). Washington, DC: Author.

Anastasi, A. (1988). *Psychological testing* (5th ed.). New York: Macmillan.

Boehm, A. E. (1985). Home observation for measurement of the environment. *Mental Measurements Yearbook 9* (pp. 663–665). Lincoln: Buros Institute of Mental Measurements of the University of Nebraska–Lincoln.

Buckingham, M., & Clifton, D. O. (2001). *Now discover your strengths.* New York: Free Press.

Buckingham, M., & Coffman, C. (1999). *First, break all the rules.* New York: Simon and Schuster.

Caldwell, B., & Bradley, R. (1984), *Home observation for measurement of the environment.* Little Rock: University of Arkansas at Little Rock.

Conyne, R. K., & Clack, J. R. (1981). *Environmental assessment and design: A new tool for the applied behavioral scientist.* New York: Praeger.

Deal, A. G., Trivette, C. M., & Dunst, C. J. (1988). Family Functioning Style scale. In C. J. Dunst, C. M. Trivette, & A. G. Deal (Eds.), *Enabling and empowering families: Principles and guidelines for practice* (pp. 179–184). Cambridge, MA: Brookline Books.

Endler, N., & Magnussen, D. (1976). *Interactional psychology and personality.* Washington, DC: Hemisphere.

Felner, R., Aber, M. S., Primavera, J., & Cauce, A. M. (1985). Adaptation and vulnerability in high risk adolescents: An examination of environmental mediators. *American Journal of Community Psychology, 13,* 365–379.

Friedman, S. L., & Wachs, T. D. (Eds.). (1999). *Measuring environment across the life span: Emerging methods and concepts.* Washington, DC: American Psychological Association.

Gallup Organization. (2000). The StrengthsFinder [Online]. Accessed Dec. 6, 2001, at http://www.gallup.org

Goh, D. S., Teslow, C. J., & Fuller, G. B. (1981). The practices of psychological assessment among school psychologists. *Professional Psychology, 12,* 699–706.

Gough, H. G. (1954). *The Home Index.* Berkeley: University of California Press.

Greenwood, C. R., Carta, J. J., Kamps, D., & Delquadri, J. (1992). *Ecobehavioral Assessment Systems Software (EBASS): Practitioner's manual.* Kansas City, KS: Juniper Gardens Children's Project.

Greenwood, C. R., Delquadri, J., & Hall, V. (1978). *The code for instructional structure and student academic response.* Kansas City, KS: Juniper Gardens Children's Center.

Holland, J. L. (1985). *The Vocational Preference Inventory.* Odessa, FL: Psychological Assessment Resources.

Holland, J. L. (1987). Some speculation about the investigation of person-environment transactions. *Journal of Vocational Behavior 31,* 337–340.

Holland, J. L. (1994). *Self-directed Search Form R* (4th ed.). Odessa, FL: Psychological Assessment Resources.

Holland, J. L., Hansen, J. C., Borgen, F. H., & Hammer, A. L. (1994). *Strong Interest Inventory applications and technical guide.* Palo Alto, CA: Consulting Psychologists Press.

Home Observation for Measurement of the Environment [On-line]. (2000). Available Dec. 6, 2000, at http://www.ualr.edu/·crtldept/home4.htm

Kerr, W. A. (1942). The measurement of home environment and its relationship with certain other variables. *Purdue Studies in Higher Education, 45,* 7–43.

Moos, R. H. (1976). *The human context: Environmental determinants of behavior.* New York: Wiley.

Moos, R. H. (1984). Context and coping: Toward a unifying conceptual framework. *American Journal of Community Psychology, 12,* 5–25.

Moos, R. H. (1991). Connection between school, work, and family settings. In B. J. Fraser & H. J. Walberg (Eds.), *Educational environments: Evaluation, antecedents, and consequences* (pp. 29–53). New York: Pergamon Press.

Mumford, L. (1968). *The urban prospect.* New York: Harcourt Brace Jovanovich.

Olson, D. H. (1992). *Family Inventories Manual.* Minneapolis, MN: Life Innovations.

Olson, D. H. (2000). Circumplex model of marital and family systems. *Journal of Family Therapy, 22,* 144–167.

Olson, D. H., Bell, R., & Portner, J. (1992). *FACES II.* Minneapolis, MN: Life Innovations.

Olson, D. H., Portner, J., & Bell, R. Q. (1982). *FACES II: Family adaptability and cohesion evaluation scales.* St. Paul: Department of Family Social Science, University of Minnesota.

Olson, D. H., Russell, C. S., & Sprenkle, D. H. (1989). *Circumplex model: Systemic assessment and treatment of families.* New York: Haworth Press.

Peterson, C., & Seligman, M. E. P. (2001). *Values in action (VIA) classification of strengths* [Online]. Accessed Dec. 6, 2001, at http://www.psych.upenn.edu/seligman/taxonomy.htm

Repetti, R. L. (1986). Linkages between work and family roles. In S. Oskamp (Ed.), *Applied social psychology annual* (Vol. 7, pp. 98–127). Beverly Hills, CA: Sage.

Schooler, C. (1999). The workplace environment: Measurement, psychological effects, and basic issues. In S. L. Friedman & T. D. Wachs (Eds.), *Measuring environment across the life-span:*

Emerging methods and concepts (pp. 229–246). Washington, DC: American Psychological Association.

Search Institute. (2000). *Search institute: Raising caring and responsible children and teenagers* [On-line]. Accessed Dec. 6, 2001, at http://www.search-institute.org

Shapiro, E. S. (1989). *Academic skill problems: Direct assessment and intervention.* New York: Guilford Press.

Steele, C. (2000, Oct.). *The importance of positive self-image and group image.* Presentation at the Positive Psychology Summit 2000, Washington, DC.

Stern, G. G. (1970). *People in context.* New York: Wiley.

Talbert, J. E., & McLaughlin, M. W. (1999). Assessing the school environment: Embedded contexts and bottom-up research strategies. In S. L. Friedman & T. D. Wachs (Eds.), *Measuring environment across the life span: Emerging methods and concepts* (pp. 197–227). Washington, DC: American Psychological Association.

Trivette, C. M., Dunst, C. J., Deal, A. G., Hamer, W., & Propst, S. (1990). Assessing family strengths and family functioning style. *Topics in Early Childhood Special Education, 10*(1), 16–35.

Walsh, W. B., & Betz, N. E. (1995). *Tests and assessment* (3rd ed.). Englewood Cliffs, NJ: Prentice Hall.

Walsh, W. B., Craik, K. H., & Price, R. H. (Eds.). (2000). *Person–environment psychology: New directions and perspectives* (2nd ed.). Mahwah, NJ: Erlbaum.

Walsh, F., & Olson, D. H. (1988). Utility of the Circumplex Model with severely dysfunctional family systems. *Journal of Psychotherapy and the Family, 4,* 51–78.

Wright, B., & Lopez, S. J. (2002). Widening the diagnostic focus: A case for including human strengths and environmental resources. In C. R. Snyder & S. J. Lopez (Eds.), *The handbook of positive psychology* (pp. 26–44). New York: Oxford University Press.

Ysseldyke, J. E., & Christenson, S. L. (1993). *The Instructional Environment System–II.* Longmont, CO: Sopris West.

Ysseldyke, J., & Elliott, J. (1999). Effective instructional practices: Implications for assessing educational environments. In C. R. Reynolds & T. B. Gutkin (Eds.), *The handbook of school psychology* (3rd ed., pp. 497–518). New York: John Wiley & Sons.

Part VII

Looking Ahead

29

The Future of Positive Psychological Assessment: Making a Difference

Shane J. Lopez and C. R. Snyder

Twenty years ago an article titled "Uncovering Hidden Resources" was published, and in the introduction the authors (Wright & Fletcher, 1982, p. 229) stated,

> It has been recognized that when the assessment of client problems did not sufficiently incorporate positive aspects of client functioning or the role of the environment, the assessment was seriously deficient. Yet this deficiency persists, and we add our voices to those who have already urged that positives as well as negatives be systematically examined with respect to both *the* person and the environment.

We add our voices to this call for a more balanced, comprehensive assessment. We do this because we believe that the *uncovering of hidden resources can make a difference in the lives of people.* That is our omnibus hypothesis.

In this final chapter we specify hypotheses that need to be tested to determine if positive psychological assessment is making a positive difference in the pursuits of some of life's fulfillments—education, meaningful work, and mental health. In addition, we present a hypothesis associated with training counselors and psychologists. We reaffirm that the quests for negative and positive information are complementary. Also, we provide the basic foundation of a model explaining the connections between positive personal and environmental characteristics and aspects of the good life.

The Negatives and Positives in Us All

Beatrice Wright, a founder of rehabilitation psychology, has framed many of the ideas associated with positive psychological assessment. In this subsequent vignette (originally presented in Wright, 1991, and reprinted in Wright & Lopez, 2002, p. 36), she emphasized the importance of finding the negatives and positives in us all.

A counselor, seeking consultation concerning the rehabilitation of a delinquent youth, presented the case of 14-year-old John. The following 10 symptoms were listed: assault, temper tantrums, stealing (car theft), fire-setting,
self-destructive behavior (jumped out of a moving car), threats of harm to
others, insatiable demand for attention, vandalism, wide mood swings, and
underachievement in school. On the basis of these symptoms, the diagnosis
on Axis I of the Diagnostic and Statistical Manual of Mental Disorders was
conduct disorder, undersocialized, aggressive, and with the possibility of a
dysthymic disorder; on Axis II, passive aggressive personality. No physical
disorders were listed on Axis III. The psychosocial stressors, rated as extreme on Axis IV, noted the death of his mother when John was a baby and
successive placement with various relatives and homes. On Axis V, John's
highest level of healthy functioning was rated as poor.

Following perusal of this dismal picture, Wright asked the counselor
whether John had anything going for him. The counselor then mentioned
that John kept his own room in order, took care of his personal hygiene,
liked to do things for others (although on his own terms), liked school, and
had an IQ of 140. Notice how quickly the impression of John changes
once positives in the situation are brought out to share the stage with
the problems. Before that, the fundamental negative bias reigned supreme.
Whereas the fact of John's delinquency had led to the detection of all sorts
of negatives about John's conduct and situation, the positives remained
unconsidered. Is this case atypical? Only in its extreme neglect of strengths,
we venture to say . . . . Notice, also, that the positives in John's case had
been neglected with respect to both personal characteristics and significant environments.

This vignette demonstrates that, despite the surface presentation of weakness,
this person has resources (personal and environmental) that change the overall
impression. As such, finding strengths makes a difference.

Positive Characteristics, Positive Lives:
Toward a Model of Healthy Psychological Growth

Operationalizing strengths and environmental resources have received increasing attention in recent years. This volume is but one example of this "movement." Now, more scholarly efforts are needed in defining and measuring
qualities of a positive life—fulfillments of the good life (e.g., love, lasting joy,
meaningful work, civic pride). Scholars must consider any associated value
judgments when identifying aspects of a positive life; failure to do so could
result in scholarship suggesting the "right way to live" rather than a healthy
way to live (see Lopez et al., 2002).

Without a doubt, the interconnections between strengths, resources,
healthy processes, and fulfillments are complex. Yet if each and every set of
psychological variables were well-operationalized, associations could be more
easily elucidated. Indeed, if more scholarly efforts were devoted to refining
measures of strengths, to creating new measures of healthy processes (e.g.,
resiliency), to validating existing measures (e.g., coping), and to developing

Figure 29.1.   A model of healthy psychological growth.

and validating measures of fulfillments, then the anatomy of the "good life" would become clearer.

Though scholars currently are drafting models of explaining how "vital living" is achieved, there is no clear conceptualization of how strengths, healthy processes, and fulfillments reverberate to produce good living. We do, however, have some ideas about how this may happen (see Figure 29.1). Notice the model represented by the delta and the arrows is embedded in an environmental context; thus all evaluations of strengths, healthy processes, and their interplay should be contextualized (i.e., considered in the context of environmental and cultural variables).

An Assumption About Strength

All people have psychological strengths and the capacity to attain optimal mental health. Our model of healthy psychological growth is grounded in this assumption. Furthermore, as the model suggests, we believe that strengths are essential for growth. Said another way, strengths are the springboards for healthy processes and life fulfillments. Without human strength, healthy processes *may not* develop and human fulfillments *may not* be attained. To borrow comments on one strength from scholars of the distant (e.g., Terence, Cicero, Gay) and recent past (Menninger, Mayman, & Pruysers, 1963, p. 417), "where there is hope there is life."

The Role of Healthy Processes

Healthy processes may be most effective if they spring from strengths. For example, it is possible that individuals who cope best with adversity also possess more potent strengths before the adversity. Healthy processes not linked to human strengths may facilitate "psychological survival" but not optimal mental health. For example, a person with little hope may cope with the daily stressors of life fairly well but not realize improved mental health. A hopeful person, however, may cope with daily insults to well-being in the same manner and turn the successful coping into increased agency for goal pursuits.

Toward a Fulfilling Life

We believe that people who have a repertoire of potent strengths and active healthy processes will create fulfilling lives for themselves. Those people will find meaning in their relationships and work; moreover, they will find benefits in adversity and face challenges with vigor. In essence, individuals who cultivate strengths and refine healthy processes may realize fulfilling lives during good times and bad.

The Interplay Between Strengths, Healthy Processes, and Fulfillments

As indicated by the arrows in Figure 29.1, there are many paths to healthy psychological growth. The straight arrow to the right of the delta (signifying change and growth) represents direct and indirect relationships between strengths, healthy processes, and fulfillments. That is, strengths are used to develop and engage in healthy processes, and these effective processes then lead to fulfillment (or healthy processes mediate or moderate the association between strengths and fulfillments). An alternative path is represented by the curved arrow pointing up (at the right of the delta). The arrow links strength and fulfillment directly, suggesting that strength may, at times, manifest itself as meaning, love, or satisfaction.

The arrows to the left of the delta reflect our views of how strengths and healthy processes are maintained. The straight arrow indicates that those who are fulfilled adapt better and in turn retain or develop new strengths. The curved arrow indicates that fulfillments may build a person's repertoire of strengths directly. This model does not account for the complexity of all of the relationships between strengths, healthy processes, and fulfillments, but we do believe that this type of theorizing needs to be undertaken. This is our current "best guess," and it should be revised (by us and by you) as our understanding of psychological growth expands.

Omnibus Hypothesis: Positive Psychological Assessment Makes a Difference

Our omnibus hypothesis—positive psychological assessment makes a difference—is based on two assumptions: (a) Data about the negative and the positive aspects of human nature can be gathered about every person; and (b) all people have psychological strengths and the capacity to attain optimal functioning. Identifying and measuring human strengths, healthy processes, and fulfillments may have a positive effect on people. Testing this hypothesis directly may be difficult given the broad definition of the independent variable (positive psychological assessment) and the dependent variable (making a difference). Though the omnibus hypothesis cannot be addressed in a rigorous manner, specific hypotheses related to aspects of positive psychological assessment and measurable positive outcomes can be examined.

Hypothesis 1: Identifying and Enhancing Strengths Improves Achievement

Adjunctive K through 12th school programs often focus on academic remediation (reading programs designed to bring students up to "standard") and on prevention of psychosocial problems (e.g., psychoeducational programs designed to prevent bullying and other forms of violence). Recently, however, enhancement programs have been developed and administered in our nation's schools.

An innovative charter high school in Philadelphia, High Tech High, has devoted a large portion of its regular curriculum to identifying and enhancing human strengths with hopes of leading students toward fulfillments including academic achievement.[1] The "treatment" involves students' completion of a strengths assessment, their participation in formal, manualized strength-enhancement programs (promoting accurate explanatory style and hope), and teachers' identification and promotion of strengths. The dependent variable of achievement is measurable and is represented by grade point average and national standardized test scores. Therefore, the effects of the strengths curriculum could be determined by gathering data on meaningful markers of academic fulfillment: changes in students' grades over their past year's performance, differences in standardized test scores (across High Tech High and other schools), and status of the "achievement gap" between White students and ethnic minority students at High Tech High.

Hypothesis 2: Managing According to Measured Strengths Leads to Meaningful, Productive Work

Analysts at the Gallup Organization have conducted two million interviews of leaders of all types (e.g., CEOs, activists, and exemplary teachers). During

---

[1] Contact Dr. Lopez for more information about this program.

construction of this monumental data set, Gallup analysts determined that "each person's talents are enduring and unique" and "each person's greatest room for growth is in the areas of the person's greatest strength" (Buckingham & Clifton, 2001, p. 215). In their book, *Now Discover Your Strengths,* a Gallup senior analyst, Marcus Buckingham, and former CEO Donald Clifton outline aspects of a strategic approach for managing according to strengths. They offer the following directives:

- You should spend a great deal of time and money selecting people properly.
- You should focus performance by "legislating" outcomes rather than forcing people to pursue one type of successful outcome.
- You should focus training time and money on educating people about strengths and figuring out ways to build on these strengths rather than on plugging "skill gaps."
- You should devise individualized ways to help people "grow" their career without necessarily promoting them *up* the corporate ladder and *out* of areas of strengths. (Buckingham & Clifton, 2001, pp. 7–8)

Applying this type of management style requires the measurement of human strength and an individualized management plan. It also requires operationalization of numerous outcomes that reflect what meaningful, productive work means to each and every employee of a team, company, or government. Given the individualized nature of the expected results of managing for strengths, case study or qualitative methods may be most appropriate for testing the hypothesis regarding the effects of positive psychological assessment and enhancement in the workplace.

Hypothesis 3: Measuring and Enhancing Strengths Improves Mental Health

Seligman (1998) asserted that "we have discovered that there is a set of human strengths that are the most likely buffer against mental illness: courage, optimism, interpersonal skill, work ethic, hope, honest and perseverance." This most certainly evokes many testable hypotheses. Akin to, but a significant departure from Seligman's assertion is the hypothesis that strengths serve to improve *mental health.* The distinction between mental illness and mental health is becoming clearer as positive psychology scholars develop theories and conduct research illustrating how illness and health are related yet orthogonal dimensions.

To test our hypothesis, it would be necessary to start by measuring human strength. Then the *routes to strengths enhancement* would have to be chosen—there are many. Universal applications (shared with all members of a team, school) of general strength-enhancement programs have been implemented. In these programs, all participants learn to be strong but particular strengths are not targeted for enhancement. Universal programs designed to enhance one strength have been used—these often are brief and focused. Programs targeting individuals low in a particular strength also may be appropriate in certain situations. Therefore, the nature of the treatment variable (i.e., type of treatment: universal vs. targeted, general strength vs. specific strengths) needs to be well-defined and empirically pitting two or more of these treatments against each other needs to be considered a viable means of testing this hypothesis.

Regarding the operationalization of the optimal mental health, much scholarly focus and fieldwork is needed to conceptualize and measure this aspect of optimal functioning. Currently, Keyes's conceptualization of flourishing (see chapter 26, this volume) and the MIDUS scales serve as one means for operationalizing optimal mental health.

Hypothesis 4: Training in Positive Assessment Improves Practice and Research

We teach what we believe, as suggested by our colleague Thomas Krieshok (2000). We believe that positive psychological assessment provides the information we need to be more helpful to people and to conduct meaningful positive psychological research. Our students pick up on this belief and run with it. Thus, our students (and, in the future, the readership of this volume) serve as the most appropriate target population for examination of this hypothesis.

Our work with our graduate students, many of whom have contributed to this volume and to positive psychology articles and books, is the intervention; their good deeds (in scholarly and practice realms) are the outcomes of interest. Testing our hypothesis (i.e., training in positive psychological assessment improves practice and research conducted by our students and others) might involve examining the extent to which our students have indoctrinated and applied the positive psychological assessment approach (independent variable). The variability in indoctrination and application would have to be determined and then students' contributions to practice and research (dependent variable) would have to be quantified and qualified. This examination of training outcome also would help us determine the effects of positive psychological assessment and practice.

Conclusion

"First you need to measure their strengths!" (personal communication, October 1999). This is the impassioned reply that Don Clifton gives when asked how to better manage, educate, or counsel people. He believes that measuring and enhancing strengths is what makes a difference in the lives of people—all people.

We have begun to use a positive psychological assessment and with this approach we have encountered fascinating new clinical and research hypotheses. These hypotheses lead us and the people we teach and counsel to discoveries about healthy processes and human fulfillment. At the heart of our "making a difference" pursuits are the discoveries about the best in all of us.

References

Buckingham, M., & Clifton, D. O. (2001). *Now, discover your strengths.* New York: Free Press.

Krieshok, T. S. (2000). We practice what we teach. *Journal of Career Assessment, 8,* 205–222

Lopez, S. J., Prosser, E., Edwards, L. M., Magyar-Moe, J. L., Neufeld, J., et al. (2002). Putting positive psychology in a multicultural perspective. In C. R. Snyder & S. J. Lopez (Eds.), *The handbook of positive psychology* (pp. 700–714). New York: Oxford University Press.

Menninger, K., Mayman, M., & Puysers, P. W. (1963). *The vital balance.* New York: Viking Press.

Seligman, M. E. P. (1998). *Building human strength: Psychology's forgotten mission.* http://www.apa.org/monitor/jan98/pres.html

Wright, B. A. (1991). Labeling: The need for greater person–environmental individuation. In C. R. Snyder & D. R. Forsyth (Eds.), *Handbook of social and clinical psychology: The health perspective* (pp. 416–437). New York: Pergamon Press.

Wright, B. A., & Fletcher, B. L. (1982). Uncovering hidden resources: A challenge in assessment. *Professional Psychology, 13,* 229–235.

Wright, B. A., & Lopez, S. J. (2002). Widening the diagnostic focus: A case for including human strengths and environmental resources. In C. R. Snyder & S. J. Lopez (Eds.), *Handbook of positive psychology* (pp. 26–44). New York: Oxford University Press.

Author Index

Numbers in italics refer to listings in reference sections.

Subject Index

About the Editors

Shane J. Lopez received his PhD in counseling psychology from the University of Kansas in 1998. As an intern at the Eisenhower Veterans Affairs Medical Center in Leavenworth, Kansas, he spent his first six months in an assessment rotation that focused on the "dark side" of human functioning. On changing rotations at midyear, he was challenged by his role of therapist to aging veterans with chronic health conditions. The pathology model offered little guidance. Thus, he rediscovered the work of C. R. Snyder and that of M. E. P. Seligman. The introduction of hope and optimism into therapy provided clients a foundation to build on rather than another roadblock to overcome. Because of this experience, Dr. Lopez decided to commit himself to the positive psychology movement.

In August 1998, he joined the counseling psychology faculty at the University of Kansas, where he teaches courses in psychological assessment and educational leadership. He is coeditor of the *Handbook of Positive Psychology*, coauthor of *Positive Psychology*, and associate editor of the *Journal of Social and Clinical Psychology*. His research foci include examining the effectiveness of hope training programs in schools (under the auspices of the Making Hope Happen Program) and refining a model and measure of psychological courage.

C. R. Snyder received his PhD in clinical psychology from Vanderbilt University in 1971. He was assistant professor in the Kansas University Department of Psychology and in 2001 was appointed as the M. Erik Wright Distinguished Professor of Clinical Psychology. He also was the director of the Clinical Psychology Program from 1975 through 2001. He has published 20 books and 220 articles and chapters. Dr. Snyder has received numerous awards for his teaching at the university, state, and national levels and for his research at the university and national levels. He has also received many research grants and has been recognized with fellow status in eight psychological societies. He is known for his theoretical advances at the interface of clinical, social, personality, and health psychology. Of particular note are his theory and research on how people react to personal feedback, the human need for uniqueness, the ubiquitous drive to excuse transgressions and, most recently, the hope motive.